Developing Skills for Business Leadership

Second edition

Edited by Gillian Watson and Stefanie C. Reissner

Chartered Institute of Personnel and Development

Published by the Chartered Institute of Personnel and Development

151 The Broadway, London SW19 1JQ

This edition first published 2014
First published 2010
Reprinted 2011, 2012, 2013

Designed and typeset by Exeter Premedia Services, India
Printed in Great Britain by Ashford Colour Press.

British Library Cataloguing in Publication Data
A catalogue of this publication is available from the British Library

ISBN 9781843983163

Chartered Institute of Personnel and Development
151 The Broadway, London SW19 1JQ
Tel: 020 8612 6200
Email: cipd@cipd.co.uk
Website: www.cipd.co.uk
Incorporated by Royal Charter. Registered Charity No. 1079797

Contents

List of figures and tables

Chapter 18

Author biographies

Gillian Watson is currently a principal lecturer in the Faculty of Business and Law at the University of Sunderland, responsible for International Development and Partnerships. She has also undertaken other senior roles in the faculty such as HRM Team Leader, Chair of the PG Board and Chair of the Applied Management, FdA and HND Board. She has led several key initiatives to enhance the learning experience for postgraduate and undergraduate students. Her current role allows her to foster co-operation and share good practice with the faculty's transnational education and other partner institutions.

Stefanie Reissner is currently a lecturer at Newcastle University Business School. She conducted her doctoral research, a cross-cultural study of organisational change and learning, at Durham University and has received ESRC-funding for her current research into storytelling in management practice. Her findings have been published in academic journals and books. Stefanie has a keen interest in supporting the learning of others and teaches study and research skills at undergraduate and postgraduate levels. She is currently Degree Programme Director for a Dual Master's Award in conjunction with Rijksuniversiteit Groningen in The Netherlands. Stefanie is a Fellow of the Higher Education Academy and an Associate Academic Member of CIPD.

Mike Ashwell, BA (Hons), FCMA, CGMA, FHEA, is a Chartered Management Accountant by background and currently Senior Lecturer in Accounting at Teesside University. As a management accountant, he worked in a variety of organisations, ranging from major multinationals to SMEs, where he undertook a number of roles both in general finance management and in the implementation of business systems and controls. Mike is currently the Programme Leader for the BA (Hons) Degree in Accounting and Finance at Teesside University Business School. He teaches on a range of Management Accounting and Financial modules, at undergraduate and MBA level, and also devises and delivers short courses designed to assist the understanding of finance by non-financial managers. Mike is currently the Chairman of the Teesside Branch of the Chartered Institute of Management Accountants, and is also a volunteer Director and Trustee of Sedgefield Development Trust.

Kevin Gallagher is a senior lecturer at the University of Sunderland. Before he joined the academic world he worked firstly as a civil engineer, spending several years overseas, then as the business development manager for a UK-based plc. Kevin is now the programme leader for BA Business and Management and teaches various business and research skills modules at both UG and PG levels. Kevin previously co-authored the CIPD textbook *Managing for Results* and is the author of the second edition of a leading UG textbook on business and management skills development. He is currently researching how students address their own research projects and dissertations.

Lesley Mearns is currently employed as a Principal Lecturer at Sunderland University in the Faculty of Business and Law. Her role is Team Leader HRM and Leadership and she is currently Programme Leader for MSc HRM. Lesley is actively engaged in research in the area of employment/industrial relations, leadership and the management of people. She is at present looking at the impact that geographical location has on the employment relationship, especially in NE England. This has included examining issues such as immigration and migration, kinship and employee mobility.

Andrew Simpson is currently Director of Accreditation and MBA Programme at Sheffield University Management School. Andrew's PhD is in Statistics from Newcastle University and he is a Fellow of the Royal Statistical Society. Andrew's research interests include operations strategy and forecasting within supply chains. He teaches on the MBA programme and is an experienced research methods lecturer at postgraduate level.

Permissions and acknowledgements

This book has been a truly collective endeavour and the editors wish to thank:

- All contributors, without whose expertise and hard work this book would not have been possible.
- The following individuals for giving their help, support, time and information:
  - Barrie Watson, member of Belbin Associates and Managing Director of CERT Consultancy and Training (www.belbin.com and www.belbin.info).
  - Mike Cockburn, Sogno Ltd. for contributing a case study based on his coaching practice (Chapter 7).
  - Preye Deinne, Rui Hu, Helen Toseland and Pak Ki Tsang for permission to use materials from their group assignment for the Managing Change module (Chapter 12).
  - Craig Smith, Flint Consulting, for allowing us insights into his exciting work, resulting in the case study 'Leading bold change™' (Chapter 12).
  - Darryl Warden and Kathryn Atkinson for contributing a case study on redeployment in a public–private partnership (Chapter 17).
  - Dr Robert Allan, Managing Director at Hapsis, for contributing a case study deriving from his consultancy practice (Chapter 17).
  - Dr Angelique Du Toit, Paul Andrew, Debbee Forster and Gabi Greiner for supplying us with case studies and raw materials for original case studies.
  - Diana Klose for permission to use the sample assignment 'HRM in Russia' (Chapter 2).
- The anonymous reviewers who helped us improve earlier drafts of this book.
- All at CIPD Publishing for their support throughout this project, particularly Katy Hamilton.
- Our long-suffering families for their patience and support.

We also wish to thank the following individuals, organisations and publishers for giving us their kind permission to use their material as acknowledged in the text where appropriate. Among these, we would like to express our particular gratitude to:

- The CIPD for extracts from *People Management*, case studies and materials from their website and other publications.
- Barrie Watson, member of Belbin Associates and Managing Director of CERT Consultancy and Training (www.belbin.com and www.belbin.info).
- Belbin Associates for the use of Belbin materials (www.belbin.com and www.belbin.info).
- Elsevier for permission to reproduce material from Benfari et al.'s article 'The effective use of power' published in *Business Horizons* (1986), Vol. 29, issue 3, pp.12–16.
- G4S for permission to reproduce their remuneration report (Chapter 14).
- Peter Cook, Managing Director of Human Dynamics, for permission to reproduce material from his books *Best practice creativity* and *Sex, leadership and rock'n'roll* (Box 16.1), reproduced with permission by Crown House Publishing Ltd.

- Penguin for permission to reproduce material from Edward De Bono's book *Six thinking hats* (Table 16.1).
- Debbee Forster and Susan Doyle (Area HRD Manager) from International Hotels Group for case study material (Chapter 17).

CIPD qualifications map

Developing Skills for Business Leadership

The content of this CIPD module is covered as follows:

Developing Skills for Business Leadership learning outcomes	Developing Skills for Business Leadership chapters
Understand, analyse and critically evaluate.	Chapter 1: Skills for continuing professional development and practice (Part 2) Chapter 2: Essential skills for postgraduate study and beyond Chapter 17: Applying skills for business leadership
Manage themselves more effectively at work or in another professional context.	Chapter 1: Skills for continuing professional development and practice (Part 2) Chapter 4: Concepts of self and self-management skills Chapter 5: Developing your professional identity Chapter 18: Consolidating leadership skills: project management and your development (Part 2)
Manage interpersonal relationships at work more effectively.	Chapter 8: Effective team-building and communication Chapter 9: Negotiation and the management of interpersonal relationships at work
Make sound and justifiable decisions and solve problems more effectively.	Chapter 7: Coaching, professional development and practice Chapter 16: Effective decision-making and problem-solving Chapter 17: Applying skills for business leadership
Lead and influence others more effectively.	Chapter 11: Leadership and team dynamics Chapter 12: Leading change and development in organisations Chapter 18: Consolidating leadership skills: project management and your development (Part 1)
Interpret financial information and manage financial resources.	Chapter 14: Interpreting financial information Chapter 15: Managing financial resources
Demonstrate enhanced IT proficiency.	Chapter 13: Introduction to quantitative data analysis

Developing Skills for Business Leadership learning outcomes	Developing Skills for Business Leadership chapters
Demonstrate an essential people management skill-set.	Chapter 6: Skills for learning, training and development Chapter 7: Coaching, professional development and practice Chapter 10: Constructive performance management
Demonstrate competence in postgraduate study skills.	Chapter 2: Essential skills for postgraduate study and beyond Chapter 3: Practical aspects of postgraduate study skills

Walkthrough of textbook features and online resources

LEARNING OUTCOMES

At the beginning of each chapter a bulleted set of learning outcomes summarises what you can expect to learn from the chapter, helping you to track your learning.

LEARNING OUTCOMES

By the end of this chapter, provided you engage with the activities, you should be able to:

- understand the qualitative difference between undergraduate and postgraduate study skills
- understand the importance of critical thinking for postgraduate study and CPD
- apply critical thinking to your studies and beyond
- access high-quality information for study tasks
- analyse and evaluate written and oral materials
- develop and justify original arguments
- apply strategies to improve your writing.

ACTIVITIES

Questions and activities throughout the text encourage you to reflect on what you have learned and to apply your knowledge and skills in practice.

ACTIVITY 1.2

Your profession – present and future

It will be useful for you as (prospective) HR professionals to get some understanding of the current state of the profession – prevalence, role, purpose, skills – and likely changes over the next few years. Imagine how the prevalence, role and purpose of the HR profession as well as your skills as a professional may change in the near future. What may the Implications be on your career and its development? You may want to discuss your analysis with a tutor, work colleague or HR expert. Again, those of you not studying for an HR-specific degree can do the same exercise for your chosen profession.

CASE STUDIES

A number of case studies from different sectors will help you to place the concepts discussed into a real-life context.

EVERYONE'S ENTITLED TO AN OPINION

CASE STUDY 1.1

The case study is about a group of students new to a university studying on a postgraduate programme in international management. The cohort group consists of 20 students with 11 different nationalities and a plethora of religious and cultural backgrounds. They had undergone development in appreciating each other's cultures, which included food, religion, cultural dress, tolerance of different societal norms, and so on. This had all helped to encourage camaraderie and a sense of working together for a common goal. The students had been tasked to complete a project in set groups of five. This type of cultural inclusivity as a learning process had worked very well in previous years.

The newcomer was male and came from the United Arab Emirates (Ali).

Not long after the introduction Ali announced to the group how he liked all things American and intended to go and live there one day. John offered a view of the US from his perspective, which included the advantages and disadvantages of having a porous border and a powerful neighbour. Ping identified Canada as a great place to live as some of her relatives had moved to Toronto and really liked it. Ali was somewhat dismissive and reacted as if he was being challenged, and disagreement grew. Tie had said he should not speak to Ping in such a way. The tutor responded

PAUSE FOR THOUGHT

Identify at least three things that you have learned by studying this chapter and engaging with the activities. How will your newly acquired knowledge and skills support your continuing professional development? What value do you expect your learning to have for your daily routines and your further career? In what area have you identified a need for further development and how are you planning to fill that gap? Address these issues in your learning journal and/or CPD log. You may also wish to discuss them with a peer, colleague, mentor or coach to aid your further development.

PAUSE FOR THOUGHT

An opportunity to reflect on your learning in the chapter and to identify further development needs.

EXPLORE FURTHER

CIPD website: http://www.cipd.co.uk

MOON, J. (1999) *Learning journals: a handbook for academics, students and professional development*. London: Kogan Page.

UNIVERSITY OF KENT CAREERS AND EMPLOYABILITY SERVICE: http://www.kent.ac.uk/careers/sk/skillsmenu.htm

EXPLORE FURTHER

Explore further boxes contain suggestions for further reading and useful websites, encouraging you to delve further into areas of particular interest.

ONLINE RESOURCES FOR TUTORS

- Lecturer's guides – practical advice on teaching using this text.
- PowerPoint slides – build and deliver your course around these ready-made lectures, ensuring complete coverage of the module.
- Additional case studies and resources for use within teaching, including checklists, sample assignments and tools.

Visit www.cipd.co.uk/tss

CHAPTER 1

Skills for Continuing Professional Development and Practice

STEFANIE REISSNER AND GILLIAN WATSON

1.1 INTRODUCTION

> A university education isn't just about getting a degree – it's about preparing you for the world beyond study. (Newcastle University, Careers and Employability Service 2013)

In an applied discipline like business and management, employers increasingly expect graduates to contribute to the organisation's success from the moment they join. While subject knowledge will undoubtedly play a crucial part in your ability to make a difference for your organisation, even more fundamental are the skills, that is, the capabilities and expertise (Leitch Review of Skills 2006), that you bring with you into your chosen career or role. Of particular importance are transferable skills, which are required for a wide variety of roles regardless of the organisation and industry in which they are being employed (Bennett 2002). Such transferable skills include the ability to manage oneself and others, to analyse and resolve problems, to negotiate, to lead and to manage change (Rankin 2003). Your programme of study will include both acquisition of knowledge and development of skills, and most universities will also offer careers and employability services to help you make the most of your learning in preparation for your future career.

However, ultimately it is your responsibility to develop and maintain the key skills required for your chosen profession during your programme of study and beyond. Unlike knowledge, which can be acquired by sitting in a lecture or reading a book, skills development takes time and typically requires interaction with other professionals. Many transferable skills are relational, with negotiation and leadership being obvious examples. In other instances, the relational nature of skills is less obvious; for example, other people's responses to our behaviour can tell us what effect we have on others. We can then reflect on whether this is conducive to the situation at hand or not – a key part of self-management.

Moreover, skills can always be developed further for even greater professional proficiency. Let us take presentation skills as an example. Most students entering a postgraduate course will be able to give an adequate presentation. By this we mean that they are able to identify a clear argument, structure the materials in a logical order, provide visuals and handouts where appropriate and speak relatively freely and fluently. Because they are able to do all of this, we suggest that they have basic presentation skills. But does this mean that they are as good as a professional speaker? Probably not. But the more presentations these students give, the more experienced they get and the better their presentations are likely to become until they get close to the standard of professional speakers. And even then, professional speakers will continually hone their already excellent presentation skills to maintain and improve them.

The same applies to other transferable skills such as the management of interpersonal relations, decision-making, problem-solving, negotiation and leadership. Once you have acquired such skills at a basic level (for instance during your programme of study), you need to develop them continually to be able to contribute to your organisation's success over time (see Routledge and Carmichael 2007). This is where continuing professional development (CPD) comes in, which is fruitfully defined as 'the maintenance and enhancement of the knowledge, expertise and competence of professionals throughout their careers according to a plan formulated with regard to the needs of the professional, the employer, the profession and society' (Madden and Mitchell, as cited in Jones and Fear 1994, p50). It involves 'a combination of approaches, ideas and techniques' that will enable professionals to manage their learning, growth and development (CIPD 2013a), including training, mentoring, coaching, networking and reflective practice.

Notice the role of employers and professional bodies in these definitions. Employers can do their part to support their employees' continuing professional development, for instance, through providing (or funding) training, mentoring or coaching. Professional bodies such as the CIPD will offer a variety of courses and networking events, and they will also monitor their members' CPD activities on a yearly basis. Recognising the importance of skills among HR professionals, the CIPD has also created the CIPD Profession Map, which explains 'what the most successful HR professionals know and do at every stage of their career' (CIPD 2013b, p2). We will introduce the CIPD Profession Map in more detail in Section 1.4 of this chapter.

Developing Skills for Business Leadership has been written in response to the increasing need for professionals to demonstrate both subject-specific knowledge and transferable skills at work. It aims to help prospective professionals in HR and cognate areas develop the key skills required for a successful and rewarding career. This introductory chapter consists of two parts. Part 1 outlines the rationale, approach and structure of this book as it seeks to support your skill-building and continuing professional development during your programme of study and beyond. Part 2 focuses on the skills required for continuing professional development in an increasingly diverse work environment. It also discusses issues pertinent to the debate about skill-building and continuing professional development from both an individual and an organisational perspective, such as competence, diversity, career development, succession planning, talent management and human capital.

PART 1: RATIONALE, PHILOSOPHY AND APPROACH OF THIS BOOK

1.2 WHY WE WROTE THIS BOOK: WHAT YOU NEED TO KNOW

As university lecturers, we have experienced the importance of skills in three key areas. Firstly, the British Government has made universities one pillar of their skill-building agenda (Leitch Review of Skills 2006), and there is increasing pressure (also from employers) to make skill-building more explicit in the curriculum (Bennett 2002). Hence, we are encouraged to reflect on the provision of skill-building measures and identify new opportunities to help our students build new and hone existing skills. While some skill-building will be integrated in existing modules, new specialist skills modules are being developed to meet the need for systematic and focused skill-building among students and professionals. It is likely that you are using this book in one of the latter.

Secondly, employers are increasingly looking for staff – both graduate and postgraduate – who can think critically and independently, analyse and evaluate complex situations, and resolve challenging problems (for example Forbes 2012, Banbury 2013).

Moreover, an increasing number of employers expect potential applicants to master such skills prior to employment (Bennett 2002). As university lecturers we are required to provide our students with the opportunities to build these skills and to hone them as part of their studies to allow them to 'hit the ground running' after graduation. This also includes creating an awareness of the skills that they possess and the ability to identify any skills gaps as well as any development measures to fill such gaps; this is an important part of managing oneself and one's career (see also Chapters 4, 5 and 18).

Thirdly and most importantly, as university lecturers we work with you, the student, on a daily basis and we know how much easier studying becomes with the right skills. All the ambition and hard work of this world will only get you so far if you do not possess the right skills to study and work smartly. It may be useful to think of skills as tools, which, if applied correctly, will make a task much easier. The trick, it seems, is to help you learn how to learn (Rawson 2000), which will allow you to adapt to constantly changing circumstances in a rapidly changing work environment. The key to this is to become aware of the skills that you already possess and those that you need to build or hone so that you can employ them more effectively in your daily work and to change and adapt as required.

As university lecturers we are also aware that students often regard skill-building as an add-on to their programme of study, particularly since skill-building has become more explicit. Do you also wonder when you will have the time to engage in skill-building? We appreciate that such concerns are very valid with many of you having to work while studying (or study while working), and many of you will also have family and other commitments to compete with your time. However, skill-building has always been an essential part of higher education, and students have always built and honed skills as part of their studies, albeit often unawares. In twenty-first-century education, skill-building has become more prominent over subject knowledge, and any skill-building initiative is designed to complement your studies and to help you study and work smarter. We therefore regard it as essential that you engage with skill-building as part of your programme of study and continue doing so once you have entered your chosen profession.

Continuing professional development will help you stay in touch with the latest developments in your profession, and it is your chance to hone the skills that you will have built at university and at the workplace to aid your individual and professional development. A positive correlation between the level of skills that a professional possesses and their employability in higher positions has long been established (DFES 2005, DIUS 2007), so if you are striving up the career ladder, you had better start building and honing the required skills. *Developing Skills for Business Leadership* is designed to help you on your journey.

The objective of this book is to help postgraduate students and those studying for CPD to develop those skills that are essential for professionalism and career progression. It covers skills that are vital for human resource professionals, such as communication, teamworking, self-management, people management, training, leadership, change management, financial, decision-making, problem-solving and postgraduate study skills. Moreover, it seeks to help you integrate any newly developed skills into your work and career, which we regard as vital at postgraduate and professional level. This is done through reflection, which is an integral part of experiential learning (Mezirow 1991) and professional practice (Schön 1983). We recognise that reflective learning comes naturally to some of you (even though you may not be aware of it), whereas it is more difficult for others. Since it has proven an effective means of learning and continuing professional development, many of the activities throughout this book require you to reflect on your learning and professional practice (where appropriate). While we appreciate that to some of you this may be both unfamiliar and at first glance ineffective, we encourage all of you to give it a try to make the most of your learning with this book. We will discuss reflective learning in more detail later in this chapter.

Please note that *Developing Skills for Business Leadership* is rooted in the Anglo-Saxon tradition of business, management and education and is targeted at individuals and groups studying in such a context. We have used much of the content and pedagogy of this book successfully with diverse and multicultural student groups in human resource-specific and more generic postgraduate programmes. Despite initial scepticism, the vast majority of our students have found them invaluable for their studies and further career development. If this book is adopted in a different cultural and educational context, teaching staff are encouraged to explore with their students how they can adapt the skills, theories and models presented here to their respective needs.

1.3 STRUCTURE AND CONTENT OF THIS BOOK

This book consists of 18 chapters, which cover a wide range of skills and which have been written by subject experts. You may find that the approach and style adopted in some chapters differ considerably from the approach and style adopted in others as the conventions in different disciplines vary. We hope that this variety of approaches and styles will enrich your learning experience with this book rather than hamper it. In particular, this book covers the following skills:

Chapter 2 – *Essential Skills for Postgraduate Study and Beyond* – focuses on essential postgraduate study skills. It has been designed to help you hone skills such as critical thinking, critical reading and critical writing, which you may have built in your undergraduate studies or at the workplace. The chapter provides background information on such critical skills as well as activities and practical advice to help you put them into practice in your studies and beyond.

Chapter 3 – *Practical Aspects of Postgraduate Study Skills* – builds on Chapter 2 by focusing on conventions of academic writing (including referencing), effective writing practice and effective exam preparation. It describes the key characteristics of effective essays and reports, dissertations and projects, and outlines the basics of academic referencing. The chapter also provides an exam guide to help you prepare smartly for your exams.

Please note: Chapters 2 and 3 both seek to make explicit some of the expectations that your tutors may have but never spell out. Engaging with these chapters is particularly important if you have not studied formally for some time or if you are unfamiliar with the Anglo-Saxon university system. We recommend that you study them before any of the other chapters in this book as the skills covered here will help you succeed in your programme of studies.

Chapter 4 – *Concepts of Self and Self-management Skills* – creates a contemporary view of time management, procrastination, personal organisation skills and managing stress. Its reflective approach will allow you to identify your constructive as well as your less helpful behaviours in your daily routine so that you can address them if you wish. The techniques discussed in this chapter will also help you to manage yourself and your career more effectively and to keep stress at a healthy level.

Chapter 5 – *Developing Your Professional Identity* – introduces the concept of professional identity, which integrates expert knowledge, skills and professional behaviours. The approach taken in this chapter, which has proven successful with many of our students, encourages you to reflect on your personality, values, emotions and norms and how they affect your behaviour at work as well as your professional success.

Chapter 6 – *Skills for Learning, Training and Development* – discusses the current context in which training, learning and staff development is taking place, identifying opportunities and constraints. This chapter examines in more detail the different roles a learning professional or trainer can take and the skills required for each role.

Chapter 7 – *Coaching, Professional Development and Practice* – provides an overview of coaching as an increasingly popular means of professional development from the perspective of human resource professionals. It helps practitioners identify the need for coaching in their organisation, select a coach for a particular coaching intervention, manage the provision of coaching services and evaluate the effectiveness of a coaching intervention.

Chapter 8 – *Effective Team-building and Communication* – discusses different types of teams and different team roles therein to aid your analysis at the workplace. In the various activities, you are encouraged to analyse and reflect upon your own experiences as a team member and/or team leader.

Chapter 9 – *Negotiation and the Management of Interpersonal Relationships at Work* – explores the political nature of organisations with regard to power and authority. It introduces effective approaches to negotiation and conflict resolution and considers bullying and harassment in organisations.

Chapter 10 – *Constructive Performance Management* – focuses on the ongoing nature of performance management. It highlights how performance management begins with recruitment and selection and continues with regular performance appraisals. The chapter also discusses how poor performance can be managed.

Chapter 11 – *Leadership and Team Dynamics* – focuses on leadership in a team environment, considering key leadership theories and how they have evolved over time. The activities encourage you to decide how you would react in a particular situation and to reflect on your own style of leadership.

Chapter 12 – *Leading Change and Development in Organisations* – introduces you to theories of organisational change and to a wide range of skills that are required to manage it successfully. It considers both business and people aspects of change and encourages you to reflect on the roles and contributions of yourself and others around you. The chapter also deals briefly with the role of facilitators and consultants in managing organisational change.

Chapters 13, 14 and 15 deal with key quantitative skills. Chapter 13 – *Introduction to Quantitative Data Analysis* – covers the basics of quantitative data analysis to aid decision-making. It considers what is meant by data and how data can be represented visually. The chapter also explains the key statistical terms required by human resource professionals. Chapter 14 – *Interpreting Financial Information* – introduces the key financial statements, explains the main accounting principles and discusses the importance of corporate governance. Detailed case examples show the mathematics behind the statements and make financial information straightforward to understand. Chapter 15 – *Managing Financial Resources* – examines the role of financial information in decision-making and business performance. It discusses in detail the business plan and its role and content, followed by an introduction to budget. The chapter also explains different types of cost (including calculation of the break-even point), cash management, performance monitoring, environmental accounting and the evaluation of capital expenditure. Moreover, it considers the key attributes of management accountants and other professionals involved in the management of financial resources.

Chapter 16 – *Effective Decision-making and Problem-solving* – introduces you to a range of techniques that can support managers' creative decision-making and problem-solving. It focuses on techniques that can help managers to look at a decision or problem from different perspectives and that can lead to new and potentially fruitful solutions. It also considers the role of groups in the decision-making and problem-solving process as well as ethical issues, and discusses how decisions can be fruitfully communicated to others.

Chapter 17 – *Applying Skills for Business Leadership* – contains a series of case studies that relate to more than one chapter of this book, giving you an opportunity to employ your newly acquired knowledge and to practise your newly gained skills in a safe environment. The case studies have been specifically written for this book and cover a range of issues that not only feature in this book but in contemporary managerial practice. They are about real organisations and real people, although the names of some of them have been disguised to respect their anonymity. The case studies vary in length, industry sector and international dimension to cater for a wide variety of learning needs.

Chapter 18 – *Consolidating Leadership Skills: Project Management and your Development* – brings together the themes and skills discussed throughout this book and consists of two parts. Part 1 discusses project management as an area in which the key skills covered in this book are needed. It illustrates through a case study how interpersonal and other transferable skills can be applied in the workplace and for continuing professional development. Special emphasis is put on how different skills are required to manage complex projects. Part 2 explores talent management from an individual perspective to demonstrate how it can enhance your career development. Its focus is strongly on your continuing professional and career development at a stage when your studies with this book are coming to an end.

Each chapter contains specifically designed activities to support your learning, many of which require you to identify, analyse and reflect on a particular issue, skill or management practice. Most chapters also include case studies to illustrate a particular skill, to give you the opportunity to practise a skill in a real-life context and to gain second-hand experience about a management situation. Towards the end of each chapter you will find a section called 'Pause for Thought', in which you are invited to identify your learning and to reflect on how you can include it in your daily practice in true CPD style (for details, please refer to Section 1.6 below). You will find that some of the key skills, such as communication, interpersonal, leadership and change management skills, feature in more than one chapter and we encourage you to explore them in more detail as you go along, alone or with your peers.

PART 2: SKILLS FOR CONTINUING PROFESSIONAL DEVELOPMENT

1.4 CONTINUING SKILLS DEVELOPMENT

We have already highlighted the need for HR professionals to continuously develop their skills during their studies and career and also the need for employers and professional bodies to support them. One way in which the CIPD seeks to facilitate its members' continuing professional development is the CIPD Profession Map, which defines the activities, knowledge, skills and behaviours that successful HR professionals demonstrate at the workplace. It is a flexible tool with multiple applications for individuals, teams and organisations. At individual level, it can be used for CPD planning and career development (CIPD 2013b) by using the My HR Map tool available to CIPD members (CIPD 2013a). At team level it can be used to diagnose areas of success and areas of further improvement (see CIPD 2012a for details on HR partnering), and at organisational level it can be used to identify skills gaps, build role profiles and develop career paths (CIPD 2013b).

The CIPD Profession Map has been divided into:

1   *Bands of professional competence:* There are four such bands relating to different stages of an individual's career. Professionals in Band 1 are typically at an early stage of their career (for example an HR assistant), while professionals in Band 4 have advanced HR roles in their organisation (for example HR director). As professionals

gain increasing responsibility in their daily work, their skills will be honed, allowing them to move up the career ladder and make the transition between bands (for example learning and development officer, organisation development practitioner, HR business partner).

2   *Professional areas:* The two professional areas of *Insights, Strategy and Solutions* as well as *Leading HR* are placed at the heart of the CIPD Profession Map because they underpin the purpose of the profession. Other professional areas include: organisation design, organisation development, resourcing and talent planning, learning and development, performance and reward, employee engagement, employee relations, and service delivery and information.

3   *Behaviours:* The CIPD Profession Map defines eight behaviours that competent HR professionals demonstrate: curious, decisive thinker, skilled influencer, personally credible, collaborative, driven to deliver, courage to challenge, and role model. Such behaviours have different manifestations depending on an individual's role, career stage and band of professional competence.

The CIPD Profession Map is visually represented in Figure 1.1.

Figure 1.1 The CIPD Profession Map

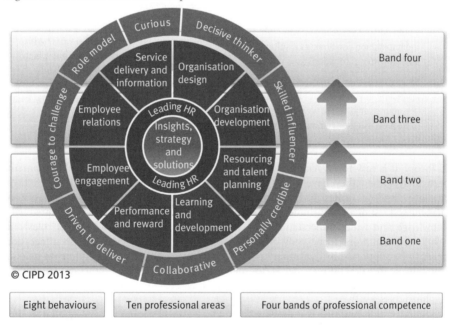

© CIPD 2013

| Eight behaviours | Ten professional areas | Four bands of professional competence |

Source: reproduced with permission from CIPD 2013b, p4

It is important to highlight that the CIPD Profession Map captures what HR professionals *actually do* in their daily practice rather than the qualifications they have – even though in many instances higher qualifications correspond to more advanced roles. Even so, prospective HR professionals can use (1) the bands of professional competence to understand at which point they may enter the profession to look for appropriate role advertisements, (2) the professional areas to determine potential specialisms within the profession, and (3) the behaviours to prepare for job interviews and assessment centres. More experienced HR professionals can use the CIPD Profession Map to manage their career more strategically by understanding which areas they need to develop before they can be considered for promotion or upgraded CIPD membership status.

We appreciate that not all of you may be studying for an HR-specific degree and that you may therefore question the value of the CIPD Profession Map for your own continuing professional and career development. While the professional areas of the Map relate to a large extent to the HR profession (not surprisingly), other professions have similar bands of professional competence (although they may not be explicitly defined) and the eight behaviours identified in the Map are relevant to other professions, too. We therefore encourage all of you to engage with this useful and practical tool.

 ACTIVITY 1.1

Exploring the CIPD Profession Map

Download the CIPD Profession Map from http://www.cipd.co.uk/binaries/profession-map-2.4-Oct-2013.pdf and study its elements carefully. Consider the following questions:

1   In which band of professional competence would you put yourself and why? What are the implications on findings a suitable position after graduation?

2   Which professional areas are most appealing to you and why? Where do you see your strengths and weaknesses? Reflect on whether you would be more

suited to a generalist or a specialist role and justify your answer. If you are not studying for an HR-specific degree, try to find out which professional areas are prevalent in your chosen profession and use them here.

3   Which professional behaviours do you exhibit in your studies and at work? Which of those come naturally to you and which did you have to acquire through hard work? What behaviours do you currently not exhibit and how could you acquire them?

In theory, it is easy to suggest that professionals engage in continuing skills development, particularly when they have access to a wide variety of CPD measures through their employer and/or professional body. In practice, however, there are a number of challenges. First of all, skill-building *per se* is not enough; skills need to be integrated with knowledge and wider understanding of the professional's identity as well as roles and relationships at work to be truly effective (see Chapter 5 for details). Such integration needs to be supported by continuing reflective practice – either as a discipline on its own (for which the practitioner needs to make time, see Section 1.6 below) and/or in conjunction with more formal development such as coaching or mentoring (for which funding is required).

Secondly, skill-building is a moving feast. Once a professional has mastered a skill to the necessary standard, other skills are likely to have come to the fore. For instance, CIPD research (2011) suggests that in addition to the skills and behaviours defined in the CIPD Profession Map, HR professionals need to gain deeper insight into their organisation and the environment in which it operates. In particular, three overlapping areas of savvy have been identified, at the heart of which HR professionals of the future need to be located:

Figure 1.2 The ingredients of organisational insight

Source: reproduced with permission from CIPD 2011, p8

Specifically, HR professionals need to have deep understanding of:

- the organisation's operations, core values and ingredients of success (*business savvy*)
- the organisation's wider environment including macro-economic and societal factors (*contextual savvy*), and
- the impact of people, culture and leadership on operations and financial performance (*organisational savvy*).

The implication is that HR professionals of the future need to have advanced analysis and synthesis skills in a variety of areas to become savvy in these areas. Moreover, the research indicates that the development of insight will increase the contribution of the HR profession as an invaluable service function to organisations, helping them develop sustainable strategies for future success (see also Chapter 11). The CIPD (2011) also highlights that being an HR professional is an increasingly uncomfortable position in the sense that they are required to challenge the status quo in an organisation and to shape future agendas, often facing opposition by those unwilling to change (see Chapter 12 for details). The implication is that HR professionals need to master more skills such as interpersonal relations, negotiation, decision-making and conflict resolution at a higher level.

 ACTIVITY 1.2

Your profession – present and future

It will be useful for you as (prospective) HR professionals to get some understanding of the current state of the profession – prevalence, role, purpose, skills – and likely changes over the next few years. Imagine how the prevalence, role and purpose of the HR profession as well as your skills as a

professional may change in the near future. What may the implications be on your career and its development? You may want to discuss your analysis with a tutor, work colleague or HR expert. Again, those of you not studying for an HR-specific degree can do the same exercise for your chosen profession.

Thirdly, the environment in which organisations operate as well as their membership and operations is constantly changing. The CIPD (2013c) highlights that increases in international trade, migration and changing demographics have led to a more diverse workforce and that advancements in information and communication technology (ICT) allow for increasingly mobile working. There are major implications on the way in which members of an organisation communicate and interact, in which decisions are made and operations are configured. Traditional means of communication, decision-making and problem-solving may no longer be effective in organisations of the future, and professionals need to find ways of enhancing their existing and developing new skills. A considerable challenge is the increasing cultural diversity in organisations, which we will explore under the next heading.

1.5 DIFFERING LEARNING AND CULTURAL TRADITIONS

Business, trade and education are becoming increasingly culturally diverse, bringing together people from different learning and cultural traditions to work, do business or learn with one another. Managing and leading a diverse workforce has become the norm (CIPD 2005), and therefore learning to work together and embrace cultural diversity is of great consequence to individuals and organisations. Recent research by the British Council and Think Global (2011) highlights the increasing importance of 'cultural agility' over qualifications or degree classification for graduate job-seekers. But let us consider the concepts of culture and diversity in more detail now.

Culture has been defined as 'a set of basic assumptions learned by a group as it solved its problems of external adaptation and internal integration, which … [is] taught to new members as the correct way to perceive, think, and feel in relation to these problems' (Schein 2010, p18). Browaeys and Price (2011, p9) add that 'culture is a structure that … fixes the framework of exchange between the people of this group … [through] adaption, integration, communication and expression'. Hence, culture influences all domains of organisational life, including the way in which individuals build relationships, relate to authority figures, set priorities, make decisions, negotiate and resolve conflict (Harvard Business School 2009). Much of the drivers of such behaviours are tacit, that is, group members take them for granted, and they can also be prejudiced. This then poses problems when individuals from many different nationalities and a wide array of cultural backgrounds come together in a professional or educational setting (Browaeys and Price 2011).

Diversity, in simple terms, is about differences between people (Harvard Business School 2009) in terms of their background, personality, physical appearance, work style, accent, ethnicity, family status, sexual orientation, religion or disability. There has been evidence suggesting that a diverse workforce can improve an organisation's competitiveness, for instance by enhancing customer care, increasing creativity and innovation, recruiting and retaining talented individuals (Özbilgin et al 2008). Similarly, studying in a diverse setting can enhance your learning experience as individuals with differing backgrounds can contribute a different angle to discussion, debate and resolution of problems. Someone starting out their career may learn from someone with work experience about structural, organisational or legislative barriers rendering a creative idea unworkable. Or someone from a privileged background may learn about life's struggles from someone coming from a disadvantaged background, having experienced discrimination or suffering from significant health issues.

However, working and learning in a culturally diverse setting can be difficult and at times confusing for those involved because there are new (albeit not always immediately recognisable) rules to master, stereotypic assumptions to cast aside and old thought patterns to discard. Harvard Business School (2009) highlights that social groups are never homogenous and that, therefore, stereotypes typically describe only part of that group. For example, Germans are generally regarded as punctual, whereas in reality there will be Germans who are persistently late for meetings or other appointments. Similarly, women generally are regarded as bad in mathematics and science, whereas in reality some of the most esteemed scientists have been women (a prime example is Marie Curie, a pioneering researcher in radioactivity). Since stereotypes tend to serve us well in most social situations, it is easy to be guided by them – even though an individual with whom we are working or studying does not conform to that stereotype. It is therefore also important to question the stereotypes we are holding.

The task (and challenge) for managers, therefore, is to create an inclusive environment, which means that managing diversity is valuing each individual for who they are – regardless of any stereotype or prejudice (CIPD 2012b). This should then be translated into equal opportunities for recruitment, development and promotion (Harvard Business School 2009), which is often easier said than done. There have been several high-profile cases in the press over recent years about the wearing of religious symbols. While a Muslim employee was allowed to wear a headscarf with her uniform, a Christian employee was prohibited from wearing a cross pendant at work by British Airways (BBC News 2006). British Airways' argument was that wearing a headscarf was an integral part of being a Muslim, but that wearing a silver cross was not essential for Christians. Others have argued that all or no employees should be allowed to wear religious symbols (such as a headscarf, turban, bangle or cross). The employee in question has now won her appeal to the European Court of Human Rights, and you can read more on the judges' complex reasoning behind the verdict (BBC News 2013).

Let us explore diversity further in an example with which the majority of you will be familiar: a typical British university in which both staff and students represent multiple nationalities, cultures and backgrounds. The British higher education system differs significantly from other systems, particularly in some Asian, African and Middle Eastern countries. Individuals from such backgrounds often face a number of barriers when studying at a British university, including language difficulties, reticence to enter into discussion and reluctance to deal with conflict. However, this creates challenges for culturally diverse learning groups, particularly as in the learner-centred view adopted at British universities group members need to interact with each other as active and engaged learners.

Hence, many programmes of study require students to work in teams that have a mix of ethnicities, genders and/or background to prepare them for an increasingly global workplace (see British Council and Think Global 2011). Acknowledging and exploring cultural difference is therefore essential as we learn and work together in multicultural groups at university and in the workplace. The following case study from our own experience teaching multicultural postgraduate student groups seeks to illuminate some cultural misunderstandings as it offers elements for debate that encourage us to understand those under-the-surface issues.

 EVERYONE'S ENTITLED TO AN OPINION

CASE STUDY 1.1

The case study is about a group of students new to a university studying on a postgraduate programme in international management. The cohort group consists of 20 students with 11 different nationalities and a plethora of religious and cultural backgrounds. They had undergone development in appreciating each other's cultures, which included food, religion, cultural dress, tolerance of different societal norms, and so on. This had all helped to encourage camaraderie and a sense of working together for a common goal. The students had been tasked to complete a project in set groups of five. This type of cultural inclusivity as a learning process had worked very well in previous years.

A new student arrived who joined one of the established groups. This particular group, now six, was made up of two British women (Jennifer and Sylvia), one

Canadian male (John), two Chinese – one man and one woman (Tie and Ping). The newcomer was male and came from the United Arab Emirates (Ali).

Not long after the introduction Ali announced to the group how he liked all things American and intended to go and live there one day. John offered a view of the US from his perspective, which included the advantages and disadvantages of having a porous border and a powerful neighbour. Ping identified Canada as a great place to live as some of her relatives had moved to Toronto and really liked it. Ali was somewhat dismissive and reacted as if he was being challenged, and disagreement grew. Tie had said he should not speak to Ping in such a way. The tutor responded immediately, realising that there was some tension. He sat with the group for about ten minutes, calming down the confused Ping and the equally confused Ali. The tutor reminded them that everyone was entitled to an opinion.

The next day the students were to continue developing their project and had arranged to meet in the coffee bar. Previously the group had split the task into several parts so that the accumulated research could be analysed and evaluated when the group reconvened the following Monday. Jennifer asked Ali if he wouldn't mind researching a particular topic over the weekend as he had not contributed to the project thus far. It was the last piece of work before the report writing commenced.

Ali declined, saying he was going out to a restaurant at the weekend with his uncle. Sylvia, somewhat annoyed, said, 'Well I'm going to the "Big Market" with some friends but it doesn't stop me doing my work for uni.' She continued, 'Why should

we do your work for you, "flash Harry"?' She was referring to Ali's 2ct diamond earring, designer clothes, and so on.

Some cultural issues such as 'the Big Market' (an area in Newcastle-upon-Tyne noted for having several bars and restaurants) and 'flash Harry' (flaunting your possessions) had been explained, and the fact that Ali's uncle lived in London was also clarified. Again, Ali reacted to the challenge with the view that women should not drink liquor and go out at night on their own. The two British women attacked him verbally in a way that he had not encountered. He was shocked and upset, saying that he was only thinking of their safety. Jennifer and Sylvia were furious at being told what they should and should not do. Ping and Tie thought the atmosphere was bad and they were going to ask the tutor if they could move to another group as they did not want to fail in the project assignment. John tried to calm them all down and tried to take some control of the situation.

Questions

1   Consider the cultural issues from each participant's perspective.

2   If you were John, what would you do now?

3   Should the tutor have seen this coming?

4   What role should the tutor take in this scenario?

5   What can you learn from this case for your future career?

6   How does this scenario compare with your current (or potential future) workplace?

Engaging in discussion about diversity or difference can mitigate disadvantage and discrimination. As a learner/individual involved in such a debate you could consider the following:

ACTIVITY 1.3

Reflecting on your background

Think about your life journey to date in a holistic sense, focusing on your family and cultural background, who you are, your route to university and/or employment, and where you believe life will take you in the future. You may find it helpful to take notes.

Now focus more deeply on the following questions and issues:

1   Describe your cultural background – what does it mean to you?

2   In what way has it impacted on your life choices?

3   What were the implications for your learning choices?

4   How many culturally diverse backgrounds are represented in your student group and/or workplace?

5   How much do you really know about those cultures, and how might you investigate them further?

Discuss the questions posed above in a multicultural group where possible – you might be surprised by what you discover!

Harnessing diversity can create a vibrant learning and working environment where difference is celebrated and individuals are respected for who they are (CIPD 2012b). Since we have considered only cultural diversity so far, let us move on to other aspects of diversity such as gender, age, religion, ethnicity, disability and sexual orientation. Canas and Sondak (2012) have identified the following five principles of diversity:

1   Expansive but has boundaries:

   ● Not limited to demographic identities such as skin colour and gender; it can embrace single parenthood and spirituality.
   ● Boundaries ensure that it can be distinguished between what constitutes diversity and what does not.

2   Fluid and dynamic:

   ● Diversity affiliation is continuously being redefined since, according to Litvin (1997), individuals are too complex to be put into clear-cut categories of diversity.
   ● Many people may associate themselves with a range of social category diversity dimensions, such as nationality, religion and disability.
   ● People can move in and out of categories: able-bodied to disabled, single parent to married, someone assumed to be straight to gay.

3   Based on differences as well as similarities:

   ● Multiple demographic characteristics influence group dynamics; they can create division when people align to a particular person or take sides. These fault lines may have a detrimental effect on morale and performance as well as make conflict more probable.
   ● People from diverse cultural backgrounds may see themselves as having similar qualities, such as being married, having children, belonging to the same religion.

4   Rooted in non-essentialist thought:

   ● In diversity debates there is a tendency to generalise the wants, needs and expectations of different individuals (for example all women want to have children, people with a disability are less effective at work). Canas and Sondak (2012) suggest that this may not be conducive to understanding diversity, and the CIPD (2012b) advocates that individuals and their fundamental characteristics are valued.

5   Directly related to how one approaches work and learning:

- This means that personal characteristics influence how individuals perceive and perform in their job as well as their capacity to learn. For example, someone who was brought up to believe that they have little talent is less likely to apply for a promotion.
- Understanding one's background and personal characteristics enables reflection on interaction with others both in and outside of a work or learning group, particularly how one can contribute to the group.
- Organisations that believe in managing through diversity will continually re-evaluate their culture, mission, strategies and business practices to maintain a positive approach towards diversity (CIPD 2012b).

ACTIVITY 1.4

Reflecting on diversity

Building on Activity 1.3 and drawing on what you have learned about potential diversity categories, consider how you would describe yourself in terms of gender, age, religion, ethnicity, disability and sexual orientation. Reflect on:

- whether all such characteristics influence your professional behaviour
- how easy (or difficult, uncomfortable, complicated) this exercise was for you and why this may have been the case

- how someone from a different background may interpret what you have written (that is, what stereotypic reactions to your diversity profile there may be)
- the potential disadvantages of categorising an individual in such a way at the workplace when it comes to managing diversity.

1.6 CONTINUING PROFESSIONAL DEVELOPMENT

Maintaining expert knowledge and competence through continuing professional development (CPD) has become a key requirement for most professionals (CIPD 2012c). CPD can help professionals keep up to date with changes to their profession, boost confidence, strengthen professional credibility and prepare for greater responsibilities, thereby increasing job satisfaction and accelerating career development (CIPD 2013f, p2). As highlighted earlier in this chapter, despite widespread support from employers and professional bodies it is *your* responsibility to engage in CPD; it is a self-managed process. Tools such as the CIPD Profession Map and online CPD logs can help you with this.

You may wonder why CPD has come to so much prominence over recent years. The CIPD (2013d) argues that CPD has benefits for both individuals in terms of career development and organisations in terms of increased productivity, efficiency and effectiveness of staff. The knowledge, experience and expertise created through continuing professional development are invaluable to an organisation because they are contextual and practical – organisations can put them to instant use. Specifically, these benefits can be summarised as shown in Table 1.1.

Table 1.1 Benefits of CPD

Benefits to individual	Benefits to organisation
Build confidence and credibility as a professional	Helps maximise staff potential by linking learning to actions and theory to practice
Earn more by showcasing your abilities and achievements	Helps HR professionals to link objectives more closely to business needs
Achieve your career goals by focusing your training and development where it is most effective	Promotes staff development, improves morale and motivation
Cope positively with change by constantly updating your skills	Adds value to the organisation as staff will consciously apply their learning to their routines
Be more productive and efficient through reflection on your learning and identification of any gaps in your knowledge, skills and experience	Supports performance appraisals

Source: based on CIPD 2013d

It is therefore not surprising that many twenty-first-century organisations support their employees' continuing professional development through organising training courses, operating mentoring schemes, allowing time off for formal study or networking, supporting their employees' formal studies or coaching financially – all of which comes at a cost. Many organisations have found, however, that increases in effectiveness and productivity coupled with improved staff satisfaction and morale outweigh their investments in CPD.

So what is CPD then? CPD is often associated with formal study, vocational training, mentoring and coaching, membership in professional bodies as well as attending lectures, workshops, professional conferences or other networking events. But more informal learning – including your reflections on professional practice, a chat to a colleague or doing a new task for the first time – may also enhance your professional knowledge and skills. You may therefore find it useful to categorise different CPD measures according to the following two dimensions – formal versus informal learning, and group versus individual learning – which have been summarised in Table 1.2.

Table 1.2 Learning situations

	Formal training and learning	Informal training and learning
Individual, cognitive learning	Formal training	Informal learning
Group, communicative learning	Learning in the classroom or other groups	Situated and reflective learning

Source: Gourlay and Bailey, as cited in Stirk and Reissner 2010, p399

Formal training might include studying on an HR-specific course while *informal learning* can take place through reflective practice. *Learning in groups* can include class discussion or group work on a programme of study or, at the workplace, it might involve an experienced colleague showing a junior colleague how a procedure works. Finally, *situated and reflective learning* can take place in conjunction with a mentor or coach (see also

Chapter 7). Despite such a variety of CPD measures at our disposal, much of what we typically put into our CPD record tends to be individual and formal learning, that is, training, often off the job. While this is undoubtedly an important part of CPD, we may learn more though informal and group learning. The difficulty with this type of learning is that we often do not have evidence for it as there are no attendance certificates or the like to demonstrate that we have learned.

Hence, it might be useful to think about CPD as 'assessing the benefit of **what you have learned** and how you will use what you have learned in your day-to-day practice' (CIPD 2012d, p2, emphasis original), irrespective of the setting (formal/informal, individual/group) in which learning took place. Many CPD logs – whether traditional paper or online versions – will provide space for both formal and informal learning.

Learning journals (sometimes also called learning logs), learning plans and personal development plans seek to make you more aware of your learning and development, help you track your learning and develop as a professional. They come in a number of formats, such as structures (as shown in Examples 1.1–1.3 below) or make use of more creative means such as diary entries, letters, blogs, and so on. For professional purposes, that is, to demonstrate to your current or a future employer what you have learned as part of your postgraduate studies, you may want to choose a more structured (and therefore professional-looking) format in the style of the following examples. The CIPD (2013f) provides online CPD resources to its members, which are structured but allow for customisation.

Example 1.1: Individual development plan

A development plan or log can be quite simple and to the point; it therefore does not have to be a daunting task to fill it in. The following log is such an example which is related to a particular concern or behaviour the individual, in this instance, wants to develop and/or change. It relates to feelings of pressure or stress at work (for further reading on the subject matter see Chapter 4).

Date	Purpose	Action required	Review
Record the instances of adding to your log. You will be able to assess how long it took to change or learn a new skill or behaviour.	*What aspects of stress or pressure would you be interested in managing more successfully?* This section will change depending on the behaviour you wish to alter.	*What action will you take?* Set out your criteria for development. Use C-SMART objectives (see Chapter 6).	State the progress you are making at timely intervals. Do you need to make changes or adjustments to your plan?
Evaluate your development. Produce a summary of your main achievements.			

This type of development plan can be accumulative; it can help you assess your progress over a period of time as well as being a document in its own right, for instance for a performance appraisal. People often make plans to achieve their goals, but as we have seen above, they must have a purpose, contain objectives and have a mechanism for prioritising and reviewing. If a plan proves unrealistic and does not match your preferred way of working, a review of the plan may be necessary. Activity 1.5 gives some suggestions for such a review process.

ACTIVITY 1.5

Review your learning plan

Taking inspiration from the example provided above, draw up a learning plan and scrutinise it by answering the following questions:

1 Do you have goals that you wish to achieve next week/month/year?

2 Do you have an unambiguous view of the priorities?

3 Do you have specific objectives?

4 Does your plan need adjustment or are you on course to achieve your stated goals?

5 When will you revisit your plan?

Such a strategic and thoughtful approach to your learning – whether in formal study or at the workplace – can help you to focus your continuing professional development and career management on what really matters to you.

Example 1.1 focused on planning individual learning; you may have to keep a group learning log to plan and record any collective learning. Example 1.2 (adapted from Bee and Bee 1977) is a straightforward log that can be used for tracking ongoing developmental learning.

Example 1.2: Group learning log (adapted from Bee and Bee 1977)

Group learning log				
Instructions: Your group should complete this log on a weekly basis, using additional sheets as required.				
Date	Background to activity/ experience	What happened?	Reflections on what your group learned	How will you apply the learning?

This group learning log will help you to track your learning as a group but it can also highlight individual group members' learning.

Personal development plans, which are quite similar in style and purpose to development plans and logs, are a versatile tool in an individual's appraisal. They can be included as an assessment for a postgraduate programme of study or form part of one's CPD process. Example 1.3 displays such a personal development plan; its composition can be adapted to the purpose for which it is used.

Example 1.3: Personal learning and development plan

Personal learning and development plan		Date:
Name:		
Overall aims	Actions required	Assessment or evaluation criteria
Main aims		
Explain the competence or business/leadership skill you intend to develop.		
Objectives (eg C-SMART)	Resources (can be fiscal or people-orientated)	Evidence

Overall comment on the process and your major achievements		
Learning/development plan agreed with: (eg line manager/tutor/self)	Commencement date:	Target end date:

We recommend that you keep track of your learning throughout your programme of study in some form of learning journal or log as this will help you to provide evidence of your learning, thereby helping you make a strong case for employment or promotion. At the end of each chapter there is a section called 'Pause for Thought', in which you are encouraged to identify what you have learned from studying the respective chapter and to consider the potential impact that this learning is likely to have on your studies and career (please refer to Section 1.7 for details).

Those of you who are in work are encouraged (or perhaps even required) to keep a CPD log that captures your learning and development needs arising from your studies or work. An effective CPD log consists of two parts (CIPD 2010): firstly, the *CPD record*, that is, a review of your learning in the past review period (usually one year) and, secondly, a *plan* of further CPD activities for the following review period (usually one year). In a good CPD log, these two parts will complement each other. There are many formats that a CPD log can take and you can find recommended templates for different professionals on the CIPD website (2013g). We have included some generic examples of CPD logs here, which can be adapted by those of you not studying for an HR-specific degree (see Examples 1.4–1.5 below).

Example 1.4: CPD template (CIPD 2010)

Part 1: Reflecting back
Q1 What do you consider were the three most important things (planned or unplanned) that you learned last year? Please also briefly describe how they were learned.
1
2
3
Q2 Please summarise the value you've added to your organisation/clients/customers over the last 12 months through your professional development.
Q3 What have been the tangible outcomes of your professional development over the last 12 months and what aspects of your work have changed as a result? Please give a brief explanation of why you've chosen to comment on these specific activities.
Q4 Who else has gained from your professional development and how?
Part 2: Moving forward
Q1 How do you identify your learning and professional development needs?
Q2 What are the three main areas or topics you wish to develop in the next 12 months and how will you achieve these?
1
2

3
Q3 What are the key differences that you plan to make to your role/organisation/clients/customers in the next 12 months?
Q4 When will you next review your professional development needs?

Example 1.5: CPD record (CIPD 2010)

Development record			
NAME:		MEMBERSHIP NUMBER:	
COVERING THE PERIOD FROM:		TO:	

This record sheet is for your guidance only – you may present your development record in any other format.

Key dates	What did you do?	Why?	What did you learn from this?	How have/will you use this? Any further action?

Development plan			
NAME:		MEMBERSHIP NUMBER:	
COVERING THE PERIOD FROM:		TO:	

Planned outcome

Where do I want to be by the end of this period? What do I want to be doing? (This may be evolutionary or 'more of the same'.)

What do I want/need to learn?	What will I do to achieve this?	What resources or support will I need?	What will my success criteria be?	Target dates for review and completion

The key to successful CPD is to embed it in your daily practice by making it a habit. Use a log and record format (hard copy/online, structured/unstructured) that works for you, unless it has been prescribed for you. All the examples of development plans/logs provided above serve the same purposes: helping you (1) keep a record of your learning and professional development, (2) evaluate your current learning and professional development, and (3) plan your further learning and professional development. They will be structured in such a way that you need to consider your learning and professional development (past, present and future) in detail and to provide evidence for it.

ACTIVITY 1.6

Getting started with CPD – for professionals

This activity is targeted at professionals in HR or a cognate area who have already engaged in CPD. If you are a prospective professional who is new to the profession, please do Activity 1.7 instead.

Take a copy of your CPD documents (plan and/or log) and answer the following questions.

1   Why have you kept these documents? Have you done it on your own accord or is it a requirement by your employer and/or a professional body?

2   Has there been an underlying theme to your continuing professional development or does it resemble something of a patchwork?

3   Does it draw on a variety of CPD measures or do you have a preference for only a few?

4   Are there any gaps? If so, what may be the reasons and what can you do about it?

Then consider whether your CPD documents actually help you both record and plan your learning and professional development and whether you are working towards a particular career goal (for example a generalist or specialist role, a career in the public or the private sector). What can you do differently to reach your goal more quickly?

ACTIVITY 1.7

Getting started with CPD – for prospective professionals

This activity is targeted at prospective professionals who are new to the profession. If you have already worked in HR or a cognate area and engaged in CPD, please do Activity 1.6 instead.

Collect a number of CPD documents (plan and/or log) and see which one would work well for you. You may want to create your own template, having taken inspiration from your collection. A good starting point may be the CIPD template specifically designed for students (CIPD 2013g).

Start populating your CPD plan, considering:

- what you need to learn and for what purpose
- what you need to do to achieve your learning goal
- what resources and/or support you may need and from whom
- how you will know that you have achieved your learning goal.

As you engage in your studies, you may want to start populating your CPD record, too, considering:

- What did you do and why?
- What did you learn?
- How will you use what you have learned?

1.7 CPD AND REFLECTIVE PRACTICE

The notion of reflection is intrinsically linked with CPD and features prominently in many CPD guides (for example CIPD 2012d). Reflection is fruitfully described as 'becoming aware of an experience, representing it and integrating it into what we already know and believe; it is also involved in reorganising our learning and in developing new understandings' (Routledge and Carmichael 2007, p105). Reflection involves stepping back in regular intervals to consider one's experiences in terms of actions, feelings and beliefs to understand them more clearly (drawing on Raelin 2001, p11). It also allows

insights into one's relationships with others (family members, friends, colleagues, bu
partners) and with one's wider organisational and societal context.

Reflection has been an integral part of learning theory for decades. A good example is
one of the best known learning theories, Kolb's (1984) learning cycle, in which reflection
constitutes one main element of the learning process alongside actual experience, rational
conclusions and emotional insights, and acting on experience. Key assumptions include
(as summarised by Vince 1998) that (1) learning is grounded in the learner's experience,
(2) that it involves interaction with others, and (3) that it is a means by which individuals
adapt to their environment. Hence, through reflection individuals can transform everyday
experiences into meaningful learning (Boud et al 1985), which can then become the basis
for further personal and professional development.

In a work context, reflection encourages professionals to take responsibility for their
growth and development, to identify the benefits of a professional development measure,
to see the value in different learning experiences, and to learn how to learn (CIPD 2013e).
Considering how learning can best be achieved can make good use of the plethora of CPD
measures available to you rather than relying heavily on one particular type. Whatever
development measure, the trick is to formalise seemingly everyday experiences so that you
can draw on them in the future. This may sound difficult, but it can be achieved by
answering a few straightforward questions (CIPD 2013e, p4) on a regular basis:

1   What have I got out of this event or experience?

2   How did I learn?

3   How will I apply it in practice?

By engaging in reflection in such a way, you will realise what skills you possess and at
what level. You can compile evidence for these skills (for example from assignments from
university or the workplace) and in that way strengthen a job application, performance
appraisal or promotion request. In short, reflection will give you the opportunity to get to
know yourself better (see also Chapter 5) and take a strategic position towards your
further career development because it is learning in action through action and reflection.
Hence, to get the most out of reflecting on your learning and its application in practice,
you could consider your longer-term career development. Specifically, you could ask
yourself (CIPD 2013e, p4):

1   What do I want to achieve?

2   What do I need to learn to achieve this?

3   How do I learn best?

By engaging with such questions and tailoring any professional development to your
ambitions, you will be able to take more control of your career (see Section 1.9 and
Chapter 18, Part 2 for details on career development). For instance, in a performance
appraisal your development needs should be discussed, and by having clear suggestions of
what kind of development you may need you can encourage your line manager to support
it. If you do not have regular performance appraisals, you can make a case for financial
support for a particular type of development instead.

You may wonder what reflection looks like in practice. In his work on the *Reflective
Practitioner*, Donald Schön (1983) revealed that practitioners will observe the processes
and benefits of their learning, formulate small-scale hypotheses, test these through further
observation (and perhaps even experimentation), and in that way create new knowledge
and skills about their behaviour and routines at work. Becoming a reflective practitioner

involves the development and integration of the following values into daily practice (drawing on Hartog 2002):

- the ability to listen and learning to hear what colleagues and subordinates are saying
- caring for subordinates and peers, perceiving them as whole individuals and supporting their learning and development
- integrating reflective practice into our daily routines that allows us to interpret what is going on at the present moment in a thoughtful manner
- adopting a critical stance to challenge the status quo and develop professional and managerial practice.

Hence, reflection will allow you to assess and, where appropriate, adapt your thinking and behaviour towards your subordinates and peers and in that way improve your professional practice (Hartog 2002). In Higgins' (2013, p1) eloquent words, such a 'process of reflecting for, in and on action, makes it possible to change our current understanding of action by framing the issue or encounter it in a different or novel way, or by improvising on new ways to solve the issue at hand'.

However, reflection is not always welcome in business environments in which busyness and action are much valued (Routledge and Carmichael 2007). Professionals with overflowing diaries may wonder about the benefits of stepping back and thinking about what is happening – if they can make time for it in the first place. Indeed, in some cultures and organisations those individuals who regularly take time for reflection may be perceived as idle because, on the one hand, the benefits of reflective learning are often difficult to assess without a mindset that is tuned into the subtleties of human learning and, on the other hand, the absence of reflective learning is often not obvious.

Yet, reflection is something that most (if not all) of us do all the time, albeit subconsciously. Have you have ever thought 'I am not happy with this, I'm doing it differently next time'? Yes? Then you have reflected on a situation, your experiences and behaviours. If you then actually did do things differently next time, you have learned reflectively as not only your thinking changed ('this is a better way of doing things in this situation') but also your behaviour (having actually done things differently). Hence, reflective practice is not a somewhat 'woolly' and unhelpful activity that wastes your time, regardless of how full your diary is (see also Bolton 2010). Instead, it is something that you already know and practise regularly; it is an essential part of human experience, learning and development.

 ACTIVITY 1.8

Reflecting on experience

Take a few moments to think about recent examples in which you have changed your thinking about a particular situation as well as your behaviour. Try to describe in as much detail as you can the situation in which this happened, what triggered your reflections (and a subsequent change in behaviour), and what effect this had on you and others.

You may also want to consider whether someone else has had any input into this process (for example, a colleague, manager, mentor, family member or friend), how this input came about (for example, as part of a conversation or you seeking their advice) and to what extent their input has shaped your decision. Can you identify a pattern here?

Most of your examples in Activity 1.8 are probably related to your ability to do something, that is, skills in relation to your studies, professional practice and/or interaction with others. Hence, because of its practical, experiential nature, reflection is particularly valuable in the development and assessment of skills (Moon 2004). Through reflection, you can identify the skills that need further development, outline discreet action and, once put into practice, assess the development of the skills in question. But reflection also allows you to understand the relationship between your emotions, cognition and action (Ghaye 2011), thereby helping you consider yourself and your professional practice in a more holistic fashion.

Hence, reflective learning is about reviewing, evaluating and where necessary adapting one's behaviour in a particular situation, making sense of this experience (Moon 2004). It works by making unplanned, emergent and experiential learning explicit (Bourner 2003) by evaluating and drawing conclusions from it (Cottrell 2003). Reflective learning involves thinking about *what* you are learning (content), *why* you are learning (rationale), and *how* you are learning (means). Importantly, reflective learning needs to go beyond description and instead focus on how you make use of your learning in your studies and/or professional practice (what Rolfe et al (2001) call the *so what* question), how you can maximise your strengths and address your key weaknesses, and how these will support or hinder your practice (what Rolfe et al (2001) call the *now what* question). Reflective learning therefore allows you to focus on your experiences and their implications on you as a person, your further development and future career.

ACTIVITY 1.9

Developing reflective practice

Select one of the examples that you identified in Activity 1.8 and consider the following questions:

1   What are you learning?

2   Why are you learning?

3   How are you learning?

4   What impact does your learning have on your professional practice?

5   How can you develop your professional practice further?

Write down your answers. You may choose to discuss them with a colleague, mentor or in a small study group.

Moreover, reflective learning allows you 'to check out your personal and professional congruence' (Megginson and Whitaker 2007, p37), that is, the extent to which who you are and what you do professionally are in tune. If you find the two elements to be congruent, you can continue to develop both your professional practice and your professional identity along the chosen track (see Chapter 5 for details). If you find, however, that the two elements are incongruent, you can explore alternative career paths, for instance with a career adviser or a coach. The earlier you realise that you are on the wrong track, the earlier you can make the necessary adjustments.

Reflective writing is a powerful means to aid professional development and practice through reflection (Hubbs and Brand 2005). Jennifer Moon (2004, p187) describes reflective writing 'as a melting pot into which you put a number of thoughts, feelings, other forms of awareness, and perhaps new information'. It is a way to express in an unstructured manner the out-of-the-ordinary things happening at work and in your life more generally with a quest to 'sort them out' (ibid).

There is no one best tool of engaging in reflective writing, although it is widely recommended that a log, diary or journal be used over a sustained period of time. Bolton (2010) explains that a log is simply a record of events, while a diary captures 'stories of happenings, hopes and fears, memories, thoughts, ideas, and all attendant feelings. They also contain creative material: draft of poems, stories, plays or dialogues, doodles and sketches' (pp127–8). The learning journal sits somewhere between the log and the diary; it records experiences and associated thoughts and feelings (ibid) and allows insights into the issues an individual is grappling with at a particular point in time (Hubbs and Brand 2005).

Reflective journal writing allows the individual to record and keep track of their experiences, thoughts and feelings over time, for instance over the course of a programme of study or between performance appraisals at work. They can go back over their reflective journal, identify patterns of interaction, and experiment with new behaviours and attitudes where appropriate. In particular, learning journals help facilitate learning, skills-building and professional development more generally in the following areas (Moon 2006):

- developing critical thinking
- allowing self-expression
- increasing ownership of learning
- enhancing problem-solving skills
- fostering communication and creative interaction.

Hence, reflective writing can help raise self-awareness and allow individuals to explore issues in their studies, at work or in other domains of their lives (Bolton 2010). It thereby allows you to assess and develop important skills for continuing and sustained professional development. The first step in reflective journal writing is to *record your experience* by describing a situation in as much detail as you can. You may want to write down everything you can remember, uninterrupted, for a particular amount of time. It may be helpful to give a title to capture what you have written.

The second step is to *question the experience* that you have recorded. Questions could include the following: why did you select the experience that you have recorded? What might be missing from your record? What did you think and feel then and how are you thinking and feeling about the experience now? What are your assumptions that influence your experience and the record?

The third step is to *rewrite the experience* in story form and from a third party's point of view. If the situation involved other people, you may want to rewrite the experience from their viewpoint. Alternatively, you may want to choose an omniscient observer. If you are a keen writer, you may want to limit the time available to focus your writing on what really matters at a particular point in time.

The fourth step is to *question the story* that you wrote in the previous step. Questions could include the following: why did you write the story in the way you did? What meaning do any metaphors or symbols have? What might be missing from the story? What are your assumptions that have influenced the story?

The fifth step is to *read the story to yourself* – ideally out loud – to help you become aware of its potential meanings and significance. Try to respond to what you have written, particularly anything that is surprising or that you find difficult. Ask yourself where this exercise has taken you. What patterns of behaviour can you identify? What does the language you use tell you about yourself and your interaction with others? Where does this lead you?

You may also want to consider working with a peer with whom you are comfortable sharing your reflections. Particularly if you lack the discipline of reflecting regularly or if you tend to struggle with answering the reflective questions outlined above, a peer can often give you fresh insights into what might be going on. If you decide to work with someone else, you need to ensure that they are positive about the process and supportive of your professional development (Routledge and Carmichael 2007).

You can follow such an in-depth process for all reflective journal writing, regardless of whether you are using it for educational purposes or for professional development. In educational settings, however, you may be given a predetermined structure (often in the form of exercises or questions, Moon 2006) to adhere to. If you are able to determine the structure of your learning journal, you may want to consider alternative writing formats (Routledge and Carmichael 2007). For instance, you may want to use commentary to reflect any internal dialogue that you may be having with yourself, you may want to use poetry to capture a particularly moving experience, or you may want to write a letter to someone explaining how you feel (and then destroy the letter rather than sending it). The use of blogs has also become popular for reflective journal writing in educational settings (Moon 2006), and many virtual learning environments have a blog function that allows you to record your experiences with more privacy than an open blog would allow.

It is important to be mindful, however, of the tensions associated with privacy in reflective journal writing – both for the 'learner' (student, coachee, mentee) and for the 'educator' (teacher, lecturer, coach, mentor). Ghaye (2011) has identified two such tensions. The first refers to the *content of reflection*, which by definition is very personal. The writer may find it difficult to strike the right balance between being honest and accurate and not being unfair or perhaps even offensive when writing about others. The second tension refers to *access to the reflection*. On the one hand, the writer has a right to privacy when divulging personal experience, but on the other an educator may need to know what has been written. In practice, the process of editing a reflective account (for instance by following a critical-reflective process as outlined above or by using a blog) will help the writer find the right balance between these tensions, meeting both their own needs and those of the educator.

In summary, reflective learning is a powerful tool for learning and personal/ professional development. Keeping a reflective learning journal does not have to be onerous; simply spending a few minutes every day or every week recording your learning and other experiences at the workplace can be a powerful exercise to realise the amount of learning you have achieved over a period of time. That said, the more you engage with your reflections, the better will be your outcomes for your professional development and practice, and this is the reason why we have included a large number of reflective exercises throughout this book. Many students find reflection difficult at first, but after one semester they begin to appreciate the value of having a record of their experience and of being able to trace their learning and development over time. We do encourage you to engage with reflection if you are not doing so already. Happy reflecting!

1.8 PRACTICAL ADVICE IN DEVELOPING EVIDENCE OF COMPETENCE FOR PERSONAL DEVELOPMENT

It can often be tricky to provide evidence for learning from informal CPD measures, and we have therefore devoted a section of this book to this. Before we embark on giving you practical advice on how to develop and gather evidence for personal and professional development purposes, however, let us make explicit the assumptions that we have made when writing this section. We have assumed that you:

- have embarked on a postgraduate programme of study or a formal CPD measure
- are reading this book to develop your current professional and/or managerial skills
- have considered your current level of competence and achievement in specific areas of your current or future work
- will need to produce a learning diary or log and possibly conduct a developmental portfolio
- will be engaged in CPD.

Tracking your professional development will require you to provide evidence for it, but it is often unclear what counts as evidence in your line of work, how you can gather it and how it can provide proof that the learning activity has been undertaken or achieved in a way that meets the key measurement or assessment criteria. Such a record of your learning can be used in a workplace context and/or for CPD purposes, which implies that your goal should be to display a range of knowledge and skills that demonstrate that you are able to meet the required level of competence. Acceptable evidence usually includes:

- documentary evidence of your work
- your own (reflective) account of your learning
- an independent authentication of your ability from mentors/peers or others involved in work with you or affected by your actions.

It is useful to break down evidence in two categories: *inherent* and *exclusive*. Inherent evidence originates in the work that you will already be involved in. For example, the learning log that we encourage you to keep while studying for this module is a powerful example of what you have learned. In contrast, exclusive evidence is specific to you and has some special meaning. It refers, for instance, to an event or development measure in which you have taken part and in which you have exhibited a particular competence; for example, some of our students attend a CIPD conference, and their ability to network may be reflected in how successful they have engaged with practitioners there.

One key purpose of keeping a learning or development log is to achieve and demonstrate competency. Sometimes you will find that a distinction is drawn between competence and competency. The CIPD (2012e) puts this as follows: '"Competency" or "competencies" may be defined as the behaviours (and, where appropriate, technical attributes) that individuals must have, or must acquire, to perform effectively at work', while '"competence" or "competences" are broader concepts that encompass demonstrable performance outputs as well as behaviour inputs, and may relate to a system of minimum standards required for effective performance at work'. Therefore achieving competence is a transitional process towards competency.

Organisations use competencies to indicate to an employee the performance level they seek. Competencies, therefore, offer a marker to the individual of the behaviours and skills that are valued, appreciated or even rewarded in the organisation, articulating not only the professional's efforts but also the way in which the required behaviours and skills are manifested (CIPD 2012e). Therefore, accumulating competence in a range of skills will enhance your overall development. Evidence of competence is gathered through (1) personal reflections, (2) products such as letters, emails and reports that you have created, and (3) statements confirming your competence from independent sources. Let us look at these in more detail.

As outlined in Section 1.5 above, reflection is a key part in learning and gathering evidence for competence and competency. Personal reflections are about the things that you have done, whether it worked or whether further action is required, and consequently to demonstrate what you would do differently, if anything. It can also establish your understanding and knowledge. Personal reflection in an ongoing learning diary can be a useful source of evidence for CPD purposes.

Evidence to demonstrate competency can also include letters, emails, reports, budgets, surveys, plans, notes, very brief and well-chosen audio and visual recordings of you in operation, minutes of meetings and so on. The main points to remember are that items of evidence must be of your own work and must be chosen selectively to demonstrate the learning outcome or the criteria that have been met. Some roles or professions may be more suited to different types of such evidence.

Finally, evidence can be provided by a third party, such as through a testimony or personal report from a line manager or client. Such evidence should reinforce that what you have done is experienced by others exactly as you have claimed. This information should come from someone who is able to comment critically and directly on your competence and/or behaviour. This may be your line manager, colleagues in your own and other departments, staff you work with or managers in other departments. From a student's perspective it could be a tutor, peer or students of another discipline. In any case, witness testimony needs to be written and explicit: 'I have always found Carla Conrad to be a very efficient manager' may be gratifying to hear but does not provide much in the way of evidence, but 'I can confirm that Carla Conrad led the successful negotiation with ABZ Direct' does.

A cautionary note if you need witnesses to write a statement: they can do this task in any way they want. To assure that what they have written is agreeable (and to minimise the effort they are making on your behalf), it may be sensible to produce a standard letter or questionnaire that can be easily completed; this also allows them to insert whatever comment(s) they wish. A brief note, a signature and a date on each item of evidence is also advisable.

To present a convincing case for your learning and professional development, you will need to provide different types of evidence for the same competency or behaviour. For example, evidence for chairing meetings might include the following:

- an email inviting participants to a meeting
- a briefing paper sent out to participants prior to the meeting and any papers about which you spoke during the meeting
- points copied onto a memory stick produced during the meeting as aide-memoires of summaries of discussion – you may need to arrange for a colleague to conduct this activity
- minutes and a letter of thanks to participants
- an email to your line manager amplifying the minutes and outlining the next steps
- witness testimony from those who participated in the meeting.

This list is not exhaustive, and it is often a good idea to add a personal reflection to explain and analyse the background to the activity, the selection of participants, what you did to ensure that everyone was encouraged to contribute to the process by which a decision was reached, and how you handled any potential or actual unhelpful arguments or digressions. This is only one example and not necessarily appropriate in your unique circumstances. In any case, evidence of your learning should meet the criteria outlined in Table 1.3.

Table 1.3 Types of evidence of learning and professional development

Terms	Explanation of terms
Sufficient	Does the evidence establish the performance criteria you claim in a number of circumstances? If you have not been able to attain enough product evidence, use a personal reflection to outline what you would do or have done in other situations. Is the evidence self-explanatory? It is best to use a personal report to explain any relevant background about the organisation or instances that led to your action, or even to guide the assessor through the documentary evidence.

Terms	Explanation of terms
Authentic	It should be clear beyond doubt that your evidence is your own work. This can be confirmed by witness testimony. Although you would not expect others to comment on product evidence at the level of detail of your personal reports, every claim of competence at elementary level (and ideally at the level of performance criteria) should be independently corroborated by your line manager or another witness. Highlight parts of teamwork which are exclusively yours and/or use a personal report to explain your contribution.
Valid	Does the evidence really relate to the competences you claim? It can sometimes be tempting to load all sorts of claims onto slender evidence and to claim, for example, that a meeting on departmental budgets demonstrates your competence in operating a budget, using resources effectively, maintaining good relations with colleagues, contributing to group discussion and problem-solving, and recording and storing information. Once again, performance criteria and range indicators are a good guide to the appropriateness of evidence against specific elements of competence. Is it worth asking yourself about an item of evidence: 'Who or what does that say more about – existing procedures or me?' If it says more about existing procedures than you, it may need some more thought to identify exactly what it is *you* do which demonstrates that you are competent.
Current	Ideally evidence is derived from what you are currently doing. What you were doing several years ago is not necessarily proof of your ability to do something similar now. Circumstances, technology and skill requirements may have changed in the meantime. You may want to draw on something you have done in the recent past. This is quite acceptable provided you can still produce the level of detail required as evidence and colleagues can recall what took place sufficiently well to corroborate your evidence.

Compiling evidence of knowledge, learning, skill and competence needs to be a deliberate and systematic process, which requires a particular attitude of mind. It can be very frustrating to know, for instance, that you are leading a team that pioneered a new initiative last year but the detail of what you did and how you did it has long since been forgotten. We therefore repeat our encouragement to keep track of your learning and development both in your studies and at the workplace.

ACTIVITY 1.10

Reflection on evidence

Referring to a recent learning or development situation and any evidence for it, answer the following questions:

- Does the evidence show that you understand the principles and concepts as well as that you acted appropriately? Again it is best to use a personal report. This allows reflection upon what you did, or the inclusion of activities from the workbooks or an assignment to demonstrate your knowledge and understanding.
- Query the level of detail: have you included too little or too much?
- Do you need to highlight parts of documents or to provide extracts or summaries to ensure that everything presented is directly relevant to demonstrating competence?

The bulk of your evidence will originate from your current studies or employment. Product evidence is obtainable from documentation that you will generate during the course of your job, such as letters, reports, proposals, budgets, performance appraisals, and so on. It is highly unlikely that every competency can be encompassed by means of inherent evidence from your current job. It is more likely that you will need to show some exclusive evidence to accomplish confirmation of all your competencies, demonstrating that you are interested in your professional and wider career development.

1.9 CAREER DEVELOPMENT

Careers are important to us as individuals because they define us, give us status, enable us to achieve personal fulfilment – or simply allow us to earn enough for a comfortable lifestyle for ourselves and our family (Jackson 2000). Many of us, therefore, aspire to develop and enhance our career in the medium and long term (Ibarra 2003). Career development is the pursuit of improving the disposition of one's working life so that the best use is made of intrinsic knowledge, skills and attributes. It is connected with the individual's capability and the environment that supports their continuing learning and professional development. It does not always imply promotional opportunities, however. Career development can make an individual's current job become more interesting or satisfying and can enable the individual to become more effective in their employment, thereby also benefiting the organisation.

Hence, career development is in the interest of both the professional and their employing organisation. It is therefore desirable to create a situation in which an individual's professional development can be supported in such a way that it aligns with the organisation's needs. Career development mechanisms, therefore, can help prioritise those development measures that will be most valuable for both organisation and employee (Elsdon 2010). As outlined above, however, career development requires an investment by both individuals and organisations, and therefore the resources necessary to aid career development need to be viewed from an organisational and individual point of view (see Table 1.4).

Table 1.4 Career development – a resource perspective

Individual	Organisational
Own talent, skills and abilities	The overall national education system The facility to develop from one professional level to the next
Own personality and professionalism	Human resource/development professionals
Personal motivation	The organisation's employee development and talent management process
Opportunity to take up learning initiatives	Consultants and other types of training and coaching initiatives
Learning aids Books, journals, etc Attending university/college, etc In-house training and development Coaching/mentoring	Financial resources to pay for development plans
The individual's professional body, for example CIPD, ACCA, CMI, CIM, etc	A well-thought-through personal/professional development planning system for each employee

Individual	Organisational
Support of peer group, family and friends	Managers in the organisation securing training and development for their staff

This table is not exhaustive but allows insight into many factors – some of which are beyond the control of individuals and organisations – that need to be in place to allow for career development. Jackson (2000) counsels that careers are being influenced by social changes (such as demographic changes), economic changes (such as economic growth or difficulties), organisational changes (such as changes in ownership or regulation) and technological changes (such as increasing automation of business processes). We could add legal changes to this list, particularly in the light of recent legislation on age discrimination (CIPD 2013h).

It is therefore not surprising that recent decades have seen changing trends to career development. Individuals are increasingly building portfolio careers with lateral job moves to build skills and expertise. There are more opportunities to move from full-time to part-time employment as one's family circumstances change. Individuals may choose to change career – it is not unknown for investment bankers to re-train as teachers or development workers in the poorest parts of the world. From an organisational point of view, work processes are being restructured to have more assignment- or project-based work (for example internal consulting and coaching roles), which also affect a traditional career trajectory (see Jackson 2000).

Let us consider career development in relation to you.

ACTIVITY 1.11

Critical reflection on your career development

Consider your career from the first time you entered employment; analyse the periods or events of critical importance for representing one of the following:

- worst growth period
- best growth period
- static period
- working for a particular company or individual
- meeting a specific individual
- participating in a particular development event
- being at the right place at the right time!

Reflect on how much of this was planned or happened by chance and how much of your career development you intend to leave to chance in the future.

You may want to discuss your findings with a colleague, mentor or study group.

Activity 1.11 may bring to light circumstances beyond our control that may support or hinder our career development; this can be a challenge. While some people happen to be in the right place at the right time or happen to know the right people to progress, others plan to be there and others again may never make it. External influences such as the state of the economy often have a role here. The last few years have witnessed testing economic times across the globe, and it is likely that the following trends will continue for some time to come:

- The labour market will continue to be volatile.
- There will be fewer jobs available.
- There is the potential for organisations to exploit more internal promotional places.

● Individuals seeking employment must show they have the ability to learn, develop and grow in their role or profession.

Crucially, the main lesson for those seeking advancement is that they will have to demonstrate an array of skills and attributes that either shows that they have potential or the requisite abilities that businesses require. This makes the acquisition of skills and a vehicle for evidencing those skills all the more important when seeking employment or promotion in the contemporary labour market. Hence, a strategic and thoughtful approach to your career development that includes development planning and keeping track of your learning and professional development greatly enhances your chances of fulfilling your goals and developing your career. You need to bear in mind that organisations that support their employees' career development rarely do so for altruistic reasons; it makes good business sense to allow individuals access to organisational resources for professional and career development. Specifically, Jackson (2000) argues that organisations not engaging in career development are less likely to attract the best qualified candidates, are more likely to suffer from skills shortages and have higher staff turnover – all of which result in lower productivity and higher recruitment and training costs. In short, the message is that organisations cannot afford not to engage in career development.

1.10 CONCLUSION

Knowledge, skills and continuing professional development are at the top of the twenty-first-century human resources agenda for a good reason: such issues help individuals and organisations to fulfil their potential and set them up for success. This introductory chapter has highlighted the importance for professionals to continuously develop and hone their skills and build their competencies. We have considered an increasingly diverse and turbulent business environment in which individuals and organisations compete for increasingly scarce resources to be spent on the continuing professional development of individuals.

But our discussion has also highlighted the importance of you taking responsibility for your professional development and wider career management, for instance by engaging regularly with CPD measures provided by your employer and/or professional body. While many such measures carry a fee (undoubtedly a luxury for some), others are part of membership in a professional body such as the CIPD or even completely free. The key to successful professional and career development is not necessarily the quantity of measures that you engage in but the quality of reflection, getting a clear idea of how you apply your learning in your daily practice and how it may shape your behaviour at work. We will build on many of the points raised here as we journey through this book and are pleased to have you on board.

PAUSE FOR THOUGHT

Identify at least three things that you have learned by studying this chapter and engaging with the activities. How will your newly acquired knowledge and skills support your continuing professional development? What value do you expect your learning to have for your daily routines and your further career? In what area have you identified a need for further development and how are you planning to fill that gap? Address these issues in your learning journal and/or CPD log. You may also wish to discuss them with a peer, colleague, mentor or coach to aid your further development.

EXPLORE FURTHER

CIPD website. http://www.cipd.co.uk

MOON, J. (1999) *Learning journals: a handbook for academics, students and professional development.* London: Kogan Page.

UNIVERSITY OF KENT CAREERS AND EMPLOYABILITY SERVICE: http://www.kent.ac.uk/careers/sk/skillsmenu.htm

REFERENCES

BANBURY, K. (2013) *Employability: an IB graduate recruiter's perspective [online].* Available at: http://www.heacademy.ac.uk/assets/documents/events/SS_assets/Blog/Lboro_Banbury.pdf [Accessed 17 September 2013].

BBC NEWS. (2006) *Woman to sue BA in necklace row [online].* Available at: http://news.bbc.co.uk/1/hi/england/london/6052608.stm [Accessed 16 September 2013].

BBC NEWS. (2013) *British Airways cross case winner Nadia Eweida 'jubilant' [online].* Available at: http://www.bbc.co.uk/news/uk-england-london-21025710 [Accessed 16 September 2013].

BEE, R. and BEE, F. (1977) *Project management: the people challenge.* London: IPD.

BENNETT, R. (2002) Employers' demands for personal transferable skills in graduates: a content analysis of 1000 job advertisements and an associated empirical study. *Journal of Vocational Education and Training.* Vol 54, No 4. pp457–75.

BOLTON, G. (2010) *Reflective practice: writing and professional development.* 3rd ed. London: Sage.

BOUD, D., KEOGH, R. and WALKER, D. (eds). (1985) *Reflection: turning experience into learning.* London: Kogan Page.

BOURNER, T. (2003) Assessing reflective learning. *Education & Training.* Vol 45, No 5. pp267–72.

BRITISH COUNCIL and THINK GLOBAL. (2011) *The global skills gap: preparing young people for the new global economy [online].* Available at: clients.squareeye.net/ uploads/dea/documents/BusinessPoll_online_TG.pdf [Accessed 1 August 2013].

BROWAEYS, M.-J. and PRICE, R. (2011) *Understanding cross-cultural management.* 2nd ed. Harlow: FT Prentice Hall.

CANAS, K.A. and SONDAK, H. (2012) *Opportunities and challenges of workplace diversity: theory, cases and exercises.* 3rd ed. Upper Saddle River, NJ: Prentice Hall.

CIPD. (2005) *Managing diversity: people make the difference at work – but everyone is different [online].* Available at: http://www.cipd.co.uk/binaries/mandivers0305.pdf [Accessed 1 August 2013].

CIPD. (2010) *Download a CPD template [online].* Available at: http:// www.cipd.co.uk/cpd/guidance/CPDrecordandplan.htm [Accessed 12 March 2010].

CIPD. (2011) *Next generation HR [online].* Available at: http://www.cipd.co.uk/hr-resources/research/next-generation-hr-insight-driven.aspx [Accessed 31 July 2013].

CIPD. (2012a) *HR business partnering,* factsheet revised December 2012 [online]. Available at: http://www.cipd.co.uk/hr-resources/factsheets/hr-business-partnering.aspx [Accessed 31 July 2013].

CIPD. (2012b) *Diversity in the workplace: an overview [online].* Available at: http:// www.cipd.co.uk/hr-resources/factsheets/diversity-workplace-overview.aspx [Accessed 31 July 2013].

CIPD. (2012c) *Continuing professional development policy, V7 [online].* Available at: http://www.cipd.co.uk/NR/rdonlyres/BBD65DDE-1471-4221-8FB6-FD520D1FFFFB/0/ CPD_Policy_v7_Jan_12.pdf [Accessed 30 July 2013].

CIPD. (2012d) *Fresh thinking on CPD: the value of what you do [online].* Available at: http://www.cipd.co.uk/NR/rdonlyres/A8614FFF-2FCA-4708-9DBC-C15A5C1A8743/0/5741_CPD_brochure.pdf [Accessed 31 July 2013].

CIPD. (2012e) *Competency and competency frameworks.* Factsheet [online]. Available at: http://www.cipd.co.uk/subjects/perfmangmt/competnces/comptfrmwk.htm?IsSrchRes=1 [Accessed 2 August 2013].

CIPD. (2012f) *Succession planning.* Factsheet [online]. Available at: http:// www.cipd.co.uk/subjects/hrpract/general/successplan.htm?IsSrchRes=1 [Accessed 2 August 2013].

CIPD. (2013a) *Learn more about My HR Map [online].* Available at: http:// www.cipd.co.uk/cipd-hr-profession/hr-profession-map/learn-more-about-my-hr-map.aspx [Accessed 31 July 2013].

CIPD. (2013b) *Profession map – our professional standards, V2.4 [online].* Available at: http://www.cipd.co.uk/binaries/profession-map-2.4-Oct-2013.pdf [Accessed 29 October 2013].

CIPD. (2013c) *CIPD mega trends: the trends shaping work and working lives [online].* Available at: http://www.youtube.com/watch?v=d6oXfMilLe8 [Accessed 1 August 2013].

CIPD. (2013d) *Benefits of CPD [online].* Available at: http://www.cipd.co.uk/cpd/benefitscpd.htm [Accessed 2 August 2013].

CIPD. (2013e) *What is reflective learning? [online].* Available at: http://www.cipd.co.uk/cpd/aboutcpd/reflectlearn.htm [Accessed 2 August 2013].

CIPD. (2013f) *Guide to CPD online [online].* Available at: http://www.cipd.co.uk/cpdonline/cpdguide.htm [Accessed 2 August 2013].

CIPD. (2013g) *Examples of CPD [online].* Available at: http://www.cipd.co.uk/cpd/guidance/examples/default.htm [Accessed 2 August 2013].

CIPD. (2013h) *Employment law FAQ: what are the forms of age discrimination and who does age discrimination legislation cover? [online].* Available at: http://www.cipd.co.uk/hr-resources/employment-law-faqs/age-discrimination-retirement-forms.aspx [Accessed 14 October 2013].

COTTRELL, S. (2003) *Skills for success: the personal development planning handbook.* Basingstoke: Palgrave Macmillan.

DFES. (2005) *Skills: getting on in business, getting on at work.* Department for Education and Skills. Norwich: HMSO.

DFES. (2007) *Curriculum diversity guide.* In collaboration with NIACE. Norwich: HMSO.

DIUS. (2007) *World class skills: implementing the Leitch review of skills in England.* Department for Innovation, Universities and Skills. Norwich: HMSO.

ELSDON, R. (2010) *Building workforce strength: creating value through workforce and career development.* Santa Barbara, CA: ABC-Clio.

FORBES. (2012) *The ten skills that will get you hired in 2013 [online].* Available at: http://www.forbes.com/sites/meghancasserly/2012/12/10/the-10-skills-that-will-get-you-a-job-in-2013/ [Accessed 31 July 2013].

GHAYE, T. (2011) *Teaching and learning through reflective practice: a practical guide for positive action.* 2nd ed. London: Routledge.

HARTOG, M. (2002) Becoming a reflective practitioner: a continuing professional development strategy through humanistic action research. *Business Ethics – A European Review.* Vol 11, No 3. pp233–43.

HARVARD BUSINESS SCHOOL. (2009) *Managing diversity: promote inclusiveness, handle conflict, tap into value.* Boston, MA: Harvard Business Press.

HIGGINS, D. (2013) Why reflect? Recognising the link between learning and reflection. In: HIGGINS, D. (ed.). *Reflective learning in management, development and education.* Abingdon: Routledge, pp1–2.

HUBBS, D.L. and BRAND, C.F. (2005) The paper mirror: understanding reflective journaling. *Journal of Experiential Education.* Vol 28, No 1. pp60–71.

IBARRA, H. (2003) *Working identity: unconventional strategies for reinventing your career.* Boston, MA: Harvard Business School Press.

JACKSON, T. (2000) *Career development.* London: Institute of Personnel and Development.

JONES, N. and FEAR, N. (1994) Continuing professional development: perspectives for human resource professionals. *Personnel Review.* Vol 23, No 8. pp49–60.

KOLB, D. (1984) *Experiential learning.* Englewood Cliffs, CA: Prentice Hall.

LEITCH REVIEW OF SKILLS. (2006) *Prosperity for all in the global economy: world-class skills.* Final Report, December 2006. Norwich: HMSO.

LITVIN, D.R. (1997) The discourse of diversity: From biology to management. *Organisation.* Vol 4, No 2. pp187–209.

MEGGINSON, D. and WHITAKER, V. (2007) *Continuing professional development.* 2nd ed. London: CIPD.

MEZIROW, J. (1991) *Transformative learning dimensions of adult learning.* San Francisco, CA: Jossey-Bass.

MOON, J.A. (2004) *A handbook of reflective and experiential learning: theory and practice.* Abingdon: Routledge Falmer.

MOON, J.A. (2006) *Learning journals: a handbook for reflective practice and professional development.* 2nd ed. London: Routledge.

NEWCASTLE UNIVERSITY CAREERS AND EMPLOYABILITY SERVICE. (2013) *Developing professional skills and experiences [online].* Available at: http://www.ncl.ac.uk/undergraduate/careers/addingtoyourdegree/#d.en.87271 [Accessed 29 July 2013].

ÖZBILGIN, M., MULHOLLAND, G., TATLI, A. and WORMAN, D. (2008) *Managing diversity and the business case.* London: CIPD.

RAELIN, J.A. (2001) Public reflection as the basis of learning. *Management Learning.* Vol 32, No 1. pp11–30.

RANKIN, N. (2003) Hard as nails? The skills that employers really want. *Competency and Emotional Intelligence.* Vol 10, No 2. pp25–8.

RAWSON, M. (2000) Learning to learn: more than a skill set. *Studies in Higher Education.* Vol 25, No 2. pp225–38.

ROLFE, G., FRESHWATER, D. and JASPER, M. (2001) *Critical reflection for nursing and the helping professions: a user's guide.* Basingstoke: Palgrave Macmillan.

ROUTLEDGE, C. and CARMICHAEL, J. (2007) *Personal development and management skills.* London: CIPD.

SCHEIN, E.H. (2010) *Organisational culture and leadership.* 4th ed. San Francisco, CA: Jossey-Bass.

SCHÖN, D.A. (1983) *The reflective practitioner: how professionals think in action.* London: Temple Smith.

STIRK, S. and REISSNER, S. (2010) Integrated IT skills. In: G. WATSON and S. REISSNER (eds). *Developing skills for business leadership.* London: CIPD, pp396–415.

VINCE, R. (1998) Behind and beyond Kolb's learning cycle. *Journal of Management Education.* Vol 22, No 3. pp304–19.

CHAPTER 2

Essential Skills for Postgraduate Study and Beyond

STEFANIE REISSNER

OVERVIEW

Critical thinking, reading and writing are the pillars of postgraduate study, managerial work and continuing professional development (CPD). While critical in other domains of our life, many of us find it difficult to critique teachers, scholars and other perceived experts at university or at the workplace. In this chapter, you will learn to understand critical methods in an educational context and to apply them to your work at university and beyond. In particular, you will learn the characteristics of an argument so that you can read and write critically, which is the basis for independent thinking, the creation of knowledge and the improvement of professional and managerial practice. Moreover, you will get useful background information on how to study smartly by following a structured process for approaching tasks during your postgraduate study and other CPD measures. You will also learn why your university tutors expect certain things from you and what the rationale behind these, at first glance perhaps strange, expectations is. The information, activities and checklists provided in this chapter will help you build a stronger foundation for your postgraduate study, managerial work and continuing professional development.

LEARNING OUTCOMES

By the end of this chapter, provided you engage with the activities, you should be able to:

- understand the qualitative difference between undergraduate and postgraduate study skills
- understand the importance of critical thinking for postgraduate study and CPD
- apply critical thinking to your studies and beyond
- access high-quality information for study tasks
- analyse and evaluate written and oral materials
- develop and justify original arguments
- apply strategies to improve your writing.

2.1 INTRODUCTION

If you are about to skip this chapter thinking that you have done all of this before, stop! Yes, the content will sound very familiar to you. Yes, you will have had plenty of practice (and perhaps even study skills training) while studying for your degree (what we call 'undergraduate degree' is a British bachelor's degree, which corresponds to Level 6 of the European Qualifications Framework (QAA 2008)). And yes, you may wonder what the point is of doing it again. Let me assure you that this chapter is *not* a repetition of what you may already know, even though its content may look very similar. Postgraduate study (what we call 'postgraduate degree' is a British master's degree, which corresponds to Level 7 of the European Qualifications Framework (QAA 2008)) and continuing professional development (CPD) differ *qualitatively* from undergraduate study, and in order to be successful as a postgraduate student you will need to hone the skills that you may already possess, particularly critical thinking.

Critical thinking is a meta-skill, that is, a skill that subsumes and enhances many other skills that competent professionals possess (Paul and Elder 2002). Metaphorically speaking, if postgraduate study and CPD is a house, critical thinking is its foundation. The application of critical thinking to other aspects of postgraduate study and professional practice, such as reading and writing, are the wall of this house (see Figure 2.1). Your aim as a postgraduate student and smart professional should be to build a strong foundation and solid walls, and this chapter seeks to help you with that.

Figure 2.1 Critical thinking in postgraduate study and CPD

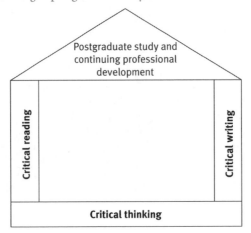

You may not be convinced yet, perhaps recalling your undergraduate student days in which critical thinking may already have featured strongly. Indeed, critical thinking, analysis and synthesis are key skills of any business and management student (QAA 2007a), but they have an even more central role for postgraduate studies (QAA 2007b). The Quality Assurance Agency for Higher Education (QAA) in the United Kingdom, for instance, puts it at the fore of their official subject benchmark statement for master's awards in business and management:

> [Skills] include: being able to think critically and be creative: manage the creative processes in self and others; organise thoughts, analyse, synthesise and critically appraise. This includes the capability to identify assumptions, evaluate statements in terms of evidence, detect false logic or reasoning, identify implicit values, define terms adequately and generalise appropriately. (QAA 2007b, p6)

So, critical thinking and appraisal as well as self-management and the organisation of thought are the official minimum requirements for postgraduate study (QAA 2007b). This means that as a postgraduate student you are expected to work at a more advanced and independent level than as an undergraduate. You will not only manage yourself and your studies more independently and professionally (see also Chapter 5), but you will also gain deeper understanding of the subject matter by scrutinising any materials through a more critical approach.

In addition, by becoming a postgraduate student, you will also become a member of a community of knowledge and scholarly activity in your chosen field. You are expected to think independently and contribute to the knowledge of your field of study by engaging in research and other thought experiments (Hart 1998). You may wonder what this actually means for you as a postgraduate student, so let me try to illustrate this qualitative difference with the following example.

Imagine that you have been given an assignment asking you to analyse the human resource function in a country of your choice. Such an assignment may feature both in undergraduate and postgraduate courses, but your tutor would expect a more advanced approach at postgraduate level, which is outlined in Table 2.1.

Table 2.1 Undergraduate and postgraduate approaches to study

Undergraduate approach	Postgraduate approach
<ul><li>Collecting information about the country (probably from the Internet).</li><li>Using some theory to understand the different aspects of the human resource function.</li><li>Describing your understanding of the human resource function employment practices in the country in question.</li><li>Identifying good and bad practice, possibly followed by some basic recommendations.</li></ul>	<ul><li>Collecting information about the country from more than one reputable source and scrutinising it for quality and veracity.</li><li>Using (and possibly integrating) different theories to understand the different aspects of the human resource function, looking at the situation from different angles and evaluating the theories for their suitability.</li><li>Describing your understanding of the human resource function in the country with the help of theory and with a clear argument and concise language, eliciting the meaning of the situation.</li><li>Identifying and evaluating practices, taking the country's wider context into account, possibly offering some thoughtful recommendations with consideration to the consequences.</li></ul>

Sounds difficult? Well, it may not be easy at first to approach such a seemingly simple task critically. To some extent, this is the point of postgraduate education; in the words of QAA again (2007b, pp1–2):

> The overall objective of master's level business and management degrees is to educate individuals as managers and business specialists, and thus to improve the quality of management as a profession. Master's degrees add value to first degrees by developing in individuals an integrated and critically aware understanding of management and organisations, and assist them to take effective roles within them.

With some practice and guidance to hone your critical skills, however, you should be able to make good progress (Hughes 2000). This chapter will provide you with exercises, activities, tips and tricks to support your learning journey towards becoming a more critical student and professional. Practice is famously the first step to mastery, so let us start off with an activity.

ACTIVITY 2.1

Analysing an assignment

If you have kept any previous assignments from your undergraduate student days, look at them again and analyse your approach in the light of what you have been reading so far. (For those of you who have not kept any assignments, please use the sample assignment 'HRM in Russia' provided on the companion website.) Read through the assignment and ask yourself the following questions:

1   What is the main argument of the assignment?

2   What does the reader learn about the topic under investigation?

3   What kind of sources does this assignment draw on?

4   How much detail is provided about the topic under investigation?

5   What is the structure of this assignment and what kind of language is used?

6   How sensible and original are the conclusions and recommendations?

I recommend you write down your answers and discuss them with a peer or in a small group, if possible. Asking such questions about a written piece of work is the first step to a more critical approach to your studies (Wallace and Wray 2011). Exercises such as this allow you to view your work with the eyes of a third party, so I expect this to be an eye-opening exercise for you. Just a few hints with regard to your answers to these questions:

1   If you cannot identify a main argument, there probably is none. Any assignment should have something to say, and it is your task to work it out before you start writing. There is a range of techniques that can help you identify your argument and present it in an effective manner; see Sections 2.3 and 2.4 below for details.

2   If you cannot answer this question, there is probably not much new or original in the assignment. Again, any assignment should have something in it that the reader can take away – and that does not have to be groundbreaking new knowledge! A well-developed argument can help you elicit the key learning points of your assignment; see Sections 2.3 and 2.4 below for details.

3   If you have used academic journal articles, conference papers, research monographs – well done and keep up the good work! If you have relied heavily on websites and textbooks, Section 2.3.1 will be of utmost importance to you. Postgraduate students are expected to draw on high-quality sources for their work to gain in-depth understanding, and your reading should reflect this.

4   The question really is whether you are looking at the topic under investigation in a superficial manner or whether the analysis digs deeper about what is going on. A superficial assignment will lack numbers and figures as well as specific examples to illustrate the main argument.

5   A good assignment has a clear structure that builds the main argument. It uses formal yet simple language and provides clear definitions of the key terms and issues. See also Chapter 3, Section 3.2 for the characteristics of effective writing.

6   The answer to this question will tell you a lot about the quality of your assignment and is closely linked to points 1, 2 and 4. It is not difficult to conclude that 'organisation A needs to improve their employment practices', but more so to specify what that improvement could look like, how it might be achieved, how much it may cost and what potential downsides are.

I encourage you to engage with Activity 2.1 and identify any areas of the assignment that you are either particularly happy or unhappy with. If you are working with a peer, tutor or in a small group, you may want to compare your notes and discuss any discrepancies of opinion. In that way, you will find out how this piece of work can be approached differently, which will give you new ideas about how to approach and develop future assignments. Activity 2.1 provided you with an opportunity to learn about your own writing (or my early student writing if you used the sample assignment 'HRM in Russia'); you may now want to look ahead to your postgraduate study with Activity 2.2.

ACTIVITY 2.2

Alternative approaches to the assignment

Consider alternative approaches to tackling the assignment that you have analysed in Activity 2.1. Again, it will be beneficial if you do this with a peer, tutor or in a small group. Here are some questions that may help you, and there are no answers apart from the ones that you come up with:

1   What could be done differently?

2   What other points could be raised?

3   What other sources could the assignment draw upon and of what quality are they? (See also Section 2.3.1 below.)

4   What level of detail could be added to the text?

5   How could the assignment be structured differently?

6   What other conclusions could be added?

Following discussion of the answers to these questions, you may wish to rewrite the assignment putting them into practice.

This exercise will allow you to step back from your own knowledge and understanding, to question it and to see it differently. It will also tell you much about your approach and your way of working and will highlight any areas for development. By knowing both your strengths and weaknesses, you can target any intervention to where it is needed most, thereby helping you study more effectively and efficiently and to enhance your capacity as a smart professional. You may also want to consider any assessment feedback in the light of these questions throughout your studies to help you develop your academic practice continuously.

The remainder of this chapter will elaborate on many of the issues raised so far. In particular, Section 2.2 will examine critical methods with a focus on critical thinking in an educational and professional context. It will provide questions commonly used to scrutinise written and oral materials in order to understand the argument comprehensively. Section 2.3 will apply critical thinking skills to reading, including the analysis of texts such as research reports and other academic literature. It will also distinguish between different sources of literature and outline how to access them. Section 2.4 will apply critical thinking skills to writing with a focus on the development and justification of original arguments. The activities and exercises will help you hone your current study skills for postgraduate study and beyond, and checklists will help you along the way.

2.2 BEING CRITICAL – THE MOTHER OF POSTGRADUATE SKILLS

Before delving into critical methods in more detail, I would like you to consider the following excerpt from an advert of a promise of extra income; it is of the kind you sometimes find on the windscreen of your car after a shopping trip. Ask yourself whether you would respond to it or what might prevent you from responding:

> Is your monthly income enough? Supplement your income by £250 – £500+ immediately and develop a passive stream of income of £2,000+ every month with no boss, control over the hours you work, no targets, no fuss and no hassle. We are looking for motivated people aged 18 or over who want freedom and control of their life to take up this fantastic opportunity.

So, what would your reaction be? Would you respond straight away? My guess is that you would not. You would probably either discard it, thinking that this offer sounds too good to be true (which it probably is), or you would scrutinise it by using questions such as 'what kind of work is this?', 'what is the risk?', 'who is behind this?', 'what is in it for them?', 'is this legal?', 'where is the catch?', 'do I have to put funds into this?' to find out more. So, if you would be cautious in this instance, you already have a critical mindset.

Unfortunately, such everyday criticality will not be enough to turn you into a critical student and professional. It does not come naturally to most of us to critique our teachers and other people whom we consider to be experts (Cottrell 2005), probably because most of us were brought up to respect them (meaning: not to question). And there may also be a fear of making a fool of ourselves to critique someone who may know better than us after all. It does not help that most scholars are experts in their fields, knowing more about a particular subject than most other people. Then there is a strong value of academic truthfulness (Wallace and Wray 2011) and quality assurance processes such as peer review to ensure that academic sources meet high standards (Oxford Dictionaries 2013). However, despite academic authors' expert status and stringent quality checks in the publication process, educational and academic materials may contain untrue assumptions, flawed reasoning, conflicting information and may even use evidence selectively to emphasise a particular point (Wallace and Wray 2011). Hence, we ought to be equally sceptical in educational and academic matters as we are in other domains of our life, asking more critical questions such as:

- Why?
- To what extent?
- For what reasons?
- How do we know this is true?
- Is there sufficient evidence for the claim?
- Does the evidence add up?
- What do we not know about the topic?
- Is there any bias?
- How reliable is the source of evidence?
- What are the authors' credentials?
- Is there a hidden agenda?
- What are the implications?

This means that as a postgraduate student you are not only allowed but *expected* to think independently, which includes scrutinising the materials that you are exposed to or working with, such as lecture and seminar content, case studies, papers and presentations – both other people's and your own (Cottrell 2005). This includes asking critical questions about the content of the material, the key terms and definitions, the underlying assumptions, the methods used to gather information, the process and approach of writing as well as the author's credentials. It also means identifying the key elements of an argument, the key learning points, benefits and advantages, but also omissions, pitfalls and disadvantages.

Hence, a critical mindset means that you do not take materials at face value and accept every point that is being made – even though the author of a text might be a well-renowned expert in their field. Neither does a critical mindset mean to reject everything that you are presented with and to be negative, bitter and disgruntled. A critical mindset means being open to accept the valuable points the author makes while being sceptical about content and approach; it 'integrates a controlled sense of scepticism or disbelief about claims, assertions and conclusions ... [and] involves interrogating existing information for strengths, weaknesses and gaps' (Borg 2008, p13). Hence, it is about a reasonable balance between 'uncritical acceptance' and 'overcritical rejection' (Wallace and Wray 2011, p5), which Paul and Elder (2002) call 'fair-mindedness'. 'What a task', you may think, 'how am I ever going to finish reading or writing anything at all?' Yes, it will take you some time to get into the habit of thinking critically, scrutinising and questioning what you are hearing, reading or writing, but it will be worth it for your postgraduate studies and further professional development as the quality of your work will improve considerably. In Bowell and Kemp's (2009, p5) eloquent words:

> If you develop your ability to analyse people's attempts to persuade you so that you can accurately interpret what they are saying or writing and evaluate whether or not they are giving a good argument ... then you can begin to liberate yourself from accepting what others try to persuade you of without knowing whether you actually have a good reason to be persuaded.

In other words, the perceived expert status of academic authors does not mean that you have to be persuaded by everything they say; indeed, many scholars do not agree with one another, and a key task for postgraduate students is to make sense of different perspectives on a subject of study, as you will find out in due course (if you have not done so already). The following activity will help you apply critical thinking to a short text, using the critical questions above.

 ACTIVITY 2.3

Critical analysis of an assignment

Print a copy of the sample assignment 'Is knowledge the only source of competitive advantage today?' provided on the companion website and scrutinise it using the critical questions listed above. Alternatively, you may prefer to work with a text that you have been asked to critically evaluate as part of your studies. You may find it useful to discuss your findings with a peer or in a small group.

Let us delve more deeply into critical methods now, beginning with critical thinking. The term 'critical thinking' has become commonplace in higher education over recent years and is sometimes seen as one of the pillars of the educational trinity of *knowledge, intelligence* and *thinking* (De Bono 1976). It is fruitfully defined as 'the process of hunting assumptions – discovering what assumptions we and others hold, and then checking to see how much sense those assumptions make. ... We do critical thinking so we can take informed actions – actions that are grounded in evidence, can be explained to others, and stand a good chance of achieving the results we desire' (Brookfield 2012, p24). By engaging in critical thinking, we can improve its quality (Fisher 2001).

Hence, critical thinking is a deep, reflective and independent form of thinking that seeks to understand the assumptions and thought structures behind a statement or argument. In other words, critical thinking is about recognising and analysing arguments, which in this context are not disagreements or verbal fights (as often referred to in everyday language), but 'attempts to persuade us – to influence our beliefs and actions – by giving us reasons to believe this or that, or to act in this way or that' (Bowell and Kemp 2009, p1). According to Hughes (2000), critical thinking involves the application of the following three key skills:

1   *interpretive skills* to identify the *meaning* of a statement

2   *verification skills* to determine the *veracity* of a statement

3   *reasoning skills* to analyse the *inferences* made in an argument.

ACTIVITY 2.4

Applying critical thinking skills

Again working with the sample assignment 'Is knowledge the only source of competitive advantage today?' provided on the companion website (or any other text of your liking), identify:

● the meaning of the text (that is, what does the author want to persuade the reader of?)

● the veracity of the text (that is, to what extent can the author be believed and why?)

● the inferences made in the text (that is, what is its conclusion?).

Through the application of such skills, critical thinking can (or should) lead to informed and thoughtful decision-making by constantly challenging the status quo in both the theory of a field of study and its professional practice (Paul and Elder 2002). Critical thinking will give you a more independent mind that is able to appreciate both sides of an argument (Wallace and Wray 2011) and that can engage in thought experiments to create new knowledge. Critical thinking will also help you approach tasks in your studies or at work in a more strategic fashion (Moon 2007). As such, it permeates many other fundamental skills that you will need as a postgraduate student and competent professional, such as advanced reading, writing, evaluation and analysis skills. The process of critical thinking contains the following elements (drawing on Brookfield 1987, Fisher 2001, Cottrell 2005, Wallace and Wray 2011):

● identifying and challenging assumptions, arguments and conclusions
● evaluating evidence that supports any points made and identifying any unsupported claims
● weighing up opposing arguments and taking supporting evidence into account
● reading between the lines and understanding deeper meaning
● recognising any flaws, hidden agendas or mismatch with other authors' arguments
● taking context, purpose and values into account
● matching authors' claims with your own knowledge and experiences
● reflecting on issues in a structured, logical and insightful way
● drawing conclusions based on evidence and reasonable assumptions
● clarifying expressions, claims and meanings
● producing logical arguments
● presenting a viewpoint clearly and with good reasoning
● exploring alternatives in a creative and reflective manner.

So, what does this mean for postgraduate study and continuing professional development? It means to be more sceptical about what you hear, read, say and write in the classroom, in independent study and in the workplace. It means to step back from taken-for-granted knowledge, question it and reflect on it, both in your own work and in the work of others. While it may not come naturally to you to be critical in such contexts, you will be able to hone your critical skills and apply them if you follow the guidance in this chapter and pursue independent study of other, specialist resources. Critical thinking will emancipate you and help you improve your work in postgraduate study and professional practice.

2.3 APPLYING CRITICAL THINKING (1): READING

Reading is an integral part of postgraduate study because you will need to build in-depth understanding of a topic to write about for assessment purposes. However, you will not have time to read everything that sounds interesting or relevant to a particular task or project. Instead, you will need to select appropriate materials for your study, access them strategically through your library, read them critically and evaluate them in the light of any claims made and any evidence presented. This process requires some thought and preparation every time you approach a new task, but it will not be a waste of time. Thorough preparation is famously half the work, and reading for academic purposes is no different. I propose the following six-stage process (see Figure 2.2), through which the remainder of this section will guide you.

Figure 2.2 The process of critical reading

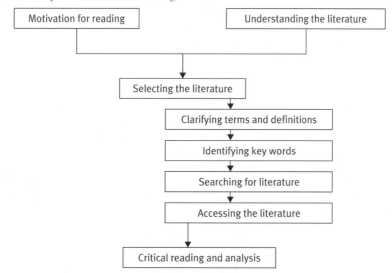

Critical reading can be time-consuming (Cottrell 2003), particularly if you do not have the necessary knowledge and skills to do it effectively and efficiently. The following headings will guide you through this process, giving you background knowledge and introducing you to smart strategies for critical reading as well as the evaluation and analysis of texts.

2.3.1 KNOWING WHY YOU READ

Before opening a book or accessing any other written source, you need to establish your motivation for wanting to read that item. Do you want to find out more about a new subject area? Are you more interested in methods and approaches? Or are you searching for the practical application of knowledge? So the very first question should be 'what do I want to get out of reading this item?' and then bear this question in mind when reading (Cameron 2007). Knowing in what way a text will inform your understanding will determine what sources will be most appropriate, and it is useful to distinguish between the following types of literature:

- *reference literature*, which provides definitions and explanations of terms and concepts
- *theoretical literature*, which develops and reports theoretical advances in a field
- *research literature*, which reports original research to deepen the understanding of a topic of interest or to test theory
- *review literature*, which reviews current theory and research in a field of study
- *methodological literature*, which suggests advances in methods of study
- *practice literature*, which focuses on practical aspects (for example of managerial work)
- *policy literature*, which reviews policies and suggests amendments.

So, if you seek to learn more about a topic, the theoretical, research and review literature is likely to provide you with the necessary information. If you seek to learn more about current practice in your field of study, the practice or perhaps policy literature will be more relevant. If you seek to learn more about approaches to gathering and analysing data in your field of study, the methodological literature will be the place to start. Hence, knowing your motivation for reading will help you search specifically for a particular type of literature. It is smart to target your reading and read different types of literature for different purposes and at different stages of your studies. For instance, an assignment in the early stages of your studies may draw on a limited number of types, while your project or dissertation is likely to draw on most if not all of them. The difficulty is that not all sources belong in only one category; a research paper, for example, will contain sections on theory, methods and original data. A better understanding of different types of literature may help you judge what category an item may belong in and which elements of the item will be most suitable for your purposes.

2.3.2 UNDERSTANDING DIFFERENT SOURCES OF LITERATURE

You will need to know your literature to make the most of your literature search for your postgraduate studies and beyond. You may have worked with many sources of literature before, but what you know from your undergraduate student days or work experience does not necessarily apply to postgraduate study. Table 2.2 outlines the nine most common sources of literature on which you will draw for your studies to find out what is already known in a subject area. Not all sources are of appropriate quality, however, which means that you will have to make an informed judgement about which materials to select for which aspect of your studies.

You need to be aware of the limitations of free materials available on the Internet, which can be accessed through everyday search engines. As a postgraduate student, you are expected to access high-quality sources that are recognised by the experts in your field of study because they have been published following peer review (Oxford Dictionaries 2013). These are usually sources that draw on original theory or research and the content of which can be trusted; examples include reference materials, journal articles and specialist books. You should always be able to identify the author and/or editor of a source as well as their affiliation and ensure that the information is still up to date (Fink 2010); this is a great challenge for web-based materials that do not come from a university's or other trustworthy organisation's website (Wallace and Wray 2011). You also need to bear in mind that *all* sources will, to a greater or lesser extent, reflect the personal choice of the author(s) or editor(s) of what is important enough to be included in that particular item. Nothing that you will read in the social sciences will represent a universal truth or a complete account, and as a postgraduate student you will be encouraged to look for different viewpoints and alternative interpretations and juxtapose them. Your critical thinking skills will help you in this process.

Table 2.2 Common sources of literature, their use and quality

Type	Definition and examples	Use in postgraduate study	Quality of information	Accessibility	Category
Reference materials.	Dictionaries, encyclopaedias.	Good starting point to learn more about a new subject area and its language.	Print and licensed online versions are usually very reliable. Beware of free web-based dictionaries and encyclopaedias (such as Wikipedia) as entries can contain false information.	Reference section of your library or online portals. Also available for purchase in hard copy or e-book version.	Reference literature.
Skills textbooks.	Focus on building transferable skills, usually practical and process-oriented.	Valuable resource for any student and professional to complement their studies and work.	Contents can usually be trusted, but level of detail may vary considerably.	Hard copies in library, increasingly also as e-books.	
Subject textbooks.	Introduction to a field of study through summary of prevalent knowledge in that field.	Useful support for course or module, good starting point for research because of detailed reference list. Generally not suitable for assignments or projects.	Contents can usually be trusted but is only an abbreviated interpretation of knowledge. Level of detail may vary.	Hard copies in library, increasingly also available as e-books.	
Journal articles.	Academic papers reporting on current research and academic debates.	Peer-reviewed academic journal articles should be the staple diet of your reading. Special issues offer debates on a particular topic.	Up-to-date information published after scrutiny by peer-review panels.	Mostly available as e-journals; some older issues may be available in hard copy in the library.	Theoretical, research, review, methodological or practice literature.

Type	Definition and examples	Use in postgraduate study	Quality of information	Accessibility	Category
Readers.	Edited books containing research reports and essays about a particular subject area.	Focused reading of sources that the editors regard as classic or topical sources. Some chapters may have been published as a journal article in their own right.	Content can usually be trusted but is only a selection of knowledge in a particular area.	Hard copies in library, occasionally also available as e-book.	Theoretical, research, review, methodological or practice literature.
Research monographs.	Report on original research with great detail about results and interpretations provided.	Detailed information about a research project.	Content is usually reliable because of peer-review procedures.	Hard copies in library, increasingly also available as e-book.	Research literature.
Conference and working papers.	Report on original research at an early stage of development.	Up-to-date knowledge in concise format and easily accessible.	Content tends to be assessed through peer review before publication.	Through university websites or specialist databases.	Theoretical or research literature.
Government and other reports.	Report on policy or other relevant issues.	Useful for background and contextual knowledge.	Content is usually reliable but may represent a particular political ideology.	Through government departments or the Internet.	Practice literature.
Internet.	Websites, often commercial.	Use Google Scholar (scholar.google.com) to search for academic sources. Otherwise, use websites sparingly, eg for company or industry information. Avoid sites that provide basic subject information and also free encyclopaedias.	Content is freely publishable without any quality procedure, hence it requires careful scrutiny. There are subject gateways, which can help you find suitable online sources; please ask your librarian for details.	Everywhere and at any time.	

The ability to develop and share knowledge within your community of scholars or practitioners depends on organised collections of knowledge – a library. Hence, your university's library will be your closest ally in your studies as a portal from which to access a wide range of high-quality sources. If you have not been to a university library for some time and think about dusty volumes stacked high on shelves – think again. Although the concept of the library as an organised collection of knowledge remains unchanged, the way in which libraries operate has altered significantly over recent years and continues to develop in accordance with technical advances. Modern libraries provide a range of services that are invaluable to twenty-first-century students, particularly at postgraduate level. In addition to the traditional hard-copy books and academic journals, you will find a wide variety of audio-visual, digital and increasingly online resources to support your study, and your library is the portal from which to access these increasingly virtual resources that are not accessible through other means. The best thing you can do at the beginning of your studies is to attend the library tour that your institution is likely to offer and spend some time in the library to familiarise yourself with the facilities and what is on offer. Moreover, Easterby-Smith et al (2002) recommend that you build a good relationship with your subject librarian, who is a highly trained specialist that will select the materials provided in the library on recommendation of teaching staff. Librarians will be able to advise you on the availability of sources and help you get materials from other libraries through a system called 'inter-library loans' (ILL). The following activity will help you get to know your library at bit better.

 ACTIVITY 2.5

Library checklist

Take the following checklist to your university's library and complete it (a blank is provided on the companion website) if you have not done so yet as part of your university's induction programme.

What are the opening hours of the library?	Most university libraries are open until late and also on weekends. However, there is not always a member of staff at hand, so check staffed hours (for example, when you need help or have to pay a fine) and access to the library outside of staffed hours.
What do I have to do to join the library?	Some universities will register you automatically for the library; in others you may have to go there and register with your student card.
Where is the helpdesk?	The helpdesk is the first point of enquiry if you need help or encounter any problems. Staff are there to help, so do ask them if necessary.
Where is the library catalogue?	Modern university libraries will have an electronic library catalogue, so identify where the computer terminals are.
Where is the reference section?	This is a section where there are books for reference purposes only (this means that any items in this section can be consulted in the library but cannot be taken out on loan). You will usually find dictionaries and encyclopaedias there together with the key textbooks of a field of study.

Is there a short loan section?	Most libraries will have a section with key resources that can be taken out on loan for a few hours or overnight. This is a great resource when revising for exams.
Where are the computers, printers and photocopiers?	Universities will give you access to their online resources via computer terminals as well as to printers and photocopiers. You may also want to check if acetate, large paper and colour printing/photocopying is available.
What do I have to do to connect my computer to the university's intranet when working in the library?	Most libraries will have the facilities to provide you with access to online resources when working on your own computer in the library. There may be specialist areas for this.
How much does it cost to print and photocopy?	You will probably be charged a small sum for each page printed or photocopied. Check for charges and the procedure on how to pay for printing and photocopying.
How many books can I take out at any one time?	There will be a maximum number of books that you can take out, so check how many they are. You may also want to check how long you can take a book out for and if it can be recalled at any time.
How often can I renew books and how do I do that?	Most libraries will restrict the number of renewals on your books, so check how often you can renew. You should also make a note of how to renew any items on loan (most libraries will offer online or telephone renewals).
How can I reserve a book?	If the source you need is out on loan or at another site, you may be able to reserve it. Check with your librarian how this works at your institution.
What are the fines for not returning books?	Most libraries will fine you if you fail to return a book on time. The amount may differ for different types of loans (for example a short loan tends to be more expensive than a standard loan).
Who is the subject librarian?	This is the specialist librarian for your subject and they are there to offer specialist guidance and advice.
Which are the relevant classification codes for my field of study?	There are different classification systems in libraries, so check which ones are likely to apply for your field of study.
Where are the relevant resources held (which site, which floor, which shelf mark)?	Many university libraries are spread over more than one floor and often more than one site. So check where you can expect to find the resources you need.
Where is the quiet study area?	Most libraries will offer an area or a room in which you can study quietly.
Can rooms be booked for group study?	Some libraries offer small rooms that can be booked for group study. So if you would like to study with your peers, this may be the place to do so.

How can I access online resources?	The availability of online materials – both academic journals and books – is increasing and for a good reason: they are easy to access when and where you want. It will be worth checking with your library how you can access these resources (the most common access systems in UK further and higher education are Athens and Shibboleth).

In addition to your university library, your local library may also stock relevant materials and is worth checking, too. If there is another university nearby, you may want to enquire what level of access is offered to visitors. There are different arrangements: some will only allow you to study on site, while others will allow you to take out a limited number of sources (online materials are usually exempt from any such arrangement, though). Members of a professional body such as the CIPD may have access to online resources as part of their membership. Working in and with libraries will give you access to a wide range of print sources and will keep down your expenses on books.

2.3.3 SELECTING AND ACCESSING ACADEMIC LITERATURE

Once you know your motivation to read and which type of literature will be most appropriate for your purposes, you can start searching for materials. 'What?' you may ask, 'I am still not reading yet? I really cannot afford to waste more time!' I know how tempting it is to roll up your sleeves, get stuck in and play things by ear, but many years of being a student have taught me that it is more effective and efficient in the long term to be strategic and follow a logical process. Thorough preparation is the key to success in postgraduate study and beyond.

You may find it useful to focus your selection of literature early on. Currie (2005), for instance, suggests you look at the research field (for example human resource management), followed by the parent discipline (for example human resource planning), sub-discipline (for example recruitment) and research subject (for example interviewing). While in some instances you will be able to identify them relatively easily, you may wish to ask your tutor or librarian for help if you are stuck. That said, I would also encourage you to follow your tutor's guidance as sometimes insights from cognate disciplines such as sociology, psychology or philosophy may be relevant to the topic that you are studying. Effective literature search and reading often strikes a balance between focus on a field, discipline and subject and openness to insights from cognate areas.

2.3.3.1 Clarifying terms and definitions

If you are new to a field of study (or if you are a non-native speaker exposed to subject vocabulary for the first time), you may want to start browsing the reference literature. You may find that a specialist dictionary and a subject textbook in a particular area are good starting points for getting to know the subject-specific language of your field of study (this is sometimes called 'jargon'). The dictionary will provide you with key definitions and the textbook will give you a broad overview of the subject, indicating how different aspects of a field of study are related. Textbooks also feature detailed reference lists, which can point you in the right direction for your literature search. Both sources will introduce you to the prevalent terminology of the field of study, which is the basis for the identification of key words and a focused search for literature.

2.3.3.2 Identifying key words

Key words describe your area of interest and may even reflect the title of an assignment, project or dissertation (Cottrell 2003); they are sometimes called 'descriptors' or 'identifiers' (Fink 2010). Key words are the terms that you will type in the library catalogue or online database to search for literature. According to Easterby-Smith et al (2002), a good set of key words is the greatest asset for your literature search, but you need to be aware that a term may refer to different things in databases originating in other (English-speaking) countries and also in different subject areas. If your search is unsuccessful, remember alternative spellings and identify synonyms of the terms you are searching for; a thesaurus will be of great help (Fink 2010).

Some search engines allow you to search for more than one term using the AND function or for alternative terms using the OR function to make your search more specific to your needs. Some search engines also allow you to search for subject areas and to exclude a term using the NOT function. So check with the search engine that you are using how to improve your searches and consult your librarian if in any doubt. Key words can feature in the title of a book or paper, in the list of key words provided in most journal articles, in the table of contents of a book or in the text as such. As a rule, if the key words feature in the title or list of key words of a source, the more relevant it tends to be.

Hart (2002) suggests that you also think about the boundaries of your topic, that is, what is relevant and needs to be included in a particular piece and what is not. Considerations such as this may be the last thing on your mind when starting a project, but it is something to be aware of from the outset. Any assignment or project will have a word limit and will therefore be limited in scope; yet, a characteristic of postgraduate assignments is their open-endedness. Many of my students complain that the word count of an assignment or project is insufficient, but in my experience even 100,000 words would not be enough for everything that could be said or that you may want to say! Hence, you will not be able to include everything that might be relevant and you will have to choose carefully what to include and what to leave out. Let me illustrate this.

Imagine you have been given a 2,000-word assignment asking you to discuss theories of motivation that are relevant to explain employee behaviour in twenty-first-century organisations. On the one hand, there are myriad theories that seek to explain motivation in employees, the earliest being Maslow's and Herzberg's, for instance. On the other hand, there is a wide range of behaviours in modern-day organisations, both desired and unacceptable. It is beyond the scope of any piece of work, let alone a 2,000-word assignment, to deal with all of that. It makes sense to focus on a small number of behaviours (for example the recent phenomenon of employees engaging in social networking during working hours) and a small number of theories to explain why this may be the case. This will allow you not only to focus your literature search and reading, but also to deal with the theories and behaviours in sufficient depth to create a critical argument in your writing and to contribute to the knowledge in your field of study in that way.

2.3.4 SEARCHING FOR LITERATURE

Once you have identified the key words of your assignment or project, you can start searching for relevant materials. Wallace and Wray (2011) recommend that you draw up a long list of possible sources, comprising items from reading lists past and present, one or two key textbooks and the names of a few journals that publish relevant papers. It is a good idea to do an initial appraisal of each item before adding it to your long list. Your long list should include both the seminal works by the key authors of your subject area and more recent work that builds on them. The question will be, however, what constitutes a seminal work and how to recognise it. As a rule, the more often you hear about an author or a book or journal article, the more important this item is regarded in the subject area. For instance, Herzberg and Maslow are widely recognised as the key authors on motivation and therefore their names will be frequently mentioned in that context. Another clue can be found in the library catalogue: the more copies of a particular book that are available and the more editions of a particular book that have been published, the more important it is regarded by those teaching the subject.

When producing your long list of potential sources, make sure you note down the full reference (that is, author, date of publication, title of book or journal article, publisher or name of journal plus volume, issue and page numbers; for details on referencing please refer to Chapter 3) together with information on how to access it. The latter includes the name of the library or library site (where applicable), the floor and the shelf mark. You may want to check availability of these items using the library catalogue and the main databases containing journal articles and conference proceedings (in business and management, these are currently *Business Source Premier*, *Emerald*, *Science Direct* and *Web of Knowledge*; in addition, the big academic publishers such as Sage, Taylor & Francis and Wiley operate databases of the books and academic journals that they publish).

Keeping track of your library search is vital as we all think that we can do without it but never quite manage. You can keep a manual log of sources that you have accessed (for instance a simple spreadsheet or database) or you may wish to use bibliographic software packages. Most universities offer access to such specialist software, and there are also free, web-based programmes available (a commonly used one is Zotero). I would encourage you to find a system that works for you early on in your studies as there is nothing more stressful than hunting for references in the last few hours before an assignment or project is due!

Currie (2005) proposes eight criteria that can be used to determine the relevance of any source you may wish to include in your written work (see Table 2.3).

Table 2.3 Evaluating the relevance of literature

Question	Guidance
1 How recent is the item?	This question does not mean that all of your data should be recent. In fact, many tutors like you to draw on seminal work in the area, which can be 20, 30, 40 years or even 100 years old and are still valid, relevant and important. However, you are expected to demonstrate your awareness of up-to-date thinking (within the last 5–10 years, for example).
2 Is the item likely to have been superseded?	To find out, compare the item with other similar items of data, note the dates and assess the degree to which they all match up. If the item is the oldest, does not match up and other theories may be taken as modern alternatives to those in the item, the likelihood is that it has been superseded.
3 How relevant is the item for the purpose of reading?	Evaluate the degree to which the item is central to your motivation for reading. If it is only marginally relevant, make a note of its details and location, and decide later whether to include it.
4 Have you seen references to this item (or its author) in other items that were useful?	If you have, study those other items to see if this one should be integrated with them. How does it relate to them? Is the item relevant enough to justify inclusion? At the early stages of your literature search, it is not advisable to discard marginal material.

Question	Guidance
5 Does the item support or contradict your arguments?	If the item supports your argument and is central to what you have to say, it will serve as evidence for your case. If it is contrary to your argument, you may still decide to use it when you are comparing and contrasting what others have said.
6 Does the item appear to be biased? Even if it does, it may still be relevant.	While not all published material provides a balanced view of the subject, what is said may be relevant to the questions you are answering. You have to decide if it fits into your argument and, if so, where. Depending on your task, you may have to justify why you included this item despite its bias.
7 What are the methodological omissions from the work? Even if there are any, it may still be relevant.	Does the item include sufficient evidence to support what is being said? Should the researcher have used different research methods and, perhaps, further methods so that the data could be cross-checked? How valuable is it to your task? Depending on your task, you may have to justify why you included this item despite its methodological omissions.
8 Is the precision sufficient? Even if it is imprecise, it may be the only item that you can find, and so may still be relevant.	Lack of precision may have occurred in the application of the data-gathering and analytic techniques. Before you use imprecise data, you have to check their validity. If you decide to use something you should point out where you think the imprecision lies. If it is the only item you could find when you did the search, try searching further for other items that support the claim. Depending on your task, you may have to justify why you included this item despite its imprecision.

Source: adapted from Currie 2005, p78

2.3.5 ACCESSING THE LITERATURE

Once you have identified how to access what sounds like the most appropriate sources, you can access them through your library or any other information portal. Where possible, scan an item before taking it out (in the case of a hard-copy book or journal article) or before printing it (in the case of an e-book or online journal article) to ensure that the item is indeed what you are looking for. It can be frustrating to locate an item that sounds exactly what you were looking for, just to find that the title is misleading and that the item is not suitable for your purposes after all. The earlier you come to realise this, the better.

One common myth among my students is that you need to start reading at the beginning of a book or paper and finish at the end. Well, it is really just a myth. The key to postgraduate study and CPD is strategic and selective reading (Cottrell 2003), always bearing in mind your motivation for reading a particular item. So, when accessing a written source for the first time, start with the **summary information**. In the case of a book, this will be the back flap, table of contents, index and list of figures. In the case of a journal article or other paper, this will be the abstract or executive summary and the list of key words. If the information there sounds promising, progress to **introduction** and **conclusion** to learn more. You may find that you have already got enough information for your purposes or that the item is not as relevant or useful as expected; if this is the case, discard it. It is a good idea to make a note of it in your literature database, though, as it is frustrating to take out an unsuitable item more than once simply because you have lost track.

If the source is relevant and suitable, you will need to select the most relevant **parts, headings and subheadings** of the book or paper. Buzan (1977) suggests that scanning the item with a focus on headings and anything that is highlighted (with figures, colour, bullet points, bigger font, bold or italic print and so on) will give you the gist of the text. Once you have selected the most relevant parts, read the **first paragraph of a section** (Cottrell 2003) as well as the last, which should contain the most important information (Buzan 1977). Bearing in mind your motivation for reading that particular item, you need to decide how you can use what you are reading and how much detail you need; this may vary from source to source. More often than not, you will read for content relating to a particular theory or research. Sometimes, it will be enough to mention briefly a particular fact, but sometimes you will have to discuss large parts of it in great depth. However, you may also wish to adopt a particular research approach used in your source or borrow elements of style that are particularly effective in your field of study. Once you have decided which elements of a source to read, you can start to read critically and in depth. But what does this mean, you may wonder?

2.3.6 CRITICAL READING AND ANALYSIS

Critical reading means to apply your critical thinking skills when selecting, reading and analysing written materials. This means to identify and evaluate the main argument of the text, asking questions such as 'what is this text about?', 'what is the purpose of this text?', 'what is the author trying to say?' (Wallace and Wray 2011). It will be useful to bear in mind the different types of literature here. As the names suggest, a theoretical piece will be written to advance theory, while a practical piece will focus on practice. Hence, you cannot expect a theoretical piece to tell you much about practice and vice versa, and you will need to bear this in mind when analysing that piece.

Critical reading is a slow process (Cottrell 2003) because you will need to read, scrutinise what you have read using the questions listed in Section 2.2 above, think over what you have read, make notes of both content and your thoughts, and maybe go back to the text to re-read a particular passage and go through the above steps again, perhaps several times. However, only such a thorough process will give you the depth of understanding that is required for the majority of tasks that you will encounter during your postgraduate studies and beyond. You are expected to know your stuff, and the type of material you will be dealing with can be difficult to grasp!

Critical reading focuses on the argument of a text and you will therefore need to understand the components of an argument and how to analyse it. It is widely recognised that an argument consists of a *claim* and a *justification* and that an unjustified claim is nothing but an opinion (for example Fisher 2001, Wallace and Wray 2011, Lapakko 2009). Let us take the following sentence, which I have seen in many student assignments: 'Organisation A is an innovative organisation.' This is an opinion. If we add a justification, such as 'because it has adopted the latest human resource management techniques', we have created a very basic argument. So, an argument is essentially a causal relationship between two pieces of information (the claim and the justification), and this causal relationship is often highlighted by the use of the following language indicators (Fisher 2001, Wallace and Wray 2011):

> because, since, for, so, hence, thus, consequently, therefore, it follows that, x demonstrates that, it must be concluded that.

This list is not exhaustive, of course, but intended to serve as a starting point for your critical analysis of text. You may want to look out for such language indicators when reading and analysing a text, but you may find that the causal relationship that you are looking for is implied in the text (Lapakko 2009). The logical strength of an argument depends not only on the extent to which the claim is justified (Hughes 2000), but also by what means – whether by facts, data or other evidence, by definitions or principles, or by causal explanations, recommendations and value judgements (Fisher 2001). Claims justified by facts, data or evidence tend to be strong (Lapakko 2009), so be aware of value judgements and unfounded recommendations, particularly if they are well presented through persuasive rhetoric (Bowell and Kemp 2009).

When engaging in critical reading, your prime task will be to determine how convincing the argument is by evaluating the claim, the accompanying justification and any evidence presented against the background of its purpose. It will be useful to identify which evidence is essential to prove a point (necessary conditions) and whether there is a range of conditions that must be met if a point is to be proven (sufficient conditions). Cottrell (2005) distinguishes the two as follows: a necessary condition can be identified through the statement 'without this, then not that…' (p109) and a sufficient condition can be identified through the statement 'if this, then that' (p110). For instance, a university degree is a sufficient condition for access to postgraduate study, while a particular degree classification, a relevant degree, finance and work experience may be necessary conditions to be admitted to the programme of your choice.

It is also the reader's task to identify the critical assumption behind an argument and to determine if it is reasonable (Lapakko 2009, drawing on Toulmin 1958). So, in the above example about the innovative organisation, the critical assumption (that is, the assumption on which the link between claim and justification depends) is that an organisation that has adopted the latest human resource management thinking can be regarded as innovative. As the term 'innovative' is defined as 'featuring new methods' (Oxford Dictionaries 2013), the argument that 'Organisation A is an innovative organisation because it has adopted the latest human resource management thinking' is probably reasonable. In contrast, the absence of such a critical assumption is often called *non sequitur*, which is Latin for 'does not follow' and which suggests that the assumptions do not support the claim part of the argument.

You can see that scrutinising a text in that way answers many of the questions outlined in Section 2.2 above. Importantly, however, you need to be in a position to take a stance about the text (Brookfield 2012). To help you with that, you may want to track the claim and justification(s) of an argument graphically through an **argument map** (Cameron 2007), which identifies the claim, justifications and evidence as well as any supporting or opposing links, as illustrated by Figure 2.3.

Figure 2.3 Argument map for sample assignment 'HRM in Russia'

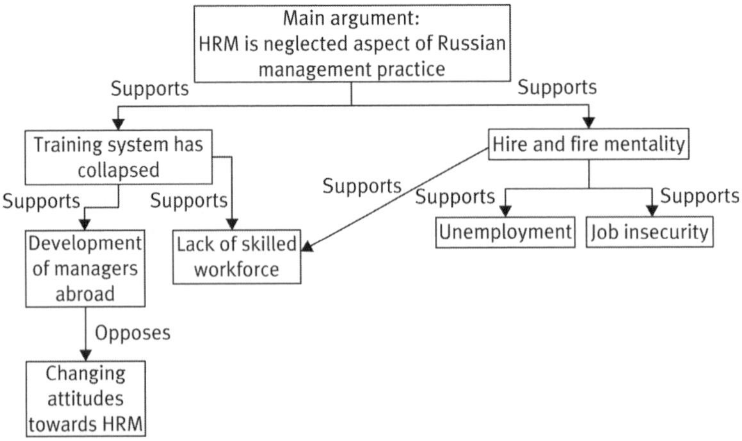

An argument map can also help you identify any flaws in the argument, of which there are many different types. Firstly, if you are left with questions like 'why?' or 'so what?' while reading a text in detail (Wallace and Wray 2011), there is likely to be something missing. So, if you are left asking 'why', the justification is weak or missing. If in the above example the argument would consist only of the claim, that is, that 'Organisation A is an innovative organisation', you would quite rightly ask why that was allegedly the case. If you are left asking 'so what?', the claim is weak or missing. If in the above example the argument would consist only of the justification, that is, that 'Organisation A has adopted the latest human resource management thinking', you may rightly wonder why this is important. In addition, it will be beneficial to examine the evidence that is provided for the justification (Lapakko 2009). In the above example, you may want to determine if the management thinking that has been adopted by Organisation A is indeed as recent as claimed or if these allegedly new ideas have indeed been applied to their human resource processes. Sometimes, a text does not provide us with clear answers to such concerns, and we may have to look for additional details or infer information that helps us assess the quality of the argument.

Other flaws in the argument are more difficult to detect, and some authors can be very good at masking a flaw in the argument through the use of deflective language (Cottrell 2005). Deflective language includes words that suggest that a claim is so obvious that it does not need to be proved, such as 'naturally, of course, clearly, obviously'. It also includes attempts by the author(s) to collude with the audience through phrases such as 'everybody knows/believes, as we all know, anyone with any sense', and so on. Such tactics tend to make the audience feel inadequate, assuming that they are not in the know or that they have not understood something properly, thereby not readily challenging or questioning the author. Critical reading will help you identify such tactics.

It is crucial that you take detailed notes about what you are reading as well as your thoughts about the text. Cameron (2007) suggests that note-taking enhances both your concentration and understanding, helps you retain what you have read and aids you with revising content. Perhaps more importantly, writing supports your thinking (Huff 2002) and allows you to create new knowledge. To support your reading and note-taking, you may want to photocopy or print relevant sections of a book or journal article so that you can highlight, cross-reference and comment on the most important parts of the text (this is also called annotation, Cameron 2007) or use a voice recorder to record your thoughts. It may be a good idea to build a comprehensive note system to keep track of what you have read and what you learned from each item (Hart 2002).

In order to enhance your understanding of what you have read, you may find it particularly beneficial to create a **knowledge web** for each subject about which you are reading. It is a collection of information that you already know about the subject and that helps you integrate (or 'trap') other pieces of information like a spider's web. A good starting point for a knowledge web is the creation of an alphabetical list (Birkenbihl 2007) at the beginning of your project, and this is how to do it. Divide a plain sheet of paper into two columns. Write the alphabet from top to bottom in the first column. Then take a minute or two to fill in the second column with relevant words, terms and concepts that you already know about the subject in question. It is important to write anything down in the order you think of it rather than alphabetically to get as full an account of your previous knowledge as possible. Feel free to write down more than one word per letter if necessary. Why not give it a try?

ACTIVITY 2.6

Creating an alphabetical list on a certain topic

Take a plain sheet of paper, fold it in half to create two columns and write the alphabet from the top down in the first column. Then allow yourself 90 seconds to jot down anything you know about 'coaching' or a subject that is close to your heart. Your time starts now.

What does your list look like? How many terms and concepts have you come up with? How many blanks are there? You may want to compare results with a peer or in a small group and fill in any more terms and concepts that you are learning in this process. You will be surprised at how quickly your alphabetical list will fill up and how easy it is to add any other terms, which can then be put into a knowledge web, as demonstrated in Figure 2.4.

Figure 2.4 Example of a knowledge web on critical skills

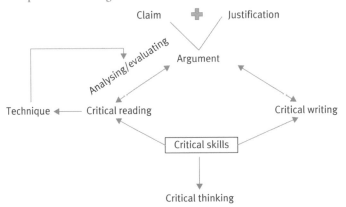

Other techniques to map your knowledge include the **sticky note technique** for which you write each key term and concept of your subject of study on an individual sticky note and then use a big sheet of paper (or a whiteboard, where available) to determine the relationship between the different elements. In that way you can move terms and concepts around until you are happy with how they relate to each other. This will help you develop deep understanding about the subject in question and link anything you read to information that you already know. If you work with differently coloured or shaped sticky notes you can create a complex picture of theory, practice, examples, and so on. Such techniques work particularly well with predominantly visual or kinaesthetic learners, so don't worry if they are not for you; there are other techniques which help you develop clarity, abstraction and theorising; a learning and teaching specialist at your institution may be able to give you further advice.

In conclusion, critical reading is an in-depth way of engaging with written materials that helps you enhance your understanding of a subject and your ability to make informed decisions. Critical reading will enable you to analyse both written and oral materials for their quality and their relevance, allowing you to make informed judgements on which sources to draw on and to what extent. This will have a major impact on your studies, particularly the way in which you approach any new task, access written texts and select materials to include in your writing. Critical reading is also the foundation for critical writing in postgraduate study and beyond. Admittedly, it is a somewhat time-consuming process if done properly, but what counts in postgraduate study is depth of your analysis, which you can only gain by working with text in great detail. Engaging with the process of critical reading will enable you to work more efficiently and effectively as you will be more thoughtful about the decisions you make and more careful in approaching your work. As a result, you will waste less time on unproductive ad hoc reading and writing.

2.4 APPLYING CRITICAL THINKING (2): WRITING

2.4.1 CRITICAL WRITING

Critical writing means to apply your critical thinking skills to your writing, which is a vital process for the creation and communication of knowledge in the social sciences. Critical writing is best perceived as the continuation of the critical reading process outlined in the previous section since you will be applying the basic understanding of argumentation that you will have built there. Critical writing is about carefully crafting the argument of your writing by determining the claim, justification and any supporting evidence in the light of the intended audience (Wallace and Wray 2011). The analysis and evaluation of arguments is at the heart of critical writing (Moon 2007), which also involves asking further questions, such as:

1   What is the critical assumption I am making? How reasonable is it?

2   Are all claims I am making supported by evidence? How credible and appropriate is the evidence supporting my argument?

3   Are my conclusions based on evidence and reasonable assumptions?

4   Have I clarified expressions, claims and the meaning of key terms and concepts?

5   Does my argument follow a logical line of thought?

6   Have I considered alternative arguments?

The point of scrutinising your work with such questions is to enhance the clarity of your writing. Asking critical questions about your work will enhance its clarity and, indirectly, its quality in various ways. Firstly, it will allow you to develop what Moon (2007) calls 'academic assertiveness', which comprises notions of challenging other authors' work, acknowledging alternative viewpoints, finding your voice and developing confidence in your writing. Secondly, your writing will be more logical and convincing because claim and justification of your argument can be clearly identified and supported by high-quality evidence. Thirdly, your writing will be more concise if you approach it in a critical fashion because you will be more thoughtful in the way you work (see also Chapter 3, Section 2). In Armstrong's (2011, p8) eloquent words: 'A useful thing to remember when you're composing your own writing is that ... your audience can't immediately interact with you in the present moment, so above all you should strive for clarity.'

2.4.2 DEVELOPING ORIGINAL ARGUMENTS

One of the biggest let-downs I encounter in student work is a lack of argument: it is not clear what the student wants to say (lack of claim) and/or why this is important (lack of justification). Hence, it is fundamental that you establish the claim and justification of your argument at the outset of a new writing project. This is often easier said than done but the analysis of text through critical reading will have given you a sound understanding of your subject and the development of a knowledge web or other techniques will have supported this. You may also wish to map out your emerging argument using an argument map (Cameron 2007, see Figure 2.3 for an example) as part of your own writing.

When thinking about an assignment or project, most of us will initially go through an unstructured thought process looking at different observations, experiences, theories and models that will lead us to a conclusion. This conclusion will then constitute the claim of our argument. For instance, in the example of the presentation on HRM in Russia (Klose and Reissner 2000), my colleague and I reflected upon what fellow students (Russian managers studying for a British MBA) told us about their work and organisation. We looked at the literature on human resource management in different countries to see if our fellow students' experiences have been validated by other sources. We developed our argument by discussing our observations and our understanding from the literature. A similar process can be applied individually by using a knowledge web, argument map, sticky note technique or by simply writing down your thoughts in a first draft that is aimed at developing your understanding.

Fisher (2001) argues that there are two approaches for the structure of reasoning which allow you to check whether your argument is logical. The first approach is about the development of a *chain of reasoning*, which consists of at least four elements that are linked by the words 'so – thus – therefore': firstly, a statement which leads to claim 1 ('so'), which is the justification for claim 2 ('thus'), which leads to the overall conclusion or claim ('therefore'). Going back to the above example, this chain of reasoning could look as follows: 'increasing globalisation requires an effective HR function in Russian firms, so Russian firms need to adapt and build an HR function, thus attitudes of Russian managers towards HR need to change, therefore there is a need for HR training and reform in Russian firms'. This chain of reasoning can be graphically presented as shown in Figure 2.5.

Figure 2.5 Arguing through a chain of reasoning

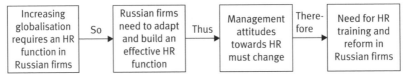

The second approach is to list a series of *side-by-side justifications* which lead to the overall claim and which are linked by 'also – furthermore – for all these reasons'. Again, going back to the example of HRM in Russia, the argument could be structured as follows: 'globalisation requires an effective HR function in Russian firms, also the previous training system has collapsed, furthermore the workforce needs new skills, so for all these reasons, there is a need for HR training and reform in Russian firms'. This structure of reasoning is graphically represented in Figure 2.6.

Figure 2.6 Arguing through side-by-side justification

An alternative approach to developing your argument and structuring it logically is the use of pyramids (Minto 2002). Every piece of writing should have one key thought (claim) which summarises other ideas (justification and evidence). Each idea will receive its own box, and all boxes will be structured to form a pyramid, in which the claim is at the top. The pyramid can consist of an indefinite number of layers, which are linked by the question 'why'. Find it difficult to picture? Again, going back to the example of HRM in Russia, our argument pyramid could look like the one in Figure 2.7.

Figure 2.7 Example of an argument pyramid

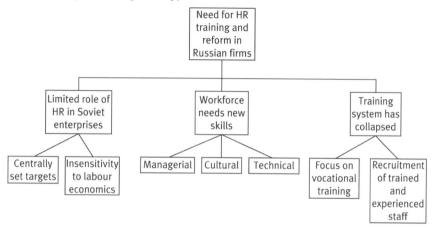

Bear in mind that writing is a creative process in which your understanding of different elements, groupings and links as represented in a pyramid is likely to change. You can build your pyramid from the top down or from the bottom up. Minto (2002) suggests that the former is usually more effective if you already know what you want to say as you can map out your claim, justifications and supporting evidence to keep you on track. The latter is usually more effective if you are unsure of your argument because you can list all the points that should feature in your writing, establish the relationship between them and draw conclusions from that. You may find it useful to build a skeleton pyramid and fill in any gaps as your reading progresses and understanding develops. If you feel restricted by writing down your pyramid on paper, try the sticky note technique again. If you find it difficult to determine the top of your pyramid – that is, the central idea of your text – ask yourself what it is that you want the reader to learn from your writing. It is often useful to write this down and simplify it until you have reached a basic sentence or question; this will be the claim part of your argument. In addition, you may want to consider how much the reader is likely to know and may want to learn as well as how much you know and may want to tell (Kaye 1989). It may also make sense to check your plan against the assignment title to make sure that you answer all the elements of the assignment question.

 ACTIVITY 2.7

Practising ways of arguing

Take an assignment question; this can be from a previous assignment, a real assignment that you are working on or a fictitious, practice assignment that your tutor has given you.

Construct one or more possible arguments in response to that assignment question using a chain of reasoning, side-by-side justification and/or an argument pyramid.

2.4.3 STRATEGIES FOR SMART WRITING

Writing is an integral part of enacting logical thinking and creativity, and it is therefore a smart move to make writing a regular habit. Contrary to your first reaction, you will not be writing for the sake of it but to explore ideas and search for answers. Writing will help you express what you are thinking, deconstruct your ideas on paper and confront them in small thought experiments. Clear writing reflects clear thinking, and this is what examiners are looking for in postgraduate work. Admittedly, this sometimes is easier said than done, but there are a number of creative techniques that you can use if straightforward 'writing things down' does not work for you. Often, you will be able to use large parts of what you have written in such an exploratory fashion for your final piece with only minor rephrasing required, and it is in these instances that regular and disciplined writing pays off.

The **bubble technique** is a good tool to think (and write) about the relationship between different aspects of a field of study or the elements of an argument or theory in a structured manner. Once you have identified the key aspects or elements of what you are going to write about, put each of them into a bubble and let the bubbles overlap. Then assign a number to each bubble and each area of overlap, as represented in Figure 2.8.

Figure 2.8 The bubble technique applied to 'HRM in Russia'

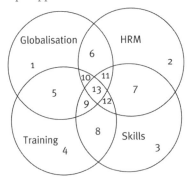

Now you can think about the different areas and relationships (there are 13 in this example) in a structured and logical manner, writing down your thoughts as well as any evidence that you may wish to provide for support. For example, number 4 will help you take stock of what you know about training in the context of your studies in general, a particular module or even a specific task. Number 8 will help you think about the relationship between training and skills, and you may want to explore what skills can be built effectively through training and what the limitations of training as a means of skills-building are. Number 13 will help you explore training and skills development in the wider context of human resource management and a trend towards globalisation. Exploratory writing in such a structured manner can be most beneficial and I encourage you to give it a go – it may well work for you!

ACTIVITY 2.8

Using argumentation techniques

Experiment with the different techniques discussed in this section to see which ones support your writing best. You may want to use an assignment as part of your study, a report for work or anything else that you are working on at present to practise critical reading and writing.

However, simply following a structured process for academic reading and writing and using different techniques to enhance your engagement with a text does not guarantee success. The vast majority of my students could achieve considerably higher grades if they followed one piece of advice, which I give them early in their studies: never, ever submit a first draft of your assignment or project. The reason for this seemingly strange piece of advice is that the first draft of any writing project serves to help you make sense of what you want to write; it very rarely offers a strong argument in response to the assessment task. Once you have determined this, you can start writing the assignment that you will submit. I know how difficult it can be to devote sufficient time on each of your assignments, ideally leaving some time in between drafts, but rewriting your first draft does not mean to start with a clear page. Thanks to word-processing we are able to move sentences and paragraphs around effortlessly, to amend, add and delete text where necessary.

I would also encourage you to consider additional ways in which to strengthen your argument. As outlined above, providing a strong justification and compelling evidence is an important way to give weight to your argument. In addition, you can make use of counter-arguments to support what you have to say, however paradoxical this may sound. According to Armstrong (2011), acknowledging alternative viewpoints in your writing and discrediting them as part of your argument is a powerful means to persuade your audience of what you have to say. You may be concerned that such tactics distract from your argument, but acknowledging and discrediting alternative viewpoints does not have to use up many words. A good language indicator for this is 'while', which contrasts two or more viewpoints; for example, 'While some discredit the need for training reform in Russian enterprises, emphasising the strong training tradition under communism, recent research reveals the need for new skills among managers and employees.' Such a few extra words can demonstrate to your audience that you are aware of the key debates in your topic of study.

Once you have finalised the second or perhaps even third draft of your assignment, checking your work thoroughly prior to submission will help you avoid the most common faults in student writing as outlined by Barrass (2002): lack of knowledge and understanding, lack of evidence, lack of logic, lack of relevance, lack of balance, lack of order, lack of originality, bias, repetition and poor organisation. These faults are more easily detected in other people's writing, which makes scrutinising your own work particularly important. If you are in doubt that you can do it entirely by yourself, why not ask a peer, a colleague, a friend or a relative to help you? There is bound to be somebody in your network of contacts who is both critical and honest and can help you improve your written work.

I find it useful to check my writing prior to submission using the **PowerPoint technique**. If you are familiar with PowerPoint or a similar computer package, this is quite simple. Put the claim of your argument on the first slide and then map the key points (justification plus evidence) on to other slides as they appear in the text. A few words for each slide are usually enough, so this exercise can be done quickly. This will allow you to check your writing for clarity of structure, causal links, and flow of argument, repetitions and omissions. Above all, it can give the confidence to submit a piece of writing that is the best that you can master at that point in time.

In conclusion, I cannot stress enough how important it is for you to get your writing just right. The reason is that an examiner cannot judge the extent of your knowledge and understanding *per se*; they can only assess the extent to which your knowledge and understanding is represented in your writing through the strength of your argument, the quality of the supporting evidence and the way in which your text is structured. If your writing is poor, the true extent of your knowledge and understanding cannot be assessed, which results in low marks and, usually, lots of disappointment. We will continue with our consideration of academic writing in the following chapter, so join us there.

2.5 CONCLUSION

Postgraduate study and CPD require you to become more independent as a learner as you are expected to think critically and work independently to create and share new knowledge with scholars and practitioners in your field of study. While your tutors will give you guidance and advice, much of your learning will come from the level of engagement in the tasks and the quality of the processes and techniques that you employ in your studies. The one skill that will allow you to do this is critical thinking, the foundation of postgraduate study and CPD. It will allow you to approach any task or project in a structured and thoughtful manner, to make decisions as to which sources to consult and which content to include, to analyse and evaluate arguments and to develop and justify your own. I encourage you to keep honing your ability to be critical when studying the other chapters in this book as your ability as a learner will improve. I also encourage you, in true postgraduate fashion, to delve more deeply into any areas that you feel may benefit from more theoretical understanding or practical application.

 PAUSE FOR THOUGHT

Identify at least three things that you have learned by studying this chapter and engaging with the exercises and activities. How will your newly acquired knowledge and skills support your continuing professional development? What value do you expect your learning to have for your daily routines and your further career? In what area have you identified a need for further development and how are you planning to fill that gap? Address these issues in your learning journal and/or CPD log. You may also wish to discuss them with a peer, colleague, mentor or coach to aid your further development.

EXPLORE FURTHER

BAILEY, S. (2011) *Academic writing for international students of business.* London: Routledge.

BRINK-BUDGEN, R.V.D. (2000) *Critical thinking for students: learn the skill of critical assessment and effective argument.* 3rd ed. Oxford: How To Books.

FOUNDATION FOR CRITICAL THINKING [website]: http://www.criticalthinking.org

FOUNDATION FOR CRITICAL THINKING [YouTube channel]: http://www.youtube.com/user/CriticalThinkingOrg

REFERENCES

ARMSTRONG, D. (2011) *Analysis and critique: how to engage and write about anything.* Course guidebook. Chantilly, VA: The Great Courses.

BARRASS, R. (2002) *Study! A guide to effective learning, revision and examination techniques.* 2nd ed. London: Routledge.

BIRKENBIHL, V.F. (2007) *ABC Kreativ: Technikenzurkreativen Problemlösung.* 4th expanded ed. Munich: Hugendubel (Ariston).

BORG, E. (2008) Understanding the nature, possibilities and challenges of academic writing. In: S. MOORE (ed.). *Supporting academic writing among students and academics.* London: Staff and Educational Development Association Ltd (SEDA).

BOWELL, T. and KEMP, G. (2009) *Critical thinking: a concise introduction.* 3rd ed. Hoboken, NJ: Taylor & Francis.

BROOKFIELD, S. (1987) *Developing critical thinkers: challenging adults to explore alternative ways of thinking and acting.* Milton Keynes: Open University Press.

BROOKFIELD, S. (2012) *Teaching for critical thinking: tools and techniques to help students question their assumptions.* San Francisco, CA: Jossey-Bass.

BUZAN, T. (1977) *Speed reading.* Newton Abbot: David & Charles.

BUZAN, T. (2000) *The mind map book.* With Barry Buzan. Millennium ed. London: BBC Books.

CAMERON, S. (2007) *The business student's handbook: learning skills for study and employment.* 4th ed. Harlow: Pearson.

COTTRELL, S. (2003) *The study skills handbook.* 2nd ed. Basingstoke: Palgrave Macmillan.

COTTRELL, S. (2005) *Critical thinking skills: developing effective analysis and argument.* Basingstoke: Palgrave Macmillan.

CURRIE, D. (2005) *Developing and applying study skills.* London: CIPD.

DE BONO, E. (1976) *Teaching thinking.* Harmondsworth: Penguin.

EASTERBY-SMITH, M., THORPE, R. and LOWE, A. (2002) *Management research: an introduction.* 2nd ed. London: Sage.

FINK, A. (2010) *Conducting research literature reviews: from the internet to paper.* 3rd ed. Los Angeles, CA: Sage.

FISHER, A. (2001) *Critical thinking: an introduction.* Cambridge: Cambridge University Press.

HART, C. (1998) *Doing a literature review.* London: Sage.

HART, C. (2002) *Doing a literature search.* London: Sage.

HUFF, A. (1999) *Writing for scholarly publication.* London: Sage.

HUFF, A. (2002) Learning to be a successful writer. In: D. PARTINGTON (ed.). *Essential skills for management research.* London: Sage, pp72–83.

HUGHES, W. (2000) *Critical thinking: an introduction to the basic skills.* 3rd ed. Toronto: Broadview Press.

KAYE, S. (1989) *Writing under pressure: the quick writing process.* New York and Oxford: Oxford University Press.

KLOSE, D. and REISSNER, S.C. (2000) *HRM in Russia: stepchild of management practices?* Presentation for module International Human Resource Management, MA International Business Administration, Newcastle Business School, University of Northumbria at Newcastle, 7 December.

LAPAKKO, D. (2009) *Argumentation: critical thinking in action.* 2nd ed. New York: iUniverse.

MINTO, B. (2002) *The pyramid principle.* 3rd ed. Harlow: Pearson.

MOON, J. (2007) *Critical thinking: an exploration of theory and practice.* London: Routledge.

OXFORD DICTIONARIES. (2013) [online]. Available at: http://oxforddictionaries.com/definition/english/peer%2Breview [Accessed 19 April 2013].

PAUL, R.W. and ELDER, L. (2002) *Critical thinking: tools for taking charge of your professional and personal life.* Harlow: Pearson.

QAA. (2007a) *Subject benchmark statements: general business and management [online].* Available at: http://www.qaa.ac.uk/Publications/InformationAndGuidance/Documents/GeneralBusinessManagement.pdf [Accessed 20 December 2013].

QAA. (2007b) *Subject benchmark statements: master's degrees in business and management [online].* Available at: http://www.qaa.ac.uk/Publications/InformationAndGuidance/Documents/BusinessManagementMasters.pdf [Accessed 12 April 2013].

QAA. (2008) *The framework for higher education qualifications in England, Wales and Northern Ireland [online].* Available at: http://www.qaa.ac.uk/Publications/InformationandGuidance/Documents/FHEQ08.pdf [Accessed 20 December 2013].

WALLACE, M. and WRAY, A. (2011) *Critical reading and writing for postgraduates.* 2nd ed. London: Sage.

CHAPTER 3

Practical Aspects of Postgraduate Study Skills

STEFANIE REISSNER

OVERVIEW

Writing is a crucial means of communication for postgraduate students and competent professionals, and it is vital that you master this skill with confidence. Building on the critical thinking skills developed in the previous chapter, this chapter explores the characteristics of effective formal writing. You will learn about what makes an effective report, essay, review, project and dissertation as well as tips and tricks from the writer's toolbox. You will also learn the basic rules of academic referencing (including the rationale for it) and how you can avoid the academic sin of sins – plagiarism. Finally, you will learn how to revise and prepare for examinations the smart way.

LEARNING OUTCOMES

By the end of this chapter, provided you have engaged with the activities, you should be able to:

- understand the characteristics and techniques of effective writing
- apply critical thinking skills to the writing of reports, essays, reviews, projects and dissertations
- reference other authors' work correctly
- revise subject knowledge for examinations.

3.1 INTRODUCTION

Writing is one of the main means of communicating new knowledge and ideas, and it is therefore a crucial skill for postgraduate students and competent professionals (Barrass 2005). Writing is both an art and a science, which means that although having a talent for writing is beneficial, you can learn to write effectively (Peck and Coyle 2012a). In academic writing, there are recognised norms that are relevant to postgraduate students and those studying for continuing professional development. This chapter seeks to help you understand what effective writing in an educational context looks like and provide advice on how you can improve your writing for academic and professional purposes. Please bear in mind that any advice provided here relates to the Anglo-Saxon tradition of education (see also Chapter 1); if you use this book in a different educational context, please ask your tutor about the relevant norms in case they differ.

Under the following headings, we will discuss generic characteristics of effective texts before moving on to specific pieces of writing. The critical skills covered in the previous chapter will enhance your learning here. In addition, we will cover the basic rules of referencing (a key aspect of academic writing) and provide details on how you can avoid plagiarism. We will finish off this chapter with a discussion of effective revision and exam techniques.

3.2 EFFECTIVE WRITING IN ACADEMIC AND PROFESSIONAL CONTEXTS

Effective writing means to communicate knowledge, understanding and skills to others in a clear and concise manner. It is a transferable skill that will enhance both formal studies and career progression (Cameron 2009). Effective writing requires understanding of arguments (see Chapter 2), structure and language as well as practice of how to construct a text. It has been compared with constructing a building (Cottrell 2013, Peck and Coyle 2012a), which requires careful planning, a logical structure, building blocks (that is, sections and paragraphs) as well as cement to stick the building block together (that is, language indicators). Since we have attended to the planning of an argument in the previous chapter, our focus here will be on the structure and language of effective writing in academic and professional contexts.

3.2.1 THE STRUCTURE OF EFFECTIVE WRITING

The structure of a text is the framework in which the argument is placed and according to which it is organised. It should follow a logical line of thought and leave the reader with no further questions (Barrass 2005). A clear structure will enhance the content of a text as it makes it easier for the reader to understand and assess what is being communicated, and it is your duty as the writer to ensure that you communicate clearly through both structure and language. While structure and language will enhance your argument, they are no substitute for a strong argument. So please do not make the same mistake as some of my students who copy the structure and language of an effective text (usually an assignment that has received a high mark) and add some mediocre content to it, thinking that they have produced a great piece of work as a result.

While in most writing assignments it will be possible to structure content in different ways, there is an expectation that academic writing follows a traditional three-part structure consisting of introduction, main body and conclusion. Let us look at the role and characteristics of each in turn.

The *introduction* states the claim part of an argument, that is, what the text is about. In a short text, such as a 2,000-word assignment, one or two paragraphs are usually enough (Peck and Coyle 2012b), and it is good practice to start with a simple and straightforward opening statement. This will encompass the argument and awaken the readers' interest (Peck and Coyle 2012a). You can even be controversial here; for instance, starting a critical discussion of organisational change with a statement such as 'change is good'. This will make the reader suspicious yet curious to learn more about what you have to say – and you have them hooked! For a longer piece, such as a 15,000-word dissertation, the narrative technique may be employed, which outlines a situation, introduces a complication and ends with a question (Minto 2002); the answer is given in the main body of the text. The advantage of such a direct opening is that it establishes a point of reference that will help the reader to follow the argument more easily (Peck and Coyle 2012a).

By the time the reader has finished with the introduction, they will want to learn more; hence, the claim part of your argument is justified in the *main body* of the text and supported by appropriate evidence (see Chapter 2 for details). It is a good idea to limit the number of points that build the argument and deal with them in depth. Where appropriate, you may want to justify why you have decided to focus on some points while leaving out others. Each point should be put under a heading (for longer texts) or a paragraph (for shorter texts), which are logically linked. By the way, it is not good practice to call this part of your text 'main part' or 'main body'; it is much more effective to devise a heading that captures the essence of your argument.

The *conclusion* summarises the argument and highlights any key points, such as what you want the reader to learn or take away for further thought or discussion. It is sometimes appropriate to include general learning points or practical recommendations, so please check your assignment brief or ask your tutor if in doubt.

Since different sections or paragraphs in a text represent different points, it is often beneficial to reinforce the structure of a text using highlighting techniques such as numbering or bullet points, the use of underlined or bold font, indentation, frames, shades and figures. Some of these may not be appropriate in a short assignment, but can emphasise the key points of your argument if used strategically and, above all, sparingly.

3.2.2 THE LANGUAGE OF EFFECTIVE WRITING

Academic writing is generally not renowned for simplicity, and even though some academic texts may be difficult to understand, you should aim for clear, concise and professional language in your own writing. Let us look at these three characteristics in more depth.

Clear means unambiguous, that is, where possible a term should have only one meaning that is clearly defined. For instance, you may have to refer to different types of organisational actors in a text. You may want to call those with management responsibility 'managers', those in administrative positions 'staff' and those in a production environment 'workers'. The reader will then be able to follow your argument without wondering what the different terms mean. In longer texts, such as dissertations, you may want to use a glossary of terms if you are using many specialist terms or abbreviations. Your tutor will be able to advise whether this is appropriate.

Concise means 'giving a lot of information clearly and in few words' (Oxford Dictionaries 2013). Concise writing is about using specific terminology and cutting out unnecessary words. Firstly, this is about avoiding unfounded generalisations and vague terminology. For instance, 'Organisation A makes huge profits' could be replaced by 'Organisation A has made profits in excess of £100,000 each year over the last five years' to make it more precise. Secondly, words that do not add to the meaning of a sentence should be avoided. For instance, the sentence, 'A psychologist called Abraham Maslow developed a theory of motivation' could be made more concise by leaving out 'a psychologist called'. Concise also means to avoid tautology, that is, expressing the same thing in different words in the same sentence (Cottrell 2005), for example 'visual image'.

Finally, *professional language* means formal and objective language in which abbreviations are used sparingly and only after introduction (Cottrell 2013). Terms such as 'huge', 'wonderful', 'great', and so on, should be replaced by more neutral or specific terminology (see above example about profits in Organisation A). Contractions such as *'wasn't', 'didn't', 'couldn't'* should be avoided since they are associated with colloquial language use (Peck and Coyle 2012b). Moreover, Orwell (1962) warns of the use of extensively used metaphors and clichés in a text; a common one in student assignments is reference to an era of globalisation in the opening paragraph. American or British spelling should be used consistently throughout a text (with the exception of direct quotations from other sources, which need to be left in their original spelling); your tutor may prefer one way of spelling over the other, so do check with them if in doubt.

Please note that it is considered bad form in academic writing to use absolute terms, such as 'always', 'never', 'all / every' because such a clear relationship can rarely be established in the social sciences, and academic writing at postgraduate level should reflect this. It is more effective to substitute such terms with 'in most instances', 'in most cases', 'generally', 'typically', 'usually', 'often', 'tend to', 'unlikely', 'rarely', 'some', 'many', 'most', and so on (Cottrell 2005). As a general rule, the language in academic writing should be more objective than in other forms of writing so that knowledge can be shared and developed further within a community of scholars and practitioners.

A further pitfall is the (however innocent) use of sexist or ageist language, which can be particularly tricky for non-native speakers. In terms of sexism, a common issue is an implied suggestion that managers are male and secretaries are female, for instance. To avoid any perceptions of sexism, the pronouns 'he' and 'she' can often be replaced by the plural 'they' or the sentence can be rephrased so that it does not require a pronoun. Roles such as 'spokesman' or 'chairman' are more appropriately called 'spokesperson' or 'chairperson'. The same principle applies to ageism, which I have recently seen in student assignments with, probably quite innocent, suggestions that, for instance, younger employees care less about their work or that older employees are less productive than younger ones. While some research may indicate one or the other, your writing should remain neutral.

3.2.3 THE INTERPLAY OF STRUCTURE AND LANGUAGE

Structure and language in a text are interdependent. Sentences are independent units in their own right, which consist of subject, verb and object and which at the same time depend on the other sentences in a text to create an argument. Often the relationship between sentences is implicit in the text, but sometimes it is effective to use language indicators to clarify the relationship between sentences. Table 3.1 summarises the most common ones (based on Cottrell 2005, 2013):

Table 3.1 Language indicators

Purpose	Examples
opening a phrase	first of all, firstly, to begin with, at the outset
adding a point	furthermore, moreover, in addition
emphasising a point	however, nevertheless, indeed, not only … but also
reinforcing a point	similarly, likewise, also, besides, in addition, as well as, furthermore, moreover, indeed
providing examples	for instance, for example, namely, particularly, notably, including
listing different points	firstly, secondly, thirdly, finally, in conclusion
presenting alternatives	it might be argued that, on the one hand … on the other hand, by contrast, alternatively, despite, even though
dealing with contrast	although, in fact, by contrast
expressing a consequence	hence, thus, therefore, as a result, consequently
concluding	in conclusion, thus we can see

Source: based on Cottrell 2005, 2013

The use of language indicators will also make the relationship between sentences, sections and chapters more explicit. They signpost the structure of the text to the audience, thereby helping the reader follow the argument more easily; this is particularly important for essays (which do not have headings) and for longer texts such as projects and dissertations.

ACTIVITY 3.1

Analysis of an effective text

Analyse an effective text, such as an academic journal article that you read as part of your studies, in relation to structure and language. What is the overall structure of this article? What role does each paragraph have? Where is the key information situated and how is it emphasised? Through which language indicators does the author help the reader navigate through the text? Which ones could you use in your own writing?

3.2.4 EFFECTIVE WRITING

Effective writing is writing with a purpose and with an audience in mind (Peck and Coyle 2012b). In postgraduate study the purpose of writing is usually to convince the audience (tutor/marker/examiner) of one's knowledge and understanding of a subject as well as the mastery of associated skills. Because of an emphasis on clarity and conciseness, each element of your writing (sentence, paragraph, section) should contribute clearly to the overall argument as outlined above. You may want to check if your university has dedicated staff to help you develop your academic writing skills.

As a postgraduate student you should aim for achieving high standards in your writing, and a few simple steps can markedly improve the work that you submit. It should be second nature for you to use the grammar and spell checker of your word processor before submitting any piece of writing. If spelling and grammar are not your strengths or English is not your first language, ask somebody to proofread the text for you. An occasional mistake will be readily excused, but many typos, unfinished sentences or grammatical errors will create an unfavourable impression in the reader's mind. More importantly, the overall quality of your work may suffer because unclear structure and language rarely communicate a clear and strong argument.

A great yet somewhat eccentric idea is to read out loud what you have written (Peck and Coyle 2012a), which I use regularly. By reading out loud, you will get a better idea of how clear the argument is, how well the sentences hang together, how well the language works and if there are any repetitions or omissions. If you struggle to read to yourself what you have written without pausing or changing emphasis, so will the reader. Take the opportunity to restructure sentences, replace words and introduce language indicators and headings to make the text clearer; this can be the difference between a decent and a good grade. Let me stress again, however, that your tutor will not be concerned about language *per se*; language is the means by which you communicate your knowledge and understanding, but without clear language, clear communication is difficult, if not impossible.

3.3 WRITING EFFECTIVE REPORTS, ESSAYS AND CRITICAL REVIEWS

3.3.1 REPORTS AND ESSAYS

The characteristics of effective writing outlined in the previous section will apply to writing effective reports and essays and will not be repeated here. Rather, the purpose of this section is to distinguish between two common formats of writing in postgraduate studies in business and management: essays and reports. Some tutors may use these terms interchangeably, while others distinguish between them and mark you down if you use the incorrect format for your assignment. So do check what your tutor expects you to do if in doubt.

A report seeks, as its name suggests, to report on something, such as a fresh look at the literature or research into practice. A good report is informative and concise and uses a formal structure with headings. It is customary to provide a list of references. While, according to Cottrell (2013), it is customary to provide acknowledgements, an abstract and a table of contents for longer reports (such as projects or dissertations, see Section 3.4 below), a 2,000-word report does not normally require these elements; if in doubt, please ask your tutor.

An essay is a formal type of writing that responds to a question or proposition 'in a logical, reasoned and evidenced manner' (Horn 2009, p292). Essays are an ideal format to explore a question in depth (Cottrell 2013) or to develop your thinking through writing (Huff 1999). Because they usually do not contain headings, each paragraph has a clearly specified role and is linked to the previous one by appropriate language indicators (see Table 3.1 above) to create a coherent narrative. Most essays will also include a list of references (see Section 3.5).

For both report and essay writing you will need to understand the assessment question, that is, which question you are supposed to answer. Barrass (2005) proposes the mnemonic SARI to help you identify the key issues: subject (what the question is about) – aspects (which aspects of the subject need to be included in your answer) – restrictions (whether the wording of the question poses any limits on what you can do) – instructions (what it is that you are expected to do, for example analyse, evaluate, compare). He also advises that you interrogate your writing by asking the what, why, how, who, when and where questions to engage critically with what you are writing.

Most reports and essays are quite short with a word limit of around 2,000–4,500 words, which means that you will be restricted in what to say. There are multiple ways of adhering to the word count, which, jointly used, can help you stay within the word limit. First of all, you should plan your answer and determine both claim and justification parts of your argument, any evidence or illustrative examples as early as possible in the writing process (Barrass 2005). Do expect, however, that the emphasis of your argument may shift as your thinking develops while writing. Secondly, this implies that in periodic intervals you need to check whether your writing is still on track or whether you have gone off a tangent. Thirdly, you should never submit your first draft (this merely establishes what you want to say) and you need to subject your writing to proper scrutiny once you have finished your second draft (that is the draft you will submit). Huff (2002) argues that you can cut out up to 50 per cent of a text without losing any meaning. Cutting out phrases that add little to your argument, such as 'it is considered', 'it should be stressed', 'to be honest', 'for obvious reasons', and so on, is a quick and easy way to cut words (see Barrass 2005).

3.3.2 WRITING AN EFFECTIVE CRITICAL LITERATURE REVIEW

A critical literature review is an integral part of a project or dissertation (see Section 3.4) and has become a popular assignment task in its own right. It is 'a comprehensive survey of published research on a particular topic. It summarises, synthesises and critically evaluates relevant research. It reveals trends and controversies, and identifies areas where further research is needed' (WDC 2013). The purpose of a critical literature review is to 'present […] a logically argued case founded on a comprehensive understanding of the current state of knowledge about a topic of study' (Machi and McEvoy 2012, p4). If part of a dissertation, it will help you to identify the main gaps in the knowledge base and to define/refine your research questions.

Hence, a critical review of the literature is an original assessment of previously published research (Jesson and Lacey 2006), in which different theories are analysed and the link between them established. It will allow you to demonstrate your understanding of the main theories and debates in your subject area (Hart 1998) as well as your understanding of the different perspectives (or paradigms) from which the topic has been approached (Jesson and Lacey 2006). That said, Machi and McEvoy (2012) stress that a literature review should be conducted with an open mind and without any foregone conclusions about what will be found. Writing a critical literature review requires you to use the critical skills discussed in the previous chapter to allow you to assess everything you read, 'weighing all data for veracity and value' (Machi and McEvoy 2012, p7).

Many students do not understand why a critical literature review is such an important part of a project or dissertation or even an assignment task in its own right. However, there are compelling reasons for this. Firstly, knowing the literature of your field of study on which you are building your project or dissertation (and to which your project or dissertation will contribute in turn) is crucial to avoid repetition and a waste of resources (Hart 1998). Since postgraduate students are expected to contribute to the knowledge in their field of study, they need to create new knowledge and therefore need to know what is already known in their subject area. Secondly, a literature review can help you identify current practice or effective methods that in turn can influence your own or that of your organisation (Fink 2010). While studies of the (academic) literature may be regarded as too abstract, they often have implications for management practice, and how better to learn about that than through the first-hand study of the literature? Thirdly, a literature review can help you to build expert knowledge about a subject for your studies or professional purposes (Hart 1998). As many of you are certainly aware, employers increasingly expect their staff to have expertise in a particular field, and the research literature is an integral part of this.

A critical literature review tells the story of what is known in a field of study by describing current knowledge, synthesising its key aspects and analysing the context of research (Jesson and Lacey 2006). To do so, you will need to categorise what you have read into broader categories and themes, determine how these relate to one another and decide on an argument that you will be making through the literature review (Machi and McEvoy 2012). A critical literature review that is appropriate for postgraduate level of study has the following characteristics (Hart 1998):

- breadth (that is, the number of theories and debates discussed)
- depth (that is, the level of detail in which the theories and debates are discussed)
- rigour (that is, the extent to which all sources were treated the same)
- clarity
- conciseness
- effective analysis and synthesis of ideas.

The latter is key: your synthesis of ideas is expected to bring new insights into the current knowledge in your subject area (Horn 2009) and, at least for a project or dissertation, to identify a gap in the current knowledge base. The foundation of a good critical literature review is your knowledge and understanding of the literature, which you will have built through wide and critical reading of original sources where possible (Jesson and Lacey 2006). Moreover, you need to engage critically with your draft literature review prior to submission to avoid the common fallacies, which include 'jumping to a faulty conclusion, presenting a conclusion without properly addressing other alternatives, misplaced causality' (Machi and McEvoy 2012, p129).

Another area of confusion among many students is what *they* are adding to what in most cases is a vast body of knowledge. To them, it seems, doing a critical literature review is merely reporting on what is known in their field of study without any input of their own and, not surprisingly, this is considered boring. However, a good critical literature review is very much about *your* interpretation of the current literature. You will strategically select and critically read what you consider the most appropriate sources, analyse and interpret them as well as synthesise their content. In addition, your critical literature review will have an argument, that is, a claim and a justification, which you create, structure and defend. A critical literature review is therefore a challenging yet exciting piece of writing. The critical reading and writing skills outlined in the previous chapter will help you to find your way in the information jungle and make good use of your time.

Jesson and Lacey (2006) provide some worthwhile tips for writing critical literature reviews, which complement Section 2.3 of the previous chapter. Firstly, a critical literature review needs to feature opposing views, and your task is to identify which schools of thought are the most common in your subject area and how they differ. Secondly, try to read as much of a source as possible as it can be a risky strategy to read summary information (that is, abstract, book flap, table of contents) only. Thirdly, scan the shelves in your library as sometimes a valuable source may be in an unexpected place. Finally, identify the theories used in a source, the conceptual variations or different schools of thought, empirical research findings, methodological issues and implications for practice (if applicable). You may want to use some of the graphical tools outlined in Chapter 2.

A good critical literature review is structured according to themes (Jesson and Lacey 2006) rather than authors (which would be more like an annotated bibliography, see Hart 1998). It has an introduction, which may outline the rationale for the review and any procedure employed. In the main body of the review, discuss each theme in turn. Within each theme, compare and contrast the prevailing schools of thought, the key authors or the most important theories. Identify any gaps in the knowledge base that need to be filled with new original research to enhance the understanding of the field of study. Each paragraph in your critical review should build on the previous one and link in with the following one, thereby creating a coherent argument. You should make good use of language indicators (see Table 3.1) to demonstrate how issues within a theme are linked as well as how the themes themselves relate to each other. The conclusion of your review should be balanced and you may want to highlight any gap in the knowledge base again. All sources cited need to be referenced; for details please refer to Section 3.5 below.

 ACTIVITY 3.2

Analysing a literature review

Writing a critical literature review cannot be taught in a classroom setting; it is something that you will need to teach yourself. A good starting point is the study of literature reviews that have been published in academic journals. The British Academy of Management (BAM), for instance, publishes a journal that is dedicated to literature reviews: the *International Journal of Management Reviews*. If you have access to this journal through your library, browse through a few articles that interest you. If you cannot access this particular journal, identify relevant articles in the top-quality journals of

your field of study (your tutor will be able to suggest a few if you are unsure). Some will publish dedicated literature reviews, but if you cannot find one, use the literature review section of a research paper instead. Analyse the articles noting the structure, language, stylistic means, references, and so on, that the authors use with particular emphasis on the synthesis of different paradigms, theories and models. Identify what works and what does not and learn the lesson. You may want to work with a peer or in a small group again as you will get different views on the matter.

3.4 WRITING EFFECTIVE PROJECTS AND DISSERTATIONS

The project or dissertation will be the most important single piece of work of your postgraduate studies, bringing together knowledge and skills that you will have learned through the taught elements of your course, empirical research and independent study. The project or dissertation will account for a considerable part of your degree (very often one-third) and will enable you to build specialist knowledge, which you can communicate to your current or any potential employer for promotion purposes. Hence, while it will be primarily an academic piece of work, it has real 'street value'. It will be a rare opportunity to design, carry out, manage and write up research into a topic of interest and make a contribution to the knowledge and debates in your subject area. This is undoubtedly a big task with many pitfalls along the way. Many skills discussed in this book, however, will allow you to approach your project or dissertation more confidently and professionally.

A project is 'a piece of research work by a ... student' (Oxford Dictionaries 2013) that is unique, focused on in-depth knowledge and based on research (Cottrell 2013). A dissertation is simply a somewhat bigger project. In postgraduate study, a project usually completes the diploma stage for those students who do not continue to the dissertation, while the dissertation usually leads to a master's degree. Both project and dissertation require good planning (White 2000) and a systematic approach (Cottrell 2013). It may be useful to divide a project or dissertation into the stages outlined in Figure 3.1.

Figure 3.1 Stages in a project or dissertation

The design stage is about deciding on a topic and devising the questions that the project or dissertation seeks to answer ('research questions'). At this stage, you will be writing your project or dissertation proposal, which is a planning document for your research (see Section 3.4.1 for details). The research stage involves the collection of background data through secondary research ('desk research') as well as first-hand data in real organisation(s) ('primary research'). The analysis stage involves the analysis and interpretation of the data collected in the research stage and may involve the creation of a tentative theory to advance the knowledge in your subject area. A detailed discussion of the research and analysis stages is beyond the scope of this chapter, but a research methods course or book will give you the necessary information. The final stage of a project or dissertation is the writing-up stage in which the work will be presented in written and sometimes also in oral format (the latter is called 'viva voce examination' or 'viva', which comes from Latin meaning 'living voice'); aspects of project or dissertation writing will be discussed in Section 3.4.2.

3.4.1 THE PROJECT OR DISSERTATION PROPOSAL

Thorough planning is vital for a successful project or dissertation, particularly at the design stage. It may be tempting to skip any preparatory work, which may not reap immediate reward, but you will be paying the price at the end of your research if you cut corners here. The first step in the project or dissertation journey is the choice of topic. Some of you may have little choice in the matter as your employer may have asked you to look into a particular issue at work. Others, however, may wonder how to come up with a topic. Here are some ideas. Firstly, think about what interests you at work, at university or in your leisure. Is there anything that annoys or fascinates you? You may want to ask your employer or colleagues if there is anything that they regard worthwhile looking into. You may want to browse newspapers, journals or listen to news programmes for inspiration and ideas. You may want to look at previous dissertations to get an idea of what other students have done; most university libraries will have copies available for reference purposes. You may also want to consider your future career path: what kind of specialist knowledge would be most beneficial for you?

If you are in the privileged yet difficult position of deciding what to write about, there are a number of techniques that can help you with this process. Try brainstorming by putting all ideas, no matter how strange they seem at first, onto a big sheet of paper. Then scrutinise all ideas and discard the ones that are unsuitable. You may want to do this in a group with peers as different people will have different ideas and take on different roles in the discussion process, which will benefit all of you. A variation of brainstorming is the sticky note technique as discussed in Chapter 2. Do not forget to write up your discussion on a sheet of paper or take a photograph so that you can go back to it later.

Currie (2005) recommends the Delphi technique, which enlists the help of groups to tackle problems in an interactive way. It is best if the group is made up of no more than six people who ideally are seated around a table. They are asked *not* to communicate with each other throughout the process. Each group member receives an A4 notepad with the problem stated on the top of the first sheet and a set of instructions (for example the criteria that your research topic must fulfil). Group members are given time to study the problem, think about it and write down a solution. After the allocated time has passed, group members are asked to pass their written solutions to the person on their right. Each reads the solution, tries to improve it and continues to pass it on. The trick is to improve on an existing solution rather than imposing one's own answer on others. The process is repeated until each solution has reached its originator. This is done in silence. At the end of this process, all final solutions (that is, improved solutions) are collated and discussed, ideally ending in consensus. You may also want to keep a notebook with ideas to which you can refer when writing your proposal or final piece of work. Do not be put off by any limiting thoughts, which we all experience from time to time. There is a dissertation topic in any field of interest if you frame it correctly.

If you come up with more than one potential topic, you will need to decide which one to go for. It is a good idea to map out the key criteria that your project or dissertation topic will need to fulfil and then rate every topic accordingly to reveal the best option. Issues you may want to consider include your level of interest, ease of access to the research setting, the amount of research already existing in this area, timeliness of your study, resources and support required, and so on. (A checklist is provided on the companion website.) It is always a good idea to discuss possible topics with a third person, for example peers, a course tutor, family members or friends, your employer or work colleagues as they may give you new ideas or refine what you already know. You may want to employ the Delphi technique again at this stage. But remember: unless your employer has decided it for you, the topic of your project or dissertation will be your decision and nobody else's. You may also want to bear in mind that the best topic for your project or dissertation is not necessarily the one that you feel most attached to; it will be the one that you will be able to do to a sufficient level of detail within the timeframe available to you.

Currie (2005) has identified the following seven criteria that a suitable research topic must fulfil:

1   *Relevance to the discipline of study* – If you are studying for a human resource management degree, for example, your project or dissertation must cover an aspect of human resource management.

2 *Topic of interest* – Writing a project or dissertation can be a long and time-consuming process, so a genuine interest in the topic will help you to deal with any problems or difficulties.

3 *Prior knowledge and expertise* – Ideally, you are already familiar with the topic through your daily work or your programme of study. This will allow you to focus more readily on what your research is about and potentially make use of personal contacts.

4 *Researchable* – Any potential research topic must relate to the academic literature in your field of study to which your work will contribute in turn.

5 *Level of study* – Your topic must allow you to achieve the standards required by your programme of study. A bachelor's dissertation differs qualitatively from a master's dissertation, and if in doubt about whether your potential topic is of an appropriate standard, please ask your tutor for advice.

6 *Research capability* – You need the skills to complete the project or dissertation, including communicating, networking, problem-solving, decision-making, and so on.

7 *Feasibility* – You need to be able to do the research within the allocated timeframe and with the resources that you have available.

Once you have a topic for your project or dissertation, you will need to focus your attention on some specific questions, which your research seeks to answer. Such research questions must be very specific to allow you to examine a particular aspect of your topic in great detail. You may be disappointed at how seemingly little you may be able to achieve as part of your research, but it is depth that your examiners will be looking for (White 2000), and in order to achieve depth within a limited timeframe, you will have to limit the scope of your investigation. So do not be disheartened if your tutor suggests that the scope of your proposed research is too big – that is quite normal. Follow your tutor's guidance and advice; they will be well qualified to advise from their own experience.

The culmination of the design stage is writing a research proposal (sometimes called project or dissertation proposal), in which you will determine the topic, scope and methods of your research. Your proposal is the map for your project or dissertation journey and its purpose is planning. Most universities will require you to produce a research proposal before embarking on the dissertation journey, but even if this is not common practice at your institution, I strongly recommend that you do it anyway. Careful planning at this stage will prevent many problems later on. Your project or dissertation proposal will answer three key questions:

1 What will your research be about ('what question')?

2 How will you go about answering your research questions ('how question')?

3 Why will this be important ('why question')?

It is not as difficult as it may sound. The 'what question' is about your topic and research questions. The 'how question' deals with the methods of data collection and analysis you plan to employ, and the 'why question' addresses whether your research is worthwhile (gap in the knowledge base as identified through your critical literature review). Your research proposal will address these three questions, often in a format similar to the one outlined in Table 3.2. Check with your tutor if there is a particular format in use at your institution and how long your proposal should be – this can range from a few hundred words to a few thousand.

Table 3.2 Elements of a project or dissertation proposal

Section	Content	Question addressed
Introduction	Outlines what the research will be about. Details the research questions to be answered in the project or dissertation.	What
Literature review	Identifies the areas of literature informing the research. Critical and analytical. Identifies gaps in knowledge base.	Why
Methods	Identifies and justifies methods of data collection. Identifies and justifies methods of data analysis. Identifies ethical issues and potential problems. Identifies how you will get access to the research setting. Outlines what the limitations of the research will be.	How
Conclusion	Summarises the key issues raised in the proposal.	
References	Provides a list of references cited in the proposal.	
Timescale	Schedules key tasks of the project.	When

A project or dissertation proposal usually follows a report format (see Section 3.3.1) and is written in the future tense. You should provide a preliminary title, your name, student number and the name of your dissertation supervisor if you have already been assigned one (White 2000). Your proposal should begin with a brief introduction, which answers the 'what' question of your proposed research. It is customary to state the research question(s) and a few sentences about the research setting.

The second section of your research proposal is usually a critical literature review (see Section 3.3.2). It should focus on the main academic theories and models, and you will be expected to actually identify the key strands of literature informing your project as well as the key authors in each field and their main propositions. In order to identify the key authors in your field of study, you will have to use the critical reading skills discussed in Chapter 2. Ideally, the literature review will identify gaps in the knowledge base of your field of study, which will allow you to justify why your research is worthwhile, thereby addressing the 'why' question.

The third section of your research dissertation proposal is usually about method and methodology, outlining how you will approach your research so as to answer your research questions ('how' question). The term 'method' refers to methods of data collection and analysis, whereas the term 'methodology' refers to the intellectual traditions which your research follows, answering broad philosophical questions such as what constitutes reliable knowledge and how we come to know what we know (Bryman and Bell 2011). Your methods, methodology and research questions should dovetail, and the language you use should reflect this. Methodological issues can be quite difficult to understand at first, so make sure that you have access to a good research methods book at all times during your project or dissertation journey and do not hesitate to ask your tutor for clarification. In terms of methods, try to be as specific as possible, for instance detailing the number of research participants (or subjects) and type and number of data collection and analysis vehicles. This will require careful planning, so take your time over your proposal.

You should also consider how you will gain access to the research setting, which may be difficult if you do not work or run your own business. You will also have to consider any ethical issues, which is always a concern when conducting research in real-life settings (Bryman and Bell 2011). Another element that some tutors like to see is the limitations of your project, that is, an awareness of what your project will not be able to find out with the methods that you are proposing. Nothing may be further from your mind at the very outset of your project or dissertation journey, but these details will allow you and your tutor to judge the potential of your proposal and anticipate any problems along the way.

A good research proposal will then provide a brief conclusion, all references and a timescale. The latter is sometimes called 'plan of work' and is an essential element of a research proposal as you will find it difficult to judge what is feasible for you to do within the available timeframe and will need your tutor's guidance. In my experience, most students do not allow enough time for data analysis, for revising drafts, for proofreading and for any unforeseen problems (like computer crashing or printer queues). In most instances, universities are not very sympathetic if you get your timing wrong, so make sure that you are realistic from the outset and follow your tutor's advice. Convention at your institution may require you to include other items, so check with your tutor if in any doubt.

It is extremely beneficial to discuss your proposal and other ideas with your peers, tutor, employer, colleagues, family members, friends, and so on, to be able to refine your plans. The most important thing is to be realistic. One of my students, for example, wanted to do research in the local Premier League football club even though he did not know anybody there. It may not be impossible to be granted access to such an organisation, but it will be extremely difficult without the necessary contacts. Another student highlighted in her proposal that she did not have much money but proposed to send out thousands of questionnaires by mail including a stamped return envelope. How she expected to finance this endeavour remains unclear. But you should get the idea. So in short, if you get your proposal right (that is, a detailed plan with realistic timing and a 'Plan B' in case something goes wrong), you have good chances of achieving good marks in your project or dissertation. Going back to my previous metaphor, if you have a good map, your chances of arriving at your destination on time are good, too.

ACTIVITY 3.3

Planning for a project or dissertation

Take any task, for instance a project or dissertation topic, an assignment brief or a project brief from work, and identify the key stages and elements. Map out what needs to be done at the different stages, what support you will need and how long you will need to complete each of them. You may also want to refer to Chapter 4 of this book for other skills that will help you in this process.

3.4.2 WRITING A RESEARCH PROJECT OR DISSERTATION

The culmination of the project or dissertation process will be your finished piece of work. Successful students start writing at the beginning of their project or dissertation journey as writing aids thinking (Barrass 2005). The structure of your project or dissertation will be very similar to that of your proposal and will answer the same three questions – what, why and how – in a report format (see Section 3.3.1). However, the purpose of your project or dissertation is different. While your proposal was about planning your research, your project or dissertation is about reporting research and is therefore usually written in the past tense. Table 3.3 outlines the typical elements of a project or dissertation, but bear in mind that the way in which your project or dissertation is structured does not necessarily reflect the way in which you approached the different tasks (the introduction is best written last).

Table 3.3 Basic elements of a project or dissertation

Chapter	Content	Question addressed
Introduction	Outlines what the research was about. Details the research questions that were answered in the project or dissertation.	What
Literature review	Critically discusses the key authors and their arguments. Best structured according to themes that are relevant to your research. Identifies gaps in knowledge base.	Why
Methods	Details and justifies methods of data collection. Details and justifies methods of data analysis. Details ethical issues and the limitations of your research.	How
Findings	Describes and discusses the key findings of your research. Best structured according to themes raised in the literature review.	What
Conclusion	Summarises the key issues raised in the project or dissertation. Determines the extent to which the research questions have been answered. Suggests areas of further research. May include recommendations or a reflective comment on your project or dissertation journey.	What, why, how
References	Provides a list of references cited in the proposal.	
Appendices (if applicable)	It is customary to provide a copy of the questionnaire or an interview schedule. Check with your tutor what they expect to be included in the appendices.	

The introduction of your project or dissertation will introduce the reader to your work by providing basic information, such as what the research was about (research questions) and where it was conducted (research setting). You may also want to provide other contextual information (for example socio-economic changes, industry changes) if relevant to your topic. It is customary to tell the reader how the project or dissertation is structured and what its conclusion is. The latter may sound strange but examiners (the prime audience of your project or dissertation) do not like surprises when marking student work. By knowing from the outset what your project or dissertation is about, what you found out and by which methods, they are in a much better position to judge the journey that you have taken. You may also want to bear in mind that the examiners are unlikely to read your project or dissertation from beginning to end. The introduction and conclusion and/or the reference list are popular starting points, and many sections of your project or dissertation may only be skimmed and scanned by the examiner. It is therefore crucial that you make clear what you have done, why you have done it and how. This is usually done by 'sign-posting', that is, telling the reader what they can expect, tell them the content and then draw out the key points of the argument. This will help the reader to stay in touch with what you have written (Peck and Coyle 2012a).

The literature review of your project or dissertation is a substantial chapter and a good opportunity to demonstrate that you can work critically and analytically. As highlighted above, a good critical literature review will outline a gap in the knowledge base that can be (however tentatively) filled by your research. This contribution may seem insignificant to you but is worthwhile in the wider context of the research and practitioner community in your field of study. If many people studied a topic in different organisations using the same approach, their work would go a long way to good theory!

Be aware, however, that not every item of written text ('literature') belongs in the literature review. The literature review focuses on academic theories, which are used to analyse the data of your research project; these are published in academic journal articles and research-oriented books. Methodological literature on how to do research belongs in the methods chapter. In contrast, government publications, company information, industry information, newspaper articles, and so on, usually constitute secondary data, which you can use to create a context for your study or as evidence to strengthen your argument. A sound understanding of different types of literature (see Chapter 2) is therefore vital for your project or dissertation.

The methods chapter (including methodology) will cover the same elements as your proposal, but in more detail. You will be expected to cover methodological issues in more depth than in your proposal and you will also need to specify what you actually did rather than what you planned to do (although it may sometimes be appropriate to contrast the two). It is customary to reflect on any ethical issues, particularly anything that has come up unexpectedly (for example an interviewee breaking down in tears) and how you handled the situation. You will also be in a much better position to judge what your research has achieved and what was beyond its scope (that is, the limitations of your research).

The findings chapter is probably the most exciting part of your project or dissertation because it is truly yours. You will be presenting findings that are unique to your study, even though they can often be generalised. But it may also be one of the most difficult chapters to write because it requires a lot of thought.

One common (and very understandable) mistake among students is that they take the data created by an analysis tool as analytical. However, any data analysis protocol will provide you with a set of descriptive data, which you will need to interpret in order to turn them into analytical data. This process of interpretation, which is usually aided by linking your data to the theories and models discussed in your literature review, is time-consuming and little is known about how you actually do it. It may be helpful to write up your results and then scrutinise what you have written with the question 'so what'; this will give you some insights into what this actually means, why it is important and how this newly created knowledge may be used by scholars and practitioners in your field of study.

The conclusion chapter will identify the extent to which the objectives of the research have been met. It will also outline the key points of your project or dissertation; it is the answer to the question of what you want your readers to learn from reading it. You may feel that your work is too insignificant to ask such a question, but it will help you to structure your thinking and present your project or dissertation in a focused and professional manner. As I explained above, your examiners are unlikely to read your project or dissertation in full as they very often do not have the time to do so, so you will have to make clear what the key points are and what you want them to learn from it. The better you do that, the better are your chances of a good grade (provided you have a strong argument of course). Some tutors expect you to outline areas for further research, that is, questions that your study has raised and that are important to follow up. You may also be expected to include recommendations or a reflective account of your learning journey; please check with your tutor if in doubt.

The list of references should contain all sources that you have cited in the main body of your project or dissertation and in the appendices. Details on referencing and compiling a reference list will be provided in Section 3.5. In addition to your reference list, you may be expected to provide a bibliography, which details all sources used for preparing your project or dissertation that you did not cite (Pears and Shields 2010). Check with your tutor what the position in your institution is.

Most projects or dissertations will contain one or more appendices, but it is by no means compulsory to include them. Appendices are commonly used as 'dumping grounds' for material that provides too much detail in the text or that does not fit anywhere. This is not the purpose of an appendix, however, and most examiners will see through such tactics. As a rule, it is customary to provide a copy of a questionnaire, a list of interview questions, an observation structure and maybe even an interview transcript. Some projects may produce large sets of statistical data or other supporting literature, which may be appropriately put in the appendix. Use appendices sparingly and appropriately; your tutor can advise on what to include and what to leave out.

It is a good exercise to spend some time browsing previous projects and dissertations to get a better idea of how they can be approached. Although the structure outlined above looks somewhat rigid, there are endless possibilities of structuring a project or dissertation. It will be down to you to analyse previous projects or dissertations and find out what effective practice is and what works for you and your research. Using the strategies for critical reading outlined in the previous chapter will help you. However, bear in mind that each project or dissertation is a unique piece of work that will require a unique approach that is appropriate for the type of work that you have done. Your tutor can advise you, particularly once you are past the early stages of the writing-up process.

 ### ACTIVITY 3.4

Analysing a project or dissertation

Identify a small number of previous dissertations, ideally from your programme of study. At most institutions you can access them via the library, learning resource centre or your tutor. Analyse them using the following questions:

- What are the research questions? How focused and detailed are they?
- What methods were used? How were they justified?
- What findings did the research reveal? How were they presented and justified?
- How analytical and critical is the presentation and justification of research results?
- Are there any recommendations? How sensible and thoughtful are they?

- What is the structure of the dissertation?
- How is the dissertation presented?
- What language is being used?
- How easy is it to follow the argument?
- How many and what kind of sources did the author cite?
- Are there any appendices? If so, how many and what has been included?
- What do I like or dislike about the dissertation?

It is important that you look at more than one dissertation, and you will soon find out what may be effective for your particular study and what your style and preferences are.

A project or dissertation will also contain a number of elements that do not belong to the main part of the text; these are called 'preliminary materials' (or 'prelims' to use publishing jargon) and include, usually in this order:

- a title page, stating the title of your project or dissertation, your name and student number, the title of the degree for which you are submitting and the name of your supervisor
- any declaration of your authorship that may be required by your institution
- an abstract/executive summary
- acknowledgements of people who helped you with your project or dissertation (such as supervisor, research participants, proofreader, and family members and friends who supported you)
- a table of contents
- a table of figures, table of tables or glossary (if applicable).

It is customary to number the pages of the prelims in Roman numerals (i, ii, iii, etc) and the main text and any appendices with Arabic numbers (1, 2, 3, etc). You may be required to add your name, student number, the title of your project or dissertation or any other information to each page, so please read the project or dissertation brief carefully and follow your tutor's advice.

It is absolutely essential that you allow plenty of time to prepare your project or dissertation for submission. This not only involves the revision of your draft manuscript, but also further editing. Even though it may sound counter-intuitive, it is usually a good idea to write what you want to write without worrying too much about the word limit. Huff (1999) suggests that text can be reduced by 30 per cent to 50 per cent without serious loss of content. However, such revision of drafts and further editing takes time and is best done in stages. It is also good practice to have your project or dissertation proofread prior to submission. You do not have to enlist the services of a professional proofreader; a family member or friend may do this for you. Your project or dissertation is such a large piece of work that you will lose track of what you have done. Although there are strategies to help you to see your work with a new pair of eyes (see Chapter 2), a third party will bring a completely new view to the project or dissertation, particularly if they are unfamiliar with the topic of study. They may be able to comment on any omissions or repetitions, point out any ambiguities, correct common typos and grammatical mistakes, and check for consistency of spelling (for example British and American English); as a matter of courtesy you should mention them in the acknowledgements. Remember that your project or dissertation should be a professional piece of work that you can be proud of and getting these seemingly insignificant things right is part of that. Please be aware that not all tutors are happy for you to have your work proofread if it goes beyond checking spelling and grammar.

3.5 REFERENCING THE WORK OF OTHERS

3.5.1 THE PURPOSE OF REFERENCING

Referencing is about identifying and acknowledging other authors' work on which you are drawing as evidence of your argument (Pears and Shields 2010) – a skill that every university student needs to master. Although primarily an academic skill, referencing has wider implications because it is essentially about being truthful about the ownership of ideas. Acknowledging any ideas taken from other authors' work is a sign of respect and is regarded as good practice in the Anglo-Saxon and Germanic university systems. Not doing so is passing off somebody else's ideas as one's own, which is essentially fraud and constitutes a serious academic offence called 'plagiarism' (Carroll 2002). Hence, by not referencing correctly, you do pass off somebody else's work as your own, whether intended or not, and commit plagiarism. You can be expected to be penalised for incorrect referencing – even if it is by mistake – and in an extreme case you may even be expelled from your programme of study. Plagiarism is so serious an offence that recently a number of German senior politicians had their doctorates withdrawn because of plagiarism and were forced to resign as a result (see Nelson 2012). In other words, plagiarism can haunt you for years to come, so do avoid it – it is not worth it. If you come from a different education system into the Anglo-Saxon or Germanic tradition, you will have to learn more about the acceptable norms and standards.

In practice, the source will be identified in the text (this is called 'in-text referencing' or 'citation'), and a list of all sources cited in the text will be compiled ('reference list'). Many students find referencing arduous and confusing, but it actually follows a logical and structured process. Several referencing systems (or referencing styles) have been developed, but the most common one in business and management studies is the Harvard referencing system, which is used in this book. It identifies a source with the surname(s) of the author(s) and the year of publication in the text, regardless of what kind of source it is. The reference list at the end of the text identifies each source unambiguously and in alphabetical order starting with the surname(s) of the author(s) and year of publication.

ACTIVITY 3.5

Exploring the Harvard referencing system

We have used the Harvard system in this book, so do take a look through the chapters and consult the reference lists for details. How many different sources have the authors drawn on? What kinds of sources are represented? How many different types of sources can you identify?

As a rule, you should reference every piece of information (including theories, models, data) that is not your own. There is only one exception to this rule, and that is common knowledge or knowledge that most people in a particular field of study will have. The difficulty is, however, to distinguish between common knowledge and specialist knowledge that needs to be referenced, particularly if you are new to a field of study. Pears and Shields (2010) suggest that you need to answer the following two questions in the affirmative to make it common knowledge: firstly, that a particular piece of information was known to you before your course of study and, secondly, that a particular idea has originated in your own mind. If you cannot answer these two questions in the affirmative (or if in any doubt), provide a reference. Many students get confused about what is their own work and what is somebody else's as a good assignment, project or dissertation will integrate other people's work in your own. Your understanding of the elements of an argument will help you to distinguish the two more easily: the claim of your argument tends to be your own ideas and the justification of the claim tends to come from already published ideas, theories, models and data in the form of evidence (a key exception of the latter is your dissertation, in which most of the justification will originate in your own research).

3.5.2 THE BASIC RULES OF REFERENCING

The practice of referencing can be confusing if a source does not conform to the norm. There are rules to govern every possibility and a good referencing guide (for example Pears and Shields 2010) will cover them all. It will be easy to memorise the rules for sources that you use regularly, and for all others consult the referencing guide, which will be an indispensable companion for your studies.

ACTIVITY 3.6

Getting hold of a referencing guide

Check with your library if there are hard copies and/or electronic versions of a good referencing guide available. At some universities, these are provided on the virtual learning environment (such as Blackboard). If you cannot easily access a referencing guide, you may want to purchase your own copy.

Under the headings below, I will outline how to reference the most common sources and exceptions used in postgraduate study and formal CPD. This list is only a brief summary; please consult your referencing guide for anything not listed here.

3.5.2.1 In-text referencing (1): paraphrased items

The most commonly used references in an academic piece should be paraphrased items, that is, you should aim to integrate other authors' ideas with your own and to put them in your own words. In the Harvard system, an in-text reference consists of the author's surname/the name of the authoring organisation, the year of publication and sometimes a page number (for example Orwell 1962, QAA 2007). If the item has been authored by two people, the surnames are separated by the word 'and' (for example Pears and Shields 2010). If there are three or more authors, it is customary to put the surname of the first author followed by *et al* (this is Latin for 'and others') to reduce the number of words (for example Saunders et al 2012).

There are three slight variations of presentation depending on where in the text the reference appears.

1   If you want to attribute a sentence or parts of it to an author:

Students should begin writing their dissertation early on (Saunders et al 2012).

Critical thinking is a minimum requirement for postgraduate study (QAA 2007).

2   If you want to include the reference as part of your writing:

Saunders et al (2012) argue that students should begin writing their dissertation early on.

The verb 'argue' is commonly used in this context, but other verbs that you may want to use are: suggest, contend, outline, highlight, point out, demonstrate, explain and the like. Never use 'write', 'say', 'think', 'feel' or 'believe' as they tend to be too weak.

3   If you need to include more than one item to justify your claim:

If you need to refer to more than one item, it is customary to list the items in chronological order by year of publication. If there is a long list of authors, which you do not want to quote, you may wish to add 'eg' before the first. For example:

Learning can be defined as a process of sensemaking, in which the learner can gain new perspectives, new ways of thinking and a new identity through interaction with others (for example Bruner 1990, Wenger 1998).

If you cannot identify the author of an item (this can happen for reports and surveys, for newspaper articles or more commonly for Internet resources) or if you are referring to a dictionary, it is customary to use the title of the item followed by the year of publication. If the year of publication is unknown, you should put 'nd' for 'no date' in lieu of the year of publication. For example:

According to Oxford Dictionaries (2013), …

Creativity enriches the life of the learner (Qualifications and Curriculum Authority, nd).

Another common source of confusion is two or more items authored by the same person(s) in one year. In these cases, it is customary to add the letters a, b, c, and so on, after the year of publication, both in the text and in the list of references to make each reference unambiguous. This could look like this:

Coaching may facilitate organisational change (Reissner 2008a).

Reissner (2008b) argues that firm context has to be taken into account when studying organisational change.

3.5.2.2 In-text referencing (2): direct and secondary quotations

There may be instances when you may wish to quote another author word-by-word; this is called *direct quotation*. In this case, you will need to provide the number(s) of the page on which it is written.

Short direct quotations (usually a sentence or two) will be put in inverted commas, for instance:

Reissner (2004, p106) argues that 'stories are not only told, but lived as they become visible and real in symbols'.

Direct quotations longer than a sentence or two will be formatted as a paragraph of their own, usually indented and without the use of inverted commas, for example:

Reissner (2004) explains the implications of narrative research on the researcher:

In most cases, though, fragmented experience is turned into a coherent explanation through story-telling, but conflictual and corrosive stories remain nevertheless. To increase the veracity and validity of the stories and their interpretations, it is crucial for the researcher/observer, as demonstrated here, to give back the stories to the story-tellers so that they can comment on them. In this way researchers can become confident about the validity of their interpretations of narratives (Reissner 2004, p110).

If you need to modify a direct quotation, you need to make this explicit. In particular, if you need to **omit parts** of a direct quotation because not every word is relevant for your purposes, use '…' to substitute the omitted text. For instance:

Reissner (2004, p106) argues that 'stories are … lived as they become visible and real in symbols'.

If you need **to add to a direct quotation**, put any added text in [ ] and the reader will know that these are your words and do not belong to the quotation. For example:

The methodological problem is to discover the most appropriate ways to record, explain and report these complex shifts in understanding [as a result of organisational change] (Reissner 2004, p110).

If you want to **emphasise** part of a quotation, put the respective words in bold or italic print or underline it and add 'emphasis added' or something similar to the reference. For instance:

> Reissner (2004, p106) argues that 'stories are not only told, but *lived* as they become visible and real in symbols' (emphasis added).

In contrast, if you want to highlight that the **quotation contains highlighted text**, add 'emphasis original' or something similar to the reference. For example:

> Transformational learning 'is the process of effecting change in a *frame of reference*' (Mezirow 1997, p5, emphasis original).

If you need to highlight that a **direct quotation contains a mistake**, leave the text and put [sic] (Latin for 'like that') after the mistake to demonstrate that it is an original mistake. For instance:

> Increasing global competitive pressures on companies are universal, but the ways in which different organisations react on [sic] them reflects the diversity of different local contexts (Reissner 2004, p101).

If you want to quote an item quoted by somebody else (secondary referencing):

Referring to an item that has been quoted by another author is called secondary referencing. It should be used sparingly and only if you cannot get access to the item in question. It is customary to add 'cited in' or 'quoted by' followed by the reference of the item where you read about it (that is, the author's surname, year of publication and page number). For example:

> Allan et al (2002, as cited in Reissner 2004, p100) suggest that the analysis of stories is a powerful tool for workplace learning.

3.5.2.2 Reference list and bibliography

All references quoted in the text, including any in the footnotes and appendices (but with the exception of secondary references) need to be provided in a list of references at the end of your text. The reference list is firstly in alphabetical and secondly in chronological order beginning with the oldest item and follows a similar process to in-text referencing. The first item provided is the surname(s) of author(s) plus initials (or the title of the item if the author has not been identified) and the year of publication (or 'nd' if this has not been identified). Any further information required depends on the type of source and will be dealt with in the following sections.

Journal articles, newspaper articles or conference papers:

In addition to the surnames of the author(s), initials and year of publication, you will need to provide the *title of the article* in inverted commas, the *title of the journal* in italics or underlined, *volume*, *issue number* and *page numbers*. All these details are usually printed on the source or listed in an electronic database. For a newspaper article you need to add the date of publication (day and month), and for a conference paper put the name of the conference in lieu of the journal title and add the date of the conference (day and month) as well as any page numbers (if published in conference proceedings) at the end. For example:

REISSNER, S.C. and PAGAN, V. (2013) 'Generating employee engagement in a public–private partnership', *International Journal of Human Resource Management*, Vol. 24, No. 14, pp2741–2759.

REISSNER, S.C. (2011) 'Stories of the unspoken', 27th *EGOS Colloquium*, Gothenburg, Sweden, July.

BOLTON, G. (1999) 'Stories at work: Reflective writing for practitioners', *The Lancet*, 17 July, pp243–245.

Books, reports or unpublished dissertations/theses:

In addition to the surnames of the author(s), initials and year of publication, you will need to provide the *title* of the book/dissertation/thesis, usually capitalised and in italics or underlined, the *edition* if it is not the first, followed by the *place of publication* (or 'unpublished') and the *publisher's name* (or the name of the degree-awarding institution). For example:

SAUNDERS, M., LEWIS, P. and THORNHILL, A. (2012) *Research Methods for Business Students*. 6th ed. Harlow: Pearson.

REISSNER, S.C. (2009) *Theory and Practice of Narrative and Storytelling in Coaching*. Unpublished MA dissertation. University of Sunderland.

Book chapters:

In addition to the surnames of the author(s), initials and year of publication, you will need to provide information on the chapter as well as the book itself. Start with the author(s) of the chapter (rather than the editors), their initials, year of publication, title of the chapter in inverted commas, followed by 'in', surnames and initials of the editor(s) followed by '(ed.)' if there is one editor or '(eds)' if there is more than one, the title of the book in italics, the place of publication, the publisher's name and the relevant page numbers. For example:

HUFF, A. (2002) 'Learning to be a successful writer', in PARTINGTON, D. (ed.) *Essential Skills for Management Research*, London: Sage, pp72–83.

Digital sources:

For digital sources it is customary to provide [online] after the title or issue number, followed by 'Available at:' and the URL. As digital content can change unexpectedly, you will also have to add the date on which you accessed it. For instance:

REISSNER, S.C. (2008a) 'Narrative and story: New perspectives on coaching'. *International Mentoring and Coaching Journal*, Vol. 6, No. 3 [online]. Available at: www.emccouncil.org, [Accessed 26 February 2009].

NELSON, S.S. (2012) 'A wave of plagiarism cases strikes German politics'. *NPR*. 24 November [online]. Available at: www.npr.org/2012/11/24/165790164/a-wave-of-plagiarism-cases-strikes-german-politics, [Accessed 21 April 2013].

There are separate rules for many more items and media, which will be included in a good referencing guide. It is important that you use one referencing system (such as the Harvard system) consistently and correctly. You also need to be aware that there are variations in presenting references in the text and in the list of references, largely depending on a publisher's house style. Please check with your tutors what their preferences are if in doubt.

3.6 EFFECTIVE REVISION AND EXAM PREPARATION

Most students wrongly assume that it is the purpose of exams to test how much information you can retain about your course and how well you regurgitate these details in the exam itself. On the contrary, exams serve the **positive** purpose of giving you the opportunity to consolidate the **ideas** you have discovered during the whole of your course of study and provide you with the chance to show the examiner how well you understand these broad, sometimes abstract concepts (Stagg and Robinson 1995, p3, emphasis original).

Despite increasing popularity of coursework, portfolios and presentations as means to assess student performance in higher education, examinations remain an integral part of assessment on many postgraduate programmes of study (Cottrell 2007). The examination period is a stressful time, which is often exacerbated by myriad myths circulating among students; these include: overestimating the extent to which one has to be gifted to be successful at exams (according to Tracy (2006), a student's innate ability to perform well accounts for only 20 per cent of the overall exam performance), a tendency to compare one's own revision with peers, fears to be regarded as stupid for not doing well, as well as assumptions about how generously (or strictly) the tutor will mark (Cottrell 2007). The reality is that, boiled down to the bare minimum, exam success consists of only three ingredients which are, to a great extent, within your control:

1   revision, revision, revision

2   preparation, preparation, preparation, and

3   your performance on the day.

By revision I mean the process by which you revise content from formal and independent study, and by preparation I mean the process of practising those skills needed to do well in the exam, which you may not use in your day-to-day study. Revision and preparation typically take place over the course of several weeks and serve as a foundation for your performance on the day of the examination. We will discuss each under the next few headings.

3.6.1 EXAM REVISION

It can be a real struggle to find the time for regular revision and detailed exam preparation when you are juggling multiple commitments. You therefore need to plan your revision, stick to your revision timetable and use techniques that will help you revise smartly and efficiently (for example Cottrell 2007). At postgraduate level, examinations tend to feature either essay-style questions that focus on analysis, evaluation and interpretation or case-study-style questions that focus on your ability to apply theoretical ideas to practical situations. Hence, in your revision you need to gain sound understanding of the subject knowledge, the ability to evaluate it and, sometimes, also to apply it. Your revision should therefore encompass class material, notes taken in class, in independent study discussions, and so on, to create a comprehensive overview of the subject materials. Stagg and Robinson (1995: 5) argue that revision encompasses four stages:

1   knowledge acquisition, for example reading through your notes

2   understanding the materials

3   memorising the information using a technique that works for you

4   testing your knowledge and understanding, for example working with exam-style questions.

If a module has been divided into different topic blocks, it is usually a good idea to revise each in their own right, particularly if you have access to past exam papers or sample questions. In this case, you can revise one unit after another to gradually build up comprehensive knowledge and understanding. The key point is to really engage with the materials, not just highlighting appropriate pieces of text (Tracy 2006). Paraphrasing and summarising different materials requires you to work with them more actively and at a deeper level of understanding. If bringing together the gist of different materials by writing them out does not work for you, why not summarise them visually, record them with a voice recorder or form a learning circle to revise with a group of peers?

The key to successful revision is to be creative and imaginative as well as strategic and resourceful (Tracy 2006), so you will need to identify what works for you. If you have not quite worked out how to best revise, you could try different methods, such as association techniques in which you link new to previous knowledge (Barrass 2002); one example is a knowledge web as discussed in Chapter 2 (Birkenbihl 2007). Another good strategy is to enlist the help of a relative or friend who is not familiar with your studies and to explain to them (without notes, of course) what the exam topic is about. If they understand your explanations, you know that you have properly understood it (Barrass 2002). Not only will thorough revision give you the knowledge you need to answer the exam questions, it will also give confidence when going into the exam. The following tips can help you make most of revision:

1   *Start to revise early* – Exams always look light years away until the week before. You will not be able to revise appropriately in such a short space of time. If you suffer from 'procrastinitis', create artificial deadlines for yourself and treat it like a real one. If necessary, work with a peer or friend who will make you stick to that deadline.

2   *Be creative* – Use auditory or visual means to help you retain information better. It is rarely effective to read your notes over and over again or to write up information over and over again; the more you engage with the material, the more you will retain.

3   *Avoid learning by heart* – While you will need subject knowledge and certain details, memorising alone will not be enough to do well as postgraduate examinations focus on the analysis, evaluation and application of knowledge rather than mere regurgitation of facts.

4   *Make the most of your time* – Try to divide your revision tasks into smaller chunks so that you can revise even in short moments of time. Try to work differently, for example by recording your revision notes and playing it while commuting to work, working out in the gym, preparing dinner or doing housework. It can also help to carry something with which you can record any unexpected thoughts (like a small notebook or an audio recording device).

5   *Stay positive and motivated* – Try working with peers and make revision interesting through the use of creative means of learning and reward.

6   *Know when you have done enough* to prevent you from losing nerve before the examination.

3.6.2 EXAM PREPARATION

Ways of studying have changed dramatically over recent years. Only a few decades ago, students relied heavily on handwriting – in the lecture theatre, in the preparation of coursework and in sitting exams. The advent of word processing, virtual learning environments and smart technology (tablets, phones) means that fewer of us use handwriting on a regular basis. In an examination, however, you will be required to write out your answers by hand, often over several hours, and this can be problematic on several fronts. Firstly, you will find it difficult to judge how much you can write within the timeframe you have, which prevents you from planning your time effectively. Secondly, you may be surprised how quickly your writing hand tires and your writing becomes barely legible, which increases the risk of the marker missing important detail. Thirdly, you may find writing by hand for a sustained period of time quite stressful because of this.

It may therefore be an idea to practise writing by hand before the exam, for instance by having a go at past exam papers or practice questions.

ACTIVITY 3.7

Practising for an examination

Sit down with an exam-like question and a timer and write your answer for the amount of time you would be allowed in the exam. Then count the number of words that you have written and analyse if your answer contains all the important details. This will give you an indication of how fast you can write and how much ground you can cover within the timeframe. You may want to be cautious with your estimate to allow for nerves on the day,

however. Prior to the exam, try to find out how many questions there will be and calculate how much time you will have on average for each question. So for example, if the allocated exam time is 90 minutes and you have to answer three questions, you will have on average half an hour for each question. It may be a good idea to spend five minutes preparing each question, twenty minutes for writing and five minutes for checking your answer. Keep practising until you are confident.

Preparation for exam success goes beyond practising writing by hand and getting a feel for timing, however. Everyday things such as eating healthily, getting sufficient sleep, working out or meditating regularly can prepare you for the added pressures of the examination period (Hamilton 1999, Tracy 2006). In addition, visualisation techniques in which you picture yourself doing well in the exam can also help you keep a positive mindset; it is a technique commonly used by athletes when preparing for competitions (Cottrell 2007).

If you experience high levels of stress or anxiety, looking after yourself becomes even more important; be gentle with yourself and take regular breaks from revision, however short (Tracy 2006). Visualisation, anchoring, breathing and relaxation techniques have been shown to successfully calm students down and get them into a more positive frame of mind as examinations approach (Acres 1998, Hamilton 1999). For some of you, such do-it-yourself approaches may not help, and it is then important that you seek professional help. Most universities have a student well-being service where special workshops on dealing with exam stress or one-to-one counselling are offered. Such services are there to support you in testing times, so please do not feel embarrassed to take them up.

3.6.3 EXAM PERFORMANCE

The third ingredient of a successful exam is your performance on the day. There are a few things that you can do beforehand to maximise your ability on examination day. Tracy (2006), for instance, recommends taking it easy on the day before to give your mind some rest. If it gives you peace of mind, you may want to read through your notes but stick to the bare minimum of further revision. Avoid working until exhaustion, go to bed early and make sure that you get the rest you need to be in top form. Also avoid any form of stress on examination day, that is, get up early, have a quiet breakfast and arrive early at university. It is much better to have a quiet cup of tea or coffee or to go for a stroll rather than rushing into the examination room just before it is locked. Make sure that you have everything you need on hand when entering the examination room (for example a drink, snack, pens or any other auxiliary means like a calculator) and lay them out in your usual fashion if that helps you stay calm.

When you get your examination paper, take time to understand all instructions. Are there any compulsory questions? Which ones are they? How many points does each question carry? Do you have to answer all questions or do you have a choice? How many questions in total do you need to answer? How much time do you have? Is there a time set apart at the beginning of the examination for any questions? Knowing the rules of the examination will allow you to focus on taking it rather than worrying about it. Tracy (2006) likens the study of an examination paper to the study of a menu in a top restaurant – you want to make sure that you do not miss a thing!

If you have a choice of question, you need to ensure that you answer the question(s) that you know best. Eliminate any questions that you know little about, unless they are compulsory. If you are unsure which questions to answer, scrutinise each possible question again and draw up a mini plan for each to help you decide which ones are likely to get you the best results. Once you have decided on the questions, you need to make sure that you know what they are. This may sound obvious, but exam questions can include a number of different aspects (Cameron 2009), which makes it easy to overlook one of them if you are nervous; take your time to be absolutely sure that you have covered all elements of the question. It is essential that you answer the actual question, not a similar one that you have prepared (Barrass 2002).

At postgraduate level, your examiners will expect a coherent and concise argument. The common strategy of starting to write down everything that you think might be relevant in the order it comes to your mind rarely works. Planning your answer will not waste time but give you an opportunity to create an answer that does justice to your knowledge and understanding. There are different approaches to planning your answers. You can either plan all questions and then deal with them one by one or you can plan a question, answer it and move on to the next (Tracy 2006). The former approach may help you decide in which order to answer the question (your favourite should be answered first), while the latter may help you manage your time more effectively as you know how much total time remains for each question.

Cameron (2009) also suggests that you can either start with a structure and fill in the content or collate information and create an appropriate structure from it. Remember that you can use visual techniques rather than linear lists if that works for you. Regardless of which approach you choose, the question, the subject knowledge that you have revised and your knowledge about your writing habits will help you make the crucial decision of how much subject knowledge, how much detail, how much theory and how much interpretation and analysis you will be able to include in your answer. You may also want to consider which points are essential to your answer and which are more peripheral to include the appropriate level of detail.

Even though examiners marking exams tend to be more generous when it comes to the presentation of your answer (Cottrell 2007), you should make sure that your answers consist of introduction, main body and conclusion. A well-structured answer communicates more effectively what you know about the subject knowledge, how well you understand it and, where relevant, how well you apply it. You should also allow control time to read through your answers again at the end and add anything that you may have missed (Barrass 2002). It is always worthwhile to start a question on a new sheet of paper or different page in your answer booklet to allow you to add any further details.

Unfortunately, things do not always go according to plan in the examination room. You may not be able to answer all questions at first glance, and the trick is to stay calm, however difficult it may be. There are various courses of action that you can take. You can start with the question(s) with which you are confident to get yourself going or you can take a big breath and read through the seemingly hard questions again (Tracy 2006). You may want to create an alphabetical list (Birkenbihl 2007) to get a starting point for your further considerations or use any of the other creative techniques discussed in Chapter 2.

If you remain calm and focused, you will find that an examination question is not as hard as you initially thought or that you know more about the topic than you expected, and then you can start planning your answer and get on with answering it. Some tutors may even be happy to accept an answer about an aspect of the examination question if you provide a sound rationale for choosing it, so focusing your answer on only part of the exam question could be your last resort.

In summary, the trick of successful examinations is to revise creatively, prepare well and remain positive, calm and confident during the examination, even though you may not have an obvious answer to a question. Breathe deeply and relax. If you have attended the classroom sessions, studied independently and done your revision, you should be able to answer the questions to a satisfactory level. Resist the temptation to go for a question without planning, monitor your timing and, above all, stay positive!

3.7 CONCLUSION

The essential skill of writing may be an art, but there are rules that you can learn and follow to improve your writing for assignments and examinations. Effective writing is effective communication of your skills and knowledge, and professional writers have a box of tools from which you can benefit for your postgraduate study, your continuing professional development and overall career. You may wonder how you can find the time to learn the tricks of the writer's trade and practise your writing, but doing so may make more efficient use of your precious time at later stages of your studies. Why produce a mediocre piece of work when you can produce a good one with minimal extra effort? You may even discover that writing is fun and that it gives deep satisfaction to communicate effectively through the written word, both at university and the workplace.

EXPLORE FURTHER

CIPD. (2011) *Preparing for examinations [online]*. Available at: http://www.cipd.co.uk/hr-resources/factsheets/preparing-for-examinations.aspx [Accessed 31 July 2013].

COTTRELL, S. (2007) *The exam skills handbook*. Basingstoke: Palgrave Macmillan.

MACHI, L.A. and MCEVOY, B.T. (2012) *The literature review: six steps to success*. 2nd ed. Thousand Oaks, CA: Corwin.

PEARS, A. and SHIELDS, G. (2010) *Cite them right: the essential referencing guide*. 8th ed. Basingstoke: Palgrave Macmillan.

REFERENCES

ACRES, D. (1998) *Pass exams without anxiety: every candidate's guide to success*. Mumbai: Jaico.

BARRASS, R. (2002) *Study! A guide to effective learning, revision and examination techniques*. 2nd ed. London: Routledge.

BARRASS, R. (2005) *Students must write: a guide to better writing in coursework and examinations*. 3rd ed. Hoboken, NJ: Taylor & Francis.

BIRKENBIHL, V.F. (2007) *ABC Kreativ: Techniken zur kreativen Problemlösung*. 4th expanded ed. Munich: Hugendubel (Ariston).

BRUNER, J. (1990) *Acts of meaning*. Cambridge, MA: Harvard University Press.

BRYMAN, A. and BELL, E. (2011) *Business research methods*. 3rd ed. Oxford: Oxford University Press.

CAMERON, S. (2009) *The business student's handbook: learning skills for study and employment*. 5th ed. Harlow: Pearson.

CARROLL, J. (2002) *A handbook for deterring plagiarism in higher education*. Oxford: Oxford Centre for Staff and Learning Development.

COTTRELL, S. (2005) *Critical thinking skills: developing effective analysis and argument*. Basingstoke: Palgrave Macmillan.

COTTRELL, S. (2007) *The exam skills handbook*. Basingstoke: Palgrave Macmillan.

COTTRELL, S. (2013) *The study skills handbook*. 4th ed. Basingstoke: Palgrave Macmillan.

CURRIE, D. (2005) *Developing and applying study skills*. London: CIPD.

FINK, A. (2010) *Conducting research literature reviews: from the internet to paper*. 3rd ed. Los Angeles, CA: Sage.

FISHER, A. (2001) *Critical thinking: an introduction*. Cambridge: Cambridge University Press.

HAMILTON, D. (1999) *Passing exams: a guide for maximum success and minimum stress*. London: Thomson Learning.

HART, C. (1998) *Doing a literature review*. London: Sage.

HORN, R. (2009) *Researching and writing dissertations: a complete guide for business and management students*. London: CIPD.

HUFF, A. (1999) *Writing for scholarly publication*. London: Sage.

HUFF, A. (2002) Learning to be a successful writer. In: D. PARTINGTON (ed.). *Essential skills for management research*. London: Sage, pp72–83.

JESSON, J. and LACEY, F. (2006) How to do (or not to do) a critical literature review. *Pharmacy Education*. Vol 6, No 2. pp139–48.

LAPAKKO, D. (2009) *Argumentation: critical thinking in action*. 2nd ed. New York: iUniverse.

MACHI, L.A. and MCEVOY, B.T. (2012) *The literature review: six steps to success*. 2nd ed. Thousand Oaks, CA: Corwin.

MINTO, B. (2002) *The pyramid principle*. 3rd ed. Harlow: Pearson.

NELSON, S.S. (2012) A wave of plagiarism cases strikes German politics. *NPR*. 24 November [online]. Available at: http://www.npr.org/2012/11/24/165790164/a-wave-of-plagiarism-cases-strikes-german-politics [Accessed 21 April 2013].

ORWELL, G. (1962) *Inside the whale and other essays*. Harmondsworth: Penguin.

OXFORD DICTIONARIES. (2013) [online]. Available at: http://oxforddictionaries.com/definition/english/peer%2Breview [Accessed 19 April 2013].

PEARS, A. and SHIELDS, G. (2010) *Cite them right: the essential referencing guide*. 8th ed. Basingstoke: Palgrave Macmillan.

PECK, J. and COYLE, M. (2012a) *Write it right: a handbook for students*. 2nd ed. London: Palgrave.

PECK, J. and COYLE, M. (2012b) *The student's guide to writing: grammar, punctuation and spelling*. 3rd ed. London: Palgrave.

QAA. (2007) *Subject benchmark statements: general business and management [online]*. Available at: http://www.qaa.ac.uk/Publications/InformationAndGuidance/Documents/GeneralBusinessManagement.pdf [Accessed 20 December 2013].

REISSNER, S.C. (2004) Learning by storytelling: Narratives in the study of work-based learning, *Journal of Adult and Continuing Education*, Vol 10, No 2, pp99–113.

REISSNER, S.C. (2008) *Narratives of organizational change and learning: making sense of testing times*. Cheltenham: Edward Elgar.

RIDLEY, D. (2008) *The literature review: a step by step guide for students*. 2nd ed. Los Angeles, CA: Sage.

SAUNDERS, M., LEWIS, P. and THORNHILL, A. (2012) *Research methods for business students*. 6th ed. Harlow: Pearson.

STAGG, G. and ROBINSON, S. (1995) *Revision and exam techniques*. Leicester: De Montfort University.

TRACY, E. (2006) *The student's guide to exam success*. 2nd ed. Buckingham: Open University Press.

WALLACE, M. and WRAY, A. (2011) *Critical reading and writing for postgraduates*. 2nd ed. London: Sage.

WDC. (2013) *Literature reviews [online]*. Writing Development Centre, Newcastle University. Available at: http://www.ncl.ac.uk/students/wdc/learning/essays/literaturereview.htm [Accessed 25 April 2013].

WENGER, E. (1998) *Communities of practice: Learning, meaning and identity*. Cambridge: Cambridge University Press.

WHITE, B. (2000) *Dissertation skills for business and management students*. London: Cassell.

CHAPTER 4

Concepts of Self and Self-management Skills

Kevin Gallagher

OVERVIEW

To be effective as a team member or a team leader you need to manage yourself. At work you will be expected to take responsibility for keeping some sense of order about your own organisation of tasks and responsibilities. You will be expected to turn up on time to meetings and to hit deadlines. If you have a managerial role, your job will often include making decisions, sometimes in tough circumstances, and handling 'disturbances'. Being in control of yourself within the workplace is an ongoing process as your work environment is often in a state of flux, which means that you too have to be dynamic in your responses. It is quite normal to feel at times that you are under pressure, but it is not good if you are constantly feeling overwhelmed by everything that is happening to you (and this includes your so-called 'work–life balance'). Stress-related illness is arguably the most insidious threat to your well-being and effectiveness in the organisation. This chapter is written with the purpose of outlining a number of self-management strategies for you to consider, perhaps try, and then reflect upon. If you are unlucky enough to have to take an extended time off work due to illness or injury, this chapter offers you some initial pointers for yourself, and those who manage you, for your successful return.

LEARNING OUTCOMES

By the end of this chapter, provided you engage with the activities, you should be able to:

- audit your time at work in terms of your technical, managerial and personal activities
- identify time-wasting activities
- recognise occasions when you tend to procrastinate
- apply strategies to improve your personal time management
- use plans, diaries and other personal organisation skills
- recognise the symptoms of micromanaging
- analyse work and personal stressors
- understand how stress management techniques can help you
- locate relevant sources of help and advice if you are returning to work after an extended absence due to illness
- apply some of these techniques to your own situation.

Within this chapter we will consider three broad areas of self-management: time management, personal organisation and stress management. These areas often overlap. In some respects time management and personal organisation may be regarded as aspects of an all-encompassing stress management. However, as time management and personal organisation are often considered in their own right as managerial skills, the distinction is used within the chapter to allow focus on specific techniques. These three areas are shown in Figure 4.1 overlapping in the 'doughnut' shape. What Figure 4.1 also shows is differing levels of sophistication which may be adopted, from 'quick-fix' to 'longer-term' strategies. For instance, a quick-fix approach for personal organisation may mean that you tidy your desk and attend to filing; a longer-term approach may mean that you analyse which items you need to file and which ones you can ignore or give to someone else. You should note that, although we are considering self-management skills, there may well be an element of personal development linked to your staff appraisal and to organisational strategies and policies. These may be linked to personal effectiveness and/or well-being.

Figure 4.1 Self-management skills approaches in the workplace

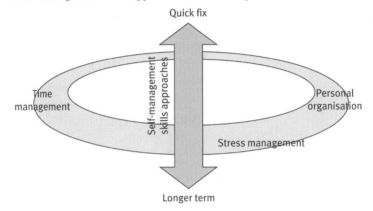

It is worthwhile spending a little more time on Figure 4.1 with regard to the merits and limitations of the 'quick-fix' and the 'longer-term' strategies. Quick-fix strategies as used in this chapter should not be seen as somehow inferior to their more sophisticated 'longer-term' strategies. The term 'sticking plaster' has sometimes been used to describe a strategy that helps the obvious symptoms but not the underlying cause of a problem, the inference being that this is a poor strategy. The view taken here is that strategies should be judged in the light of what is appropriate for that particular set of circumstances, and that often it is not a case of 'either/or' but a mix of strategies. For instance, performing some simple breathing exercises before a presentation is an example of a quick fix, but this should be coupled with a long-term series of presentational opportunities designed to gradually build confidence.

The chapter begins with a section on time management, followed by a section on personal organisation. It is aimed at those who currently have to juggle a whole range of operational and/or managerial tasks and responsibilities. Both of these sections are relatively brief, focusing on one or two techniques but providing an overview for further reading. We will be spending most of our time in this chapter on stress management. There is an overwhelming mass of information on stress – which is indicative of its prevalence and negative impact. However, there have been a number of recent advances in how stress is best tackled in the workplace, linked to ongoing government-funded and/or university-led research in the UK. We shall consider these as they have implications for both individual well-being and associated corporate welfare strategies.

4.2 TIME MANAGEMENT SKILLS

Why is time management so important for managers? The answer is twofold: in the short term it allows tasks to be accomplished more effectively (doing the right things) and efficiently (optimal use of time). In the longer term it enables managers to feel some sense of control in an often turbulent environment and thus helps them to avoid burnout through stress.

Consider a day in the life of a typical manager: this is probably most easily explored through reference to influential studies carried out by Henry Mintzberg (1997), who put forward the concept of managerial roles. He argued that in a typical day's work, a manager had to adopt a range of different managerial personas, grouped into what he described as 'interpersonal', 'informational' and decisional'. These could, for instance, include acting as a 'leader' (for example directing staff – an interpersonal role), a 'disseminator' (for example briefing staff members – an informational role) or a 'disturbance handler' (for example resolving a problem situation – a decisional role). In such a managerial world managers did not spend significant amounts of time on any one task but, rather, they were involved throughout the day in a series of activities which sometimes demanded the ability to be extremely mentally agile. Pedler et al (2007, p251) refer to this as the 'helicopter' ability. This scenario would seem to reflect reality for many managers. In itself it presents a challenge. However, you will be well aware that on those days when you feel under pressure, other factors will also impact upon how you feel and cope with the work situation. If you have outside work commitments or pressures, these have a habit of adding to your level of pressure (notice we have not yet used the term 'stress', as we shall see that the point at which pressure becomes stress varies amongst individuals).

ACTIVITY 4.1

Personal time audit

To manage your time you first of all need to be aware of how you spend it. One way to do this is simply to keep a work diary and note the time you spend on various activities. In the light of what we have just discussed you are asked to go a stage further than this and complete the following daily chart (Figure 4.2) over several days. You will notice that you have been asked to categorise your activities under various headings, including Mintzberg's ten managerial roles (Mintzberg 1990). When Mintzberg first published this concept in the *Harvard Business Review* (August 1975) it heralded a new realism of what it was *really* like to be a manager. In a sense it was the equivalent of 'a day in the life of a typical manager', and it was far from the cosy traditional model of managerial functions (for example, planning, organising, leading and controlling). The ten roles, sub-divided into the three broad categories of interpersonal roles, informational roles and decision roles, are briefly listed below and should be sufficient to allow you to categorise your managerial activities. Mintzberg's original article, as given in the references, is recommended further reading.

The following interpersonal roles:

- figurehead – for example, as the head of your department, representing your company at ceremonies, and so on
- leader – giving direction to others in your organisation (includes delegating and developing others)

- liaison – acting as a communication link with others outside of the vertical chain of command.

The following informational roles:

- monitor – keeping an eye open for relevant information – an active scanning approach
- disseminator – giving relevant information to staff, for instance in staff briefings and emails
- spokesperson – speaking on behalf of the organisation to outsiders.

The following decisional roles:

- entrepreneur – making things happen, using initiative to get things done
- disturbance-handler – resolving issues which have not gone to plan, handling arguments
- resource-allocator – deciding how to apportion limited resources (staff time, budgets, equipment, materials)
- negotiator – formal and informal bargaining (for instance with own staff, with customers).

You may be carrying out some of these roles simultaneously, so do not expect your total time for activities in the day to tally with your actual working day. Also, do not think because you do not have the title of manager, that you do not carry out some or all of the managerial roles that Mintzberg describes (for instance, as a lecturer in a university I lead a module team of other tutors but at other times I am engaged purely with teaching).

Figure 4.2 Time management audit

					Categorise activity (may use more than one)												
					Managerial roles (mark X)												
Date	Activity description	Time start	Time finish	Activity duration	Figurehead	Leader	Liaison	Monitor	Disseminator	Spokesperson	Entrepreneur	Disturbance handler	Resource allocator	Negotiator	**Own operational/technical task**	**Social/break**	Comment

After you have completed your time management audit, take a moment to reflect upon where you spend your time. Here are a few typical questions that you may wish to ask yourself:

1. Where am I spending my time? Is this consistent with my job role?
2. Are there any obvious time-wasters?
3. As a manager, am I spending too much time on non-managerial tasks that someone else could do?
4. Do I seem to be spending a lot of time in peripheral meetings?

You may want to discuss your answers with a trusted colleague, mentor or coach.

4.2.1 EAT YOUR FROG!

If you find the image of eating a live frog repulsive, this phrase is likely to be memorable and effective! I first came across this in a personal development presentation by one of my part-time management students working for a major insurance company. She had been introduced to this technique during in-house training delivered by time management consultants and it seemed to be working very well for her. The phrase is used by a prodigious writer of self-help books, Brian Tracy, in the book of the same name *Eat That Frog* (Tracy 2013). The message is simple but effective: tackle your biggest, most important jobs first. The idea is that once you have done this the rest of the day will seem relatively easy. It suggests that we sometimes put off doing important but unpleasant or difficult tasks and keep ourselves busy on lesser but more pleasant ones.

4.2.2 DON'T WAIT FOR INSPIRATION!

In a similar pragmatic vein to the previous advice, Rowena Murray (2005) advises writers at university 'not to wait for the mood'. Waiting for inspiration will not get that report written! She suggests setting aside time on a regular basis, preferably in a comfortable environment, and then committing pen to paper. Usually, ideas will start to flow after a while. However, you should note that researching and planning for the report also count as activities in the writing process. The important thing is to do some writing on most days.

4.2.3 POINTERS TO A DEEPER APPROACH?

You may note that the 'eat that frog' and 'don't wait for inspiration' techniques may work for you as 'quick-fix', pragmatic solutions. You will note that both are, in essence, psychological approaches. In the case of 'eat that frog' this is demonstrated by the way it hooks your imagination with the image of the frog and the resultant 'buzz' of achieving a big, important task. With the 'don't wait for inspiration' technique the effect is to lessen the overall fear of starting a large task by taking it in small chunks and of pushing through your initial reluctance to start a task. So, it may not be too much of a surprise to learn that recent psychological research has been shedding further light on our motivation to engage with our work, under the general heading of 'procrastination' studies. In the following section we will outline some of this recent research and its links with time management, personal organisation and stress.

4.3 PROCRASTINATION – OR 'I'LL DO IT IN THE MORNING'

If you look in the Oxford English Dictionary (2006, p811) you will find the following definition:

> **Procrastinate**: *verb*: delay or postpone action

> Original Latin: procastinare 'defer until the morning'

It would be simplistic to think that effective time management and personal organisation are achieved solely through knowing what to do, though ignorance of proven techniques may certainly act as barriers to our success. It is rather like living a healthy lifestyle: most of us know what to do – it is the doing that is the problem! Much of this is down to our psychological approach; for instance, Seo (2009, p911) refers to Lay and Schouwenburg's (1993) definition of procrastination as '*unnecessarily delaying activities that one ultimately intends to complete, especially when done to the point of creating emotional discomfort*'.

Nor do we necessarily grow out of this tendency. In one series of studies some 70 per cent of American college students experienced frequent delays in starting and/or completing tasks but as many as 20 per cent of 'normal adult men and women in everyday life' also suffered from this (Ferrari et al 2005, p1). This prompted the writers to suggest that procrastination could be due to particular circumstances (for example, completing college coursework on time) but they were more concerned with 'persons who … chronically engage in task delays as a maladaptive lifestyle' (Ferrari et al 2005, p2). As though to add insult to injury, the same writers go on to tell us that 'chronic procrastination is a complex phenomenon involving more than time management difficulty'. It all sounds rather drastic, doesn't it? You can almost hear yourself saying, 'What – me? Leading a maladaptive lifestyle? Sounds almost criminal!' Yet, as we shall see, in many instances we obstruct our progress with obstacles of our own making.

4.3.1 SOME INTERESTING PROCRASTINATION POINTS

According to Ferrari et al (2006, p29):

1   People in negative moods tend to procrastinate 'in situations where there are interesting (as opposed to boring) stimuli nearby'.

2   Generally people procrastinated on tedious tasks (but not all people, indicating other factors in play).

3   Procrastinators also tend *not* (my italics) to focus on future tasks needing attention.

4   Procrastinators are often busy with other tasks which are irrelevant to the target task.

E-breaks

Baker and Phillips (2007, p705) raise the very pertinent issue of taking breaks while on the computer by accessing emails – what they term e-breaks as 'they function like a coffee break'. Some individuals (e-breakers) tended to access the email when they should have been doing more important tasks – in other words, they were procrastinating. Also, while taking sufficient breaks may be considered beneficial, Baker and Phillips (2007, p707) point out that an e-break is not as relaxing as a normal coffee break and they suggested that e-breakers might also take their usual coffee breaks as well.

 ACTIVITY 4.2

Late again?

Take a few minutes to make a (brief!) list of activities that you habitually find yourself putting off or finishing late. Think also of specific examples. How did you feel about the nature of these tasks and of the circumstances of your examples? Have you any explanation for why you delayed or were late in completing your tasks?

4.3.2 PROCRASTINATION AND GOALS

We are often encouraged by senior managers or team leaders to 'buy in' to what we are doing, whether this is routine or some new project. The implication is that by becoming self-motivated we will do a better job. In motivational terms we talk of intrinsic motivation as opposed to extrinsic motivation: intrinsic motivation is concerned with our personal achievement needs – we want to do something for the psychological boost that doing gives us; extrinsic motivation concerns factors which influence our behaviour through external rewards and punishments – for instance to gain a pay rise, to please our boss (see Deci 1975). The suggestion researchers have considered is that perhaps if we are really motivated we will procrastinate less. And, perhaps those people who have goals which are intrinsic are less likely to procrastinate than those people who have extrinsic goals. Studies by Saddler and Buley (1999) with college students did, in fact, support the view that extrinsic goals were consistent with procrastination.

Further research by Elliott and McGregor (2001) and Seo (2009) proposes, however, a more complex framework between procrastination and goal achievement, based around (a) our motives for achieving our goals and (b) whether or not we viewed them in a positive or a negative way. In terms of achieving our goals we may strive either for 'mastery' or 'performance': 'mastery' is said to occur when we can achieve the task to some given level – for instance being able to swim 50 metres. This level of competence may be considered as absolute (therefore, it is a set standard) and/or may also be regarded as a measure of our own (internal) standard and subsequent improvements measured against this; by contrast, 'performance' considers our competence compared with that of others (for example, first or second in a race). The researchers suggested that mastery versus performance was one dimension (rather confusingly given the name 'definition') of a 2 x 2 grid which they called the 2 x 2 achievement goal framework. The other dimension (which they named more clearly as 'valence') related to if we viewed the goal in a positive or a negative way: if we set out to achieve success this was seen as positive and was labelled as 'approaching success' or more simply 'approach'; if we set out to achieve the goal with our prime motive being to avoid failure, this was regarded as negative and was labelled 'avoidance'. The researchers could now draw their grid of four quadrants, identify each one, and discuss four types of achievement goal. These are listed below:

1   *Mastery-approach goal* – The individual measures the goal in absolute or personal terms. They find that the tougher the goal is, the more challenging it is for them personally and they will use self-development methods to full effect.

2   *Performance-approach goal* – The individual references themselves against others, so it is competitive in this sense but still views success as the main aim.

3   *Mastery-avoidance goal* – This is sometimes seen in people who measure themselves against previous ability; for instance, the person who wishes to prove that they are still 'up to the mark', 'still got what it takes'. They fear not being able to do things they used to do when they were younger/fitter/more expert. They do not want to make basic mistakes. 'They are not ambitious in terms of self-improvement' (Seo 2009, p912).

4   *Performance-avoidance goal* – Individuals do not wish to be embarrassed in front of others. They do not wish to be last.

Seo (2009, p916) uses this 2 x 2 grid to explore how people's achievement goal orientations might impact upon their procrastination behaviour and has arrived at the following findings:

1   Both mastery-avoidance and performance-avoidance goals are positively related to procrastination. In other words, if you fear failure you are more likely to procrastinate, no matter if you are comparing yourself against your own standards or against those of others.

2   Procrastination is negatively related to the mastery-approach goal. In other words, if you adopt a mastery-approach strategy, you are unlikely to procrastinate. Good news!

3   However, avoidance goals (which are related to procrastination) have a greater impact on the individual than mastery goals. Not so good news.

This leads Seo (2009, p917) to the important statement:

> The results of the present study suggest that the way in which individuals interpret these task features positively or negatively is more important than the task-related features themselves. If students are helped to set positive expectations about a task, interventions designed to decrease students' procrastination might be more successful.

ACTIVITY 4.3

I will ask a question this time! (Is this you?)

Scenario

Imagine that you have been invited to attend a prestigious talk given by a renowned expert in a field of study that you are passionate about – in fact you have been carrying out some research of your own on the very topic which is being debated (think of such a topic now – or you might recall a situation similar to the one which is now described). You are attending with other work colleagues, some of them very senior in your organisation. You follow the speaker's presentation rapt with attention. The speaker finishes with the words 'and I would be delighted to answer any questions you may have'. After the applause there is an embarrassing silence. The person with the 'roving mike' anxiously glances around the packed auditorium, seeking to home in on the first raised hand. You have your question – you are burning to ask it. But dare you? In front of all these people, your boss ... and the prestigious speaker? Or will you put off asking your question this time? (once again?).

Task

Make a list of pros and cons for asking the speaker the first question.

Would it make any difference to you if you asked the second or subsequent question?

Now analyse your answers in terms of Seo's (2009) four types of achievement goals (that is, mastery-approach, performance-approach, mastery-avoidance and performance-avoidance).

4.3.3 CAN PROCRASTINATION EVER BE A 'GOOD THING'?

Some people say that they work best under pressure. They deliberately do not do something at the earliest opportunity but wait until they feel they need to do it. There is some research in support of this: Chu and Choi (2005) suggest that this behaviour is consistent with 'active procrastination', a different sort of delaying behaviour compared with the more usual concept of procrastination, which they termed 'passive procrastination'.

Active procrastinators enjoyed the challenge they got from working to tight deadlines and the sense of achievement in hitting submission dates (note: they delayed yet still hit the target deadlines). By comparison 'passive procrastinators' performed poorly as deadlines approached – to the extent of giving up on occasion, and often did not hit submission dates as they had underestimated the time required for task completion.

Active procrastinators had a high level of self-belief in their ability to achieve their goals (what is known as 'self-efficacy', see Bandura 1977 for further details). Later work by Choi and Moran (2009, p208) speculated that active procrastinators were very good at re-prioritising and handling the time they had available to them in a highly flexible manner. They suggested that occupations that had tight deadlines and unexpected interruptions (such as management consultants, professors, software engineers) favoured such a flexible approach. It could therefore be argued that this is a very effective time management strategy in certain situations but one that requires a very skilled practitioner!

ACTIVITY 4.4

Active procrastinator?

Can you think of a time when you acted as an 'active procrastinator', deliberately delaying an activity but ultimately achieving it by the deadline? If so, what are your thoughts now on your strategy? Is it an approach you would use again and if so in what circumstances?

If you have never acted as an 'active procrastinator', suggest possible reasons why you have not done so.

4.3.4 GUARDING AGAINST THE DAMAGING EFFECTS OF PROCRASTINATION

From our previous discussion we can summarise some general rules to help protect us from the worst effects of procrastination. You may also wish to use these as general guidelines for any staff who report to you, or people you are training/developing:

1   Free yourself from interesting distractions!

2   Restrict your use of e-breaks.

3   Think of ways to make tedious tasks more enjoyable.

4   Repeatedly ask yourself, 'Is what I am doing really important or should I be doing something else?'

5   Adopt an 'approaching success' strategy in yourself and others by encouraging and rewarding undertaking personal challenges, regarding mistakes as an inevitable part of learning, celebrating subsequent learning and success. Add further 'mastery goals' to whatever it is you are doing.

6   Reduce 'avoidance' strategies in yourself and others by not personalising mistakes, feeling humiliated to make mistakes. If you tend to worry that you cannot cope with a new task, ask for further guidance. If you manage people like this, give them more guidance and encouragement.

4.4 PERSONAL ORGANISATION SKILLS

Personal organisation skills are exactly that – personal. What suits one person may not suit another. Having said this, there is a requirement for some sense of *order* in our lives. One of the founding figures of management theory, Henri Fayol (1949) had this to say of order, as one of his 14 principles of management (Fayol 1949, revised by Gray 1987, p77): 'The formula for order is … a place for everything and everything in its place … a place for everyone and everyone in his [or her] place.' Time management, as previously discussed, is one aspect of personal organisation, and in its own way gives a sense of order to how we spend our time. Other areas of our working lives that we organise include how we store and access information and how we arrange our personal working space. We will briefly outline these. However, a more fundamental organisation skill for team leaders and managers is the ability to delegate certain aspects of their job roles. This has direct links with stress management as it allows otherwise overloaded managers to focus on their major contributions to the organisation. Some people attempt to do this but cannot fully release the reins and end up by meddling in the detail of tasks supposedly delegated to their staff, a situation sometimes referred to as 'micromanagement' (White 2010).

4.4.1 EVERYTHING IN ITS PLACE...

Look on the Internet under 'declutter your life' and you will find a host of articles with titles such as 'Ten ways to get rid of clutter' – the majority of them written by self-appointed experts, much of it based on their personal experience or anecdotal tips. The sheer number of articles suggests that clutter is a very real problem. It seems to make sense to keep things where you can easily find them; that there comes a point beyond which you cannot easily locate information in a disorganised filing system, that you can even 'lose' something on a messy desk. Written by specialists Theo Theobald and Cary Cooper (2007), the book *Detox Your Desk: Declutter your life and mind* gives a very practical ten-day 'detox' programme, based on the following steps (Theobald 2007), which you may notice go beyond the simple notion of tidying your desk:

1   Clear the clutter.

2   Wipe as you go.

3   Hydrate – keep a clear mind by avoiding dehydration.

4   Stop! – stop doing the things that do not matter.

5   Set your own standards.

6   Make a change a day.

7   Stop self-sabotaging.

8   Volunteer for extra – for example, help someone else out – they will repay you.

9   Curb your fear of success.

10   Do the daunting – do not put off doing things.

 ACTIVITY 4.5

Detox focus

Jot down your feelings about this list. Is there any particular area(s) which needs your immediate attention? How will your sense of well-being and/or your performance change once these areas have been addressed?

4.4.2 SCHEDULES, PLANS AND DIARIES

Where would we be without schedules and plans? It is not easy to keep detailed information in our heads; also, to convey that information to other people is much more difficult without something written down. However, as useful as schedules and plans are, the *planning process* is arguably of greater importance. Thinking through the logical sequence of activities and allocating resources (for example staff, materials, equipment, budgets) is an essential management task; monitoring events against the plan as they unfold allows the manager to retain control by applying the necessary corrective actions – which may include an element of re-planning. It is of little use to create a plan and then to consign this to a dusty shelf! One word of advice on plans in this regard: as they are often subject to change make sure that *each revision is clearly labelled*, either by date of issue or by revision number. Then make sure that everyone is given the updated plan to work to. (This advice applies to all quality documentation.) We can create plans for ourselves and for the tasks we are working on. Both types of plan should help us to make the most effective use of our time.

4.4.2.1 Daily 'to do' lists

Daily 'to do' lists may be something that you already write. They are useful as a means of firstly collecting together all of the things that you need to accomplish. You should then prioritise your list. One way to do this is to categorise them as 'must do', 'should do', 'would like to do'. Another way is to list them as 'important' and 'urgent': important things are those which are the few but vital tasks – they may or may not require immediate action; things which require immediate action are the urgent ones which will not wait. Occasionally you will have to deal with tasks that are both important *and* urgent – clearly these should be tackled as a priority.

4.4.2.2 Planners and diaries

On a longer-term basis you may find it useful to use some sort of weekly/monthly planner, inserting key work-related dates. To be useful it must be readily accessible. You should be able to easily add to your planner and make appropriate changes. This may be done electronically, especially if you need to share diary availability with others in your organisation.

4.4.3 DELEGATION AND MICROMANAGEMENT

At a more fundamental level we are sometimes in the position (and this is usually the case for team leaders and managers) to be able delegate some tasks to others in our organisation. This side of our personal organisation is not always clearly defined so we may have scope to pass some tasks and responsibilities on to others. The advice of Tannenbaum and Schmidt (1986, p129), as given in a classic article in the *Harvard Business Review*, still holds true: although we may delegate responsibility for certain tasks, we are still *accountable* for them. By delegating tasks we can help others develop their skills and at the same time allow us more time to focus on other, more important, central aspects of our job roles. By doing so we may be able to alleviate stress created by task overload. However, implicit in delegation is the question, 'Should managers participate with subordinates once they have delegated responsibility to them?' (Tannenbaum and Schmidt 1986, p129). Tannenbaum and Schmidt recommend that managers may participate but should do so in a member role rather than an authority role.

Managers who say that they have delegated but then meddle unnecessarily with the detail of supposedly delegated tasks may be said to be acting as *micromanagers*. White (2010, p71) states:

> At its most severe level, micromanagement is a compulsive, behavioural disorder similar to other addictive patterns. People who micromanage generally do so because they feel unsure and self-doubting.

White (2010, p72) goes on to describe 'symptoms' of this 'disease'. The following list outlines the main characteristics of micromanagers:

- oversee their workers too closely
- are control freaks
- go alone to their boss's office as they do not wish subordinates to gain credit
- demand frequent status reports from others but often cause delays themselves as they are so busy
- stretch themselves too thin and take on too many projects
- hate mistakes, seldom praise, consider their employees incompetent.

The advice given in *Management Today*'s 'Brainfood' section (2009, p18) goes some way to counter this approach under the heading of 'Do it right: Dynamic Delegation', as shown below:

- Delegate for the right reason (not to simply offload tasks).
- Delegate to the right people.
- Brief thoroughly.
- Define results but not method.
- Give them the tools that they need to do the job.
- Keep an eye on how they are doing but resist the temptation to grab the reins back at the first sign of trouble.

ACTIVITY 4.6

Micromanager

To what extent do you agree with the earlier statement of White's (2010) that micromanagement is a 'disease'? Do you recognise these traits in others at work? If you have a management responsibility for others, take an honest look at yourself – do you recognise any of these micromanagement 'symptoms' in yourself? Finally, how much do you think that the work context/situation influences your/others' ability to delegate?

4.5 STRESS MANAGEMENT SKILLS

4.5.1 STRESS – AN INTRODUCTION

Stress is likely to become the most dangerous risk to business in the early part of the twenty-first century.

These are the alarming words of the Health and Safety Executive (HSE) as reported by the CIPD (2009). In the same report the HSE stated that 'one in five workers' and some '5 million in the UK … reported feeling extremely stressed at work'. This does not, of course, mean that 5 million people are off ill with stress – but as many medical conditions are stress-related, it is still a shocking statistic. Further, in terms of absence and sickness, the CIPD's *Absence Management* survey of 2008 showed the problem was increasing amongst organisations (CIPD 2009). We shall explore the meaning of stress within this section, but for now a useful way to think of what it means is that repeated exposure to certain pressures may cause some people to feel '*emotionally anxious and exhausted*' (Boyd et al 2009, p199).

The general state of awareness regarding linkages between stress and work is part of a larger awareness of the mental health of the nation. A programme called 'Foresight' has been established by the Government Office for Science and has published a report entitled 'Mental capital and wellbeing: Making the most of ourselves in the 21st century' (Government Office for Science 2008). Again it is worth noting how common mental ill-health is amongst the general population. For instance, the above report (p21) states:

Many people experience mental ill-health: for example, about 16% of adults and 10% of children are affected by common mental disorders such as depression and anxiety at any one time. However, whilst all disorders are best detected and treated early, many go undiagnosed or are only treated when advanced, and when the impacts are severe for the individual and families.

One more set of statistics to consider is:

In 2000

– depression cost more than £9 billion for England and that depression/anxiety was the single most important cause of workplace absenteeism in the UK
– over half a million instances of stress resulted in absences from work, costing UK employers £3.7 billion each year (Foresight 2007).

Stressful conditions at work can exacerbate tendencies towards depression and anxiety-type illnesses. From all of the above, understanding and reducing unnecessary stress would therefore appear to be an eminently sensible strategy for managers to adopt within their workplace for both their staff and themselves. However, as we have work and personal lives, we must firstly appreciate that there are strong connections between them.

4.5.2 EFFECTS OF MULTIPLE WORK AND FAMILY DEMANDS

Figure 4.3 is an attempt to show in simplistic terms how work and personal (that is, outside of work) pressures *may* compound within the individual. This may seem a fairly intuitive conclusion but verification through research is limited; Melchior et al (2007, p573) state that 'the cumulative effects of multiple work and family demands are not well known, particularly for men', but concluded in their article (2007, p580) that 'Men and women who experience high levels of work and family demands are at increased risk of psychiatric sickness and absence'. Figure 4.3 is therefore for discussion purposes rather than a statement of fact.

Figure 4.3 Potential combination effects of personal life and work life in an individual

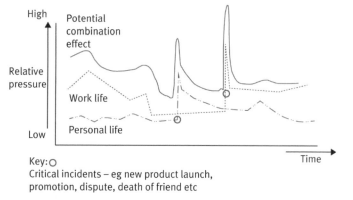

Critical incidents

Also in Figure 4.3 you will see the inclusion of 'critical incidents' which can give rise to pressure spikes. Some of these are, as you would expect, upsetting events such as a dispute or the death of a friend, but others are what we might want – for instance, the launch of a new product, or a personal promotion. This approach reflects studies by Holmes and Rahe (1967), who give a range of life events in a scale, placing the death of a spouse at the top with a value of 100, followed by other events including divorce (73), fired at work (47), change in residence (20), and so on. You should note that the pressure effect you experience may range from one of excitement to one of stress. However, as we shall see, what stresses one person may be easily accommodated by another.

4.5.2.1 Storing of stress over time

Figure 4.3 also shows the overall fluctuation in terms of the overall pressure on the individual. It would appear to show a fairly healthy response in that the effect on this particular individual does reduce when the pressure abates. However, you should be aware that there is evidence to show that the effects of stress can be cumulative over time (Sun et al 2007) – in other words, your body does not always return to its unstressed former state after each stressful challenge is encountered but stores up tension somehow and then the next stressful event builds on top of this; this is the basis for the concept of analysing how many stressful events you have encountered in a specific time (for instance a year) and inferring from this a cumulative stress load. In certain conditions we may even become sensitised and struggle to cope with pressures which we previously handled with ease.

ACTIVITY 4.7

Personal pressures

Identify typical personal and work critical incidents and their associated pressures for yourself over the last year. What are the implications on your level of well-being? Would you benefit from any remedial action? If so, what may this be? You may want to discuss this with a tutor or mentor.

4.5.3 STRESS MECHANISMS

4.5.3.1 Fight/flight

The classic model of stress (Selye 1976) describes a natural response of our bodies to a perceived threat. Our ancestors in Stone Age times might, so we are told, have been faced with the fearsome prospect of a confrontation with a sabre-toothed tiger (why this particular animal features so prominently is open to discussion, but those fangs surely must have something to do with it!); faced with the tiger, our ancestor would have had two choices – fight or run (flight). In such circumstances our bodies produce a powerful cocktail of hormones and chemicals that include raising our blood pressure and diverting blood to our muscles ready for action. Some time later, after either killing the tiger or managing to evade it by running away and climbing the nearest tree, our ancestor's bodily state would return to its previous resting state. Fortunately we do not have to fight or run away from tigers today, but the downside is that we still experience the same fight/flight reaction for other perceived threats. Rarely are these life-threatening, but they often have the ability to trigger some or all of the fight/flight reaction. Sometimes this can give us a certain 'edge' which improves our performance – such as the slight feeling of unease/ excitement before giving a presentation – but at other times can be a nuisance and actually detract from our performance. A further consideration is the cumulative effect of what are, in effect, relatively small stressors over the course of the working day but which can lead to a pooling of stress hormones in our bodies, which have no effective way to quickly release them – unlike the case of our ancestor, who could expend considerable energy in either fighting or running, effectively dissipating them.

4.5.3.2 Stressors at work

As outlined above, what is felt by one person as something which is uncomfortable, demanding or threatening is not necessarily felt by someone else. All jobs have demands of the individual; by their very nature they must – also all jobs have a role to be played and specific responsibilities. Typical stress factors are:

- hours worked (it is interesting to note that in the UK we work some of the longest hours in Europe – some 3 million people work more than 48 hours per week (Meade 2009))
- intensity of work
- challenge of tasks/situation
- change situations
- deadlines for task completion
- control over outcomes
- support from others
- responsibility for outcomes
- responsibility for others
- team relationships
- supervisor and subordinate relationships.

In certain cases there may be a tension caused by too many different demands being placed on the individual (role overload) and in others a person may have two or more roles that conflict (for instance a manager may have to discipline someone in one situation but may wish to help them in another) – role conflict.

As mentioned previously, the mere presence of these factors does not automatically mean that an individual feels overwhelmed by them. One explanation is proposed in the effort–reward imbalance (ERI) theory, which considers over a period of time the benefits (or otherwise) of an individual taking on a demanding job role, as outlined by the following defining statement:

> Effort–reward imbalance describes the perceived mismatch of spent efforts and received rewards in the workplace … A situation where an employee is investing overtime hours into completing projects with tight deadlines, but has poor career prospects and fears of being laid off, would be an example of a harmful imbalance. An extended period of harmful imbalance can cause strain reactions that may contribute to various physical and psychological illnesses (Hyvönen et al 2010, p407).

 ## ACTIVITY 4.8

Effort–reward imbalance

Do you agree with the above statement by Hyvönen et al (2010)? Discuss with a colleague, using examples if possible to support your case.

This is clearly heavily influenced by how we *think* about our jobs. However, many other factors are relevant. For instance, research on a large sample of Chinese employees (Sun et al 2007, p344) looked at the biological impact (the 'allostatic load') upon the body of chronic (that is, long-term) stress and reported that 'at 35 years, the scores began to rise sharply until age 65'. So, the implication is that we need to be better at managing our stress as we age, if we are to avoid illness.

Overcommitment to your job can be a problem, too. If you are ambitious, looking for esteem from others and have a strong need to control, you may be unable to withdraw from work (Hyvönen et al 2010, p407, quoting earlier research) and this can lead to burnout – physical and mental exhaustion and a cynical attitude to work.

4.5.4 WELL-BEING — IT'S NOT ALL NEGATIVE!

If you have the impression so far that all pressure is bad for you, that is hardly surprising, for until relatively recently most studies focused upon people who were suffering from stress-related illnesses, with the emphasis being upon avoiding such consequences. However, as the CIPD (2009, p2) points out, 'It is healthy and essential that people experience challenges within their lives that cause pressure and, up to a certain point, an increase in pressure can improve performance and the quality of life.' Some researchers are now focusing on improving well-being of employees who are not already sick. This is a positive approach seeking to improve working lives. It may not be very fashionable to admit to others that, actually, you quite like certain aspects of your job, that at times you rather enjoy the stimulation of the challenge and indeed gain a significant amount of satisfaction, even pride from a job well done. This is the opposite side of the coin to burnout: it is called 'engagement'.

A model of work pressure that is consistent with this more balanced approach is the job demands–resources model. This reinforces the view that demands are only negative if they are excessive and introduces the concept of job resources as follows:

Job resources is defined as those physical, psychological, social or organizational aspects of work context that:

1   reduce the health-impairing impact of job demand,

2   are functional in achieving work goals, and

3   stimulate personal growth development, and learning (Van den Broeck et al 2008, p278).

So, if you have access to these job resources you should be better able to cope with the demands of the job, and hence more likely to avoid feeling stressed. However, Van den Broeck et al (2008) go further to suggest that there is a motivational process at work, that of work engagement. This motivational process appears to meet what they refer to as 'the "ABC": Autonomy, Belongingness, and Competence' (Van den Broeck et al 2008, p279). In other words, being in control of what you have to do at work (Autonomy), feeling part of a community (Belongingness), and feeling that you are doing a skilled job (Competence) are all motivational factors. These lead to individuals feeling more satisfied with their jobs and, when combined with a resourceful environment, enable people to not only handle the pressures of their jobs but to grow psychologically through them.

This approach has obvious links to job design: if we can design jobs (Hackman and Oldham 1976) that are interesting, meaningful, provide us with feedback from others and allow us to achieve our potential we can provide ABC factors. This is far from being a 'quick-fix' method. It may mean a fundamental rethinking of job roles.

 ACTIVITY 4.9

Your ABC

Using your present (or a previous) job, assess it using the ABC factors outlined above. What conclusion can you draw from this analysis? If you are feeling dissatisfied with your findings, have you any thoughts on how your job might be improved?

4.5.5 AM I A WORKAHOLIC?

ACTIVITY 4.10

Workaholic quiz

Take a little time to consider the questions listed below:

Do you:

- Work 50–60 hours per week?
- Work very hard?
- Think about work even when not working?
- Sometime have arguments with your partner that you are working too much?
- Find it difficult to 'switch off'?
- Feel guilty taking your lunch break/all of your lunch break at work?
- Feel there is always much more to do, even after working hard?
- Have little time for socialising outside of work?
- Frequently not take all of your holiday entitlement?
- No longer have sufficient time for your favourite hobbies/sports?
- Love your job?
- Feel energised and stimulated by your work?

If a lot of your answers to these questions have been 'yes', alarm bells should ring: you may be a workaholic or on the slippery slopes towards becoming one!

Consider the following definition of workaholism:

> Workaholism (is) an irresistible inner drive to work excessively hard … workaholism includes two elements: a strong inner drive and working hard … a compulsion (Schaufeli et al 2009, p156).

Workaholism when defined like this is an addiction. It is obsessive. The addict feels compelled to work, feels uncomfortable when not working. The 'addict' may even realise that this sort of behaviour is likely to isolate them from family and friends and is damaging their physical and mental health through their inability to 'switch off' and relax – yet is still unable to resist the urge to work. In such cases work does provide some respite and satisfaction (though surprisingly little, according to some researchers, as outlined by Schaufeli et al 2009, pp158, 166) but this does not last long and the 'addict' is soon looking for their next 'fix'.

Schaufeli et al (2009, p166) tell us that many theorists distinguish between 'good' and 'bad' forms of workaholism and refer to the work of Buelens and Poelmans (2004), who investigated the idea that some workaholics were 'happy hard workers'. (However, their particular study did not support this theory.)

Given that some organisational cultures exhort people to work hard, to work long hours, to skip breaks and always be available on text or email, it is easy to see how susceptible individuals may succumb to workaholism. Indeed, their behaviour may be regarded in their companies as 'normal' or even as a role model for others who wish to succeed.

For those who fear that they are taking their work to extreme limits and are in danger of becoming 'workaholics', read on for strategies which go beyond the obvious ones (such as ensuring that you take sensible breaks during the working day and taking all of your holiday entitlement). Many of these can be listed under the heading of 'switching off'.

4.5.6 CALMING AND COPING STRATEGIES

It should be said at this point that if you have been feeling really stressed over a prolonged period of time, you should discuss matters with a trained counsellor or your doctor, who will be able to help you. Your goal should be to recover and then learn to recognise symptoms of stress in yourself and able to apply appropriate coping strategies in the future. Self-awareness, knowledge of what to do and your own self-belief in applying these techniques (what the theorists call 'self-efficacy') are invaluable friends. In fact Boyd et al (2009, p199) state that 'some researchers suggest that the coping style or strategy used may be more important to individual well-being than the presence of the stressor itself'. The following strategies outline some of the work literature (in particular) on dealing with stress in the workplace. Some go further and suggest, in a positive sense, how to improve well-being in the workplace.

4.5.6.1 Calming fight/flight response

Breathe!

One of the ways to manage stress is to hit the physiological 'relax' button after an unexpected threat has triggered your fight/flight response; alternatively you could activate this in advance of and during a planned experience. The simplest of these is simply to deliberately take a series of slow, deep breaths, which counters your natural tendency to tense up under pressure. Control of the breath is one of the fundamental devices used in the much deeper form of relaxation found in meditation and is well documented in guided self-help manuals (for example Williams et al 2007). Another way, if you have sufficient time, is to burn off some of those stress hormones by taking some exercise, such as a brisk walk outdoors, away from the immediate work situation. Even getting up from your desk and going to the work cafeteria is helpful.

ACTIVITY 4.11

Office yoga

There are many short video clips available on YouTube which will show you how to perform simple breathing exercises and yoga stretches. This clip (http://www.youtube.com/watch?v=4Dxay4McVP8andNR=1) demonstrates some easy but highly effective exercises you can perform in your office and are particularly good at relieving the tension build-up you might be experiencing from sitting too long at your desk or operating a computer. These are the sort of exercises that you could easily adapt to your own working situation (without needing to refer back to the video) so that they become part of your normal work routine. Have a relaxing stretch!

4.5.6.2 Relaxing music

Music can help you to relax after a stressful day, but according to recent research (Labbé et al 2007), it is important that it is the right type; typically, music was best selected by the individual and with a relaxing feel to it (classical quoted). Heavy metal music appears to have the reverse effect – you can be left feeling more stressed after listening to it.

4.5.6.3 Winding-down time – weekends and holidays

This advice will probably sound like the sort of thing your mum might have told you – but it seems mum was right in this case (Rook and Zijlstra 2006). Your body needs time to re-establish its normal unstressed state after each work day – so do not expect to relax if you are still doing work-related tasks at home or (worse?) ruminating over work matters. Good-quality sleep is really important. The traditional weekend break gives you time to recover, Saturday being the most beneficial day, and this effect is carried forward into the working week, but its effects soon fade. Holidays are also beneficial but research indicates that pre-vacation stress levels tend to return within three days (you probably already knew this too!) (Rook and Zijlstra 2006, p233).

4.5.6.4 Coping strategies

Coping may be defined as 'behavioural and cognitive efforts to deal with stressful situations' (Ben-Zur 2009, p87). These behaviours and thinking may take various forms but may be broadly categorised into either 'problem-focused coping' or 'emotion-focused coping'. According to Lazarus (1993, p239), 'the function of problem-focused coping is to change the troubled person–environment relationship by acting on the environment or oneself'. Or to put it another way, some people attempt to handle their stress by looking for ways to improve their situation. Here are two examples to illustrate this approach: (1) if you are feeling stressed because your office is a mess, you reorganise it; (2) if you are feeling stressed because you feel you do not know enough about a particular aspect of your job, you enrol on a training programme.

Of course you do not have to adopt this strategy. Take the previous example of your messy office; you could simply decide to *avoid* facing the mess – or having to tidy it up (quite literally an 'avoidance' strategy) by doing the bulk of your work somewhere else. Alternatively, you could adopt a different way of thinking about the so-called 'mess'; people who do this may say that they know exactly where things are – in other words, there is an order of sorts which is apparent to them. This really is to deny that the problem exists at all. Both of these strategies are emotion-focused coping strategies, as described by Lazarus (1993, p239), who writes: 'The function of emotion-focused coping is to change either a) the way the stressful relationship with the environment is attended to (as in vigilance or avoidance) or b) the relational meaning of what is happening, which mitigates the stress even though the actual conditions of the relationship have not changed … for example denial or distancing.'

Deciding which approach to take – problem focused or emotion focused – is sometimes your choice, but you cannot always change things. There is a well-known prayer (of contested origin) which reflects this dilemma, and whether you are of a religious disposition or not, has a certain ring of truth to it:

> God,
>
> Grant me the serenity to accept the things I cannot change;
>
> The courage to change the things I can;
>
> And the wisdom to know the difference. (Anon)

Thus, if you have made a mistake, you can try to retrieve the situation through some action and, if successful, will reduce your stressful feelings. However, some mistakes cannot be corrected. It may be useful then to think about the 'mistake' as an 'experience' from which you will learn and which will guide you in the future.

4.5.6.5 Emotional support – it's good to talk!

It would seem that even project managers (who, unsurprisingly, often use problem-focused strategies to handle stressful situations) most frequently used emotional support as a coping strategy. They talk to others about what is happening on their project, vent their frustrations with the project and other people, and seek advice and a friendly ear (Richmond and Skitmore 2006, pp8, 15, Aitken and Crawford 2007). The research reinforces what to many of us sounds so obvious – if you are stressed or anxious, it usually helps to talk to someone.

Depending upon who you talk to, you might even gain more than emotional support; the other person may be able to offer you advice on how to solve your problem. They might tell you of a time when they had a similar experience and how they approached it. They may remind you of your strengths and abilities and that encourages you to a plan of action; there is evidence that people with a high self-belief (self-efficacy) use more problem-focused strategies (Boyd et al 2009, p200). In many cases it is useful to be able to use problem- and emotion-focused strategies in tandem.

4.5.7 GET ACTIVE!

It is official! Exercise is good for both your physical and mental health, according to the Government's Foresight Project, Mental Health and Wellbeing. To quote from Section 4 of the report:

> Moderate activity seems to be most beneficial, with sessions lasting more than 30 minutes, a few times a week. However, benefits were also seen in studies prescribing relatively low intensity and duration of physical activity … Low impact physical activity such as stretching, toning and yoga may be effective in reducing depressive symptom and increasing psychological wellbeing (Hendrickx and Van der Ouderaa 2008).

The report goes on to explain that research has shown that these effects may be due to a number of reasons: they provide individuals with a positive 'mastery' method for self-improvement (a problem-focused, self-efficacy approach) whereby they feel in control of managing their stress levels; increased social interaction with others; increased production in the brain of serotonin, whose depletion is linked to depression; and increased levels of endorphins, which reduce pain and give a feeling of euphoria.

4.5.7.1 Green exercise – or 'gone fishing'

Getting outside to the natural environment and green space has also been linked to better well-being. Researchers are now starting to combine this with the effects of exercise and look at activities such as walking, cycling, horse-riding, fishing, canal-boating, and conservation activities. Pretty et al (2007, p211) state that in their study 'it was found that green exercise led to a significant improvement in self-esteem and total mood disturbance (with … tension anxiety improving post-activity)'.

 ACTIVITY 4.12

Back to nature

What sorts of natural environment appeal to you? How might you access this natural environment on a more regular basis? Are there any activities you enjoyed in the past and might want to do again? Are there any activities which you have not yet tried but would like to learn more about?

4.6 RETURNING TO WORK AFTER EXTENDED SICK LEAVE

4.6.1 IT WON'T HAPPEN TO ME

No one likes to think that they are going to fall sick or have a serious injury and have to take an extended time off work. However, at some point this is likely to happen to you or one of your work colleagues. Coping with the illness itself may be trying – but often, so is your eventual return to work. While much of the advice given earlier in this chapter may prove useful, you should be aware that returning to work after long-term sickness can have demands of its own. You may feel isolated and apprehensive; you may well benefit from the support of others. In this section you will consider a real-life example. This concerns the case of someone who returns to work after treatment for cancer. Of course, there are many types of significant illness and injury, both physical and mental, that can lead to people taking time off work. Sometimes ill-health is chronic (that is, continues indefinitely) and sometimes the individual may experience recurring episodes of alternate good and bad health. Each illness requires its own approach. That said, there are certain practices and principles that you and your organisation can follow to make your return to work more successful. Some of these are down to your own self-management, while others require actions from your organisation. There is an emphasis these days on encouraging people to go back to work after illness or injury, if they can do so. In the UK since 2010 doctors sign 'fit notes' ('Fit note – Department for Work and Pensions – Inside Government – GOV.UK', nd), which state that you are either 'not fit for work' or 'may be fit for work', with the proviso that the organisation may need to consider making adjustments to your work role/situation to allow this to happen.

 RETURNING TO WORK AS A CANCER SURVIVOR

CASE STUDY 4.1

John worked for the local university. In his mid-fifties he had been shocked when he was diagnosed with prostate cancer.* He decided to go for surgical treatment, which involved the removal of his prostate. This might provide a complete cure but it was possible that further treatment would be required. Before his operation he had been a fit, active person; but in the days and weeks that followed, his world changed from that of an independent individual to one of being a hospital patient and, subsequently, a recovering cancer survivor. He had thought that after his operation he could spend his recuperation time working on his laptop: the reality was that tiredness and pain would restrict him for much of the first month, and work was the last thing on his mind. He felt that he should just be able to 'bounce back', but soon found that recovery and strength came slowly – something which he struggled to

accept. Once discharged from hospital, his wife gave him an incredible amount of love and support at home for the first two weeks – but then she had to return to work herself; luckily, a very good friend (an old walking buddy) visited him each day, bringing him the daily papers and sharing lunch. Driving for the first six weeks was out of the question. However, he was determined to regain his former mobility; with his wife and friend he went on walks most days, from a few hundred yards at first, gradually working up to a few miles after six weeks. Gaining confidence in his physical ability was a slow process. He still felt shattered at the end of each day. His emotions were that of a rollercoaster – the expected lows and (surprisingly) the occasional highs. But, buoyed by his wife and friends, including his workmates who he had met up with, he gradually felt that he was getting 'back to normal'. Frustratingly, though, he still found sitting in a chair for any length of time to be one of the most uncomfortable aspects of his recovery – and bearing in mind the sedentary nature of his job, this would be restrictive if it continued. As for any traces of remaining cancer, John would be tested every three months at first and further treatment was possible, if needed. So John was, in effect, a 'cancer survivor'.

John had always regarded his work as a big part of his life; it provided purpose, sense of identity, financial security, interest and routine. He enjoyed working on new projects and interacting with others. He had soon tired of day-time television and felt bored. After a few months of recovery he was itching to get back to work, but apprehensive of his ability to cope with the full demands of his job. However, help was at hand; he talked to the occupational health nurse at his university and his team leader, and it was agreed that he could work on a 'phased return' basis for his first three months back at work. This was tailored to his particular needs; he would teach fewer classes; he would be limited to one-hour sessions with breaks in between; he would be excused from long periods of sitting at meetings. His GP agreed the phased return-to-work strategy and signed John's 'fit note'. John found the first month back at work to be a lot more tiring – both physically and mentally – than he had envisaged, but felt that psychologically it was the right thing for him to do. He was pleased to be back with his old work friends. Gradually, his strength and stamina returned and he was given more work after his phased return ended (although he felt reassured that he could ask for a review to extend this, should he still feel unable to do more). A year after his operation he felt more or less back to

his former health and was even starting to think about engaging in some of the work initiatives he had previously enjoyed doing. At the same time, he had reviewed his work–life balance and was ensuring that he built in sufficient time for relaxation, exercise and holidays.

The prostate gland is only found in men. It's about the size of a walnut and gets a little bigger with age. It surrounds the first part of the tube (urethra) that carries urine from the bladder along the penis ('The prostate gland', 2013).

Prostate cancer generally affects men over 50 and is rare in younger men. It's the most common type of cancer in men. Around 37,000 men in the UK are diagnosed with prostate cancer each year ('Prostate cancer', 2012).

… everyone with cancer is classed as disabled under the Equality Act, or the Disability Discrimination Act (DDA) in Northern Ireland, and is therefore protected by these Acts. An employer can't discriminate against you because you've had cancer. The employer has a duty to make 'reasonable adjustments' to workplaces and working practices to make sure that people with a disability are not at a disadvantage compared to other people. An example of a reasonable adjustment might include:

- *allowing some flexibility in working hours*
- *allowing extra breaks to help an employee cope with fatigue*
- *temporarily allowing the employee to be restricted to 'light duties'*
- *allowing working from home*
- *allowing 'phased (gradual) return' to work after extended sick leave.*

('Work after cancer treatment', 2010)

ACTIVITY 4.13

Case Study 4.1 followed the real-life experience of John (not his real name), his illness, recovery and phased return to work. John's story is not uncommon – many people get cancer at some point in their lives and, increasingly, more of them are able to return to work after treatment. Every person who gets cancer has their own experience; however, the case study raises issues which many people are faced with. This article uses web references from Macmillan Cancer Support. Here are some questions which you might wish to think about:

1   What do you think are the challenges facing the employee after long-term sick leave? (You may wish to consider the case of John, or other long-term sickness cases – for instance, stress-related illnesses.)

2   What do you think are the challenges for those involved in designing the 'phased return to work' approach (for example occupational health nurse and team leader) for returning employees?

You may want to discuss your answers with a peer, a mentor or in a small group.

4.7 CONCLUSION

Self-management skills are a 'must have' for anyone at work. As with any set of skills, you may already have a natural aptitude for them – for instance you might already consider yourself to be a good organiser and you may be the sort of person who rarely gets stressed, even under pressure. However, the majority of people will benefit greatly from developing these skills through practising the sorts of techniques outlined in this chapter. By managing your work–life balance you will certainly be more effective at both home and work – and perhaps even improve your general well-being in the process.

KEY LEARNING POINTS

This chapter has highlighted some key learning points, which may be summarised as follows:

- Through analysing where you spend your time, you may plan for time management improvement.
- Sometimes you just have to get on and do things, regardless of your mood.
- People put off doing things for a range of reasons – understanding this helps you to plan your action strategy.
- Organisation is probably an underrated skill: even simple use of diaries and schedules or having a clutter-free work environment will make you much more effective at work.
- Delegation is a difficult but important skill, allowing you to focus on your main job role, while developing others at the same time.
- Managing stress at both home and work is essential for our general well-being. It should never be underrated as the statistics show it is one of the major factors of absence and sickness.
- We need to be aware that we can use a range of problem- and emotion-oriented methods to manage our stress – and be prepared to apply them as necessary.
- Returning to work after extended sick leave can be difficult, but there are recognised avenues that you and your employer can take to ease your return.

PAUSE FOR THOUGHT

Identify at least three things that you have learned by studying this chapter and engaging with the activities. How will your newly acquired knowledge and skills support your continuing professional development? What value do you expect your learning to have for your daily routines and your further career? In what area have you identified a need for further development and how are you planning to fill that gap? Address these issues in your learning journal and/or CPD log. You may also wish to discuss them with a peer, colleague, mentor or coach to aid your further development.

EXPLORE FURTHER

Here are some more ideas for you to consider:

To look at the Government's Foresight project on mental health and well-being, go to the following website: http://www.foresight.gov.uk/OurWork/ActiveProjects/Mental%20Capital/ProjectOutputs.asp [Accessed 28 July 2013].

And, here are two case studies of companies which have implemented health and well-being strategies for their staff – complete with cost–benefit analyses:

http://www.hse.gov.uk/business/casestudy/astrazeneca.htm [Accessed 28 July 2013]

http://www.hse.gov.uk/business/casestudy/portlondon.htm [Accessed 28 July 2013].

A very interesting area to look at which is receiving a lot of attention at the moment is the concept of 'mindfulness'. This can be a good technique to use if you have difficulty in 'switching off' your mind from work. Mindfulness techniques train your mind to focus on the here and now, rather than dwell on the past or worry about the future. To find out more, you could look for YouTube videos featuring Jon Kabat-Zinn (he is also in the reference list, see Williams et al 2007).

Go to the following link on YouTube to see a clip with Professor Cary Cooper, one of the UK's leading experts on stress management: http://www.youtube.com/watch?v=-oapmDhrkUU [Accessed 28 July 2013]. Make notes of what he says about:

1   the role of managers for the health of those in their departments

2   how flexible working arrangements can help manage stress

3   stress and well-being audits in organisations.

The HSE (Health and Safety Executive) gives useful advice on how organisations should tackle stress in the workplace at: http://www.hse.gov.uk/stress/standards/downloads.htm [Accessed 28 July 2013].

The following link gives valuable advice from the CIPD (requires membership) on various issues concerning absence management: http://www.cipd.co.uk/hr-resources/employment-law-faqs/absence-management.aspx [Accessed 28 July 2013].

REFERENCES

AITKEN, A. and CRAWFORD, L. (2007) Coping with stress: dispositional coping strategies of project managers. *International Journal of Project Management.* Vol 25, No 7. pp666–73.

BAKER, J.R. and PHILLIPS, J.G. (2007) E-mail, decisional styles, and rest breaks. *Cyber Psychology and Behavior.* Vol 10, No 5. pp705–8.

BANDURA, A. (1977) Self-efficacy: towards a unifying theory of behavioral change. *Psychological Review.* Vol 84, No 2. pp191–215.

BEN-ZUR, H. (2009) Coping styles and effect. *International Journal of Stress Management.* Vol 16, No 2. pp87–101.

BOYD, N.G., LEWIN, J.E. and SAGER, J.K. (2009) A model of stress and coping and their influence on individual and organizational outcomes. *Journal of Vocational Behavior.* Vol 75, No 2. pp197–211.

BUELENS, M. and POELMANS, S. (2004) Enriching the Spence and Robbins' typology of workaholism: demographic, motivational and organizational correlates. *Journal of Organizational Change and Management.* Vol 17, No 5. pp440–58.

CHOI, J.N. and MORAN, S.V. (2009) Why not procrastinate? Development and validation of a new active procrastination scale. *The Journal of Social Psychology.* Vol 149, No 2. pp195–211.

CHU, A.H. and CHOI, J.N. (2005) Rethinking procrastination: positive effects of 'active' procrastination behaviour on attitudes and performance. *The Journal of Social Psychology.* Vol 145, No 3. pp245–64.

CIPD. (2009) *Stress at work: work-related stress [online].* Factsheet, revised June. Available at: http://www.cipd.co.uk/subjects/health/stress/stress.htm?IsSrchRes=1 [Accessed 3 March 2010].

DECI, E.L. (1975) *Intrinsic motivation.* New York: Plenum.

ELLIOT, A.J. and MCGREGOR, H.A. (2001) A 2 x 2 achievement goal framework. *Journal of Personality and Social Psychology.* Vol 80, No 3. pp501–19.

FAYOL, H. (1949) *General and industrial management.* London: Pitman: Revised and updated by Irwin Gray, Belmont, CA: David S. Lake Publishers. 1987.

FERRARI, J.R., MASON, C.P. and HAMMER, C. (2006) Procrastination as a predictor of task perceptions: examining delayed and non-delayed tasks across varied deadlines. *Individual Differences Research.* Vol 4, No 1. pp28–36.

FERRARI, J.R., O'CALLAGHAN, J. and NEWBEGIN, I. (2005) Prevalence of procrastination in the United States, United Kingdom, and Australia: arousal and avoidance delays among adults. *North American Journal of Psychology.* Vol 7, No 1. pp1–6.

FIT NOTE – Department for Work and Pensions – Inside Government – GOV.UK. (nd) Available at: http://www.gov.uk/government/organisations/department-for-work-pensions/series/fit-note [Accessed 28 July 2013].

FORESIGHT. (2007) Mental capital and wellbeing. *PMSU Lunchtime Seminar.* 11 October.

GOVERNMENT OFFICE FOR SCIENCE. (2008) *Foresight mental capital and wellbeing project. Final Project Report - Executive Summary.* London: The Government Office for Science.

HACKMAN, J. and OLDHAM, G. (1976) Motivation through design of work: test of a theory. *Organizational Behavior and Human Performance.* Vol 16, No 2. pp250–79.

HENDRICKX, H. and VAN DER OUDERAA, F. (2008) *State of Science Review: SR-E24: the effect of physical activity on mental capital and wellbeing.* The Government Office for Science.

HOLMES, T.H. and RAHE, R.H. (1967) The social adjustment rating scale. *Journal of Psychosomatic Research.* Vol 11, No 2. pp213–18.

HYVÖNEN, K., FELDT, T., TOLVANEN, A. and KINNUNEN, U. (2010) The role of goal pursuit in the interaction between psychosocial work environment and occupational well-being. *Journal of Vocational Behavior.* Vol 76, No 2. pp406–18.

KELLY, W.E. (2002) Anxiety and the prediction of task duration: a preliminary analysis. *The Journal of Psychology.* Vol 136, No 1. pp53–8.

KELLY, W.E. and JOHNSON, J.L. (nd) Time use efficiency and the five-factor model of pesonality. *Education.* Vol 125, No 3. pp511–15.

LABBÉ, E., SCHMIDT, N., BABIN, J. and PHARR, M. (2007) Coping with stress: the effectiveness of different types of music. *Applied Psychophysiology and Biofeedback.* Vol 32, No 3/4. pp163–8.

LAZARUS, R.S. (1993) Coping theory and research: past, present, and future. *Psychosomatic Medicine.* Vol 55, No 1. pp234–7.

MANAGEMENT TODAY. (2009) Brainfood: do it right: dynamic delegation. *Management Today.* September 18.

MEADE, G. (2009) EU fails to curb Britain's work hours opt-out. *The Independent.* 28 April [online]. Available at: http://www.independent.co.uk/news/world/europe/eu-fails-to-curb-britains-work-hours-optout-1675368.html [Accessed 3 May 2010].

MELCHIOR, M., BERKMAN, L.F., NIEDHAMMER, I., ZINS, M. and GOLDBERG, M. (2007) The mental health effects of multiple work and family demands. *Social Psychiatry @ Psychiatric Epidemiology.* Vol 42, No 7. pp573–82.

MINTZBERG, H. (1990) The manager's job: folklore and fact (HBR Classic). *Harvard Business Review.* Vol 68, No 2. pp163–76.

MINTZBERG, H. (1997) *The nature of managerial work.* Harlow: Prentice Hall.

MOORCROFT, R. (2009) Delegation, not relegation. *Manager.* Autumn. pp4–5.

MURRAY, R. (2005) *Writing for academic journals.* Maidenhead: Open University Press.

OXFORD UNIVERSITY PRESS. (2006) *Compact Oxford English dictionary for students.* Oxford: Oxford University Press.

PEDLER, M., BURGOYNE, J. and BOYDELL, T. (2007) *A manager's guide to self-development.* 5th ed. Maidenhead: McGraw-Hill.

PRETTY, J., PEACOCK, J., HINE, R., SELLENS, M., SOUTH, N. and GRIFFIN, M. (2007) Green exercise in the UK countryside: effects on well-being, and implications for policy and planning. *Journal of Environmental Planning and Management*. Vol 50, No 2. pp211–31.

PROSTATE CANCER. (2012, 1 May) Document. Available at: http://www.macmillan.org.uk/Cancerinformation/Cancertypes/Prostate/Aboutprostatecancer/Prostatecancer.aspx [Accessed 28 July 2013].

THE PROSTATE GLAND. (2013, 1 January) Document. Available at: http://www.macmillan.org.uk/Cancerinformation/Testsscreening/ThePSAtest/Theprostategland.aspx [Accessed 28 July 2013].

RICHMOND, A. and SKITMORE, M. (2006) Stress and coping: a study of project managers in a large ICT organization. *Project Management Journal*. Vol 37, No 5. pp5–16.

ROOK, J.W. and ZIJLSTRA, F.R. (2006) The contribution of various types of activities to recovery. *European Journal of Work and Organizational Psychology*. Vol 15, No 2. pp218–40.

SADDLER, C.D. and BULEY, J. (1999) Predictors of academic procrastination in college students. *Psychological Reports*. Vol 84, No 2. pp686–8.

SCHAUFELI, W.B., BAKKER, A.B., VAN DER HEIJDEN, F.M. and PRINS, J.T. (2009) Workaholism, burnout and well-being among junior doctors: the mediating role of conflict. *Work and Stress*. Vol 23, No 2. pp155–72.

SELYE, H. (1976) *The stress of life*. New York: McGraw-Hill.

SEO, E.H. (2009) The relationship of procrastination with a mastery goal versus an avoidance goal. *Social Behaviour and Personality*. Vol 37, No 7. pp911–20.

SUN, J., WANG, S., ZHANG, J.Q. and LI, W. (2007) Assessing the cumulative effects of stress: the association between job stress and allostatic load in a large sample of Chinese employees. *Work and Stress*. Vol 21, No 4. pp333–47.

TANNENBAUM, R. and SCHMIDT, W.H. (1986) Excerpts from 'How to choose a leadership pattern'. *Harvard Business Review*. Vol 64, No 4. p129.

THEOBALD, T. (2007, 6 October) Clear thinking. *Guardian* [online]. Available at: http://guardian.co.uk/money/2007/oct/06/work [Accessed 24 April 2010].

THEOBALD, T. and COOPER, C.L. (2007) *Detox your desk: declutter your life and mind*. Chichester: Capstone Publishing.

TRACY, B. (2013) *Eat that frog*. San Francisco, CA: Hodder Paperbacks.

VAN DEN BROECK, A., VANSTEENKISTE, M., DE WITTE, H. and LENS, W. (2008) Explaining the relationship between job characteristics, burnout, and engagement: the role of basic psychological need satisfaction. *Work and Stress*. Vol 22, No 3. pp277–94.

WHITE, R.D. (2010) The micromanagement disease: symptoms, diagnosis, and cure. *Public Personnel Management*. Vol 39, No 1. pp71–6.

WILLIAMS, M., TEASDALE, J., SEGAL, Z. and KABAT-ZINN, J. (2007) *The mindful way through depression: freeing yourself from chronic unhappiness*. New York: Guildford Press.

WORK AFTER CANCER TREATMENT. (2010, 30 September) Document. Available at: http://www.macmillan.org.uk/Cancerinformation/Livingwithandaftercancer/Lifeaftercancer/Workaftercancer.aspx [Accessed 28 July 2013].

CHAPTER 5

Developing your Professional Identity

STEFANIE REISSNER

OVERVIEW

Simply having specialist knowledge and subject-specific skills will not be enough in a very competitive environment to convince employers that you are the right person for a job or promotion. Employers are increasingly looking for individuals who can demonstrate a broad repertoire of professional attributes that make them effective as soon as they join the organisation. This chapter aims to set the context for such developments by looking at how you can become adept at knowing how and when to use your knowledge and skills in the best way in professional situations, thereby developing the behaviours that are expected of a professional in your chosen field – what we call your professional identity.

LEARNING OUTCOMES

By the end of this chapter, provided you engage with the activities, you should be able to:

- understand the concept of professional identity and how it relates to effectiveness in the workplace
- understand how organisations communicate the professional behaviours that they expect from their employees and how individuals learn to conform
- apply self-awareness in a practical way to critically evaluate your own professional behaviours and those of others.

5.1 INTRODUCTION

The term 'professional' is often associated either with highly esteemed careers such as doctors, teachers and lawyers or with professional standards such as those of the CIPD. However, being a professional does not automatically mean behaving in a professional way in the workplace, irrespective of whether a role is defined or regulated by explicit standards of professionalism. What being professional means can be fruitfully explored by considering the medical profession. Doctors will have studied for several years both at university and in practice to be able to work as a doctor; they are highly qualified professionals. They will use universally recognised procedures to diagnose illness (such as blood tests and scans) and to treat it (such as medication or physiotherapy). But why, then, are most doctors regarded as experts in their field while others (albeit a small minority) as charlatans?

ACTIVITY 5.1

Being professional as a doctor

Make a list of the main characteristics of a bad doctor.

Now list some of the characteristics of a good doctor.

Your 'bad' list may include some of the following:

- does not listen to the patient explaining their symptoms
- is dismissive of the patient and/or patronising towards them
- fails to conduct recognised tests to diagnose an illness
- fails to prescribe the necessary medication at the right dose
- prevents the patient from seeing a specialist where necessary
- decides about the treatment regime without involving the patient.

Your 'good' list may include:

- takes time to listen to the patient
- interacts with the patient with respect and empathy
- uses recognised tests to diagnose an illness
- prescribes the right medication at the right dose
- refers the patient to a specialist where necessary
- discusses the treatment regime with the patient.

These examples show that the difference between these individuals is not in their medical knowledge or their 'tools' (that is, diagnostic tests and medication), but in the way they behave. The same applies to anyone in any job or profession – from those that require no formal qualification (such as a waiter, cleaner or call centre operative) to those that are highly regulated, such as the medical profession. There is increasing recognition that there is more to expert knowledge and subject-specific skills and that professional associations have an important role in fostering professionalism at the workplace. For example, the Royal College of Physicians and Surgeons of Canada introduced the CanMEDS competency framework in 2005 to inculcate in undergraduate medical students 'ethical practice, profession-led regulation, and high personal standards of behaviour' (Frank 2005, as cited in Sanders 2010, p99). The framework includes traits such as altruism, integrity, honesty, compassion, morality, self-awareness and self-assessment, and is currently updated to include (among others) patient safety (Royal College of Physicians and Surgeons of Canada 2013). Similarly, the CIPD Profession Map, introduced in 2010, includes eight behaviours that effective HR professionals have, including curiosity, credibility and courage to challenge (CIPD 2013a; see also Chapter 1 for details). Such attributes are unique to each individual and largely determine whether they will become a competent and respected professional (Slay and Smith 2011).

This has important implications for you: when you complete your postgraduate studies you will have been assessed to the same level of expert knowledge and subject-specific skills as the rest of your cohort (as defined by the learning outcomes of your programme of study). However, how good a professional you become in whatever field you choose will depend upon how your knowledge and skills interact with your behaviours. Of course, this is very personal and unique to you, such that it defines your professional identity, that is, 'one's professional self-concept based on attributes, beliefs, values, motives, and experiences' (Slay and Smith 2011, p86). Although you can be taught about the elements that make up this identity (tools such as the CIPD Profession Map are one way of doing so), it is down to you to develop self-awareness, engage in reflection and commit to the continuing development of your professional identity throughout your career. This is particularly pertinent when starting out your career and when changing careers (for example Ibarra 1999).

The aim of this chapter is to explore the concept of professional identity and its impact on your professional life. Specifically, we will consider the building blocks of professional identity and the importance of self-awareness in developing it. We will then discuss in more detail the role of personality, values, emotions and norms before considering how individuals learn to become part of an organisation or profession. As you move throughout your career, you may want to refer to the conceptualisation of professional identity presented here as part of your continuing professional development.

5.2 EXPLORING PROFESSIONAL IDENTITY

The concept of identity is rooted in psychology but has been adopted by organisational scholars to understand how individuals operate in the workplace (Kenny et al 2011). The various aspects that contribute towards an individual's identity are complex and include personality traits, motives, values, defence mechanisms and attachment styles (McAdams 1996). There is also evidence that identity is constructed and reconstructed through experience (most notably in groups), thereby integrating a reconstructed past, perceived present and anticipated future (for example Ibarra 1999). This means that one's identity is not 'set in stone' but that it evolves and adapts to different situations in the workplace. We will see later in this chapter that this is important in terms of our ability to adapt to different roles, work environments and careers.

Despite such malleability, in work settings identity is regarded as 'the relatively stable and enduring constellation of attributes, beliefs, values, motives, and experiences in terms of which people define themselves in a professional role' (Ibarra 1999, pp764–5, drawing on Schein 1978). Understanding your professional identity allows you not only to make sense of who you are at work but also how others perceive you within your professional role on the basis of your behaviours. This is particularly pertinent for newly qualified professionals as they are being socialised into the profession, that is, as they begin to understand the professional and/or organisational demands upon them. Any incongruence between what a role demands and how you see yourself as a professional can lead to problems with fulfilling that role effectively (Arthur et al 2009). In essence, then, understanding your professional identity means that you are able to question who you are in a professional context and also to understand who your organisation wants you to be.

We have already discussed the importance of the interaction between your expert knowledge, your subject-specific skills and your behaviours at the workplace. A good professional will ensure that all three elements work in harmony to fulfil their role effectively. While it is relatively easy to ensure that we have the appropriate knowledge and skills for any given job, it is more difficult to determine what appropriate professional behaviour means, how it can be controlled and, where necessary, adapted. To be able to do so, we need to understand what determines our behaviour.

 ACTIVITY 5.2

Reflection on behaviour

Think about an incident when someone's behaviour has shocked or surprised you. (You can use yourself as the example.) Note down the circumstances of the incident and what the person did.

Then reflect on why they might have behaved in that way. List anything that you think may have helped determine their behaviour.

Many things can affect an individual's behaviour in different situations, but some that you may have noted are:

- *Personality*: For example, someone with a placid personality may surprise you by behaving aggressively when there is a dispute.
- *Values*: Someone with moral or religious values that differ from your own may make decisions that you find difficult to understand.
- *Emotions*: We all act in different ways according to the emotional state we are in at the time. When we are angry, upset or distressed we can say or do things that we might later regret. Understanding our emotions and being able to step back from them is one of the fundamental elements of emotional intelligence (Goleman 2005).

Personality, values and emotions are a good place to start when trying to understand professional identity because most of us will be able to recognise the potential effects on our behaviour at work. However, Sanders (2010) includes a further element that may not have occurred to you when you were thinking about the question: norms. By this she means the accepted standards of behaviour within a profession or organisation (see Ibarra 1999). Norms are an important element of professional identity because of the potential problem of incongruence, as mentioned earlier. In the remainder of this chapter, we will explore in more detail how personality, values, emotions and norms affect our use of expert knowledge and subject-specific skills and how they ultimately influence our effectiveness as professionals. We can visualise these elements as part of the DNA that determines professional identity by forming the bonds between skills and knowledge:

Figure 5.1 Conceptualising professional identity

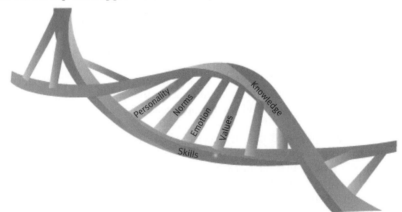

Source: reproduced with permission from Sanders 2010, p101

Before we examine each of the four binding elements of this model in turn, let us consider how professional identity may be manifested in practice.

TONY

CASE STUDY 5.1

Tony had spent nine years in the army, his only job since leaving school at the age of 16. Although he loved the job and was proud that he had done well, he decided to leave because he had a young family and no longer wanted to spend long periods away from them. He had gained a lot of experience and developed many skills in his army career so he felt fairly confident of securing a good job in civilian life. However, this proved to be difficult, and after many months of searching he found a position as a production line supervisor in a food processing factory, which was rather less than he had hoped for.

Most of the people that Tony had to manage were immigrant workers with a limited grasp of the English language. Tony found it frustrating when he asked them to do something and they did not respond in the way he wanted them to. When they did not do what he had asked, he tended to shout at them until they eventually 'got the message'.

Tony's production line did not always meet company targets, and as a result he was frequently subjected to questions and criticism from his manager. Tony usually responded to these sessions in the same way as he did with his staff – by shouting – which resulted in target reviews becoming regular weekly confrontations.

By this stage Tony was desperate to find another job and realised that he needed to do something to increase his chances, so he enrolled on a part-time business and management degree, which he hoped would tell him all he needed to know about management. However, he soon realised that it was not meeting his expectations at all. Instead of lecturers telling him all the theory he needed to know, he was being asked to spend some of the time with a group of peers (who, like

him, were all in junior management jobs), discussing and sharing their experiences and interpretation of the theory. He did not consider his fellow students to be sufficiently expert to be able to offer him the right answers. Despite his misgivings, Tony attended all classes and group discussion sessions, but he rarely contributed. He managed to pass all assignments, but achieved poor marks, the feedback indicating that his work was too descriptive and insufficiently analytical.

Six months after joining his degree programme Tony was at work late one Friday afternoon, engaged in one of his regular shouting matches with his manager. He got so angry that he stormed out, slamming the door behind him, determined to go home. Then, halfway to the car park he stopped as his colleagues in his learning group at university came into his mind. Recently they had been discussing conflict in the workplace and he began thinking about the things they had said. He realised then that his way of handling difficult situations was probably wrong and that he had to do something about his behaviour if he was ever going to do well. He returned to his manager's office and apologised (much to the manager's astonishment) and asked if they could start afresh. From that day he worked to change his behaviour and within six months he was promoted.

Consider:

- Why do you think Tony behaved the way he did when he started his new job?
- What effect do you think his behaviour had on his staff and on his performance in the job?
- Why do you think he initially behaved the way he did during his studies?
- What was it that changed Tony's behaviour?

In our conceptualisation of professional identity (see Figure 5.1) we are considering how behaviour can be affected by personality, values, emotions and norms, so let us look at each of these to see if they offer an explanation of Tony's behaviours.

Starting with **norms**, Tony had been in the army for nine years, and this was the only job he had ever had. The army norms that he was used to meant that when he asked his staff to do something he expected them to obey his 'orders' without question. When they did not do so (albeit because they did not understand) he became angry, frustrated and responded by shouting. Tony's mistake was to assume that what had worked well for him in the past would work just as well in the present. He did not appreciate that in assuming a new role he must adapt to the social norms and rules of the new workplace, including behaviours and patterns of interaction (Ibarra 1999). Tony was unable to change the norms of the factory, so to be effective *he* would have to change to become congruent with his new work situation.

In terms of **emotions**, Tony was clearly disappointed with the job, and so he may already have been feeling some underlying frustrations. When staff did not respond to his requests his frustration emerged as anger. However, in reacting in this way Tony was probably only exacerbating the problem. The emotional behaviour of a manager has important effects on organisational climate (Momeni 2009), and failure of managers to empathise and manage their own emotions can be costly for the organisation due to poor productivity (Kiel and Watson 2009). For this reason the study of emotions in the workplace, particularly emotional intelligence (EI), has become a pertinent issue in business and management (Goleman 2005), with many leadership programmes placing emphasis on emotional awareness, control and management. We will look at these later in this chapter to help you avoid making the same mistake as Tony.

What does the case tell us about Tony's **personality**? The anger response would indicate that he was quite an aggressive person, but could also point to other features. Tony clearly was not a natural 'people person' who thrives on interactions with others, so is there anything that he could do to interact more effectively with his subordinates? While much of our personality is determined by our genes, a large part is formed through interaction with our environment throughout life (Nolen-Hoeksema et al 2009). In other words, while Tony may never become a natural 'people person', he can modify his behaviour to interact more effectively with both his subordinates and superiors – and evidently he has been able to do so.

We know little of Tony's **values**, but we do know that he gave up a job he loved for the sake of his family, so we can assume that family values meant a great deal to him. If he felt that he had made a mistake in leaving the army because he could not find a job that enabled him to support his family in the way he wanted to, that may have exacerbated his feelings of frustration, and consequently affected his behaviour.

In summary, Tony's **behaviour** was clearly adversely affecting both his relationship with his staff and superiors as well as his overall job performance. We can imagine that his staff were feeling miserable, fearful and unhappy – working in a strange country with a different culture and for a boss who shouted and seemed angry all the time. No wonder their performance was poor, and Tony had to explain low production figures to his manager each week. The same features again adversely affected his performance when Tony joined his university programme. Having been used to authority figures in the army telling junior ranks exactly what to do, Tony found it difficult to accept when his lecturers, the 'authority figures' at university, did not behave in this way. This time his anger and frustration were manifested in his withdrawal and refusal to co-operate because here he was not in a position to tell others what to do. Despite this being a less aggressive response than he showed at work, it nevertheless upset his peers and affected how they worked together.

So, what was it that made Tony finally decide that his behaviour needed to change? Although he had not been actively engaging in class discussions when he attended university, he clearly had been listening to the different viewpoints offered by others, and eventually he began to realise that there were different ways of doing things. He started to become aware of the detrimental effect that his own behaviour was having on himself and others. Most importantly, he resolved to do something about it. The change did not happen overnight, but Tony began to reflect regularly on his own behaviour and performance, and proactively addressed anything that he felt was standing in the way of him doing a good job. This helped him to make the shift from being a professional soldier to a professional manager, that is, he fundamentally changed his professional identity in line with his career move (see Ibarra 2003). The key to Tony making such changes was **self-awareness**, a concept that we will be using as a starting point for our exploration of the professional identity model introduced above (see Figure 5.1).

5.3 DEVELOPING PROFESSIONAL IDENTITY

Self-awareness means 'having conscious knowledge of one's own character, feelings, motives and desires' (Oxford Dictionaries 2013) and helps us understand how our personal characteristics and actions affect both ourselves and others. As in Tony's case above, becoming self-aware can help us improve our behaviours, make better decisions and improve our judgement at the workplace. Since it would be impossible to look at all aspects of self-awareness here, we will concentrate on the four elements that are at the heart of our professional identity model – personality, values, emotions and norms.

5.3.1 PERSONALITY IN THE WORKPLACE

ACTIVITY 5.3

Reflection on personality

'Julia has a great personality.'

'Ummar doesn't have the right personality for a sales job.'

We often hear people saying something like this, but what does it mean? Think about the statements and note down what you would understand from them about these two individuals.

Personality is one of those concepts that is used frequently, yet difficult to define. Kenny et al (2011, p3) argue that personality refers to an individual's unique and distinctive cognitive structures and processes that are difficult to change. In other words, personality is something deeply personal that will remain stable over time. One problem with personality in the workplace is that blanket judgements are impossible because different personalities are more appropriate for certain roles. Our interpretation of Julia's personality, for instance, will depend on what we consider to be 'great', that is, whether we are drawn to people who are quiet and thoughtful or to people who are gregarious, outgoing and fun. It may be easier to interpret Ummar's personality from the statement above because there is an external reference to a particular type of job. Common traits appropriate to a sales job might include being outgoing, assertive, confident and communicative. We might assume then that Ummar does not display these traits. If we return to Julia, we may understand a little more about her personality if we knew the circumstances in which the statement was made. If it was made by a member of an interview panel who was selecting someone to lead a holiday tour to Ibiza, the gregarious, fun Julia might be considered 'great'. However, if the statement was made in the context of looking for someone to manage a care home, we may be more inclined to favour the quiet, thoughtful Julia.

In addition to personal or organisational preferences, cultural perspectives may also affect our judgement on others. For example, most Western nations value individuals who are independent, self-assertive and motivated to achieve, while most non-Western cultures place much less value on these characteristics, particularly for females (Browaeys and Price 2011). Depending on the cultural context in which an individual's personality is judged, it may be regarded as conducive for a particular role or not. The value of considering personality as one element of professional identity is that understanding our personality can help us find roles in which we can thrive and avoid those that may make us feel unhappy and stressed. We may also be able to identify which parts of our personality we can adapt to a role to help us improve effectiveness in the workplace (Ibarra 2003).

Over the decades, there has been an intense desire by psychologists to understand personality, and much research has focused on personality traits. One of the most prevalent theories remains the 'five-factor model of personality', commonly known as 'the big five', which has been extensively applied to the workplace (for example Howard and Howard 2010). The following five widely accepted personality traits are at the heart of this theory (as summarised by Barrick and Mount 1991):

1   *extraversion* – sociable, gregarious, assertive, talkative, active

2   *emotional stability* – anxious, angry, embarrassed, emotional, worried, insecure

3   *agreeableness* – courteous, flexible, trusting, good-natured, co-operative, forgiving, soft-hearted, tolerant

4   *conscientiousness* – careful, thorough, responsible, organised, planful

5   *openness to experience* – imaginative, cultured, curious, original, broad-minded, intelligent, artistically sensitive.

Individuals can score high or low on this taxonomy, so that these five personality traits can provide a differentiated understanding of their personality. Research has found that one's personality can have significant effects on their career satisfaction and achievement, specifically high conscientiousness, low neuroticism, low agreeableness, high extraversion and high openness to experience (Judge et al 1999).

Another well-researched and commonly used model of personality is Myers-Briggs Type Indicators (MBTI), which is an application of Carl Jung's psychology type theory (Jung 1971). Jung's work was developed further into the following four dimensions (Myers-Briggs Foundation 2007).

1   *extraversion (E) versus introversion (I)* to describe if an individual focuses on the outer or their inner world

2   *sensing (S) versus intuition (N)* to describe if an individual focuses on basic information or prefers to interpret it

3   *thinking (T) versus feeling (F)* to describe if an individual focuses on logic and consistency or on people and their specific circumstances

4   *judging (J) versus perceiving (P)* to describe if an individual prefers structure over openness.

The resulting 16 personality types (each represented by the corresponding four letters) indicate an individual's preferences across these dimensions and not their actual behaviours. This is fruitfully illustrated through the example of left- and right-handedness. While left-handed people prefer to use their left hand and right-handed people prefer to use their right hand for tasks such as writing, they can learn to use the other hand if required. Behaviour preferences based on our personality type are no different as we can learn to behave differently if required, for instance, by our role at work.

It is important to remember that in both models the dimensions are somewhat broad and that personality is complex. So while we may be able to identify an individual as exhibiting a particular trait, they are also likely to demonstrate traits across the other dimensions. In other words, neither model is perfect but both offer an opportunity to raise awareness of our personality characteristics (as well as that of others). In this way, they can give us some insight into how we behave in different organisational environments and contexts and whether our behaviour is conducive to that situation.

 ACTIVITY 5.4

Exploring personality at work

You can do this activity with either the 'big five' or with MBTI, or, if you wish, with both. Access a detailed description of the respective model in a textbook or on the Internet (unless you have access to a full questionnaire). Give yourself a score of 1 to 5 for each trait, where 1 means 'not much like me' and 5 means 'very much like me'.

Alternatively, you can take one of the free personality tests that are available online. Examples include http://www.learnmyself.com (by a not-for-profit organisation which offers personality tests without requiring you to sign in as a measure of precaution, see Stirk and Reissner 2010) and http://www.bbc.co.uk/science/humanbody/mind/index_surveys.shtml

What does your personality profile look like?

Next, ask at least three people who know you well to complete the same assessment for you. You may find it informative to ask people who know you in different environments, such as family members, friends, work colleagues, associates in sports or leisure teams, and so on.

 ACTIVITY 5.5

Reflection on your personality profile

Reflect on what the results tell you about your own perception of your personality characteristics and how you appear to others. Are the results similar or are there significant differences? Is there anything that surprises you? Reflect on any differences and analyse why different aspects of your personality emerge in different situations. You may wish to work with a trusted colleague, friend or mentor.

To summarise, personality has an important function in the workplace because it can determine which roles we are most comfortable with, which roles we may excel in and how much fulfilment we can achieve in our career (for example Judge et al 1999). While we cannot change our personality *per se*, we can adopt behaviours that are appropriate to our respective roles and organisational contexts to aid our long-term career development as a key part of professional identity.

5.3.2 VALUES

Recent corporate scandals, large-scale bankruptcies as well as reports of fraud and corruption (see Wikipedia 2013 for a list of examples) have brought the importance of values in business organisations to the fore. Protest movements such as Occupy have begun to question 'what is important, right, good, and desirable' (Gabriel 2008, p312) in business in the light of increasing social divides between the developed and the developing worlds as well as between the 'haves' and the 'have-nots' in most societies around the globe. While we may feel that as individuals there is little that we can do to make a difference to such big issues, our own values and resulting behaviour at work can make our team, department and/or organisation a better place. Let us consider this in the example of Ethan's dilemma (Case Study 5.2).

 ETHAN'S DILEMMA

CASE STUDY 5.2

Ethan was taking a short break from preparing an important tender for his design company. It had been intensive work – the contract was worth £2 million, and his boss was relying on him to do a good job. He was almost done. By the end of the afternoon he should have the tender document completed and ready to show his boss. He was quite pleased to have it completed two days ahead of schedule, and he felt justified in taking an hour out of the office to relax and unwind in the nearby gym. The gym was quiet at that time and he was the only person in the changing room after he had showered. He noticed a plain leather folio lying on the bench. Clearly someone must have left it behind, but there was nothing on the outside of the folio to indicate who that might be, and so he opened it to see if it offered any clues.

To a mixture of horror and delight Ethan realised that it contained a rival bid for the same contract that he was working on. The bid belonged to a small design company nearby. He knew a couple of the guys there and spoke to them occasionally in the gym, but he had had no idea that they were also bidding for this tender. He could not remember if he had ever spoken to them about his own tender. Ethan started to feel a little bit angry. What if he had inadvertently mentioned something to these guys from the other company that had helped them to put together their tender? He racked his brains to try to remember anything he had said, but he just could not recall. He had been so stressed recently that he found he was

forgetful about lots of things – the tender was the only thing on his mind. There was only one thing to do: he had to read their document to see if it was similar to his own.

Ethan read the document with growing dismay. He realised that it was considerably superior to his, containing one particularly inventive idea that was bound to secure them the contract. If he let this go ahead, all his hard work would have been for nothing. What was he to do? Ethan mulled over the options in his mind. He guessed the easiest thing would be to leave the folio where it was and forget he had ever seen it. But then, he knew that this other company would win the tender. What would his boss say to him if he failed? And what if someone else came into the gym and read the document as he had done, but then they took it away and used it to prepare another rival bid; there were still two days to go, so it could be done. What would happen if his boss ever suspected that he had known of this rival bid and did nothing about it? When this company was awarded the bid the tale of them nearly losing it because someone had left it in the gym would inevitably get out and become an industry legend. He could smuggle the folio out of the gym and dispose of it discreetly so that the other firm could not submit, but then they probably had copies anyway.

Then another thought occurred to Ethan. He felt guilty at first, but then the idea started to grow on him. He could leave the folio where it was, but he could go back to amend his own tender. He could use this other company's idea but improve on it so that his own company was almost certain to win. Who would know that it had not been his idea in the first place? His boss would be so pleased that he might even be awarded a junior partnership, something he had aspired to for years. His wife would be really proud. The bigger salary would come in really handy too – his daughter was due to go off to university soon and it would be good to know that he could provide for her without worrying about money. No one would ever find out that he had stolen the idea, would they? And anyway, how can ideas be 'stolen'? Everyone was free to have their own thoughts, and he was just as likely to have a good idea as the next man. What if someone *did* find out though? The gym has a swipe card system, so there would be a record of him being there at the same time as the folio. His boss would not mind – he would probably slap him on the back and say 'well done!' But what would his wife and daughter think of him?

Ethan then remembered something else. He had heard a rumour that this other firm was not doing too well and that there was likely to be redundancies unless they secured a good contract in the near future. If he used their idea and they did not win this tender, would he be responsible for some of their staff losing their jobs? But honestly, if they were stupid enough to leave their ideas lying around did they deserve to be in this business anyway?

Oh, this was such a difficult one! Ethan wished he had never left the office that morning!

ACTIVITY 5.6

Exploring Ethan's dilemma

Discuss with a group of colleagues what Ethan should do.

Does your group reach a consensus?

If there are differences of opinion, why?

What do you think are the conflicting values that are creating Ethan's dilemma? (Suggestions to guide your discussion are provided on the companion website.)

Ethan's dilemma results from a conflict between his personal values, that is, the 'principles of standard of behaviour; one's judgement in life' (Oxford Dictionaries 2013). Values help us decide what is right or wrong and what course to take in life, determining our behaviour in complex situations (for example University of Kent Career Advisory Service nd). We all have a set of values that derive largely from our background, upbringing and (moral) education. Very often our values will conflict with one another and in such circumstances it will be the values that we hold most dear that will determine what we do.

ACTIVITY 5.7

Personal values

Make a list of the things that you value most. Write down as many as you can. (You may need to come back to your list several times as different things occur to you.) Once you think you have got a complete list, try to rank them in order of importance. Keep this list for future reference.

Understanding our personal values is also important because they are an indicator of our underlying motivations and career aspirations. Particularly when making important career decisions our values can guide us towards a particular role (for example becoming an employment lawyer to help employees who have been treated unfairly) or organisational context (for example a not-for-profit organisation that works for the benefit of the local community or a disadvantaged group of people). It is important to bear in mind that, like personality, values are not necessarily 'set in stone'. While some values will remain important throughout our lives (such as honesty and fairness), other values may change as our life circumstances change. For example, someone just leaving full-time education may value independence and career success, while later family values may become more important, perhaps leading an individual to taking a part-time job to allow them to spend more time with their loved ones.

 ACTIVITY 5.8

Reflection on values

Can you think of any examples where your personal values have affected the career decisions that you have made? Have your values guided you towards a particular career, organisation or role? To what extent have you been able to live your values in that setting?

We have begun this section with reference to values in the wider business environment and the organisations operating therein, and I would like to come back to that before moving on. Like individuals, organisations are also guided by values, and there is, of course, a strong relationship between individuals and organisations. Not only do individuals create a set of values in founding an organisation, they continue to shape the organisation's values through their everyday behaviour and the decisions they make, for instance in relation to reward and recognition (CIPD 2013b). Managers appear to have a particularly important part to ensure that everyone (including themselves) behaves in accordance with the organisation's values. Recent research conducted by the CIPD, for instance, reports on cynical reactions by employees if behaviour incongruent to organisational values is tolerated. This is particularly pertinent in organisations in which branding advertises values; examples include the British retailer John Lewis promoting 'value, quality and choice' (John Lewis nd) or the Cooperative Bank's slogan 'good with money' (The Cooperative nd).

In summary, values are a vital element in an individual's professional identity, guiding them towards 'important, right, good, and desirable' (Gabriel 2008, p312) career choices, decisions and behaviours in the workplace. However, there can be instances when one's values are in conflict with one another and when it is difficult to decide what the best course of action is. In such situations, the values that are most important to you will determine your decision. In group settings (for instance as part of a project team), this often becomes more complex as different individuals hold dear different and potentially competing values, and reference to organisational and/or professional values or norms may be required (see Section 5.3.4 below).

5.3.3 EMOTIONS

Traditionally, individuals have been regarded as leaving their feelings at home when departing for work (Gabriel 2008). The publication of Fineman's (1993) seminal book *Emotion in Organizations* and the subsequent popularisation of the concept of emotional intelligence (EI) by Daniel Goleman have raised interest in matters of emotion. There is now widespread recognition that an individual's ability to recognise and regulate their emotions aids cognitive performance (for example Lam and Kirby 2002) and that there is a business case for soft skills such as EI (CIPD 2010). Before we delve more deeply into the role of emotions and emotional intelligence in the workplace, take some time to consider your emotional responses (Activity 5.9).

ACTIVITY 5.9

Reflecting on emotions

Think back to a time when you have had a heated argument with someone you care about. Have you said or done something that you have later regretted? What was it? What did you do next? How did the other person react? What were the consequences?

Chances are that your answer to the first question is 'yes'. We all do irrational things and make inappropriate decisions when emotions are high. In the middle of an argument it is difficult to see the other person's point of view; if we are convinced that we are right we tend to get more and more angry if they will not accept our argument. Later, when we have calmed down and had time to reflect, we can often start to accept some of the points they were making. What we do next is all-important. Do we stubbornly refuse to admit that we might have been wrong, or do we apologise and then talk through the issue in a more even-tempered way? Sometimes the things we do or say when we are emotional may have irreversible effects. For example, we might say such hurtful things to our partner that they decide that they no longer want a relationship with us, or we may be so excited by a new project that we volunteer to be part of the team, only to realise later that we do not really have the necessary skills or the time to do the job well. Has something like that happened to you?

One of the most important aims of developing self-awareness is to be able to avoid such situations happening in a professional context, which means to control our emotional reactions to the extent that we are able to make rational judgements when it matters. This is by no means an easy task because our emotions often take us by surprise and can easily get out of hand. The notion of EI can help you with this since it allows you to recognise and manage emotions in yourself and others. Goleman (2005) argues that having a high emotional intelligence quotient (EQ) can be more important than high IQ in determining professional success. Specifically, in his research managers with comparatively low IQ but high EQ have been more successful than those with superior IQ but inferior EQ. This does not mean, however, that EQ and IQ are opposites; everyone has a mix of both.

A basic requirement for developing EI is to understand emotions in others, so let us consider Karen (Case Study 5.3).

CASE STUDY 5.3

KAREN

Karen has worked for a medium-sized haulage company for the last ten years and was promoted to supervisor three years ago when the company was doing well. However, over the last two years business has declined because of an economic downturn, and for the last six months there have been rumours of redundancies. This reached a head two months ago when a new director was appointed at head office. The new man is known to have a reputation for turning ailing companies around by cutting costs and streamlining operations. An announcement has been made that the new director will visit the site at which Karen works the following week and will be requesting meetings with individual staff. On Friday afternoon Karen receives an email instructing her to go to the director's office at 11am next Wednesday.

How do you think Karen will feel?

On Monday the director commences a series of meetings with a number of staff.

News quickly gets around that some have been told that they will lose their jobs, while others are told that they are being reassigned. Some are keeping their jobs without change. There seems to be no pattern to the decisions.

How will Karen feel now? What effect do you think this situation will have on her job performance?

At 10:30am on Wednesday morning Karen receives an email to say that her meeting is delayed for one hour, without any explanation.

How will she feel now?

When Karen finally meets the director he tells her that he is delighted to inform her that she will be keeping her job. In fact, he wants her to take over from one of the senior supervisors who is being 'let go'. He seems surprised that Karen doesn't seem more pleased.

How is Karen feeling now?

Karen would undoubtedly have been feeling a great deal of **anxiety** when she first heard of the planned meeting with the boss. She may have feared the worst and assumed that if the boss wanted to speak to her it would mean bad news about her job. This anxiety may or may not have increased after news spread on Monday about the first meetings when she realised that some people were being given good news. The **uncertainty** of the situation was likely to be affecting her job performance; she would be preoccupied with thinking about what was going to happen – after all, she had had six days to worry about it. Her attention to detail would decline and she would be prone to making mistakes. She may also be **upset** about what is happening to her colleagues, some of whom may be her friends.

When the day of her meeting finally arrives and Karen finds that it is inexplicably delayed, another emotion may emerge: she is likely to feel **anger** because such treatment is disrespectful and inconsiderate and the least she could expect is an explanation for the delay and, better still, an apology. In an angry state Karen is much less likely to be accepting of anything that is proposed to her, which could explain why she does not seem pleased when the director tells her that her job is safe. Hence, although she will surely feel **relief** that her job is safe, she may already have misgivings about working for someone who has so little regard for their employees' feelings. In addition, if she is being asked to take over from someone who is being dismissed, she may feel **guilt** – a common emotion of 'survivors' of redundancy situations.

ACTIVITY 5.10

Handling crisis

You will agree that in Karen's case the situation was not handled well. Discuss in a small group how you would have handled it if you were the director in charge. You may wish to refer to the CIPD website for best practice in such instances.

Even though few of us will encounter such stressful situations on a regular basis, understanding how emotions affect behaviour can increase our emotional self-awareness and our ability to keep our emotions under control when required. We can do this by following three steps (drawing on Ashkanasy and Daus 2002, Goleman 2005, Momeni 2009):

1   recognising emotions

2   understanding emotions

3   controlling emotions.

1) Recognising emotions: Few of us regularly devote much time to thinking about how we are feeling, and throughout the day we may go through a range of emotions without ever noticing or appreciating how they are affecting our behaviour. But how can we ever hope to control our emotions if we do not know what they are? The first step, then, must be to actively think about what we are feeling in different situations. As an exercise, you may want to pause and think about your emotions at regular intervals throughout the day (for example when arriving at the office, when taking your lunch break and when leaving the office). It will soon become a habit to think about how you are feeling and reflect on how your emotions affect your behaviour at work.

2) Understanding emotions: Once we have learned to recognise different emotions, we need to know what triggers them, that is, what make us angry, excited, jealous, unhappy, and so on. We also need to know how we respond when we are feeling that way, how our emotions affect our behaviour towards those around us and how they respond to us. In some instances, we may be in a position to prepare for situations in which others may 'push our buttons' to help us prevent emotions from running high when remaining calm would be more beneficial.

3) Controlling emotions: Once we recognise and understand our emotions, we are well on the way towards having control over our emotions. Now it is important to develop personal strategies for emotional self-control. Reflection is very important here as it requires us to take a step back from a situation and to see it from a different perspective (see also Chapter 7). Our view of situations can change as emotions subside, so we need to consider not only how we felt about a situation at the time, but also later on when, perhaps, we are embarrassed about an angry outburst (as Tony was in Case Study 5.1). I would encourage you to engage with Activity 5.11 as a means to develop control over your emotions when letting them out may not be conducive to resolving an issue at work.

ACTIVITY 5.11

Exploring emotional control strategies

As a first step towards constructing your own emotional control strategies, keep a 'critical incident' log (Goodwin 1995) for a month to develop your emotional self-awareness. Whenever something non-routine or unexpected happens (it may be something that either involves you directly or that you observe in others), note down in your log:

At this moment I am feeling:

I feel this way because:

Because I feel this way I did:

Because of the way I behaved this happened:

Remember that you can have mixed emotions; try to capture everything you are feeling when you make your entries in your log.

At the end of the month review your entries. Are there any surprises or revelations? Is there anything you would do differently now that you have had time to reflect? Can you identify what situations trigger an emotional response that may not be constructive at the workplace or help your career?

You may also consider how your emotions about these incidents have changed over time. To what extent have you been able to let go emotionally? Why may this be the case?

Please note that the point of this exercise is not to encourage you to suppress your emotions. Suppressing one's emotions can have detrimental effects on one's health, and it is important to recognise when it is conducive to a work situation to show one's emotions and when it is not. Emotional intelligence can help you decide and also allow you to let out your emotions after holding them back in a stressful situation at work.

In summary, while it is increasingly acceptable to bring one's emotions to work rather than leaving them at home (see Gabriel 2008), showing them is not always conducive to the situation at hand. Your task as a professional is to recognise when it may be more important to negotiate as calmly and objectively as you can and when it may be appropriate to let your emotions show; emotional intelligence is a key part of self-management as well as of managing others (CIPD 2010). Hence, as you gain management responsibility it becomes increasingly important to recognise emotions in others and to deal with them appropriately, as our discussion of Karen's case has shown.

5.3.4 NORMS

Norms, the standard expected patterns of social behaviour (drawing on Oxford Dictionaries 2013) in the workplace, are the final element in our exploration of professional identity. Norms are widely considered to be a crucial element in social interaction and are viewed 'as natural, righteous, and self-obvious' (Gabriel 2008, p204) by those involved. Norms govern societies, professions and organisations. At both the societal and organisational level, norms are often captured by the term 'culture' and by what individuals from that society or organisation take for granted in interaction with others. At the professional level, there appear to be certain expectations of professionals and their behaviours, which I would like you to reflect upon in Activity 5.12.

ACTIVITY 5.12

Professions

Write down three words that come immediately to mind to describe each of the following individuals:

- police officer
- teacher
- journalist
- doctor.

Sanders (2010) explains that whenever she has asked groups of students to complete this activity, the same or similar words appear to describe each of these individuals:

- Police officers are typically described as: authoritarian, firm, trustworthy, honest, safe, judgemental.
- Teachers are most often described as: caring, educated, interested, fair, nurturing.
- Journalists tend to be described as: inquisitive, creative, ruthless, biased, relentless, 'selective with the truth'.
- Doctors are usually considered to be: intelligent, educated, caring, trustworthy, honest, dependable.

Were any of your words included here?

There are two interesting points to note here. Firstly, the fact that many different individuals come up with the same words to describe a profession suggests that there is some kind of externally recognised identity to it. People broadly know what it means to be a doctor or police officer, and so on, on the basis of generally recognised norms of that profession. Secondly, many of the words used describe behaviours, for instance authoritarian, caring, inquisitive.

These points raise further important questions. If certain professions have recognisable identities defined by behavioural norms, does that mean that only those people with a professional identity to match can do well in that profession, or does it mean that one's professional identity is somehow shaped by the profession that they have entered? Then, if we join a profession, how do we know what behaviours are appropriate? Job descriptions will list the knowledge and skills required for specific roles but generally do not describe behaviour.

Most of us will try to select a job or profession that we believe suits us, but because there are many external variables that affect our career choice, mistakes are easily made. We may be guided by our parents (and perhaps even their unfulfilled career ambitions) or follow career advice that portrays the chosen profession inaccurately. Some of us may select a profession because we know someone who is enjoying and doing well in it, but fail to take into account that this person may be very different from us in terms of personality and values. Hence, inappropriate career choices often do not become evident until someone has been in a profession for some time. Whatever the influences on our career choice, sometimes by the time we realise that a profession is not for us we have invested so much effort into it that we feel we cannot change. For example, in the UK a typical doctor will have studied for five years to gain an undergraduate degree and completed two years of foundation training before they are fully qualified. Any specialisation will take several years on top. What would responses be if such an individual announced that, actually, the medical profession is not for them after all? While this may be a stark case, similarly costly mistakes can usually be avoided if you understand what the professional and/or organisational norms are.

ACTIVITY 5.13

Exploring organisational norms

Determine a small number of organisations for which you might want to work once you have finished your postgraduate study. From publicly available material (such as corporate website, annual report, social media profiles, job descriptions) identify what the respective organisations' norms are and what kind of behaviour would be expected from newcomers. Have you found anything that has confirmed your initial choice of organisations?

Organisational norms are not necessarily homogenous since different professionals working within an organisation may subscribe to the specific norms of their profession. For instance, in an accounting department, individuals will be governed by the norms of the accounting profession (for example integrity, objectivity, due care, confidentiality, see CIMA nd). In a marketing department, individuals will be governed by the norms of the marketing profession (for example integrity, honesty, confidentiality, see CIM 2012). In an HR department, individuals will be governed by the norms of the HR profession (for example curiosity, credibility, courage, collaboration, see CIPD 2012). But how would you know as a newcomer to a profession? Let us discuss this in Activity 5.14.

ACTIVITY 5.14

Exploring professional norms

Discuss in a small group in what ways professions typically present behavioural norms.

Common ways in which professions explicitly communicate their expected standards of behaviour (behavioural norms) include 'professional standards' (a term commonly used in health care and education), 'professional ethics' (a term commonly used in accounting and engineering), 'professional code of practice' (a term used by a wide variety of organisations) or 'professional competency statement' (a good example is the CIPD Profession Map). Such documents and frameworks are designed to define acceptable behaviours and prevent the abuse of power. Again, the medical profession offers a good example for this. Doctors are expected to act solely for the patient's benefit. It would not be acceptable for a doctor to perform a procedure simply for the sake of research or to try out a new operating technique. Although patients are commonly used in research studies and experimental procedures, these practices are tightly controlled by being subject to ethical review and formal permissions, both from members of the profession and the patient.

Adherence to professional standards is often crucial because some organisations will make membership of the respective professional body a binding requirement. In some professions, individuals cannot practise legally unless they are registered by a recognised body (for doctors in the UK this would be the medical register of the General Medical Council, and other countries operate a similar mechanism). In other, less strictly regulated professions such as HR, membership in a professional body may be an organisational prerequisite. In fact, it is increasingly difficult for graduates to find a position in HR without any CIPD-recognised qualification or membership status. Membership in professional bodies requires individuals to engage in continuing professional development

(CPD), which is usually monitored on an annual basis to ensure that individuals remain at the top of their profession. Now that we have examined how we can start to identify the explicit norms of behaviour within a profession or organisation, let us explore the tacit rules of behaviour, that is, those that are not specified in written form. How might we understand these?

5.4 BECOMING PART OF A PROFESSION

 ACTIVITY 5.15

Learning the rules

Think back to a time when you have joined a new group or organisation. It may be a new school or college, a new club, a new job, or being introduced to a new group of friends. What have your experiences been?

Becoming part of a new organisation or profession, that is, learning appropriate mannerisms, attitudes and social rituals, is commonly called 'socialisation' (Ibarra 1999). At first, newcomers do not understand the language (jargon), jokes and reference to past events. They will learn through repeated observation and reflection over time to make sense of the group, its norms, values, insider knowledge and informal hierarchy (Louis 1980) – neither of which is easily grasped, explicitly defined or actually written down; they are tacit. Tacit knowledge in organisations and its implications on everyday practice has been widely researched over the last 25 years.

Despite considerable disagreement of how tacit knowledge is best defined, researchers are largely in agreement that it is acquired through intensive personal experience and observation in the absence of direct instruction and that its acquisition is highly correlated with career success (Insch et al 2008). Of course, sharing and transferring tacit knowledge will never be simple because by its very nature it cannot easily be articulated. However, understanding how tacit knowledge develops and transfers can help us identify the mechanism by which we can learn organisational know-how and integrate more quickly into new group or organisational settings. In a seminal study, Nonaka (1990) identified the following three processes of knowledge transfer:

1   *Tacit to tacit* – communicating tacit knowledge through action, observation and reflection (Baumard 1999). A good example is an apprentice who is being *socialised* into the respective trade.

2   *Tacit to explicit* – conversion of tacit knowledge into explicit knowledge is effected through *articulation*; for example, discussion about the way a problem should be tackled will gradually tease out tacit knowledge to form an explicit strategy or plan of action.

3   *Explicit to tacit* – individuals make newly acquired explicit knowledge part of their toolkit and can access it without conscious thought. Such *internalisation* can be encouraged through a process of reflection on action (Schön 1983).

According to Sanders (2010), socialisation, articulation and internalisation are important processes in the development of professional identity, much of which constitutes tacit knowledge. Specifically, *socialisation* may be achieved by engaging collaboratively with others by allowing us to observe who is who in the group and how things are done. *Articulation* can occur by talking through problems and issues, both in formal meetings and more informal communication. *Internalisation* occurs through reflection and allows us to use knowledge instinctively. Knowledge must become part of our individual 'know-how' that provides the toolkit with which we operate on a day-to-day basis. These processes are visualised in Figure 5.2.

Figure 5.2 Learning processes for tacit knowledge acquisition

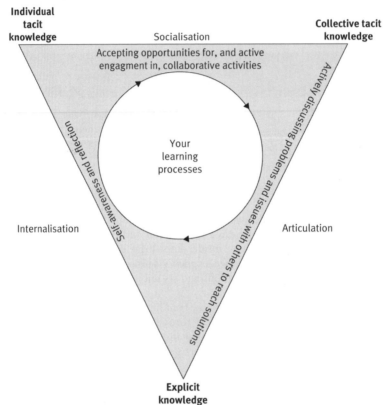

Source: reproduced with permission from Sanders 2010, p124

The model suggests that we can all play an active part in making professional and/or organisational knowledge (including values and norms) *our* knowledge by engaging in socialisation, articulation and internalisation. Undoubtedly, some of you will find a natural preference for one such process and struggle with another (see our discussion of personality in Section 5.3.1). Whichever your preference, interaction, collaboration and reflection together with self-awareness are important means to create and maintain the elements of professional identity – expert knowledge and subject-specific skills as well as the four binding elements of personality, values, emotions and norms. While this may sound abstract at present for those who have not yet decided which profession and/or organisation they would like to work in, I would expect that your ability to understand these elements will help you utilise them in a way that supports your continuing professional development and success as you begin to embark on your chosen career.

5.5 CONCLUSION

The acquisition of expert knowledge and subject-specific skills is only part of becoming and being a professional. Another, increasingly important part is the interaction between knowledge, skills and your behaviour – that is, your professional identity. If you understand your personality, values and emotions together with the prevalent professional and/or organisational norms, you are likely to find a fulfilling role and experience career success. While this may come naturally to some, for most it requires constant effort to become more aware of oneself and others in the group or organisation to ensure that your professional identity is evolving in such a way that it supports your performance and development in your professional role.

PAUSE FOR THOUGHT

Identify at least three things that you have learned by studying this chapter and by engaging with the exercises and activities. How will your newly acquired knowledge and skills support your continuing professional development? What value do you expect your learning to have for your daily routines and your further career? In what area have you identified a need for further development and how are you planning to fill that gap? Address these issues in your learning journal and/or CPD log. You may also wish to discuss them with a peer, colleague, mentor or coach to aid your further development.

EXPLORE FURTHER

CIPD. (2013) *Profession map – our professional standards V2.4 [online].* Available at: http://www.cipd.co.uk/binaries/profession-map-2.4-Oct-2013.pdf

UNIVERSITY OF KENT CAREER ADVISORY SERVICE, *Analysing your career values.* Available at: http://www.kent.ac.uk/careers/Choosing/values.htm

REFERENCES

ARTHUR, M., INKSON, K. and PRINGLE, J.E. (2009) *The new career: individual action and economic change.* London: Sage.

ASHKANASY, N.M. and DAUS, C.S. (2002) Emotion in the workplace: the new challenge for managers. *Academy of Management Executive.* Vol 16, No 1. pp76–86.

BARRICK, M.R. and MOUNT, M.K. (1991) The big five personality dimensions and job performance: a meta-analysis. *Personnel Psychology.* Vol 44, No 1. pp1–26.

BAUMARD, P. (1999) *Tacit knowledge in organisations.* London: Sage.

BROWAEYS, M.-J. and PRICE, R. (2011) *Understanding cross-cultural management.* 2nd ed. Harlow: FT Prentice Hall.

CIM. (2012) *Code of professional standards [online].* Available at: http://www.cim.co.uk/Files/codeofprofessionalstandards10.pdf [Accessed 15 July 2013].

CIMA. (nd) *Professionalism, ethics and conduct [online].* Available at: http://www.cimaglobal.com/Professional-ethics/ [Accessed 15 July 2013].

CIPD. (2010) *Using the head and heart at work: a business case for soft skills [online].* Available at: http://www.cipd.co.uk/binaries/Head%20and%20heart%20guide%20FINAL.pdf [Accessed 12 July 2013].

CIPD (2012) *The HR profession map – our professional standards, V2.3.*

CIPD. (2013a) *Profession map – our professional standards V2.4 [online].* Available at: http://www.cipd.co.uk/binaries/profession-map-2.4-Oct-2013.pdf [Accessed 29 October 2013].

CIPD. (2013b) *Balancing the pay equation [online].* Available at http://www.cipd.co.uk/pressoffice/press-releases/balancing-the-pay-equation-150413.aspx [Accessed 12 July 2013].

ERIKSON, E.H. (1968) *Identity: youth and crisis.* New York: W.W. Norton & Co.

FINEMAN, S. (1993) *Emotion in organizations.* London: Sage.

GABRIEL, Y. (2008) *Organizing words: a critical thesaurus for social and organization studies.* Oxford: Oxford University Press.

GOLEMAN, D. (2005) *Emotional intelligence: why it can matter more than IQ.* New York: Bantam.

GOODWIN, C.J. (1995) *Research in psychology: methods and design.* New York: Wiley.

HOWARD, P.J. and HOWARD, J.M. (2010) *The owner's manual for personality at work.* 2nd ed. CentACS.

IBARRA, H. (1999) Provisional selves: experimenting with image and identity in professional adaptation. *Administrative Science Quarterly.* Vol 44, No 4. pp746–91.

IBARRA, H. (2003) *Working identity: unconventional strategies for reinventing your career.* Boston, MA: Harvard Business School Press.

INSCH, G.S., MCINTYRE, N. and DAWLEY, D. (2008) Tacit knowledge: a refinement and empirical test of the academic tacit knowledge scale. *The Journal of Psychology.* Vol 142, No 6. pp561–79.

JOHN LEWIS. (nd) *Value, quality and choice [online].* Available at: www.johnlewispartnership.co.uk/csr/our-customers/value-quality-and-choice.html [Accessed 13 July 2013].

JUDGE, T.A., HIGGINS, C.A., THORESEN, C.J. and BARRICK, M.R. (1999) The big five personality traits, general mental ability, and career success across lifespan. *Personnel Psychology.* Vol 52, No 3. pp621–52.

JUNG, C. (1971) *Psychological types.* Princeton, NJ: Princeton University Press.

KENNY, K., WHITTLE, A. and WILLMOTT, H. (2011) *Understanding identity and organizations.* London: Sage.

KIEL, L.D. and WATSON, D.J. (2009) Affective leadership and emotional labour: a view from the local level. *Public Administration Review.* Vol 69, No 1. pp21–4.

LAM, L.T. and KIRBY, S.L. (2002) Is emotional intelligence an advantage? An exploration of the impact of emotional and general intelligence on individual performance. *The Journal of Social Psychology*. Vol 142, No 1. pp133–43.

LOUIS, M.R. (1980) Surprise and sense making: what newcomers experience in entering unfamiliar organizational settings. *Administrative Science Quarterly*. Vol 25, No 2. pp226–51.

MCADAMS, D. (1996) Personality, modernity, and the storied self: a contemporary framework for studying persons. In: M. TENNANT (2006) *Psychology and adult learning*. Abingdon: Routledge, pp53–7.

MOMENI, N. (2009) The relation between managers' emotional intelligence and the organizational climate they create. *Public Personnel Management*. Vol 38, No 2. pp35–48.

MYERS-BRIGGS FOUNDATION. (2007) *MBTI Basics [online]*. Available at: http://www.myersbriggs.org/my%2Dmbti%2Dpersonality%2Dtype/mbti%2Dbasics/ [Accessed 11 July 2013].

NOLEN-HOEKSEMA, S., FREDERICKSON, B.L., LOFTUS, G.R. and WAGENAAR, W.R. (2009) *Atkinson and Hilgard's introduction to psychology*. 15th ed. Andover: Cengage.

NONAKA, I. (1990) Managing innovation as a knowledge creation process. In: P. BAUMARD (ed.) *Tacit knowledge in organisations*. London: Sage, p24.

NONAKA, I. (2007) The knowledge creating company. *Harvard Business Review*. Vol 85, No 7/8. pp162–71.

OXFORD DICTIONARIES. (2013) *[online]*. Available at: www.oxforddictionaries.com [Accessed 11 July 2013].

ROYAL COLLEGE OF PHYSICIANS AND SURGEONS OF CANADA. (2013) CanMEDS *[online]*. Available at: http://www.royalcollege.ca/portal/page/portal/rc/canmeds [Accessed 11 July 2013].

SANDERS, G. (2010) Developing your professional identity. In: G. WATSON and S. REISSNER (eds) *Developing skills for business leadership*. London: CIPD, pp97–128.

SCHÖN, D.A. (1983) *The reflective practitioner: how professionals think in action*. London: Temple Smith.

SLAY, H.S. and SMITH, D.A. (2011) Professional identity construction: using narrative to understand the negotiation of professional and stigmatized cultural identities. *Human Relations*. Vol 64, No 1. pp85–107.

STIRK, S. and REISSNER, S. (2010) Integrated IT skills. In: G. WATSON and S. REISSNER (eds) *Developing skills for business leadership*. London: CIPD, pp396–415.

THE COOPERATIVE. (nd) *The Cooperative bank, insurance, investments [online]*. Available at: http://www.goodwithmoney.co.uk [Accessed 12 July 2013].

UNIVERSITY OF KENT CAREER ADVISORY SERVICE. (nd) *Analysing your career values [online]*. Available at: http://www.kent.ac.uk/careers/Choosing/values.htm [Accessed 12 July 2013].

WIKIPEDIA. (2013) *List of corporate collapses and scandals [online]*, updated 29 April 2013. Available at: http://en.wikipedia.org/wiki/List_of_corporate_collapses_and_scandals [Accessed 12 July 2013].

CHAPTER 6

Skills for Learning, Training and Development

GILLIAN WATSON

OVERVIEW

This chapter seeks to give you a relevant view of learning and related issues as they affect the individual and the organisation in which they work. We will consider the fundamental strategies such as analysing need, delivery methods and evaluation. There are also wider implications for organisations to contend with, for example decisions as to whether to develop or buy in talent. Relevant skills are required to enable both the learner and the facilitator to benefit from learning and development initiatives. We also discuss the various roles in developing others and highlight in what scenarios they may be used as well as reviewing the role of the learning professional. The tenet of this chapter is to enable you to develop the relevant skills so as to enhance your ability to develop others and/or to get your point across when presenting – all necessary skills for people in, or aspiring to be in, a leadership role.

LEARNING OUTCOMES

By the end of this chapter, provided you engage with the activities, you should be able to:

- raise your awareness of current training, learning and development issues
- conduct an analysis of learning provision
- analyse individual and departmental training/learning needs
- evaluate learning provision
- improve your presentation skills
- understand the business imperatives linked to development issues
- support organisational effectiveness through learning initiatives.

6.1 INTRODUCTION

Learning and development is a broad and varied subject and not all aspects can be covered here. However, what we can achieve is a discussion of how learning and development impact on organisations and their employees. We will consider the skills and techniques they could employ in relation to the strategic development of staff. In fact, skills in producing the business-case argument are significant in maintaining and realising relevant staff development in any organisation. The chapter also seeks to show the relationship between development and enabling you to develop skills of the learning professional. The position here is to refer to learning as a continuum where we exhibit aspirations to enable changed behaviours, encourage self-directed learning and increase capacity and performance.

There are many terms that may be employed to depict an ongoing learning process; one that looms most prominent is 'life-long learning': the premise here is that we are encouraged to continue with different forms of learning through our lives. Case Study 6.1 asks you to form an opinion regarding whether we should actually always seek or encourage individuals to learn.

 DOROTHY

CASE STUDY 6.1

The case study is narrated from Julia's perspective.

Dorothy is a line supervisor over a group of process workers in a factory which manufactures and packs pharmaceutical products; she works in one of the packing halls. Her working life began in the same factory when she left school at 15; she has never married and was the daughter who stayed at home to look after her parents and disabled brother. Indeed, her life seems to have been one of dedication to her family and her job. She is a friendly and kind individual who I (Julia) have known since I was a girl as we lived in the same village until Dorothy and her family moved to a small town six miles away so that there were better facilities to help Paul (her disabled brother). Dorothy is approximately 15 years older than me and she is aware that I work at the college as a lecturer in the larger town some 25 miles to the south; I have also been involved in training and development for her organisation. I see her quite often at local events and in the local supermarket; the following conversation took place at one of those venues.

Dorothy: Julia, Julia I've got something I need to ask you!

Julia: Dorothy, what is wrong, you seem somewhat agitated?

Dorothy: They are making me go on a training course and I don't want to go. I just do not see the point of it. What can I do to get out of going?

Julia: You have been on training courses before and your organisation has been giving five days training a year as a matter of course to workers for a long time. In fact, they have a very good record of developing staff. Why all of a sudden do you not want to be part of it?

Dorothy: I retire in three weeks! There is no real benefit to me or them; I know all there is to know about packing pills and, let's face it, things are not going to radically change in the next three weeks. My manager says I have to go.

Julia: Let's have a coffee and consider your options.

We discussed her predicament and I ascertained that Dorothy usually enjoyed the training events and joked it was better than 'working' as they, the learners, were supplied with drinks and lunch over the course of the two-day programme of study. She thought it was usually quite a good experience.

I admitted to being confused as to why Dorothy just does not go and enjoy the training programme and see it as a 'thank you' for all her years of loyal service.

Dorothy finally confided to me that she had a trainee and did not want to leave her.

Questions

1   What dynamics are motivating Dorothy's position?

2	How should Julia advise Dorothy? What are her options?	5	Consider the organisation and its development policy.
3	Are Dorothy's managers acting in her best interest?		
4	Should Dorothy have been given advice about retirement?		

6.2 GROWING TALENT

Every organisation will advocate that they aspire to attract the 'best' people. The issue is that they have varying ways of actually realising that goal. One approach is to buy in the 'talent' by recruiting new people; another is to develop people from within the organisation. This approach will only concentrate on the latter. It is critical, therefore, for an organisation which intends to grow their own talent to be fully aware of its skill gaps as well as its learning and training needs. This should enable planned activities to take place, not only to ascertain how the gaps may be filled but also what method or type of development will be employed. The problem remains, however, as these issues have been a somewhat short-term interpretation of actual requirements rather than part of continuing sustainable strategic developments. Butler (2010) suggested: 'Our professional engagement should be with issues of sustainability and substance.' This strategic point of view was seen as a defensive measure as well as a pathway to facilitate future development.

The process taken in regard to developing talent, could, as we move forward in the future, be more co-operative where attitudes to enhancing and enabling the workforce are in synergy with organisations who are aware of the need to grow the talent for the future. This also allows for a subtle change in focus from training to learning, which as a development tool has greater emphasis on the individual and how they can be engaged, motivated and prepared for a range of learning experiences at the workplace. This therefore connects the development of learning capabilities with the more progressive skills development, which organisations now recognise as necessary for their survival and growth.

Therefore, this chapter refers to 'learning' in a wider context than 'training' as the former relies on the transfer of development on a more permanent basis that encompasses the build-up of capabilities, and attributes which have the potential to support and enhance the career of the individual learner. This is not to denigrate 'training' as it has a vital role in considering the immediate need of the individual, department or organisation, which focuses in a specific area that assists the overall development strategy. It is not enough for organisations to provide learning and training opportunities. Employees must be willing to learn, to transfer and use any newly acquired knowledge and skills for the greater good of themselves and others in the organisation.

6.2.1 CIPD LEARNING AND TALENT DEVELOPMENT SURVEY – AN INTRODUCTION

The CIPD survey of *Learning and Talent Development* (2012) in the UK (which has been conducted by the CIPD since 1998) has given a relevant and erudite view of the situation in which organisations see themselves in relation to developing their staff in the current economic climate. In this particular year (2012) it was sent out to 21,122 organisations with 766 responding, a response rate of 3.6 per cent. The replies to the survey came from a wide variety of organisations that were categorised as 'manufacturing and production' (47 per cent), 'private services' (28 per cent) and 'non-profit' (10 per cent). Large organisations with more than 1,000 employees were well represented at 46 per cent of those responding compared with 53 per cent in 2011, therefore indicating less bias to larger employers. A third (32 per cent) were respondents with fewer than 250 employees. An interesting point from this year's survey was that 41 per cent of returns stated they had offices in more than one country, although the majority (86 per cent) had their headquarters in the UK.

It must be stated at the outset that this study relates to a year where 'recession and re-balancing have had far-reaching impact on the private sector' (CIPD 2012). This has been coupled with ongoing pressure in the public and not-for-profit sectors, particularly on cost and delivery. Undeniably the economic environment offers many difficulties where, the survey suggests, learning and talent development exists in a 'resource-light/challenge-rich' (CIPD 2012) dynamic. It is therefore not surprising that the organisations surveyed reported in-house development programmes and coaching by line managers as the most effective practice, followed by on-the-job training; these methods are seen as lower-cost development activities and thus reflect the 'resource-light' imperative (denoting that resources are tightly monitored and often quite limited). However, even though e-learning is not seen as a universal remedy or solution, we need to question whether its rise is caused by economic considerations and not because professionals see it as the most appropriate learning and development approach.

6.2.2 CURRENT TRENDS

A fundamental impact on changes in learning and development is an adjustment of priorities to amalgamating coaching, organisation development and performance management to advocate synergy in the pursuit of organisational change. Moreover, an increase of 50 per cent in e-learning is anticipated in the public sector coupled with less classroom instructor-led development, whereas in other sectors they foresee a 20 per cent increase in e-learning and a 25 per cent decrease in facilitator-led learning.

6.2.2.1 Talent management

One of the more worrying features of the piece is that fewer companies than in the previous year intend to carry out talent management pursuits. This may herald a shift in emphasis as it is also revealed that only two-fifths of these development activities cover all staff, with most organisations opting to concentrate on senior employees. Another major aim for most organisations is that they intend to continue developing high-potential individuals and grow future leaders and senior managers. The most effective development methods in this context are considered to be coaching and in-house programmes of study. Interestingly, a key finding of the survey shows that 60 per cent of organisations contend that talent management pursuits are effective, while only 15 per cent consider them to be ineffective. The emphasis here is that the majority of respondents believe that developmental procedures can create advantages to their organisations.

6.2.2.2 Leadership and management skills

Many of the surveyed organisations believe that there is a shortage of leadership and management skills, even among their senior staff. Some offer additional development to newly promoted managers while others do not on the grounds of a lack of necessity or for budgetary and time-related reasons. An additional concern is the lack of evaluation practices, with a distinct dearth of relevant and recognised techniques being employed, for example, organisational/engagement surveys or 360-degree feedback.

However, organisations do report that there is an intention to have the funds for more development in leadership skills with specific emphasis on performance management (see also Chapter 10), people management (see also Chapter 11) and change management (see also Chapter 12). Such learning typically features an attempt to improve managers' strategic thinking and encourage an outlook on the future (foresight). Thus, it is assumed a standard of behaviour in leadership roles will be realised and consequently lead to the attainment of organisational objectives.

Given that 40 per cent of respondents conduct their business in several countries, development for managers with international responsibility is also of importance. Typical development methods include international conferences and conference calls, which are regarded as enabling cross-border coaching and mentoring (CIPD 2012). In addition, a prominent method for large organisations is company-wide talent management programmes, and staff who are considered to have high potential may benefit from this practice.

Diagnostic tools are frequently used to analyse team development and learning needs, including widespread use of Belbin's team roles and Honey and Mumford's learning styles questionnaire. Other systematic processes such as 'Plan – Do – Check' (CIPD 2012) were also prominent.

6.2.2.3 Innovation and creativity

A category of learning and development that differed appreciably between sectors was innovation and creativity. Significantly, private organisations see the development of innovation and creativity to be critical to their growth and survival, whereas this aspect was not as prominent in public organisations. The central issue here is innovative strategies are seen as enabling organisations to deliver faster and more efficiently to their customers (CIPD 2012).

6.2.2.4 Learning and talent development in the future

Finally, there is a disquieting trend concerning the annual budget for learning and development. More than half of the organisations in the survey revealed that their financial situation had deteriorated and that, therefore, spending on development is declining. The public sector is the worst hit, with expenditure being reduced in 75 per cent of the respondent organisations.

Although the survey (CIPD 2012) highlights many unsettling issues there are general lessons to be learned, particularly because of financial constraints, managers in overall charge of learning and development will be required to be realistic and level-headed in regard to what can be achieved. The 'resource-light/challenge-rich' (CIPD 2012) dynamic referred to earlier is certainly becoming the norm for learning and development professionals to manage.

 ACTIVITY 6.1

Discuss your views of the *Learning and Talent Development* survey.

1   From the overview of the *Learning and Talent Development* survey above, consider how your own organisation (or an organisation with which you are familiar) is managing development. Do you see any similarities to the sectors represented here?

2   Review the organisation's use of different approaches to learning and development (choose three from the list below) and consider their benefits and limitations:

- coaching
- mentoring
- e-learning
- innovation and creativity

- diagnostic tools are frequently used to analyse team development and learning needs
- on-the-job training

- facilitator-led learning
- international conferences
- conference calls
- other (please specify).

6.3 AN INCREASINGLY DIVERSE WORKFORCE

All too often the debate regarding sustainability, employability and skill concentrates on the views of employers and the Government (see Leitch 2006), and neglects to involve the workforce. The CIPD (2008) survey *Who Learns at Work?* sought to include workers in the debate, and therefore the findings are worthy of examination. Of those respondents who do not receive training on a regular basis, 24 per cent worked in the private sector, and 11 per cent and 12 per cent respectively in the public and voluntary sectors (CIPD 2008). Those respondents employed by large organisations were more likely to receive training than those employed by small firms (that is, firms with 20 or fewer employees). However, out of those questioned (751 individuals), 18 per cent had not received training in the previous year. Out of the 751 individuals, the largest group (27 per cent) who had not received training were aged over 55. Those in the lowest economic groups accounted for the same percentage (27 per cent) of those who (as in the case of the over-55s) did not have the opportunity to train.

These factors are worrying from a diversity perspective (see Chapter 1). The survey (CIPD 2008) notifies us that most frequent forms of delivery are off-the-job training (64 per cent) which takes place in classrooms or meeting areas. Training delivered on the job was enjoyed by 51 per cent of respondents; here the researchers did not discriminate between employer-led or externally led deliverers. A constructive characteristic of this survey (CIPD 2008) was that the data showed an increase in employees receiving training from their line managers rising from 21 per cent in 2005 to 36 per cent in 2008. Training or coaching from someone else rose from 20 per cent to 23 per cent and training by electronic methods ('e-learning') rose from 18 per cent to 26 per cent. This suggests that:

- Increasingly line managers need to exhibit a breadth of development skills.
- More line managers than ever before need to be aware of coaching or mentoring initiatives and be prepared to engage in this activity.
- The somewhat obvious connotation, however, is that less direct, face-to-face facilitator-led activity is taking place.
- E-learning continues to grow.
- Organisations use a range of integrated learning methods (blended learning).
- There are some definite questions regarding opportunities for employees aged over 55; it may have been feasible to ask if the training policy aligned with any diversity policy in the organisations surveyed.
- Line managers as well as the learning professionals need to be knowledgeable and gain experience in a wide range of learning techniques.
- And, possibly, to have the ability to persuade others that learning and development is necessary and meaningful is a valuable communication skill to acquire.

6.4 THE LEARNING AND DEVELOPMENT PROCESS

Learning and development must be delivered as part of an overarching strategic development. Several writers (for example Harrison 2002, Reid et al 2004) offer a model for such development; the adaptations in Figures 6.1 and 6.2 draw from those sources.

Figure 6.1 Organisational development strategy

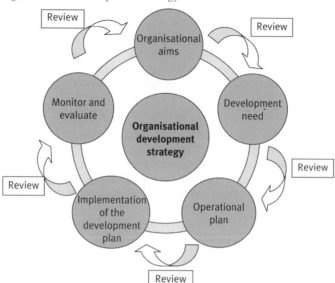

From an organisational perspective it is vital that a clear development strategy is devised and that there are adequate opportunities to monitor, review and evaluate. This strategy should be established upon a definitive identification of need linked to the organisation's aims and strategic objectives. However, for the purposes of this text we will concentrate on the operational aspects of such a plan.

Figure 6.2 Operationalising the learning process

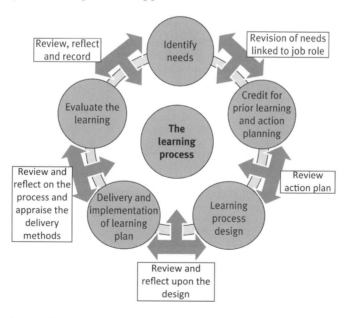

A central focus of contemporary organisations is sustainable performance, and to accomplish this organisations must create effective processes to organise the development of their staff (see Figure 6.2). These processes and plans should be monitored and reviewed continuously so that the organisation's learning and training needs can be met. Core elements of this process are the identification of learning and training needs, crediting prior learning and creating action plans, designing and planning the learning, delivering and implementing the plan and critically evaluating the whole process. We assume, therefore, that organisations are undergoing perpetual change and their learning and development practices will transform and adapt accordingly.

6.4.1 LEARNING NEEDS ANALYSIS

The identification of leaning and training need is aligned to the analysis of the gaps in skill and knowledge. Such an analysis should identify individuals who will need to learn and/or train to have the required competencies for present and future performance. The issue of identifying need is really a process that enables the organisation to fill any development gaps. This can involve both formal and informal provision encompassed in a course of action that delivers opportunity for learning and one that allows individuals to gain relevant experience. The CIPD (2009a, p1) suggests learning needs analysis to be a 'health check on skills, talent and capabilities in the organisation'. They go on to say it is a 'systematic gathering of data to find out where there are gaps in the existing skills knowledge and attitudes of employees'. The overall aim of this data-gathering is to enable learning professionals to produce a plan so that ongoing business capacity can be maintained and potentially exceeded.

Methods of data collection include *problem-centred analysis* as well a process that assesses the individual's competency and performance with that for the role profile or key tasks. A *performance-centred approach*, therefore, reviews problems or difficulties experienced by individuals or those within a department or organisation as a whole. It considers whether the problem is because of a skill gap, in which case the reason would be identified. A *profile or comprehensive analysis* takes a broad-brush approach and is used in some cases when people are new to a job or when new jobs have been created because of changed strategic imperatives. *Key task analysis* relates to a particular or critical task that related to the overall job or role held by an individual. Harrison (2002, p269) suggests: 'Job training analysis is a process of identifying the purpose of a job and its component parts, and specifying what must be learned in order for there to be effective work performance.' The learning gap may be in one of three areas in Figure 6.3.

Figure 6.3 Components of the learning gap

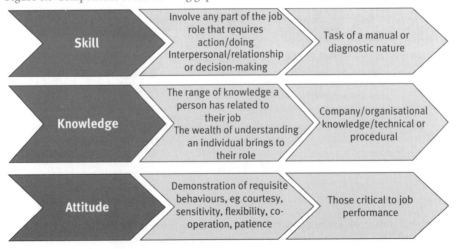

All of the components in Figure 6.3 have relevance to the development of skills required by the organisation and to the methods used in the delivery of learning and training. Table 6.1 sets out an overview of the types of data collection methods that may be employed, the KSA (knowledge – skills – attitude) required of the learning/training professional and where it is most typically used (adapted from Harrison 2009).

Table 6.1 Analysis of data collection methods

Comprehensive or profile analysis	• Examination of all tasks in the job role usually compartmentalised into skills, knowledge and attitudes. Measuring objectives, standards and frequency of performance. • KSA = time-consuming – requires skill • Typically used for: manual repetitive tasks, unchanging tasks; could have many job-holders in the organisation.
Problem-centred analysis	• Definition of the problem that requires learning or training interventions. Finding what initiated the dilemma and the characteristics of the problem and the KSA relevant to the issue. Can be combined with key task analysis. • KSA = requires good interpersonal and communication skills as the job-holder should be involved in the analytical process. • Typically used when: intervention is urgent, job-holder needs help in a limited area of development.
Key task analysis	• Proficiency in certain performance levels are critical to the job overall. Requires focus on an area of the learner's job specification; the intervention will only focus on those tasks. • KSA = requires good interpersonal and communication skills as the job-holder should be involved in the analytical process. Analysis carried out on a regular basis. • Typically used where: tasks vary and have non-critical component, job has a wide variety of tasks, intervention needed in key tasks. • Also when the job changes in content, priorities, emphasis and skill level.
Competency-based analysis	• Analysis is both job- and person- related. • Clearly defined standards of performance can relate to one or more groups in an organisation. • Need to relate interventions to a national standard, for example NVQ. • When the main problem is to identify the core behavioural attributes needed to perform across a job sector. • Use of a competency framework. • KSA = needs meticulous analytical skills, patience and resilience, along with good interpersonal and communication skills. • Typically used when: a statement of the general role or category of the job is needed, for example managerial at first-line level. A breakdown of the role in discrete parts is needed. Statement of competence needed. A criteria for the measurement of competency is required.

Learning, and personal development undertaken by individuals in organisations should result in an improvement in their performance. However, it should also be cost-effective and measurable.

6.4.2 CREDITING ACHIEVEMENT

For learning and training to be cost-effective, the needs analysis must be integral to the individuals, job and organisational status. However, most interventions tend to be directed at individuals and their immediate workplace, thus the benefits tend to be more localised. We need to keep in mind that training is not carried out in a 'tabula rasa' or neutral environments. 'Tabula rasa' is Latin for 'scraped table'; it often refers to one having a 'clean slate' or the mind of a newborn. Organisations are therefore far removed from the concept of 'tabula rasa', as they are environments with their own distinctive histories and cultures, formal structures, technology, reward systems and work practices (see also Chapter 9). All these have an impact on the relationships within an organisation, on how employees are selected for further development, on how information is disseminated and on how learning/training is perceived and supported.

Individuals also come with a raft of previous learning achievements; these may include NVQs, degrees and/or a professional accreditation. Therefore, whatever development individuals embark upon, we do not start with a clean slate. On the one hand, models of training are rooted in educational practices where knowledge and skills are closely linked (see Chapter 1 for details). The formal educational system aims to equip individuals with the ability to learn, for example, to change a situation and act autonomously. On the other hand, in organisations individuals are often expected to modify their behaviour to support the organisational aims and objectives, for example, to become part of the system (see Chapter 5). Therefore, individuals need to feel part of the system. One aspect of this is the recording of their achievements, recognising their prior learning and creating personal learning action plans for ongoing development.

Recognition of prior learning and achievement ensures that individuals feel valued and see the organisation as supporting their professional development, for instance through formal programmes of study. Such programmes may involve attendance or distance learning through a university, and these will align with the Quality Assurance Agency's mapping across programmes. However, no formal agreement actually exists between various awarding bodies and, therefore, it can be problematic if a potential student wishes to use recognised credits when applying for a higher education programme (Moon 2002). That said, most universities in the United Kingdom will try to accredit prior achievement/learning to allow for wider participation in a bachelor's or master's degree. Furthermore, universities will recognise qualifications from overseas students following internationally recognised guidelines (for instance, the European Qualifications Framework is recognised by the OECD).

6.4.3 DESIGNING LEARNING EXPERIENCES

We need to establish the link between other elements of the learning/development cycle. Firstly, we analysed development need linked to the job/role an individual possesses and how setting learning objectives helps to clarify precisely the purpose and expected outcome of learning. Secondly, when designing learning or training events, we must consider the current accomplishments of the learner. However, as we have indicated previously, there are many methods of engaging the workforce in a range of learning initiatives. Table 6.2 categorises some of the methods that enable the design of learning to take place.

Table 6.2 Design methods

Learning strategy	Design methods used
Instruction – work-based	At the workplace: ● The learner may have needed preparation time; this will have taken place before the trainer-led development. ● Assemble the necessary learning materials and aids. In terms of resources, machinery may need to be available for on-job development. ● For simple tasks, the key point will need to be emphasised and learner progress catalogued.
Managerial – work-based	● May take the form of coaching from a senior individual or an external consultant. Preparation will take place with the learner reflecting on an aspect of their job role. ● Other examples may include work-shadowing good practice. ● Key learning point will be agreed and a learning plan developed.
Focused in-company experience	● Designed using existing company initiatives; may be in or out of the department. In short, a planned experience that supports the individual's ongoing development: for example special project or assignment, new product development, problem-solving group and the like. These activities, backed by the organisation, are most likely to allow a convincing transfer of learning. Coaching and mentoring may also factor in the overall learning design.
Regular in-house courses	● Most large organisations have in-house learning and training programmes. Here the design may factor in refreshing the learner's awareness of new techniques or general updating. ● These may also include in-house discussion forums, conferences and/or tele-conferencing calls to another part of the organisation. ● Other in-house programmes may be designed to fit a particular qualification or standard, for example NVQs. ● Computer-based design may also feature; this would take a process of progressing from one unit to another until all elements have been successfully completed. ● Key learning points are firmly organisationally based, although most individuals will be capable of transferring this knowledge to other work settings.
Blended learning	● Many definitions of this method exist. However, the main consideration is that the learning is designed using more than one method of delivery, for example a distance learning programme may use the following: – computer-based – Internet/intranet-focused package – lecture – seminar – discussion with tutor – DVD. ● They are usually cost-effective and utilise in-house experience with externally developed packages. ● Key reason for using this design is that it can harmonise an individual's learning preferences with appropriate delivery methods; it also expands and enhances development opportunities for all employees.

Learning strategy	Design methods used
A planned external organisational experience	• This involves planned visits to external partners, for example suppliers, customers, other parts of the organisation (overseas). May be resource-intensive so the design must conform closely to the development need as well as the organisational imperatives. • Here the transfer of knowledge may largely depend on the value the learner places on the experience.
External courses	• All organisations are bombarded with external literature advertising courses they categorise into (a) the short 'quick hit' variety run at an external venue – usually staffed by consultants, and (b) the longer term – possible part-time programme which will end in a qualification. • The design therefore is external: the organisation's input is to decide whether it fits into an agreed learning plan and, if so, to allocate resources.
Self-oriented learning	• Here the learner is reliant on their own management and design skills to facilitate their own development, albeit these may be linked to the individual's work role. Also in some organisations staff may be actively encouraged to self-manage their learning, although in this circumstance it must be supported by an organisational culture which values development and learning. • A CPD-recording system is of value here (see Chapters 1 and 18).

Table 6.2 has sought to show a range activities and methods that could be used to augment the design process. A further example of a step-by-step design structure may help here, as illustrated in Figure 6.4.

Figure 6.4 Six-step design structure

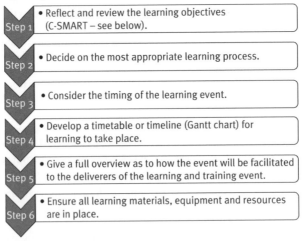

Step 1 • Reflect and review the learning objectives (C-SMART – see below).

Step 2 • Decide on the most appropriate learning process.

Step 3 • Consider the timing of the learning event.

Step 4 • Develop a timetable or timeline (Gantt chart) for learning to take place.

Step 5 • Give a full overview as to how the event will be facilitated to the deliverers of the learning and training event.

Step 6 • Ensure all learning materials, equipment and resources are in place.

(See Table 6.4 for an overview of C-SMART.)

It is always preferable to ensure such step-by-step design features are present in any learning design structure that you may undertake. Used as a checklist they help organise the design process and ensure certain elements are not omitted. The process itself is used to enable us to move to the next stage, and it also ensures the previous stages in the learning cycle have been used correctly.

ACTIVITY 6.2

Review design steps

Either

1   Review the design steps of a course or programme with which you are familiar.

or

2   Consider an aspect of behaviour (managerial, administrative, shop-floor) taking place in an organisation of your choice and think how it can be improved. Design a learning process to enable improvement to take place.

6.4.4 LEARNING AND BEHAVIOURAL OBJECTIVES

Writing behavioural objectives is an important part of learning design. However, contemplating in which learning domain they occur is worthy of purposeful reflection. We refer here to knowledge, skills and attitudes (see also Figure 6.3), which are manifest in the cognitive, psychomotor and affective domains respectively. Table 6.3 gives an overview of the type of behavioural objective that may be accomplished in a particular learning domain.

Table 6.3 Learning domain descriptors

Learning domain	Description
Cognitive (knowledge)	This domain relates to the development of the intellect that embraces conceptual skills, which in its basic form includes recall of data and recognition of facts and patterns. The basic forms must be acquired before the latter-stage categories can be undertaken and more advanced categories can be mastered.
Psychomotor (skills)	This involves the use of motor skills: physical movement and co-ordination. To achieve good psychomotor skills the learner needs to practise; measurements applied to this type of learning are the execution of speed, accuracy, distance and procedures. Again, these skills may increase in complexity the more proficient the learner becomes.
Affective (attitude)	This domain is positioned within an emotional context, the way in which we handle or cope with events. It involves our feelings, values, appreciation, enthusiasm, motivation and attitudes (see also Chapter 5). All are vital as an array of developmental opportunities used to acquire leadership skills.

Learning development objectives are an essential part of the training process; they allow both the learner and the trainer to assess whether the learner behaviour has changed in the light of the development process. In writing a learning objective the trainer is required to describe what the learner will have achieved at the end of the training or study period. They help to set targets for achievement; therefore, guidelines on how to write objectives for use in organisations and formal study is an important skill a manager should acquire. 'SMART' objectives are often used, and some managers or trainers might add 'C' to form 'C-SMART', thus: Challenging, Specific, Measurable, Achievable, Relevant and Time-bound/defined. Arguably, adding the C – challenging – helps to focus the intellect on the more stimulating and exacting form of a SMART objective.

Table 6.4 C-SMART objectives

C-SMART	Written in terms of what the individual should be able to do
Challenging	Allowing the learner a good level of challenge and enabling them to engage in activities that are both stimulating and motivating.
Specific	The objective should be as specific as possible. It should describe what the individual should be able to do or demonstrate after the training or learning event.
Measurable	Written so that an explicit (yes or no) answer can be given as to whether the objective has been attained or not.
Achievable and Agreed with the individual learner	By definition they should be achievable yet challenging and describe what the individual is currently unable to accomplish. They should not demoralise; to be precise, not too far removed from what a trainee will be capable of undertaking. Learning objectives can be a negotiated/agreed process between the learner and the trainer or line manager. Some appraisal systems operate a process where the appraisal concludes with a set of agreed development objectives, albeit in many cases the appraisee is responsible for the first draft.
Relevant	Relevant to both the needs of the individual and the department/organisation, whereby the achievement of the learning objectives will enhance performance and be a factor in the attainment of the organisational target.
Time-bound	Learning objectives are often rendered useless if they are open-ended; it removes the learner's sense of urgency and thus their motivation to achieve. Therefore a target time or date should be set whereupon the learner should be able to carry out the task, test, assessment, demonstration, and so on.

 ACTIVITY 6.3

Writing learning objectives for a learning event

From the insight you have gained thus far, practise writing a set of learning objectives for a learning session on either:

1   a briefing for your team who are meeting a new overseas client

2   a departmental change, for example merging with another department

3   a situation in your own practice.

You may choose to do this task in groups or on an individual basis. Compare and contrast your attempts with others in the study group.

6.4.5 LEARNING DELIVERY OPTIONS

A learning professional must be aware of the level at which the learning is pitched/aimed. If a first-year nursing student, for example, was due to access a lecture and had joined the midwifery module by mistake, they would be very aware that the relevant learning and underpinning had not yet taken place for the full value of the learning to be apparent. Yet, another equally important factor is whether the training is on a one-to-one basis or delivered in heterogeneous groups. The overview in Table 6.5 endeavours to raise awareness of a number of learning and training options that may be available, although this is not an exclusive compilation.

Table 6.5 Overview of learning options

Learning options		
Description of the learning	**Delivery method**	**Advantages and disadvantages**
One-to-one: tell–show–do	Sitting with 'Nellie': involves the trainee sitting alongside an experienced worker and observing the relevant behaviour before trying it out for themselves. Often also described as the 'tell–show–do' method.	Usually more sophisticated approaches are adopted; however, this does introduce a trial- and error- process that enables the trainee to learn from experience, have one-to-one guidance and to acquire basic skills. Caution is needed here as the new operative takes on the skills of the existing worker, including all their mistakes or shortcuts. In other words, the learning professional needs to be credible and truly skilled at the work.
One-to-one: coaching (see also Chapter 7)	Coaching: an individual with their senior manager or more likely an external consultant. Work-related events and developments can form a basis for reflection and monitoring of personal improvement. Because of the direct work relationship the impact can be immediate and enhancing for both the individual and the department. Executive coaching is also delivered on a one-to-one basis, although this is usually through a planned personal and professional development process for senior managers and is delivered, in most cases, through engaging an external consultant.	Advantages include: ● Remedial training can be offered if the required performance is not being achieved. ● Taking on a new challenge, the individual may need assistance to meet the range of new work or extended skill set. ● Job enhancement to stretch the individual's abilities and attributes. ● Consolidation of a range of developments or courses already experienced or achieved; the individual is encouraged to put the new skills into practice. Disadvantages: ● The main disadvantage here is cost, that is, the line manager's or a consultant's time must be budgeted as part of the overall training cost. ● If there is no follow-up process, the initiative/skill set can be diminished.

Learning options		
Combination 'blended learning': project assignment (see Chapter 18)	Project assignment has increasing worth as a training method, however it is not readily recognised as a direct development process. The projects therefore should be chosen so that the individual's capabilities can be stretched but not over-stretched. The task may involve addressing a particular problem or a relevant enhancement and enrichment. Fundamentally to enable this type of initiative to become successful, organisations must conscientiously adhere to the values and concepts involved in this type of development, notably as part of the prevailing culture of continuing enrichment. This level of development can be internally costly, and some organisations take the view that to hire a consultant to do the task or to send the trainee on a course on 'project management' would be the less expensive option.	Advantages: ● Involves the individual with their coach or development manager in addressing a work-related issue. ● Can be used as part of a master's degree programme where active research methods are being used to construct the dissertation. ● Allows the learner to acquire a considerable breadth of skills (see Chapter 1). ● Can try new methods, be creative, review a change-related initiative, be a change agent, for example pilot project. ● Has the potential to be career-enhancing. Disadvantages: ● Problematic unless you have the full backing of the management hierarchy as the project may extend over many departments. Problems also occur unless you have: ● Relevant level of understanding from staff in the various departments. ● Good preparation and planning and regular reviews. ● Good access to the senior/strategic manager who is your guide or mentor for the life of the project (it may be your line manager). ● A guide that possesses the right skill set. ● The relevant awareness of the personal demands project work can create; and are prepared to acquire new skills.

To add, the CIPD (2010b) highlights the use of e-learning and blended learning by describing them thus (p16):

● e-learning: 'developed online development topics, with exercises and diagnostic tools which are accessible to all'; and
● blended learning: 'main focus on blended learning increasing the use of e-learning and e-packages for mandatory training, for example induction, risk management'.

Table 6.6 Overview of group learning

Learning options: learning in groups		
Description of the learning	**Method**	**Advantages and disadvantages**

Learning in groups:	There are many methods associated with learning in groups. The method chosen will depend on the desired learning outcomes, for example if we take location; if a group discussion was to take place you would not locate it in a busy coffee bar as it would be extremely difficult to hear over the background noise.	Generic advantages:
		
		● Large numbers of people can be trained in one place.
		● The specialist, lecturer or facilitator can impart new ideas or techniques to a large group.
		● Cost-effective.
		● Issues can be discussed.
		● People can support and learn from each other.
		● The merits of new ideas can be analysed and evaluated.
		
		Generic disadvantages:
		
		● Problematic if the learners are not progressing at the same speed; a compromise rate is often found.
		● Restrictive issues which are often present in a heterogeneous group:
		
		  – Motivational differences (some individuals may not want to take part).
		  – Some people have different learning preferences and may not want to learn in a group environment – seriously minimises the effectiveness of the group's ability to learn.
		  – Some may have personal reasons why active participation alongside others is felt to be uncomfortable.

Problem-solving groups	Case study-based	● Ensures the group have an opportunity to practise/simulate experience of a certain technique or incident and to discuss the outcome with the facilitator ● The plenary is important as it allows the group to discuss the different solutions, challenge other groups' results or to evaluate the different methods of approaching a particular problem. ● Some participants may refute the reliability or credibility of the facilitator or the finding of another group.

Learning options: learning in groups		
Discussion group	Usually easy to find a forum for discussions to occur. If the groups are quite small in number, it allows the more reticent members of the group to feel comfortable to discuss their ideas.	• Enables a more focused discussion to take place, possibly as a follow-up to a previous session, a lecture or in preparation for a tutorial. • Useful for work groups to consider applying their learning to the work environment in a reflective style.

Planned activities	The process by which each activity is undertaken can be reviewed, for example self-analysis and observation or group analysis and observation.
	
	The role of the observer is significant, even though choosing the observer can pose problems. However, if the observer role can be interchanged between the individuals in the group taking part in the activity, it can be a powerful learning tool.
		There are various forms of this type of activity, for example:
		
		• A simple task non-job-related.
		• A complex task which is job-related, possible in two or more phases:
		
		  – plan and construct relevant objectives
		  – operationalise the plan and evaluate the outcome.
		
		An advantage in playing the observer role is that it gives the individual a chance to observe the activities more closely, which will enable them to analyse and evaluate the various events much more successfully. Remember, the observer has more of an overview than those taking part in the activity.
		The observer must give relevant feedback to the participants.

Table 6.6 has specified relevant learning options for groups, showing a range of methods and types of activities that can be employed.

ACTIVITY 6.4

Group interaction

Plan a group interaction to brainstorm the (choose one):

● re-design of a local wine-bar
● best use for office space in an inner-city facility
● outdoor team-building activity that would be suitable for a group of newly appointed first-line managers.

1   What features can you agree upon?

2   What features are unacceptable to all the participants?

3   Who emerged as leader of the group and why?

6.4.6 DELIVERING LEARNING

It would be futile to suggest 'there is one right way' to deliver learning. However, some facilitator-led learning will be delivered by using one method repeatedly, and often these approaches are destined to disappoint. Likewise, learners are diverse; they will have differing learning styles, various motivations and attitudes to learning, and they will come from a range of educational backgrounds. They may possess diverse cultural and national identities that may mean their educational experiences will again be varied; therefore, some overseas students/employees may be used to didactic methods rather than a more participative approach common in the Anglo-Saxon education system (see also Chapter 1). Hence a more blended approach may be sensible, particularly in the modern globalisation-driven business community (Simmonds 2003). It is necessary to consider the needs of the learner. Simply put: to enable learning to take place it should be learner-centred.

Figure 6.5 Retention rates against particular forms of delivery

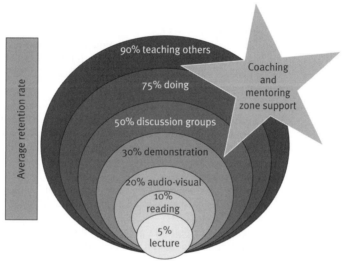

Whetton and Cameron (2007) cite research by the NTL Institute for their view of learning retention; Figure 6.5 is an adaptation of their configuration. It gives the average retention rate a trainer can expect from the learning methods cited in the text. The emphasis, however, is on the 'teaching others' figure: it suggests that by teaching/training others, one can gain a greater level of insight into the subject matter. There is also prominence given to coaching and mentoring; these are the interactive relationship-building approaches favoured by advocates of learner-centred training.

One of the keys to delivering a successful learning and training programme is planning. Hours spent in preparation will be deemed worthwhile when, after the evaluation of the event has taken place, it is deemed worthwhile by the audience.

6.4.7 EVALUATING LEARNING PROVISION AND INITIATIVES

In the current business environment learning professionals will find that there is a renewed imperative for evaluating learning, as the money spent on it will need to be justified. It is always an easy option for organisations to cut their development budget. However, if value to the organisation be can proven, the decision-makers are more likely to continue developing their staff. There are many and varied other reasons why evaluation should be carried out on any development programme, some of which are indicated below.

Table 6.7 gives an overview of how each element of the evaluation process can be completed (drawing on the work of Hamblin 1974, Bramley 1991, and Reid et al 2004).

Table 6.7 Evaluating learning initiatives

Evaluating learning initiatives	
Why should we evaluate development programmes?	• It will give an indication as to whether the training objectives have been met and if any additional learning or remedial action is warranted. • It will give feedback to the facilitators regarding their performance (although this can be controversial), methods and the learners' opinion about the whole experience. • It may sanction the tutors to make changes to the programme to initiate (ongoing) improvements. • From the individual learner's point of view, it will allow them to evaluate in-progress achievements as part of their continuing development. • From the organisation's standpoint, it enables a review of their expenditure on training and an opportunity to judge the outcomes. This may ameliorate the tendency of organisations to see training as intangible.
Who should carry out the activity?	• A crucial decision. Any hint of favouritism or bias could invalidate some very good work (results) or render the training worthless. Therefore, no single-person evaluation is advisable (Tracey 1968). • Tolerance, care and sensitivity should also be considerations when giving feedback. • Involve the learners (for example 'happy sheets', longer forms that are designed to collect data to enable the whole programme to be evaluated). • From the organisation's perspective, the line manager and the employee should make it part of an appraisal and co-operate together in evaluating the benefits. • Others may be involved, for example external consultant, evaluator, examiner, development manager, and so on.
What elements should be evaluated and when should this task be completed?	• Levels 1 and 2 are the most straightforward to evaluate; they concentrate on the opinions of the trainees as to the content and methods used in the training and learning realised by the trainees. • Level 3 – the perceived or actual change in the trainee's behaviour after the learning and training period has ended. • Level 4 – has the training had a beneficial effect on the work of the department, for example measurable improvement? • Level 5, which is probably the most difficult to evaluate – has the learning and training programme had a positive effect on the organisation as a whole? This may link directly to issues of enhanced profitability or survival.

What kind of measurement tools will be used?	• Varying methods of measurement will be needed depending upon the level and type of learning and training undertaken.
	• Timing the measurement tool to coincide with the staged completion of the training is advisable; for example the 'happy sheet' is often used at the end of a course. Further evaluation is necessary when the trainee is back in the workplace using the new techniques, although trainees may not know for several weeks whether their new learning has been helpful.
	• At Level 1 of evaluation it is reasonable to use a questionnaire, interview, group discussion, individual interview or written report by the trainer.
	• At Level 2 evaluation tools may be part of the assessment process – phase test, final test, concluding examination, project, case study, exercise, structured activities, take part in a discussion. All of these techniques can be used to assess how the learner is progressing during or at the end of the course. The trainer would make an assessment of the learner's development.
	• Level 3 concentrates upon improved job performance. Before and after measurements can be taken if the training was in an operational area of work.
	• The higher up the organisational structure the trainee is, the more complex the evaluation can be. The point of the training may have been about reflecting on a new behavioural technique. The measurement of success may be simply by questioning superiors or colleagues about the changes in behaviour, although the malfunction of the learned behaviour may not materialise for some time.
	• Generally, the more care that has been taken over the assessment of need, the greater thc possibility of effective evaluation.
	• Levels 4 and 5 are notoriously difficult to evaluate as the evaluation is dependent on several individuals who will all have an opinion regarding levels of improvement. Evaluation is therefore carried out more on a general scale, for example through an organisational survey. Another recognisable method is seeking evidence from other internal sources, for example fewer customer complaints, employers hold a favourable attitude to training, greater profitability, higher organisational profile of the development, performance, appraisal, internal promotion (you may think of others).

ACTIVITY 6.5

Critical evaluation

1   Using Section 6.4.7 above, critically evaluate a course, short training programme or conference you have attended during the past year.

2   Consider an area of behavioural development you would like to enhance, for example presentation skills.

• Compile a suitable development programme for 'using presentations as a tool of persuasion'.

• Create the learning outcomes and justify your plan – outline the methods to be used.

• How would this be evaluated?

TRAINING NEEDS ANALYSIS AT SOUPSTOCK LTD

Introduction

Soupstock Ltd is a canning factory that employs 150 people. Staff are employed in four departments: production, stock control, HR and administration, and maintenance. The majority of staff work in the production department on the factory floor.

Analysing training needs

A new human resource development manager, Jill Collins, has recently been appointed. The board has decided that its organisational objectives for the next five years are to improve quality and reduce wastage. Jill's first function was to consider how the organisational objectives could be met through training and development of staff. She therefore set about establishing employees' training needs.

Jill started by examining the human resource plan, which set out the human resource needs of the organisation for the next five years. She was able to see from this that particular areas, such as stock control, were expecting an increase in staffing levels in years two and three. Jill approached the managers of each department to discuss their jobs and what, if any, succession plans they had in place for key staff, including themselves. She found that only one department had a plan in action for ensuring that if staff left or were promoted, there would be other staff available to take over their duties; this was the HR and Administration department.

Her next job, then, was to identify key positions and key staff in the organisation and consider the training needs of staff likely to take over critical positions in the organisation if the current incumbents left. While she was collecting the above information from managers, she witnessed an incident which was very useful in her analysis of training needs. There was an accident in the production bay, where a hand-operated fork-lift landed on the operator's foot. Luckily the operator was wearing steel-capped boots so no real injury other than some bruising was caused. However, Jill was able to determine that the incident was caused because the operator had insufficient experience in using the equipment, as she normally worked in another part of the factory. This had occurred as the process of 'borrowing' staff from one part of the organisation to another in busy times was common. Staff generally had no problem with this – indeed they enjoyed the change of work; however, staff were often not trained in the procedures of that particular area. As they were called upon only in busy times, there was no time to train them properly during these periods. Nevertheless, for Jill, this incident demonstrated a clear training need. In particular she felt that health and safety could be jeopardised if individuals had not received full training. This incident provided very useful information on the training needs of individuals that may not have come to light otherwise.

Next, Jill used the computerised information system to retrieve data on departmental targets and production levels as well as wastage levels. As she was not familiar with the particular system, an administrative assistant helped her to find the information required. From this information she was able to identify where targets were not being met and, again, in talking to the managers and staff in those areas, establish what the problems might be and if training or development might help. The organisation had a formal appraisal system that operated once a year. Managers and their staff met individually to set performance targets and discuss training needs. By examining the formal appraisal and development plans that were written by the manager, and signed by the employee,

Jill was able to find out individual areas where staff needed training. Once she had identified the training needs she was able to organise supervisors to meet with their staff on a one-to-one basis and agree personal objectives for training. Within these personal objectives, one had to be related to improving quality. Individuals' training needs were then established and a training and development plan was written for the employee. From then on, meetings were regularly held between the manager and the employee every quarter to discuss progress.

Questions

Answer the following questions, then discuss them with other members of your tutor group.

1 The above case emphasises different sources of information that can be used to analyse training needed. Identify the methods that Jill used to gain this information.

2 How might Jill now organise and analyse the training needs further?

Author: Deborah Hicks-Clarke, Manchester Metropolitan University

Source: adapted from CIPD 2012, reproduced with permission

 HOW DO WE KNOW WHAT THEY NEED?

Layla has inherited a new team at Creative Consultants and they come with a reputation for being quite dysfunctional, having worked for three different managers over the last 18 months. Most of the team have been at the organisation for over seven years and are confident in their abilities to perform their roles and are technically very competent in using the firm's technological equipment. One of Layla's initial concerns is regarding the technology as she feels that it is now quite outdated – and is no longer used widely by their competitors. There is also a risk that their customers' expectations may change and that new customers will be looking for suppliers who make use of the latest technology as a means of improving their processes and outputs.

There are some excellent individuals within the team and overall they are successful, particularly in winning new contracts (though they are not always successful in re-tendering to existing clients). Over the next year the organisation will be going through an extensive change programme which will impact on the way that the team operates and the services that they can offer to their clients. As a head of department Layla is tasked with undertaking a learning needs analysis for the department; as she will be 'bidding' against other managers in the organisation, she will need to provide a robust analysis and demonstrate the potential return on investment that the organisation may gain if they invest in appropriate learning and development interventions.

As a starting point Layla asks all members of the team for a copy of their last performance review documentation so that she can reflect on the development needs that were identified. In theory this would give her a good starting point by identifying individual needs and mapping against her future plans. Unfortunately when she receives the documentation she is very disappointed to see that most of the development sections are blank.

Your task

1   How can Layla engage her new team to participate in the process of analysing their learning needs?

2   Advise Layla on how to undertake a learning needs analysis which captures needs at individual employee level. Design at least six

questions which she could use as part of the process and make a list of supporting evidence that she could gather.

3   What should she do to identify learning needs at a team level? Refer to any evidence or data that she could gather to support this process.

Source: adapted from CIPD Case Studies Extra with permission

6.5 ROLES OF LEARNING PROFESSIONALS

A learning professional is someone who may have had a variety of roles and myriad actual job-related skills in the development field. Certainly the complexity of the tasks related to development can be both expansive and eclectic. Therefore the role related to the learning professional or the development manager can have a different meaning in a number of organisations. These roles can range from a direct deliverer, an HR generalist who has some accountability for staff development or performance, an internal or external consultant, a line manager, a training administrator (high- or medium-level job role) or a director of learning and development (Johnson and Geal 2009).

Figure 6.6 Role and skill elements of the learning professional

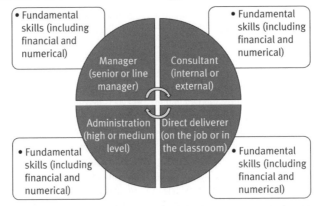

Source: drawing on Bureau of Training (1970) as cited in Johnson and Geal 2009, p49

There are some fundamental skills that a learning professional/trainer should possess, which include a good level of intellect as well as relevant knowledge and synthesis of the materials – in short, attributes that enable them and others to perform. They would also be expected to possess good numerical and communication skills and require personal qualities that allow them to relate to others in order to facilitate learning, always remembering that the reason we encourage staff to engage in training is to ensure that they learn and, consequently, develop. The requirement of the learning professional/trainer therefore is to learn and develop into a well-rounded professional in order to progress their own career. Table 6.8 elaborates on Figure 6.6 by expressing the type of behaviours and practical tasks each of the roles could include.

Table 6.8 Developing the learning professional

Developing the learning professional	
Administrator	• The role may include the production of a range of paperwork: – training notes – joining instructions – course lists – letters to: venue – clients – suppliers. • Could act as clerical assistant to the trainer, consultant or manager • Manage the library – loan of learning materials • Manages the learning interface – officiates over the rules of attendance and certification • Problem-solver and handler – everyone needs information or help – NOW! Skills of: insightfulness, reliability, dealing with people
Direct deliverer or trainer	Need a systematic approach to the task; therefore, initially they develop skills in: • conducting learning needs analysis • defining entry-level behaviour • producing learning objectives. Designing the learning event using the appropriate delivery methods: • delivering the event and assessing the results • initially trainers train from their own experience – pass on their skill to others • teach what is new – trainees do as they are instructed • present information – albeit that the information may be complex • devise experiential learning opportunities • lead the group in facilitating learning. These events above may need a complex set of skills where the trainer is in effect managing the learning.
Consultant: learning professional	Some consultants take qualifications to achieve formal consultant status, for example MA, MSc, PhD. Conduct organisational development. Design and process elements of the training function. Run assessment centres. Conduct psychometric tests. Become a personal coach. Conduct executive coaching. Show empathy – build relationships – be credible. Become a change agent.

Developing the learning professional	
Manager: learning professional Plus all of the above	A well-rounded learning professional skilled in all the areas mentioned above, plus: • They have developed management and leadership skills. • They have become someone who plays a vital role in the organisation and is an advocate for the development function.

Source: drawing on Johnson and Geal 2009

Table 6.8 focuses on the elements necessary to accomplish the tasks of development as well as some of the skills. The items we have highlighted are numerous, and to become proficient and experienced in them will take time and practice. However, they do serve as a focus for the aspiring learning professional.

ACTIVITY 6.6

Skills development

Consider Table 6.8 as an opportunity to reflect on the skills that you already have and those that you intend to acquire. Use it as a checklist for part of your continuing professional development process. Incorporate your results into your learning log and/or CPD log.

ACTIVITY 6.7

Training and/or learning in organisations

To give you an overall perspective as to how learning is managed in your organisation (or an organisation with which you are familiar):

1   Evaluate whether some of the roles and attributes mentioned in Table 6.8 are present in the department/wider organisation in which you work or study.

2   Consider if the roles are largely accomplished by line managers.

ACTIVITY 6.8

Government provision

For those reading this text that are *not* familiar with UK systems and are from another EU or overseas country, this may be an opportunity for you to review what provision your government is making to help train the workforce. Carry out an Internet search and list the initiatives and support processes in which your government is engaging.

Review the questions in Activity 6.7 in light of your investigation.

6.6 PRESENTATION SKILLS

6.6.1 EFFECTIVE PRESENTATIONS

In organisations, individuals' success depends to a large extent on their ability to organise and present ideas confidently, to stay in focus and to show enthusiasm and clarity. Oral presentations, whether formal or informal, can be a powerful communication tool, helping to inform or persuade others. At the same time, oral presentations provide immediate feedback. However, just like everything else in life, variables such as resources, time, audience and the place may determine the outcome, thus skilful presentation may contribute to our success.

6.6.2 PREPARING FOR A PRESENTATION

The grid in Table 6.9 helps to serve as a checklist as part of the preparation process.

Table 6.9 Preparing for a presentation

The first step in preparing an effective presentation at the right pitch begins with getting to know the audience. Knowing the audience or the make-up of the audience may make a difference between being successful or failing to get your message across. The presenter needs to seek answers to the following questions:	
Who is the audience?	Technical experts, generalists, mixed audience
What is their knowledge and skills?	How much background to introduce
What are their preferences?	Formal or informal presentations
What is the size of the audience?	What facilities are available? What time?
What are their attitudes?	Interested, hostile, indifferent
What are their demographics?	Men, women, mixed audience Young and inexperienced Position in the organisation
The second step is to help the presenter to establish **their** credentials by asking the following questions:	
What is the purpose of the presentation?	General purpose: to inform, to persuade, to entertain Specific purpose: whom to influence, how, when and where
What message is to be delivered?	Is a response desirable?
Is the speaker an expert and is their knowledge essential for audience to learn?	How authoritative is their knowledge? Do they have all the important and up-to-date information/figures, and so on?
How do they feel about the presentation?	Enthusiastic, indifferent, reluctant? Always remember that it is difficult to sell an idea or a product we do not believe in.
The third step is to develop a credible and realistic key idea. This should be in a form of a statement, which is then periodically repeated and supported by the main body of presentation.	

It is relevant for all presenters, learners and listeners to be alert to the fact that unfocused presentations can be confusing; the audience, therefore, are then likely to lose interest or, worse, not realise the true intent of the presentation. To emphasise this, on occasion salespeople hide the purpose of their presentation by stating that: while they do not want to sell anything, they are concerned about the consequences of the audience not having what the presenter has to offer or *is* actually selling. This is clearly unethical behaviour and indicates that presentations may not always be to the learners'/listeners' advantage.

 ACTIVITY 6.9

Building presentation skills (1)

You have been asked to give a five-minute presentation on one of the following:

1   Interview for a job in another department.

2   Ask for a pay rise.

3   Brief two new employees on the key operating procedures in your department.

6.6.2.1 Generic presentation

Presentations may take a number of different formats, although a generic presentation consists of the following three parts:

1   introduction

2   main body

3   conclusion.

Key words such as: the *next* important …, *another* reason …, *to conclude*, … act as bridges and are important in progressing ideas, promoting clarity, emphasising key points and keeping the audience interested (see also Chapter 3). These should refer to both recent and the next idea, showing relationship between the two.

Table 6.10 Introduction

The **purpose** of an introduction is to get attention from the audience who may not **be** interested in the topic. Often on-the-job presentations have an audience whose attendance is mandatory. It is therefore vital to build a rapport with the audience by convincing them that the presentation is worthwhile and that they would find it interesting. An introduction should last about one-fifth of the whole presentation and consists of the following steps:
The **opening remarks** should put the audience in a good mood and get their attention.
If the speaker was not introduced and is not known to all present, they need to establish their credibility and demonstrate their competence.
The introduction is concluded by briefly outlining the major purpose for the presentation using a short summary format.

ACTIVITY 6.10

Building presentation skills (2)

Prepare an introduction for the following topics. Each presentation should last no more than eight minutes:

1   Getting funding for an interesting and, from your point of view, important conference.

2   Your department is planning to upgrade the software you are currently using and you were asked to introduce different products for the employees to choose from.

3   Introduce new safety procedures after a recent accident.

4   Lead a discussion on reducing employee absenteeism.

Table 6.11 The main body

Presenters often find the opening statements of the main body difficult. Thus, if the audience and the topic are familiar, only a brief background may be needed instead of a formal introduction. By now, the presenter should have the audience's attention, although the interest has to be retained. This requires pitching the tone at the right level, the remarks must be related to the topic at hand and the topic has to build seamlessly onto the introduction. Adler and Elmhorst (2002) suggest a number of steps for opening statements of the main body:
Involve the audience by asking them a question and establish its importance.
Lead the audience into the topic by telling them a story.
If appropriate, present a quotation, making sure that it is relevant.
Make a startling statement, although be sure not to offend your audience.
Refer to the audience by mentioning their needs, concerns or interests.
Use humour. A timely joke or an amusing remark may be effective in retaining attention, making a point and/or making the audience like the speaker more. Once again, humour must be appropriate to the topic and to the occasion. Risky jokes of all kinds are not worth the laugh they generate; remember, humour does not always travel across cultural boundaries.
When the opening part is completed, the speaker may concentrate fully on the key topic of the presentation. The main points in the body of the presentation should be stated in complete sentences and should support the key topic. The body of the presentation should not exceed five points, and each point should contain only one idea. The main body may be presented with the following approach:

- **The ideas must be presented in chronological order.**
- **The ideas must be topical, spatial and focused.**
- **If appropriate, the 'cause–effect' approach can be used.**
- **If appropriate, the 'problem–solution' approach can be used.**

ACTIVITY 6.11

Building presentation skills (3)

Plan an opening sentence for the following presentations:

1   A discussion on the topic of 'what your organisation expects from graduates'.

2   An appeal for involving your organisation with the local community.

3   The second in a series of five talks on uptake of new technology in your organisation.

4   The management has announced a round of redundancies.

Table 6.12 The conclusion

The conclusion should include the following two parts:
● The restatement of the purpose of the presentation and a summary of the main points.
● The conclusion or a closing statement. People usually remember the beginning and the end of the presentation, thus strong closing remarks help the audience to remember the presentation favourably. The closing statement may, if appropriate, challenge the audience to take action. The above listed opening statements to the main body of presentation may work well too.

ACTIVITY 6.12

Building presentation skills (4)

Use the topics from the previous activity and prepare concluding remarks.

All presentations follow more or less this basic structure. On establishing a purpose and a statement of the purpose, the first step in the preparation is to compile a list of all points that need to be covered by the presentation. These then have to be organised into parts as suggested in this chapter. After the main body is developed, the introduction and conclusion should be added, using transitions for clarity and progression. Presentations must be focused and logical if they are to be understood, persuasive and establish the speaker's credibility.

6.7 CREATING VALUE

As individuals we place worth and value on every enterprise or activity in which we engage; therefore it is no surprise that organisations do the same. The difference is that organisations must justify their actions to chief executives and stakeholders, whereas individuals have only themselves to answer to. One of the worst conditions of any economic 'belt-tightening' is the lack of understanding regarding the worth and value of the role learning and development performs in an organisation. Consequently managers of the development function or those at line-manager level may need to justify, advocate and persuade decision-makers of the worthwhile contribution development makes to the existence and well-being of the organisation.

Therefore, the art of promoting and even marketing the development function is worthy of debate, as conveying the relevant business case for any development is an overriding factor of contemporary organisational life. A CIPD study (2007a) suggests that because of the global rethink about the direction and purpose of organisations, learning and talent development has never been more important. However, again there will need to be justification, as organisations do not always make the relevant connection that learning and development has had an impact on organisational success. Activity 6.13 brings this issue to the fore and asks you to relate the questions to your own organisation.

ACTIVITY 6.13

Creating an impact

Consider the following questions, originally posed by the CIPD study (2007a), and relate them to your organisation. Answer them honestly (or if you do not know the answers, try to find out and share them with others as to whether or how you could justify development).

- Would you know how to demonstrate the impact of a customer service programme, for example, to your marketing department?
- Could you defend a coaching programme that may be considered by your managing director as 'nice to have' in terms of its bottom-line impact?
- Do you really know how the costs and benefits of e-learning compare with other methods when your finance director says, 'Why don't we just give everybody a DVD? It's a tenth of the cost'?
- Do you know what methods and approaches are considered most effective? Is it classroom training, is it blended learning, e-learning? (CIPD 2007a)

The report (CIPD 2007a) emphasises the need to show 'relevance, alignment and measurement' and cites the example of the finance department of a local authority, which illustrates a process of measurement and rationalisation that can be defended (see Table 6.13).

Table 6.13 Promoting the value of learning in adversity

Measuring the value of learning: council finance and resources department	
What matters to the organisation	Measurement option(s) (for different staff groups)
How is learning contributing directly to the achievement of our organisational targets?	Time taken to gain competence, data for finance centre staff Proportion of employees with required competence level Customer feedback data on handling of council tax bills Employee engagement data measured by staff survey/Gallup questions Number of individuals able to move into key positions Council member satisfaction with finance function The number achieving professional qualifications (ACCA, and so on)

Measuring the value of learning: council finance and resources department	
To what extent are employees achieving their performance targets?	Achievement against performance appraisal targets for council budget
How cost-effective are the learning and training opportunities we provide?	Employee reaction and learning data (levels 1 and 2 evaluation) Management feedback data
What economic benefits does our investment in training provide?	Cost–benefit data for specific learning interventions measured against costs and productivity: – SAGE training – Advanced Excel – Accounting technician stage modules.
Is learning contributing directly to the achievement of HR targets?	Performance data on relevant HR targets; for example: – absence – retention – number of internal promotions.

Source: adapted from CIPD 2009b, p12

ACTIVITY 6.14

Organisational development strategy

1   Adapt Table 6.14 to align with a department in your organisation, or one with which you are familiar; ensure you link your table to the current organisational development strategy.

2   Can you now offer justification for any expenditure on development?

3   Prepare a presentation to senior management for a new/essential learning initiative.

Organisations should be alert to the need for relevant identification of skill gaps or learning needs as this may illustrate the appropriate improvement or development practices that should be implemented. As part of this whole deliberation of learning and development we continue to advocate continuous professional development (Lucas 2012, p580), as this assists organisations and individuals alike in affirming their commitment to the acquisition of an eclectic, practical and constructive breadth of skills. Skills can, on the one hand, improve performance levels for the organisation and, on the other, enable individuals to become more employable, thereby enhancing their career prospects.

Hence, 'employers who invest in their own staff are best placed to save money, improve staff motivation and increase employee retention' (Parry, quoted in CIPD 2009b, p2). In other words, knowledge-led learning companies are best placed to not only preserve their business but also extend their capacity. They do this by developing talent, which enables the organisation to exploit its human capital, which in turn furnishes the organisation with the wherewithal to compete in current and future markets. In a CIPD study (2009b, p1) the following suggestions are made in order to help learning professionals/managers argue a case for development:

- putting the relevance and impact of learning and development (L&D) at the centre of the business, therefore building the business case for effective learning and development

- helping to connect the importance of L&D with key people in the business by ensuring that you can align your approach to the organisation's goals and objectives
- helping you to prove the most effective measures and metrics to help consolidate the impact of L&D on the business.

6.8 CONCLUSION

This chapter has given, what we hope you will consider as, a well-founded view of the challenges facing the learning and development arm of any business. It has also alluded to the skills learning professionals need to be effective. Principally, we have painted a picture of the current business environment and how the need for accurate research, information, valuing people and good presentation skills are essential when advocating the importance of learning and training to decision-makers in the business. In any development situation we should take account of the process of development the managers and leaders of the learning and development function have undergone to become learning professionals.

PAUSE FOR THOUGHT

Identify at least three things that you have learned by studying this chapter and engaging with the activities. How will your newly acquired knowledge and skills support your continuing professional development? What value do you expect your learning to have for your daily routines and your further career? In what area have you identified a need for further development and how are you planning to fill that gap? Address these issues in your learning journal and/or CPD log. You may also wish to discuss them with a peer, colleague, mentor or coach to aid your further development.

EXPLORE FURTHER

CIPD. (2012) *Learning and talent development*. Survey report. London: CIPD.

QCF Readiness Programme [online] available at: http://www.qcda.gov.uk/qualifications/qcf/58/.aspx

Review your government's website on their development initiatives.

Visit the Quality Assurance Agency website: http://www.qaa.ac.uk

REFERENCES

ADLER, R.B. and ELMHORST, J.M. (2002) *Communicating at work: principles and practices for business and the professions*. 7th ed. New York: McGraw-Hill.

BRAMLEY, P. (1991) *Evaluating training effectiveness.* London: McGraw-Hill.

BUTLER, M. (2010) The talent of the future. *People Management Online.* Available at http://www.peoplemanagement.co.uk/pm/articles2010 [Accessed 30 March 2010].

CIPD. (2007a) *The value of learning.* Research report in collaboration with the University of Portsmouth. London: CIPD.

CIPD. (2007b) *Learning and the line: the role of line managers in training, learning and development.* London: CIPD.

CIPD. (2008) *Who learns at work? Employees' experiences of training and development.* Survey report, March. Online version also available at: http://www.cipd.co.uk/surveys [Accessed September 2013].

CIPD. (2009a) *Identification of learning needs.* Factsheet. London: CIPD.

CIPD. (2009b) *Promoting the value of learning in adversity.* London: CIPD.

CIPD. (2010a) *Overview of CIPD surveys: a barometer of HR trends and prospects [online].* Available at: http://www.cipd.co.uk/surveys [Accessed 30 Sept 2013].

CIPD. (2010b) *Innovative learning and talent development.* London: CIPD.

CIPD. (2012) *Learning and talent development.* London: CIPD.

HAMBLIN, A.C. (1974) *Evaluation and control of training.* Maidenhead: McGraw-Hill.

HARRISON, R. (2002) *Learning and development.* London: CIPD.

HARRISON, R. (2009) *Learning and development.* London: CIPD

JOHNSON, B. and GEAL, M. (2009) The complete trainer. *Training Journal.* November. pp48–52.

LEITCH. (2006) *Prosperity for all in the global economy – world class skills. Final report; HM Treasury Leitch review of skills.* Online version also available at: http://www.dcsf.gov.uk/furthereducation/index.cfm?fuseaction=content.view&CategoryID=21&ContentID=37 [Accessed September 2013].

LUCAS, A. (2012). Continuous professional development – friend or foe? *British Journal of Midwifery,* Vol 20, No 8, pp576–581.

MOON, J. (2002) *An exploration of theory, practice and professional development.* London: Routledge Falmer.

REID, M.A., BARRINGTON, H. and BROWN, M. (2004) *Human resource development: beyond training interventions.* 7th ed. London: CIPD.

REYNOLDS, J. (2002) *How do people learn?* London: CIPD.

REYNOLDS, J. (2004) *Helping people learn: strategies for moving from training to learning.* London: CIPD.

SIMMONDS, D. (2003) *Designing and delivering training.* London: CIPD.

TRACEY, W.R. (1968) *Evaluating training and development systems.* New York: Harper & Row.

WHETTON, D.A. and CAMERON, K.S. (2007) *Developing management skill.* Upper Saddle River, NJ: Pearson.

CHAPTER 7

Coaching, Professional Development and Practice

STEFANIE REISSNER

OVERVIEW

Business coaching has become a popular means of professional development, and HR professionals have a pivotal role in contracting, managing and evaluating coaching services on behalf of their organisation. Hence, they need to have a thorough understanding of what business coaching is, when it is fruitfully applied and what difference it can make to the performance of both individual and organisation. In this chapter, you will gain the necessary understanding of business coaching as a means of professional development to enable you to make informed decisions about the possibilities that it can offer to your organisation. We will be taking the perspective of HR professionals when attempting to define coaching, explaining the coaching process and identifying reflective learning as the key mechanism behind coaching as a means of professional development.

LEARNING OUTCOMES

By the end of this chapter, provided you engage with the activities, you should be able to:

- understand what coaching entails and how it differs from related concepts such as mentoring and counselling
- make an informed decision as to whether coaching is an appropriate method of professional development in a given situation
- select a business coach for a specific coaching intervention
- apply key coaching skills in your managerial practice
- evaluate the effectiveness of a coaching intervention for both individual and organisation.

7.1 INTRODUCTION

Recent years have seen increasing emphasis on professional development and practice, and, consequently, advanced methods of staff development such as coaching have gained in importance (CIPD 2012a). While in the past the availability of coaching was largely restricted to professional sports people and senior business executives (for example Peltier 2001), it is nowadays available to a wider group of individuals at the workplace, including front-line employees (see Warden 2010, Du Toit and Reissner 2012 for examples). Hence, not only may you be offered coaching as part of your own personal and professional development, but also as an HR professional you are likely to take an active role. For example, you may be involved in buying, contracting, managing and evaluating coaching services (CIPD 2008) and building a business case for coaching in your organisation (Tulpa 2007). You may coach subordinates as part of a managerial role ('manager as coach', see Ellinger et al 2010) or you may even become a trained coach within your organisation (internal coach, see CIPD 2012b).

With the increasing popularity of business coaching, however, a number of difficulties have surfaced. Firstly, despite a drive towards professionalisation (CIPD 2008), the emerging coaching industry is not regulated like traditional professions, which means that anybody can work as a coach without training or experience (McMahon et al 2006). While there are a number of rigorous training programmes for business coaches run by universities or respected private training providers, at present there is no one recognised qualification. Despite opportunities for accreditation by, for instance, the European Mentoring and Coaching Council (EMCC), the Association for Coaching (AC), the International Coach Federation (ICF) and the Association for Professional and Executive Coaching and Supervision (APECS), it can be difficult for HR professionals to identify which coach is sufficiently qualified and experienced for the required work in their organisation (for example CIPD 2008).

Secondly, business coaching as an emerging discipline draws on a diverse heritage with roots in sports coaching, psychology, education and other social science disciplines (for example Bachkirova et al 2010). Business coaches, therefore, often draw on an eclectic mix of tools and techniques, some of which have been long recognised (such as Myers-Briggs Type Indicators or neuro-linguistic programming), while others have somewhat esoteric connotations but nonetheless can achieve effective outcomes (see McMahon and Archer 2010 for examples). Each coach will have built a specific coaching toolkit that is informed by their philosophy of human development. HR professionals need to be able to recognise which philosophy and toolkit may be most promising for their purposes, taking into account the specific circumstances of a coaching intervention.

Thirdly, the services of a business coach can be expensive, and consequently some organisations have established an internal pool of trained coaches to cut the costs of buying external coaching services. Indeed, research conducted by the CIPD (2011) found that the majority of coaching among their sample is conducted by line managers or other internal coaches. While internal coaching has proven a successful means of raising the quality of interactions between managers and subordinates and subsequently improving performance (see Warden 2010), there remains debate among practitioners and scholars alike as to whether a member of an organisation can indeed be an effective coach therein (see EMCC 2012a for details); there is a risk that the internal coach's familiarity with the organisation may lead them to be blinkered or biased (Bachkirova et al 2010). However, adoption of a balanced approach between internal and external coaching (for example Cunningham 2007) may allow organisations to cater for a wider range of individual learning needs and styles. HR professionals need to be able to strike the right balance between internal and external coaching when selecting a coach.

Hence, given the current popularity of business coaching and the associated complications outlined above, HR practitioners need to understand what business coaching is, what skills are required and how it works (CIPD 2012a). They also need to be able to select the right coach (internal or external) for a coaching intervention, manage the coaching process on behalf of the organisation, and evaluate what difference the coaching intervention has made for both coachee and sponsoring organisation (CIPD 2008). This chapter seeks to give you the necessary background knowledge and understanding to enable you to make more informed decisions about coaching as an advanced means of professional development. We will be taking the perspectives of an HR professional involved in buying, managing and evaluating coaching services or, where appropriate, that of a line manager using coaching techniques to support the development of their subordinates (for example Anderson et al 2009).

This chapter has two main parts. The section following this introduction seeks to define what business coaching is and what place it has in modern-day organisations. Given the wide variety of approaches to business coaching (see Cox et al 2010 for details), it will not be possible to offer one encompassing definition. However, I will endeavour to give you a working definition of business coaching that covers its main aspects (see Association for Coaching 2013). We will also consider how business coaching may differ from associated concepts such as mentoring and counselling/therapy, with which there is considerable overlap but which have other, distinct functions in organisations. The second part of this chapter will guide you through a typical coaching process from preparation to follow-up, as outlined in Figure 7.1. This will give you the necessary understanding of coaching to guide your practice as an HR professional and/or line manager.

Figure 7.1 The coaching process

You may find it useful to re-read the section on reflective practice provided in Chapter 1 (see Section 1.6) since reflection is one of the key mechanisms behind coaching (eg EMCC 2012b). Understanding why coaching works will help you promote it as a means of professional development in your organisation where appropriate (see also Section 7.3.1). Moreover, reflection is an integral part of coaching supervision (see Section 7.4.3 for details) and can aid the professional development of coaches (Garvey et al 2009). HR professionals need to understand the importance of supervision and ongoing professional development of coaches to manage coaching within their organisation effectively.

7.2 DEFINING COACHING

7.2.1 WHAT IS COACHING?

Despite the increasing popularity and importance of business coaching as a means of professional development, two main areas of confusion persist. Firstly, there is a lack of clarity of what business coaching actually is and what it entails in practice. This is partly due to a wide variety of definitions and conceptualisations of business coaching, ranging from fairly directive to more open-ended and non-directive approaches (Bachkirova et al 2010). Each of these is informed by a distinct perspective of learning and development, and they all have appeal to organisations in line with their vision, values and culture (Brockbank and McGill 2006). Hence, diversity in approaches to business coaching is important to cater for a wide range of development needs in a wide variety of organisations.

Such diversity, however, is a challenge for those seeking a clear definition of business coaching and unambiguous understanding of what it entails. The following bullet points jointly capture a widely shared understanding of what business coaching is, what it seeks to achieve and what outcomes it can have if successfully employed (drawing on

Association for Coaching 2013, Bachkirova et al 2010, CIPD 2008, 2012a, Garvey et al 2009):

- Coaching is a non-directive development process that seeks to improve the coachee's performance and effectiveness at the workplace.
- Coaching involves structured and thought-provoking interactions between coach and coachee that seek to give the coachee feedback and work towards achieving a particular goal for both coachee and organisation.
- Coaching involves the short-term use of strategies, tools and techniques to promote sustainable change in the coachee's attitude, cognition and behaviour that is desirable for both coachee and organisation.

In practice, the coachee usually determines in interaction with the coach (and sometimes the sponsoring organisation) the area(s) which they feel a need to work on and negotiates with the coach which strategy, tool or technique might be most fruitful to pursue (non-directive) (see Section 7.3.3 for further details). The coach is a guide and facilitator, a critical friend who 'holds up the mirror' for the coachee as part of the coaching process (Melrose 2010) to aid their self-awareness and long-term professional development (structured and thought-provoking interactions) (see Sections 7.4.2 and 7.6 for details). The term 'critical friend' needs to be taken literally in this context – the coach facilitates the coachee's development by challenging their preconceptions and by giving them support to recognise their strengths to build on them as well as their weaknesses to overcome them where applicable (feedback on strengths and weaknesses).

 ACTIVITY 7.1

How coaching works

Watch the video clip on YouTube provided by WellCoaches (2008) on 'how coaching works' (http://www.youtube.com/watch?v=UY75MQte4RU). Consider the role of the coach, the role of the coachee and how they interact. What does this tell you about coaching? How does this portrayal of coaching relate to what has been discussed in this chapter so far? Where applicable, how does this portrayal tally with your own experiences of coaching?

Business coaching builds on a number of distinct assumptions (see Rogers 2004 for details). Firstly, the coachee is perceived to have the resources to deal with their problems, and these resources are unlocked in interaction with the coach. Secondly, despite a focus on the workplace, business coaching takes into account the coachee's whole life experiences. Thirdly, while the coachee will 'set the agenda' for the interaction with their coach, coach and coachee are equal partners in the coaching process. Despite such differences from other types of professional development, business coaching is closely related to other, more mainstream notions of learning in that it is also influenced by (drawing on Brockbank and McGill 2006, pp98–9):

1   the **context** in which it takes place

2   the **coachee**, their motivation and propensity to engage with coaching

3   the **coach**, who facilitates the coaching intervention.

Hence, in terms of context the **organisation**'s vision, values and culture will affect the availability of coaching, the type of coaching that is being sponsored and also what outcomes will be expected from a coaching intervention (see Table 7.3 for details).

ACTIVITY 7.2

Availability of coaching

Consider the following questions, ideally with reference to a specific organisation. Discuss with others the implications of your answers on employees, managers and the wider organisation.

1 Who should receive coaching?

2 Which employee groups should be invested in?

3 Will coaching be restricted to individuals of a certain level of seniority?

4 Will coaching be provided only in relation to certain development activities?

5 Will there be a limit on the number of hours available to each individual?

6 Will internal or external coaches be used?

7 How will the success of the coaching intervention and value for money be measured and evaluated?

Source: CIPD 2008, p21, reproduced with permission

According to Rhodes et al (2004, p24) 'the needs and aspirations' of the **coachee** can also constrain the quality of coaching at the workplace. In other words, the coachee and their prior experiences with professional development will affect the openness with which they engage with coaching and the seriousness with which it will be approached. The effectiveness of business coaching is often limited if the coachee does not appreciate the need for coaching and subsequently does not engage in self-directed learning suggested by the coach (see Wilson 2007). A discussion of identifying the need for coaching is provided in Section 7.3.1 below.

Finally, the knowledge, skill and expertise of the **coach** will affect the quality of the outcomes of a coaching intervention for both the individual coachee and organisation. A knowledgeable, skilled and experienced coach will work effectively with their toolkit to establish trust and rapport with the coachee and engage in deep and thought-provoking interactions that 'turn the coachee's focus inside' (Wilson 2007, p8, drawing on Gallwey). The selection of a business coach, the skills required from a business coach and evaluation of a coaching intervention are discussed in more detail in Sections 7.3.2, 7.4.2 and 7.5 respectively.

7.2.2 HOW DOES COACHING DIFFER FROM MENTORING AND COUNSELLING?

The second area of confusion relates to how coaching differs from related notions such as mentoring, counselling (for example Stone 1999) or other forms of psychotherapy (Hart et al 2001, Rogers 2004), which is partly due to its rich and diverse heritage as outlined above. Indeed, it can be very difficult to distinguish between these concepts in practice as they can all be classified as forms of 'one-to-one helping' (Megginson and Whitaker 2007, p77) and as a coach may have a counselling/therapy background. To aid the creation of clearer boundaries between these concepts, the CIPD (2008, p11) has provided the following characteristics that are more prevalent in coaching than in mentoring or counselling/therapy:

- Coaching is based on the premise that the coachee is psychologically healthy and does not require medical intervention (unlike counselling/therapy).
- There is an assumption that the coachee is self-aware or able to develop self-awareness (unlike mentoring).

While coaching and mentoring are often dealt with in tandem, scholars and practitioners alike contend that there is a difference between them. Table 7.1 summarises the key differences between coaching and mentoring as identified in the literature (drawing on Hay 1995, as cited in Brockbank and McGill 2006, p80; Rosinski 2004, as cited in Garvey et al 2009, p21; Stone 1999).

Table 7.1 Distinctions between coaching and mentoring

	Coaching	Mentoring
Orientation	Short term and specific	Long term and broad
Role of 'helper'	Facilitator	Adviser
Tools	Asking probing questions Non-judgemental listening	Giving advice Establishing networks
Focus	Enabling the coachee to discover new meanings and direction	Exchanging experiences with the mentee

Table 7.1 emphasises the assumptions that (1) the coachee has the capacity to resolve the issue on which they are working and (2) the coach is but a facilitator of the coachee's learning and development (Rogers 2004). Hence, the interaction between coach and coachee, which is characterised by working through challenging questions, differs from the interaction between mentor and mentee, which is characterised by giving advice and opening doors. The implication is that business coaching tends to address deep-seated perceptions, attitudes, behaviours and beliefs, and consequently leads to more sustainable learning and development. Business coaching is typically employed when addressing interpersonal or managerial skills, such as communication, knowledge-sharing, staff engagement and conflict resolution (Anderson et al 2009), and it is often necessitated by change in the coachee's professional life, such as promotion or career move (CIPD 2012a).

Similarly, there is some overlap between coaching and counselling/therapy as both seek to increase the client's self-awareness and bring about profound and sustainable change to the client's life. Both draw on a similar skill-set of non-judgemental listening, asking probing questions to clarify the issue for the client, and working with them towards a solution (Hart et al 2001). Table 7.2 summarises the key differences between coaching and counselling/therapy as identified in the literature (drawing on Hart et al 2001; Hall and Duval 2004, as cited in Hawkins and Smith 2006, pp36–7; CIPD 2008; Rogers 2004; Stone 1999).

Table 7.2 Distinctions between coaching and counselling/therapy

	Business coaching	Counselling/therapy
Starting point	High performance	Feelings of deficiency
Orientation	Prospective – present and future	Retrospective – past injuries
Scope	Narrow focus on performance improvement at the workplace	Broader focus and greater depth to understand root causes behind performance issues at the workplace
Role of 'helper'	Facilitator	Therapist
Focus	Enabling the coachee to discover new meanings and direction	Resolving psychological issues

	Business coaching	**Counselling/therapy**
Stakeholders	Representatives of the sponsoring organisation may be involved in contracting and evaluation (see Sections 7.3.3 and 7.5)	Organisational representatives are normally not involved

Due to the fluid boundaries between coaching, mentoring and counselling/therapy, business coaches need to be aware of the limits of their interventions and of situations when the coachee may benefit from long-term support by a mentor or when they may require referral to a therapist. In the latter case, the coaching intervention should be interrupted until underlying psychological issues have been dealt with (for example Rogers 2004). It can be very easy for a business coach to unwittingly stray into the territory of therapy and potentially cause harm for coachee, organisations and themselves. In Clutterbuck's (1998, p53) eloquent words: 'the most dangerous person in the organisation is the one who is unaware of his or her limitations'.

There are two implications. Firstly, for **HR professionals** it is imperative that coaches are selected wisely, as a well-qualified and experienced coach who has regular, high-quality supervision is more likely to recognise their limits and refer the coachee to a therapist if necessary. Secondly, for **line managers** coaching their subordinates, it is imperative that they recognise and act upon common signals that point towards the coachee needing help from a therapist. These, according to Rogers (2004), include frequent and intense crying, recurrence of a problematic relationship (usually with a close family member), dominating fear (such as the fear of rejection or loss of control), or unacknowledged catastrophe or trauma in the coachee's life. Line managers need to be sensitive in the way in which they pursue such a situation further and may want to consult HR professionals for expert advice.

ACTIVITY 7.3

Coaching, mentoring or therapy?

Study the following scenarios. Consider for which coaching would be an appropriate means of development and justify your decision. You may want to consider what other forms of professional development might be used instead of or in conjunction with coaching:

1   Imagine you are a line manager in an HR department and are conducting a performance appraisal with Sarah, one of your subordinates. Sarah has just finished a postgraduate qualification in HRM, and her dissertation was about workforce diversity. You were pleased with Sarah's performance in her programme of study and are keen to give her further development opportunities. As part of the performance appraisal, you suggest to Sarah that she build a taskforce to enhance workforce diversity within your organisation. While Sarah seems flattered by this offer, you can sense her anxiety about it. How can you support Sarah's transition into the new role?

2   Imagine you are an internal coach for a large organisation, and a departmental manager contacts you to address performance issues of one of his team members. During your initial conversation with the manager, you find out that the individual in question used to be the star performer of the team but that his performance has decreased since being promoted to a team leadership role. You sense that the manager is angry about the lack of performance, feeling let down by his subordinate. What will you do?

3   Imagine you are coaching Chris, who has been referred to you by the team leader to resolve some performance issues. When

first meeting Chris, you pick up overwhelming feelings of helplessness, powerlessness and misery, which have a profound negative impact on Chris's performance and interaction with colleagues. How do you respond to the situation?

7.3 PREPARING A COACHING INTERVENTION

7.3.1 DECIDING ON COACHING AS AN APPROPRIATE INTERVENTION

Business coaching is firmly rooted in a gap analysis model common in human resource development (HRD), which assumes that the individual lacks a key quality required for the successful fulfilment of their role (Garvey et al 2009). It is therefore not surprising that it is sometimes portrayed as a tool through which organisations can 'sort out' what is perceived as a 'difficult employee'. In other words, business coaching is sometimes perceived as a tool through which an organisation can change an individual's cognition and behaviour at the workplace in a predefined manner. Thankfully for ethical business practice, coaching is not a tool for manipulating organisational actors in such a way, and there is a risk that attempts to shape individuals into the organisation's mould will backfire to the detriment of the organisation. Executive coach Dr Angelique Du Toit reflects on one of her coaching assignments in Box 7.1.

Box 7.1: Manipulation? No, thank you

I was approached by a large multinational organisation to work with one of their rising stars. As an American-owned company they felt the individual in question, a German woman, needed to soften her direct approach to be more in keeping with the company's culture. During the coaching intervention, the coachee realised that she would need to compromise her values and identity if she allowed herself to be shaped into the organisation's cultural mould. That was a step too far for her, and she decided to resign. The organisation had lost one of its most talented managers.

ACTIVITY 7.4

Reflecting on the limits of coaching

In a small group, discuss the scenario described by Dr Du Toit in Box 7.1. What are your thoughts in relation to:

1   the organisation's desire to change the individual's approach?

2   the coachee's decision to resign?

3   the open-endedness of coaching?

What (if anything) could HR professionals have done to prevent such a scenario?

As with all training and professional development, HR professionals have to determine the development needs of potential coachees (see Rhodes et al 2004) and to assess whether coaching is indeed the most appropriate means of professional development for them. The CIPD (2008) counsels that coaching is not a panacea for all professional development needs and that it needs to be chosen wisely for the benefit of individual, team and organisation as part of wider talent management (CIPD 2013).

As a generic rule (see also Chapter 6 for a discussion of training and learning in organisations), knowledge is best acquired through formal learning methods such as short courses, in-house training and/or degree programmes, and the same applies to basic work-related skills (for example working with a new computer program, preparing reports and presentations). Mentoring is usually a good option when an individual requires longer-term nurturing (Megginson and Clutterbuck 2005), for instance when an employee moves into a new role and would benefit from the guidance and advice of a more experienced colleague.

Business coaching is typically offered to individuals who have high potential but need a bit of support to fully achieve that potential, very often in relation to leadership at functional or senior management level. For instance, individuals in a management role may need to identify ways through which to manage their time more effectively and/or cope with multiple pressures (stress management) that go beyond basic time and stress management techniques offered in courses. Business coaching can help them identify both situations in which they struggle to manage time or stress levels and situations in which they manage them successfully (see Rogers 2004 for examples). Working with a coach can aid deeper understanding of the underlying issues, such as anxiety to delegate work or to say 'no' to additional work, and subsequently find a lasting solution.

Decisions as to whether coaching is an appropriate development intervention for an individual need to be seen in the wider organisational context, including business strategy, organisational culture and resource allocation (see also Section 7.2.1 above). Knights and Poppleton (2008, p39) have identified seven factors that determine how business coaching is typically employed in an organisation (see Table 7.3).

Table 7.3 The coaching context

Factor	Description	Key questions for HR professionals
Business priorities	Long-term strategic objectives and short-term imperatives driven by external factors or stakeholders	• What are the current priorities for the organisation? • What impact may business priorities have on who is offered coaching and how objectives are set? • How might coaching support the organisation's effective response to those priorities?
Organisational culture	Identification of what kind of coaching is congruent with the organisation's culture and readiness to experiment at the boundaries	• How would you describe the culture of the organisation? • What works well and less well in this culture? • What is the difference that coaching is supposed to make in this culture? • What are the implications of these questions for where and how coaching is offered? • What type of structures, systems and processes will work well and still model the changes in culture we wish to support?

Factor	Description	Key questions for HR professionals
Learning and development climate	Degree of cynicism or acceptance of learning and development, position and reputation of learning and development function in the organisation, perceived success of previous learning and development interventions	• How do organisational actors respond to learning and development interventions? • How is the HR or learning and development function perceived in the organisation?
Perception of coaching	Based on assumptions and/or prior experiences	• What experience do organisational actors have of coaching? • Are these experiences positive or negative? • What assumptions do they hold about the purpose of coaching? • What assumptions do they hold about the form that coaching might take? • Are there any influencers who have a positive experience of coaching? How can they be used to create a positive perception of coaching more widely in the organisation?
Coaching purpose	Clear and overarching purpose for coaching, which is shaped by business priorities and shapes the availability of coaching in the organisation	• What is the role of coaching as opposed to other interventions? • What is the definition of coaching for our organisation at this time?
Available resources	Budget to buy in services from an external coach, access to appropriately skilled internal coaches	• What is the purpose of coaching? • What are the constraints in terms of resources? • What mix of coaching resources is available and affordable for us? • What, if any, time limits exist in respect of the coaching offer?
Degree of sponsorship	Support from senior management for high-profile coaching interventions	• What is the senior team's experience and understanding of coaching? • What role are they willing to play in supporting coaching? • What do we need to do to build their sponsorship? • How do we make the most of the support for coaching within the senior team? • Who are the key leaders and influencers within different parts of the organisation?

Source: Knights and Poppleton 2009, pp39–42, reproduced with permission

ACTIVITY 7.5

Is coaching the right means of development?

With an organisation with which you are familiar in mind, answer the questions provided in Table 7.3. From your answers, identify how

coaching may be fruitfully employed in the organisation in question. You may want to discuss your findings in a small study group.

7.3.2 SELECTING THE RIGHT COACH

Once a decision has been made that coaching is an appropriate development intervention for an individual, HR professionals need to be able to select the right coach for the assignment in question. While in some instances the coachee can decide largely independently which coach they would like to work with, it is often decided more centrally within the organisation the services of which coach to employ (for example CIPD 2008). Given the unregulated nature of the emerging coaching profession, the wide variety of approaches to coaching and the importance of selecting a qualified and experienced coach, this is not an easy task. To aid HR professionals' selecting a good coach for a particular coaching intervention, Hall (2009) provides a list of dos and don'ts (see Box 7.2 for details).

Box 7.2: Selecting coaches: The Dos and Don'ts

Do:

- Dig deep in your questioning methods. You are trying to understand what the coach brings to their practice and how that fits with objectives.
- Ensure the coach has a clear understanding of the purpose of coaching within the context of your organisation.
- Think carefully about taking on coaches who insist on using their own coaching assessment tools – they should be able to adapt to an organisation's tools.

Don't:

- Consider coaches who can't outline what they can achieve.
- Take on coaches who name individuals they have worked with, but beware those who aren't able to name any clients.
- Assume experience counts for everything.
- Accept qualifications at face value.
- Consider a coach who does not undertake independent supervision.

Source: reproduced with permission from Hall 2009, p33

Hence, Hall (2009) not only emphasises the contextual nature of coaching (that is, that a coaching intervention needs to fit with the organisation's vision, mission and approach to professional development, see also Section 7.3.2), she also cautions HR professionals against taking the qualifications, experience and expertise of potential coaches at face value. HR professionals need to ensure not only that the potential coach understands the organisational context and the nature of the coaching assignment but also that they have the right level of qualification and expertise for the job. Other factors that HR professionals typically take into account when selecting a coach include the coach's track record, approach and style, adherence to professional standards, supervision and continuing professional development, knowledge of the organisation/industry sector (*The Coaching Study 2004*, cited in McMahon et al 2006, pp183–4), the coach's availability and any work they have done with a direct competitor (Zeus and Skiffington 2000). Activity 7.6 can further assist HR professionals in assessing the fit between organisation and coach.

ACTIVITY 7.6

Congruence between organisation and coach

Step 1

Map the key characteristics of the coaching approach that would work well in your organisation. On each of the dimensions below, mark a cross where your ideal approach sits. This can be used as part of the 'ideal coach profile' when selecting a coach (see Step 2).

Step 2

Ask the coach to discuss their approach with regard to the dimensions below, perhaps even marking it on the diagram. All of these dimensions could be turned into questions to gain greater understanding of the coach's approach, for example 'to what extent does the individual lead the agenda?'

Directive	Non-directive
Individual leads the agenda	Organisation leads the agenda
Holistic	Specific
High personal content	Low personal content
High business content	Low business content
Developmental	Remedial

Source: CIPD 2008, p16, reproduced with permission

In addition to determining the fit between the coach (that is, the philosophy and toolkit) and the organisation (for example strategy, culture, learning climate), the match between coach and coachee is a further important consideration. O'Broin and Palmer (2010a) outline that traditionally coach and coachee were matched on the basis of factors, such as gender, age and cultural background as well as personality, albeit with mixed outcomes. Indeed, if coach and coachee have very similar personalities, they may work well at a personal level. However, their blind spots may match, thereby weakening the effectiveness of the coaching relationship (see Section 7.4.1 for details). On the other hand, a mismatch between the personalities of coach and coachee can lead to irritation and frustration – a powerful barrier to the effectiveness of a coaching intervention (Zeus and Skiffington 2002).

7.3.3 CONTRACTING

'No coaching should begin without an agreed contract' argue Brockbank and McGill (2006, p174), and this blanket statement refers to the work of both external and internal coaches. This may sound odd, and you may ask why internal coaches would be concerned with setting up a contract, given that they are typically employed by their organisation to do coaching solely or as part of their role. The term 'contracting' is somewhat ambiguous as it refers to both negotiation of a (legal) contract between coach and sponsoring organisation *and* the setting of ground rules between coach and coachee (moral contract). Importantly, such a contract does not have to be a bureaucratic process that results in a written contract (Megginson and Clutterbuck 2005), even though in practice the coaching contract is usually in writing. A verbal contract is also legally binding when the coach receives payment for their services (McMahon et al 2006), and a moral contract will also exist in the absence of a written contract (O'Broin and Palmer 2010a).

As an HR professional, you are one of four key stakeholders in the coaching process together with the coach, the coachee and the line manager (see Figure 7.2), and part of your role is to manage the relationships between them (CIPD 2008). There are, of course, instances when one individual has more than one role, such as when a line manager coaches their subordinate (for example Anderson et al 2009), and extra care needs to be taken in distinguishing between different roles and managing the respective relationships in such instances.

Figure 7.2 Stakeholders in business coaching

Source: CIPD 2008, p19, drawing on Hay 1995; reproduced with permission

Hence, as an HR professional you may become involved in managing a coaching intervention in relation to three stakeholders. Firstly, you may support the line manager in identifying a need for coaching in relation to a particular individual (see also Section 7.3.1). Secondly, you may represent the sponsoring organisation when negotiating contractual details with a coach and when managing the coaching intervention on the organisation's behalf (legal contract). Thirdly, you may also advise the coachee about the process of coaching, the relationship with the coach and potential outcomes of the coaching intervention (moral contract).

To understand in more detail what is involved in 'contracting', it may be useful to think of three elements: (1) administrative, (2) professional and (3) psychological (Reed 2010). Administrative elements are covered largely through negotiations between coach and sponsoring organisation (typically represented through HR professionals) as part of the legal contract. Professional and psychological elements tend to be of more relevance to contracting between coach and coachee (moral contract). In practice, however, there is considerable overlap, as Table 7.4 demonstrates.

Table 7.4 Contracting in coaching

	Coach–organisation	Coach–coachee
Administrative (contractual details)	Purpose of coaching Number of sessions Length of sessions Frequency of sessions Payment Evaluation of coaching	Goal of coaching Number of sessions Length of sessions Frequency of sessions Location of sessions Cancellation of sessions Evaluation of coaching
Professional (relationship)	Focus of coaching Competences Expertise	Competences Expertise Working together Establishing purpose Creating trust
Psychological (understanding)	Subconscious messages of what coaching is really about	Subconscious messages of what coaching is really about Mutual and reciprocal expectations of coach and coachee

Source: drawing on Brockbank and McGill 2006, O'Broin and Palmer 2010a, Reed 2010

The administrative and professional elements are somewhat self-explanatory as they deal with practical issues ranging from number, length and frequency of sessions, payment and evaluation to competences, expertise and ways of interacting. It is not uncommon for these elements to be put into a written and legally binding contract. What is being stipulated at the contracting stage will set the parameters for the coaching intervention from the purpose, goal and focus of the coaching intervention to the creation of trust between coach and coachee. It is the last point at which meaningful changes to the fundamentals of the coaching intervention can be made, and therefore constitutes an important step in the coaching process.

The psychological element is more difficult to grasp for anyone who has not been involved in coaching. Even if all parties agree to the coaching contract, this does not preclude differences in understanding and interpretation. In other words, it is easy for the parties involved in contracting to have certain assumptions of how coaching works and what the (legal and moral) contract entails, without there being a shared understanding (for example Megginson and Clutterbuck 2005). While a coach should have had some training and experience allowing them to identify some of the other parties' assumptions, HR professionals need to do their part (Hall 2009). They need to listen 'not only to the words but also to what is behind the words, and even to the spaces between the words' (Whitworth et al 2007, pxxi) during the contracting stage to identify and resolve potential misunderstandings at an early stage.

An effective coach will try to make previously taken-for-granted assumptions explicit and, where appropriate, include them in the (legal) contract. They will use their *listening skills*, picking up on the client's language, and paraphrase what they are hearing (for example Rogers 2004) in negotiating both the legal and moral contracts. They will also use their *questioning skills* to negotiate the foundations for working with the coachee, considering, for instance, their expectations of themselves and each other, the responsibilities they have towards themselves and each other, what factors or circumstances might prevent them from working well, and how they might overcome any difficulties (Megginson and Clutterbuck 2005).

ACTIVITY 7.7

Contracting for an effective coaching relationship

Listen to the podcast provided by the *Centre for Creative Leadership* (2013) (http://www.ccl.org/leadership/podcast/

transcriptTheCoachingRelationship.aspx) and consider the implications of the advice provided on the different stakeholders in the coaching process (see Figure 7.2).

7.4 THE COACHING INTERVENTION

7.4.1 THE COACHING RELATIONSHIP

Strictly speaking, the coaching relationship begins at the contracting stage (moral contract) in which the coachee will start to define the goals that they want to achieve through the coaching intervention and to outline the benefits and drawbacks of achieving these goals. The coachee will highlight who is responsible for achieving these goals and which support they may need from others. The coachee will also consider how they will know when the goals have been achieved (The Strengths Foundation 2011). I have chosen to include the coaching relationship in the discussion of the coaching intervention as the goals and the ways of working between coach and coachee may alter in sustained interaction during the coaching process (Megginson and Clutterbuck 2005).

The coaching relationship is the foundation of coaching (Flaherty 2010) as well as a key determinant of its effectiveness (O'Broin and Palmer 2010b). Indeed, both content and process of coaching are influenced by interpersonal relationships (Palmer and McDowall 2010). In terms of content, the coachee may be focusing on their relationship with others in the workplace when working on their interpersonal, team management or leadership skills. In terms of process, the relationship between coach and coachee (and often also other stakeholders, see Figure 7.2) will determine the effectiveness of their interaction and, subsequently, the effectiveness of the outcomes. Coaching is unlikely to be successful if the coaching relationship is not constructive for coach and coachee or the goal of the coaching intervention.

Yet, at the same time the coaching relationship is unique because it is influenced by the personalities of coach and coachee, their life experiences and their perceptions of coaching (Zeus and Skiffington 2002). It is also dynamic, a 'complex adaptive system' (O'Broin and Palmer 2010b, p28), as coaches can shape the coaching relationship through the use of skills such as giving the coachee complete attention, listening actively and empathetically, and pacing the coaching sessions appropriately to enhance the way in which they interact with the coachee. Other tools include reframing (that is, allowing the coachee to think about a situation differently and in a less emotionally charged way, see Cusack 2010), and there are myriad other strategies, tools and techniques that coaches can use to enhance the coaching relationship (see McMahon and Archer 2010 for examples).

The coaching relationship differs from other interpersonal relationships in a professional context through higher levels of mutual trust, mutual respect and 'mutual freedom of expression' (Flaherty 2010, p48). A coach has a unique professional relationship with the coachee; they are a critical friend who seeks to facilitate the coachee's learning and professional development within the boundaries defined through the coaching contract. Except in situations when a line manager coaches a subordinate, the coach remains outside of the coachee's immediate work environment and is therefore perceived as neutral and more trustworthy (see Simmel's notion of 'stranger', Levine 1971).

7.4.2 COACHING SKILLS

'Coaching is essentially a conversation – a dialogue between a coach and a coachee – within a productive, results-oriented context' (Zeus and Skiffington 2000, p3). This eloquent description of coaching has two implications on the skills required by business coaches. Firstly, business coaches need an *inter-disciplinary skill set* that includes listening, questioning and other interpersonal skills to establish and maintain the dialogue highlighted above. Secondly, business coaches also need awareness of the wider environment in which the organisation operates, its structures, systems and decision-making processes (see CIPD 2008). Moreover, business coaches also benefit from situated understanding of the philosophical underpinnings of coaching in relation to what a human being is and how human beings relate to one another, what truth is and how one can know it, and what role language, observation and interpretation have in the coaching relationship (Flaherty 2010). HR professionals may want to identify the quality of the coach's contextual knowledge at the selection or contracting stage (see Sections 7.3.2 and 7.3.3 above).

At a basic level, a coach's most important skill is *active listening*, in which they give the coachee their full attention, noticing not only words and language but also tone of voice and facial expressions, posture and gesture (Zeus and Skiffington 2000). Active listening also means that the coach uses silence to let the coachee talk about what they feel is important without interrupting (Cook and Poole 2011).

However, listening is not an end in itself; rather it is both starting point and foundation for the coach's analysis, interpretation and synthesis that allows them to understand possible root causes for the client's issues (Flaherty 2010). Business coaches will also try to identify what values drive the coachee and whether there is any incongruence between their needs and their current situation (Zeus and Skiffington 2000). In practice, effective business coaches will receive what the coachee is saying, reflect on and make sense of what they are hearing, and then rephrase what they have heard to ensure that they have understood the intended meaning (Cook and Poole 2011).

Asking probing questions is another key skill of a business coach, particularly as they seek to challenge the coachee to reconsider assumptions and perceptions. Business coaches will use a broad spectrum of questions, ranging from factual questions (for example, 'how many members are in your team?'), over explanatory questions (typically starting with 'why'), hypothetical questions (usually starting with 'what if' or 'suppose'), alternative questions (in which the coachee has a choice of answers) to summary questions (in which the coachee seeks to discern the categories with which the coachee makes sense of their experience) (Cook and Poole 2011). Each type of question will add to the coaching intervention with factual questions giving the coach a better general understanding while summary questions tend to address deeper cognitive issues.

Interpersonal skills, such as giving feedback and negotiating goals and plans (Zeus and Skiffington 2000) are inherent in the coaching intervention as is emotional intelligence to identify barriers to an effective coaching relationship (Zeus and Skiffington 2002). Moreover, effective business coaches are rigorous in their analysis, patient with the coachee, consistent in their approach, yet creative and flexible (Flaherty 2010). They will also be able to be empathetic, authentic, flexible and resourceful in their approach to professional practice (Zeus and Skiffington 2002).

So far, this section has focused on the skills that business coaches typically use to facilitate the coachee's professional development. However, as coaching is situated and contextual, there is a need for organisational actors more generally to contribute personal, interpersonal and relational skills to the coaching process (see Rhodes et al 2004 for a discussion). As part of the coaching intervention, the coachee needs to listen to the coach, ask for clarification if necessary and engage actively in making sense of the coaching relationship. It is the coachee after all who seeks to resolve the issues that prevent them from achieving their potential, and that is not possible without their input.

7.4.3 COACHING SUPERVISION

The notion of supervision comes from the realm of therapy where counsellors and other helping professionals are required to meet regularly with an experienced practitioner to 'review their work with clients, their professional development, and often their personal development as well' (Mulhauser nd). Please note that a supervisor in this context is an independent practitioner who offers a professional service to the therapist, not a superordinate as the term usually denotes at the workplace. The same principle applies to supervision of coaches.

In coaching practice, supervision means that coaches discuss their professional practice (particularly any difficulties or dilemmas) with another coach. Rogers (2004, p169) expresses this as follows: 'A supervisor offers a space and place where professional concerns can be discussed with a more experienced practitioner. Supervision operates on coaching principles – that is, the supervisee brings his or her agenda to the sessions and the supervisor works without giving advice.' According to Hawkins (2007), coaching supervision has three elements:

1 *coaching* the coach in relation to their practice

2 *mentoring* the coach in relation to their continuing professional development

3 ensuring the *quality* of the coach's professional practice through an external and independent practitioner.

Coaching supervision is important for coaches at all stages of their career (Rogers 2004). In the early stages, coaches benefit from being able to share their concerns with another coach and get the necessary support to resolving them (professional development through mentoring, see Hawkins 2007). In the later stages of their career, coaches usually benefit from being challenged in their practice to prevent them from becoming over-confident or complacent (continuing professional development and quality assurance, see Hawkins 2007). Coaching supervision can also help the coach alleviate stress and cope with other professional pressures (Rogers 2004). Like coaching, it is a reflective and exploratory process that helps coaches to raise awareness of their interaction with the coachee and gain a better understanding of the dynamics that shape the coaching relationship (Hawkins and Smith 2006).

ACTIVITY 7.8

The importance of coaching supervision

Watch the video clip on YouTube provided by Dr Patricia Bossons (2012) from Henley Business School (http://www.youtube.com/watch?

v=GHSovtwUfJE) and consider the extent to which coaching supervision can enhance a coach's professional practice. You may want to discuss your findings in a small group.

CASE STUDY 7.1

COACHING, SUPERVISION AND REFLECTION

This case study was kindly provided by business coach Mike Cockburn from Sogno Ltd.

All names in the case study itself have been changed to maintain confidentiality.

I was part of a development team working with a service company dealing with a UK-wide client base through a regional management structure. There were five coaches on the project, which was led by a coaching consultancy headed up by Nick, a long-term colleague and friend of mine. I knew most of the other coaches/facilitators, having worked with them on a range of projects before. The project was a large-scale, ongoing development programme for about 60 of the organisation's high-potential managers who had access to a series of development workshops and one-to-one coaching sessions to enable them to personalise and apply their learning.

In the coaching contract we had established with the learning and development manager that while the company was funding the project, each individual coachee would be 'the client' and the coaching conversations would be completely confidential. However, within this context we also established that we would collaborate as a coaching team, in order to:

- Identify generic corporate learning needs which would drive the origination of content for the development workshops.
- Provide reflective support for each other.
- Explore and resolve any dilemmas that may arise.

As we got to know the organisation we discovered it had an extremely results-driven, competitive culture, which ultimately presented me, and my colleagues, with a challenging ethical dilemma.

One of my coaching clients, Graham, was the finance manager in one of the operating divisions, and in one of our coaching sessions he outlined an issue to me that he was struggling to resolve. Two of his colleagues in the division's senior management team had confided in him that they were cultivating a multi-million-pound contract in secret. They had kept this information from the division's MD and the company's senior management as they felt their involvement could jeopardise the deal and also would lead to others taking the credit for their work. They had taken Graham into their confidence and then insisted that he maintain secrecy. He needed to work out what to do and he had to make a decision quickly, because if the senior management team found out about the contract from other sources he would be put in a very awkward position.

We spent some time exploring the consequences of different courses of action and, although he felt his colleagues had put him in a no-win situation, he came to the conclusion that he had to let his line manager know what was happening. My guiding principles, especially in sensitive situations like this, are never to give advice (the client must come to their own conclusions) and never to intervene in the communication process inside the organisation. With my support the client needs to work out what is best for them and then decide when, how and to whom they need to communicate to achieve the best outcome.

This situation also presented me with an ethical dilemma as one of my colleagues, Amanda, was the coach of the sales manager, one of the individuals involved in the 'secret' contract. I rang my supervisor to talk through possible scenarios and concluded, although there was no obvious 'right answer', that I should first inform Nick as the project manager of the coaching team so that he was in the picture and we could explore options together. We decided that the best way forward was to manage this between the two of us and for me to ensure Graham had all the support he needed in dealing with the potential fallout from the announcement to his boss.

We decided not to tell Amanda for the following reasons:

- We only had one side of the story – Graham's version.
- If we had informed Amanda, she would have been party to information that she couldn't share with her client as it had come to light in a confidential coaching session with Graham. This would be likely to have a detrimental impact on her relationship with her client for no benefit.

We did discuss the situation in our end-of-project review and Amanda, who is a very experienced and insightful coach, appreciated the sensitivity of the decision and felt it was the best option to take.

I think the way this scenario played out highlights the challenges of the coaching process in a team coaching environment, with multiple individual clients within a single organisational client. The contracting process becomes multifaceted with a complex series of overlapping contracting relationships. In the example above there was:

- the relationship between Nick's business and the organisational client
- the relationship between the coaches and Nick's business
- the relationship between the individual coaches on the coaching team
- and of course the relationship between the individual clients and their respective coaches.

So a lot of thought needs to go into the definition and recording of the contracting arrangements, although even then it is difficult to draft something that will cover every eventuality. My mindset around this is that the contracting process lays the foundation for what becomes a living,

organic relationship that needs to grow and develop as the coaching process develops.

I think the scenario demonstrates how big an impact the culture in the client organisation can have on the effectiveness of coaching. We were unaware at the start of the extent of the internal pressure to compete, and the influence it was having on behaviours in the business and the subsequent erosion of trust.

The fact that the members of the coaching team knew each other and had worked together before served us well on this occasion as there was a high level of trust and professional respect between us. This enabled us to reach a best-case outcome. Without this the risks of negative fallout in our team would have been considerably heightened.

That said, I have worked on several multi-coach, team-based projects in the past and problems have been rare, but as soon as you scale up beyond a single one-to-one relationship, the challenges of contracting become progressively more challenging.

Questions

1 Taking the perspective of an HR professional, consider the extent to which similar dilemmas may be encountered in other coaching assignments. You may wish to focus your discussion on internal coaching and the multiple relationships therein.

2 Bearing in mind what you have learned about coaching in this chapter, discuss the extent to which Mike, client Graham and project manager Nick have taken the right decision. Given the circumstances, would you have come to the same decision? If so, why? If not, why not?

3 Reflecting on the case study (and, where applicable, your

own experience of coaching), consider the importance of contracting and supervision.

What lessons can you learn from Mike Cockburn's experience?

7.5 EVALUATING COACHING

The CIPD (2008, p7) stresses that 'rigorous evaluation of coaching is crucial' for both organisations (CIPD 2010) and the coaching profession (Phillips 2006). Particularly in testing economic times, organisations need to ensure that all resources are spent wisely. Recent experience has shown that the budget for training and professional development is often among the first expenditure to be cut if an organisation needs to tighten its belt (CIPD 2012c). To make a stronger business case for advanced means of professional development such as coaching (Tulpa 2007) and to gain more widespread commitment to such means (Zeus and Skiffington 2002), HR professionals need to evaluate the impact of coaching on both individual and organisation. In the eloquent words of the CIPD (2010, p5): 'coaching cannot claim a unique contribution to organisational performance and impact if its practitioners and champions assume its value rather than prove it'.

However, recent CIPD surveys have shown that coaching is rarely effectively evaluated (see CIPD 2010 for a summary and interpretation), and one reason may be that HR professionals are overwhelmed by the myriad potential benefits that coaching can have for individual, team and organisation. According to Bresser and Wilson (2007), such benefits include:

- *individual level*: enhanced self-awareness, increased performance, higher motivation and commitment, better work-related skills, enhanced clarity and purpose
- *team level*: clearer vision, improved performance, better team spirit
- *organisational level*: reduced absenteeism, enhanced ability to change and improved organisational performance.

Hence, it can be a challenge to attend to such a multitude of factors when evaluating the effectiveness of a coaching intervention. While decisions about which factors to evaluate will depend on the purpose and context of the coaching intervention, HR professionals need to be clear about what they are evaluating, why they are evaluating it, and how a particular factor can be evaluated (Zeus and Skiffington 2002). Common means to evaluate coaching include happy sheets, key performance indicators (KPIs), return on expectations (ROE) or return on investment (ROI), and anecdotal evidence (CIPD 2010). Yet, some remain sceptical that coaching can be evaluated effectively at all: 'It's absurd to even try to measure so abstract and evanescent an intervention as coaching' (response to the CIPD *Taking the Temperature of Coaching* survey 2009, cited in CIPD 2010, p7).

Despite such debates, the CIPD (2010, p7) is adamant that the evaluation of coaching is 'not rocket science'. To be effective, evaluation of coaching must be relevant for and aligned with wider business strategies and objectives (see also Knights and Poppleton 2008). The CIPD (2010, p15) proposes an integrated thinking tool called OPRA to evaluate coaching that considers ownership (people and organisation), positioning (context and purpose), resourcing (make/buy and manage costs), and assessment/ evaluation (contracting and results) to 'ensure that the process is grounded in credible insights and organisational data'. HR professionals are encouraged to consider the questions summarised in Table 7.5.

Table 7.5 Evaluating coaching with OPRA

Ownership	Is coaching sponsored by senior managers? Is coaching used in some parts of the organisation but not others? What is the frequency of coaching? What is the reach of coaching within the organisation?
Positioning	What change do we want to see through coaching? What do we expect coaching to deliver? What is the purpose of coaching? How does coaching fit with the organisation's culture? How does coaching fit with overall organisational priorities? Does coaching need to be linked to other professional development initiatives? Is the learning and development climate of the organisation conducive to coaching?
Resourcing	How is coaching bought and paid for? What resources does the organisation have to deliver coaching? What is the ratio between internal and external coaching? How much coaching capability does the organisation have internally? How is this maintained and developed?
Assessment/ evaluation	How is coaching evaluated?

Source: CIPD 2010, reproduced with permission

Business coaching can be evaluated qualitatively through success stories of coaching and quantitatively in relation to predefined key performance indicators at individual, team and/or organisational level (CIPD 2010). In terms of qualitative measures, Leedham's (2005) research suggests that the coachee's feelings and behaviours after the coaching intervention, increased clarity and focus as well as better use of reflective practice are common indicators, and these may be typically expressed anecdotally. Despite criticism of anecdotal evidence, the CIPD (2010) stresses that a large amount of anecdotal evidence of the benefits of coaching can add contextual detail to other, more numeric factors.

That said, quantitative evaluation may be more convincing for stakeholders seeking a clear return, and measures can include an increase in new business, improvements in customer service, enhanced productivity at an organisational level and improvements in decision-making or enhanced ability to deal with stress at personal level (Zeus and Skiffington 2000). In addition, the CIPD (2010, p12) proposes the use of psychometric analysis, performance appraisal tools such as 360-degree feedback, individual diagnostics (such as MBTI, learning styles, Belbin), team diagnostics and performance data, employee surveys and HR systems data (relating, for instance, to absence, retention, development).

In summary, a coaching intervention is fruitfully evaluated within its unique organisational context and through a number of means (CIPD 2010) to take into account the benefit for individual, team and organisation. The outcomes of a coaching intervention for the individual may be questionable if they did not perceive it as constructive despite organisational measures pointing to the contrary. Similarly, the outcomes of a coaching intervention for the organisation are questionable if no signs of performance improvement can be detected even though the coachee may be very pleased with it. The evaluation of coaching will always be difficult and controversial, and HR professionals are encouraged to develop a system that works for their organisation.

ACTIVITY 7.9

Evaluating coaching in practice

With a specific organisation in mind, consider the questions posed in Table 7.5. On the basis of your answers, what could a good system for evaluating coaching in this organisation look like? What factors would be measured? Why, when and how?

7.6 CONCLUSION

Coaching has become a popular means of professional development over recent years, and HR professionals have an active role in buying, contracting, managing and evaluating coaching services on behalf of their organisation (CIPD 2008). They need to understand what coaching is, when it can be fruitfully employed and how its outcomes can be evaluated. However, coaching is also surrounded by ambiguity and uncertainty, which derives largely from a rich heritage and a wide variety of approaches in practice. Such ambiguity is important to allow you to appreciate the manifold uses of coaching in organisations, and it is hoped that you will have gained a good foundation for further exploration of coaching in the context of your organisation.

PAUSE FOR THOUGHT

Identify at least three things that you have learned by studying this chapter and engaging with the exercises and activities. How can coaching enrich professional development in your organisation? How can reflection aid your own professional development? What are areas of professional development and practice that you can address yourself and what are the areas for which you may need the support from others? Address these issues in your learning journal and/or CPD log. You may also wish to discuss them with a peer, colleague, mentor or coach to aid your further development.

EXPLORE FURTHER

Professional coaching bodies

Association for Coaching (AC): http://www.associationforcoaching.com

Association for Professional and Executive Coaching and Supervision (APECS): http://www.apecs.org

European Mentoring and Coaching Council (EMCC): http://www.emccouncil.org

International Coach Federation (ICF): http://www.coachfederation.org

CIPD online tools

CIPD. (2008) *Developing coaching capability: how to design effective coaching systems in organisations*. Online tool [online]. Available at: http://www.cipd.co.uk/hr-resources/practical-tools/design-effective-coaching-systems-organisations.aspx [Accessed 1 February 2013].

Resources

BOLTON, G. (2010) *Reflective practice: writing and professional development.* 3rd ed. London: Sage.

MOON, J.A. (2006) *Learning journals: a handbook for reflective practice and professional development.* 2nd ed. London: Routledge.

REFERENCES

ANDERSON, V., RAYNER, C. and SCHYNS, B. (2009) *Coaching at the sharp end: the role of line managers in coaching at work.* London: CIPD.

ASSOCIATON FOR COACHING. (2013) *Coaching defined [online].* Available at: http://www.associationforcoaching.com/pages/about/coaching-defined [Accessed 4 February 2013].

BACHKIROVA, T., COX, E. and CLUTTERBUCK, D. (2010) Introduction. In: COX, E., BACHKIROVA, T. and CLUTTERBUCK, D. (eds). *The complete handbook of coaching.* London: Sage, pp1–20.

BOSSONS, P. (2012) *Coaching supervision: what it is and why it is needed [online].* Available at: http://www.youtube.com/watch?v=GHS0vtwUfJE [Accessed 8 March 2013].

BRESSER, F. and WILSON, C. (2007) What is coaching? In: PASSMORE, J. (ed.). *Excellence in coaching: the industry guide.* London: Kogan Page, pp9–25.

BROCKBANK, A. and MCGILL, I. (2006) *Facilitating reflective learning through mentoring and coaching.* London: Kogan Page.

CENTRE FOR CREATIVE LEADERSHIP. (2013) *The coaching relationship.* Podcast [online]. Available at: http://www.ccl.org/leadership/podcast/transcriptTheCoachingRelationship.aspx [Accessed 1 February 2013].

CIPD. (2008) *Coaching and buying coaching services [online].* Guide. Available at: http://www.cipd.co.uk/hr-resources/guides/coaching-buying-coaching-services.aspx [Accessed 1 February 2013].

CIPD. (2010) *Real-world coaching evaluation: a guide for practitioners [online].* Available at: http://www.cipd.co.uk/binaries/5350_Real_World_Coaching_guide.pdf [Accessed 8 March 2013].

CIPD. (2011) *The coaching climate [online].* Survey report, September. Available at: http://www.cipd.co.uk/hr-resources/survey-reports/coaching-climate-2011.aspx [Accessed 1 February 2013].

CIPD. (2012a) *Coaching and mentoring [online].* Factsheet, revised August 2012. Available at: http://www.cipd.co.uk/hr-resources/factsheets/coaching-mentoring.aspx [Accessed 1 February 2013].

CIPD. (2012b) *Learning methods [online].* Factsheet. Available at: http://www.cipd.co.uk/hr-resources/factsheets/learning-methods.aspx [Accessed 17 January 2013].

CIPD. (2012c) *Learning and talent development: annual survey report [online].* April. Available at: http://www.cipd.co.uk/binaries/5688%20LTD%20SR%20report%20WEB.pdf [Accessed 8 March 2013].

CIPD. (2013) *Identifying learning and talent development needs [online].* Factsheet revised February 2013. Available at: http://www.cipd.co.uk/hr-resources/factsheets/identifying-learning-talent-development-needs.aspx [Accessed 8 March 2013].

CLUTTERBUCK, D. (1998) *Learning alliances.* London: IPD.

COOK, M.J. and POOLE, L. (2011) *Effective coaching.* 2nd ed. New York: McGraw-Hill.

COX, E., BACHKIROVA, T. and CLUTTERBUCK, D. (eds) (2010) *The complete handbook of coaching.* London: Sage.

CUNNINGHAM, I. (2007) Why managers shouldn't do all the coaching. *People Management.* Vol 13, No 2. p60.

CUSACK, J. (2010) Reframing. In: MCMAHON, G. and ARCHER, A. (eds). *101 coaching strategies and techniques.* Hove: Routledge, pp179–281.

DU TOIT, A. and REISSNER, S.C. (2012) Experiences of coaching in team learning. *International Journal of Mentoring and Coaching in Education.* Vol 1, No 3. pp177–90.

ELLINGER, A.D., BEATTIE, R.S. and HAMLIN, R.G. (2010) The 'manager as coach'. In: COX, E., BACHKIROVA, T. and CLUTTERBUCK, D. (eds). *The complete handbook of coaching.* London: Sage, pp257–70.

EMCC. (2012a) *Summary of internal coaching research documents [online].* Available at http://emccuk.org/wp-content/uploads/2013/01/Internal-coaching-research-Summary-Report.pdf [Accessed 4 February 2013].

EMCC. (2012b) *Reflective practice pack [online].* Available at http://emccaccreditation.org/wp-content/uploads/2012/08/EMCC-Reflective-Practice-Pack-August-2012.docx [Accessed 4 February 2013].

FLAHERTY, J. (2010) *Coaching: evoking excellence in others.* 3rd ed. Burlington, MA: Elsevier.

GARVEY, R., STOKES, P. and MEGGINSON, D. (2009) *Coaching and mentoring: theory and practice.* Los Angeles, CA: Sage.

HALL, L. (2009) Coaching: the highlights. *People Management.* Vol 15, No 1. pp32–5.

HART, V., BLATTNER, J. and LEIPSIC, S. (2001) Coaching versus therapy: a perspective. *Consulting Psychology Journal: Theory and Practice.* Vol 53, No 4. pp229–37.

HAWKINS, P. (2007) Coaching supervision. In: PASSMORE, J. (ed.). *Excellence in coaching: the industry guide.* London: Kogan Page, pp203–16.

HAWKINS, P. and SMITH, N. (2006) *Coaching, mentoring and organizational consultancy: supervision and development.* Maidenhead: Open University Press.

KNIGHTS, A. and POPPLETON, A. (2008) *Developing coaching capability in organisations: research into practice.* London: CIPD.

LEEDHAM, M. (2005) The coaching scorecard: a holistic approach to evaluating the benefits of business coaching. *International Journal of Evidence-based Coaching and Mentoring.* Vol 3, No 2. pp30–44.

LEVINE, D.E. (ed.) (1971) *Georg Simmel on individuality and social forms*. Chicago, IL: University of Chicago Press.

MCMAHON, G. and ARCHER, A. (eds) (2010) *101 coaching strategies and techniques*. Hove: Routledge.

MCMAHON, G., PALMER, S. and WILDING, C. (2006) *Achieving excellence in your coaching practice*. London: Routledge.

MEGGINSON, D. and CLUTTERBUCK, D. (2005) *Techniques for coaching and mentoring*. London: Elsevier.

MEGGINSON, D. and WHITAKER, V. (2007) *Continuing professional development*. 2nd ed. London: CIPD.

MELROSE, P. (2010) Hold up a mirror and the client will do the rest. In: MCMAHON, G. and ARCHER, A. (eds). *101 coaching strategies and techniques*. Hove: Routledge, pp22–4.

MULHAUSER, G. (nd) Counselling and therapy supervision. *Counselling Resource: Mental Health Library [online]*. Available at: http://counsellingresource.com/lib/therapy/aboutcouns/supervision/ [Accessed 25 February 2013].

O'BROIN, A. and PALMER, S. (2010a) Building on an interpersonal perspective on the coaching relationship. In: PALMER, S. and MCDOWELL, A. (eds). *The coaching relationship: putting people first*. Hove: Routledge, pp34–54.

O'BROIN, A. and PALMER, S. (2010b) Introducing an interpersonal perspective on the coaching relationship. In: PALMER, S. and MCDOWELL, A. (eds). *The coaching relationship: putting people first*. Hove: Routledge, pp9–33.

PALMER, S. and MCDOWELL, A. (2010) The coaching relationship: putting people first; an introduction. In: PALMER, S. and MCDOWELL, A. (eds). *The coaching relationship: putting people first*. Hove: Routledge, pp1–8.

PELTIER, B. (2001) *The psychology of executive coaching: theory and application*. New York: Routledge.

PHILLIPS, L. (2006) Prove coaching really works. *People Management*. Vol 12, No 11. p15.

REED, J. (2010) *The importance of contracting in coaching*. My Life Gym Blog, 23 November. Available at: http://www.mylifegym.co.uk/blog/?p=41 [Accessed 4 February 2013].

RHODES, C., STOKES, M. and HAMPTON, G. (2004) *A practical guide to mentoring, coaching and peer-networking*. London: RoutledgeFalmer.

ROGERS, J. (2004) *Coaching skills: a handbook*. Maidenhead: Open University Press.

STONE, F.M. (1999) *Coaching, counselling and mentoring: how to choose and use the right technique to book employee performance*. New York: Amacom.

THE STRENGTHS FOUNDATION. (2011) Three tips for establishing a coaching contract, The Strengths Blog, 26 February. Available at: http://www.thestrengthsfoundation.org/3-tips-for-establishing-a-coaching-contract [Accessed 4 February 2013].

TULPA, K. (2007) Coaching within organizations. In: PASSMORE, J. (ed.). *Excellence in coaching: the industry guide*. London: Kogan Page, pp26–43.

WARDEN, D. (2010) Guardian angel. *Coaching at Work*. 27 April. pp38–40.

WELLCOACHES. (2008) *How coaching works [online]*. Available at: http://www.youtube.com/watch?v=UY75MQte4RU [Accessed 4 February 2013].

WHITWORTH, L., KIMSEY-HOUSE, K., KIMSEY-HOUSE, H. and SANDAHL, P. (2007) *Co-active coaching*. 2nd ed. Mountain View, CA: Davies-Black Publishing.

WILSON, C. (2007) *Best practice in performance coaching: a handbook for leaders, coaches, HR professionals and organizations*. London: Kogan Page.

ZEUS, P. and SKIFFINGTON, S. (2000) *The complete guide to coaching at work*. Sydney: McGraw-Hill.

ZEUS, P. and SKIFFINGTON, S. (2002) *The coaching at work toolkit: a complete guide to techniques and practices*. Sydney: McGraw-Hill.

CHAPTER 8

Effective Team-building and Communication

GILLIAN WATSON

OVERVIEW

Teamwork is a common feature of contemporary organisations and it is critical for today's and tomorrow's managers to understand how they form and perform and how they can be led effectively. This chapter discusses the key theories of building, managing and working in teams, with a particular focus on team roles and the behaviours and skills of individual team members. It also considers the need for communication and giving feedback in a team context. This chapter ends with a discussion of conflict in teams, including the emergence of conflict and different ways of handling it.

LEARNING OUTCOMES

By the end of this chapter, provided you engage with the activities, you should be able to:

- identify various stages in group/team development
- evaluate a range of methods to aid team-building and development
- critically evaluate the worth of team role when compiling a team
- explain how a virtual team works and what leadership skills may be employed to manage such a team
- evaluate the need for interactive communication and feedback in teams
- understand the emergence of conflict in teams and how it can be managed.

8.1 INTRODUCTION

Groups and teams are naturally occurring features in organisations as the notion of organisation itself implies that several individuals work towards a common goal. All members of a group, team or organisation bring in their personality, life stories and prior experiences, which often results in complex group, team or organisational dynamics. Ideally, these group dynamics lead to improved organisational performance (Jackson and Carter 2000). To achieve its maximum potential, a group or team is more than just a collection of individuals. A group or team is a collection of individuals in which there is *social interaction*, a relatively stable pattern of *relationships* and the sharing – and working towards – a *common goal*. In most instances, however, groups and teams are made up of very diverse individuals – individuals of different age, gender, background (including nationality and culture) who have different knowledge, skills, views and agendas. While such diversity is undoubtedly the strength of groups and teams, it is also often the source of confusion, irritation and conflict (see also Chapter 1).

This chapter introduces you to the theory of working in groups and teams. We begin by distinguishing between groups and teams and examine what it means to work as part of a group or team. We then consider what needs to be done to build a team as well as the different roles that individuals take in teams. We also discuss how team role theory can be applied in practice to build and develop teams and introduce the notion of the virtual team. We end this chapter with a discussion of communication (including feedback) and with consideration of conflict in team situations.

8.2 WORKING IN GROUPS AND TEAMS

8.2.1 DISTINGUISHING GROUPS AND TEAMS

Groups and teams have long been common types of working in organisations. There is a number of theories on why humans tend to live and work with others, which Clegg et al (2005) summarise as enhancing the safety of individuals in evolutionary terms as well as the need to belong that the 'social animal' called human seems to have. From an organisational perspective, there are significant similarities between groups and teams; for instance, they comprise different members that ideally complement each other, they perform different tasks and roles, and they can contribute significantly to organisational effectiveness and efficiency. This may be the reason why the terms groups and teams are often used interchangeably. There are, however, significant differences between groups and teams, so let's consider both terms/concepts in detail.

8.2.2 WORKING IN GROUPS

Groups consist of a number of members who perceive themselves and recognise each other as being part of that group. In mutual interaction, group members define the boundaries of the group and the ground rules (Schein 1988). Group members contribute individually to the group's common goal, and the evaluation of their performance depends on their individual contributions. There are different types of groups. Formal groups, that is, groups that are intentionally created to achieve certain goals, can be permanent (for instance to head a department or unit) or temporary (such as committees and taskforces). The creation of formal groups often leads to the emergence of informal groups which are dynamic, inventive and can transform organisations into a living, functioning and goal-oriented entity and could therefore be harnessed by team leaders to support the attainment of organisational goals (Luthans 2005). Formal and informal groups are often regarded as distinctly separate entities, but all formal organisations tend to give rise to informal groupings that eventually resemble formal groups and refer to them as the emergent organisational structures (for example McKenna 1999). Informal groups can enhance the effectiveness of organisational structure, lighten managers' workload, fill gaps in managers' knowledge and skills, improve communication and provide a safe outlet for sharing thoughts and feelings.

ACTIVITY 8.1

Analysing informal vertical groups

Consider an informal vertical grouping in the workplace, with which you are familiar. Can you identify what characteristics form part of their bond? Also reflect upon an informal group of which you have been a member using the characteristics of power in informal groups. To what extent have they:

- enhanced the effectiveness of organisational structures?
- lightened the managers' workload?

- filled gaps in managers' knowledge and skills?
- improved communication?
- provided a safe outlet for emotions?

Have you been aware of any of these processes taking place? Does our work environment and culture support any of these working practices? Compare and contrast those elements you believe are working and those that are not. Why might this be the case?

Individuals take on specific roles in groups, and Allcorn (1985) identified three types of such roles: group task roles, group maintenance roles and self-oriented roles. In more detail, group task roles focus on productivity and the development and achievement of organisational goals. Group task roles usually involve:

- *facilitating*: setting goals and procedures for problem-solving activities
- *seeking information*: initiating discussions, seeking ideas and viewpoints from others
- *disseminating information*: offering suggestions, information and own viewpoints
- *co-ordinating and monitoring of activities*
- *energising or motivating* the group to achieve higher levels of output.

Group maintenance roles, in contrast, focus on fostering open and positive relationships between group members. In this set of roles, group members act as:

- *encouragers* to create a friendly interpersonal atmosphere and encourage others
- *harmonisers* to mediate in conflict situations
- *gatekeepers* to keep information flowing and facilitate participation
- *standard-setters* to propose and negotiate standards for group members to adopt
- *observers and followers* can provide useful feedback, and willingly follow given direction.

Finally, self-oriented roles refer to each group member's individual needs and personal agendas, which can move the group on or have a negative impact on the group's cohesiveness. In particular:

- *Aggressors* can be excessively competitive, thus they are likely to devalue contributions from others.
- *Blockers* can be negative and resist agreed-on decisions.
- *Recognition-seekers* crave attention and work primarily to further their own position in and beyond the group.
- *Dominators* tend to control the group by means of flattery or giving orders.

Allcorn (1985) suggests that the categories are self-contained and mutually exclusive and that different group members take on a distinct role. However, while groups need to contain a balanced mix of all the three types of roles, it would be more realistic to conceive that each individual in a group possesses a combination of all three role types. For example, a facilitator may be at the same time an encourager and a recognition-seeker. This makes it difficult to objectively evaluate someone's role effectiveness. Moreover, group size is another key contributing factor to group performance. The relationship between group size and group performance is an inverted 'U' shape: as a group grows, so does the level of performance. At some point, the critical mass of group effort exceeds the task needs. At this point, a phenomenon called 'social loafing' or 'self-limiting behaviours' comes into play, and individuals begin to withdraw by exerting less effort than they would if working alone (Clegg et al 2005).

Hogan et al (1994) observed a number of senior management teams during decision-making and identified a number of reasons for managers' self-limiting behaviours. They found that the presence of someone with more expertise was the major reason for managers' self-limiting behaviour (73 per cent), followed by a presentation of a compelling argument (62 per cent), lack of belief in their own ability (61 per cent) and unimportant and meaningless decisions (58 per cent). Almost half of the study participants gave in to team pressure to conform (46 per cent). While these results are somewhat outdated, we can safely assume that similar dynamics are in place today. Self-limiting behaviours or failure to participate in decision-making reduce the group member's ability to offer the kind of dynamic leadership that organisations need to succeed.

8.2.3 WORKING IN TEAMS

Teams can be defined as 'a group whose members have complementary skills and are committed to a common purpose or set of performance goals for which they hold themselves mutually accountable' (Greenberg and Baron 1997, p270). Hence, a team depends on both individual and team contributions, and its members take collective responsibility for the results. The notion of collective responsibility thus seems to be the key issue that qualitatively separates teams from groups, and team members enter into a psychological contract with each other that group members do not (Clegg et al 2005).

There have been major changes over the years in the way in which teams are being perceived, created and evaluated. The following four general types of teams have long been identified (Aranda et al 1998):

1   *Management teams* inspire and integrate the work of the organisations, such as creating a vision, refining the organisational culture and improving morale, carrying out major change initiatives and improving the organisation's image.

2   *Task teams* tend to be cross-functional teams (that is, their members come from different functional units within the organisation) that work on projects for a defined but often extended period of time.

3   *Work teams* are self-contained work units that are responsible for manufacturing a particular product or delivering a particular service.

4   *Parallel teams* work independently but in parallel to the organisational structure and focus on problem-solving or seeking organisational opportunities.

Teams have many advantages, but also many disadvantages, which are summarised in Table 8.1.

Table 8.1 Advantages and disadvantages of teamwork

Advantages	Disadvantages
Team decisions may deliver a wider choice of solutions.	Team meetings can be costly; it is a hidden cost although important enough to affect the organisation's effectiveness.
Team participation may lead to higher commitment and ownership of outcomes.	Pressures to conform may lead to premature decisions and result in poor leadership.

Advantages	Disadvantages
Team discussions increase feedback and can decrease timing in communication.	Personal agendas may lead to conflict and poor quality of outcomes.
Team membership is known to increase overall effort.	Extreme cause of cohesiveness may lead to 'groupthink'.

Source: drawing on Haynes 2008, Hall 1991 and Janis 1972

 ACTIVITY 8.2

Reflecting on your experiences of teamwork

Analyse, using your own experiences, the points made in Table 8.1 regarding advantages and disadvantages of teamworking. Would your evaluation differ if your role in the team was that of a team member or a team leader? Discuss this with others – does their experience differ from yours?

Early research on team dynamics linked team cohesiveness with stability and higher productivity. Communication in cohesive teams was found to be more frequent and more satisfying, and team members were found to be more participative when they held similar values. Less cohesive groups experienced more difficulty in enforcing standards of behaviour amongst their members. The key factor influencing their productivity, however, was the teams' performance norms. Highly cohesive teams with high performance norms were found to be highly productive, and their performance levels dropped when they adopted lower performance norms. Highly cohesive teams with low performance norms were by far the poorest performers (Bartol and Martin 1991, Mullen and Cooper 1994). But what makes an effective team?

Traditionally, organisations have used productivity to measure both individual and team effectiveness, but there is increasing scepticism as to whether such measures remain appropriate in an uncertain and rapidly changing business environment. For instance, task teams need to be flexible, operate within shorter planning and production cycles and often with changing targets. In addition, it has been recognised that different organisational theories perceive and evaluate teams differently, even though competency in problem-solving, technical know-how and the maintenance of relationships within the group have been found to be widespread criteria to evaluate team performance.

Aranda et al (1998), for instance, identified three types of skills that enhance team productivity. These are team problem-solving skills, team interpersonal skills and task problem-solving skills. Table 8.2 summarises the tasks and outcomes associated with each of these skills.

Table 8.2 Skills and tasks that enhance team productivity

Skill	Tasks include	Outcomes
Team problem-solving	Identifying alternatives Making and justifying decisions Putting plans into practice	Critical thinking Creativity
Team interpersonal	Encourage communication between team members Consult team members in the decision-making process Analyse and synthesise information	Facilitating Supporting

Skill	Tasks include	Outcomes
Task problem-solving	Gathering, analysing and communicating data Prioritising	Analysing Synthesising Discovering

Source: drawing on Aranda et al 1998

Ideally, a team comprises individuals with a wide range of such skills to tap into each other's strengths and to achieve increasingly complex tasks in an increasingly uncertain work environment. Hence, team members should be selected on the basis not only of the skills that they already possess but also on their willingness and ability to learn new skills. This poses a challenge to managers and other organisational decision-makers who have traditionally selected team members based on position and proximity, that is, seniority, association or location. It is also common practice to use the same team over and over again, which results in the team taking the same or similar actions and arriving at the same or a similar outcome. This has far-reaching implications on organisations. Firstly, new organisational problems require fresh thinking that established teams are unlikely to create and, secondly, there is a reluctance to develop potential new team members that might bring in new knowledge, skills and ideas. It is therefore imperative that current and aspiring managers know how to build effective groups and teams, which is what we will discuss in the following section.

8.3 POINTS TO CONSIDER WHEN BUILDING A TEAM

There is much written about team-building, possibly because teams infrequently perform as well as they might or up to their managers' expectations; therefore we constantly strive to find the factors that make a difference – always, it would seem, trying to redefine our community of practice in relation to building the perfect team. Some dynamics (Kruyt et al 2011) that could aid this practice are discussed in this section, which are: (1) acquire the appropriate associates, (2) ensure teams concentrate on their own work, and (3) be conscious of the team evolution and energy.

8.3.1 ACQUIRE THE APPROPRIATE ASSOCIATES

'Acquire the appropriate associates' may be an obvious sentiment. However, while it is probably the most neglected activity managers use to configure a team, for the most part it is a critical element that impinges on the team's performance. It is important that the department head takes the crucial decision in deciding what contribution to the organisation the team as a whole and each individual should make. Sharing the vision or team remit contributes to the synergy in aspirations and potential achievement the team can make.

8.3.2 CONCENTRATION ON THEIR OWN WORK

Teams need focus and, therefore, the team leader needs to be able to create the circumstances that help enforce the team parameters, their culture and work ethic. To ensure this happens, part of the team leader's role is to ensure that priorities are devised and met. This may include deciding on what tasks individuals embark upon, those that are collective activities, those that are monitored and activities that are to be curtailed. The aim here is to maintain focus and not have work that drags on too long or that takes the team away from their priorities, as this can render the team dysfunctional. Team associates need to be aware of their responsibilities – personal and collective – and have a relevant series of performance directives which are transparent and consistent.

8.3.3 EVOLUTION AND ENERGY

This area concerns how the team develops, how they work together, who works with whom, who collaborates well with others and who is recurrently absent, all adding to the team's overall dynamic and whether they function well together or whether there is incongruence. The team's ability to operate is linked to their energy and motivation, their ability to take ownership of events and their ability to collaborate and communicate. The team may therefore exhibit commitment to each other and the tasks at hand, engendering trust and a need to achieve as a team. Dysfunctional elements such as disagreements, deep-rooted interests, organisational politics and outside interference can all add to problems that could result in a lack of commitment and performance (see also Chapter 9).

Every team has distinctive elements and will have support systems and challenges which they must work out for themselves. Areas of development for a newly formed team may include learning to rely on or trust each other, and developing a workable culture and communication process. A nascent level of satisfaction and even pride in their work may help to bring a team together.

8.4 BUILDING GROUPS AND TEAMS

We have seen that organisations require teams that are fluid and functional, and that possess a mix of interpersonal, technical and problem-solving skills and the ability to form and re-form in order to respond to changing organisational needs. It has long been established that groups and teams go through different developmental stages that are relatively predictable. Probably one of the best-known models of group and team development is Tuckman's (1965) five-stage model of forming, storming, norming, performing and adjourning.

Figure 8.1 Developmental stages of groups and teams

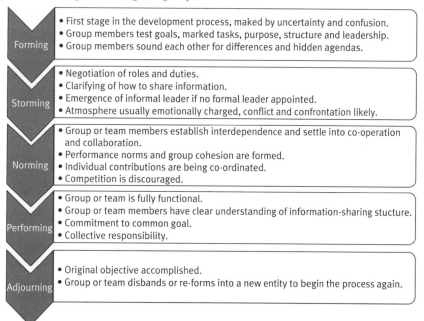

Source: drawing on Tuckman 1965, Quinn et al 2003

Tuckman's (1965) model demonstrates that the road to an effective group or team is bumpy. It is satisfying for individuals to know that they contribute to a group or team and achieve outcomes that they would not be able to achieve on their own. It is also desirable for organisations to have effective groups and teams that perform well and contribute to its success. However, it often seems that the ideal of effective groups and teams overshadows the difficulties and conflicts that groups and teams have on their journey to operating effectively. Current and aspiring managers must therefore have the necessary skill and understanding to facilitate the building of groups and teams to help them to achieve their potential. The team leader's role is paradoxical in that they have to demonstrate a strong personal vision while having to balance the task and group/team maintenance by allowing group or team members to lead and take responsibility themselves (Quinn et al 2003). Micromanaging and allowing some group or team members to shine at the expense of others can have detrimental effects on team productivity and cohesion.

ACTIVITY 8.3

Reflecting on your group or team

Consider a group or team of which you are a member, either at the workplace, at university or in your leisure. Reflect on your experiences as a member and determine if they tally with Tuckman's (1965) model. Can you identify a particular moment or event when your group or team moved from one stage to another? Were you aware of that happening? Can you think of any evidence to demonstrate this?

8.4.1 TEAM ROLES

After our discussion of group and team development, let us now focus on the different roles that team members take on. (We focus on teams rather than groups because teams have clearer roles and a more strategic approach to their creation rather than groups; however, this discussion may also be helpful when considering group issues.) When leading a team, we need to consider how teams are created or what types of behaviours may be required. The work of Meredith Belbin is important here, as a team-based management approach is constantly advocated in many contemporary organisations. Gunduz (2008) considers this to be the second industrial revolution and indicates that it may also be a milestone on the road to increased organisational productivity.

Organisations use whatever means possible at their disposal to ensure competitive advantage; in order to achieve this they need to be flexible and they need teams that are able to identify activities and associated resources (including people) to react quickly to environmental requirements. Therefore, a well-run, well-managed team should bring with it certain positive aspects that are acceptable to all members and fit into the organisation's strategic imperatives (Ozbilgin 2005). The team leader's task is to create the right team atmosphere, make-up of the team, team attitude and behaviour so that the team role concept (Benne and Sheats 1948, Bales and Slater 1955, Belbin 1981, 2007, Watson and Gallagher 2005) can work successfully. Therefore, a review of what Belbin's work offers to the team leader in order to build a team is relevant to contemporary practice.

Team role theory advocates that people interact with others in different ways and exhibit different behaviours. Belbin (1981, 2007) identifies different roles that team members take, which partly depend on their personality and partly on the team dynamics. These roles can be classified into three different sets of roles – task-related, team-related and individual- or thinking-related. Table 8.3 provides details about the different team roles Belbin's work distinguishes and the characteristics that individuals possess and display.

Table 8.3 Team roles

A) Task-related team roles		
Team role	**Strengths**	**Weaknesses**
Shaper	Challenging, dynamic, goal-oriented, has drive and courage.	Prone to provocation, often offends people's feelings.
Implementer	Disciplined, organised, efficient, turns ideas into actions.	Somewhat inflexible, slow to respond to new possibilities.
Completer finisher	Accurate, conscientious, meticulously prevents error.	Inclined to worry unduly, reluctant to delegate.
B) The team- or social-related team roles		
Team role	**Strengths**	**Weaknesses**
Resource investigator	Extrovert, enthusiastic, communicative, explores opportunities, develops contacts.	Over-optimistic, loses interest once initial enthusiasm has passed.
Co-ordinator	Calm, confident, clarifies goals, promotes participative decision-making.	Can be seen as manipulative, offloads personal work.
Teamworker	Co-operative, caring, diplomatic, sensitive, a good listener, averts friction.	Indecisive when faced with tough decisions.
C) The individual- or thinking-related team roles		
Team role	**Strengths**	**Weaknesses**
Plant	Creative, imaginative, unorthodox, solves difficult problems.	Ignores incidentals, too pre-occupied to communicate effectively.
Monitor evaluator	Logical, analytical discerning, judges accurately.	Lacks drive and ability to inspire others.
Specialist	Single-minded, motivated by the pursuit of knowledge.	Contributes on a narrow front, dwells on technicalities.

Source: drawing on Belbin Associates 2006 and Belbin 2007; printed with kind permission of Belbin Associates. For further information and access to updated material, please follow the links provided to www.belbin.com and www.belbin.info

Belbin (1981, 2007) makes many distinctions, for example: the need for different team roles being prevalent at various stages of the team's existence, that high-performance teams need a balance of team roles, that individuals show signs of behaviours in many of the roles and that an overall individual profile can be produced for each team member through team role tests. These tests seek to assist existing teams, help to form new teams and to be used as a recruitment or promotion tool. Belbin's team role tests assess dominance, intelligence, introversion/extroversion and anxiety/determination, and arguably we all have these attributes in our make-up in varying degrees. It is the combination of behaviours and attributes that are the key to determining the individual's place in the team and possibly how they are valued or whether they are 'engaged performers' (Stevens 2010) – ostensibly, whether an individual is motivated to want to feel they belong in the team. The leadership skill in these investigations is to achieve the best fit for the work-related elements and the most attuned social combination. Again, this joining of people's attitudes and behaviour into a team can prove successful and is highly valued when the team engages and performs well.

8.4.2 THE TASK–TEAM–INDIVIDUAL MODEL

Figure 8.2 Task–team–individual model

Source: drawing on Adair 1986, Belbin Associates 2006, Belbin 2007; printed with kind permission of Belbin Associates. For further information and access to updated material, please follow the links provided to www.belbin.com and www.belbin.info

Adair's (1986) model enables us to see a more focused context in the differentiation between one role grouping and another:

- The 'task'/'action striving' grouping will use individuals from both the other grouping in the team to start or complete a task; this is a driving force that gives the team energy.
- The 'team' grouping focuses on the interrelationship within a team and socialisation that can be present in the team because of those 'team'/'socially relating' individuals within it.
- The 'individual'/'thinking' grouping, on the other hand, would contribute from what they view as a feeling of self-worth, which in itself emanates from their own particular way of thinking, cognitive style, attitude or specialist ability.

These attributes will enable them to accomplish tasks in their own way. Overall the characteristics of all the groupings contribute to the whole; in essence, there needs to be a balance of all the roles for the team itself to be successful. The way we interrelate with others in the team does concur with our tendency to behave in a certain way, principally because certain roles are prevalent in our team role profile. Team role tests offer the opportunity to the individual to assess their overall profile, and to review what are their most preferred as well as their least preferred roles in the team. Critically, identifying an individual's team role (Belbin 1996, 2007) enables us to:

- improve self-awareness and personal effectiveness
- foster mutual trust and understanding between work colleagues
- engage in team selection and team-building
- match people to jobs more effectively.

There is prevalence for contemporary organisations to use in-house trained Belbin assessors and consultants from private practice or higher educational institutions to conduct the Belbin analysis with their staff teams. An important point to note is that all Belbin-trained assessors/consultants will advocate the pitfalls of relying on self-reporting alone. Moreover, they would actively seek corroboration of the individual's behaviour from their colleagues so as to avoid the team role profile just becoming a self-fulfilling exercise, open to faking and therefore somewhat unreliable, thereby acknowledging that self-perception can be skewed; for example, we may be unaware of how we are perceived by others. In amalgamating various sources of data collection, a normalising of the results occurs, enabling the Belbin group to assert that this test has validity and reliability. It is worth emphasising that the Belbin assessment itself is attempting to enable us to analyse behaviour rather than personality, as in a psychometric assessment – although our personality is part of our overall make-up and is a constituent part of our behaviours and attitudes (see also Chapter 5), which is elaborated upon in Figure 8.3.

Figure 8.3 Underlying factors to team role behaviour

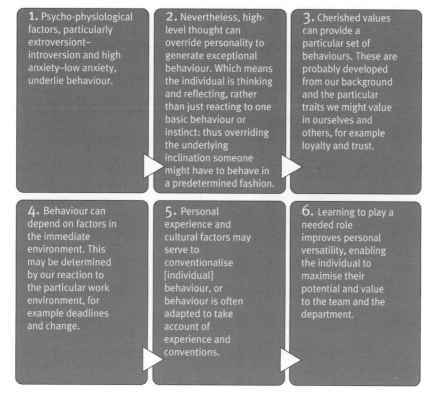

Source: in Watson and Gallagher 2005

Developing a team is a quite complicated process. However, if conducted accurately, it will lead to the norming stage (Tuckman 1965) or a pattern of society within the team, what Belbin (1996, 2007) describes as 'a personality propensity, modified by the thought process, modified still further by personal values, governed by perceived constraints, influenced by experience and added to by sophisticated learning'.

ACTIVITY 8.4

Applying your team role profile

If you are fortunate enough to have a personal team role profile, reflect on the result. Try to establish what you and your team intend to do with it. How can it be used effectively? How can relevant personal development strategies be part of the overall outcome? How will you make the most of this knowledge, remembering that roles in your profile could be classified thus (for personal development purposes): least preferred, manageable, preferred (see Figure 8.4)?

Figure 8.4 Classification of team roles

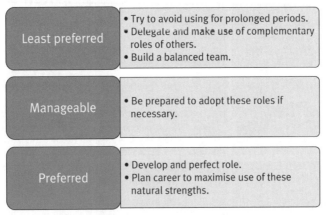

Source: drawing on Belbin Associates 2006, Belbin 2007; printed with kind permission of Belbin Associates. For further information and access to updated material, please follow the links provided to www.belbin.com and www.belbin.info

Figure 8.4 demonstrates that Belbin's team roles can play a significant part in evaluating personal development and career development choices. The point here is that awareness has been raised and therefore a three-tier decision-making process can exist regarding developmental decisions. The individual will need to make personal decisions, but the team, department and the organisation as a whole will need to make strategic decisions on how and why teamworking is of value to the organisation and how to utilise their talented individuals. This new awareness also enables the team leader and team members to discuss roles that are manageable, preferred and least preferred; for example, the individual has the choice of developing and maximising their strengths and enhancing areas that are least preferred. Indeed, it may serve to change a team member's job role in the team.

8.4.3 TEAM ROLE THEORY IN PRACTICE: MATCHING PEOPLE TO JOBS

Team role profiles can support recruitment and promotion decisions as the team leader has the option of recruiting the person that fits the demands of the job as well as having a relevant 'fit' within the team. While the conventional recruitment process considers the eligibility for a job linked to the relevant entry criteria, Belbin's work suggests that performance criteria and suitability of candidates should also be taken into account when recruiting, selecting or promoting candidates (see Figure 8.5).

Figure 8.5 Entry and performance criteria

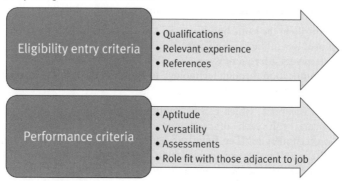

Source: drawing on Belbin Associates 2006, Belbin 2007; printed with kind permission of Belbin Associates. For further information and access to updated material, please follow the links provided to www.belbin.com and www.belbin.info

There are several crucial elements to consider in selecting an appropriate candidate. At the beginning of the selection process, the manager defines the job or project and compiles a job requirement assessment. In addition, certain team members compile a job observation survey and a job suitability report, which then assesses whether a candidate is suitable for the job in question. When selecting a candidate for a particular project or role, managers and those in roles of responsibility must consider not only entry criteria such as skills, experience and qualifications, but also suitability criteria such as aptitude, temperament and behavioural tendencies, which Belbin's test assesses. In particular, entry criteria are vital in actually securing an interview and requisite qualification will always be an essential part of the recruitment process.

However, these criteria do not guarantee that the new recruit will be successful in the job and suitability criteria will reduce the 'leap of faith' present in any recruitment decision. Given that the assessment of suitability criteria has been developed through using observation of behaviour with data-reporting variables such as self and others, the 'suitable' candidate can emerge. Belbin (1996) confides that he would always want to make a case for backing a suitable candidate rather than an eligible one. His argument is that the candidate that hitherto may not have been deemed eligible can have their level of eligibility enhanced through executing a personal development plan, although, as always in today's organisations, the cost of this development would have to be worthwhile. Cannall (2009, p1) puts this as follows: 'Team selection is not an exact science … A mix of types is necessary, as is a mix of skills.'

To build a diverse balanced team, other more important considerations are worthy of note: there needs to be a flow of readily available candidates with the right prerequisites and the relevant diversity of talent and measure of team roles. Each person on the team would have their own reciprocal role, with a given purpose or terms of reference to achieve results; this would therefore be used to assemble the 'perfect' team.

8.5 VIRTUAL TEAMS

The concept of the 'virtual team' was created out of the Internet revolution and the transformation of many subsequent business practices, such as e-business, e-learning and the overall e-economy, which arguably forced businesses to put aside their time-honoured, erstwhile practices and look for a new way of dealing with the globalisation of their business (Townsend et al 1998). Technology companies in particular realised that the way they communicated had to change. Therefore, the challenge was to harness the positive aspects of teamworking and translate it into a work team that:

- was not necessarily in the same building
- was not – probably – in the same country
- meet face to face very infrequently
- relies on communication through technology to maintain the fundamental nature or spirit of their co-operation.

The virtual team was born, which can be defined as 'geographically dispersed members who communicate with each other using some variant mix of information and communication technologies' (Lee-Kelly and Sankey 2008, p52). Often, virtual teams are created to realise a new project or development, but this does not diminish its worth or negate the challenges that teamwork generally brings. If anything, virtual teams are more complex than other, more traditional types of team due to geographical and temporal distance (Lipnack and Stamp 2000, Townsend et al 1998), 'boundary spanning, life cycle and member roles' (Bell and Kozlowski 2002). Cannall (2009, p1) suggests that the virtual team 'may need to communicate by telephone, e-mail and teleconferencing rather than face-to-face. Managing them is particularly difficult, not least because remote working can exacerbate misunderstanding.' Leadership skills can be the critical factor in managing a virtual team; therefore, we must investigate what the key issues are which can support success or condemn the team to failure. Technological processes are critical to the existence of a 'pure virtual team' (Arinson and Miller 2002) and fundamental to influencing how the team works. Therefore, the team leader in this instance relies on the organisation investing in the appropriate technology to support virtual teamworking.

Cascio and Shurygailo (2003) suggest there are four categories of virtual team: teleworkers, remote team, matrixed teleworkers and matrixed remote team, as defined in Figure 8.6. According to Cascio and Shurygailo (2003), a further other variable is time and shift-working; however, this will be salient to the particular organisation and therefore is not included here.

Figure 8.6 Forms of virtual teams

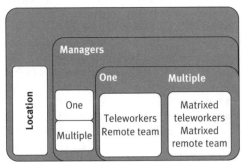

Source: drawing on Cascio and Shurygailo 2003

Organisations may create hybrid forms of virtual teamworking to suit their requirements. Agreement has not yet been reached about the skills involved in leading a virtual team. One view suggests that managers or leaders of a virtual team need have no particular leadership style (Cascio and Shurygailo 2003); the other view extols that any remote leader has little or no control over the virtual team (Kostner 1996, as cited in Lee-Kelly and Sankey 2008). This would suggest that the team's well-being and performance relies on the team for voluntary control and therefore its members need to be self-motivating and to some extent self-managed individuals. In any case, leading a virtual team requires exceptional co-ordination and communication skills, and team leaders and those aspiring to become team leaders in future need to have self-determination in extending their skills.

Let us consider the leadership or co-ordination of virtual teams in more detail. The matrix in Table 8.4 shows practical approaches that the potential leader of a virtual team may need to adopt in their management technique and to take account of creating structure, culture and rules or plans by which the team will adhere.

Table 8.4 Co-ordinating virtual teams

Shared goals	Clear roles and regular performance feedback are important and need to be explicit.
Standard operating systems	Clear timeframes for replying to communication media, and working in a congruent manner, for example how team meetings will operate.
Using appropriate technology	Telecommunications, Internet, email, groupware, Skype, video-conferencing, mobile phones, intranet.
Appropriate communication	Face to face when necessary, for conveying appropriate verbal and non-verbal information (Skype or web cam could be utilised here). Remember: email is relevant for simple tasks.
Building and maintaining interpersonal relationships	Team-building activities, possibly together at one venue – this is linked to training the workforce to work together, virtually. Also they need to learn how to work and interact in a cohesive and trustworthy manner and, importantly, to respect each other's cultural differences.
Selection	Ensure careful consideration is given to team-fit when selecting staff; also be clear about the skill level required in each area of the work, for example technical and interpersonal skills.
Maintaining levels of creativity	Motivate staff – ensure they have attainable goals.

Source: drawing on Axtell et al 2004, Watson and Gallagher 2005

A particularly neglected area of communication when managing virtually is listening, and Williamson (2009) advocates we should 'listen to silences'. She contends that we need to listen, with care, to every team member when they are on the telephone – remembering that there may not be a facility to use Skype or a web cam, which in itself makes it important to be vigilant to the nuances in the speed, quality and pitch in the voice as well as the silences within the conversation, especially critical in alleviating any potential problems the member of staff may be experiencing. Figure 8.7 may help illustrate this point.

Figure 8.7 The importance of listening

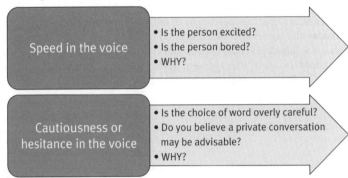

Source: drawing on Williamson 2009

ACTIVITY 8.5

Listening

In groups answer the questions posed by Figure 8.7. You may need to do this as a role-play exercise if you have limited experience of working in a virtual team. Suggest, analyse and discuss your own thoughts as to the problems a virtual team leader may encounter. Consider how you would detect any problems and how you would deal with them.

The following section will help illuminate many factors relating to group/team communication.

8.6 INTERACTIVE COMMUNICATION IN TEAMS

Communication has long had a key role in an organisation's effectiveness, and it is therefore not surprising that managers spend much time communicating with others (Mintzberg 1989). Current and aspiring managers need to develop and hone their communication skills to make use of a wide range of different methods to communicate more effectively. Written communication through emails, proposals, reports and oral communication through presentations, interviews, negotiations, mediation, coaching and so on are all indispensable devices for managerial communication.

Face-to-face and telephone communication/Skype is fast, personal and offers immediate feedback. However, face-to-face communication can be costly, time-consuming and there is often a need to follow it with a document. Written communication occurs through different media, offers the sender an advantage to formulate the message prior to sending, can be widely disseminated and provides a record.

8.6.1 SUCCESSFUL COMMUNICATION PATTERNS

There is an argument that 'successful communication patterns' (Pentland 2012) contribute much to the achievement of a team. Interestingly, Pentland maintains that the talent or skill of an individual member contributes less to team success. It is the elements of communication between team members that make a difference. There are also certain features of successful teams that Pentland's (2012) research revealed:

- Everyone on the team talks and listens in roughly equal measure, keeping contributions short and sweet.
- Members face one another, and their conversations and gestures are energetic.
- Members connect directly with one another – not just with the team leader.
- Members carry on back-channel or side conversations within the team.
- Members periodically break, go exploring outside the team, and bring information back to the team.

If we consider how a team member may adhere to these ideals, it is reasonable to suggest that the key is how they communicate. It is not on just one level; it encompasses several. For example, as a description of someone who exemplifies the points made above, they would have the following characteristics: they actively circulate, engage their associates in short, high-energy dialogue, communicating equally with team members while persuading all to voice their opinion on an issue. These people are not necessarily gregarious or assertive personalities; they are comfortable when engaging others and most of all they are active listeners. Pentland (2012) describes them as 'charismatic connectors'. In fact, this depicts a team player who is well connected to their team yet is engaged in probing data from outside the team. Essentially, though, the discussion illustrates an adept communicator committed to their team.

8.6.2 COMMUNICATION PROCESSES

Regardless of the type of team and the way in which a team was built, team members have to communicate to engender the team dynamic and team culture that enables the team to be successful. Therefore, the communication medium may vary quite dramatically, as can the time taken to effect the interaction. Shannon and Weaver (1949, cited in Chandler and Munday 2011) have deliberated upon this issue and, in one of their earlier and much-used versions of their theories, considered the process by which we interconnect. The process is also useful in facilitating any analysis of the communication, particularly if meaning has been misinterpreted, although it must be stated that this is considered a linear process. The process involves a consideration of:

- the source of the communication
- the method we use to encode the message
- the channel employed, which includes the symbols and signals
- the manner by which we decode the message
- a reflection of how a person receives the communiqué.

Figure 8.8 depicts how a communication can be employed.

Figure 8.8 Source–channel–receiver

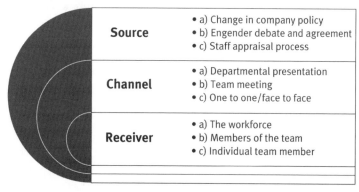

Source	• a) Change in company policy • b) Engender debate and agreement • c) Staff appraisal process
Channel	• a) Departmental presentation • b) Team meeting • c) One to one/face to face
Receiver	• a) The workforce • b) Members of the team • c) Individual team member

From Figure 8.8, it is clear that each element becomes more focused as we near the receiver; undeniably, the whole communication process stands or falls on the receiver's interpretation of the message being conveyed. It is, however, essential we bear in mind the importance of:

- *encoding the message*: the manner by which the sender (source) translates their ideas into symbols
- *decoding the message*: the receiver construes the message they think the sender desires to convey
- the *symbols* (gestures, words, pictures)
- the *signals* (that is, the tacit signposts inherent in the message) that all interplay.

Of fundamental significance in our attempts to communicate in the workplace can be the accurateness, appropriateness or possibly the truthfulness of the sender's message; the sender's calculation of how the message will be received may also have bearing on the outcomes and on the quality of the interaction.

ACTIVITY 8.6

Using a communication process

Consider the a, b and c scenarios highlighted in Figure 8.8:

1   Discuss in your groups a process that would enable the receiver to interpret the message in the way that the source intended.

2   Discuss how the message may be misinterpreted – pay particular attention to the encoding, decoding as well as the symbols and signals employed.

3   Reflect upon an incident you have encountered where the receiver misinterpreted the message. What was the outcome?

- Analyse why this occurred.
- How could the communication have been improved?

8.6.3 APPROACHES TO TEAM COMMUNICATION

Approaches to team communication can consist of the following consideration: the *purpose* for communicating, the *audience* (the make-up of the team) and the available *resources*. In other words, the communicator must know their purpose for the communication but not assume that the team would automatically share it. The message must be specific to the issue at hand, enabling the vocabulary and the amount of detail expressed to be determined by the audience's needs. To ensure a suitable match, the following questions must be answered:

- How much do the team members know about the subject?
- Are they likely to agree with the presented position or advice?
- What kind of advice have they heard recently on this topic?
- How did they react?

The scope of the communication should then be confined within the resource boundaries, such as time, money, energy and available information.

Both oral and written communications are supported by non-verbal elements. Non-verbal communication is not coded into words, but consists of kinesic behaviour, proxemics, paralanguage and object language, and it would be difficult to imagine any type of interaction without it:

- *Kinesic behaviour* conveys feelings about discussed issues through body movements, posture and facial expressions.
- *Proxemics* refers to the impact that distance and space has on interaction. It varies from imposing degrees of formality or intimacy on situations.
- *Paralanguage* refers to vocal aspects of words, such as timbre, pitch, tone, laughing and yawning.
- *Object language* refers to the communicative aspects of the personal and physical environment, such as appearance, materials, furniture layout, architecture and similar.

8.6.4 COMMUNICATION FEEDBACK

When communicating, 'noise' is always present, threatening to distort the meaning of the message. The reasons for noise are many, such as the chosen medium, sender may poorly articulate and receiver may not be a good listener. Inserting feedback into communication is useful; it acknowledges that the message was sent and received. There are three types of feedback: informational, corrective and reinforcing:

- *Informational feedback* is a non-evaluative response indicating that a message was received and includes additional information.
- *Corrective feedback* challenges or corrects the original message.
- *Reinforcing feedback* is a response that a message was received.

For communication to be effective, a total listening environment must be created where a message is heard, non-verbal cues observed and hidden aspects of a message are not missed.

As organisations become larger and/or more complex, flattening of organisational structures becomes a necessity. This needs to be supported by integrated horizontal communications. Historically, horizontal communication was evident in informal networking activities such as socialising and politicking (see also Chapter 9), although there is need for integration into the formal organisational structure. Giving social support operates well within one level, but fails in upward or downward communications. However, organisations remain comfortable with such vertical, that is, 'downward' (management to employees) communication. Vertical communication is directive and purposeful, although for teamwork to be effective, communication must move to more horizontal interaction (Bell and Kozlowski 2002, Maznewski and Chudoba 2000, Graetz et al 1998).

There are four reasons for integrated interactive communication (Luthans 2005):

1 *Task co-ordination*: for teamwork to be effective and to stay on course, team members must regularly meet and discuss the work in progress.

2 *Problem-solving*: the team members use their problem-solving skills to approach a given problem or opportunity, and to know how to minimise potential crisis situations. A number of techniques can be used, such as brainstorming, the best and worst scenario, and so on.

3 *Information-sharing*: the team decides on how to access necessary information.

4 *Conflict resolution*: the team will meet to share feedback and develop techniques to resolve inherent conflicts arising from their activities.

ACTIVITY 8.7

Giving and receiving feedback

In order to practise giving feedback, write a short evaluation about yourself. Then select someone you consider as 'safe' and friendly, although not someone you are close to. Ask them to do the same. Place yourself in the other person's shoes (use empathy and ask yourself how it feels to be that person), and then read their self-evaluation. Arrange a joint session with the person at a place and time where you will not be disturbed. Swap your self-evaluations and give the other person feedback on it.

Consider the following:

1   Did you check that the other person was in the right frame of mind to hear your feedback?

2   Were you able to say what you wanted to say? What response did you get?

3   Did you have a clear idea of what you wanted to accomplish before the meeting?

4   How were you affected by the feedback you received?

5   Would you make any changes in the future?

Like other managerial skills, giving and receiving feedback requires self-awareness, and it is therefore not surprising that many organisations offer training in giving and receiving feedback, often as part of the appraisal process (see also Chapter 10). In addition to the knowledge of how to give and receive feedback, the giving and receiving of feedback requires constant practice, and we encourage you to take every opportunity to practise this vital skill.

8.7 CONFLICT IN TEAMS

As we have seen in previous sections of this chapter, teams do not just happen; they need commitment, investment and training as well as knowledge about effective team-building. It must be emphasised that teamwork is destined to fail in many organisations in which team activities are not rewarded and in which mistrust, negative feelings and unresolved conflicts are rife. The result of ineffective or failed teamwork is often conflict. Indeed, there is evidence that 20 per cent of management time is spent on resolving conflict (Haynes 2008).

One view of conflict, the *unitary perspective*, considers an organisation to be a happy family, with loyal employees that pull together in harmony to achieve the organisation's goals. Conflict tends to be explained in terms of poor communication, personality clashes or the work of troublemakers. Managers who claim that their work units run smoothly and without conflict are either: exceptionally self-aware, skilful communicators or, more likely, they suppress conflict. Due to their very nature, suppressed conflicts do not allow resolution and therefore stifle any meaningful interaction between individuals and groups with often major impact on overall staff morale and productivity. Conflicts may arise from a variety of reasons, such as differences in personal communication styles, levels of inarticulateness, hidden agenda or status. Workplace norms and patterns of communication (values, assumptions, self-image) can lead to individuals' or groups' insecurity and fear, which in turn may result in a variety of defensive types of behaviour (Argyris and Schön 1996).

Another view of conflict, the *pluralistic perspective*, accepts conflict as an inherent part of the organisation. Conflict situations can and do arise from the organisational structure, the size of the workforce, standardisation of jobs, and increased levels of hierarchy. The word 'conflict' conveys negativity and things being out of control, although conflicts can and often bring benefits by fostering creative thinking in seeking resolution. Hatch (1997), for instance, argues that a low level of conflict is often associated with poorly focused, unmotivated and ill-integrated teams, while a high level of conflict leads to a lack of co-operation, distraction from the overall goal and hostility. Hence, the trick for managers and team leaders is to find and encourage a healthy level of conflict that can produce cohesive, productive and co-operative teams. Such an approach requires all parties to jointly identify the sources of a problem, to agree on what the problem is and to seek different solutions.

Teams do have minor disagreements that over time may have led to conflict (Open University 1985, as cited in Senior and Fleming 2006, p221). Many conflicts begin with a simple misunderstanding, followed by different values, viewpoints and interests of the parties involved, which can lead to interpersonal differences when emotions such as irritation, anger and frustration come into play. There are different conflict-handling styles, ranging from the avoidance of conflict through competing, compromising and collaboration to accommodating (Thomas 1976). Each manager or team leader will have their own style, and different situations and context will require different styles of dealing with conflict.

ACTIVITY 8.8

Team behaviour and attributes

1   Reflect upon a team with which you are familiar or have been a part of and review their behaviour and attributes:

- Do they have complementary skills?
- Are they committed to a common purpose?
- Do they share performance goals?
- For what does each individual hold themselves accountable?

- Do all members participate fully in the team's activities and team meetings?
- Who offers team members feedback on their contributions?

2   Discuss which behaviours and attributes are more conducive to a harmonious and productive team environment.

8.8 CONCLUSION

Team-building can be enthralling, enjoyable and even exasperating at times. The theoretical and practical situations discussed in this chapter were assembled to assist you in developing the necessary skills to participate and bring together individuals effectively under the banner of 'teams'. We have emphasised the need for an enlightened view of team roles and an individual's self-worth within the team. We have highlighted the need to be more sensitive to the nuances of co-ordinating a virtual team. We have discussed the vital role communication has in teamwork and discussed conflict in teams.

Groups and teams have long intrigued scholars of management and organisations as well as management practitioners, but there is still a long way to go to create effective teams reliably and consistently. One reason for this may be the sheer complexity of human interaction to which team members bring their personality, life stories and prior experiences, which often results in complex group, team or organisational dynamics. The challenge for managers and team leaders is to turn a group of often diverse individuals into cohesive and functioning teams; team leadership is discussed in Chapter 11 of this book.

PAUSE FOR THOUGHT

Identify at least three things that you have learned by studying this chapter and engaging with the activities. How will your newly acquired knowledge and skills support your continuing professional development? What value do you expect your learning to have for your daily routines and your further career? In what area have you identified a need for further development and how are you planning to fill that gap? Address these issues in your learning journal and/or CPD log. You may also wish to discuss them with a peer, colleague, mentor or coach to aid your further development.

EXPLORE FURTHER

See http://www.youtube.com/watch?v=OOai178ZiiQ for an excellent YouTube video clip in which Meredith Belbin discusses team role theory in an international context

BELBIN ASSOCIATES: http://www.belbin.com or http://www.belbin.info

BELBIN, R.M. (2007) *Management teams: why they succeed or fail.* London: Elsevier Butterworth Heinemann.

CANNALL, M. (2009) *CIPD Factsheet – Team Working*, rev. August 2009. London: CIPD.

REFERENCES

ADAIR, J. (1986) *Effective teambuilding.* Aldershot: Gower.

ALLCORN, S. (1985) What makes groups tick. *Personnel.* September. pp52–8.

ARANDA, E.K., ARANDA, L. and CONLON, K. (1998) *Teams: structure, processes, culture and politics.* New York: Prentice Hall.

ARGYRIS, C. and SCHÖN, D.A. (1996) *Organizational learning II.* Reading, MA: Addison-Wesley.

ARINSON, L. and MILLER, P. (2002) Virtual teams: a virtue for the conventional team. *Journal of Workplace.* Vol 14, No 4. pp166–73.

AXTELL, C., WHELLER, J., PATTERSON, M. and LEACH, A. (2004) From a distance. *People Management.* 25 March. p39.

BALES, R.F. and SLATER, P.E. (1955) Role differentiation in small decision-making groups. In: PARSONS, T. and BALES, R.F. (eds). *Family socialisation and interaction process issues.* Glencoe, IL: Free Press, pp259–306.

BARTOL, K.M. and MARTIN, D.C. (1991) *Management.* International ed. New York: McGraw-Hill Irwin.

BELBIN, R.M. (1981) *Management teams: why they succeed or fail.* London: Heinemann.

BELBIN, R.M. (1996) *Team roles at work.* London: Butterworth Heinemann.

BELBIN, R.M. (2007) *Management teams: why they succeed or fail.* London: Elsevier Butterworth Heinemann.

BELBIN ASSOCIATES. (2006) Cert UK. barrie.watson@belbin.info

BELL, B.S. and KOZLOWSKI, S.W.J. (2002) A typology of virtual teams. *Group and Organisation Management.* Vol 27, No 1. pp14–49.

BENNE, K.D. and SHEATS, P. (1948) Functional roles of group members. *Journal of Social Issues.* Vol 4, No 2. pp41–9.

BRADLEY, L.K., ROSEN, B., GIBSON, C.B., TESLIK, P.E. and MCPHERSON, S.O. (2002) Five challenges to virtual teams success. *Academy of Management Executive.* Vol 16, No 3. p67.

CANNALL, M (2009) *CIPD Factsheet – Team Working.* Rev. August. London: CIPD.

CASCIO, W.F. and SHURYGAILO, S. (2003) E-leadership and virtual teams. *Organisational Dynamics.* Vol 31, No 4. pp362–76.

CHANDLER, D. and MUNDAY, R. (2011) *A dictionary of media and communication.* Oxford: Oxford University Press.

CLEGG, S., KORNBERGER, M. and PITSIS, T. (2005) *Managing and organizations.* London: Sage.

GRAETZ, K.A., BOYLE, E.S., KIMBLE, C.E., THOMPSON, P. and GARLOCH, J.L. (1998) Information sharing in face-to-face teleconferencing and electronic chat rooms. *Small Group Research.* Vol 29, No 6. pp714–43.

GREENBERG, J. and BARON, R.A. (1997) *Behavior in organizations.* New York: Prentice Hall.

GUNDUZ, H.B. (2008) An evaluation of Belbin's team roles theory. *World Applied Science Journal.* Vol 4, No 3. pp460-9.

HALL, R.H. (1991) *Organizations.* 4th ed. Harlow: Prentice Hall.

HATCH, M.J. (1997) *Organization theory: modern symbolic and postmodern perspectives.* Oxford: Oxford University Press.

HAYNES, G. (2008) *Managerial communication: strategies and applications.* 4th international ed. New York: McGraw-Hill Irwin.

HOGAN, R., HOGAN, J. and ROBERTS, B.W. (1994) What we know about leadership. *American Psychologist.* Vol 49, No 5. pp493–504.

JACKSON, N. and CARTER, P. (2000) *Rethinking organisational behaviour.* Harlow: FT/ Prentice Hall.

JANIS, I.L. (1972) *Victims of groupthink.* Boston, MA: Houghton Mifflin.

KRUYT, M., MALAN, J. and TUFFIELD, R. (2011) Three steps to building a better top team. *McKinsey Quarterly.* No 1. pp1–3.

LEE-KELLY, L., and SANKEY, T. (2008) Global virtual teams for value creation and project success. *International Journal of Project Management.* Vol 26. pp51–62.

LIPNACK, J. and STAMP, J. (2000) *Virtual teams*. 2nd ed. New York: Wiley.

LUTHANS, F. (2005) *Organizational behavior*. 10th international ed. New York: McGraw-Hill.

MAZNEWSKI, M.L. and CHUDOBA, K.M. (2000) Bridging space over time. *Organization Science*. Vol 11, No 5. pp473–92.

MCKENNA, E. (1999) *Business psychology and organisational behaviour*. London: Taylor & Francis.

MINTZBERG, H. (1989) *Mintzberg on management*. New York: Free Press.

MULLEN, B. and COOPER, C. (1994) The relation between group cohesiveness and performance. *Psychology Bulletin*. Vol 115, No 2. pp210–32.

OZBILGIN, M. (2005) *International human resource management: theory and practice*. Basingstoke: Palgrave.

PENTLAND, A. (2012) The new science of building great teams. *Harvard Business Review*. Vol 90, No 4. pp1–11.

PETZINGER, T. (1999) *The new pioneers: the men and women who are transforming the workplace and marketplace*. New York: Simon and Schuster.

QUINN, R.E., FAERMAN, S.R., THOMPSON, M.P. and MCGRATH, M.R. (2003) *Becoming a master manager: a competency framework*. 3rd ed. Chichester: Wiley.

SCHEIN, E.H. (1988) *Organizational psychology*. 3rd international ed. New York: Prentice Hall.

SENIOR, B. and FLEMING, J. (2006) *Organizational change*. 3rd ed. Harlow: FT/Prentice Hall.

STEVENS, M. (2010) Public sector 'intellectually but not emotionally engaged'. *People Management*. 26 January [online]. Available at: http://www.peoplemanagement.co.uk/pm/articles/2010/01/public-sector-intellectually-but-not-emotionally-engaged.htm [Accessed 26 May 2010].

THOMAS, K.W. (1976) Conflict and conflict management. In M.D. DUNETTE (ed.). *Handbook of industrial and organizational psychology*. Chicago, IL: Rand McNally, p900.

TOWNSEND, A., DEMARIE, S. and HENDERSON, A. (1998) Virtual teams: technology and the workplace of the future. *Academy of Management Executive*. Vol 12, No 3. pp17–29.

TUCKMAN, B.W. (1965) Developmental sequence in small groups. *Psychological Bulletin*. Vol 63, No 6. pp384–99.

WATSON, G. and GALLAGHER, K. (2005) *Managing for results*. 2nd ed. London: CIPD.

WILLIAMSON, B. (2009) Managing virtually: first, get dressed. *Business Week*. 17 June. p19.

CHAPTER 9

Negotiation and the Management of Interpersonal Relationships at Work

LESLEY MEARNS

OVERVIEW

Managing within contemporary organisations is becoming increasingly difficult due to the many internal and external changes which are occurring, such as the expansion of globalisation, the financial crisis and the evolution of new technologies and new managerial practices. Today's managers need a broad range of skills and capabilities; they must be able to handle a diverse workforce and to negotiate complex and diverse interpersonal relationships within the modern workplace. Managers also need to have the capability to successfully negotiate and manage the boundaries of the employment relationship, to positively utilise power and authority within the organisation, to resolve conflicts and to monitor and control bullying in the working environment.

The manager–employee relationship is the foundation upon which a successful organisation evolves and gains competitive advantage. Unfortunately, however, many organisations fail to develop, train and support their managers in order to ensure that they have the necessary skills to construct and develop a strong and meaningful employment relationship which will underpin and support employee morale, motivation and ultimately organisational performance. This chapter, therefore, argues that the manager–employee relationship has a major impact on the performance and behaviour of the workforce. It highlights the importance of managers to the development of a constructive and positive employment relationship. At the same time, however, it questions why so many organisations fail to provide adequate training, development or support to their managers in order to develop and nurture this vitally important relationship (Renwick 2003).

Research has demonstrated that one of the main reasons that people leave their employing organisations is because the relationship between their managers and themselves has broken down. In fact, Potter-Efron (2003) suggests that in general employees don't leave organisations, they leave line managers. This is a matter for concern as there is a growing body of evidence which suggests that there is a positive correlation between high employee turnover and organisational performance and employee motivation (Allen 2008). Therefore, the ability to engage, motivate and retain talented employees is an important part of a contemporary manager's role. The present chapter encourages students to explore the important role that managers play by effectively developing their interpersonal skills and their ability to constructively negotiate a positive employment relationship.

The development of the skills and capabilities to successfully manage the employment relationship within contemporary organisations, however, does not take place in a vacuum; certain aspects of organisational behaviour as well as interpersonal dynamics need to be considered. For example, there is

…and the role of power, authority and politics within organisations. Managers must …uses within organisations as well as the impact they can have on the employment …e ability to negotiate and manage interpersonal relationships, therefore, becomes an …set to any modern-day manager.

LEARNING OUTCOMES

By the end of this chapter, provided you engage with the activities, you should be able to:

- understand the role and use of power and authority within an organisation
- appreciate the role and importance of organisational politics in securing human resource management objectives
- identify effective approaches to conflict resolution
- understand the skills necessary to manage workplace bullying
- apply and use negotiation skills effectively
- understand the role and importance of consultation.

9.1 INTRODUCTION

Organisations are made up of a diverse range of individuals whose central employment purpose is to help the company achieve its business strategies while earning a living for themselves. These employees are all individuals who have been moulded by their education, personal life and working experiences (see also Chapter 5). They all require individual motivational stimulation, performance management and understanding in order to work effectively and meet organisational targets.

It is therefore the responsibility of the manager to ensure that these objectives are achieved through, for example, the encouragement and reinforcement of acceptable behaviours, knowledge and understanding of each employee and the positive use of power and authority. This chapter focuses on the role and management of power, authority and organisational politics together with the skills and competencies required to negotiate with employees and effectively manage a variety of interpersonal working relationships in order to ensure that organisational performance is improved. The discussion provided here informs other chapters in this book, most notably Chapters 8, 11 and 12.

9.2 POWER AND AUTHORITY

Power and authority emerge in an organisation at the time it introduces any formal hierarchy, that is, the introduction of an organisational structure, policies and procedures which attempt to control the behaviour of employees and promote organisational performance. Power and authority are therefore seen to enable managers to ensure that their subordinates behave effectively and in accordance with the strategic plans of the organisation (Clegg et al 2008). As will be apparent in the following paragraph, power and authority are important features within an organisation and require serious consideration by contemporary managers.

According to Schieman and Reid (2008), power within organisations is related to the ways in which certain individuals possess and control organisational resources and employees. Many theorists have explored various aspects of organisational power and its impact on employees and workplace relationships, for example trust (Kramer 1999), anger (Sloan 2004), workplace violence (Folger and Baron 1996), absenteeism (Geurts et al 1999), workplace commitment (Blader and Tyler 2003), and morale and productivity (Weakliem and Frenkel 2006).

Authority is a concept most inextricably linked with power (Salamon 1998, p69) and often linked to a formal position in the organisation. Fayol (1956, p21), for instance, states that 'authority is the right to give orders and the power to exact obedience'. Hence, authority has been legitimised by the organisation and is given to a manager as part of their position as a manager. Its relationship with power is often conceptualised thus: authority can only be achieved through the use of power and that positive power cannot be exercised without authority. Therefore, the main reason that power and authority are used within organisations is to make sure that all employees abide by the rules and regulations that have been put in place to ensure the smooth running of the business and a positive employment relationship. Early theorists in the study of power and authority, French and Raven (1959), identified five power sources within organisations.

Table 9.1 Sources of power (1)

Type of power	Source of power
Legitimate	The leadership and the management receive the authority to use power within the employment relationship from their position within the hierarchy. This allows them to gain obedience and conformity from the workforce.
Reward	This source is gained as the employees see that the manager has the power to reward their behaviour within the workplace and will thus conform in order to benefit from the compensation.
Expert	Expert power is founded on the perceived ability of the manager's expert knowledge and skill in a given area.
Referent	This source of power is founded on the personal attributes of the individual manager in the sense that they generate respect among their workers and employees are able to identify with their goals.
Coercive	Coercive power is based on the fear that the manager can inflict punishment on those workers who do not conform to the wishes of the manager.

Source: adapted from French and Raven 1959

Benfari, Wilkinson and Orth (1986) add three more.

Table 9.2 Sources of power (2)

Type of power	Source of power
Information	The ability of a manager or a leader to exert influence based on the beliefs of followers that the manager/leader has access to information that is not public knowledge.
Affiliation	The ability of a manager or a leader to exert influence based on the beliefs of followers that the leader has a close association with other powerful figures on whose authority they are able to act.

Type of power	Source of power
Group	The ability of a leader to exert influence based on the beliefs of followers that the leader has collective support from a team or group.

Source: Benfari et al 1986, reproduced with permission

Whatever the power base, it is important that employees accept a manager's 'right to manage' to ensure the effective performance of the organisation without the need to use coercion or disciplinary measures, which could lead to demotivation or even deviant employee behaviour, such as workplace bullying. Harbison and Myers (1959, p19) highlight that managers can be viewed as ineffective unless they are able to exert power and authority. As such it is important for modern managers to develop the skills necessary to effectively obtain and use both power and authority within the workplace to ensure that (1) they can support and develop employees in carrying out the roles that have been assigned to them, and (2) they have the necessary characteristics, skills and behaviours to perform effectively. It is also vitally important that managers ensure that employees have the opportunities to develop professionally and progress their career. The management of a positive employment relationship will result in an improvement of organisational performance.

Kotter (1977, p125) suggests that power and authority have become much more complex as organisations have developed and that, as such, it has become more difficult for managers to achieve their aims and objectives through a total reliance on formal power and authority. He adds that there has been a shift in the traditional use of power and authority within contemporary organisations and that managers now increasingly need to use power and authority to 'influence' and 'encourage' conducive employee behaviour.

Hence, modern managers must have the skills to influence, negotiate and persuade employees rather than using power and authority as a means to 'command and control' the employment relationship. Kotter (1977, p126) concludes that many managers 'perform significantly below their potential because they do not understand the dynamics of power and because they have not nurtured and developed the instincts needed to effectively acquire and use power' in the modern workplace. Consequently, contemporary managers need to realise that characteristics and expectations of employees have changed (George 2011). For example, it has been suggested that younger individuals such as those belonging to Generation Y do not respond positively to more traditional command and control behaviours.

Therefore, perhaps there is a need for modern managers to look at the changing role and use of power and authority in the workplace. George (2011) concludes that managers need to change their approach to the use of power and authority. Specifically, they need to consider how these aspects can be transformed to support an approach to management which emphasises that 'over the long term, organisations filled with empowered employees who collaborate to serve customers will consistently outperform hierarchical organisations', that is, organisations that rely heavily on traditional command and control behaviours based solely on power and authority (George 2011).

As indicated above, power and authority continue to play an important part in modern organisations, and this is partly due to their impact on the allocation of resources as 'represented in salaries, in promoting opportunities and in control of tasks, people, information and new areas of business' (Pettigrew 2002, p45). While power is linked to political processes in organisations, it can be used in a positive way to improve the employment relationship as well as improving organisational performance (Pfeffer 1992). Therefore, in order to be an effective manager, Farnham (2011) highlights that it is necessary to know how to manage and use power positively. Pfeffer (1992) suggests seven ways in which managers can utilise power effectively within organisations:

1   **Goals:** Identify your goals. What is it you are attempting to achieve?

2   **Individuals:** Identify which individuals are important and influential in helping you to achieve your goals.

3   **Opinions:** What are their opinions likely to be? How will they feel about what you are attempting to do?

4   **Power bases of others:** What are the power bases of others and which of them is more influential in the decision?

5   **Personal power base:** What is your personal power base and how much influence do you have? What bases of influence can you develop in order to obtain more control over the situation?

6   **Strategies and tactics:** Which strategies and tactics for exercising power are likely to be the most effective as well as the most appropriate considering the situation?

7   **Action:** Based on the above considerations, which action is the most appropriate in achieving the goals?

It is at this point that politics can become an aspect of organisational behaviour and it is where managers need to become aware of its existence. Organisations are fundamentally political entities in which individuals, teams, groups and managers engage in 'political game-playing' in which various stakeholders compete to gain access to increased resources or more power and authority (Mintzberg 1985). Politics, then, has a negative impact on the manager–employee relationship (Pfeffer 1992) as it results in political behaviour which is divisive and conflictive and frequently sets individuals and groups up against formal authority and accepted organisational ideology, causing instability and conflict. Hence, politics is a form of power which is illegitimate as it is not 'formally authorised, widely accepted or officially certified' (Mintzberg 1985, p134).

Ferris et al (2005, p127), however, reject this negative view of politics and suggest that organisational politics, if managed effectively, has the 'ability to effectively understand others at work, and to share such knowledge to influence others to act in ways that enhance one's personal and/or organisational objectives'. Seen in the second way, politics can be used by managers to help develop important interpersonal relationships and build a strong and empowered workforce which is founded on a positive employment relationship.

ACTIVITY 9.1

Reflection on political behaviour

Consider the political behaviour that exists in organisations.

- Have you encountered any kind of political activity within an organisation that you are familiar with?
- Describe what happened and explain why you regard the situation as politically charged.

- In what ways did such behaviour impact on the employment relationship?
- Do you think the situation was successfully managed? If not, why not? Explain your answer.

Political behaviour often emerges when other forms of influence are absent or weak. However, it can also be caused by other forms of influence, for example when a particular department (which has been created through formal authority) promotes group processes that benefit their insular interests at the expense of the needs of the whole organisation. Mintzberg (1985, p134) identified 13 political games which he argues are played to 'resist authority per se, counter such resistance, build a power base, defeat a rival or change the organisation'. For example, he highlights the game of 'insurgency' in which the central stakeholders (usually unskilled blue-collar workers) come together to form small groups. They tend to reject authority and question its legitimacy in 'controlling their working environment'. Their behaviour towards managers is generally antagonistic. This then results in a poor employment relationship which is difficult to manage. Another political game which Mintzberg (1985, pp135–6) identifies is around the allocation of budgets. The main stakeholders are the various line managers who vie for resources in order to build their power base. Their behaviour does not, however, tend to be hostile and usually co-exists with authority.

ACTIVITY 9.2

The role of power

Reflecting on the first part of this chapter, consider the role that power plays in our personal as well as professional lives. Think about people that you regard as being powerful; they can be political or social leaders, business people or just leaders you are familiar with in society. Answer the following questions.

1   What is it about them that makes them powerful?

2   How do they demonstrate their power?

3   What is it about their use of power that makes you notice them?

4   Do they have a formalised position of power?

In small groups:

● Reflect on your list and try to identify any commonalities between the individuals you have chosen.

● Do you think that it is possible to learn and develop these traits?

● If so, how could this be achieved?

Now that you have practised identifying power in others, let us consider its practical aspects through a further activity.

ACTIVITY 9.3

Role-play

Divide into groups of approximately five and allocate team members to take on the following roles:

● Peter Frost, Managing Director
● Anne Hayward, Financial Director
● Tom Scott, Human Resource Manager
● Observer 1
● Observer 2

Study the brief below and prepare for the part that you will adopt in this role-play (approximately 10 minutes).

The company is a large advertising organisation which has been struggling to perform in the present economic climate. The human resource management department have undertaken a large study to investigate the causes of the decline in organisational performance. They have come to a number of conclusions and have made the following recommendations:

- There is a shortage of staff who have the appropriate knowledge, skills and ability to maintain the levels of performance required in this very competitive climate. It is therefore recommended that the organisation invests in a programme of training and development which will enhance the knowledge, skills and capabilities of the workforce.
- The policy of no recruitment, which has been in force in response to the global economic climate, has resulted in a general shortage of workers. This has also led to demotivation of current staff and a general low level of morale throughout the organisation. It is therefore recommended that the organisation begins a programme of recruitment and selection of talented workers who could contribute to the performance of the organisation. It is also recommended that the company invests in team-building activities which would help re-energise the workforce and ultimately improve performance.

Clearly these recommendations have cost implications for the organisation.

Anne Hayward, the financial director, is concerned that the company is still not performing as well as it should and that profits are still below those in 2007. Anne is worried that any expenditure should have quantifiable results and thus requires evidence that any investment will result in increased profits. Anne has a lot of influence at board level and needs to be persuaded of the benefits of any investment.

Peter Frost, the managing director, is generally receptive to suggestions about how to improve the performance of the organisation; however, he is also aware that he is accountable to the shareholders.

In response to the findings Tom Scott has requested a meeting with Peter Frost and Anne Hayward to discuss the situation and to propose that the company invests in the recommendations to improve organisational performance.

Each character should consider the issues involved in the case and think about how they are going to negotiate a successful outcome. The observers should take notes and be prepared to feed these back at the end of the role-play.

The role-play should last approximately 20–30 minutes.

Once you have concluded the role-play, you should consider the following points:

1   What power was/could have been exerted during this role-play and by whom?

2   Was there an opportunity for any political activity to have taken place during this negotiation process?

3   What was the outcome?

4   Could it have been handled in any other way?

9.3 NEGOTIATION

Human beings learn to negotiate from an early age. Every time we want or need something, we negotiate; we put forward our case and the other party outlines theirs. We debate, argue and make concessions until, hopefully, we reach an agreement (and get what we want). It is, therefore, not just a skill which is used in an organisation but also in our social lives – for example, pay rise negotiation, budget allocation, deciding what time to meet up with friends, what food to eat or even where to go on a rainy day. Negotiation is generally thought to be a compromise which is aimed at benefiting our interests as much as possible. It therefore is often associated with conflict resolution within organisations and occurs 'when people with differing needs or goals are prevented – or perceived that they are being prevented – by others in achieving these needs or goals' (Browaeys and Price 2008, p301). More simply argued, it is the 'process of resolving conflict through compromise'.

Kellogg et al (2006) have suggested that new forms of organisation are emerging with flatter, more informal structures, networked and more flexible forms. Such new organisational forms require the use of a different approach to the use of power and authority and thus management behaviour, interpersonal and negotiation skills. As a result it is likely that conflict within organisations will become more frequent in the future since such organisational structures redistribute power to different levels and roles throughout the organisation. As such, the ability to negotiate and the interpersonal skills needed to manage negotiation are becoming one of the most important elements for contemporary managers to master (Volkema et al 2013). Understanding the numerous approaches to negotiation and conflict resolution is therefore vital to a successful manager.

From the above, it is clear that the ability to effectively communicate and engage in a range of interpersonal skills is becoming essential for managers to negotiate, resolve conflict and maintain a good employment relationship. Managers must be able to present structured arguments in many different ways, for example in a face-to-face environment, through the telephone, email or even in a formal letter. They must be emotionally intelligent (Goleman 2005) in the sense that they are able to recognise, understand and manage their own emotions as well as those who are in an opposing position. Goleman (1998, 2005) highlights that individuals have a number of competency domains that assist them when they engage in the process of negotiation, for example, self-awareness, self-management, social awareness and relationship management.

It is important to remember that negotiation is not always between a manager and an employee or even between two individuals. It can include a number of individuals or groups within an organisation, for example a trade union negotiating with senior managers for an increase in the wages of its membership or employees, negotiating for a much-needed training and development programme, and so on. There are clearly many reasons why people may wish to negotiate, and it is important to appreciate that there are a number of ways in which negotiation can be approached (see Figure 9.1). For example, there could be competition over scarce organisational resources, disagreement over responsibility, power and authority, allocation of rewards, equality or even just individual differences. Many authors have, therefore, argued that negotiation is a difficult skill to learn due to the amount of power and politics that operate within many modern organisations (Luthans 2005).

The process of negotiation is generally broken down into two very different approaches (Walton and McKersie 1965, Dibben et al 2011):

1   **Distributive negotiation**, which is generally an adversarial approach that aims at winning the process at the expense of the opposition – a win–lose scenario.

2   **Integrative negotiation**, which generally focuses on a problem-solving approach and generally aims at achieving a win–win scenario.

An example of *distributive negotiation* would be that of buying a car. The seller will ask for a specific price, for example £2,500, and the buyer will generally offer a lower price, say £1,500. The buyer and seller will then engage in a period of negotiation which will (hopefully) conclude with the buyer purchasing the car at an agreed sum, say for example £2,200. In this example the seller has lost £300 in the process of negotiation and the buyer has gained £300 on the original purchase price. It is, therefore, a win–lose scenario.

The second approach, that of *integrative negotiation*, could be that of a negotiation between a trade union and an employer. The trade union wants the employer to increase the wages of the workforce and the employer does not want to increase wages; however, they do want to increase productivity. The trade union and the employer will engage in a process of negotiation and an agreement is made in which the employees gain a pay rise (win for the trade union) and in which the employers also gain because the pay rise is linked to increased productivity (so they also win).

Figure 9.1 Process of negotiation

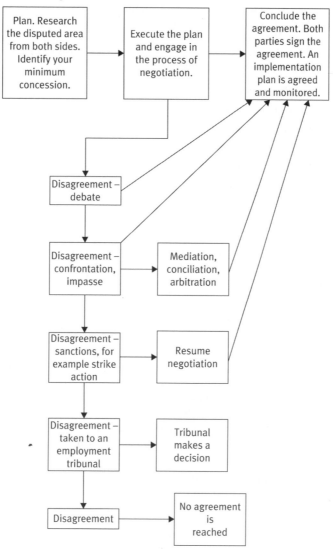

In many situations within the workplace there is evidence that both approaches have been used in order to solve the conflict. Dibben et al (2011) add a third approach, which is very negative and on the whole is destructive for both the individual employee and the organisation:

3   **Destructive negotiation**, which happens when neither party are prepared to compromise and they would rather lose their employment and/or business than reach agreement. This rarely happens and results in a lose–lose situation.

An example of destructive negotiation can occur when the workforce is seeking a pay rise and the organisation is unprepared to award this. If neither side is prepared to compromise, industrial action could take place. A good example is the 1984 miners' strike in the UK, when neither the miners' union nor the Government at the time were prepared to compromise. This resulted in the closure of many mines and severe hardship on the mining community (a lose situation). The UK Government lost a thriving mining industry, which had a negative impact on the economy of the UK (again a lose situation).

Whichever approach is adopted, Dibben et al (2011) have argued that negotiation goes through three distinct phases, which must be effectively managed to ensure that an appropriate outcome is reached. They add that each stage is very different and creates unique challenges that require certain specific skills (Nel et al 2005).

1   preparation for the negotiation

2   conducting the negotiation

3   concluding the negotiation.

A fourth stage could also be added here in which the manager reflects on the experience and considers whether or not the objectives have been achieved and if not, why not?

9.3.1 PREPARATION FOR THE NEGOTIATION

Consider the following points:

- **Integrative vs. distributive vs. destructive:** It is very important to spend time considering your position before engaging in any form of negotiation. It would be wise to know whether you intend to seek an integrative, distributive or destructive solution as this will have an impact on what skills you use and could frame the manner in which you approach the task.
- **Aims, objectives and interests:** Consider what you want to achieve through the process of negotiation. What is the best outcome? What is the minimal deal that you will accept? What is the minimum you think that the other party(ies) will settle for?
- **Information:** What information do you have that could strengthen your position during the negotiation process? What information would it be useful to obtain? This should include information about the demands/needs of the other party(ies).
- **Advantages and disadvantages:** What are your strengths and weaknesses? What are the strengths and weaknesses of the other party(ies)?
- **Strategy:** Consider what strategy you are going to use during the process of negotiation. Consider what strategy(ies) the other party(ies) may utilise in the process in order to be prepared for any eventuality.

As indicated above it is essential to ensure that negotiators know what areas are important to them. They should be able to identify where they are willing to make concessions and where they are not. Contemporary managers must be very clear about their aims and objectives and try to understand the aims and objectives of the other party(ies). Many negotiations fail because those involved with them do not come fully prepared and are not ready to attempt to reach an agreement. It is a good managerial strategy to be able to identify the minimum point to which you will agree.

Wertheim (2007) has outlined a number of points that should be considered before the onset of the negotiation process:

1   What is the minimum that can be accepted in order to resolve the conflict?

2   What is the maximum that can be requested without becoming too unreasonable?

3   What, realistically, is the maximum that can be given away without causing too much hardship?

4   What is the minimum which can be offered without appearing unreasonable?

Consider and attempt to predict the answers that the other party may have to the above questions.

Fisher and Ury (2011) acknowledge that the negotiation process should be planned and prepared for but that sometimes the other party refuses to negotiate or agree. They therefore proposed the concept of best alternative to a negotiated agreement (BATNA). It has been suggested that BATNAs are critical to negotiation because it is not possible to make an informed decision without knowing what the alternatives are. For example, if you were offered a used car for £5,000 but there is an even better one at another dealership for £3,500, the £3,500 car is your best alternative to a negotiated agreement (BATNA). In other words, if the seller of the first car does not drop the price, you will walk away and buy the alternative. Hence, if the suggested agreement is better than your BATNA, you should accept it. If the deal is not an improvement on your BATNA, perhaps it is time to reopen negotiations or, alternatively, 'walk away'. Having a BATNA or 'fall-back plan' improves an individual's negotiating power in the sense that if it has been possible to identify a good alternative, concessions can be kept to a minimum.

ACTIVITY 9.4

Best alternative to a negotiated agreement

Consider what you would do if you did not receive an attractive job offer from a company you had applied for a job with. Their offer did not meet your expectations. What will you do and why? Will you take another job? Will you widen your search for alternative employment? Will you seek to improve your educational qualifications? Which option is the most realistic?

It is important to remember, however, that negotiation within organisations generally involves people or groups with whom you will have to work on a continuing basis and, therefore, it is important that a working relationship is maintained on conclusion of the negotiation process. Dibben et al (2011) highlight that when engaging in negotiation, it is important to restrict the number of people on each side who become involved. This will limit the number of opinions being debated at the same time, thereby reducing the possibility of misunderstandings as well as reducing the amount of time the process is likely to take. It could also be advisable to limit the number of issues which will be included in the negotiation process. Too many debatable areas could prevent the possibility of reaching an agreement in a reasonable timeframe. Dibben et al (2011, p173) add that the chances of reaching an agreement are improved when the areas open for negotiation are 'concrete and quantifiable rather than abstract and intangible'.

9.3.2 CONDUCTING THE NEGOTIATION

It is usually good practice to appoint a chairperson, if possible from an independent department or even an external individual, to oversee the process and to ensure that the negotiations stay focused on relevant issues. It may also be advisable to consider the structure of the meeting and the possible timeframes to be observed by both parties. Once the practicalities of the process have been established, it is time to begin the negotiation. Each side of the argument needs to be given the opportunity to present its ideas and proposals. Each side should listen carefully to the other and request further information if required. The debate should then focus on obtaining as much information as possible, clarifying areas of uncertainty and investigating areas of concern. The discussion will probably include proposals and counter proposals, concessions, rejections, demands, impasses, threats and final offers. It could lead to stronger action such as the imposition of sanctions or strike action taking place. Eventually, in theory, agreement is achieved and the organisation continues to perform.

However, in practice a number of unforeseen problems are likely to be encountered. Many of these are the result of poor managerial negotiation and interpersonal skills. For example, in some negotiation processes individuals can personalise the arguments and 'attack' the individual making the point. It is therefore vital, although at times incredibly difficult, to ensure that individual personalities and emotions are separated from the issues which are being discussed to prevent emotional and personal reactions. If personal issues are allowed to penetrate the negotiation, it could damage the process, create problems within the employment relationship and cause problems in coming to any satisfactory negotiated agreement. Any such issues may jeopardise a manager's ability to manage. The negotiation process is therefore often emotionally charged and requires a great deal of interpersonal and negotiation skills as well as professionalism in the sense that those engaged in the negotiation must understand and be able to maintain a respectful and courteous manner. Aggression and hostility generally do not facilitate or support a positive employment relationship.

Although it is natural that as negotiators we focus on our own interests, a valuable skill for a negotiator is the ability to understand the opposing party's point of view as well as the underlying reasons for the conflict of opinions. A skilled negotiator will attempt to identify commonalities' between the opposing viewpoints and attempt to minimise the differences which exist. Wertheim (2007) suggests that the main reason why negotiation tends to fail is that the parties involved focus too much on the distributive approach and seek a win–lose situation rather than looking for a compromise and a solution which would please both parties. Therefore, it is important that a good manager spends time reflecting on trying to appreciate the position of the other party and to seek, where possible, an agreement which could be used to transform the distributive discussion into the integrative win–win approach. If the negotiator can integrate the objectives and requirements of both parties, both sides are much more likely to agree while at the same time maintain a good working relationship.

 ACTIVITY 9.5

Negotiating a better mark

Consider a situation in which you have been given a low mark at college which you do not believe was appropriate. How would you handle the situation?

- Would you go to your tutor and state that the reason for the bad mark was poor and ineffective teaching?

What sort of reaction do you think that you would get from this confrontation? How helpful do you think the tutor would be in advising you how to gain an improved mark as a consequence of your reaction?

- Would you go to the tutor and ask for an explanation for the poor mark and advice on how you could improve the grade?

Do you think the reaction would be different from the one above? Explain your reasons for this.

9.3.3 SUCCESSFUL CONCLUSION OF NEGOTIATION PROCESS

Assuming that the opposing parties are able to come to an agreement, it is necessary to set out clearly what they have agreed to. It is good practice for this to be put in writing and signed by both parties in order to bring closure to the debate as well as avoiding disputes emerging in the future. A signature from the parties concerned demonstrates a commitment to the solution which has been agreed. It is also useful that consideration is given to how the agreement will be implemented and monitored.

ACTIVITY 9.6

Negotiation in a recruitment scenario

As head of the human resource management department you have interviewed a number of potential candidates for a position as senior quantity surveyor. You and the interviewing panel have identified someone who would fit well into the engineering department. He demonstrated his technical capabilities at the interview and you felt that he could become a key member of the engineering team. However, the potential employee requested a salary that would, in your opinion, compromise the integrity of the pay structure within the organisation as it was 25 per cent higher than other senior employees. The economic situation of the organisation is difficult at the moment; however, you believe that this individual could make a positive contribution to organisational performance and therefore profitability. If you agreed to pay the required salary, it would have a negative impact on the bonuses of the existing staff, which you believe they deserve this year. However, you have been looking for an individual with the skills, competencies and experience that this individual has for over three months.

Task:

1 Analyse the power sources at play within this situation.

2 Think about your negotiation strategy.

3 Identify the key elements of the negotiation process.

Not all negotiations reach a successful conclusion that is acceptable to all parties. In this case alternative dispute resolution (ADR) methods may be adopted (Podro and Suff 2005). ADR methods have become more common as a result of pressure from both policy-makers and practitioners in relation to increasing costs (Podro and Suff 2005). ACAS (Podro and Suff 2005) has described ADR as a number of processes which engage the services of a third party who is responsible for bringing together the two disputing parties in order to resolve their differences without having to resort to legal action.

Perhaps the most common ADR is **mediation**. This is a confidential service which acts as a third party within the negotiation process. It is generally brought in when the negotiation process has broken down and an impasse has been reached. The role of the mediator is to look at the whole negotiation process, examining the issues and the areas of debate. The mediator will attempt to resolve arguments and disagreements which may have occurred between the negotiating parties. The mediator is generally a professional who is trained in the area of problem-solving and effective communication techniques. Mediators are able to offer advice and make suggestions; however, the role of the mediator is to facilitate an agreement between the two opposing parties, not to conclude an agreement for them (Gospel and Palmer 1993). Although meditation involves an agreed settlement, the final decision remains in the hands of the parties to the negotiation and not the mediator.

There are a number of occasions when it may be necessary for management to bring in the services of a trained, professional mediator:

- when the area of negotiation is based on two opposing and conflicting views
- when there has been conflict between the parties in the past and the possibility that some issues may have been left unresolved

- when the opposing parties do not trust each other, which gives rise to adversarial and hostile emotions
- when there is a significant requirement that positive working relationships are maintained for future business performance
- when the areas in dispute are of a sensitive, emotional, hostile or political nature.

If the dispute or negotiation is restricted to an individual employee and their employing organisation, occasionally another form of ADR is used – **arbitration**. Arbitration is a technique which is used to resolve issues outside the legal system; however, it is binding on both conflicting parties and constitutes a legally binding contract. In the UK arbitration is usually undertaken by ACAS, which is charged with preventing and resolving issues related to the employment contract. It aims to decide cases more quickly than if they were to go through a formal legal process; however, they do attempt to ensure that their conclusions are consistent with those of an employment tribunal. Both sides of the dispute are required to agree to take the case to arbitration and, once this agreement has been signed by both parties, an employment tribunal is no longer able to hear the case. Once a decision has been made, there are only a limited number of grounds for challenging their decisions and appeals are restricted.

A third source of intervention in the negotiation process is that of **conciliation**. This generally occurs when the organisation and another party within the organisation are in dispute. It is a voluntary process which seeks to reach agreement from both parties without reference to an employment tribunal; however, it is necessary that both sides agree to participate. Conciliation is similar to mediation in the sense that it could be used when an employee wishes to complain about specific actions of their employing organisation which could be referred to an employment tribunal. It is very different from arbitration as it lacks authority to request any evidence or interview any witnesses. Further, it cannot make decisions or any awards for compensation. Therefore, it is generally only used in minor cases where perhaps channels of communication have broken down.

CASE STUDY 9.1

COLLECTIVE BARGAINING ROLE-PLAY – CAPITAL STEEL NORTH-EAST

Divide into two groups. One group will take on the role of the management in the negotiating process and one group will represent the trade union position. Read the relevant brief. Prepare for the negotiation process. Engage in the negotiation process.

Management brief

Every year between September and November, the trade unions (Community and Unite) put together and submit a joint annual pay claim. This document serves as a focus for negotiations over the general terms and conditions of the employees within the company. It is also viewed by management as an opportunity to

negotiate any changes that they see as necessary. Management is represented by the organisation's Human Resource Management Department, while the employees are represented by both of the trade unions.

This year, due to the economic climate, the pay negotiations are taking place in an unstable environment, which has been made worse by increased competition and by the fact that the organisation is threatened by a growing number of takeovers amongst steel manufacturing companies. As a result the organisation's shareholders as well as the board of directors are keen to be viewed as having tight control over unnecessary expenditure, and pressure is being placed on the Human Resource Management negotiators to make efficiency savings. They have been told specifically that the board of directors will not sanction an increase in pay that adds any more than the average UK wage increase of 3.5 per cent to the wages bill. However, 2.6 per cent is the maximum figure and should not be the starting point for any negotiations with the trade unions. In reality, the Human Resource Management Department will be judged by senior management on their ability to minimise the cost of this year's annual pay agreement while, at the same time, maintaining a good employment relationship. It has been suggested that the Human Resource Management Department also seeks ways in which savings can be made, particularly in relation to areas such as overtime costs.

Relations with the trade unions to date have on the whole been fairly good. Over the last 15 years, as a result of changes to employment legislation, management have been able to dominate the negotiation process and have forced through many changes. Unfortunately, this has had an increasingly negative impact on employee morale. Absence rates have increased alongside working hours and the intensification of the work itself. The last couple of years have seen an increase in industrial action, which would have been unthinkable four years ago. Industrial action would be costly for the organisation and disastrous for public relations so should be avoided at all costs.

The Human Resource Management negotiators are therefore facing a difficult task of limiting pay increases, increasing efficiency, while at the same time maintaining the morale of the staff and the employment relationship. They need to remember that any deal agreed with the unions must be one that will be acceptable to the board of directors as well as the shareholders.

Trade union brief

Every year between September and November, the trade unions (Community and Unite) put together and submit a joint annual pay claim. This document serves as a focus for negotiations over the general terms and conditions of the employees within the company. It is also viewed by management as an opportunity to negotiate any changes that they see as necessary. Management is represented by the organisation's Human Resource Management Department, while the employees are represented by both of the trade unions.

Relations with management have on the whole been fairly good. Although over the last 15 years, as a result of changes to employment legislation, management have been able to dominate the negotiation process and have forced through many changes. Unfortunately, this has had an increasingly negative impact on your membership and employee morale has in general decreased. Absence rates have increased alongside working hours and the intensification of the work itself. Over the last five years employees have seen a reduction in their pay in real terms and are keen to see an increase which is well above the inflation rate of 2.6 per cent as well as gaining more job security.

The trade union members would like their negotiators to ensure that work schedules are adjusted in such a way that improvements are made to improve their work–life balance so they can enjoy a more 'normal' home and working life. The employees are dissatisfied and feel in a stronger position than they have been for a number of years due to the shortage of skilled workers in the industry. The trade union negotiators also feel more confident given that trade union membership is increasing and that the industry has seen evidence that trade union members have been prepared to engage in industrial action recently.

Despite these positive signs, the trade unions are aware that their members are concerned about job insecurity, especially as the organisation is located in an area of high unemployment. Therefore, the negotiators should be aware that while employees may support some resistance, prolonged industrial action is probably an unreasonable expectation.

The trade union negotiators need to remember that any agreement arrived at with management must be one that will be supported by the majority of trade union members at Capital Steel North-East.

Reflection on learning

1   Did the agreement that you reached meet the minimum requirements of the group you were representing? If not, why not?

2   Consider the skills that were needed to reach the agreement.

3   Do you think that the process could have been organised more effectively?

9.4 BULLYING AND HARASSMENT IN THE WORKPLACE

As highlighted above the process of negotiation does not always work and can lead to conflict. If conflict is not dealt with quickly and effectively, it can quickly become personalised and could move into harassment and bullying. Harassment and bullying have a very negative impact on the employment relationship as well as on organisational performance, and more personally can cause problems for the mental and physical health of the employees concerned.

The CIPD (2011) has stated that conflict in the workplace is now a major concern for many organisations and therefore managers as the organisation's representatives. Conflict has existed in the workplace for generations; however, it has become more prominent due to the changing approaches to how we believe that people should be managed. This is well reflected in the example of the contemporary HR philosophy that people are an organisation's most valuable asset. The increasing belief that organisations should look at the needs of employees in relation to areas such as health and well-being, work–life balance, engagement and empowerment have all helped push the issue of conflict management, bullying and harassment up the managerial agenda.

Although often used interchangeably, bullying and harassment are distinct terms. For example, bullying is defined by Gennard and Judge (2010, p485) as 'offensive, intimidating, malicious or insulting behaviour, an abuse of power through means intended to humiliate, denigrate or injure the recipient'. Whereas the CIPD (2010) has suggested that harassment is unwanted behaviour which is brought about by a particular individual characteristic which results in the violation of an individual's dignity or creates an intimidating, hostile, degrading, humiliating or offensive environment for an individual.

Although generally speaking many people assume that negotiation and conflict within organisations tends to be restricted to groups of employees, managers or collective groups such as trade unions, this is not always the case. Individual managers and colleagues negotiate on a daily basis in relation to their roles, training and development, work–life balance, and so on, and sometimes these negotiations break down and conflict occurs, which can easily lead to bullying and harassment. If this conflict results in the development of negative behaviour, it is important that it is dealt with immediately and effectively in order to ensure the health, well-being and productivity of employees.

Conflict between individuals and groups should be managed constructively and consistently to gain and maintain employee commitment, loyalty and support for the development of organisational performance as well as to prevent bullying and harassment. Fox (1966, 1974) proposes three approaches that managers can use to define and understand conflict within the employment relationship. This, he argues, helps to explain how they approach conflict in the workplace and, to some extent, its management.

The first view, *unitarist*, states that conflict is dysfunctional and is a result of 'trouble-makers' such as trade union representatives or perhaps because of poor communication. Conflict, according to this approach, is therefore irrational and therefore 'bad' for organisational performance.

The second view, *pluralism*, recognises that conflict is an inevitable part of the employment relationship. This view is founded on the belief that employers and employees have different priorities. For example, employers seek to maximise employee output while minimising wages and employees want to maximise wages while controlling work input. In this approach, managers need to seek a balance between the two opposing positions. Sometimes it may require the involvement of a third party, for example a trade union. However, from this perspective trade unions are not seen as a negative part of the employment relationship; in fact, they are viewed as having a legitimate role in representing the interests of their membership. The manager's role in this approach is to develop a working relationship with the trade union representatives in order to enable them to negotiate within the employment relationship and to minimise negative conflict.

The final view adopts a *Marxist* perspective, which argues that conflict is inevitable as it is the result of employees' exploitation by the owners of capital. This perspective, however, rejects trade unions and their role in the employment relationship as they are viewed as being an instrument used by managers to control the workplace. Conflict will only be resolved when capitalism is overthrown and organisations are controlled by the proletariat. This is not a view that is commonly held by managers.

Rees and French (2011) add another approach and argue that conflict is mainly preventable and that co-operation between employers and employees is in fact normal as they work together to meet organisational performance targets. However, in this approach managers act proactively and design and enforce policies and practices which ensure employee performance while taking account of the employer's expectations. This approach necessitates managers, ensuring that they work *with* employees through mechanisms such as involvement and participation schemes in order to gain and maintain commitment and loyalty.

The CIPD reinforces the belief that managers and leaders need to develop effective ways of managing employees to ensure that both collective and individual conflict is positively controlled. This implies that managers should be prepared to intervene at the first opportunity when they realise that there is a risk of bullying and harassment. The CIPD reiterates that although lively interaction should be promoted, as it is key to innovation and creativity, it is essential that mutual respect is reinforced and that certain standards of behaviour should be maintained by all employees within the workplace (CIPD 2008, p4). It is difficult to gain respect from the workforce if managers have (or appear to have) condoned negative patterns of behaviour over a period of weeks, months or even years.

Therefore, the CIPD suggests that although intervention in conflict can be daunting for some individual managers, it is one of their central roles, both in relation to organisational performance as well as in maintaining the health and well-being of their staff. If managers ignore conflict in whatever form or any other unacceptable behaviour within the workplace, such as bullying and harassment, the problems will escalate to disciplinary or grievance action. To prevent this from occurring, it is suggested that this requires good communication, interpersonal and managerial skills, which have been highlighted throughout the chapter.

On occasions, managers are not in a position to deal with conflict, bullying and harassment and may wish to seek the involvement and advice of the human resource management department and/or trade union representatives. It has been suggested that there is a very fine line between managerial control and actual bullying, which is why without the development of interpersonal skills and organisational support for those involved, accusations of bullying and harassment can increase and organisational performance become restricted (Zapf and Gross 2001).

Einarsen et al (2010) present a conceptual framework which highlights the main variables that should be considered by those responsible for preventing workplace conflict and in particular bullying and harassment. They argue that a distinction should be made between the nature of the causes of the bullying behaviour displayed by the bully and those of the 'victim'. The framework highlights the importance of considering the perceived behaviour of those who witness such behaviour as well as those who are actively involved. Einarsen et al also suggest that managers and leaders should consider a number of important areas when managing such a delicate issue, such as the impact on the organisation, the victim, the perpetrator, the witnesses and consequently the culture of the organisation as a whole.

As already stated, the best way to deal with issues of bullying, harassment and conflict at work is quickly and informally. This limits possible costs to the organisation and helps to reduce damage to working relationships which could occur if a more formal disciplinary/grievance route is followed. The UK Government, in an attempt to reduce harassment and bullying in the workplace, has introduced the Equality Act 2010 and the Employment Act 2002. Both pieces of legislation attempt to reduce conflict within the workplace by encouraging organisations and individual employees to resolve and manage conflict within the workplace rather than seeking the involvement of an employment tribunal.

The Health and Safety Executive has estimated that bullying and harassment in the workplace accounts for approximately 50 per cent of all stress-related workplace illness in the UK. This, they suggest, equates to about 80 million lost working days and about £2 billion per year. The CIPD (2005) has argued that organisations could also incur costs such as loss of time, increased staff turnover and absenteeism, low morale and employee commitment. They concluded that one of the main reasons why workplace stress and bullying has increased is ineffective managers, which they suggest is due to managers lacking the necessary confidence, interpersonal and professional skills required to recognise and deal with the problems as they emerge in the workplace (CIPD 2008, 2011).

However, as suggested earlier, the damage to organisations as a result of the failure to manage harassment and bullying in the workplace is not restricted to financial costs. Workplace conflict can have much wider implications, such as the human costs, low morale, motivation, employee health and well-being and, consequently, reduced performance and productivity, which could, if not addressed by managers, lead to legal action (CIPD 2008). There are many forms that bullying can take within the organisation; for example, intentionally copying emails that are important about someone to others who do not need to know; a manager treating one or more members of staff unfairly in relation to others; the misuse of managerial power or supervision; making threats or comments about another's job security without good reason.

Harassment is slightly different in that in some countries, such as the UK, there are specific categories of workers who have legal protection due to certain characteristics. These are age, disability, gender reassignment, race, religion or belief, sex and sexual orientation. As an example, harassment could be based on the fact that a manager failed to prevent the frequent teasing and humiliation of an employee because of their age, ethnic background, a disability or other features that make a workforce diverse (see also Chapter 1). Another example could be that the same manager, by failing to prevent the teasing and humiliation, allowed an offensive office environment to emerge in which people felt degraded.

The Employment Tribunal Service has claimed that they have experienced a 52 per cent increase in bullying and harassment cases over the last few years, and suggest that organisations need to ensure that they have clear and robust procedures and policies in place and that these must be followed effectively by managers throughout the process. If not, it is argued, organisations will find themselves ill-equipped to defend such claims. They conclude that these issues are too costly for organisations to just ignore. A survey carried out by the CIPD (2006) stated that 19 per cent of employees had experienced bullying and harassment in the workplace over a two-year period. Unison (2003) adds that 47 per cent of the workforce had witnessed bullying occurring.

Although it is generally agreed that most organisations today have introduced policies and procedures which address issues such as bullying and harassment at all levels within the organisation, it is clear that in many circumstances they are not working. This may be because organisations and their managers, who on the whole are not equipped with the relevant interpersonal skills or knowledge of appropriate policies, are not following the set procedures. This, together with the fact that they are generally failing to take action as soon as issues begin to emerge, has encouraged the development of conflict in many workplaces. For managers to become effective in reducing conflict, they need to learn how to address the complexities of interpersonal relationships and build confidence in their own abilities to manage. In part it has been suggested that they are failing to 'manage' employee expectations and the psychological aspects of bullying and harassment as well as its impact on all individuals involved – the victim, witnesses and the bully/harasser (Einarsen et al 2010).

If managers are not able or willing to intercede informally as the conflict emerges, there are two choices that can be made. Firstly, the managers may decide to take disciplinary action against a specific employee or group of employees. This usually occurs when there are issues surrounding competency and capability to undertake their specified job or if managers feel that there has been any inappropriate behaviour or infringements of the rules in relation to acceptable behaviour within the workplace. The ultimate stage of disciplinary action would be dismissal. However, misconduct, which is what this section of the chapter is focusing on, is generally dealt with through a process of disciplinary warnings. However, extreme cases such as gross misconduct, which could include behaviour such as theft, assault, and so on, could lead to immediate dismissal without a period of notice.

The second choice of action could be for an employee or group of employees to put in a formal grievance claim. The causes of the grievance sometimes only highlight the more visual aspects of the latent conflict which is occurring within the organisation. Dibben et al (2011) suggest that many grievance claims are founded on the failure of management to deal quickly with potential sources of conflict which then escalate and spread, becoming less easy to detect and therefore to manage.

As already stated, failing to address conflict that results in harassment and bullying at an early stage can result in individualised or collective action, which may be costly in legal and financial terms. Dibben et al (2011) have further highlighted that poorly managed conflict which has escalated to become a discipline and grievance issue can also have an impact on organisational performance and lead to:

- low morale, motivation and poor interpersonal relations
- a lack of co-operation and teamworking
- poor performance
- behavioural problems among the workforce

- high staff turnover
- increased absenteeism
- non- or low co-operation in relation to implementation of organisational change.

Many countries have developed frameworks and legislation in order to deal with conflict in the workplace. For example, Sweden introduced legislation on victimisation at work in 1993; Southern Australia approved anti-bullying legislation in August 2005. In 2004 the Canadian province of Quebec introduced workplace bullying legislation, and the province of Saskatchewan made workplace bullying illegal in 2007; the Republic of Ireland introduced the Safety, Health and Welfare Act in 2005 from which the Code of Practice to prevent bullying was developed. In the United States, although 35 per cent of employees have reported experiencing bullying at work, no anti-bullying legislation has yet been passed; however, at present, 16 states are considering it (Healthyworkplacebill.org 2013).

Bearing this in mind, managers should consider the organisation's location and ensure that it is meeting both its legal and moral obligations in order to ensure that employees remain happy, motivated and productive. In order to achieve this there is a need for managers to carry out a few basic tasks to manage conflict effectively and maintain a positive employment relationship:

- Identification at an early stage of any issues that could cause conflict within the workplace – any such issues should be managed as quickly as possible to try to minimise any potential conflict, for example chatting informally with the individuals concerned, communication and management of employee expectations on a regular basis.
- If it has not been possible to prevent the conflict occurring, it may be necessary to begin more formal procedures. All the facts should be investigated, including considering if there are any personal reasons which might have contributed to the 'problem'. Notes and evidence must be documented.
- Statements should be taken from those concerned, including any relevant witnesses. Always ensure that another senior member of staff is present, perhaps a member of the human resource management team.
- Some sort of formal hearing would need to be arranged in order to explore the issues and evidence. The employee should also be allowed to take a colleague or trade union representative with them to any formal meeting and should be allowed to talk to them and even address the meeting if necessary.
- Clarification is sought from those involved in the conflict that they fully understand what is happening and that they accept their role and responsibilities in relation to the claim of conflict. They should also be asked if they agree to the suggested action which is proposed to resolve the conflict and improve the situation.
- Management should then outline the conclusion that they have arrived at and be able to explain to those concerned the reasons the decision has been made. They should also highlight any mitigating circumstances that have been taken into account.
- Following any formal meeting, the conclusion should be confirmed in writing. If any support is being offered, this should be outlined, for example training and development or counselling.
- The 'victim(s)' should also be offered support, for example counselling.
- The employee(s) should be given the opportunity to appeal against the decision.

ALISON

 CASE STUDY 9.2

Alison, who had been recently appointed to the department of human resource management within a large manufacturing plant, decided after months of harassment and, in her opinion, bullying from a work colleague to submit a formal letter of complaint to her line manager. She cited a number of issues; however, the main focus of her complaint was the aggressive nature of many of the emails she received from her colleague as well as the sheer quantity of them.

She highlighted in her letter that she had pointed out to her colleague that she felt that the emails were overly aggressive and that she felt offended by the content and, in particular, the suggestion that she lacked the capability to undertake her job effectively. Alison supported her complaint with a number of emails and

suggested that there were a number of witnesses who would be able to support her claims.

Task

1   How should Alison's line manager deal with this complaint now that she has formally submitted it?

2   What processes should be followed to ensure that a thorough and fair investigation is undertaken?

3   Following an investigation, what would you advise her line manager to do to ensure that the department could work effectively again?

4   Can you suggest how this situation could have possibly been prevented or managed more effectively?

 ACTIVITY 9.7

Reflection on practice

Reflect on Case Study 9.2 and consider whether, in your experience, this reflects management's behaviour in managing the workforce. Do managers in your experience seek to ensure that conflict does not occur, either between individuals in the workplace or between line managers and subordinates? If so, do they do this at an early stage as the problems begin to emerge? What advantages and disadvantages does this have?

9.5 CONCLUSION

This chapter has reviewed issues such as power and authority, negotiation and conflict in contemporary organisations and how each has an impact on organisational performance. It has demonstrated that interpersonal and managerial skills are essential to the efficient functioning of modern organisations and that the organisational leadership needs to invest time and money in supporting and developing these. The chapter has highlighted that a 'good' manager must have the ability and the necessary skills to intercede at an early stage in order to address issues of conflict at all levels within the workplace. It has further demonstrated that organisations need to have clearly communicated and managed policies and procedures in place to make sure that managers are effectively supported and that issues are dealt with quickly and efficiently. Throughout the chapter it has been emphasised that all managers need to develop effective interpersonal skills to manage and control power and authority, manage negotiations and limit negative conflict.

PAUSE FOR THOUGHT

Reflect on what you have read and the activities that you have engaged in within this chapter and identify at least three things that you have learned. How will you apply this newly acquired knowledge and skill to your personal continuing professional development? Do you think that the issues raised in this chapter will encourage you to develop any areas in which you feel you may require support? Address these issues in your learning journal and/or CPD log. If necessary you could discuss your thoughts with colleagues, a mentor or a coach.

REFERENCES

ALLEN, D.G. (2008) Retaining talent: a guide to analysing and managing employee turnover. *SHRM Foundation Effective Practice Guidelines Series.* pp1–43.

BENFARI, R.C., WILKINSON, H.E. and ORTH, C.D. (1986) The effective use of power. *Business Horizons.* Vol 29, No 3. pp12–16.

BLADER, S. and TYLER, T.R. (2003) What constitutes fairness in work settings? A four-component model of procedural justice. *Human Resource Management Review.* Vol 12. pp107–26.

BROWAEYS, M.J. and PRICE, R. (2008) *Understanding cross-cultural management.* Harlow: FT/Prentice Hall.

CIPD. (2005) *Bullying at work: beyond policies to a culture of respect.* London: CIPD.

CIPD. (2006) *How engaged are British employees?* Annual survey report. London: CIPD.

CIPD. (2008) *Recruitment, retention and turnover.* Annual survey report. London: CIPD.

CIPD. (2010) *Equality Act 2010.* Factsheet. London: CIPD.

CIPD. (2011) Managing conflict is 'top of the agenda' says CIPD. *Personnel Today.* 3 March.

CLEGG, S., KORNBERGER, M. and PITSIS, T. (2008) *Managing and organisations: an introduction to theory and practice.* London: Sage.

DIBBEN, P., KLERCK, G. and WOOD, G. (2011) *Employment relations: a critical and international approach.* London: CIPD.

EINARSEN, S., HOEL, H., ZAPF, D. and COOPER, C.L. (2010) The concept of bullying at work: the European tradition. In: S. EINARSEN, H. HOEL, D. ZAPF and C.L. COOPER (eds). *Bullying and emotional abuse in the workplace: international perspectives in research and practice.* London: Taylor & Francis, pp3–39.

FARNHAM, D. (2011) *Human resource management in context: strategy, insights and solutions.* London: CIPD.

FAYOL, H. (1956) *General and industrial management.* London: Ditman and Sons.

FERRIS, G.R., DARREN, C., TREADWAY, R.W., KOLODINSKY, W.A., HOCHWARTER, C.J., KACMOR, C.D. and FRINK, D.D. (2005) Development and validation of the political skills inventory. *Journal of Management.* Vol 31. pp126–52.

FISHER, R. and URY, W. (2011) *Getting to yes: negotiating without giving in.* New York: Penguin.

FOLGER, R. and BARON, R.A. (1996) Violence and hostility at work: a model of reactions to perceived injustice. In: G.R. VANDENBOS and E.Q. BULATAO (eds). *Violence on the job: identifying risks and developing solutions.* Washington, DC: American Psychological Association, pp51–85.

FOX, A. (1966) Industrial sociology and industrial relations. *Research Paper No 3 Royal Commission on Trade Unions and Employers' Associations.* London: HMSO.

FOX A. (1974) *Beyond contract: work, power and trust relations.* London: Faber and Faber.

FRENCH, J. and RAVEN, B.H. (1959) The bases of social power. In: D. CARTWRIGHT (ed.). *Studies of Social Power.* Ann Arbor, MI: University of Michigan Press.

GENNARD, J. and JUDGE, G. (2010) *Managing employment relations.* London: CIPD.

GEORGE, B. (2011) The power of leadership groups for staying on track [online]. Harvard Business School. 6 September. Available at: http://hbswk.hbs.edu/item/6801.html [Accessed 13 August 2013].

GEURTS, S., RUTTE, C. and PEETERS, M. (1999) Antecedents and consequences of workhome interference among medical residents. *Social Science and Medicine.* Vol 48. pp1135–48.

GOLEMAN, D. (1998) *Working with emotional intelligence.* New York: Bantam Books.

GOLEMAN, D. (2005) *Emotional intelligence.* New York: Bantam Books.

GOSPEL, H.F. and PLAMER, G. (1993) *British industrial relations.* London: Routledge.

HARBISON, F. and MYERS, C. (1959) *Management in the industrial world.* New York: McGraw-Hill.

HEALTHYWORKPLACEBILL.ORG (2013) The healthy workplace bill – workplace bullying legislation for the US [online]. Available at: www.Healthyworkplacebill.org [Accessed 18 August 2013].

KELLOGG, K.C., ORLIKOWSKI, W.J. and YATES, J. (2006) Life in the trading zone: structuring coordination across boundaries in post-bureaucratic organisations. *Organisational Science.* Vol 17. pp22–65.

KOTTER, J.P. (1977) Power, dependence and effective management. *Harvard Business Review.* Vol 55, No 4. pp125–36.

KRAMER, R.M. (1999) Trust and distrust in organizations: emerging perspectives, enduring questions. *Annual Review of Psychology.* Vol 50. pp569–98.

LUTHANS, F. (2005) *Organizational behavior.* New York: McGraw-Hill.

MINTZBERG, H. (1985) The organization as a political arena. *Journal of Management Studies.* Vol 22, No 2. pp133–54.

NEL, P., SWANEPOEL, B., KIRSTEN, M., ERASMUS, B. and TSABADI, M. (2005) *South African employment relations: theory and practices.* Pretoria: Van Schaik.

PETTIGREW, A. (2002) Strategy formulation as a political process. In: S. CLEGG (ed.). *Central currents in organization studies II – contemporary trends.* London: Sage pp43–9.

PFEFFER, J. (1992) Understanding power in organisations. *California Management Review*. Vol 34, No 2. pp29–50.

PODRO, S. and SUFF, R. (2005) *Alternative dispute resolution*. Policy discussion paper. London: ACAS.

POTTER-EFRON, R.T. (2003) *Working anger: preventing and resolving conflict on the job*. Oakland, CA: New Harbinger Publications.

REES, G. and FRENCH, R. (2011) *Leading, managing and developing people*. London: CIPD.

RENWICK, R. (2003) Line manager involvement in HRM: an insider view. *Employee Relations*. Vol 25, No 3. pp262–80.

SALAMON, M. (1998) *Industrial relations: theory and practice*. Hemel Hempstead: Prentice Hall.

SCHIEMAN, S. and REID, S. (2008) Job authority and interpersonal conflict in the workplace. *Work and Occupations*. Vol 35. pp296-326.

SLOAN, M. (2004) The effects of occupational characteristics on the experience and expression of anger in the workplace. *Work and Occupations*. Vol 31, No 1. pp38–72.

UNISON. (2003) *Bullying at work guidelines for UNISON branches, stewards and safety representatives*. London: UNISON.

VOLKEMA, R., KAPOUTSIS, I. and NIKOLOPOULOS, A. (2013) Initiation behaviour in negotiations: the moderating role of motivation on the ability–intentionality relationship. *Negotiation and Conflict Management Research*. Vol 6. pp32–48.

WALTON, R. and MCKERSIE, R. (1965) *A behavioral theory of labor negotiations*. New York: ILR Press.

WEAKLIEM, D. and FRANKEL, S. (2006) Morale and workplace performance. *Work and Occupations*. Vol 33, No 3. pp335–61.

WEIGHTMAN, J. (2004) *Managing people*. London: CIPD.

WERTHEIM, E. (2007) *Negotiations: an overview*. Ft Leavenworth, KS: The US Army Command and General Staff College.

ZAPF, D. and GROSS, C. (2001) Conflict escalation and coping with workplace bullying: a replication and extension. *European Journal of Work and Organisational Psychology*. Vol 10, No 4. pp369–73.

CHAPTER 10

Constructive Performance Management

LESLEY MEARNS

OVERVIEW

In today's competitive environment it is vitally important that organisations effectively manage employee performance. In order to achieve this they must ensure that their leaders and managers are able to constructively criticise their subordinates, identify training and development needs and recognise potential barriers to individual performance including personal family issues as well as organisationally focused problems.

This chapter highlights the importance of modern managers constructively managing the performance of employees. It outlines the key skills which an effective leader and/or manager will require, at each stage in the employment relationship, in order to successfully and constructively manage the performance of all employees throughout the organisation.

LEARNING OUTCOMES

By the end of the chapter, provided that you engage with the activities, you should be able to:

- recognise the importance of identifying performance-related issues among the workforce
- understand the core management skills involved in the management of employee performance
- identify the role and purpose of selection, appraisal and disciplinary interviews in relation to managing workforce performance
- understand the importance of effectively planning and preparing for the recruitment and selection process
- explain how to prepare for and conduct interviews in a variety of situations
- comprehend the role of induction within the performance management process
- understand why it is important for organisations to develop appropriate performance management procedures and ensure that they are implemented effectively.

10.1 INTRODUCTION

There is a lot of dissatisfaction among senior managers with the actual functioning of many performance management systems (Moullakis 2005, Mercer 2002, Stoskopf 2002). In fact Morgan (2006, p22) has argued that 'too many companies are finding that their performance management systems are falling short of expectations'. Aguinis and Pierce

(2008) have laid the blame for this failure at the feet of managers, who have been unable to effectively put performance management policies into practice. This chapter will, therefore, examine the skills required by an organisation's management in ensuring that their workforce's performance is effectively managed.

The competitive and increasingly international environment in which most modern organisations now operate means that they have to constantly review the external environment in order to remain competitive. For example, they must assess industrial developments, consider the economic environment, update their technological capabilities as well as review and evaluate the skills and competencies of their workforce on a continual basis. All this requires organisations to have an experienced and knowledgeable leadership as well as a skilled management team who are able to effectively manage the performance of the workforce and to maximise productivity of the organisation.

Armstrong and Baron (2005) argue that performance management is not the sole responsibility of managers; it should include all employees, who should strive to fulfil the strategic aims of the business as well as their personal career goals. Marchington (2012, p225) highlights that performance management should be a continuous process which 'links together performance, motivation, individual goals, departmental purpose and organisational objectives'; these, in turn should be overseen by management but engage the workforce. Biron et al (2011) agree; however, they argue that employees require tangible 'signposts' in order to become motivated and recognise the link between their own aims and objectives and those of the organisation, thus improving their performance. Srivastava and Lurie (2001) argue that this can only be achieved through clear communication so that employees understand what is expected of them. However, several researchers have argued that it is how the performance management system is implemented and managed that makes a crucial difference to its success (Hazard 2004, Haines and St-Onge 2012). Hazard (2004) suggests that if management 'get it wrong' in the sense that it becomes merely a 'tick-box' exercise, it can become a burden rather than an inspirational motivational tool.

Organisational culture, which is reflected in policies and procedures, also plays a significant part in helping employees understand what is expected of them (see also Chapter 5). For example, work–life balance policies such as flexible working patterns can signal to employees that their employers care about employee well-being, which in turn could improve commitment, engagement and performance. Haines and St-Onge (2012) suggest that there is strong evidence to suggest that strong and positive organisational culture increases employee engagement, which in turn produces more positive performance management outcomes. Elicker et al (2006) add that as well as a positive culture which engages the employees, it is important for the leadership and the management to seek to create a good employment relationship, which they again argue is associated with a more effective performance management system.

However, it is important to recognise that much of the research that has been conducted into effective performance management has been restricted to the West (Selvarajan and Cloninger 2012). This has perhaps handicapped an emerging entity of contemporary managers who seek to control the performance of an increasingly international and multicultural workforce. The role and skills of modern management are, therefore, changing as organisations increasingly expect them to manage in a cross-cultural and international environment, which again requires the development of new managerial skills (Selvarajan and Cloninger 2012).

From the above it is clear that effective performance management not only requires the co-ordination and integration of a number of human resource management practices but also requires a wide range of managerial skills and competencies which include an appreciation and an understanding of many of the skills covered elsewhere in this book, such as emotional intelligence, interviewing techniques, coaching, mentoring, reflection, interpersonal communication skills, cultural awareness, and so on. Therefore, the chapter will encourage and support the exploration and development of these aspects.

The chapter does not attempt to cover every aspect of all performance management systems; however, it will focus on the central skills which are believed to be essential in order to maintain the effective performance of employees and consequently the organisation (see Figure 10.1). The chapter is, therefore, divided into a number of key areas, outlined briefly below, which seek to enhance awareness of these skills as well as encouraging the reader to reflect on personal experiences and identify areas where they can develop and improve their own competencies.

Figure 10.1 Key components of effective performance management

Performance management begins at the start of the employment relationship and continues throughout an employee's employment within the organisation. The chapter will therefore outline the importance of recruiting and selecting the 'right' person for the job and the role of management as an organisational gatekeeper. It will focus on the skills required in identifying and selecting an appropriate employee who will add value to the organisation. This will include the ability to effectively interview candidates as well as being able to manage the expectations of the 'selected' employees as they begin working within the organisation. It will highlight the value of effectively managing the induction process and the interpersonal and communication skills required by management to ensure employee performance is supported and maximised from an early stage of employment within the organisation.

The second section of the chapter centres on the management of the appraisal process. Appraisals are often seen as the main way of managing employee performance as it is a process which should allow an honest and open conversation between (usually) the line manager and the employee, which is essential to ensure effective organisational performance (Pichler 2012). Selvarajan and Cloninger (2008) suggest that performance appraisals are the *most* important aspect of the management of people and the achievement of organisational goals in that they provide the opportunity to motivate, encourage and develop employees on a regular basis. Guest (1997) states that performance appraisals are an integral part of all organisations as they enable the organisation to operate effectively and achieve its strategic goals. Therefore, ensuring that performance appraisals are effectively managed is essential for organisational success. It is argued here that appraisals should be a positive and motivational experience for all concerned; it should be a constructive experience which enhances the performance as well as increasing the productivity of the organisation. Thus, the chapter will explore the skills that an effective manager will need to ensure that the underlying philosophy of the appraisal system is understood and the importance of its effective implementation is vital to ensure an improvement in employee performance.

A third area which contributes significantly to organisational performance is the management of employees who underperform and fail to meet expected targets for a range of reasons, for example, a broken or damaged psychological contract, de-motivation, lack of skill or ability, laziness or perhaps non-compliance with the employment contract. As in most areas of management, it is important to address poor performance, for whatever reason, at an early stage and informally to prevent it from escalating and becoming a much more serious disciplinary issue, which would be time-consuming for all concerned as well as having a negative impact on employee performance.

The chapter concludes by highlighting the importance of effectively managing employees' performance throughout their tenure in order to maximise overall organisational productivity as well as employee satisfaction and staff morale.

10.2 RECRUITMENT: THE ROLE OF THE ORGANISATION'S 'GATEKEEPER'

Performance management should be a central feature for any organisation, large or small, and as such should be a central management task. However, there are many aspects which integrate and contribute to the effective management of people. Leatherbarrow et al (2010, p223) suggest that although performance management has been around for as long as people have needed to work together, the actual term is relatively new. They suggest that it has emerged from the human resource management theory that argues that the success of an organisation is the outcome of the behaviour of their 'most valuable assets', their employees.

From the above it is clear that modern managers must ensure that they have the knowledge and skills to enable them to identify the necessary competencies that are required by the organisation to enable them to realise their business strategy *before* they even begin to engage in the recruitment and selection process. Sutherland and Wocke (2011) emphasise that it is the ability and skills of management to identify the most appropriate employees which drives a successful organisation. Therefore, 'getting it wrong' will 'reduce organisational effectiveness, invalidate reward and development strategies, are frequently unfair on the individual recruit and can be distressing for managers who have to deal with unsuitable employees' (Pilbeam and Corbridge 2006, p142).

It has been argued that attracting, retaining and effectively managing talented employees can provide the organisation with a sustainable competitive advantage (Michaels et al 2001, Boxall and Purcell 2008). As competition between organisations for skilled employees intensifies, the 'war for talent' becomes significantly more important in ensuring both current and future organisational performance. The effective planning and management of the recruitment and selection process is therefore essential if an organisation is to improve its performance and increase its competitive advantage. However, it should be acknowledged that this is not an easy task and will be influenced by the kind of knowledge, competencies, skills and personal attributes of the management (Sutherland and Jordaan 2004) as well as those that are required by the organisation. For example, skilled and competent managers will be able to attract and encourage suitable candidates, who will improve organisational performance.

Boxall and Purcell (2008) highlight that one of the most important aspects of the recruitment and selection process is having competent managers who are able to plan and manage the process in line with organisational strategies and resources. A successful appointment creates a match between the capabilities and inclinations of potential candidates with the demands and goals of the organisation (Dale 2003). In support, the CIPD (2011) emphasises the importance of management planning their employment needs in line with the business strategy and their resources. Their study demonstrates that organisations that engage in workforce planning are able to flourish as they tend to attract, develop and retain employees who are able to meet the developing business strategies while at the same time maintaining their competitive advantage.

The CIPD (2010, p4) defines workforce planning as 'a core process of human resource management that is shaped by the organisational strategy and ensures the right number of people, with the right skills, in the right place, at the right time to deliver short- and long-term organisation objectives'. It is therefore important that management begin the process by analysing the organisation's business strategy. Managers, therefore, must carefully access the human requirements which will be necessary to ensure that the business strategy is achieved. An audit of the necessary human resource skills, competencies and knowledge is required to assess the ability of the organisation to meet its present and future needs. It should include both qualitative and quantitative data which is kept by the organisation. This information will highlight employee numbers, skills, competencies and geographical location as well as indicating shortfalls or areas of concern which may require management to begin the recruitment and selection process, engage in training and development or even performance management procedures.

Generally, the analysis of the data together with workforce planning should be done in partnership with the organisation's leadership, the human resource management department as well as line managers. On a practical level, workforce planning should also include consideration of the available organisational resources. However, Gilmore (2013, pp91–2) highlights that achieving a balanced input from these stakeholders 'can be challenging'.

The following section will focus on the skills needed for the identification of 'talented' employees as well as the recruitment and selection process from the perspective of maintaining and improving organisational performance. This is important for any organisation as the CIPD states that the cost of the recruitment and selection process is approximately £8,000 for senior managers and £3,000 for other less prestigious employees (Heap 2012). Therefore, it is in the best interests of the organisation to 'get it right' first time around.

Recruitment and selection can be divided into three main areas: (1) attracting the 'right' talent for the organisation, (2) selecting the most appropriate candidate(s) who match the knowledge, skills and competencies of the available position(s) and (3) management of the selected candidate into the organisation through mechanisms such as the management of expectations, the induction process, mentoring, training and development.

Many theorists view recruitment and selection as being interlinked areas (Bratton and Gold 2012, Foot and Hook 2011) where one feeds directly to the other and the end result is the employment of the 'best' candidate for the job (Gilmore 2013). However, it is argued that although this may be the most rational approach to employing the most talented employees, it does not always occur in practice, mainly due to *poor preparation* and *weak managerial knowledge and skills*. Pilbeam and Corbridge (2010) state that the traditional approach to recruitment and selection is one which is systematic and carefully planned. Leatherbarrow et al (2010, p123) suggest that a majority of managers, engaged in recruitment and selection, traditionally use the 'systematic recruitment cycle' as a tool to identify the 'right person for the job'. They divide the cycle into six stages:

Stage 1 – Identify the need to recruit an employee.

Stage 2 – Gain permission to fill the vacancy.

Stage 3 – Undertake a thorough job analysis.

Stage 4 – Write a job description and a person specification based on the analysis.

Stage 5 – Consider the methods that are available to advertise the vacancy. Choose a method which is most suitable for the position you are trying to fill.

Stage 6 – Publicise the vacancy in a way which will attract a pool of talented employees from which they can choose the 'best person for the job'.

10.2.1 BEGINNING THE PROCESS

A systematic approach to the recruitment and selection process should begin with the identification of a need to recruit. Once this has been achieved, managers need to ensure that they have both the permission of senior management as well as the necessary resources to recruit an employee to fill the post. It is at this stage that Leatherbarrow et al (2010) suggest that a full review of the nature of the vacancy and the strategic requirements of the organisation is undertaken. For example, the organisation needs to conduct a full job analysis as well as a review of the organisation's business strategy. This is extremely important, as many organisations merely seek to replace an employee who has left the organisation, without considering the full requirements of the organisation's business strategy. This is a common mistake and tends to lead to the recruitment of inappropriate personnel lacking the necessary skills and competencies to meet the evolving requirements of the organisation.

10.2.2 THE JOB ANALYSIS

A thorough job analysis will include management ensuring that they have gathered all the relevant information about the job from the existing employee and all those who worked with the post-holder to ensure the data is current. The evaluation should include information about the roles and responsibilities of the position and the aims and objectives of the job. Other information should include performance measures. The next stage in the recruitment process will probably be collated by HR practitioners, who will produce a job descriptor. Traditionally the job descriptor will contain the following information:

- an indication as to where the job fits within the organisation and how it contributes to the organisation's business strategy
- a brief summary and an outline of the purpose of the job
- an outline of the job's key roles and responsibilities, which should be grouped together under specified areas central to the job.

The Advisory, Conciliation and Arbitration Service (ACAS) (2011a) has suggested that the job descriptor should be written concisely, should provide an overview of the job and highlight the main areas of responsibility and competency. Blenkinsopp and Zdunczyk (2005) highlight that there is often a mismatch and a vagueness between job expectations and reality, and that this is the reason for much of the failure within the recruitment and selection process in practice.

Once this has been undertaken, management need to carry out a full review of the current labour supply in order to identify potential capabilities which could be realised through investment in areas such as training and development. If there are no suitable candidates internally, management must look externally to meet organisational resourcing needs and ensure the effective performance of the organisation. ACAS (2010) suggests that, in order to maintain organisational performance and avoid compulsory redundancies, management need to undertake this kind of review on a regular basis and ensure that it is integrated with other human resource management (HRM) activities. The next stage is for management to put together a detailed person specification which not only matches the present needs of the organisation but also considers the requirements of the future business strategy. This should be taken from the job descriptor and should highlight the specific skills, competencies and experience which will be required of the ideal candidate. It will also provide the selection criteria against which management will assess each candidate.

ACTIVITY 10.1

Recruitment criteria

You are an HR manager and you have asked to become involved in the recruitment of a new member of your team, an employment relations specialist. Consider and outline in the table below the person specification criteria that you believe is relevant to such a position and suggest ways in which you might assess/test potential candidates during the selection process.

Company Name	ABC Construction Ltd.		
Job Title	Employment Relations Manager		
Department	Human Resource Management		
	Essential Requirement	**Desirable Requirement**	**Method of Assessment**
Qualifications			
Professional Qualifications			
Experience			
Knowledge and Skills			
Interpersonal Skills			

Once you have done this, discuss your ideas/thoughts in small groups. Discuss any conflicts that you may have had in your group. Are there any improvements that you could make to the methods you have identified to ensure that you will select the 'right person for the job'?

10.2.3 ADVERTISING A VACANCY

Once it has been established that there is a need to externally recruit a new member of staff, consideration should be given to the means of attracting and filtering appropriately qualified and experienced candidates. The CIPD (2012a) highlights the top four recruitment methods used by modern organisations as: organisational website, recruitment agencies, employee referral schemes and commercial job boards (see Table 10.1). Gilmore (2013, p98) argues that the aim of the recruitment process is to achieve 'a balance between attracting suitable candidates and not incurring an excessive cost'. However, the focus of effective recruitment should be to attract appropriately qualified candidates in relation to their professional capabilities, their working experience and interpersonal qualities, from which to make a selection. Advertising in the newspapers, once the most popular method to attract potential employees, is now in decline (Heap 2012) and is increasingly being replaced by online applications (see Table 10.1).

Table 10.1 Most effective methods for attracting applications, by year and industry sector (per cent)

	2010	2011	2012	Private sector	Public sector	Not-for-profit
Own corporate website	63	59	61	46	57	75
Recruitment agency	60	54	53	74	59	20
Employee referral scheme	35	29	35	31	52	10
Commercial job boards	33	27	32	26	37	17
Specialist journals/trade journals	31	27	29	18	24	42
Local newspaper advertisement	36	32	26	23	20	38
Professional networking, eg LinkedIn	14	16	22	18	31	8
Speculative applications/word of mouth	24	25	20	24	24	11
Search consultants	22	15	20	37	20	9
Jobcentre Plus	23	25	20	22	15	26
Apprenticeships	12	11	17	31	11	21
Links with schools/colleges/universities	18	13	16	22	18	11
Secondments	11	11	10	6	8	15
National newspapers	16	11	10	6	3	25
Social networking, eg Facebook	3	4	8	6	9	5

Source: CIPD 2012a, reproduced with kind permission

Cober and Brown (2006), for example, have stated that 50 per cent of new hires in their study in the USA were sourced from the Internet. It is clear from Table 10.1 that the Internet now plays an important part in the recruitment and selection process in many organisations; however, it should be noted that there are still a significant number of organisations who are not yet using online recruitment. In fact, there is evidence to suggest that those who use online recruitment tend to use it in conjunction with other techniques. Parry and Wilson (2009) conclude that although online recruitment has become well established and that it has in part changed the way management recruit employees, it has not had the overwhelming impact that many researchers predicted.

 ACTIVITY 10.2

Exploring advertising outlets

Consider and identify three types of jobs which could be suitably advertised on a company website. Write down the justification for this decision and share it with your colleagues. Identify three positions which it would be inappropriate to advertise on an organisation's website. Explain your decision.

Gilmore (2013) argues that the movement towards online recruitment is evolving and that it now includes social media sites such as Twitter, Facebook and LinkedIn. She perceives this as a new movement which is attempting to target a specific pool of employees who are now increasingly communicating through this form of media. Specifically Heap (2012) suggests that many organisations rank professional networking sites such as LinkedIn highly in recruitment and selection, and as increasingly proving effective media for attracting 'talented' workers. In fact, there is significant data available which suggests that the use of online social networks has now become ubiquitous within the process of recruitment and selection (Vick and Walsh 2010). Ollington et al (2013) highlight that there were 500 million users of Facebook in 2011 (an increase of 100 million from the previous year), demonstrating that more and more prospective employees are interacting in a virtual environment. This, they suggest, provides managers with access to a wide range of socialising outlets on which they can access and view prospective employees' profiles, seeking an array of information which is not available using more traditional recruitment methods.

However, Vick and Walsh (2010) have argued that these changes have not all had a positive impact on the recruitment and selection process. They highlight that some of the changes have increased the pressure on management in that they are expected to produce more detailed information about candidates in a drastically reduced timeframe. It can also create problems in respect to the number of applications that could be generated from unsuitably qualified applicants. Therefore, managers need to ensure that correct screening processes are in place to ensure that they do not waste valuable time sifting through inappropriate applications. Parry and Wilson (2009) warn that online recruitment is, by comparison with other methods, resource-intensive and suggest that it is better suited to some particular industrial sectors and specific job types. They add that position within the hierarchical structure of the organisation also plays a significant part in the appropriateness of online recruitment. Hence, contemporary managers need to acquire and develop a wider range of skills, for example the ability to use information technology, be competent researchers, and so on.

As well as online recruitment, telephone and Skype interviews have increased in popularity (Marchington and Wilkinson 2012, p214). This may be linked to the growth in the use of call centres and flexible workers, who need to demonstrate competence in these areas in order to effectively perform their jobs.

ACTIVITY 10.3

Examining job adverts

Spend some time looking through the various media sources which could be used to advertise a vacancy. Look at the way they are set out. What information do they include about: (a) the vacancy; (b) the person? Do they include any other relevant information which relates to the position? Do they provide any information about the employing company which could be used by potential applicants in deciding whether the job would be appropriate?

Therefore, the choice of which recruitment method to adopt together with the amount of resources available will be influenced by the vacancy to be filled and its hierarchical position within the organisation. For example, an organisation that needs to recruit manual unskilled workers may seek to recruit from a local job centre or place local adverts in the press, which would have comparatively low recruitment costs. However, recruitment for a professional manager is much more likely to use sources such as professional journals (a good example for HR specialists and managers is *People*

Management), organisational websites and the national press, which are more resource-intensive, in order to generate a pool of possible employees.

It is clear that there are a variety of different recruitment methods available to management (Gilmore and Williams 2013, Marchington and Wilkinson 2012, Rees and French 2011). There is no intention in this chapter to describe each and every method. The aim is to highlight the importance of ensuring that the management responsible for the recruitment and selection of the workforce have the necessary skills. In today's dynamic business environment it is vitally important that management have the skills, competencies and capabilities to recruit and retain a talented workforce which will provide them with a competitive advantage. They must ensure that they recruit and select the 'right person for the job' as well as having them in place and functioning effectively at the 'right time'. An important point to take from this chapter is that effective and competent management will be able to increase the validity and reliability of their choices through reflection, research and planning.

As with recruitment, the selection process has many methods available to it. However, good practice suggests that a range of selection methods should be adopted when trying to identify the 'ideal candidate(s)' (Gilmore and Williams 2013, p176). With this in mind, only a selection of the most popular methods will be identified and analysed together with the skills that management will be required to master in order to carry them out effectively.

10.3 SELECTION

As organisations are increasingly operating in a global context, it is important that management recognise that variation does exist between different countries and cultures. For example, it has been suggested that the UK and the USA tend to favour using a formal interview process, whereas other countries such as Germany, France and the Netherlands focus on assessment testing (Newell and Tansley 2001). China, the Middle East and Mexico predominantly use personal and family connections in the recruitment and selection process (Brewster et al 2007). This therefore has implications for management in the sense that different skills and competencies may be required in different geographical locations and within different cultures (Harzing and Pinnington 2011, Manroop et al 2013).

The accuracy of using one single approach is limited (Roberston and Smith 2001). Marchington and Wilkinson (2012) therefore advocate combining one or more selection methods in order to improve the accuracy of identifying a suitable candidate. Wilk and Cappelli (2003, p122) note that utilising a range of methods increases the information available on the skills, competencies and capabilities of the various candidates, providing a wider, more informed basis for selecting the most appropriate candidate.

10.3.1 THE APPLICATION FORM

Gilmore (2013) argues that the application form and CV submission continue to be the most widely used selection methods in a majority of organisations. It should be noted, however, that recent legislation in the European Union has forced organisations to consider what information they are requesting as well as what details may be retained for future use. It is therefore important that managers are fully aware of the relevant legislative framework in the country in which they are recruiting and selecting employees to make sure that their procedures do not breach the law. This is often the point at which those responsible for the selection of employees should seek specialist support and advice.

The application form is used to enable those responsible for the selection of employees to compare and contrast the abilities, qualifications and experiences of each candidate effectively. The information sought on the application form should relate to the education, competencies and working experiences of each candidate and it should correspond to the job and person specifications which are set out in the advertisement. ACAS (2010) states that the information requested on the forms should be easy to understand and realistic in nature. ACAS (2010) highlights a number of advantages of using an application form:

- It makes comparing and contrasting each candidate much easier as the same information is sought from each candidate. CVs may not provide all the required information and can be difficult to compare as each applicant provides a range of information.
- They can be useful in providing a mechanism through which to undertake an initial filter when set against identified criteria.
- The quality and ability in which the form has been completed can give some indication as to the applicant's suitability for the position. For example, if written communication or presentation skills are essential for the position, the application form can provide an indication of some of these skills and competencies.
- The application form also provides the management with a written record in the candidate's own hand of their qualifications and abilities.

However, as with most approaches to selection, there are disadvantages:

- Care should be taken by those who formulate the application forms that too much or irrelevant information is not sought from potential employees. The forms should seek information which is relevant to the position advertised and should relate to the person and job specifications in the sense that it should concentrate on areas such as experience, knowledge and competencies that will be required to undertake the job.
- Some potential applicants may dislike completing forms or have a disability which may deter them from filling in the application form. For example, some individuals who are very experienced may find the forms inadequate and frustrating as they are not able to demonstrate their full capabilities within the restrictive confines of the application form. Alternatively, those with only a limited amount of experience or qualifications may feel inadequate as the form may have many empty spaces. Equally someone with a disability, for example dyslexia, may struggle to read and complete the application form effectively. In each scenario the organisation may be losing out on the opportunity to employ a valuable and experienced individual who would have the ability to 'do the job' well.
- It has also been suggested that application forms, especially if not planned and written effectively, just add another layer and time to the selection process without adding sufficient value.
- Unless planned carefully by specialists, application forms can inadvertently become discriminatory in nature. For example, they could ask the applicant to complete the form in their own handwriting. This could be an issue if written communication is not relevant to the position advertised, in that it could discriminate against those whose first language is not English or who may have poor literacy skills.
- Any question which seeks information such as marital status, ethnic origin or date of birth is illegal unless it is there for legal requirements or to meet codes of professional practice. In this case, it should be clearly stated and placed on a different sheet of paper or on a tear-off section (ACAS 2010). Candidates should be told that this information is voluntary and does not form part of the formal selection process.
- In the UK the Data Protection Act 1998 and the subsequent Codes of Practice must be taken into account throughout the recruitment and selection process, and there may be similar requirements in other countries. If the organisation intends to retain any information, either manually or through information technology, applicants must be informed and told for what purposes it is being retained and for how long.

- There is evidence that candidates are not always honest when they complete an application form (Schorr Hirsch 2007) and thus the application form should only be viewed as a starting point in the selection process.

Hence, it becomes clear that organisations that utilise an application form for selection purposes need to make sure that they are prepared to investigate fully the claims made by prospective candidates in order to ensure the reliability and validity of the information that is provided. Suff (2008) highlighted this problem and suggested that a high percentage of respondents had agreed that applicants had either been dishonest or had included inaccuracies on their application forms, reinforcing the importance of management checking the information provided on the application forms through the use of other selection processes.

ACTIVITY 10.4

The application form in practice

ACAS (2011b) has produced an advisory booklet relating to the retention and storage of personal employee data. Access this booklet on the Internet via the following link (www.acas.org.uk/index.aspx?articleid=717) and look at the example application forms. Critically analyse these forms. One could be used for a middle management or specialist position and the other for a clerical or manual position.

- Consider how you could adapt one or both of these forms to recruit an HR specialist in employment law.
- In groups of two or three, draft a job specification and a person specification for the position.
- What advertising methods would you use? Be prepared to explain your answer.
- What other selection methods might you consider in order to identify your ideal candidate?

10.3.2 THE SELECTION INTERVIEW

McCarthy et al (2010) and Bye et al (2013) have concluded that in Western countries the employment interview is the most popular method of selecting employees. They are viewed as providing the channel through which both the employer and the potential employee exchange information as well as having the opportunity to meet and begin to develop the psychological contract which will become an important part of the performance management system. Lipsmeyer and Zhu (2011), however, question the value of an employment interview where there is a culturally diverse applicant pool, which, they argue, is becoming more likely given the expansion of international organisations and the migration of workers. Macan (2009, p215) highlights that contemporary managers should ensure that they remain alert to the possibility that they may fail to recruit the best person for the job because they have not considered aspects such as cultural stereotyping or culturally biased recruitment methods. Silvester and Chapman (1996) emphasise that failure to understand the nature and purpose of the interview could lead managers to reject suitable candidates simply by misunderstanding cross-cultural differences.

ACTIVITY 10.5

Reflection on practice

Students should read the paragraph below and consider the cross-cultural differences and their potential impact on the information which has been obtained by the British manager.

A British national senior manager who was employed in the Middle East was asked to conduct an interview in which the performance of a trainee teacher was to be evaluated after an observed session in order to determine their suitability for promotion. The first question was along the lines of 'how did you feel your teaching session went?' The British manager expected that the trainee teacher would follow the UK model of 'this went well, but I would like to develop X'. However, the trainee teacher responded, 'It was perfect; I could not have done anything differently.'

In small groups consider:

- How could the manager have achieved his aims and objectives more effectively?
- What advice would you give him in order for him to manage this employee's performance more effectively?

Dipboye et al (2004) have argued that the most effective interview to use in the recruitment and selection process is the structured interview because it improves reliability and validity. The reason for this is that each candidate is required to address the same questions and issues in the same order, therefore making it easier to compare and contrast the responses as well as increasing its legal defensibility (see Table 10.2). They add that structured interviews are more reliable at predicting future performance than other interviewing techniques, especially if they are founded on a thorough job analysis and person specification. Therefore McCarthy et al (2010) state that unstructured interviews are less likely to identify the best candidate as they do not tend to produce reliably scored information. Indeed, unstructured interviews tend to encourage subjective analysis, which is based on things such as appearance, manners and even on how similar to the interviewer each candidate is instead of seeking evidence of potential job performance (Hunter and Hunter 1984).

Table 10.2 Comparison of traditional and structured interviews

Traditional interview	Structured interview
Loosely structured	Highly structured
Emphasises candidate characteristics	Emphasises job-related behaviour
Dynamic interchange – amendment of overall agenda	Consistency predominates
Sequence of questions often haphazard – ad hoc format	All candidates asked identical questions or the same number of questions from a predetermined base
Closed questions	Open questions
Limited information	Encouragement of in-depth probing
Answers jotted down	Answers scored on checklists and rating scales
Content frequently unrecorded	Systematic recording
Evaluations often subjective and impressionistic	Structured evaluations

Traditional interview	Structured interview
Social encounter with potential for stereotyping and bias	Formal encounter with limited capacity to establish rapport

Source: adapted from Walley and Smith 1998, as cited in Beardwell 2011, p223

Dipboye et al (2004) have suggested that the interview design and structure can be summarised into a three-dimensional model, which would include:

1   how the interview related to the job itself

2   the standardisation of the process

3   the structured use of the data to evaluate the interviewees.

Huffcutt (2011) expands this and identifies a number of constructs that should be examined in the employment interview:

● cognitive ability
● personality
● job knowledge
● job experience
● education and training
● situational judgement
● social skills
● emotional intelligence
● self-discipline
● interpersonal presentation
● teamwork
● personal and demographic characteristics.

However, Manroop et al (2013) have questioned the extent to which it would be possible to accurately measure some of these constructs, especially in a cross-cultural environment. Roberts and Campbell (2006) have highlighted that in general managers who are engaged in interviewing tend to judge the potential employees based on their own cultural assumptions and communicative styles. Therefore, it is essential that management become aware that cultural differences between themselves and the interviewee can lead to interactional problems and miscommunication (Gumperz 1999).

 ACTIVITY 10.6

Measurement of individual traits

Consider the constructs identified by Huffcutt (2011) above.

In groups, go through each construct and identify a way in which management could successfully measure this construct during the selection process. What impact (if any) do you think a cross-cultural applicant pool would have on the methods you use?

The aim of the interview is to identify and appoint the candidate(s) best suited to the job(s), whatever their cultural background is. However, in order to achieve this it is important that the potential employees are given as much information about the position as possible in order for them to consider how they think they will 'fit' into the organisation, as well as the extent to which the organisation will meet their 'needs' in relation to their career and developmental plans (see also Chapters 1 and 5). It should be noted that managers must be aware that they need to carefully manage the expectations of potential employees at this stage as they are building on the foundations of the psychological contract which, if the appointment is made, will become an important element in their motivation, performance and commitment to the organisation.

The selection interview will impart both conscious and unconscious information to both the interviewee and the manager. Consciously, from the employer perspective, information about the job, terms and conditions of employment, organisational structure, career development opportunities, and so on, can be given to the potential employee. At the same time the manager can obtain verification of working experience, qualification and competencies. It is perhaps important at this stage to highlight that the potential employee will be formulating their own opinions of the organisation. They will be gathering information which will not only relate to the specific job but will give an indication of areas such as organisational culture and career progression opportunities, which will help inform the decision to accept or reject the position if offered.

An important management skill is, therefore, to ensure that the impressions that potential employees pick up at this stage in the selection process are positive to ensure that, if successful, talented candidates will accept the position that is being offered. Therefore ensuring that managers have the 'right' interviewing and communication skills is essential both to the selection process as well as in relation to the management of performance.

There are a number of core skills which managers are required to have when conducting an effective interview:

- planning and preparation
- verbal communication skills, including areas such as interpersonal behaviour, formulating and asking probing and informative questions
- non-verbal communication skills and the ability to demonstrate as well as interpret areas such as body language
- effective listening and observational skills
- record-keeping ability such as note-taking
- ability to handle and rank information received against a predetermined scale
- decision-making.

The CIPD (2009) highlights that it is important for organisations to ensure that those involved in interviewing employees should be given formal interview training. Unfortunately, Chapman and Zweig (2005) suggest that in practice a majority of these managers do not received appropriate training and consequently fail to appoint the 'right person for the job'. As demonstrated above, the selection interview is undertaken by most organisations; however, their structure and content vary from institution to institution and from position to position. For example, some organisations operate a very unstructured format in which questions will flow with very little structure to it, much more reflective of a conversation between two people. Others prefer a highly structured framework in which all questions are predetermined and asked to all candidates in the same order in an attempt to ensure the validity and credibility of the process. Each approach should be an attempt to measure the qualifications, competencies and experience of each candidate against some assessment criteria.

In order to conduct an effective interview, whether structured or unstructured, a manager must make sure that they are fully prepared. This requires managers to gather and analyse as much background information as possible about the candidate and the position to which they are being recruited. For example:

- present and future organisational requirements

- details about all the candidates, including their qualifications, competencies and experience
- an understanding of the assessment criteria against which the interviewers will be measuring each candidate.

Once this has been achieved, time must be given to planning and preparing for the interview itself:

- What questions will be asked?
- What information will be needed from the candidates?
- Ensure that the questions and their context are not going to discriminate against either an individual applicant or any particular group of potential employees.
- How many stages will there be to the selection process?
- What other selection methods will be utilised, if any?

ACTIVITY 10.7

Planning and preparation for an interview

1   Consider a time when you have been invited to an interview. Reflect on the amount of research that you undertook in relation to the:

- skills and competencies that were required for the position
- the qualifications and experience that was sought

- the nature and reputation of the employing organisation.

2   How much time did you spend considering the possibilities of career progression or development opportunities?

Spend a few moments with your group comparing and contrasting each other's results.

10.3.3 THE SKILLS REQUIRED TO EFFECTIVELY MANAGE THE INTERVIEW PROCESS

Once all the planning and preparation has taken place, it is time to consider communication skills. As highlighted earlier, the interview should focus on gathering and imparting important information in relation to the criteria identified in the job and person specification. The interview will do this both verbally and non-verbally, making effective communication an essential management skill. It has been argued that these skills can be divided into a number of key areas:

- empathy
- questioning
- negotiating
- listening
- observation of non-verbal communication
- recording information against the identified criteria
- discussion, analysis and decision-making
- ability to provide constructive feedback.

10.3.3.1 Empathy

For a candidate to perform effectively at an interview, it is important that they feel as relaxed as is reasonably possible, therefore building some kind of rapport and having the ability to emphasise their key strengths. Beardwell (2011) has suggested that a job interview is a time of anxiety and nervousness for both parties; however, it is probably more stressful for the potential employee. Good interpersonal and communication skills will help to establish some kind of rapport with the candidate and it can help to establish a positive atmosphere in which a constructive interview can be conducted. If the potential employee feels more at ease, they tend to be more forthcoming with the information that could be important in trying to decide which of the candidates is the most suitable for the position (Torrington et al 2011). Here are some common areas which the interviewers should consider:

- The interviewers should always speak first.
- They should smile, look self-assured, relaxed and confident.
- Begin with talking about harmless exchanges such as the 'weather'. This will enable both the interviewees and the interviewers to communicate with each other without the answers being important to the selection process.
- Outline clearly the format of the interview process and any itinerary that may apply for the day.
- Ensure that the interviewee has understood and is in agreement with what has been explained to them.

10.3.3.2 Questioning skills

There is a wide range of different approaches to asking questions. However, Beardwell (2011) has stated that the area of 'questioning' can be divided into broad categories of open, closed and probing questions.

Open questions are the ones which cannot be answered simply with a 'yes' or 'no' response; they require some level of qualification or explanation. It has been suggested that open questions tend to begin with 'what', 'why', 'how' or 'where' (Beardwell 2011, p219), although at times they may ask the interviewee to give an example of how they have handled a particular situation. Such questions are generally used to elicit information which relates to their ability and competence. An effective interviewer will allow the potential employee to undertake most of the talking.

Closed questions are those to which the candidate is only required to give a 'yes' or 'no' response. This type of question is not thought to be suitable within a selection interview as it restricts the flow of information and can stilt the dialogue so that it prevents 'any useful exchange of information' (IRS 2003, p154), thus creating a strained atmosphere in which valuable information is overlooked. It is useful to note that occasionally closed questions can serve a purpose; for example, they can be used to clarify ambiguous statements.

 ACTIVITY 10.8

Open and closed questions

Read the questions below and highlight which ones are open questions and which are closed ones:

- How long have you been employed within your current organisation?
- Are you able to work as part of a team?

- Can you give me an example of a time when you have worked effectively without supervision?
- Could you outline how you would go about managing a culturally diverse team?
- Do you enjoy working within the department in which you are employed?

Probing questions on the other hand allow the interviewer to explore issues or confirm information outlined in, for example, the application form or CV. However, these questions need to be supported and developed through the use of supplementary enquiries in an attempt to obtain more detailed information of specific areas of the application. Explorative questions are required in most selective interviews to ensure that the candidate is not concealing information which may be relevant to the position. The number of probing questions will be influenced by the purpose of the interview and the amount of information that the preparatory research has unearthed during the planning stage. Skilful probing during the interviewing stage can sometimes lead to potential employees disclosing information that they may have preferred to have kept hidden. A skilled interviewer will be able to identify an unintentionally divulged piece of information and have the ability to move 'swiftly on' so as not to embarrass the candidate.

How a manager asks and responds to questions is therefore important as the information that they gather and subsequently used in relation to the recruitment and selection of a talented workforce will have a direct impact on the performance of the organisation as a whole.

10.3.3.3 Negotiation skills

Negotiation is an important aspect of every sphere of our lives, whether it be social, family or in the workplace, and negotiation skills are essential for all managers within an organisation (please refer to Chapter 9 for details). In order for the interviewee or the interviewer to achieve their aims and objectives, it is important that a process of negotiation is entered into. The interviewer may decide that they need to present their terms and conditions and see to what extent the interviewee is prepared to accept them. Negotiation is therefore an important skill which needs to be maintained between two, perhaps diverse, parties. Although negotiation is generally associated with the management of conflict within the workplace, it will also occur during the selection process and the management of performance.

As outlined in the previous chapter, there are two main approaches to the negotiation process: distributive and integrative bargaining. The first approach, *distributive bargaining*, adopts the perspective that there will be a win–lose situation; the other, *integrative bargaining*, suggests that there will be a win–win position (Walton and McKersie 1965). It is the integrative bargaining that management should strive to achieve in their selective interview process in that both sides seek to achieve a mutually beneficial result. The successful negotiator has certain abilities such as communication skills, power and interpersonal capabilities. Goleman (2005) argues that successful negotiators are 'emotionally intelligent', which in laymen's terms means that they are able to understand and manage their own and other individuals' emotions (CIPD 2009). This therefore means that emotionally intelligent negotiators are able to interpret the interview process and will be able to influence the outcome through their skills. The emotionally intelligent negotiator will be able to work towards an agreement that will be acceptable to both sides, that is, the interviewer and the interviewee. The skilled negotiator should realise that the psychological contract is being developed at this stage, and they must realise that commitment and loyalty need to be established and managed from this point forward.

10.3.3.4 Listening skills

Asking the right questions at the right time will only help those involved in the selection process gather information if they 'listen' to what is being said and take note of the content of what is being outlined. Beardwell (2011) highlights that quite often the quality of the information provided at the interview can be diminished because the interviewers tend to focus on the questions that they are going to ask rather than the ones they have just asked. She explains that listening is an important skill and suggests that this is much more than just hearing. She states that hearing means 'paying attention to what is being said and how it is being said' as well as observing 'the non-verbal signals that accompany the message' (Beardwell 2011, p220). In fact it means that the listener has to be much more perceptive in the sense that they need to become aware of the non-verbal signals that are displayed at the same time as the words that are spoken. The listener must therefore be aware of what is not said and ask questions in order to help understanding in relation to these areas. Beardwell (2011) calls this active listening; it results in a better appreciation of what the interviewee is saying. Robbins and Hunsaker (2009) suggest that the active listener must display certain behaviours:

- Eye contact must be maintained throughout the conversation.
- There must be a demonstration of interest in what is being said, for example, appropriate facial expressions must be made.
- Body language is important and inappropriate actions should be kept to a minimum, for example, distracting gestures or any indication of boredom.
- Interest should be shown by the listener, for example, asking the speaker to demonstrate what they mean by specific statements.
- The speaker should not be interrupted and interest can be shown by summary statements.
- The interviewer should not undertake too much talking; for example, it has been argued that the interviewee should be allowed to talk for approximately 80 per cent of the time.
- The listener should be aware of all non-verbal communication, which includes body language and facial expressions.

Beardwell (2011) has suggested that 'active listening', which is an essential managerial skill, should at all times display signs of understanding the speaker. This can be demonstrated through the use of reflection and summary (Torrington et al 2011). Summaries can serve two purposes: they can indicate that the listener has 'heard' what is being said by showing that the main points have been noted; it also gives the speaker the opportunity to correct any information which the listener has 'mis-heard'. It is further suggested that the most efficient listeners are able to manage 'silence' in the sense that most people are uncomfortable with long silences and will seek to fill it. However, a truly effective listener will allow silences to emerge as they provide the space for new messages to emerge as well as the opportunity for both parties to think about the conversation (Torrington et al 2011).

10.3.3.5 Non-verbal communication

Communication is not confined to what is spoken; it includes non-verbal communication such as body language. Some have even suggested that 90 per cent of the way humans communicate is non-verbal (Quilliam 1995) and as such should be taken very seriously. Specifically within the interviewing process it is felt that an awareness of an individual's body language is important for two reasons (Huffcutt 2011). Firstly, it is important to show outward signs of interest in order to encourage the interviewee to divulge important information which could assist the interviewer in the selection process. Secondly, non-verbal signals from the interviewee could be useful to the interviewer in determining interest as well as indicating areas where further exploration is required.

Eye contact is believed to be essential both from the perspective of the interviewer as well as the interviewee. It helps build rapport as well as displaying empathy and attentiveness. However, Torrington et al (2011) have argued that the ability to maintain 'good' eye contact is very hard to achieve and highlight that there is a very thin line between showing attentiveness and staring intently. The skill is to demonstrate enough eye contact to reinforce interest in the subject; however, the contact must be interrupted occasionally so as not to indicate 'obsessiveness'.

10.3.3.6 Recording information and note-taking

It is important within the selection process that notes must be taken, especially as the aims and objectives of the interview focus on the recruitment and selection of the most appropriate person for the position within the organisation. In order to achieve this, it is necessary to make sure that accurate notes are taken to ensure that the decisions which are made are informed and based on information which was obtained throughout the recruitment and selection process.

ACTIVITY 10.9

Stop and think

Think about the notes that you take throughout a lecture which supplement the lecture slides. Do you consider that these add value to the learning process? Do they help you understand the nature of the lecture and the information which is being provided? Do they help you to remember what has been discussed?

Despite the undoubted value of note-taking, the notes should be kept to a few key words or points during the interview itself so as not to distract the interviewee. However, these notes should be supplemented immediately after the interview. Again this reinforces the need to prepare for the interview in the sense that the interviewer should know what areas to note down and what information may be irrelevant.

10.3.3.7 Discussion, analysis and decision-making

It is important throughout the recruitment and selection process to ensure that discussions take place between all those involved in the selection process. They need to be very clear on the skills and competencies that are required for the organisation, both now and in the future. They must be able to analyse the data that is presented to them in the form of application forms and CVs as well as selection methods such as the interview. Finally, they must have the ability to make decisions. It should be emphasised again that the central aim of the interview is to select the 'right person for the job'; in other words, to select or reject potential candidates and identify potentially talented workers who will improve the overall performance of the organisation. Beardwell (2011) argues that if decisions are made effectively, they can contribute to the performance of the organisation. Unfortunately, evidence seems to indicate that in practice decisions are based on inappropriate judgements, inaccurate and partial data (Walley and Smith 1998).

10.3.3.8 Constructive feedback

An area that is often forgotten by management as well as the academic books that support them is the need for constructive feedback. Constructive feedback is essential in all stages of performance management and should therefore be part of the selection process. Unsuccessful candidates should be given the opportunity to learn from 'failure' in the sense that they need to understand the reasons why. Therefore, constructive feedback should be based on the overall 'performance' of the potential candidate, including the application form, the interview process and any other selection method which has been undertaken. This feedback should enable the candidate to understand why they have not at this stage met the requirements of the position and realise what areas they need to improve in.

Robbins and Hunsaker (2009) suggest that constructive feedback should be divided into a number of specific areas, such as:

- Be specific about the areas that you feel are worthy of praise or criticism. This is important as it allows the candidates to identify areas where they have strength as well as areas which require attention.
- Be selective in the number and issues that will be targeted for feedback. It should be noted that there is only so much criticism that one person can take at a time. Armstrong and Baron 2005, p336) state that too much criticism causes the potential employee to withdraw and stop 'listening', thus the feedback will not be constructive.
- Armstrong and Baron (2005) suggest that the focus should be on what can be changed and improved in relation to practical aspects of the selection process, for example job-related issues rather than areas such as personality traits or personal characteristics.
- In general, Robbins and Hunsaker (2009) have argued that the most constructive feedback is given as close as possible to the interview when issues are clear in the mind.

As this chapter's focus is on performance management, there is neither time nor justification for spending a lengthy period of time describing and analysing various individual selection methods, details of which can be found in most standard human resource management books. However, a sound introduction to the importance of interviewing skills is a significant skill that must be mastered by those wishing to effectively manage employee performance throughout the employment of an employee. For example, it is required in the recruitment and selection process, the continuous management of employee performance through tools such as appraisal and the management of performance through disciplinary and grievance interviewing, and so on.

10.4 EFFECTIVE MANAGEMENT OF PERFORMANCE

Effective management of employees begins *before* they set foot within the organisation and continues until they leave the organisation's employment. This is vitally important to the overall performance of the organisation as it establishes a framework and sets expectations for the future employee and effectively establishes the psychological contract which must be managed and maintained throughout an employee's employment if performance is to be enhanced. As the human resource management literature suggests, commitment and loyalty are essential ingredients for positive employee motivation and, therefore, workforce and organisational performance, which must be managed effectively by the leadership and management.

10.4.1 INDUCTION – MANAGING THE EXPECTATIONS OF THE SELECTED EMPLOYEE(S)

Newly appointed employees are at their most vulnerable during their first few weeks of their employment (Butler 2008); therefore, the central aim of the induction process is to help them settle into their positions and support them to enable them to quickly become performing employees (Mestre et al 1997). It has been argued that the first 100 days are critical in determining whether or not an employee will remain in the organisation (Fritz and Vonderfecht 2007). A well-managed induction process reduces the amount of time that it takes for a new employee to feel commitment to the organisation and achieve a good level of performance (Derven 2008, D'Aurizio 2007). This was demonstrated by Scottish and Southern Energy, which saw their customer satisfaction rating doubled to 80 per cent after they introduced a 'good' induction programme (Pollitt 2007).

Induction, therefore, should be a time when the organisation's managers welcome the new employee(s) into the organisation. It is a time when information relating to performance standards and expectations can be given to the employee, the organisational culture should be imparted to them as well as the company's policies and procedures, and there should be an attempt to socialise them within the organisation (Marchington and

Wilkinson 2012). This is important as it helps support the new employees as well as ensuring that they are able to perform effectively from an early point in their employment.

ACAS (2010) emphasises that there are many organisational benefits to be gained by effectively managing the induction process:

- The employee is more relaxed and settled.
- The employee will be more open to initial training and development.
- Retention of new employees is higher in organisations that effectively induct their new employees.
- There is strong evidence to suggest that there is a positive correlation between induction and employment/industrial relations.

The CIPD (2012b) suggests that the aims and objectives of induction should be to ensure that new employees are integrated into the organisation. They add that research has demonstrated that 'tailor-made induction programmes' result in higher retention rates and improved organisational performance. The CIPD (2012b) states that a 'good' induction programme should contain the following elements:

- a detailed outline of the position that the employee has been placed in, together with the job requirements and performance standards
- an outline of the terms and conditions of employment
- some form of practical orientation, that is, a guided tour of the site including highlighting where the facilities are located
- an organisational orientation which shows clearly where the employee 'fits' into the organisational chart and how their role supports the organisation's business strategy
- it is also good practice to introduce the new employee to key staff, including senior employees
- information relating to the organisational policies and procedures in relation to areas such as health and safety (this is required under British law), discipline and grievance
- it is also useful to include a brief outline of the organisation's history, its mission statement, its core values and culture together with an outline of its key products and services.

The CIPD (2010) highlights that employees whose performance expectations are not managed at the induction stage often fail to fully understand either the organisation itself or indeed their position within it. This, they argue, leads to:

- weak integration into the team within which they are to work
- low morale and motivation, especially for the new employee
- reduced productivity levels
- poor organisational performance.

In some cases the new employee will decide to leave the organisation, which in turn results in:

- additional recruitment and selection costs
- loss of valuable management time in relation to the recruitment and selection process
- demotivation and loss of employee morale among the remaining employees
- possible damage to the organisation's reputation and credibility.

Despite the evidence above, Marchington and Wilkinson (2012) have emphasised that while organisations spend billions of pounds on recruitment and selection, they quite often fail to effectively manage the induction process, which ultimately has a negative impact on performance (Butler 2008). This is of concern as the induction process should be an integrated part of the performance management within an organisation and must be viewed as part of an employee's continuous development.

Table 10.3 Induction table

Pre-employment	joining instructions proof of the right to work in the UK (if not already done during recruitment) conditions of employment company literature
Health and safety	emergency exits evacuation procedures first aid facilities health and safety policy accident reporting protective clothing specific hazards policy on smoking
Organisation	site map – canteen, first aid, post, and so on telephone system computer system organisation chart – global organisation chart – departmental company products and services security pass car park pass security procedures Official Secrets Act Data Protection Act/Freedom of Information Act
Terms and conditions	absence/sickness procedure working time, including hours, flexi-time, and so on arrangements for breaks holidays/special leave probation period performance management system discipline procedure grievance procedure Internet and email policy
Financial	pay – payment date and method tax and National Insurance benefits pension/stakeholder pension expenses and expense claims
Training	agree training plan training opportunities and in-house courses CPD and personal development plan career management
Culture and values	background mission statement quality systems customer care policy employer brand

Source: CIPD 2010, reproduced with kind permission

ACTIVITY 10.10

Induction skills

Considering the points above, in small groups, design an induction programme for the employment relations specialist who was appointed following Activity 10.1. The company is a large logistics organisation which was established in Sweden in 1892. Be prepared to present your programme together with justification for what you are proposing.

The skills that are required for the induction process generally reflect many of those needed throughout all aspects of performance management in the sense that planning and preparation are key areas. The early stages of the employment relationship are an important 'gateway' to the organisation and need the presence of a skilled line manager in order to successfully integrate the new employee into the team and the organisation. Again communication, verbal and non-verbal, skills are essential in ensuring that the new recruit understands the information which is being given to them from a legal perspective, but also in relation to performance standards and expectations. Management must remember that the induction process is in part aimed at gaining commitment and loyalty with the purpose of maximising organisational performance. Glendinning (2002) argues that managers play a major role in the induction process and suggests that there is strong evidence to support the claim that organisations whose management are committed to induction and recognise that it is an important part of the performance management system are more successful.

10.5 APPRAISAL – THE ONGOING MANAGEMENT OF EMPLOYEE PERFORMANCE

The induction process should form the foundations upon which management builds and establishes the performance standards and expectations of the organisation. The performance appraisal, however, is often considered one of the most important aspects in the management of employee performance (Selvarajan and Cloninger 2008). Chiang and Birtch (2010) argue that there are many advantages to ensuring that appraisals form an effective part in the management of performance. They suggest that it is an opportunity for the manager:

- to clarify the expected performance standards and to measure the extent to which these have been achieved over a period of time
- to allocate rewards as well as indicating any talented employees
- to highlight training and development needs
- to discuss career progression
- to counsel the employees if required
- to give constructive feedback, which may include negative aspects of their performance
- to establish future aims, objectives and targets
- to motivate the employee and increase their morale
- to improve communication.

Again, in order to be able to successfully manage the appraisal process, the manager must have a range of knowledge, competencies and interpersonal skills. The appraisal process must be prepared for and planned carefully in that the manager should engage in a range of information-gathering techniques in order to ascertain the extent to which each employee has achieved their performance targets. This is important as the manager must be able to identify relevant rewards, training requirements, promotion opportunities or the need to begin discipline or incapability measures in order to manage the performance of the organisation effectively.

Marchington and Wilkinson (2012) suggest that managers need to decide the criteria against which each employee will be measured. These criteria should be drawn from the job and person specifications and linked to the department's and, ultimately, the organisation's strategic objectives. Armstrong and Baron (2005) add that, in their opinion, there are five specific elements to a performance appraisal:

1   The ability to measure employee performance in relation to the extent to which they achieve the agreed performance standards and targets.

2   The communications skills required to provide constructive feedback.

3   The competency and confidence to provide positive reinforcement of good practice.

4   The ability to engage in discussion and debate in relation to individual and organisational performance.

5   The ability to negotiate and reach agreement in relation to what is to be undertaken by both management and employee in order to improve individual and organisational performance.

Considering the above, it is clear that managers must be able to conduct research and analyse the data to clarify the context against which the performance appraisal will be evaluated. Beardwell (2011) argues that the performance appraisal must be based on 'hard' evidence in order to validate it and to ensure that the process is perceived as being fair. In fact, Piggot-Irvine (2003) warns that if the research has not been thoroughly undertaken, the process will be seen as inequitable and perhaps even subjective.

A majority of managers are not sufficiently committed to the underlying philosophy of the appraisal system or are not adequately prepared (Soriano 2007), which is perhaps why they are often viewed as unsuccessful and in some cases demotivating. Roberson and Stewart (2006) argue that the performance appraisal serves as a means for giving feedback to employees which should result in improved performance. However, Selvarajan and Cloninger (2008) highlight that for employees to feel motivated and committed, they must perceive the performance appraisal as being fair and accurate and that the targets agreed are realistic. Therefore, management must determine the factors that are specifically related to improving employee performance in order to elicit positive employee reactions, which will ultimately motivate and improve performance (Selvarajan and Cloninger 2009).

The performance appraisal should be viewed as a strategic part of the employment relationship and, if not conducted effectively, can be viewed as a 'paper exercise' or even unnecessary by some. McMahon (1999) states that a key skill is the ability of management to create a relaxed atmosphere in which the employee feels able to talk freely about their employment experiences, their work-based achievements along with their developmental requirements. As with many areas in performance management, like the selection interview, an important skill during a performance appraisal is the ability to ask relevant and informative questions and listen to the answers (Armstrong and Baron 2005).

However, unlike the selection interview, the appraisal questions should focus on the individual employee's experiences, opinions and emotions within a defined period of time within the workplace, usually the period since the last appraisal. On a practical level Beardwell (2011, p235) suggests that the appraiser should refrain from asking probing questions which, for example, begin with 'why', as it is seen as confrontational and could have a negative impact on the performance appraisal process. Questions that begin with words such as 'what' can be used to encourage the individual employee to 'identify their own solutions to issues and to determine future actions' (Beardwell 2011, p235).

As with the selection interview the appraiser should demonstrate the ability to listen and again should allow the appraisee to monopolise the conversation. For example, it is suggested that the appraisee should be allowed to talk for approximately 80 per cent of the time. Beardwell (2011) suggests that the manager should engage in 'active' listening in that they should not only use their ears but should observe facial movements and body language as well as listening to the tone and volume of their voices while answering questions.

As highlighted earlier, silence can be a good tool in that it provides time for employees to reflect on what has been said to date as well as to consider their answers or issues that they may wish to raise. A skilled manager should use the period of silence to observe the appraisee's body language in order to anticipate what they are thinking. Also the manager could use the time to reflect on the appraisal and consider which areas could need further questioning or even research. Beardwell (2011) suggests that summarising what has been discussed is useful to both the appraiser as well as the appraisee, especially at the end of the review, as it allows both parties to clarify their understanding of the meeting and the targets which have been agreed.

Another important management communication skill is the ability to give constructive feedback. Gillen (2007) suggests that this feedback can be divided into two areas. Firstly, the manager should give feedback on the individual's workplace performance and, secondly, suggestions and expectations about future performance. It should be noted that management tend to find giving positive feedback is much easier than anything negative. Robbins and Hunsaker (2009) suggest that negative feedback can be problematic as there is the possibility that it could cause offence or it could become a demotivating factor if not managed constructively. Beardwell (2011, p238) states that management should engage in open, honest and constructive feedback as it ensures that problems or potential problems are confronted and managed rather than avoided.

Once a 'problem' has been identified and analysed, managers can develop a suitable course of action which should enable the organisation to effectively manage its performance. The appraiser should make sure that they do not attempt to impose their will on individual employees as management should ensure that they engage the workforce and obtain their loyalty and commitment through persuasion rather than force. Managers need to have the ability to analyse the situation and consider performance objectives which align themselves with the strategic objectives of the organisation. It has been suggested that effective objectives should be C-SMART (Locke and Latham 1990):

C	Challenging
S	Specific or Stretching
M	Measurable
A	Achievable or Agreed
R	Realistic
T	Time-bound

The objectives should be jointly agreed between the appraiser and the appraisee. In this way management can attempt to gain employee 'buy-in' and obtain commitment and loyalty to the organisation. In order to set effective objectives, it is necessary to be able to explain the performance standards which the organisation expects and be able to relate them to the organisation's strategic objectives as well as the employee's capabilities (Locke and Latham 1990).

10.6 MANAGING POOR PERFORMANCE

According to Russell (2010), 'poor staff performance is one of employers' most common complaints. Managers faced with difficult conversations about standards and potentially litigious staff often avoid dealing with it or don't handle it very well. But ignoring the issue can demotivate other staff, so tackle poor performance firmly.' Performance management, however difficult, must also address the underperformance of employees within the organisation. This is vitally important to ensure that employees are being treated in a fair and equal way in order to reinforce managerial and organisational expectations. Underperformance can be identified in a number of ways (ACAS 2011a); for example, it could be:

- the failure to meet the expectations of the job
- the non-compliance with workplace regulations, policies and procedures
- unacceptable behaviour in the workplace
- disruptive, aggressive or negative behaviour that has a negative impact on colleagues.

Equally, the explanations for a failure to perform at an appropriate level are varied (ACAS 2011a). For example, it could be because:

- The employee does not understand what is expected of them in relation to organisational goals or standards.
- There are cultural misunderstandings which make performance expectations unclear.
- There are interpersonal differences between one or more colleagues.
- The capabilities of the employee do not match the requirements of the job that they are undertaking.
- The employee does not have the knowledge or skills required to do the job.
- The performance management system has failed.
- There is low personal morale and motivational levels.
- The organisation has a poor working environment.
- The employee has personal issues, such as physical or mental problems.
- The organisation has a bullying culture.

Whatever the reason for the underperformance, it must be dealt with quickly and appropriately to prevent an escalation of the problem, which may require more serious disciplinary action. However, an important point to remember when considering dealing with underperformance is that the courts appear to indicate that a poor-performing employee needs time to remedy the situation (Churchman 2001).

Thus, Wilton (2011, p383) has suggested that the focus for management should be on improving future performance rather than punishing or dwelling on the past. Some organisations have introduced capability procedures that are totally separate from the disciplinary route. The capability approach of supporting improvements in performance is consistent with the underpinning philosophy of human resource management, which believes in investing and developing human capital to improve organisational performance (see also the discussion of the CIPD Profession Map in Chapter 1). In doing so, Risher (2003) states that managers must be prepared to speak openly and honestly with the underperforming member of staff as well as be prepared to acknowledge that their own behaviour may have contributed to the situation.

Managing underperformance may be challenging (Wilton 2011, p383); however, with clear policies and procedures in place and skilled and willing managers, this problem can be addressed. Armstrong and Baron (2005, p344) state that 'managing underperformers is a positive process which is based on feedback throughout the year that looks forward to what can be done by individuals to overcome performance problems and, importantly, how managers can help'. If poor performance is allowed to continue unabated, it undermines the overall validity of the performance management system within an organisation. Therefore, for performance management to be successful, managers must ensure that they manage within a climate of fairness, openness, ongoing communication and fundamental support. The skills required by management therefore focus on areas such as interpersonal communication, the ability to give constructive feedback, reflection and listening.

ACTIVITY 10.11

Managing poor performance

Consider the following situation:

A small veterinary practice, the owner-manager and three supporting vets in a North Yorkshire practice recruited a newly qualified junior veterinary surgeon. The probation period was for three months. It quickly became apparent that the junior vet lacked key skills and that the supporting nursing staff frequently had to help out rather than being able to undertake their own tasks. The owner-manager, although recognising that there was potentially an issue,

failed to deal with it. Four months later the junior vet made a number of serious mistakes during routine operations that led to the death of a number of animals and potential legal action from their owners.

In groups discuss:

- how this situation had occurred
- what action should have been taken by the owner-manager and at what stage
- what action should now be taken to prevent any more 'mistakes'.

Russell (2010) argues that there are a number of stages which management need to engage in to manage poorly performing staff:

1   Management must ensure that they assess the capability of the employee to undertake the position to which they have been recruited. This means that they should monitor and assess the employee's skills, ability, aptitude and knowledge in relation to their role on a continuous basis. Poor performance is reasonable grounds for dismissal provided that a fair capability procedure or disciplinary procedure has been followed.

2   Clear standards must be communicated to the employee to ensure that they know what the organisation's minimum standards for performance are. Management must ensure that there are clear rules and guidelines which outline acceptable performance. If these are not clear – and if the case is ever taken to an employment tribunal – there could be problems.

3   Management should make sure that feedback is provided on a regular basis. The feedback should be objective. If an employee is believed to be failing to achieve adequate levels of performance, an effective manager must meet with the employee on a regular basis (every two to three months). This is important as it allows the manager to manage the expectations of the employee and reinforce the policies and procedures of the organisation.

4   It is important that management take action quickly. Delaying a response or ignoring the situation could make the situation much worse as well as have a negative impact on other employees.

5   Russell (2010) also highlights that it is important to focus on the facts as hopefully this may prevent the situation from becoming personal. Focusing on evidence will help management to build an accurate picture of the employee's performance. Thus a meeting between the manager and the employee should be conducted professionally and provide examples of poor performance which will be supported with evidence. A performance improvement plan (PIP) should be agreed between the manager and the employee that outlines how employee performance will be improved and what support, if any, will be provided.

6   An important part of this process will be to allow the employee time to improve. Russell (2010) recommends approximately two to three months; however, it would depend on the task and the level of performance. If there is insufficient improvement made within this timeframe, it would be appropriate to move to a more formal capability process. The performance improvement plan should continue to remain in place.

7   The final point to note is that the employee should understand that the manager has the right to manage poor or failing performance. If this is not understood (and sometimes even when it is), some employees may respond to their performance being challenged by claiming a grievance and citing bullying and harassment. Russell (2010) has suggested that when this occurs, many managers simply abandon the process and the poor performance is allowed to continue. In an attempt to avoid this, managers need to ensure that the employees understand that they have a right and a duty to manage, especially when they have evidence that the employee has failed to attain specified performance targets. It may even be good practice to ask an employee why they think that they are being bullied and harassed.

However, it is important that constructive criticism is given to ensure that organisational performance is maintained. Management need to make sure that all employees appreciate and understand exactly what is expected of them. They need to be able to communicate performance targets, management expectations and managerial measures. Despite this, Swinburne (2001) suggests that in general managers tend to avoid confrontation with poor performers until it becomes unavoidable or it becomes a disciplinary issue. She adds that giving regular 'constructive feedback reduces the need to challenge and discipline people' as well as encouraging organisational support and training. Swinburne (2001) also argues that there are a number of things that managers can do in order to improve the quality of the feedback. For example, managers should make sure that they are speaking courteously to the employee in the sense that they should be aware of their tone of voice, words used and body language. Managers should also ensure that they constructively frame their criticisms and make sure that even though they are being critical, the employee should be able to identify some positive areas for development. Finally, managers should make sure that the poor-performing employee has the opportunity to respond to the criticisms, either for clarification or defence. If used in this way, even criticism can be seen in a positive light in that it is contributing to the performance of the organisation.

10.7 CONCLUSION

This chapter has attempted to outline some of the many skills which managers need to effectively manage the performance of their employees. It has emphasised in particular the importance of preparation, planning, research, analysis, communication and interpersonal skills in the successful management of organisational performance. It has suggested that, in general, many managers do not practise these skills and therefore fail to maximise the overall performance of the organisation.

 PAUSE FOR THOUGHT

Identify at least three things that you have learned by studying this chapter and engaging with the activities. How will your newly

acquired knowledge and skills support your continuing professional development? What value do you expect your learning to have for your daily routines and your further career? In what area have you identified a need for further development and how are you planning to fill that gap? Address these issues in your learning journal and/or CPD log. You may also wish to discuss them with a peer, colleague, mentor or coach to aid your further development.

EXPLORE FURTHER

CIPD. (2009) *Selection and interviewing*. Factsheet. February. London: CIPD.

CIPD. (2010) *Workforce planning: right people, right time, right skills*. London: CIPD.

CIPD. (2011) *Resourcing and talent planning*. Annual survey report. London: CIPD.

CIPD. (2012a) *Resourcing and talent planning*. Annual survey report. London: CIPD.

CIPD. (2012b) *Induction*. Factsheet. London: CIPD.

REFERENCES

ACAS. (2010) *Recruitment and induction*. London: ACAS.

ACAS. (2011a) *Job evaluation: considerations and risks*. Advisory booklet. London: ACAS.

ACAS. (2011b) *How to manage performance*. London: ACAS.

AGUINIS, H. and PIERCE, C.A. (2008) Enhancing the relevance of organisational behaviour by embracing performance management research. *Journal of Organisational Behaviour*. Vol 29, No 1. pp139–45

ARMSTRONG, M. and BARON, A. (2005) *Performance management: the new realities*. 2nd ed. London: CIPD.

BEARDWELL, J. (2011) Interviewing and managing performance. In: G. WATSON and S. REISSNER (eds). *Developing skills for business leadership*. London: CIPD.

BIRON, M., FARNDALE, E. and PAAUWE, J. (2011) Performance management effectiveness: lessons from world leading firms. *International Journal of Human Resource Management*. Vol 22, No 6. pp1294–1311.

BLENKINSOPP, J. and ZDUNCZYK, K. (2005) Making sense of management mistakes. *Career Development International*. Vol 10, No 5. pp359–74.

BOXALL, P. and PURCELL, J. (2008) *Strategy and human resource management*. New York: Palgrave Macmillan.

BRATTON, J. and GOLD, J. (2012) *Human resource management theory and practice*. 5th ed. Basingstoke: Palgrave Macmillan.

BREWSTER, C., SPARROW, P. and VERNON, G. (2007) *International human resource management*. 2nd ed. London: CIPD.

BUTLER, K.H. (2008) Getting employees to stay onboard instead of jumping ship. *Employee Benefit News.* January.

BYE, H., HORVERAK, J., SANDAL, G., SAM, D. and VANDE VIJVER, F. (2013) Cultural fit and ethnic background in the job interview. *International Journal of Cross Cultural Management.* pp1–20.

CHAPMAN, D. and ZWEIG, D. (2005) Developing a nomological network for interview structure: antecedents and consequences of the structured selection interview. *Personnel Psychology.* Vol 58, No 3. pp673–702.

CHIANG, F. and BIRTCH, T. (2010) Appraising performance across borders: an empirical examination of the purposes and practices of performance appraisal in a multi-country context. *Journal of Management Studies.* Vol 47, No 7. pp1405–16.

CHURCHMAN, P. (2001) Managing poor performance. *New Zealand Business.* p24.

CIPD. (2009) *Selection and interviewing.* Factsheet. February. London: CIPD.

CIPD. (2010) *Workforce planning: right people, right time, right skills.* London: CIPD.

CIPD. (2011) *Resourcing and talent planning.* Annual survey report. London: CIPD.

CIPD. (2012a) *Resourcing and talent planning.* Annual survey report. London: CIPD.

CIPD. (2012b) *Induction.* Factsheet. London: CIPD.

COBER, R. and BROWN, D. (2006) *Direct Employers Association recruiting trends survey.* Washington, DC: Booz Allen Hamilton.

DALE, M. (2003) A *manager's guide to recruitment and selection.* 2nd ed. London: Kogan Page.

D'AURIZIO, P. (2007) Onboarding: Delivering on the promise. *Journal of Nursing Economics,* Vol 25, No 4. pp228–9.

DERVEN, M. (2008) Management onboarding. *Journal of Training and Development.* April. pp49–53.

DIPBOYE, R.L., WOOTEN, K. and HALVERSON, S.K. (2004) Behavioral and situational interviews. In: J.C. THOMAS (ed.). *Handbook of psychological, industrial and organisational assessment.* Hoboken, NJ: Wiley. pp297–326.

ELICKER, J.D., LEVY, P.E. and HALL, R.J. (2006) The role of leader–member exchange in the performance appraisal process. *Journal of Management.* Vol 32, No 4. pp531–51.

FOOT, M. and HOOK, C. (2011) *Introducing human resource management.* 6th ed. Harlow: FT/Prentice Hall.

FRITZ, L.R. and VONDERFECHT, D. (2007) The first 100 days. *Journal of Healthcare Executive.* Vol 22, No 6. pp8–14.

GILLEN, T. (2007) *Performance management and appraisal.* London: CIPD.

GILMORE, S. (2013) Recruiting and selecting staff in organisations. In: S. GILMORE and S. WILLIAMS (eds). *Human resource management.* Oxford: Oxford University Press.

GILMORE, S. and WILLIAMS, S. (2013) *Human resource management.* Oxford: Oxford University Press.

GLENDINNING, P.M. (2002) Performance management: pariah or messiah? *Public Personnel Management.* Vol 31, No 2. p161.

GOLEMAN, D. (2005) *Emotional intelligence*. New York: Bantam.

GUEST, D. (1997) Human resource management and performance: a review and research agenda. *International Journal of Human Resource Management*. Vol 8, No 3. pp263–76.

GUMPERZ, J. (1999) On international sociolinguistic method. In: C. ROBERTS and S. SARANGI (eds). *Talk, work and institutional order: discourse in medical, mediation and management Settings*. Berlin: Mouton De Gruyter.

HAINES, V. and ST-ONGE, S. (2012) Performance management effectiveness: practices and context. *International Journal of Human Resource Management*. Vol 23, No 6. pp1158–75.

HARZING, A. and PINNINGTON, A. (eds) (2011) *International human resource management*. 3rd ed. London: Sage.

HAZARD, P. (2004) Tackling performance management barriers. *Strategic Human Resources Review*. Vol 3, No 3.

HEAP, N. (2012) *Resourcing and talent planning*. Annual survey report. London: CIPD.

HUFFCUTT, A. (2011) An empirical review of the employment interview construct literature. *International Journal of Selection and Assessment*. Vol 19, No 1. pp62–81.

HUNTER, J.E. and HUNTER, R.F. (1984) Validity and utility of alternative predictors of job performance. *Psychological Bulletin*. Vol 96. pp72–98.

IRS. (2003) *IRS best practice in HR handbook*. Croydon: LexisNexis.

LEATHERBARROW, C., FLETCHER, J. and CURRIE, D. (2010) *Introduction to human resource management: a guide to HR in practice*. London: CIPD.

LIPSMEYER, C. and ZHU, L. (2011) Immigration, globalisation and unemployment benefits in developed EU states. *American Journal of Political Science*. Vol 55, No 3. pp647–64.

LOCKE, E. and LATHAM, G. (1990) New directions in goal-setting theory. *Current Directions in Psychological Science*. Vol 15, No 5. pp265–8.

MACAN, T. (2009) The employment interview: a review of current studies and directions for future research. *Human Resource Management Review*. Vol 19. pp203–18.

MANROOP, L., BOEKHORST, J. and HARRISON, J. (2013) The influence of crosscultural differences on job interview selection decisions. *International Journal of Human Resource Management*. Vol 24, No 8.

MARCHINGTON, L. (2012) Performance management. In: M. MARCHINGTON and A. WILKINSON (eds). *Human resource management at work*. 5th ed. London: CIPD.

MARCHINGTON, M. and WILKINSON, A. (2012) *Human resource management at work*. 5th ed. London: CIPD.

MCCARTHY, J.M., IDDEKINGE, C.H.V. and CAMPION, M.A. (2010) Are highly structured job interviews resistant to demographic similarity effects? *Personnel Psychology*. Vol 63. pp325–59.

MCMAHON, G. (1999) A lovely audience. *People Management*. 25 March.

MERCER. (2002) *Effective performance management practices*. New York: Mercer Human Resource Consulting.

MESTRE, M., STAINER, A. and STAINER, L. (1997) Employee orientation: the Japanese approach. *Journal of Employee Relations*. Vol 19. pp443–56.

MICHAELS, E., HANDFIELD-JONES, H. and AXELROD, B. (2001) *The war for talent*. Boston, MA: Harvard Business School Press.

MORGAN, R. (2006) Making the most of performance management systems. *Compensation and Benefits Review*. Vol 38, No 1. pp22–7.

MOULLAKIS, J. (2005) One in five workers actively disengaged. *The Australian Financial Review*. Vol 10. p10.

NEWELL, S. and TANSLEY, C. (2001) International uses of selection methods. *International Review of Industrial and Organisational Psychology*. Vol 16. pp195–213.

OLLINGTON, N., GIBB, J. and HARCOURT, M. (2013) Online social networks: an emergent recruiter tool for attracting and screening. *Personnel Review*. Vol 42, No 3. pp248–66.

PARRY, E., and WILSON, H. (2009) Factors influencing the adoption of on-line recruitment. *Personnel Review*. Vol 38, No 6. pp29–46.

PICHLER, S. (2012) The social context of performance appraisal and appraisal reactions: a meta-analysis. *Human Resource Management*. Vol 51, No 5. pp709–32.

PIGGOT-IRVINE, E. (2003) Key features of appraisal effectiveness. *International Journal of Educational Management*. Vol 17, No 4. pp170–8.

PILBEAM, S. and CORBRIDGE, M. (2006) *People resourcing: contemporary HRM in practice*. Harlow: FT/Prentice Hall.

PILBEAM, S. and CORBRIDGE, M. (2010) *People resourcing and talent management*. 4th ed. Harlow: FT/Prentice Hall.

POLLITT, D. (2007) Scottish and Southern Energy slashes staff attrition. *Human Resource Management International Digest*. Vol 15, No 17. pp14–17.

QUILLIAM, G. (1995) *Body language*. Godalming: Carlton Books.

REES, G. and FRENCH, R. (eds) (2011) *Leading, managing and developing people*. London: CIPD.

RISHER, H. (2003) Refocusing performance management for high performance. *Compensation and Benefits Review*. Vol 35, No 5. pp20–30.

ROBBINS, S. and HUNSAKER, P. (2009) *Training in interpersonal skills*. 5th ed. London: Pearson.

ROBERSON, Q.M. and STEWART, M.M. (2006) Understanding the motivational effects of procedural and informational justice in the feedback process. *British Journal of Psychology*. Vol 97, No 3. pp281–98.

ROBERTS, C. and CAMPBELL, S. (2006) *Talk on trial: job interviews, language and ethnicity*. Research Report No 344. London: Department for Work and Pensions.

ROBERTSON, I. and SMITH, M. (2001) Personnel selection. *Journal of Occupational and Organisational Psychology*. Vol 74, No 4. pp441–72.

RUSSELL, K. (2010) How to address poor performance. *People Management*. 25 November.

SCHORR HIRSCH, M. (2007) Getting to the truth of the matter. *People Management*. Vol 13, No 9. p46.

SELVARAJAN, T.T. and CLONINGER, P.A. (2008) The importance of accurate performance appraisals for creating ethical organisations. *Journal of Applied Business Research*. Vol 24, No 3. pp39–44.

SELVARAJAN, T.T. and CLONINGER, P.A. (2009) The influence of job performance outcomes on ethical assessments. *Personnel Review*. Vol 38, No 4. pp398–412.

SELVARAJAN, T.T. and CLONINGER, P.A. (2012) Can performance appraisals motivate employees to improve performance? A Mexican study. *International Journal of Human Resource Management*. Vol 23, No 5. pp3063–84.

SILVESTER, J. and CHAPMAN, A.J. (1996) Unfair discrimination in the selection interview: an attribution account. *International Journal of Selection and Assessment*. Vol 4, No 2. pp63–70.

SORIANO, K. (2007) Appraisals seen as a 'box-ticking' exercise. *People Management*. 3 December.

SRIVASTAVA, J.N. and LURIE, L. (2001) A consumer perspective on price matching refund policies: effect on price perceptions and search behaviour. *Journal of Consumer Research*. Vol 28. pp296–307.

STOSKOPF, G.A. (2002) Taking performance management to the next level. *Workspan*. Vol 45, No 2. pp28–30.

SUFF, R. (2008) Background checks in recruitment: employers' current methods. *IRS Employment Review*. 17 April.

SUTHERLAND, M. and JORDAAN, W. (2004) Factors affecting the retention of knowledge workers. *South African Journal of Human Resource Management*. Vol 2, No 2. pp112–23.

SUTHERLAND, M. and WOCKE, A. (2011) The symptoms of and consequences to selection errors in recruitment decisions. *South African Journal of Business Management*. Vol 42, No 4. pp23–32.

SWINBURNE, P. (2001) How to use feedback to improve performance. *People Management*. 3 December.

TORRINGTON, D., HALL, L., and TAYLOR, S. (2011) *Human resource management*. 7th ed. Harlow: FT/Prentice Hall.

VICK, B. and WALSH, D. (2010) Happy about LinkedIn for recruiting [online]. Available at: http://deswalsh.com/book/lifr.pdf [Accessed 7 August 2013].

WALLEY, L. and SMITH, M. (1998) *Deception in selection*. Chichester: Wiley.

WALTON, R. and MCKERSIE, R. (1965) *A behavioral theory of labor negotiations*. New York: McGraw-Hill.

WILK, S. and CAPPELLI, P. (2003) Understanding the determinants of employer use of selection methods. *Personnel Psychology*. Vol 56, No 1. pp103–24.

WILTON, N. (2011) *An introduction to human resource management*. London: Sage.

CHAPTER 11

Leadership and Team Dynamics

Gillian Watson

OVERVIEW

Leading a team can be a considerable challenge as there are complex team dynamics at play that need to be handled skilfully. This chapter seeks to help you to understand and apply the attributes and skills required to lead successfully in the team environment in order to enhance the team's performance. Building on our discussion of teamwork in Chapter 8 and the political organisation in Chapter 9, we will focus on team leadership and, in particular, on leadership, delegation, chairing meetings and co-ordinating discussions, resolving conflict between team members as well as on decision-making.

LEARNING OUTCOMES

By the end of this chapter, provided you engage with the activities, you should be able to:

- understand the key aspects of leadership in a team environment
- apply people's skills to the management of staff in work teams
- understand how team leadership can enhance performance
- understand the characteristics of effective meetings
- apply appropriate modes of handling conflict.

11.1 INTRODUCTION

Teams have a central role in organisations as they can improve the creative and innovative potential of an organisation as well as its overall performance. But teams do not just happen; they need to be purposefully created and constantly maintained through social relationships. Although all team members are collectively responsible for the working and outcome of their team, the team leader has a particular role to play. They have to lead by example, manage the collective processes and resolve conflict whenever necessary within the constraints of the organisation's rules, procedures and control structures. In many instances, the team leader faces a balancing act between ensuring that tasks get done and maintaining the team's morale and productivity. There are different styles of leadership that team leaders can employ to do so and it is their responsibility to choose the right approach for a particular situation.

'People skills' such as fostering collective effort, building cohesion and morale in teams and effectively resolving interpersonal conflicts are an intrinsic part of the team leader's role. An experienced team leader is able to relate well to others, to build trust, manage conflict, promote participation and to design and chair meetings. Very importantly, team leaders are responsible for developing leadership skills within their team, thus contributing to the development of staff within their organisation. Effective team leaders engage with and empower their employees and in that way reduce dissonance between individuals and groups within the organisation. More importantly, quality team leadership through engagement with others is a significant predictor of performance in organisations (Alimo-Metcalfe et al 2007). However, such a style of team leadership needs to be supported by the organisation's culture and systems (Alimo-Metcalfe and Bradley 2008).

It has become accepted wisdom to distinguish between management and leadership. *Management* is generally associated with efficiency, planning, procedures, regulations and control. *Leadership*, in contrast, is associated with providing direction, guidance and vision (Gabriel 2008). The latter is sometimes connected to self-knowledge (Boyatsis et al 2008), as the Greek oracle temple in Delphi had inscribed upon it 'know thyself'. Boyatsis et al (2008) argue that understanding oneself is a precursor to understanding one's dreams and aspirations, without which one cannot create a vision for a team nor lead convincingly.

Throughout history, the study of leadership has employed different methodologies that reflect the prevalent thinking in different periods of time. However, the focus was invariably on a leader's personal characteristics, such as charisma. Greek themes help us again when remembering the term 'charisma' as it comes from classical Greek, meaning 'gift', and traditionally charismatic leaders were seen to derive their authority from their personal qualities such as self-confidence and their ability to communicate with others. In organisations, charismatic leaders help to develop a vision, energise action by setting high expectations and enable others to become effective. The concept of charismatic leadership remains a popular subject in management writing and even among managers.

However, there are other approaches to leadership that have long been identified, and this chapter will provide you with an overview of the most important ones. We will also look at team decision-making, effective conduct of team meetings, team problem-solving and handling conflict in a team environment.

11.2 APPROACHES TO LEADERSHIP

Leadership, good or bad, is often cited in general conversation and the media as the cause for a positive or negative performance by the organisation. You only have to view the leadership of any football club to realise how tenuous the position really is. Notwithstanding Sir Alex Ferguson, formerly manager of English football club Manchester United, whose longevity is now legend, most football club managers do not survive for over 30 years in the job; they are used as modern-day scapegoats for failure to achieve expectations and results. Likewise, heads of industry may lose their positions through lack of performance in the marketplace. Heads of governments also suffer from the ups and downs of the economy as its shifting position may mean 'boom' in one parliament and 'bust' in another. The leader who we embrace as a hero or honour as a statesmen is a rarity.

The cogent or rational point of view, however, prevails in most organisations as we distinguish between (1) what a leader can achieve in a particular business environment with a distinct workforce, and (2) what is unfeasible or impractical at a specific moment in the organisation's history. We tend to view leadership behaviour, therefore, as part of the most significant stimuli an organisation may possess while recognising that it is not the only factor that leads to success.

Theorists have often created distinct demarcations between leaders and managers in organisations. For example, managers may have been seen as defending the status quo, traditionally maintaining the organisation and what it stands for. Leadership, on the other hand, has been linked to transition and change, exhibiting a more vibrant agenda that energises their organisations. Whetten and Cameron (2011) describe this as leaders 'doing the right things' and managers as 'doing things right'. They contend that in today's business environment such clear distinctions should no longer apply as leaders must be seen as good managers and managers as showing relevant leadership behaviours to be deemed successful. Managers no longer have the confident position of maintaining the equilibrium; they must be active in progressing their teams/organisations forward by making the appropriate decisions, in other words 'do the right things'. Whetten and Cameron (2011, p560) state: 'No organisation in a post-industrial, hyper-turbulent, twenty-first-century environment will survive without individuals capable of providing both management and leadership.' Consequently, leading and managing in a contemporary workplace requires skills which are synonymous to both undertakings.

Another less conventional thought is postulated by Quinn (2004), who argues that we display leadership behaviours on a transient basis, that is, not all the time. Notwithstanding someone's position in an organisation, they may assume a definite attitude or frame of mind that elevates them into displaying leadership attributes. Therefore, this notion corresponds with the idea that mangers ought to also be leaders or undeniably show leadership behaviours when that is justified or necessitated. Although these theories are questionable, Quinn's (2004) main contentions are that 'anyone can be a leader' and that 'most of the time none of us are leaders'. However, this does lead us into the judgement that leadership is not something we are born with; rather, it becomes a set of attributes we can develop.

11.3 HISTORICAL VIEW OF LEADERSHIP

There have been many attempts over the last decades to understand what leadership is and how leaders can be distinguished from followers. The *trait approach* to leadership was one of the earliest attempts to shed light on the mysterious and somewhat nebulous concept of leadership. It suggests that leaders have particular personality traits that distinguish them from the rest of the population, which has given it the nickname 'great person theory' (Barker 2001). The traits that have been identified (as summarised by Clegg et al 2005) include:

- self-confidence
- a drive for achievement
- honesty, integrity
- the ability to motivate people towards a common goal
- intelligence
- creativity
- the ability to adapt.

While certain traits have been identified as being present in good leaders (House et al 2004), there is no evidence to suggest that leaders are born. In fact, it is far more likely that leaders gain their skill and knowledge over time. Moreover, trait theory holds little predictive value, since leaders can be only understood in the context in which they operate. A leader may be excellent in one organisation and fail in another, and again, football managers are a good example.

The trait approach to leadership was followed by the *situational approach*, in which leadership is regarded as emerging from the situation. In a formal group, an appointed leader achieves their legitimacy from the position they hold, while emergent leaders achieve their authority from the group members (Brown 1965, Turner 1991, Gross 1993).

The *behavioural approaches* attempt to identify behaviours associated with leadership. Likert (1961) studied patterns of behaviours that result in effective group performance and identified two basic orientations that leaders engage in to influence their subordinates: relationship-oriented and task-oriented behaviours. Relationship-oriented leaders build trust, show respect and generally care about their employees. These leaders are concerned with developing good relations with their subordinates and in return tend to be liked and respected. Task-oriented leaders, on the other hand, are primarily concerned with employees performing at their best so that the job gets done. Both leadership behaviours are independent variables, thus supervisors can be high or low on both orientations.

Fiedler's (1971) theory of leadership, also known as the *contingency theory*, incorporates the situation and the group as key variables in effective leadership. The leader's effectiveness is seen as contingent upon the situation, and it is the situation that determines if a leader is successful. In Fiedler's contingency model, the following variables are considered as the key determinants of leadership effectiveness:

- The *relations structure* determines how much workers like and trust their leader.
- The *task structure* determines the extent to which employee tasks are made clear, and how positive the situation is for effective leadership.
- The *position power structure* (legitimate, reward and coercive power, see Chapter 9 for details) determines a leader's ability to influence. When the leader's position power is strong, their leadership effectiveness becomes more influential.

Fiedler's model purports to identify situations in which different managers have the opportunity to perform at their best. The preferred leadership style is relatively stable (Adamson 1997), and managers are likely to be effective when:

- They are placed in situations that suit their leadership style; or
- The situation is adapted to fit the manager's leadership style.

Fiedler's contingency model further proposes the following steps of an effective influencing approach:

1   clearly defined job outcomes

2   rewards for high performance and goal attainment must correlate with employees' value

3   obstacles to effective performance must be removed

4   confidence in employee's ability must be shown.

Transformational leadership focuses on the basic difference between leading for stability and leading for change. In particular, effective leaders are able to recognise and guide organisational changes (Burns 1978). Transactional leaders, on the other hand, are known for their use of reward and coercive powers to encourage high performance from employees.

The *collective or substitute leadership approach* assumes situations where the need for leadership is superfluous (Sims 1987). Collective leadership arises from accepting the following:

- characteristics of the employees with their skills, experience and motivation
- characteristics of the context in which work is interesting, challenging and satisfying
- employee empowerment or self-managed work teams, and
- awareness that there is not always the need to directly exert influence over others.

11.4 A FRAMEWORK FOR LEADING DYNAMIC TEAMS

At this stage the chapter will review several leadership attributes that are an amalgamation of many skills that arguably constitute the elements necessary to enable successful leadership and team management behaviours. A framework for developing such attributes is provided in Figure 11.1.

Figure 11.1 A framework for leading dynamic teams

Whether an individual is leading a top team or leading as a middle/first-line manager, these criteria will be useful as the skills needed are relevant to all. Table 11.1 helps extrapolate and categorise some of these issues.

Table 11.1 Extrapolation of the framework for leading dynamic teams

Extrapolation of the framework for leading dynamic teams	
Creating an affirming team dynamic	<ul><li>create a dynamic and encouraging interaction</li><li>assure consideration and empathy among team members</li><li>identify and shape the strength of the team</li></ul>
Prepare the team	<ul><li>review the good performances and practices within the team</li><li>representational/critical incident</li><li>team identity</li></ul>
Communicate innovation	<ul><li>create a vision of the team identity</li><li>foster credibility</li><li>think creatively</li></ul>
Engender dedication and responsibility	<ul><li>employ social attitude</li><li>facilitate team/company-wide commitment</li><li>step-by-step strategy of success</li></ul>
Consolidate the team's community of practice	<ul><li>facilitate team development</li><li>grow 'human capital' and talent</li><li>create goals and capture and monitor the team's progress</li></ul>

11.4.1 CREATING AN AFFIRMING TEAM DYNAMIC

The main focus here is to engender a positive and affirming attitude within the team. This is much harder than it might first appear as the tendency in most managed environments is to focus on the negative rather than the positive: leadership is being shown when the affirming dynamic is prevalent. Baumeister et al (2001) suggested that a critical, disapproving standpoint (which, alas, many managers take) is counterproductive as it has a prolonged negative influence on both individual and team. Their research recommended that 'bad' stimulus is more powerful than 'good', indicating that leaders need to be tenacious when intending to concentrate on optimistic and encouraging phenomena rather than allowing inconveniences, pressures and impediment to cloud and obscure the team's behaviours. An exemplar of affirming behaviour is presented by Mahatma Gandhi:

> Keep your thoughts positive, because your thoughts become your words. Keep your words positive, because your words become your behaviour. Keep your behaviour positive because your behaviour becomes your habits. Keep your habits positive because your habits become your values. Keep your values positive, because your values become your destiny. (Source: http://goodreads.com, Accessed 30 September 2013)

Therefore, in order to attempt to engender and 'create an affirming team dynamic', the following three factors may help in realising that goal.

1   **Create a dynamic and encouraging interaction**
    Baker et al (2003) maintain that people they describe as 'positive energisers' have the ability to enable others to achieve enhanced results as well as being high-achievers themselves. These individuals do not show negativity such as neglecting to engage, exhibiting self-centeredness, lacking in enthusiasm and suffusing an aura of pessimism or disapproval. They do, however, exhibit behaviours that are self-motivating, offer supportive comments to colleagues and create good interpersonal relationships. They are respected and trusted, and are accommodating and open-minded pragmatists. In short, they offer other team members a role model to follow, they form friendships within the group and are often seen to be rewarded by their managers.

2   **Assure consideration and empathy among team members**
    In order to show empathy, an individual must first understand the issues at play. We encounter situations every day in our working lives where managers do not show consideration, forgiveness or compassion for their workforce. We all have lives outside work as well as inside the organisation that can impinge on our ability to do the job; we feel anguish, encounter prejudice or unfairness, have failed relationships and have difficulties coping. All those problems and more besides may need to be dealt with by the team leader. The team needs a solid platform on which to build; therefore, before this can take place, creating an assuring, considerate even empathetic environment may support the overall team dynamic.

    Leadership is always carried out within a particular context where the team leader seeks to influence people and events to ensure organisational goals are met. Ford (2010) adds to this debate by asserting that leadership is personal and that some of the prevalent influencing factors are psychosocial and the leader's own sense of self. Therefore, a level of what Goleman (1998) describes as 'emotional intelligence' is needed. He explains the five components of 'emotional intelligence' as: self-awareness, self-regulation, motivation, empathy and social skills (see also Chapter 5). All of these competencies are potential contributors to the leader's involvement and commitment to the team dynamic.

However, this is not to infer that all team leaders can display such positive attitudes and behaviours. In fact, most of us rarely work in an environment where such behaviours are commonplace. However, team members do benefit from surroundings where there is a climate of concern and empathy for workers, and it is a worthy developmental goal for practising and aspiring leaders.

3 **Identify and shape the strength of the team**
There are many techniques regarding identifying and shaping a team, and some of those perspectives are mentioned in Chapter 8. Here, however, the main factors under discussion are in relation to engaging and assessing expectations: characteristics that are in many respects shaping the team to play to their strengths. This involves new and innovative ways of working and, above all, it involves thinking and actions that help transmit an 'out with the old and in with the new' attitude.

11.4.2 PREPARE THE TEAM

The team leader needs to actively engage the team in preparation for changing work processes, new product development or to enhance existing performances. Whichever the issues, team leaders need to prepare the team for a range of eventualities.

11.4.2.1 Review good performances and practices within the team

One of the methods of identifying what the team does or is capable of doing is to evaluate performance, specifically assessing the team performance with standards that are considered to be high and of good quality (please refer to Chapter 10 for a discussion of performance management). Essentially, the team leader would engage in instilling best practice into all the work practices related to the team and consequently in preparing team members to surpass those benchmarks. However, those elevated practices do need to be appropriate and able to be reached.

11.4.2.2 Representational critical incident analysis

In many respects this element is about creating a critical incident that the team remembers as helping to represent their moving ahead as a team rather than just being a group of individuals (see also our discussion in Chapter 8). It may be represented in a positive affirming manner, for example it could be an award (either external or internal) or it could be that the team are trusted to take on a new project within their department. Whatever the incident, the team leader must ensure it is marked either by an emblem of some kind that is hung on a wall or by a visual representation on each member's workstation.

11.4.2.3 Team identity

The concept of team identity is not new; however, it is one of those ideals to which we often return in our attempts to instil connections, that is, the social glue that enables the team to form good work relationships. It can be considered motivational as it also unites individual goals with that of the team. The notions that 'we are in this together' and 'we are working for each other' are those that should prevail.

11.4.3 COMMUNICATE INNOVATION

Here the emphasis is on 'making a difference' by showing that the team is successful and capable of tackling whatever the future holds. The team leader therefore should communicate values, the vision for the future and that the team is able to innovate. It shows a desire to drive creative ideas which will have a positive impact upon the department or organisation.

11.4.3.1 Create a vision of the team identity

The issues here relate to how the team views itself, and how they are perceived by others. In essence, are they communicating what they stand for?

Firstly, we should be clear how the term vision is being used here. The vision includes the values and guiding ethics and principles that dictate the team's behaviours. The vision should generate meaningful guidelines for the team to follow and provide an optimistic outlook in which members can believe. These ideals are more than just goals or targets set for a mission statement; they are intended to enable the team to think about themselves in a more positive manner. This in turn will help cement team identity. For a discussion on individual professional identity, please refer to Chapter 5; you may wish to consider the implications on team identity.

11.4.3.2 Foster credibility

Maslow (1954) included 'belonging' in his hierarchy of motivation and achievement, establishing that we all desire to 'belong' to something or someone. This need is powerful; however, the object of that desire must hold credibility. The notion of credibility connects the team to: upholding its 'core values' as well as communicating an uncomplicated, unpretentious message. It is not only what the team believe of them, but also what others in the organisation believe about the team.

11.4.3.3 Think creatively

Encouraging innovative thinking and allowing creativity to flourish is a key aspect of leading a dynamic team. Therefore, this section seeks to give practical suggestions as to how the team might explore 'thinking creatively' about the team. It is important to consider two distinct ways in which we think. Neuroscientists maintain we think with the right- and left-brain viewpoint; they attribute certain ways of thinking to each.

The right side of the brain, which controls the left side of the body, is the artistic, non-rational cognitive domain that commands intuition, imagination, emotions as well as creativity. Left-brain thinking is deemed to control deductive, logical and numeric thinking that helps us with rational analysis and mathematical problem-solving; it also controls the right side of the body – although both must act together to enable complicated and creative endeavour to take place. Consider the grid in Activity 11.1; it depicts right- and left-brain thinking.

 ACTIVITY 11.1

Statements showing right-/left-brain thinking

It is largely accepted wisdom that we think with both hemispheres of the brain. In groups or your work teams, discuss and make a judgement of the statements in the grid – decide whether they have been devised from a right or left side of the brain standpoint.

Statements	Left side	Right side
Define the organisation's notable strong point		
Do we have any strategic advantages? If so, what?		
What are the significant problems that we must deal with?		

Does anything stand in the way of change for the better?		
Define the foremost resources that we need.		
What information do we require?		
What indicates top performance?		
Indicate what constitutes our greatest level of performance.		
Tell us the legends and significant memories that define us.		
Indicate an analogy that allows us to see a vision of what the future might hold for the organisation.		
What icons or pictorial elements help to indicate our core values?		

11.4.4 ENGENDER DEDICATION AND RESPONSIBILITY

The dedication, ethical beliefs, passion and level of responsibility we bring to our jobs are often determined by our personal attitudes but also by the values we consider to be core to the organisation's overarching philosophy (see also Chapter 5).

11.4.4.1 Employ a social attitude

There is a fine balance to be struck here that the team leader must take into account. On the one hand, the company will be urging the accomplishment of the team's aims, while simultaneously leadership is being shown when the interpersonal relationships in the team are central to their core values. This links to how people feel concerning their working lives: are they contented, happy, invigorated or enthusiastic about their situation? The more positive the outlook of members of the team, the more likely it is that this in turn can generate commitment. Therefore, promoting a good social network or attitude within the team may help achieve wide-ranging team goals.

Goleman (1998, cited in Torrington et al 2011) suggests emotional competencies are pertinent here, for as well as highlighting self-awareness, self-regulation and motivation, he also construes empathy and social skills to be significant. From Goleman's five aspects of 'emotional intelligence', the following two are relevant here:

- *empathy* – considering employees' feelings alongside other factors when decision-making
- *social skills* – friendliness with a purpose, being good at finding common ground and building rapport.

Hence, leaders who employ a social attitude have the potential to be good at collaborating with others, find ways to influence, and have the talent to display a variety of interactive practice that ultimately bolsters their team's achievements.

11.4.4.2 Facilitate team/companywide commitment

Organisations have a diverse assortment of methods by which they choose to communicate with their workforce in order to gain commitment. This may be manifested in a top–down scenario or a set-piece performance where a very senior individual (or groups of senior managers) briefs a large gathering of staff. Nevertheless, the team leader needs to ensure information flow and that there is reciprocity in commitment to the overall goals. Some methods of achieving this include:

- team email, a round-up of team and company news

- suggestion box, by which new and/or innovative ideas can be aired
- attitude surveys, in which many organisations engage, albeit as a company-wide process; it usually offers an insight into how workers truly feel as it is often conducted anonymously
- consultation, to which organisations resort after a dispute rather than consulting if or when changes are deemed necessary – consulting team members before a potential problem occurs is perhaps more in keeping with employing a social attitude. Indeed, taking this notion forward would indicate that the team would even be consulted in order to aid managerial decision-making (see also Chapter 16 on problem-solving and decision-making).

11.4.4.3 Step-by-step strategy of success

We all want to be successful; however, success needs to be built and then consolidated. Accepted wisdom tells us that there is no such thing as overnight success. Hence, the step-by-step method helps create incremental elements of achievement that promote successful outcomes. To initiate this, the team leader would select a step, idea or process that either the team all agree and want or that is easy to achieve. The team then works towards the first aim. If successful, the team leader initiates the next aim, and so on.

Figure 11.2 Steps to success

The process builds on the team's successes, empowering ongoing achievement and in so doing creating a culture where the team expects to achieve and they are acknowledged for their efforts.

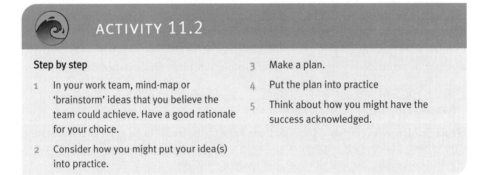

ACTIVITY 11.2

Step by step

1 In your work team, mind-map or 'brainstorm' ideas that you believe the team could achieve. Have a good rationale for your choice.

2 Consider how you might put your idea(s) into practice.

3 Make a plan.

4 Put the plan into practice

5 Think about how you might have the success acknowledged.

11.4.5 CONSOLIDATE THE TEAM'S COMMUNITY OF PRACTICE

Much of the discussion in this section so far has concentrated on enabling the team leader to build and enhance the achievements of the team. However, creating a well-functioning team needs active and focused participation of all team members. Their community of practice therefore must be coherent and to some extent synchronise with whatever goals and aspirations, to which collectively, the team embraces.

Here the term 'community of practice' is used to express the desire of most individuals to belong to a group or team where they feel valued in relation to their particular expertise. Perhaps this is a goal we all strive to achieve. Conceivably, it is also a component of a community of practice (Wenger et al 2002) that when actioned it will enable a fit between both personal motivators and professional norms.

11.4.5.1 Facilitate team development

As HR tasks (including staff development) continue to be dispersed to line managers/team leaders, the task of deciding who takes up development opportunities is part of that role (for a more detailed discussion of training, learning and development, please refer to Chapter 6). Leadership of teams may also carry the expectation that mentoring and/or coaching the members may be part of that role, which is discussed in more detail in Chapter 7.

Two essential issues worthy of emphasis here are: (1) the need for targeted team development and (2) personal and professional development plans linked to team goals. Figure 11.3 highlights some of the valuable development issues that can be accomplished; both elements are complementary.

Figure 11.3 Essential issues in team development

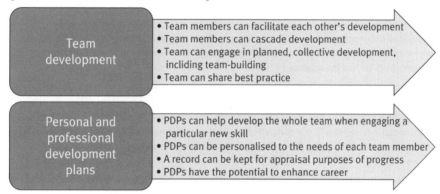

Teams need constant development opportunities to enable them to continue enhancing their skills; as they do this they create a high-performing and dynamic culture.

11.4.5.2 Grow human capital and talent

Organisations use the human capital at their disposal, which indicates they use the skills and talents of the workforce to enhance the business. To enable this they either develop existing talent or hire new members. When relating these matters to teams, there is no exception. The human capital of the team, therefore, is the foundation of quality performances, growth and enhancement, which has an impact upon the future potential of the organisation. In essence it can facilitate longevity. Team members working in such an environment learn to act on their own initiative, are motivated, creative and are able to take on leadership roles themselves.

11.4.5.3 Create goals and capture and monitor the team's progress.

As well as many of the aspects of team enhancement we have discussed thus far, it is necessary to also have mechanisms for measuring and monitoring progress. Quite simply, this enables the team leader and their managers to assess how well the team is performing.

Performance indicators and an array of measurement tools have become an essential part of organisational life. This can be achieved by:

1   Ensuring that there are performance indicators that address two outcomes that stipulate the end results which are desirable to achieve – they link to the core element of a particular job or project; essentially they address the outcome that is required.

2   Selecting a measurement tool, that is, ensuring that data is collected at the relevant times and in the most appropriate manner – elements may include time of delivery (of a project or report, etc), speed and accuracy (in production or service delivery), and the quality of their work as well as the speed would be in synergy.

3   Creating goals, monitoring and assessing progress of the team or its individual members are linked to their professional development. We could call it a signpost where overall achievement is calculated, possibly by the end of three months.

Team members will rightly expect to be remunerated for their work, particularly any work they do on top of their contractual agreement. The CIPD survey *Aligning Strategy and Pay* (2012) reveals relevant links to pay, reward and development (see Box 11.1).

Box 11.1: HR outcomes

Our results imply that transparency of pay arrangements in respondent organisations was associated with more positive employee relations climates. Organisations with good ER climates were also more likely to operate performance-related reward schemes but have lower median total earnings for non-management grades.

For labour productivity, our findings show that organisations with better productivity than competitors are more likely to use competencies and skills as pay progression criteria for non-management grades. Organisations that have seen labour productivity increase in the past three years are also more likely to use competencies as pay progression criteria for managers. However, they were also more likely to have lower median total earnings for non-management grades.

Source: reproduced with kind permission from CIPD 2012

The passage in Box 11.1 endorses the need for measurements and performance indicators to assess not only developmental progress but also recommendation for adequate reward and pay.

 ACTIVITY 11.3

Leading dynamic teams

Discuss the following questions, preferably in groups:

1   Do we always need leadership in teams?

2   Consider a team in which you have worked: does the team leadership you experienced coincide with any of the scenarios proposed above?

3   Did the team in which you were a member engage in specific team-building? Why or why not?

4   What measure or performance indicators are used in your organisation? Consider the merits and limitations of this system.

11.5 EMPOWERING THE TEAM

Empowerment can be of benefit to managers, since empowered employees feel they are an integral part of the organisation. This then increases employees' motivation levels, which reflects back on the manager by releasing them from controlling to concentrate on other activities. This notion of empowering and engaging staff conforms to Alimo-Metcalfe et al's (2007) research of how staff perceive the quality of leadership displayed by their team leaders. These are categorised as having three dimensions: engaging with others, visionary leadership and leadership capabilities (Alimo-Metcalfe et al 2007, Alimo-Metcalfe and Bradley 2008). Table 11.2 sets out to show the 'how' or by 'what' method these dimensions could be addressed as well as the effect they would have on a staff team.

Table 11.2 How staff perceive the quality of leadership

Dimension	'What'	'How'	Effect on the team
Leadership capabilities	• Understanding and using overall strategy to achieve goals and objectives. • Ensuring clarity of roles. • The goals and/or targets and criteria of success. • Establishing, maintaining and being committed to high standards of service delivery and quality outcomes. • Having well-thought-out systems and procedures that support the effective use of resources.		• Motivation, job satisfaction, strong sense of team effectiveness.
Visionary leadership		• Having a clear vision of what the team was aiming for. • Being sensitive to the agenda of a wide range of stakeholders. • Inspiring them with the team's passion and determination.	• Significantly positive effect on motivation, and on aspects of well-being, a sense of fulfilment. Also the researchers reported this approach reduced stress and exhaustion.

Dimension	'What'	'How'	Effect on the team
Engaging with others		<ul><li>Concern for the needs of staff.</li><li>Empowering them by trusting them to take decisions.</li><li>Listening to others' ideas and being willing to accommodate them.</li><li>Finding time to discuss problems and issues despite being very busy.</li><li>Support others by coaching and mentoring.</li><li>Inspiring all staff to contribute fully to the work of the team.</li><li>Actively promoting the achievements of the team to the outside world.</li></ul>	<ul><li>Significantly affected all aspects of positive attitudes to work, and all aspects of well-being, a strong sense of team spirit backed by the organisational culture.</li></ul>

Source: adapted from Alimo-Metcalfe and Bradley 2008

The importance of engagement and the need for a supportive organisational culture highlighted in Table 11.2 are supported by Boyatsis et al (2008), although their research leads them to advocate the importance of optimism, honesty and emotional intelligence (Goleman et al 2002) as leadership attributes, which, they add, can be learned. However, their current thinking is endorsing and even encouraging managers to become 'resonant leaders' (Boyatsis et al 2008), the opposite of which is dissonance. Obviously, dissonant environments would be classed as negative places to work in which, they suggest, emotions such as fear, anxiety, anger, pessimism and individualism would abound. In such environments, leadership would be characterised as command and control, possibly micro-management and a lack of trust. However, in environments where resonant leadership is practised we could expect 'powerful collective energy that reverberates among people and supports higher productivity, creativity, a sense of purpose and better results' (Boyatsis et al 2008, pp8–24). Boyatsis et al (2008, pp8–24) further suggest that 'resonant leaders need to know what inhibits effective individual and team performance and how to address these issues. In other words leadership requires emotional and social intelligence and a deep understanding of social systems – and the people in them – must work together to achieve complex and challenging goals'.

Leading teams, therefore, is complex, challenging and engaging. To be successful, it requires positive participation from team members and their managers alike.

11.6 PARTICIPATIVE DECISION-MAKING

The participative management approach used in organisations today reflects the values embraced by the world's developed democratic societies. The concept of democracy became a basis for the human relations management model after Elton Mayo's research at the Western Electric Company between 1924 and 1934 (also known as 'the Hawthorne Studies') became generally known and accepted. The human relations model focuses on the following three areas of group functioning: (1) commitment, (2) cohesion and (3) morale, where the key values are participation, consensus-building and conflict resolution. Participative decision-making should be evident in the following areas:

- the decision-making processes
- decisions about who should participate, to what extent and when
- effectively managed meetings.

Supervisors constantly face decisions regarding their own and their subordinates' work by deciding when it is appropriate and to what degree to involve employees in the day-to-day operations. The boundaries of the decision-making process are determined by the overall organisational structure and the degree of authority a manager holds. In terms of competitive advantage, participative decision-making offers two broad benefits to organisations. Firstly, the front-line employees possess detailed knowledge concerning their work and thus have the competency to take decisions. Secondly, the more information is shared among employees, the better the decision-making outcomes.

In Figure 11.4, the decision-making process is expressed as a bipolar continuum with the *individual decision-maker* (control orientation) positioned at one extreme end and the *participative decision-making* at the other. At the control-oriented end decisions are made by the top management without involving the employees. At the opposite end decisions are made by employees. In reality, participative decision-making always takes place within the boundaries determined by management (Lawler 1992).

Figure 11.4 Decision-making in organisations

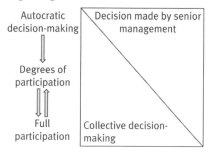

There is no general agreement on whether managers functioning as individual decision-makers are more or less effective than functioning as members of decision-making teams. The collective knowledge of a team is diverse and exceeds that of any individual. Team decision-making offers more approaches to decision-making, but team consensus takes longer to reach and high team cohesiveness has been found inherently problematic. Further, pooled judgements of non-experts were found less competent than those of a best-qualified team member and team members were found to accept risk and uncertainty more readily than individual decision-makers. There is a general belief that greater participation in decision-making increases the acceptance of the final choice (Janis 1982, Campbell 1968, Stoner 1968, Tattersall 1984).

An example of individual decision-making is Roger Carr, chairman of Cadbury, the British confectionery company founded in Birmingham in 1831. Carr negotiated a hostile takeover bid by the American Kraft Foods and secured a 'good' price for the company and recommended that the shareholders accept the settlement. In an interview, he stated that, as a chairman, he was employed and paid by shareholders to get the best deal for them, and in modern financial markets, £11 billion is considered a good deal. The winners of this deal are the senior managers, who will get pay-offs or bonuses; the fund managers, whose performance (and therefore remuneration) will be boosted by a short-term blip as a result of selling out to a hostile bidder; and the bankers and lawyers, who have made bumper fees (over £200 million) out of the whole business, 'as per usual' (Corrigan 2010). The likely losers are Cadbury employees losing their job, the UK taxpayers that will finance the redundancy benefits, and Kraft Foods, who took on considerable debt to finance the takeover. Cadbury's chairman confirmed to the BBC that job losses are inevitable. Workers past and present voiced their concerns, with some describing the move as 'a disgrace'; while others believe the brand's profile could grow in the US (BBC News, Corrigan 2010).

ACTIVITY 11.4

Managing the Kraft Foods takeover of Cadbury

You are a newly appointed line manager at Kraft Foods. You have been briefed to use the concept of participative decision-making during the process of streamlining Cadbury operations in line with those of Kraft Foods.

- Where shall you begin?
- What do you need to know?
- Who do you need to talk to?

You already have a fair understanding of how your unit feels about the changes and also of the overall morale among your staff.

- What do you need to achieve?
- How will you go about it?

Write a short in-progress report to your superiors stating your objectives, actions and times of implementation.

Then answer the following questions:

1. How difficult did you find the activity?

2. How easy was it to use the participative approach in this particular situation?

3. What interpersonal skills did you find most useful?

4. What in particular did you find difficult?

5. How useful were your past experiences?

Using Figure 11.4, decide where you position yourself in managing the above situation. Remember, there are both advantages and disadvantages in involving employees in the decision-making process. The approach cannot be arbitrative, but depends on the context of socio-cultural values, the nature of the workforce and the external environment.

GROUP DECISION-MAKING AT A GLASS MANUFACTURING COMPANY

CASE STUDY 11.1

Douglas McDougal, a manufacturing line manager, was sent by his medium-sized glass manufacturing company to attend a week-long workshop on participative leadership organised by a well-known and respected training consultancy. Douglas was impressed by the 'hands-on' style of delivery and was active during group discussions and decision-making activities. The workshop's main message was that employees, given the opportunity, would responsibly discuss, and then arrive at, quality decisions.

On return, Douglas decided to follow the principles he had learned at the workshop, and called a meeting with his employees. He frankly discussed the recent low production levels, which he attributed both to the recently introduced new working practices and needing to upgrade the present manufacturing equipment. Without increased production output, the company was unlikely to have a future in today's fierce global competition. After having presented all the possible scenarios on the future of the company, he left his employees to discuss and to decide among themselves what steps are to be taken to remedy the situation. Douglas was confident that the group would find a rational solution that would lead to increased production, and thus ensure the company's future.

After a discussion lasting several hours, Douglas was presented with the group's unanimous decision. The unit's decision was that the working conditions were already far too demanding and, since they were given the authority to decide their own standards, they were making a reduction in output by 5%. Douglas found the decision deeply disappointing, since even the present level of production output would fail to deliver a fair profit on the owner's investment. Without implementing radical changes the

company's future was uncertain. He felt let down and placed in a 'no-win' position since he could not present the decision to the company owners.

Before taking a course of action, Douglas called the workshop organisers to discuss the situation.

Questions

1   What do you think happened at the group meeting?

2   Should Douglas have anticipated the group decision-making outcome? Justify your answer.

3   Given the current situation, was Douglas right to use participative decision-making in this way?

4   What would be your advice to Douglas? Be specific in your suggestions and justify your decision.

Research suggests that team decision-making is beneficial in unpredictable, non-routine and one-off situations, while individual decision-making is more appropriate in routine and recurring situations. Harrison (1995) proposed the following six steps for the full utilisation of both individual and team decision-making strengths:

1   The combined knowledge of team members is superior in setting organisational objectives.

2   In searching for alternatives, pooled individual efforts offer a wide variety of options.

3   The collective judgement is best utilised in evaluating options proposed by individuals.

4   In situations of high risk, the team decision is likely to be accepted as a result of participation of those who will be affected by its consequences.

5   Decisions made by both individuals and teams must be implemented by individual managers, who are then responsible for the outcomes.

6   Follow-up and control procedures also must be carried by individual managers at the point of implementation.

11.7 LEADING MANAGEMENT MEETINGS

Team decision-making more often than not takes place during meetings, even though meetings are not always very popular among staff. Meetings are conducted to inform, instruct and persuade. Barrett (2006, p213) states that 'meetings matter because that's where an organisation's culture perpetuates itself'. Meetings can take many forms and are the settings for communicating strategy, management planning, organising and resolving problems. As meetings take up a significant amount of working time, they need to be effective and productive.

ACTIVITY 11.5

My recent meeting ...

Remind yourself of a recent meeting that you attended and answer the following questions about the meeting:

1 What was the topic of the meeting?

2 Who chaired the meeting?

3 Did you receive an agenda prior to, or at the beginning of, the meeting?

   ● What were the ground rules?
   ● How were the ground rules presented?
   ● Were you satisfied with the procedure?

4 What preparations did you make for the meeting?

5 Did you contribute to the discussion? Was contribution encouraged?

6 Was the meeting well structured?

7 What decisions were taken? Did you agree with them?

8 Were the participants satisfied with the meeting?

9 How was the meeting concluded?

10 Were any follow-up measures proposed?

11 If you chaired the meeting, what differences would you make?

In order to conduct meetings effectively, you need to be able to determine if a meeting is an appropriate forum for your activity in the first place and if it will deliver the desired outcome. Barrett (2006) suggests the four-step approach for small-group meetings in organisations:

1 Deciding if a meeting is the appropriate forum, and when it should take place.

2 Planning a meeting.

3 Conducting a meeting.

4 Managing problems and conflicts.

1 **Deciding if a meeting is the appropriate forum:** One of the first considerations is the purpose, the audience and the desired and likely outcomes. The following questions have to be answered before the next step can take place:

   ● Is a meeting necessary and what is to be accomplished?
   ● Are there other, more suitable alternatives?
   ● What is the expected outcome from the meeting?

2 Once the above questions have been satisfactorily answered, the **meeting can be planned**. The following questions need to be answered:

   ● *Selecting the appropriate participants* – the selected attendees must have an important stake in the outcome of the decision, and contribute towards the meeting objectives' outcomes in terms of diversity and expertise.
   ● *Information and materials needed for the meeting* – an in-advance prepared and distributed agenda with supporting information increases the likelihood of achieving the meeting's planned outcomes.

- The *items on the agenda* to be included need to follow from the objectives. The time for each must be realistic and not allowed to overrun.
- The *place, settings and timing* for the meeting must be appropriate for the purpose. Seating arrangements can be critical in determining the flow of interaction. Holding a meeting in an office carries a different message from using a dedicated room. For example, the organisation's culture may play a part and in some organisations the most senior member of staff in the meeting may always be seated at the head of the table, while others are seated according to rank. If disagreements or hostilities are expected, key individuals can be interspersed around the room to prevent forming power groups, and so on. Timing too is important, and attendees' schedules and commitments should be taken into account.

3   **Conducting a meeting:** For a meeting to be productive, the following activities must take place:

- The meeting must start on time, participants must be introduced to each other if they do not know each other already, the agenda must be presented and any actions agreed on the previous meeting must be discussed. The roles and responsibilities of the leader, the facilitator, the minute-taker and the time-keeper must be determined ahead of or at the beginning of the meeting. The agenda of the meeting must be followed. However, an organisation's culture will often determine the format of a meeting, the decision-making process and the discussion.
- The standing ground rules for each meeting needs to be established. The number of interruptions must be minimised and valid contributions to be encouraged. Again, different organisational cultures may determine whether active participation and contributions are encouraged. Table 11.3 provides a checklist for conducting an effective meeting. Box 11.2 summarises a number of problem-solving activities commonly used by teams. These are a creative way of dealing with unusually complex or politically sensitive problems.

Table 11.3 Checklist for conducting an effective meeting

Checklist issue	Related issue	Tick off when completed
Start on time	Promptness is valued by members of the meeting	
Introduce	The leader The facilitator The minute-taker The time-keeper	
Review the agenda	Check for any relevant adjustments	
Introduce all those attending	Where necessary If the members of the meeting all know each other, this is not necessary If the meeting consists of many employees, this is too time-consuming and inefficient	
Follow the agenda	Deviation can cause annoyance and interrupt the 'flow' of the meeting Also there may be some preparation needed for new or unlisted agenda items	

Checklist issue	Related issue	Tick off when completed
Eliminate or at least minimise interruptions	If the meeting is being conducted in a 'virtual' environment or by Skype, minimise background noise Avoid members conducting aside conversations Unnecessary fidgeting – tapping pens, rustling papers	
Encourage participation	The level of participation depends on – the organisational culture, the purpose of the meeting	
Conclude the meeting	Review the decisions which have been reached Assign tasks or activities which are to be carried out	
At the end of the meeting	Action and responsibilities agreed on at the meeting are to be assigned to appropriate individuals Summarise the meeting, including the assigned deliverables Jointly agree on the date of the next meeting Close the meeting	
After the meeting	Distribute the meeting minutes in a timely manner Follow up on actions in-progress	

Box 11.2: Problem-solving activities for teams

There are many useful activities available to teams for generating new ideas. The activities range from relatively simple ones such as *brainstorming* – a fast generation of an exhaustive list of ideas – to relatively complex ones such as *the scenario*, an evaluation of a preferred alternative at the end of strategic decision-making (see also Chapter 16).

Some of the activities have their basis in the *means end analysis (MEA)* using a general heuristic strategy of gradual reduction in distance between the current situation and the current goal. The major aim of this heuristic is to reduce a problem into manageable parts that are then dealt with by trying different methods, and incorporating progress checks that indicate if the problem-solvers are on the right track (Simon 1979). Another approach is a *state-space theory* developed for use when one situation requires to be changed into another. Here the solution takes a sequence of action akin to travelling along tree branches towards the desired goal (Garnham 1988).

The advantages of team problem-solving activities are two-fold: efficiency and creativity. Efficiency is gained through encouraging teams to work together using a common approach and arriving at a joint solution, which is likely to save time and money (Barrett 2006). Creativity utilises knowledge, intellectual abilities and personality characteristics, such as self-confidence and an ability to handle criticism (Godfrey 1986).

1   **Brainstorming** is a technique intended to produce new ideas and solutions to problems new to the organisation by simulating creativity and encouraging group members to build on the contributions from others (see also Chapter 16).

Session 1:

- Team members are presented with a problem.
- The team members then generate ideas with brief explanations.
- Each idea, however risky or impractical, is recorded for all to see.
- No evaluating comments are allowed.
- Each member is asked to generate as many ideas as possible.

Session 2:

- The alternative ideas are evaluated for their usefulness.
- The team members then end up with a few realistic alternatives.

Brainstorming is unlikely to provide resolutions to problems; it provides a few realistic alternatives for further consideration.

2   **The nominal group technique (NGT)** is used in a later stage of brainstorming by offering a means with which to identify a problem and select appropriate criteria for evaluating alternatives.

- The team convenes to address an issue.
- Each individual writes a list of ideas. The activity is timed.
- Team members present their ideas to the rest. This could be done anonymously if appropriate.
- All the ideas are recorded for all to see.
- More ideas are generated from the shared list.
- A discussion of the ideas on the list takes place.
- Team members then anonymously rank the presented ideas.
- The generation-discussion-vote may take place until a decision is reached.

The nominal group technique offers an advantage in using anonymity for generating ideas (and/or voting), thus minimising the negative effects of power and status differences between members.

3   **The Delphi technique** is similar to the nominal group technique and is used to gather judgements from experts in the forecasting process. This technique uses questionnaires for generating and evaluating alternatives and is often deployed when experts are geographically dispersed. (For a discussion of quantitative analysis, please consult Chapter 13.)

4   Techniques, such as the **SWOT** (strengths, weaknesses, opportunities and threats), **from–to** (current–desired future situation), **force-field** (current–desired future situation, and driving–restraining forces) analyses attempt to deal with organisational change (see Chapter 12). They evaluate the current position against the desired new state against the organisation's background of strengths (or drivers), weaknesses (or restraining forces) and the impact of the external environment. The objective of the exercise is two-fold: to seek new opportunities and to effectively manage the change.

5   **Opposition** and the **scenario** analyses force the team members to evaluate both the risks and benefits inherent in the preferred. The outcome of the evaluation then determines the future action to be taken.

11.8 MANAGING A MEETING IN PRACTICE

A prescriptive approach to holding a meeting as suggested above may look like an attempt at micromanaging. This may well be the case, but we all will have attended badly managed meetings, which wasted valuable organisational resources and left us feeling dissatisfied. Well-structured meetings, on the other hand, tend to finish on time, encourage fuller participation and have more productive outcomes.

ACTIVITY 11.6

Managing a meeting about organisational practices

For this activity form a group of up to six members. Enact a meeting for the following scenario and employ any participative decision-making skills that you think can be used safely in this situation.

You have been selected to chair a quality task team meeting. The task team was formed to discuss and make suggestions about policies and procedures dealing with employees doing personal business during office hours. Over the past few months, senior management became aware that some employees spend a substantial amount of time doing personal business from work. They came to a conclusion that this accounts for substantially decreased output. When the unit managers were approached about the problem, some responded that their employees would reasonably argue that some personal business can be done only during office hours, thus it wouldn't be fair to expect them to take personal leave for sorting out things that usually take only a few minutes. Other managers dismissed the concern, saying that the amount of time lost is not worth worrying about. What is more, they argue, taking any punitive action would likely result in negative feelings towards the organisation.

In your meeting, discuss the following issues:

1   How can you monitor and change staff behaviour?

2   How can you improve working practices to ensure employee productivity generally?

Once you have conducted the meeting, reflect on the following issues:

● How did you prepare for the meeting?
● How did you run the meeting?
● What happened during the meeting?
● Did all taskforce members participate in the meeting?
● Did your team propose any follow-up measures?
● Would you run future meetings differently? If so, what would you change?

Running an effective meeting does not come naturally; it is a learned skill. A meeting is effective when well structured and mindful of the participants' time. Effective meetings result in higher-quality solutions, thus can improve participants' morale. Let us return now to Barrett's (2006) four-step model.

Conflicts occur when values, norms, beliefs and attitudes of individuals and groups clash. In such situations of interdependence when departments and individuals have incompatible goals and interests but cannot accomplish tasks independently, individuals can experience both internal and intrapersonal conflict. Other conflict situations may arise when having to choose between two equally desirable options, when outcomes carry both positive and negative consequences, or when having to choose between two or more negative outcomes (Lewin et al 1939).

Sometimes problems discussed at meetings turn into conflict. When this happens, the meeting must be interrupted and the conflict has to be negotiated there and then, if it is not to spill into the working environment. Conflicts are an inherent part of both organisational and private lives and are not always dysfunctional but can be positive by acting as agents of change (see also Chapter 9). In organisations, conflict arises mainly from organisational structures and communication errors and is common: managers spend up to half of their working time on dealing with conflict.

Conflict progresses through a number of stages (Quinn et al 2003):

Stage 1: Conflict is latent: the situation is set up for conflict, for example due to the organisational structure, although neither party senses the conflict.

Stage 2: There is a perception of a potential conflict by one or both parties. This could be cognitive and/or emotional, where the concerned individuals or groups become aware of their differences. The other party gets the blame and emotional reactions such as hostility, frustration, anxiety and pain take place.

Stage 3: Cognitive and/or emotional feelings turn into action, where conflict becomes overt, and action is taken to resolve the conflict either explicitly or implicitly. This may be demonstrated as aggressive behaviour, both verbal and physical. At this stage the conflict can be resolved only if both parties are positive (see also Chapter 9).

Stage 4: Functional resolution of the conflict fosters a better understanding, improved quality of decision, increased attention to creativity and innovation, and, most importantly, positive self-evaluation. Dysfunctional outcomes include continued anger and hostility, reduced communication, destruction of team spirit, and snowballs into new conflicts.

11.9 TEAM EFFECTIVENESS AND CONFLICT

Conflict situations in a team can be rooted in a wide gambit of human emotions felt by one or more of the members. These emotional states can include: resentfulness, anger, hurt feelings and defensiveness, to name but a few, that in turn can lead to friction, mistrust, ego clashes, tension and open personal disagreement (Jehn 1997). A team experiencing relationship conflict (Guetzkow and Gyr 1954) may become dysfunctional. The imperative for the team leader is to have the necessary people skills to turn relationship conflict into task conflict or to design the team so that the likelihood of relationship conflict does not emerge. As outlined in Chapter 8, Belbin's (1993, 2008) team role theory may be utilised to compile a potentially effective team.

However, not all team leaders have the luxury of designing their team. This is why the more constructive task conflict is crucial to developing team cohesiveness. For many in leadership roles, managing task conflict (or managing an open debate) is thought of as difficult and potentially risky. The essence of managing task conflict over a period of time (Jehn and Mannix 2001) is to have the team focus on a particular project, plan or task. They can then debate the merits of one method for achieving the team's goals over another, thus offering an outlet for tension and for the most part avoiding personalising an argument (see also Chapter 9).

A major element of team cohesion is to agree on the common goals and to share the vision; however, it is only by sharing the vision that a team can become homogeneous. Agreeing common goals helps to define the ground rules or decisions on how the team will operate, whereas creating or sharing a vision can enlist 'buy-in' to where the team wants to be and what they all want to achieve. This is where a skilled leader would employ factors that promote collective interest, for instance an attempt to instil and communicate a common identity leading to a team culture, be aware of shared threats, harmonise jobs/work, encourage relationships and friendships within the team and also with other, similar teams. The latter can help to ensure that the team is not isolated and thus can avoid the harmful effects of 'group think' (Janis 1982).

To handle conflict effectively, Thomas (1976) developed a conflict-negotiating approach involving different levels of assertiveness (that is, degree to which a party is concerned with their own interest) and co-operation (that is, degree to which a party is concerned with the other party's interest). Each of the resulting five conflict-handling modes, which are discussed in more detail in Table 11.4, will have its use in handling different conflict situations.

Table 11.4 Conflict-handling modes

Mode	Criteria	Explanation	Appropriate use
Avoidance	● Low assertiveness ● Low co-operativeness	● Recognises but does not address the conflict, thus satisfies neither party. Both parties withdraw and put up a barrier. Avoidance is useful during the 'cooling-off' period, although the conflict remains unresolved. Later all the problems tend to surface again, and important management issues will not be addressed.	● When an issue is trivial. ● When there is no chance of satisfying own concerns. ● When potential disruption outweighs the benefits. ● When gathering information supersedes immediate decision. ● When others can resolve the conflict more effectively. ● When issues seem tangential and symptomatic of other issues. ● When cooling down.
Accommodation	● Low assertiveness ● High co-operativeness	● Act only to satisfy the other party's concerns by preserving harmony, and avoiding disruptions. Accommodation exploits the individual's willingness to sacrifice personal needs, although is useful in the short term. In the long term, it stifles creativity and innovation.	● When wrong-footed. ● When issues are more important to others. ● When building social credits for later use. ● When minimising losses after being outmatched and losing. ● When harmony and stability are very important. ● When learning from mistakes.

Mode	Criteria	Explanation	Appropriate use
Competing	• High assertiveness • Low co-operativeness	• Satisfies one party's own goals only, relies on authority structures and formal rules, and is used in 'win–lose' situations. Competing can be appropriate for quick and decisive action, but limits creativity and new ideas.	• When quick, decisive action is needed. • When unpopular actions need implementing. • When issues are vital to the organisation's interests. • Against those who take an advantage of non-competitive behaviour.
Collaborating	• High assertiveness • High co-operativeness	• Concerns both with own and others' interests. There are no underlying assumptions of fixed resources and giving something up in order to gain. It offers a 'win–win' situation, is good for cohesion and morale, but may not always work.	• When seeking an integrative solution. • When the objective is to learn. • When sharing insights. • When gaining commitment. • When working with negative feelings.
Compromising	• Medium assertiveness • Medium co-operativeness	• Is first in the solution approaches, depends on giving up something in order to get something else, and neither party wins or loses.	• When goals are not worth the effort to disrupt. • When dealing with an equal opponent. • When seeking temporary settlements to complex issues. • When seeking expedient solution under the time pressure. • As a back-up when collaboration fails.

Source: drawing on Thomas 1976, 1977

We have seen that these five conflict-handling modes can be used to approach a wide range of conflicts in organisations. One problem we may face, however, is that we tend to be blind to our problems and often resist resolving personal conflicts. Although painful, we may sometimes find ourselves prolonging the conflict by refusing to see the other person's point of view. However, the approaches in Table 11.4 can be learned and require practice, which will enhance our ability to deal with conflict both in our professional and private lives more constructively. It becomes clear from Table 11.4 that the collaborative approach is the only one of the five styles that can create a genuine 'win–win' situation beneficial to all parties involved (see also Chapter 9).

11.10 CONCLUSION

Leading and managing people in a team context can be motivating, interesting and at times exasperating. It requires a diverse set of people skills to deal with the individual team members' expectations, behaviours and emotions, to encourage participation and creativity and to deal with conflict. This skill set operates at different levels – the strategic, the operational and the personal – and team leaders have to work very hard to build these very diverse skills required to lead effectively. We also have to remember that team leadership and team dynamics do not happen in a vacuum, but that they are influenced by the organisation's culture, dynamics, rules, systems and procedures.

Hence, a leader can be extremely effective and successful in one organisation, while failing miserably in another. Nevertheless, an effective leader in a wide range of contexts will be confident, honest, intelligent and creative; they will have a drive for achievement and the ability to motivate others and to adapt. Generally effective leaders will also be emotionally intelligent, being able to read different team situations in order to identify and manage emotions.

PAUSE FOR THOUGHT

Identify at least three things that you have learned by studying this chapter and engaging with the activities. How will your newly acquired knowledge and skills support your continuing professional development? What value do you expect your learning to have for your daily routines and your further career? In what area have you identified a need for further development and how are you planning to fill that gap? Address these issues in your learning journal and/or PDP log. You may also wish to discuss them with a peer, colleague, mentor or coach to aid your further development.

EXPLORE FURTHER

BELBIN ASSOCIATES: http://www.belbin.com, http://www.belbin.info

REFERENCES

ADAMSON, I. (1997) Management consultants' intervention styles and the small organisation. *Journal of Small Business and Enterprise Development.* Vol 4, No 2. pp55–65.

ALIMO-METCALFE, B. and BRADLEY, M. (2008) Cast in a new light [online]. *People Management.* 24 January. Available at: http://www.cipd.co.uk/pm/peoplemanagement/b/weblog/archive/2013/01/29/castinanewlight-2008-01.aspx [Accessed 16 October 2013].

ALIMO-METCALFE, B., ALBAN-METCALFE, J., SAMELE, C., BRADLEY, M. and MARIATHASAN, J. (2007) *The impact of leadership factors in implementing change in complex health and social care environments.* Department of Health NHS NIHR SDO project 22/2002.

BAKER, W., CROSS, R. and WOOTEN, M. (2003) Positive organisational network analysis and energising relationships. In: K.S. CAMERON, J.E. DUTTON and R.E. QUINN (eds). *Positive organisational scholarship: foundation of a new discipline.* San Francisco, CA: Barnett-Koehler, pp328–34.

BARKER, R.A. (2001) The nature of leadership. *Human Relations.* Vol 54, No 4. pp469–94.

BARRETT, D.J. (2006) *Leadership communication.* Singapore: McGraw-Hill.

BAUMEISTER, R.F., BRATSHAVSKY, E., FINKENAUR, C. and VOHS, K.D. (2001) Bad is stronger than good. *Review of General Psychology.* Vol 5. pp323–70.

BBC NEWS [online]. Available at: http://bbc.co.uk/news

BELBIN, R.M. (1993) *Team roles at work.* London: Butterworth-Heinemann.

BELBIN, R.M. (2008) *Management teams: why they succeed or fail.* 2nd ed. Oxford: Butterworth-Heinemann.

BOYATSIS, R., MCKEE, A. and JOHNSTON, F. (2008) *Becoming a resonant leader.* Boston, MA: Harvard Business School Press.

BROWN, R. (1965) *Social psychology.* New York: Free Press.

BURNS, J.M. (1978) *Leadership.* New York: Harper and Row.

CAMPBELL, J.P. (1968) Individual versus group problem solving in an industrial sample. *Journal of Applied Psychology.* Vol 52, No 3. pp205–10.

CIPD. (2012) *Reward management: aligning strategy and pay.* Annual survey report supplement 2012. London: CIPD.

CLEGG, S., KORNBERGER, M. and PITSIS, T. (2005) *Managing and organizations.* London: Sage.

CORRIGAN, T. (2010) [online] Available at: http://www.telegraph.co.uk/finance/comment/tracycorrigan [Accessed 19 January 2010].

FIEDLER, F.E. (1971) Validation and extension of the contingency model of leadership effectiveness. *Psychological Bulletin.* Vol 76, No 2. pp128–48.

FORD, J. (2010) Studying leadership critically: a psychological lens on leadership identities. *Leadership.* Vol 6, No 1. pp1–19

GABRIEL, Y. (2008) *Organizing words.* Oxford: Oxford University Press.

GARNHAM, A. (1988) *Artificial intelligence: an introduction.* London: RKP.

GODFREY, R.R. (1986) Tapping employees' creativity. *Supervisory Management.* Vol 31, No 2. pp17–18.

GOLEMAN, D., (1998) What makes … a leader. *Harvard Business Review.* Nov–Dec. pp93–102.

GOLEMAN, D., BOYATSIS, R. and MCKEE, A. (2002) *Primal leadership.* Boston, MA: Harvard Business School Press.

GROSS, R.D. (1993) *Psychology: the science of mind and behaviour.* 2nd ed. London: Hodder and Stoughton.

GUETZKOW, H. and GYR, J. (1954) An analysis of human conflict in decision making groups. *Human Relations.* Vol 7. pp367–81.

HARRISON, E.F. (1995). *The managerial decision making process.* 4th ed. Boston, MA: Houghton Mifflin.

HOUSE, R.J., HANGES, P.J., JAVIDAN, M., DORFMAN, P.W. and GUPTA, V. (eds). (2004) *Leadership, culture and organizations: The GLOBE study of 62 societies.* Thousand Oaks, CA: Sage.

JANIS, I.L. (1982) *Groupthink.* 2nd ed. Boston, MA: Houghton Mifflin.

JEHN, K.A. (1997) A qualitative analysis of conflict types and dimensions in organisational groups. *Administrative Science Quarterly.* Vol 42, No 3. pp530–57.

JEHN, K.A. and MANNIX, E.A. (2001) The dynamic nature of conflict: a longitudinal study of intragroup conflict and group performance. *Academy of Management Journal.* Vol 4, No 2. pp238–51.

LAWLER, E.E. (1992) *The ultimate advantage: creating the high-involvement organisation.* San Francisco, CA: Jossey-Bass.

LEWIN, K., LIPPITT, R. and WHITE, R. (1939) Patterns of aggressive behaviour in experimentally created social climates. *Journal of Social Psychology.* Vol 10. pp271–99.

LIKERT, F.E. (1961) *A theory of leadership effectiveness.* New York: McGraw-Hill.

MASLOW, A. (1954) *Motivation and personality.* New York: Harper and Row.

QUINN, R.E. (2004) *Building the bridge as you walk on it.* San Francisco, CA: Jossey-Bass.

QUINN, R.E., FAERMAN, S.R., THOMPSON, M.P. and MCGRATH, M.R. (2003) *Becoming a master manager: a competency framework.* 3rd ed. Hoboken, NJ: Wiley.

SIMON, H.A. (1979) Information processing theory of human problem solving. In: W. ESTES (ed.). *Handbook of learning and cognitive processes.* Vol 5. Hillsdale, NJ: Laurence Erlbaum.

SIMS, H.P. (1987) Leading workers to lead themselves. *Administrative Science Quarterly.* Vol 32, No 1. pp106–28.

STONER, J.A.F. (1968) Risky and cautious shifts in group decisions. *Journal of Experimental Social Psychology.* Vol 4. pp442–59.

TATTERSALL, R. (1984) In defence of consensus decision. *Financial Analysts Journal.* Vol 40, No 1. pp55–67.

THOMAS, K.W. (1976) Conflict and conflict management. In: M.D. DUNNETTE (ed.). *Handbook of industrial and organisational psychology.* New York: Wiley.

THOMAS, K.W. (1977) Toward multi-dimensional values in teaching. *Academy of Management Review.* Vol 2, No 3. p487.

TORRINGTON, D., HALL, L., TAYLOR, S. and ATKINSON, C. (2011) *Human resource management.* 8th ed. Harlow: Prentice Hall.

TURNER, J.C. (1991) *Social influence.* Milton Keynes: Open University.

WENGER, E., MCDERMOTT, R. and SNYDER, W.H. (2002) *Cultivating communities of practice: a guide to managing knowledge.* Boston, MA: Harvard Business School Press.

WHETTEN, D.A. and CAMERON, K.S. (2011) *Developing management skills.* 8th ed. Upper Saddle River, NJ: Prentice Hall.

CHAPTER 12

Leading Change and Development in Organisations

STEFANIE REISSNER

OVERVIEW

Organisational change is widely regarded as a constant reality and its management as a key challenge. The stakes are high, it seems: if an organisation does not change, its future prosperity and even survival may be under threat. Yet, managing organisational change is a complex task that involves two main aspects: (1) the *business processes* that govern an organisation, including strategic and operational considerations, and (2) *cultural aspects* such as the roles and relationships of organisational actors (that is, all those working for an organisation). In contrast to other accounts of organisational change, this chapter focuses on the interplay of the business and people aspects as well as the skills and key tools that managers and employees will need to manage organisational change. It will also consider the potential benefits and pitfalls of consultant involvement in organisational change.

LEARNING OUTCOMES

By the end of this chapter, provided you engage with the activities, you should be able to:

- understand the key aspects of organisational change
- appreciate the importance of the context of change
- apply business skills to the management of change
- apply people's skills to the management of change
- understand when consultants can support organisational change.

12.1 INTRODUCTION

ACTIVITY 12.1

Perceptions of change

What comes to mind when you hear the term 'organisational change'? Are you dreading the mere mention of it or are you excited about what is to come? Why do you think you react the way you do? What are your

> experiences with organisational change? Take a few minutes to jot down some thoughts; you   will need them later for the activities of this chapter.

Organisational change involves the complex interplay between (1) *business processes* that can be designed and implemented and (2) the *meanings* that organisational actors (that is, those working for an organisation) attribute to it. Hence, it can only be understood and managed through the experiences of those involved (Dawson 2003a). The challenge is that organisational change means different things to different people. For some, it is an exciting opportunity to turn around an organisation or parts of it, to make their name or just to do something new. For others, change means unsettling times, a break with routines and old truths, and the fear of pay-cuts and redundancy (see Reissner 2010, 2011). Due to the major differences in which organisational actors understand and experience change, managing it is a difficult task.

Organisational change is often employed as a rigid and controlling process of renewal, and it is therefore not surprising that the majority of change initiatives fail (for example Meany and Pung 2008, as cited in Armenakis and Harris 2009). In order to succeed at managing organisational change, managers and change agents need to focus their attention more on reading the context of change and respecting the organisation's history and culture; this requires a complex set of skills, including analysis of business processes, self-awareness and people skills.

This chapter explores the key aspects of organisational change and some essential strategies for its management by focusing on both business and people aspects. Business aspects of organisational change are discussed in Section 12.2 below. Despite increasing recognition of the limits of stage models of change (for example Reissner et al 2011), it may be useful to consider change as comprising five stages, which include contextual issues that affect the organisation and the way it changes. Section 12.3 examines people issues including an understanding of organisational actors' perceptions, experiences and skills. I will introduce key tools to raise awareness in individuals and teams to support change and development within organisations. In Section 12.4, I will bring business and people aspects of change together and discuss issues of leadership, agency and sustainability of organisational change. Each section is complemented by activities to help you understand yourself and your role in organisational change.

12.2 BUSINESS SKILLS FOR CHANGE

12.2.1 CONCEPTS OF ORGANISATIONAL CHANGE

Organisational change has been understood in a multitude of ways and is regarded here as 'a process by which an organisational entity alters its form, state, or function over time' (Stevenson and Greenberg 1988, p742). This definition comprises anything from systematic continuous improvement (Drucker 1999) to fine-tuning activities to major programmes of transformation (Dunphy and Stace 1993). It comprises change that has been planned as well as change that has emerged naturally (Wilson 1992). It also comprises change programmes that are reactive as well as those that anticipate external changes (Dawson 2003b). The processual nature of organisational change makes it a dynamic and fluid phenomenon that involves a unique mix of factors. Despite representations to the contrary common in the popular management literature, there is no fool-proof recipe for managing organisational change. The good news is that studies of organisational change have identified factors that increase the likelihood of successful change management (or, put differently, the absence of which increases the risk of failure). Drawing on Plant (1987), Kotter (1995) and Murray and Richardson (2003), these factors are summarised in Figure 12.1.

Figure 12.1 Key factors in organisational change

The first factor in this process consists of the detailed analysis of (1) the organisation's context (that is, its external and internal environment) to establish any opportunities and threats to the organisation and (2) the change challenge to create a detailed understanding of what the change programme seeks to establish; this is vital to provide strategic direction.

The second factor includes the formulation of a change vision and mission (Plant 1987), the creation of a shared understanding of the change challenge (Murray and Richardson 2003), a sense of urgency (Kotter 1995) as well as change strategies and tactics, all of which will increase its chances for success (Ulrich 1997). This is usually done by a change team (Kotter 1995) whose task is to prepare the organisation for change (Armenakis et al 1993) and to manage the change process.

The third factor focuses on communicating the vision, mission and urgency of the change programme to the organisational actors to develop a shared understanding of what lies ahead (Murray and Richardson 2003). It is vital that communication at this stage goes beyond written materials or a single meeting. Kotter (1995) emphasises that change programmes need to be communicated in a way that reflects their importance and urgency within the organisation over a sustained period of time to capture the hearts and minds of those affected and to get their involvement in making change happen.

The fourth factor comprises the implementation of the change programme. Ideally, this happens in stages with clearly defined milestones so that each stage can build on the momentum of the previous one. It is important to build in flexibility, both in design and implementation (Ulrich 1997) to respond to any unforeseen circumstances.

The fifth factor is concerned with institutionalising the change programme to make it an established part of the way in which an organisation operates; this is the key to sustaining change and preventing the organisation from falling back into previously familiar (and now ineffective or counterproductive) ways of working.

Throughout the process it is crucial to the potential success of a change initiative to remove any obstacles and barriers (such as structural and cultural issues) and to speed up decision-making in the communication, implementation and institutionalisation phases (Murray and Richardson 2003). This will require a detailed action plan, changes to policies and practices and sustained commitment from all organisational actors, with HR professionals having a crucial role (Hughes 2010, CIPD 2013).

Despite a visual representation to the contrary, the proposed model is *not* to be understood as a neat, linear series of actions. It would be wrong to assume that an organisation consists of a homogenous mass of individuals who journey along at the same speed. Some may move along more quickly while others lag behind and require more time to come to terms with the realities of change. Moreover, the boundaries between the steps are fluid in that it is often difficult to determine when the majority of organisational actors move from one step to another. This creates difficulties for managers, change agents and associated professionals, who have to judge which intervention is required for which group of organisational actors at which time.

Effective communication of any change programme, both as a factor in its own right and an ongoing activity, is a vital ingredient for the management of change. Scott and Jaffe (1989) recommend the following strategies: firstly, organisational actors should initially be addressed in person and be given an opportunity to raise their voice and have their questions answered. Written communication (such as newsletters or blogs) can be a useful means of further communication to support the ongoing change process. Armenakis et al (1993) suggest that external information such as reports by government departments, think tanks or professional associations may also support the message that the change team seeks to communicate. Secondly, organisational actors should be informed about all aspects of the change programme, particularly those changes that may have a negative impact on their working lives. The change team may want to encourage questions to minimise the amount of uncertainty among organisational actors; this may help reduce resistance. Thirdly, the change team should express their feelings as this will often reflect what other organisational actors think and feel; this can be a powerful tool to build rapport and provide a bond between different groups in the organisation (Scott and Jaffe 1989). The most powerful message of all, however, will be the change team's actions (Armenakis et al 1993). The key to successful organisational change, it seems, is to make it happen in a joint effort.

ACTIVITY 12.2

Identifying a change issue

Identify a change issue in your organisation, which you are involved in or contribute to. This can be anything from the introduction of a new computer system to a major restructuring exercise. Describe the change programme in detail, including what it is expected to achieve, who initiated it, how it is being implemented,

how long it will take to accomplish, how the key stakeholders have reacted to it, and so on. You may also want to consider your role, perceptions and experiences of this change programme. Please write down your answers as this exercise is the first step of a reflective process, which will continue throughout this chapter.

12.2.2 CONTEXT OF CHANGE

A prerequisite for the successful management of change is the understanding of the organisation's context, which consists of its external and internal environment. The *external environment* comprises social, political, economic, technical, legal factors as well as industry, supply chain, market and other considerations (such as geographical location or the country's education system). The *internal environment* comprises the organisation's history and culture, the organisational actors' skills, roles and relationships, their expectations, hopes and fears, values and beliefs (see also Chapter 5). It is important to bear in mind that these contextual factors are often in flux, which can make their interpretation, analysis and management difficult. One key task of managers and employees involved in shaping organisational change is the analysis of the organisation's present context (Plant 1987) as well as any anticipated changes in its external and internal environment, and there is a wide range of tools and techniques available.

A popular tool for the analysis of an organisation's external environment is PESTEL[1] (Johnson et al 2010), which is an acronym for political, economic, social, technological, environmental and legal factors. The central premise of this model is that small changes in its environment can have a major impact on the organisation (Carruthers 2009). For each category, the key factors influencing the organisation are listed, identified as being an opportunity or threat and rated according to how strong an impact that factor is expected to have on the organisation. It may also be a good idea to compare the current state of the PESTEL environment with an anticipated future one so that the key factors can be identified and their impact on the organisation evaluated in more detail. PESTEL provides an overview of the wider environment in which an organisation operates and is likely to be useful in most change situations. More importantly, such analysis can help an organisation to anticipate changes in their wider environment and be proactive (Carruthers 2009). Depending on where the stimulus for a change initiative originates, more specific analysis of the competitive forces in an industry, marketplace, distribution channels and sources of finance will have to be conducted. A detailed discussion of these is beyond the scope of this chapter. Suffice to say that techniques originating in strategy such as five forces analysis (Porter 1980), life cycle analysis and growth-share matrix, in finance (breakeven analysis, cost–benefit analysis, profit analysis and ratio analysis) and in marketing (such as 3 Cs or 4 Ps) are widely used.

The analysis techniques mentioned above will often involve statistical and other quantitative data for analysis (see also Chapter 13). The advantage of using established analysis techniques such as the ones mentioned above is that they break a phenomenon into its constituent parts for detailed examination through a structured approach. However, such techniques will rely to a large extent on the *interpretation* of information and forecasts, and any results will therefore be subjective. Hence, such analyses are best conducted in a team setting or in conjunction with a consultant to get a more balanced view of the situation and to get expert knowledge where appropriate. Additionally, the relatively rigid factors of established analysis tools can hinder understanding of how different factors are linked to others within a model or how different models may complement each other. It is also important to bear in mind that analysis tools are unlikely to provide a definitive answer about which course of action to take, and managers and change agents will need to employ their decision-making tools (see Chapter 16). Nevertheless, such techniques will allow managers to think in a more structured manner and focus their attention on the key factors expected to impact on the change programme and the organisation's future prospects.

An organisation's internal environment is essentially about its culture, which can be defined as organisational members' 'patterned ways of thinking, feeling and reacting' (Kluckhohn 1951, p86). These derive from an organisation's history and heritage and are usually taken for granted by organisational actors. As they are reflected in various domains of an organisation's fabric, these are made explicit in models such as the cultural web, which consists of six interrelated elements that define the paradigm in which an organisation operates (Johnson and Scholes 1992). These are:

1   *stories* or the events and characters of the past, which are still talked about today and other rhetoric means to bring other, impersonal organisational aspects to life

2   *rituals* and routines or daily actions and behaviours that are regarded as acceptable within the organisation – they are often described as 'the way things are done here'

3   *symbols* or visual representations of what the organisation stands for (such as the company logo, dress code, any displays and organisation-specific jargon)

---

1 Several abbreviations are commonly used, including PEST, STEP, PESTLE, STEEPLE, but the principles of the analysis remain the same.

4   *organisational structure*, both as defined on organisational charts and as lived out in daily interaction

5   *control systems* to manage finance, quality, rewards and acceptable behaviours

6   *power structure*, or who matters in the organisation, regardless of their formal position.

For analysis purposes, each element is considered in its own right and in the present time. The cultural web can be employed at different levels of an organisation, such as functions, divisions, departments or other sub-units as well as the organisation as a whole. It is often a good idea to determine which aspect is crucial for each element, that is, which aspect would create the biggest difference if it was changed or taken away. (For instance, the performance of a department would suffer if George retired because he knows everything about the organisation. Without George, nobody would know where to look for information or whom to ask. George is therefore in a position of great knowledge within that department, and there may be ways of sharing that knowledge more widely.)

Then, the analysis can move on to what the organisational culture should be after successful completion of the change programme to determine an appropriate course of action. (For instance, the language used to address each other might incorporate less swearing and show more respect to individuals instead. Such a step would address rituals and symbols that are central to a department's way of working.) The cultural web is usually graphically represented in overlapping bubbles, which can be modified in size, position and level of overlap according to the relative importance of each element.

Tools such as the cultural web can help break down organisational culture into smaller parts to aid detailed analysis; however, the outcome will differ depending on who conducts the analysis and at what time. It is therefore imperative to establish the views of a multitude of organisational actors to create a shared understanding of the change initiative (Murray and Richardson 2003). It is usually beneficial to seek the views of organisational actors from different departments, backgrounds and positions to get a picture that reflects reality, although it may unearth some uncomfortable truths for managers. You will also need to be aware that many of the deeper issues involved here, such as organisational actors' values and beliefs, may be difficult to surface (see also Chapter 5). External parties such as independent researchers, facilitators or consultants are often in a better position to make such tacit issues explicit than organisational actors themselves.

The external and internal environments of an organisation are interdependent entities, and there is usually a strong link between an organisation's environment, particularly the industry in which it operates, and the type of culture it has established. Plant (1987), for instance, suggests that organisations that receive slow feedback from their environment (such as government departments, education institutions, public utilities, pharmaceutical and heavy industry) tend to be procedural and bureaucratic, whereas organisations that receive fast feedback from their environment (such as IT, retail, sales, construction and entertainment) tend to be more dynamic and agile. Each type of culture has to be appropriate for the environment in which an organisation operates, and each change programme has to be appropriate for the organisational context. The analysis of an organisation's context will determine the 'substance of change' (Dawson 2003a, p47). This term comprises a range of factors, such as:

- *content* of change
- *timeframe* in which change needs to be completed
- *criticality* of change to the prosperity and survival of the organisation.

Let us consider what the substance of change might look like in practice in Case Study 12.1.

LUFTHANSA

CASE STUDY 12.1

In the 1990s, reduced demand for air travel and fierce competition triggered deregulation and liberalisation of the European airline industry (Captain and Sickles 1997). German carrier Lufthansa was unresponsive and complacent, the prevailing attitude being 'We are the German Airline Company, state-owned and a prestige organisation. They will never let us die' (Kar 2009). In 1992, while being privatised, Lufthansa suffered cash insolvency with cash resources to sustain only two weeks of operations.

Lufthansa embarked on a stringent change initiative called 'Program 93'. The first phase (1992–95) focused on *operative reconstruction* through reduction of capacity and workforce and the sale of assets. The second phase (1993–96) focused on *structural reconstruction* through restructuring and optimisation of

business processes. The third phase (1994–99) focused on *strategic reconstruction* through completion of privatisation and the establishment of co-operation across the organisation (European Foundation for the Improvement of Living and Working Conditions 2002).

As a result, net losses of €373 million in 1992 transformed into pre-tax profits of €1.28 billion in 1998. Moreover, by 1998 passenger numbers had increased by 6.8 million and 70 per cent of seats were filled (Bruch and Ghoshal 2003). Lufthansa has continued to adapt to a changing operating environment.

Source: adapted from student work and reproduced with permission by Preye Deinne, Rui Hu, Helen Toseland and Pak Ki Tsang

---

 ACTIVITY 12.3

Lufthansa

Analysing Case Study 12.1, identify the content, timeframe and criticality of change at Lufthansa in the 1990s. You may want to work on your own or in a small group.

Moreover, the *depth of change*, that is, whether the change programme works at operational, strategic, cultural or paradigmatic level, is an important consideration when planning and designing organisational change. Murray and Richardson (2003) argue that each of these levels has a different purpose and is best achieved with a particular set of measures. At the operational level, change is often sought to achieve efficiency through measures like restructuring. At the strategic level, change tends to focus on increasing the organisation's effectiveness, for instance by adapting the product portfolio. At the cultural level, change seeks to modify organisational actors' values, beliefs and attitudes through new leadership, for example. Finally, change at the paradigmatic level seeks to secure organisational survival through a complete redefinition of purpose.

There are two implications: firstly, each type of change has a specific focus, and there are specific tools to help accomplish it. This is contrary to the popular change management literature that will often advocate a change tool, which, allegedly, is effective in all circumstances. Those planning and designing organisational change need to be mindful of the contextual nature of change as discussed above and consider carefully whether the latest change tool will indeed help their cause. Secondly, the more fundamental the change programme, the more difficult it will be and the longer it will take to achieve it. For example, an organisation fighting for survival, such as Lufthansa in the 1990s (see Case Study 12.1) will take longer to bring about change than an organisation that simply introduces a new computer system to enhance operations.

In summary, the analysis of an organisation's context will determine what kind of change programme will be required and what measures are likely to yield the best results. Each change initiative will be unique in the type of opportunities and threats coming from the external environment, in the type of organisational response that will be appropriate given the organisation's history and culture and in the ways in which a change programme will be implemented. Managers frequently look for straightforward answers when facing complex situations, but there are no recipes for managing change successfully. The key skills required for organisational change are numerical skills (such as finance and statistics, see Chapters 13, 14 and 15), analysis, synthesis and evaluation (see Chapter 2), and interpersonal and communication skills (see Chapters 8, 9 and 11).

ACTIVITY 12.4

Contextual analysis

Drawing on the change issue that you identified for Activity 12.2, determine which factors in the organisation's external or internal environment were central to the initiation, implementation and outcome of the change programme. You may want to draw on the models introduced above to aid your analysis and work with a peer or in small groups.

12.3 PEOPLE'S SKILLS FOR CHANGE

12.3.1 SENSEMAKING – THE KEY TO SUCCESSFUL CHANGE

The definition of organisational change provided in the previous section lacks one crucial element: the *personal dimension* of organisational change, that is, organisational actors' perceptions and experiences. Organisational change is best understood as socially constructed (Reissner 2008), which means that organisational actors ascribe meaning to change, which derives from their knowledge, experiences, values and beliefs. The creation of meaning (or sensemaking, Weick 1995) is intensely personal and will differ between groups and individuals. However, it is central to the way in which organisational actors think and behave in times of organisational change (Reissner 2008), and therefore needs to be taken into account when planning, designing and implementing it. This is often easier said than done because many of the factors that determine the meaning of change are tacit. Internal analysis tools such as the cultural web (Johnson and Scholes 1992) can provide some insights into how change may be interpreted by organisational actors.

ACTIVITY 12.5

Reactions to change

Consider the following questions: how do you react to change in your personal and professional life? Do you embrace change with open arms or are you more sceptical and reluctant to do things differently? You may want

to draw on your experiences with change with   down your answers; you will need them later
the change issue identified above and write   on.

Organisational actors are often hesitant at first to commit to a programme of change and
you may understand why this is the case. However, in many instances their perceptions,
attitudes and behaviours change over time and many will take an active role in making
change happen. This can be after initial communication by the change team or once a
change programme has begun. In my research (Reissner 2008), one manager described
this process beginning with disbelief and ridicule about the change programme, assuming
that something like that just could not work. However, as the first results became evident,
an increasing number of organisational actors started to acknowledge that there may
indeed be something worthwhile in the initiative and began to show more commitment
towards the change programme. As further results became evident, organisational actors
began to take the new way of working for granted and even started to question those who
remained unconvinced. Such a process moving through three stages is graphically
illustrated in Figure 12.2.

Figure 12.2 Making sense of change

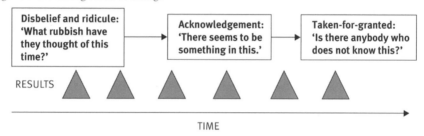

Source: drawing on Reissner 2008

The two imperative factors in this process seem to be time and results. Few organisational
actors will be convinced about the need for change merely by hearing about it from their
managers, and initial scepticism is often important as a safeguard against rash decisions.
While good communication may convince organisational actors to give the change
programme a chance (Kotter 1995, Murray and Richardson 2003), they need to see results
as they go along to commit more fully and over a sustained period of time (Reissner
2008). Importantly, organisational actors need time to reflect on and make sense of any
interim results. The achievement of targets will therefore enhance the credibility of a
change programme, and it is therefore imperative that it be implemented in steps or
phases.

12.3.2 UNDERSTANDING ONESELF

One major complaint among organisational actors is that change is being done to them
and that they have little input into what is happening. In an ideal world, every
organisational actor would have input into a change programme and would be fully
committed to its successful implementation and sustainability; change would really be a
joint effort (see Kotter and Rathgeber 2006). However, most organisations do not operate
in an ideal world. Many change programmes will be conceived with only marginal
consultation and involvement by front-line employees, particularly in the early stages.
While organisational change may be an unpleasant reality for those involved which is
beyond their control, with some self-awareness they can change their reaction to change.

Throughout this book we have attempted to help you increase the level of self-awareness, that is, awareness of your personality, skills and expertise as well as your contributions to your team and wider organisation. The activities in this chapter will further support your learning journey.

I have already introduced the Myers-Briggs Type Indicators (MBTI) briefly in Chapter 5, a method that analyses personality in four dimensions (Myers-Briggs Foundation, nd). The first dimension is about where we draw our energy from. Extravert individuals (E) tend to get a buzz out of crowds, while introvert individuals (I) tend to recharge their batteries on their own. The second dimension is about what we pay attention to and how we come to know. Sensing individuals (S) rely on their experience, while intuitive (N) individuals focus on possibilities and patterns. The third dimension is about a preference of how to make decisions. Thinking individuals (T) prefer structure, while feeling individuals (F) rely on personal values and empathy in their decision-making. The fourth dimension is about one's lifestyle. Judging individuals (J) are drawn to structure and organisation, while perceiving individuals (P) are flexible and spontaneous. Each personality type is represented as four letters (one from each dimension), which are made up by the dominant characteristics that an individual exhibits. The MBTI framework is non-judgemental, that is, each personality type is as valuable as any other (or, put differently, none is better than any other), and it is inappropriate to use MBTI or similar models to put individuals in rigid boxes and expect particular behaviours from them.

In the context of organisational change, MBTI can help explain our responses. Drawing on the first two dimensions discussed above, Cameron and Green (2004) distinguish between four types of organisational actors and their preferred way of dealing with organisational change. The introvert or thoughtful types will focus on observation, analysis and theorising, while the extravert or action-oriented types will want to experiment and implement. The intuitive or innovative types will focus on what is new while the sensing or realist types will be drawn towards stability and the status quo. In particular, the thoughtful innovator (IN) will excel in generating new ideas for the organisation's future, drawing on their ability to analyse and synthesise information. The action-oriented innovator (EN), in contrast, will excel at implementing change with a team of others drawing on their creative potential. The thoughtful realist (IS) will carefully consider which aspects of the organisation need to remain untouched and which areas need to change. It is the person who will quietly observe what is going on and caution against any rash action. The action-oriented realist (ES) will focus on improving the status quo in a practical manner.

Armed with such knowledge, organisational actors can ask what they can bring to a change programme to make its accomplishment a joint effort. The contributions of each organisational actor to the change effort will of course depend on their position, role, qualifications and skills as well as self-awareness. Those in managerial positions may get involved in planning, designing and implementing change, conducting analyses and gathering information, or championing a particular part of the change programme. Those not in managerial positions may support the change initiative by continuing to give their best in their daily routines. Every organisational actor will have personal characteristics or skills that are valuable for change in their immediate team or wider organisation. These may look insignificant but can have a big impact on morale and ways of working. The challenge for the change team will be to know who the individuals with the biggest contribution may be and to find ways to involve them in the change programme.

12.3.3 UNDERSTANDING THE TEAM

Like individuals, teams can contribute to organisational change, and the key question should be: 'what can we bring to the change programme?' A team is a group of people who work together towards a particular goal, who determine the structure of the team and who negotiate rituals and traditions, and each team member has a role to fulfil (Luft 1984). Knowledge about the role which each team member fulfils is crucial to achieve maximum performance and satisfaction, particularly about those roles that do not appear on any official list or chart (see also Chapter 8). The trick is to identify the characteristics and skills of each team member and their contribution to the team to raise awareness. There is a simple yet powerful exercise to surface such otherwise often hidden characteristics and skills, which is as follows. Team members ideally sit in a circle or square; this is purely for practical reasons. Each team member takes a sheet of paper, writes their name at the bottom and passes it to the person sitting on their right. The person receiving their neighbour's sheet writes something they value about that person, starting at the top, fold over what they have written to make their contribution anonymous and pass it on to the person sitting on their right. This continues until the sheet of paper reaches the person whose name it bears. It is imperative to focus on the positive contributions of each team member rather than complaining about each other's faults and weaknesses. If team dynamics allow, team members may be willing to share what has been written about them, which helps make the different contributions explicit and take appropriate action. In the context of organisational change, this exercise may be used to distribute any tasks required for the initiative or to put forward names for a role to be filled. It is vital that this process takes place in a safe and trusting environment and that it remains positive and non-judgemental throughout.

Knowledge of models such as MBTI can also support the analysis of team situations, particularly if a team has been newly created, if roles within the team are to be redistributed or if there is conflict. An understanding of different people's preferences in behaviour can help other team members appreciate, for instance, why Paula always asks questions about the practicalities of a team's ideas for change. It is vital in such circumstances to remain non-judgemental, as it is Paula who provides a reality check for potentially unworkable ideas, and such a contribution can be crucial for the success of a change programme. The trick is twofold: firstly, to be aware of one's own and each other's characteristics and skills, and secondly, to appreciate rather than condemn differences.

Knowledge of personality types can also explain why reactions to organisational change can differ considerably from team member to team member. Murray and Richardson (2003) suggest that 20 per cent of employees will actively support any change programme, while 70 per cent remain uncommitted (it is they that are often perceived to resist change) with the remaining 10 per cent opposing any changes as a matter of principle. You may be able to see the connection to Cameron and Green's (2004) application of MBTI to organisational change discussed above. The action-oriented types are more likely to support a change programme, while the thoughtful types are more likely to remain uncommitted. You can also see that realists may be more suitable for analysis roles while innovators may be more suitable for design roles within the change process. The understanding of why team members react in a particular way can help you make these issues explicit, discuss them and decide on a course of action. The challenge, however, is often to find the time and space to do so.

In summary, the key skills involved in the people aspects of organisational change are self-awareness, appreciation of different traits, skills and roles and understanding of how individuals and teams can contribute to a change effort. Other important skills include communication, analysis, synthesis and evaluation. Analysis and synthesis are likely to be based on qualitative factors deriving from reflection, observations and experiments that will be more difficult to capture than quantitative factors. Tools such as MBTI are frameworks to understand and express some of the often tacit issues involved here. However, any initiative to raise self-awareness among individuals and teams requires authentic commitment and a culture that enables and supports such a process.

12.4 MANAGING CHANGE

12.4.1 CHANGE AGENCY: DRIVING CHANGE

Let us now combine business and people aspects of organisational change and consider further pertinent issues in the management of organisational change. Business and people aspects are best regarded as interdependent entities that need to complement each other if a change programme is to succeed. Business aspects tend to be relatively easy to analyse, manage and control, but people aspects can develop a life of their own that are difficult to predict and manage. If business and people aspects develop in different ways, the success of a change programme will be severely compromised. Figure 12.3 is a graphic representation of the process of organisational change and highlights potential interaction of the business and people aspects as change unfolds. For instance, the announcement that a change programme is to be launched is likely to be met with disbelief or ridicule, while communication about the need for change may move some organisational actors to acknowledge its importance. Results in the implementation stage are likely to convince more organisational actors of the benefits of the change programme.

Figure 12.3 Business and people aspects of change

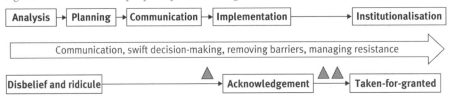

Figure 12.3 also illustrates that it often takes a while to get organisational actors on board and that the change team may have to adapt their approach to the communication and implementation of change. Change agents, the drivers of organisational change that provide direction and are involved in all stages of the change process, require a wide range of business and people skills. These include clarity, flexibility, tolerance of ambiguity, interpersonal skills, motivation, enthusiasm, sensitivity and political awareness (Buchanan and Boddy 1992) as well as credibility, trustworthiness, sincerity and expertise (Armenakis et al 1993). In addition, good change agents will have excellent communication skills and high levels of self-awareness (Plant 1987), which means that they will know when to trust themselves and when to trust others, when to talk and when to listen. Good change agents also find the right balance between the consensus required to implement change and the creative potential of difference that fosters innovation (Olson and Eoyang 2001) – all of which are required to provide strategic direction.

There are a number of different approaches to change agency. Caldwell (2003), for instance, distinguishes between change agents that are senior managers, change agents that are middle managers, teams of change agents and external change agents (for example consultants). Each approach has advantages and disadvantages, and the organisation's context and substance of change will determine which one will be most appropriate. Regardless of the approach, the human resources function in an organisation will ideally have a central role in supporting organisational change due to its detailed knowledge of the organisation and its context as well as the range of skills available among HR professionals (CIPD 2013). According to Ulrich (1997), four roles appear to be particularly important to support and facilitate organisational change:

1   *strategic partner* – aligns human resource strategies and practices with the overall business strategy and the way it is being executed

2   *administrative expert* – designs, implements, maintains and evaluates human resource systems

3   *employee champion* – builds skills and capabilities to manage organisational change and communicates employees' concerns and needs to management

4   *change agent and consultant* – drives change in the organisation and identifies other groups within and outside of the organisation that can drive change.

Hence, change agency is rarely about one person doing all the work, even though in many instances there will be a visible figurehead. More often, change agency is about collaboration and teamwork between different parts of an organisation and perhaps also outside parties such as facilitators and consultants. Poole (2004) even suggests that actions taken by someone behind the scenes may prove fundamental to the success of a change programme, and that factors originating in an organisation's external environment (for example, a change in government policy or an economic downturn) may limit change agents' ability to drive organisational change. Nevertheless, sound analysis of the organisation's context and the substance of change as well as multiple initiatives and a focus on the work that promises the best results may support change agents' work (Shepard 2005).

12.4.2 MAKING CHANGE STICK

One key challenge for managers is to institutionalise change and sustain any improvements that an initiative may have achieved as all too often organisations slip back into established routines. The problem is, however, that there has been little research into the sustainability of organisational change (Buchanan et al 2005), which could inform managerial practice. Nevertheless, there are several factors that are likely to determine whether a change programme can be sustained in the medium or longer term. Many change programmes are destined to fail from the outset due to a lack of realistic analysis, planning, design and implementation, and in such instances it is positive for the organisation's future prosperity that they fail early on. Other, more promising change programmes are often easier to sustain if the difficult issues are tackled first (so that organisational actors do not perceive change to get harder over time), if management commitment remains the same or increases over time, and if a change programme is perceived to be tackling problems rather than symptoms (Senge et al 1999). In short, any change initiative needs to be properly thought through, have a strong rationale that is being communicated to all organisational actors and have the buy-in from organisational actors to be sustainable.

Sustainability also requires commitment by the majority of organisational actors to do things differently on a permanent basis (Lewin 1951) and needs to be supported by managers and change agents (Kotter 1995). Cameron and Green (2004), for instance, highlight the paradoxical nature of reward systems in this context. While teamwork and collaboration are highly desirable features in many organisations, reward systems often focus on the best-performing team member. The same applies to innovation and creativity (where rewards are reaped for making no mistakes) as well as employee involvement (which is often coupled with tight operational and financial controls). Such a mismatch is counterproductive and needs to be eradicated. Hence, changes in organisational actors' behaviour as well as structures, systems, policies and procedures that govern life in an organisation are essential to making change stick (Plant 1987). Early involvement of key organisational actors in the change programme through clear and focused communication can also help sustain organisational change (Kotter 1995). It is imperative that the change team pay attention to the steps of the change process outlined above as well as those that may be specific to their organisation. As there is no recipe for successful organisational change, a change programme must be evaluated against expectations from time to time to detect and tackle any mismatch at an early stage. Implementing and sustaining organisational change successfully is a joint effort by all organisational actors and therefore requires an approach that reflects the collectiveness of the process.

ACTIVITY 12.6

Agency and sustainability of change

Relating to the change issue you worked with above, consider agency and sustainability. Who are the drivers of change? Is there a change team that has been specifically appointed for the task? What skills, characteristics, experiences and background do they have?

What part does the HR function play in designing, planning and implementing the change programme? How likely is it that the organisation slips back into its old ways? Again, you may want to draw on the models discussed above and share your ideas with a peer or in a small group.

12.4.3 UNDERSTANDING RESISTANCE TO CHANGE

ACTIVITY 12.7

Resistance to change

One common complaint among managers and change agents is that employees resist change. Why do you think this is the case? Referring to the change situation above, identify the forms

of resistance that organisational actors employ as well as any reasons for resistance. What kinds of issues feature on your list? Are they understandable or are they unreasonable?

Although associated behaviour is often difficult to distinguish, there is a big difference between non-commitment and resistance (Murray and Richardson 2003). A non-committed employee will initially remain neutral and get on with their work, while an employee who opposes change may do so actively, for instance through non-compliance. To an outsider, their behaviours may look identical and both employees may be perceived to resist change. However, the non-committed employee may yet have to be convinced of the value of the change initiative to gain their full commitment, whereas it will be more difficult to convince employees opposing change.

Resistance to change, whether real or perceived, is often due to a lack of knowledge and information (Plant 1987), particularly about the substance of change (Dawson 2003a), and this, in turn, is often due to a lack of appropriate communication by the change team (Kotter 1995). In such circumstances, it is understandable that organisational actors remain initially cautious. The trick, it seems, is to get sufficient backing to create the momentum to start off change and to win an increasing number of organisational actors through results (see Reissner 2008).

Other common reasons for resistance are the perceptions and assumptions of organisational actors that have been shaped by bad experiences with organisational change, which is sometimes called 'change fatigue' (Hughes 2010). Rather than engaging in open conflict, organisational actors often disengage from the change process and demonstrate high levels of energy and creativity to counteract change in their organisation. According to Keen (1985), common initiatives include reducing the change agent's credibility and influence, bringing in representatives from different functions to reduce the impact of plans, and keeping a low profile. However, resistance to change is not limited to employees as often management pays lip-service to change rather than making it happen through active leadership (Cockman et al 1999). The challenge for the change team is to identify such behaviours and address them appropriately, which is often done more successfully with outside help (see also Section 12.5 below).

One tool to investigate the balance of power, to identify the key organisational actors as well as the opponents and allies in change is force field analysis (Lewin 1947). It starts off with a description of the current and desired state and tries to identify how a situation will develop without any action. Then, all driving and resisting forces will be listed and rated according to strength. It is important to scrutinise this list to see if these forces are valid, if they are critical to the success of the change programme and if they can indeed be changed. A tool that can complement force field analysis is what Plant (1987) calls 'key relationship mapping'. It involves asking four questions about a proposed change programme, which are:

1   Who are the *winners*?

2   Who are the *losers*?

3   Who has *information*?

4   Who has *power*?

It is important to bear in mind that both force field analysis and relationship mapping deal with the perceptions of those involved. Those employees who perceive themselves as winners of change may need little convincing, but it may be more difficult to convince those employees who perceive themselves as losers. It may be useful for the change team to view the change process and its implications for organisational actors through their employees' eyes as managers and employees tend to have different views of change. Management tend to focus on the opportunities and benefits of a change programme, while employees tend to focus on the threats and disruptiveness associated with change (Strebel 1996). The result is often a breakdown in communication, difficulties in implementing a change programme and a lack of tangible results, which will further reduce the credibility of the change programme and increase any resistance that may have developed. To increase the chances of success, managers need to examine the reciprocal obligations and commitments between the organisation and its employees and to balance the needs of different organisational actors (Duck 1993). Any intervention may be fruitfully targeted at those with information and power, as it can make a big difference to convince an organisational actor who is well respected by their peers to participate more actively in the initiative. However, dealing with people, particularly in the context of organisational change, needs to be done with utmost sensitivity and respect.

Several barriers to organisational change have been established that go beyond resistance. Carnall (2007, drawing on Adams 1987) suggests that there are five areas which can potentially block a change initiative. Firstly, *perceptual blocks* are about the way in which organisational actors perceive the change effort and include the inability to view a situation from more than one viewpoint or the inability to identify a problem in a complex scenario. Secondly, *emotional blocks* are about the way in which organisational actors feel about change and include fear of failure, inability to cope with ambiguity and an overcritical attitude towards any suggestions for change. Thirdly, *cultural blocks* are about the norms, values and beliefs that are acceptable in an organisation and its wider context. These include, for instance, a tension between reason and intuition and between tradition and change. Fourthly, *cognitive blocks* are about the way in which language impacts on perception and include a lack of flexibility and creativity in the implementation of change as well as a lack of information. Finally, *environmental blocks* are about the support for a change initiative within an organisation and include a lack of acceptance of alternative or deviant points of view.

In conclusion, organisational change is often a minefield. A multitude of issues, both external and internal, need to be taken into account when planning, designing and implementing a change initiative. An almost infinite number of factors can make or break any change programme, some of which can be anticipated and some of which are beyond the control of those involved. Managing organisational change is less about methods, tools and techniques and more about trust, respect, honesty and transparency. It is the organisational actors that will (and will have to) make change happen together, but often it is worthwhile seeking outside help.

ACTIVITY 12.8

Barriers to change

Drawing on your change issue, what are the barriers to change in that instance? How can they be overcome? You may want to work with a peer or in a small group again and draw on the issues discussed in this section.

12.5 CONSULTING FOR CHANGE AND DEVELOPMENT

Throughout this chapter I have referred to the possibility of seeking external support in diagnosing and implementing organisational change, and I would like to discuss consultant involvement further before drawing this chapter to a close. Managers and other professionals need to decide at different points in a change programme whether it would benefit from the services of a consultant. While consultancy services have recently come under scrutiny (for example Sorge and Van Witteloostujin 2004), there is no doubt that the management of organisational change can benefit from consultant support to provide new perspectives on both business and people aspects of change (for example Armbrüster and Glückler 2007).

Consultants can have multiple and at times shifting roles in a change programme, including (1) *expert*, who contributes knowledge, skills and expertise, (2) *problem-solver*, who helps improve performance issues, and (3) *facilitator*, who supports the whole change process from analysis to design, implementation and evaluation (Myers et al 2012). More specifically, consultants can be involved in planning, organising, directing and controlling, in being a leader, figurehead, spokesperson, negotiator and troubleshooter (Wickham 2004).

Recent research suggests that the impact of consultant work on organisations is often exaggerated (Sturdy 2011), and there are a few pitfalls that client organisations need to be aware of when involving a consultant in the management of change. Firstly, consultants are not always responsible for the outcome of the task or project for which they provided advice (Kubr 2002). Secondly, despite efforts to devise a system of certification (International Council of Management Consulting Institutes 2004–08) consulting is an unregulated profession, which means that everybody can call themselves a consultant and provide consultancy services. Thirdly, consultants can usually only be held liable for gross negligence or fraud but not for erroneous professional judgement (Kubr 2002). Hence, organisations seeking the help of a consultant need to select them carefully.

ACTIVITY 12.9

Consulting for change

Referring to the change issue identified above, consider the involvement of consultants, both actual and hypothetical. If consultants are involved, what role do they have? What style do they use? How successful is their intervention?

If consultants are not involved in this instance, consider how the scenario would differ if they were involved. What type of consulting would be most appropriate? What would help the organisation most with the change issue?

Nevertheless, a range of innovative and creative approaches to consulting for change have been developed over recent years. Their aim is to help managers and change agents facilitate learning and development in the organisation and make change reality. One such approach is the Leading Bold Change™ programme (ISB Worldwide 2007–2009) that is being delivered to organisations across the globe. It is based on Kotter and Rathgeber's (2006) fable 'Our iceberg is melting', a development of Kotter's (1995) eight-step model that works with story, image and metaphor (see Reissner et al 2011 for a discussion). The fable is about a colony of penguins which discovers that its habitat is under threat and accordingly adapts its way of life. It includes both business and people aspects of organisational change and allows participants to explore the opportunities and challenges of change in their own organisation in a creative and playful way. Craig Smith, consultant at Flint Consulting, who has been delivering Leading Bold Change™ to many high-profile organisations in the UK and continental Europe since 2008, explains in Case Study 12.2.

LEADING BOLD CHANGE™

CASE STUDY 12.2

'Organisational change is often over-rationalised. Managers know exactly what to do in terms of business: They know all the important figures, they do all the relevant analyses, they collate all the right measures, they employ all the right strategies and tactics to make change happen. But there comes a point when they realise that they are missing a trick; they are struggling to engage people's hearts and minds in what they are doing. This is the point when they come to us for help. At the beginning of such an assignment there will be a lot of consultation work, in which we try to establish what they want to achieve and if *Leading Bold Change*™ is the right thing for them.

'The story is extremely valuable in helping managers to understand what it means to develop a sense of urgency for a change programme, what it means to

communicate change effectively, what it means to remove obstacles. It allows them to detach themselves from their own organisation and explore these issues in the context of the fable. The workshop material requires participants to engage very deeply not only with the theory of change that underlies the story, but more importantly with the practice of change in their own organisation – issues of power, authority and credibility in particular. It helps them to reveal previous blind spots, to understand how their organisation ticks and what they need to do to progress with their own change programme.

'The characters of the book epitomise commonly found characters and roles in organisations. There is NoNo, who refuses to believe the need for change and works hard to sabotage the change effort – and there is also the change team – Fred, who is curious, observant and creative; Louis, who is patient, conservative and respected; Alice, who is tough and practical; the Professor, who is fascinated by interesting questions and analysing information; and Buddy, who is liked and trusted by everyone. These six characters demonstrate the leadership qualities of task-orientation, people-orientation, proactivity and reactivity. As part of the workshop, participants are asked to identify themselves with one of the characters of the change team, which helps to make the composition of the management team in their organisation explicit. I often find that technical manufacturing firms have a high share of Professors and Alices and not enough individuals like Buddy and Louis to make change happen. This means that they focus on micro-management rather than providing direction through a vision. Once participants have realised this they can take appropriate action to establish a better balance of characters in their change team to fill all necessary roles.

'We also explore the character of NoNo, his motivations and his behaviour, and participants then identify the NoNos in their own organisation – in terms of people as well as systems, processes and procedures, cultural barriers, resource limitations, etc. Common issues that participants mention include cultural barriers, such as complacency and the refusal to believe in the need for change, and reward and performance management systems that are not or are no longer appropriate. The trick is to go beyond NoNo's negativity and explore what managers can do to overcome such barriers and make change happen; it is a bit like a force field analysis. We also analyse what the characters in the book do that works, focusing on the positive, and an exploration of what behaviour can be expected in their own organisation if things are going according to plan. We then identify actions that will make an immediate difference in the organisation and that participants can introduce after the workshop to keep the momentum going.

'The beauty of "Our iceberg is melting" and the *Leading Bold Change*™ workshop is that it is creative, personal and practical. It disrupts people's mindsets and understanding of change. It covers a wide range of issues, ranging from business issues to leadership issues to people's issues that change agents are confronted with in their daily work. It also gives the management and, more importantly, the *leadership* of change a structure, a language and a meaning that participants can transfer to their own organisation. *Leading Bold Change*™ allows participants to engage more deeply with the issues raised by the book on its own, and rather than feeling like attending a "course", they actually come to do a day's work – work for which they normally don't have the time.'

This illustrative case study demonstrates that organisational change can be supported holistically through an approach in which business and people aspects of change interact, thereby providing important links between the two. It is also an approach that provides a structure in which organisational actors can explore the theory, practice and meaning of change in their own organisation, for their team and themselves.

ACTIVITY 12.10

Leading Bold Change™

Reflect on Case Study 12.2 and discuss with a peer or in a small group the advantages and potential pitfalls of such an approach to supporting organisational change. You may want to consult the following YouTube clip to get insights into what the programme involves: http://www.youtube.com/watch?v=HnGJyl3LQmQ

12.6 CONCLUSION

Organisational change is often seen as the biggest challenge that managers are currently facing, and with good reason. On the one hand, it is an impersonal phenomenon consisting of business processes that need to be re-engineered, while on the other hand, it is a very personal affair that provokes intense emotional reactions among organisational actors. It is the people aspects that can make or break a change initiative, and although they are difficult to manage they must be aligned to business aspects for change to be successful. The management of the business aspects of change requires different skills from the management of people aspects, and therefore organisational change is often best managed by a change team that encompasses individuals with different strengths.

Organisational change ideally focuses on the improvement of an organisation, in particular on creating a culture that encourages and supports learning and development for its future survival and prosperity. There are many pitfalls in designing, planning and implementing organisational change, some of which can be avoided by taking into account the experiences, perceptions and wisdom of organisational actors. Others may be more difficult to predict and manage, and often organisations would benefit from the support of consultants to facilitate change.

Through the activities in this chapter, I have attempted to help you reflect about your own experiences with and reactions to change and bring them together with other, more impersonal aspects of organisational change. To be successful, organisational change is a joint effort, and each organisational actor has to contribute their unique skills and capabilities. This, however, requires a high level of self-awareness, both as individuals and in teams. The theories presented and discussed above will provide a framework for analysis and interpretation and will provide a language to express otherwise tacit issues. The challenge is to increase organisational actors' self-awareness despite time pressures and excessive workloads. This is where HR professionals have a fundamental role: they can champion organisational change and facilitate it through formal and informal development measures. By providing new experiences for organisational actors, which lead to new perceptions and behaviours, HR can be instrumental in making change happen and in developing the organisation for sustained prosperity and success.

ACTIVITY 12.11

Change and continuing professional development

Revisit the change issue that you identified at the beginning of this chapter and identify how your understanding of change has developed. How can you contribute to the success of change in your organisation? You may want to add your reflections to your CPD log.

> **❚❚ PAUSE FOR THOUGHT**
>
> Identify at least three things that you have learned by studying this chapter and engaging with the exercises and activities. How will your newly acquired knowledge and skills support your continuing professional development? What value do you expect your learning to have for your daily routines and your further career? In what area have you identified a need for further development and how are you planning to fill that gap? Address these issues in your learning journal and/or CPD log. You may also wish to discuss them with a peer, colleague, mentor or coach to aid your further development.

EXPLORE FURTHER

KOTTER, J.P. and RATHGEBER, H. (2006) *Our Iceberg Is melting: changing and succeeding under any conditions.* London: Pan Macmillan.

NICKOLS, F. (2010) *Change management 101: a primer [online].* Available at: http://www.nickols.us/change.pdf

REISSNER, S.C. (2008) *Narratives of organisational change and learning: making sense of testing times.* Cheltenham: Edward Elgar.

REFERENCES

ARMBRÜSTER, T. and GLÜCKLER, J. (2007) Organizational change and the economics of management consulting: a response to Sorge and van Witteloostuijn. *Organization Studies.* Vol 28, No 12. pp1873–85.

ARMENAKIS, A.A. and HARRIS, S.G. (2009) Reflections: our journey in organizational change research and practice. *Journal of Change Management.* Vol 9, No 2. pp127–42.

ARMENAKIS, A.A., HARRIS, S.G. and MOSSHOLDER, K.W. (1993) Creating readiness for organizational change. *Human Relations.* Vol 46, No 6. pp681–703.

BEER, M. and NOHRIA, N. (2000) Cracking the code of change. *Harvard Business Review.* Vol 78, No 3. pp133–41.

BRUCH, H. and GHOSHAL, S. (2003) Unleashing organizational energy. *MIT Sloan Management Review.* Vol 45, No 1. pp45–51.

BUCHANAN, D. and BODDY, D. (1992) *The expertise of the change agent.* Hemel Hempstead: Prentice Hall.

BUCHANAN, D., FITZGERALD, L., KETLEY, D., GOLLOP, R., JONES, J.L., SAINT LAMONT, S., NEATH, A. and WHITBY, E. (2005) No going back: a review of the literature on sustaining organizational change. *Journal of International Management Reviews.* Vol 7, No 3. pp189–205.

CALDWELL, R. (2003) Models of change agency: a fourfold classification. *British Journal of Management.* Vol 14, No 2. pp131–42.

CAMERON, E. and GREEN, M. (2004) *Making sense of change management: a complete guide to the models, tools and techniques of organisational change.* London: Kogan Page.

CAPTAIN, P.F. and SICKLES, R.C. (1997) Competition and market power in the European Airline Industry: 1976–90. *Managerial and Decision Economics.* Vol 18, No 3. pp209–25.

CARNALL, C.A. (2007) *Managing change in organizations.* 5th ed. Harlow: Pearson.

CARRUTHERS, H. (2009) Using PEST analysis to improve business performance. *In Practice.* Vol 31, No 1. pp37–9.

CIPD. (2013) *Change management [online].* Factsheet. Available at: http://www.cipd.co.uk/hr-resources/factsheets/change-management.aspx [Accessed 26 July 2013].

COCKMAN, P., EVANS, B. and REYNOLDS, P. (1999) *Consulting for real people: a client-centred approach for change agents and leaders.* 2nd ed. London: McGraw-Hill.

DAWSON, P. (2003a) *Understanding organizational change: the contemporary experience of people at work.* London: Sage.

DAWSON, P. (2003b) *Reshaping change: a processual perspective.* London: Routledge.

DRUCKER, P. (1999) *Management challenges for the 21stcentury.* New York: Harper Business.

DUCK, J.D. (1993) Managing change: the art of balancing. *Harvard Business Review.* Vol 71, No 6. pp109–18.

DUNPHY, D. and STACE, D. (1993) The strategic management of corporate change. *Human Relations.* Vol 46, No 8. pp905–20.

EUROPEAN FOUNDATION FOR THE IMPROVEMENT OF LIVING AND WORKING CONDITIONS. (2002) *Pacts for employment and competitiveness: case studies, Lufthansa AG [online].* Available at: http://www.eurofound.europa.eu/areas/industrialrelations/pecs/pdf/english/pecs_lufthansa.pdf [Accessed 26 July 2013].

HUGHES, M. (2010) *Managing change: a critical perspective.* 2nd ed. London: CIPD.

ISB WORLDWIDE. (2007–2009) [online] Available at: http://www.isbworldwide.com/training.html [Accessed 29 March 2010].

JOHNSON, G. and SCHOLES, K. (1992) Managing strategic change: strategy, culture and action. *Long Range Planning.* Vol 25, No 1. pp28–36.

JOHNSON, G., WHITTINGTON, R. and SCHOLES, K. (2010) *Exploring corporate strategy.* 9th ed. Harlow: Pearson.

KAR, P. (2009) *A tale of two airlines... [online].* Available at: http://www.business-standard.com/article/opinion/pratip-kar-a-tale-of-two-airlines-109071300056_1.html [Accessed 5 May 2013].

KEEN, P. (1985) Information systems and organization change. In: E. RHODES and D. WIELD (eds). *Implementing new technologies: choice, decision and change in manufacturing.* Oxford: Blackwell, pp361–73.

KLUCKHOHN, C. (1951) The study of culture. In: D. LEHNER and H.D. LASSWELL (eds). *The policy sciences: recent developments in scope and methods.* Stanford, CA: Stanford University Press, pp85–101.

KOTTER, J.P. (1995) Leading change: why transformation efforts fail. *Harvard Business Review.* Vol 73, No 2. pp59–67.

KOTTER, J.P. and RATHGEBER, H. (2006) *Our iceberg is melting: changing and succeeding under any conditions.* London: Pan Macmillan.

KUBR, M. (ed.) (2002) *Management consulting: a guide to the profession.* 4th ed. Geneva: International Labour Office.

LEWIN, K. (1947) Frontiers in group dynamics. *Human Relations.* Vol 1, No 1. pp5–41.

LEWIN, K. (1951) *Field theory in social science: selected theoretical papers.* London: Tavistock.

LUFT, J. (1984) *Group processes: an introduction to group dynamics.* 3rd ed. Palo Alto, CA: Mayfield.

MURRAY, E.J. and RICHARDSON, P.R. (2003) *Organizational change in 100 days: a fast forward guide.* Oxford: Oxford University Press.

MYERS, P., HULKS, S. and WIGGINS, L. (2012) *Organizational change: perspectives on theory and practice.* Oxford: Oxford University Press.

MYERS-BRIGGS FOUNDATION. (nd) *MBTI basics [online].* Available at: http://www.myersbriggs.org/my%2Dmbti%2Dpersonality%2Dtype/mbti%2Dbasics/ [Accessed 11 July 2013].

OLSON, E.E. AND EOYANG, G.H. (2001) *Facilitating organizational change: lessons from complexity science.* San Francisco, CA: Jossey-Bass/Pfeiffer.

PLANT, R. (1987) *Managing change and making it stick.* London: Fontana Paperbacks.

POOLE, M.S. (2004) Central issues in the study of change and innovation. In: M.S. POOLE and A.H. VAN DE VEN (eds). *Handbook of organizational change and innovation.* Oxford: Oxford University Press, pp3–31.

PORTER, M.E. (1980) *Competitive strategy.* New York: Free Press.

REISSNER, S.C. (2008) *Narratives of organisational change and learning: making sense of testing times.* Cheltenham: Edward Elgar.

REISSNER, S.C. (2010) Change, meaning and identity at the workplace. *Journal of Organizational Change Management.* Vol 23, No 3. pp287–99.

REISSNER, S.C. (2011) Patterns of stories of organisational change. *Journal of Organizational Change Management.* Vol 24, No 5. pp593–609.

REISSNER, S.C., PAGAN, K. and SMITH, C. (2011) 'Our iceberg is melting': story, metaphor and the management of organizational change. *Culture and Organization.* Vol 17, No 5. pp417–33.

SCOTT, C.D. and JAFFE, D.T. (1989) *Managing organisational change: a guide for managers.* London: Kogan Page.

SENGE, P., KLEINER, A., ROBERTS, C., ROSS, R., ROTH, G. and SMITH, B. (1999) *The dance of change: the challenges of sustaining momentum in learning organizations*. London: Nicholas Brealey.

SHEPARD, H.A. (2005) Rules of thumb for change agents. In: W.L. FRENCH, C.H. BELL Jr. and R.A. ZAWACKI (eds). *Organization development and transformation: managing effective change*. 6th ed. Boston, MA: McGraw-Hill Irwin, pp336–41.

SORGE, A. and VAN WITTELOOSTUJIN, A. (2004) The (non)sense of organizational change: an essay about universal management hypes, sick consultancy metaphors, and healthy organization theories. *Organization Studies*. Vol 25, No 7. pp1205–31.

STEVENSON, W.B. and GREENBERG, D.N. (1988) The formal analysis of narratives of organizational change. *Journal of Management*. Vol 24, No 6. pp741–62.

STREBEL, P. (1996) Why do employees resist change? *Harvard Business Review*. Vol 74, No 3. pp86–92.

STURDY, A. (2011) Consultancy's consequences? A critical assessment of management consultancy's impact on management. *British Journal of Management*. Vol 22, No 3. pp517–30.

ULRICH, D. (1997) *Human resource champions: the next agenda for adding value and delivering results*. Boston, MA: Harvard Business School Press.

WEICK, K.E. (1995) *Sensemaking in organizations*. Thousand Oaks, CA: Sage.

WICKHAM, P.A. (2004) *Management consulting: delivering an effective project*. 2nd ed. Harlow: Prentice Hall.

WILSON, D.C. (1992) *A strategy of change: concepts and controversies in the management of change*. London: Thomson.

CHAPTER 13

Introduction to Quantitative Data Analysis

ANDREW SIMPSON

OVERVIEW

The use of data underpins much of modern management decision-making. As a manager you will often be asked to make decisions based upon data presented to you, or early in your career to prepare data for others to present. The skills of quantitative data analysis can be complex. This chapter gives you an introduction to the techniques that will prove useful in your professional life and during your academic studies.

LEARNING OUTCOMES

By the end of this chapter, provided you engage with the activities, you should be able to understand:

- the nature of data
- graphical representations of data
- measures of typicality and variability
- basic statistical testing
- forecasting models.

A series of activities throughout this chapter will build into a case study, where you collect and analyse data on your class as a way of building your learning.

13.1 INTRODUCTION

We live in an increasing data-rich world, where organisations collect data routinely through manual and technology-assisted means. This data is often not used effectively by organisations; however, for many it is a source of their competitive advantage. This data can provide the basis for many decisions, for example, where to locate a new store, how many checkouts to have, what products to stock and when to stock them and how many staff to have on a particular shift. Without good analysis of the data, such decisions are made in an ad hoc manner that can be sub-optimal. While detailed analysis is often done by specialists, it is important for managers and other professionals to understand the tools and techniques of statistical analysis, along with the limitations of these if they are to use them effectively.

Managers will use data and the statistics generated from it to inform their decisions, justify their actions and to plan for the future. The use of data will either reinforce current actions and objectives or provide new opportunities that can lead to new strategic choices. Data and statistics, however, are not neutral; they can be misused intentionally or otherwise by organisations to justify positions or points of view. The old adage phrase should always be recalled, 'there are lies, damn lies and statistics'. A more chilling view was provided by Winston Churchill: 'I gather, young man, that you wish to be a Member of Parliament. The first lesson that you must learn is that, when I call for statistics about the rate of infant mortality, what I want is proof that fewer babies died when I was Prime Minister than when anyone else was Prime Minister. That is a political statistic' (cited in Fairlie 1968, pp203–4). While such deliberate misuse of statistics is rare, all statistics contain an element of subjectivity. For example, who do we sample? How are we defining what we are measuring? And then, which tests do we perform on the data? All of these allow us to potentially reach conclusions that we seek.

This chapter is designed to provide an overview of the fundamental principals of data and statistics and is aimed at readers with limited or no prior knowledge. If you are interested in the topics presented, there are a plethora of books on business statistics available that will give you a deeper understanding of the topic (see 'Explore further' at the end of this chapter for examples).

13.2 DATA

The first step of any statistical analysis is to collect the data to analyse, and this data needs to be quantitative or quantifiable. In many organisations this is done automatically, through such tools as EPOS (electronic point of sale) or websites. However, there is also much data that is collected manually, for example date of birth and educational history, although this is frequently stored electronically in the organisation's information system. Data can also be collected through surveys, such as staff satisfaction surveys. It needs to be remembered that not all data is quantitative; much is indeed more qualitative, for example customer complaints. However, there are statistical tools that allow us to quantify such qualitative data to allow analysis.

Some data is clear and unambiguous, for example someone's age or height, or the length of time it takes to take a call in a call centre. These can all be measured using universally accepted metrics. However, not all data is quite so clear-cut. If we consider Churchill's quote again, how can the young man he is talking to prove that fewer babies died when he was prime minister? The ambiguity arises through the terminology baby and infant mortality. What is a baby and what is an infant? The *Concise Oxford English Dictionary* defines a baby as 'very young child, esp. one unable to walk' (1979). This is hardly a precise definition as children learn to walk at different ages. The term infant is equally ill defined: it can refer to a child of one to twelve months, a child of zero to 36 months or, in English law, to anyone who is not of full legal age, that is, a minor, so this is anyone under 18 years of age. This lack of precision in definition of the terms used would allow the young man to choose a definition of infant that produced statistics that showed that fewer babies died when Churchill was prime minister.

Aristotle said, 'It is the mark of the educated man to look for precision in each class of things just so far as the nature of the subject admits' (2004, p1094b). It is therefore important to clearly define the phenomenon you are interested in and to measure it very clearly. This clear distinction in definition allows you to make comparisons between data collected from multiple sources. This might seem like an academic debate; however, even when considering something as simple as unemployment, the UK Government provides two measures of this, the ILO measure and the claimant count; these provide distinctly different numbers and yet are both equally valid measures of unemployment. So if you were looking at the unemployment levels in two locations when deciding to site a new call centre, it would be important to ensure that you used the same measure for both.

Some phenomena that we might be interested in might not be easily measured. We call these 'concepts', and we look for a 'measure' or 'measures' that allow us to quantify the phenomenon. In HRM we might be interested in employee satisfaction, but can we measure this directly? You might well say we can ask employees if they are satisfied so we can easily measure this and many organisations do. However, is this really a clear measure? Is one person's satisfaction the same as another's dissatisfaction? Will people answer honestly, especially if they fear for their job or are trying to make a point to management? Also the timing of the asking of the question could have an impact on the answer: who is at their best at 16:00 on a Friday afternoon, or having just taken a call from an irate and rude customer? To overcome this we need to look for a more objective measure for employee satisfaction or, ideally, multiple measures to allow for less room for error. In this case, such measures include turnover rates of employees, levels of unauthorised absence or even sickness. All of these could be indicative of high or low employee satisfaction and therefore are better and more objective ways of measuring this concept.

Data can come in one of two basic forms: it can be *continuous*, that is we measure it on an interval scale (in practice this means they have decimal places), for example, height, weight, time and so on. It can be *discrete*, when we measure it in whole numbers. This can take several forms, things we can count such as the number of employees we have. It can also be used to quantify qualitative data; if we can place things into categories, the numbers in each of these categories can be counted. For example, we can categorise our workforce into managers and others, then count the number in each of these categories. Discrete data can also include what we call *ordinal* data. Ordinal data is data that is given a number only for comparison purposes; this is common in many situations. For example, you might be asked to state how satisfied you are as an employee on a scale of one to five. If you answer four, this does not mean you are twice as satisfied as someone who answered two, only that you are more satisfied. The form of the data is critical in assessing the statistical analysis we can undertake with it.

 ## ACTIVITY 13.1

Exploring data

Think what data you could collect from your colleagues in the class. For example, their height, their ages, their country of origin, their views of the module, and so on. For each piece of data you could collect, discuss what kind of data this is. Is it continuous, discrete, categorical or ordinal? Collectively agree a set of questions and undertake a survey of your class to collect this data.

13.3 STATISTICAL ANALYSIS

As a manager you will often be required to present information to your colleagues and managers. Often you will need to include numerical data within your analysis. For example, as an HR manager you might have to present turnover rates or employee satisfaction. A marketing manager might present on the success of a marketing campaign, while a production manager might present on the efficiency of the operations. In order to present this data correctly you will need to understand basic statistical techniques. You should bear in mind that many people are not comfortable with numerical data – this might include you! The techniques presented below will help you present this data correctly.

13.3.1 GRAPHICAL APPROACHES

The first stage of much statistical analysis is to provide some form of graphical representation of the data. This allows us to make quick, if not necessarily accurate, comparisons. It also allows us to potentially identify possible relationships in the data. Graphical representations effectively summarise the data we have. They are powerful tools as they can be easy to interpret, even for a reader who knows little about the data, and can convey a large amount of information. Software has meant that these can easily be produced by almost anyone. The most common software used for undertaking statistical analysis includes SPSS and Minitab.

The simplest form of graphical presentation is to present a table which summarises the data. If we are interested in the make-up of our staff in the call centre in Newcastle, we can extract this from our personnel database and summarise in a table, as shown in Table 13.1.

Table 13.1 Staff at Newcastle call centre

Employment category	Number	Percentage
Managerial	12	3.6%
Supervisors	25	7.4%
Customer service representatives	300	89%
Total	337	100%

This table clearly shows the absolute numbers of staff in the Newcastle call centre and, by including the percentage of each grade, it shows the relative numbers in each category as well. Including the percentage is a useful tool if we wish to compare one call centre with another. If we look at Table 13.2, where we have included data for the Sheffield call centre as well, we can start to make comparisons between the two centres.

Table 13.2 Staff at Sheffield call centre

	Newcastle		Sheffield	
Employment category	Number	Percentage	Number	Percentage
Managerial	12	3.6%	15	2.9%
Supervisors	25	7.4%	31	6%
Customer service representatives	300	89%	470	91%
Total	337	100%	516	100%

Sheffield is clearly a larger centre, with 516 employees against Newcastle's 337. This difference in size makes it impossible to make direct comparisons if we look at the absolute numbers; Sheffield has more employees in all categories. However, if we look at the percentage of employees in each category, the table starts to tell another story. Sheffield has only 2.9% of its employees as managers, while Newcastle has 3.6%, and a similar situation can be seen for supervisors. This suggests a difference between the two call centres, and from a managerial standpoint such differences are interesting and worth investigating. The first question we should ask is: do these call centres do the same tasks? If not, we should perhaps not assume that they need the same level of supervision.

However, if they are doing the same task, why is it that Sheffield is managing with relatively fewer supervisors and managers than Newcastle? It is possible to calculate that Sheffield has 15 customer service representatives per supervisor and Newcastle has 12. Does this mean that Sheffield is more efficient? That it has better trained staff who need less supervision? The data as presented does not answer these questions but it allows you to ask them. Data when presented needs to be interpreted by a manager to turn it into information and that will be your task as a manager. In this case you will need to ask these questions, as well as many others.

Categorical, discrete data can also be presented as a pie chart (Figure 13.1) or bar chart (Figures 13.2 and 13.3); these both contain precisely the same data; however, this more visual form of presentation might be more appropriate for presentations where simple graphics are often best.

Figure 13.1 Pie chart of staff roles in Newcastle call centre

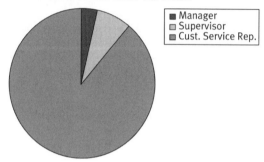

Figure 13.2 Bar chart of roles for Newcastle call centre

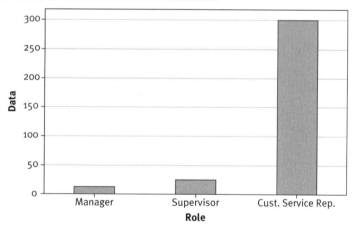

Figure 13.3 Bar chart showing both call centres in proportional terms

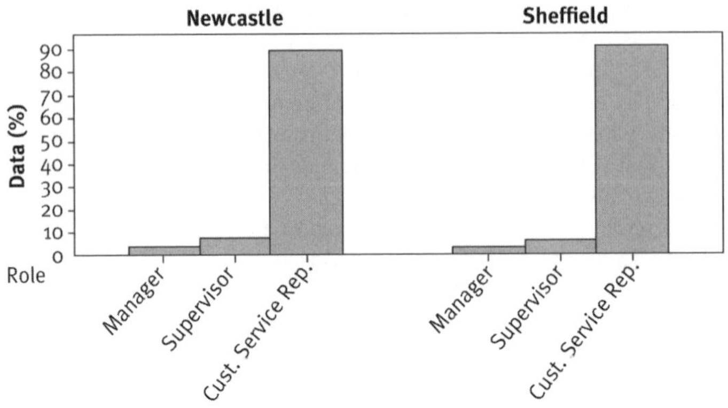

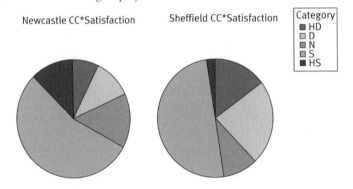

The difference between Figures 13.2 and 13.3 is that the latter shows the percentages in each category while Figure 13.2 only shows the absolute numbers.

Ordinal data can be displayed in the same ways. The company asked all employees to fill in an employee satisfaction survey. One question was as follows:

How satisfied are you in your work?

Highly dissatisfied	Dissatisfied	Neutral	Satisfied	Highly satisfied
1	2	3	4	5

Again these responses can be represented in a table, pie chart or bar charts.

Table 13.3 Results of employee satisfaction survey

Centre	HD (1)	D (2)	N (3)	S (4)	HS (5)	Total
Newcastle	25	36	50	185	41	337
	7.5%	10.7%	14.8%	54.9%	12.1%	100%
Sheffield	77	119	50	258	12	516
	15%	23%	9.7%	50%	2.3%	100%

Figure 13.4 Pie charts showing employee satisfaction for Newcastle and Sheffield

Figure 13.5 Bar charts showing employee satisfaction in Newcastle and Sheffield

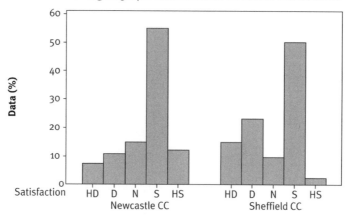

Again presenting the relative figures allows the manager to compare the level of satisfaction between the two call centres. It is clear from the percentages that the staff in Sheffield appear less satisfied in their work than those in Newcastle. In this case this is also apparent from the absolute numbers, but it is always good practice to look at the percentages. Later in this chapter, we will look at more sophisticated ways of looking for the differences between the two call centres.

As a manager, you might start to assemble the two sets of data presented so far. We have seen earlier that the Newcastle call centre has higher levels of supervision of the customer service representatives and here we have seen that generally the staff are more satisfied in their work. This is not proof that there is a causal link between the two; however, as a manager it would be worthy of further investigation.

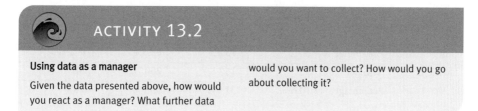

ACTIVITY 13.2

Using data as a manager

Given the data presented above, how would you react as a manager? What further data would you want to collect? How would you go about collecting it?

Continuous data has to be presented in a slightly different format where data is grouped. The data can still be presented in a table; however, this time it is called a frequency table, or relative frequency table if percentages are included. Table 13.4 shows a relative frequency table for the annual pay including commission for the customer service representatives in Newcastle.

Table 13.4 Salaries at Newcastle call centre

Salary	£10,000–15,000	£15,000–20,000	£20,000–25,000	£25,000–30,000
Number	20	40	205	35
Percentage	6.7%	13.3%	68.3%	11.7%

This can also be presented as a histogram, which is similar to a bar chart but used for continuous data. Here the bars join each other to represent the continuous nature of the scale (Figure 13.6).

Figure 13.6 Histogram showing salaries in the Newcastle call centre

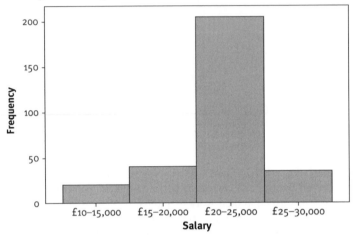

This clearly shows us that the majority of staff in Newcastle earn more than £20,000 per annum. Looking at the data for Sheffield, we can again make a comparison between the two call centres (see Table 13.5 and Figure 13.7).

Table 13.5 Salaries at Sheffield call centre

Centre	Salary	£10,000–15,000	£15,000–20,000	£20,000–25,000	£25,000–30,000
Newcastle	Number	20	40	205	35
	Percentage	6.7%	13.3%	68.3%	11.7%
Sheffield	Number	50	150	250	20
	Percentage	10.6%	31.9%	53.2%	4.3%

Figure 13.7 Histograms of salaries in both Newcastle and Sheffield call centres

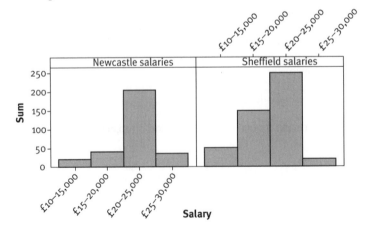

In both call centres the majority of staff earn more than £20,000; however, in Sheffield we can see that a sizable minority (42.5%) earn less than this, whereas in Newcastle this is only 20%. If we consider this in conjunction with the data in Table 13.3 on employee satisfaction, this might provide an alternative explanation for the difference between the two call centres. Rather than the level of supervision being related to satisfaction, it might actually be that the fact that the staff in Newcastle earn more increases their level of satisfaction.

The graphs presented here are produced using Minitab, one of many commercially available statistical packages. Microsoft Excel, to which many people have access, has limited statistical functionality and is not recommended for undertaking real statistical analysis.

ACTIVITY 13.3

Working with data

With the data you collected in Activity 13.1, discuss in groups how you would present each

of these pieces of data graphically. As homework you can produce a set of graphs of this data.

13.3.2 SUMMARISING DATA

Graphical presentation of data is a good starting point to an analysis; however, in many cases it is not sufficient in itself. It is necessary to try to summarise the data numerically. Generally we are concerned with two things: what is typical of the data? And how much does it vary? These two parameters can tell us much about the data we have.

There are three common measures of typicality: the **mean**, the **median** and the **mode**. Other measures exist but tend only to be used by statisticians in particular circumstances and will not be considered here.

The *mean* is the measure you will be most familiar with; it is colloquially called the average. It is calculated by adding up all our data points and dividing this sum by the number of data points we have. The following data represents the number of days' unauthorised sickness absence taken by 10 members of staff in the Newcastle call centre.

2, 5, 7, 1, 0, 2, 3, 4, 2, 0

The mean number of days of absence would be:

(2+5+7+1+0+2+3+4+2+0) / 10 = 26/10 = 2.6 days

Since we have more than 10 employees in the call centre, these 10 represent a sample of the population, that is, the whole call centre. This mean is therefore a sample mean, which mathematically we represent as $\overline{X}$. When we have the whole population, which is rare, the population mean is represented by μ.

$\overline{X}$ is used to represent the variable we are interested in – in this case the number of days taken on sickness absence. The formula for calculating the mean can be written as:

$$\overline{X} = \frac{\sum X}{n}$$

Here Σ is the Greek capital letter sigma and simply means take the sum of all the variables X, and n is the number of observations we have in our sample. Nobody calculates the mean by hand anymore; even basic calculators have a function to calculate this, as do all statistical packages.

It is worth noting that while 2.6 days' absence is the typical value, nobody actually takes 2.6 days; they take anywhere between zero and seven days. Since this is a sample of a total of 337 employees, we can use this sample mean to estimate what is typical of all employees at the Newcastle call centre. Samples need to be unbiased and representative (for more details see Wisniewski 2010) if they are to be used to represent the whole population. A sample of 10 from 337 is unlikely to be representative or unbiased. However if it were, this would tell us that typically an employee in the Newcastle call centre takes 2.6 days per year of unauthorised sickness absence.

The mean is the most commonly used measure of typicality; however, it is not always the most appropriate. Let us consider the following data set:

2, 5, 7, 1, 0, 2, 3, 4, 2, 0, 51

This data includes one more data point, an individual who has taken 51 days' unauthorised absence. This unfortunate individual has a major effect on the mean, which is now 7. There are only two individuals with seven or more days' absence and so the mean looks less typical of the data. The mean can be affected by either relatively very small or very large numbers, which are referred to as *outliers*. Large samples are less affected, and so the advice is generally to try to use as large a sample as is practicable.

The *median* is simply the middle point in the data if they are placed in ascending order. The median is generally most useful with small samples, especially if the data contains outliers. If we consider our previous data set for sickness absence days, in order they read:

0, 0, 1, 2, 2, 2, 3, 4, 5, 7

If there are an odd number of data points, the median is simply the one that lies in the middle. Here we have an even number of data points so the median is the value that lies halfway between the fifth and sixth data point (2 and 2) so the median is also 2. There are formulae available for calculating the median; however, again, all statistical packages will do this for you. You simply need to know what it represents.

The median can be less affected by outliers; if we consider the second data set again:

0, 0, 1, 2, 2, 2, 3, 4, 5, 7, 51

The median will be the sixth data point as this is in the middle of our data and this is still 2. In this case it could be argued that the median is more typical of our data than the mean. Good practice says you should calculate both, and the summary statistics produced by many packages do this for you.

The final measure of typicality is the *mode*. This is simply the most common value in the data, that is, the one that appears most often. Looking at the previous data set, the mode in both cases is 2, as this appears three times. It is possible to have more than one mode. For example:

2, 5, 7, 1, 0, 2, 3, 4, 2, 0, 51, 0

In this case both 0 and 2 appear three times, so these are both modes and this is called being bi-modal. Again, most statistical packages will calculate the mode when appropriate.

The mode is most useful when considering data such as that in Table 13.3. While technically speaking it is not sensible to calculate the mean or median of this kind of ordinal data, it is common in practice to calculate the mean anyway. Looking at this data for both Newcastle and Sheffield the modal value is 4 (satisfied). If we calculate the means, they are 3.53 and 3.01 respectively. This reflects the fact that a large proportion of Sheffield's employees registered dissatisfaction with their work; however, both means are slightly above 3 (neutral).

Good practice suggests that when looking at a data set, the calculation of all three measures of typicality is sensible as these might show interesting information.

There are also three measures of variability: the **range**, the **interquartile range** and the **standard deviation**. All three measures are useful in the workplace. As with measures of typicality it is sensible to calculate all three for any set of data, where meaningful.

The *range* is simply the difference between the largest data point and the smallest. If we consider the original data set of unauthorised sickness absence days, the largest number is 7 and the smallest is 0, hence the range is 7. The range gives you a quick indication of how much the data varies. The range, like the mean, is affected by outliers. If we look at the second data set, the largest is 51 and the smallest is 0, hence the range is 51. This limits the usefulness of the range; however, it is still a simple and easily understood measure of variability. All statistical packages will calculate the range as part of their basic functions.

The *interquartile range (IQR)* is calculated in a similar manner to the median. The median is halfway through the data and is sometimes referred to as the second quartile (Q2). If the ordered data is divided into four equal proportions, rather than two as with the median, we have a first and third quartile (Q1 and Q3). These represent being 25% of the way through the data and 75% of the way though the data. The interquartile range is simply the difference between these two values. It represents the middle 50% of the data, and hence can be regarded as being the range that is typical of the majority of the data.

Looking at the original data on unauthorised sickness absence, Q1 = 1 and Q3 = 4, hence IQR = 3. The IQR is less affected by outliers than the range, so looking at the second data set, Q1= 1 and Q3 = 5, hence the IQR = 4.

Statistical packages will calculate this for you. They also will produce another form of graphical representation of the data, called the box and whisker diagram. The box and whisker diagram (boxplot) shows the minimum and maximum values as well as the median and the interquartile range. Figure 13.8 shows the box and whisker diagram for the first data set.

Figure 13.8 Box and whisker diagram of unauthorised absence at the Newcastle call centre

Box and whisker diagrams are useful to allow you to see if the data is roughly symmetrical, that is, does it have similar differences between the box and the minimum and maximum, and is the median in the middle of the box? If it is symmetrical it suggests that the data is evenly spread. If the box is closer to the minimum or the maximum, the data is less spread out in this direction. For example, in Figure 13.8 the bottom of the box is closer to the minimum, indicating that the data is closer to the minimum and not evenly spread around the mean.

Box and whisker diagrams are also very useful for making simple comparisons between data sets. Figure 13.9 shows the box and whisker diagrams for total unauthorised absence for 2011 for both the Newcastle and Sheffield call centres.

By placing both plots on the same graph it is possible to easily see the differences between the two centres. It appears from these that Sheffield has a higher level of unauthorised absence than Newcastle.

Figure 13.9 Box and whisker diagram of unauthorised absence at both the Newcastle and Sheffield call centres

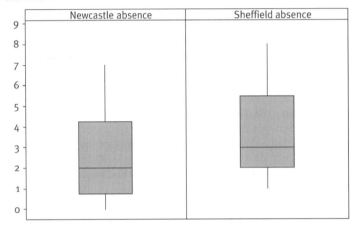

The final measure of variability is the *standard deviation*. The standard deviation is in effect the mean of the differences that data points are from the mean. The standard deviation (*s*) of a sample is calculated using the following formula:

$$s = \sqrt{\frac{\sum_{i=1}^{n}\left(x_i - \overline{x}\right)^2}{n-1}}$$

Here *n* is the number of data points you have in your sample.

All statistical packages will calculate this for you. Smaller standard deviations show that the data does not vary much around the mean of the sample; larger values show the data varies more from the mean. This is a mean of the variation from the mean, and for reasonably large samples it is not affected by outliers.

Table 13.6 shows the calculation done by hand for the first data set on unauthorised sickness absence. Remember the mean, $\overline{X} = 2.6$.

Table 13.6 Unauthorised sickness absence

	Data (X)	Data – Mean $\left(x_i - \overline{x}\right)$	(Data – Mean)^2 $\left(x_i - \overline{x}\right)^2$
	2	−0.6	0.36
	5	2.4	5.76
	7	4.4	19.36
	1	−1.60	2.56

	Data (X)	Data – Mean $\left(x_i - \overline{x}\right)$	(Data – Mean)^2 $\left(x_i - \overline{x}\right)^2$
	0	–2.6	6.76
	2	–0.6	0.36
	3	0.4	0.16
	4	1.4	1.96
	2	–0.6	0.36
	0	–2.6	6.76
Totals	**26**		**44.76**

Fitting these numbers into the formula:

$$s = \sqrt{\frac{44.76}{9}} = 2.21$$

If we repeat the calculation for the second data set we get a value of $s = 14.74$. This shows the effect of the large outlying value.

The measures of typicality and variability allow us to say much about the data we have. They tell us what is typical or average about our data and how much variability there is in the data. These are useful ways of summarising the data we have and are standard techniques used when presenting data. The mean and the standard deviation underpin much of basic statistics and allow us to start to think about how we compare sets of data against each other or against a target.

ACTIVITY 13.4

Exploring typicality and variation

With the data you collected in Activity 13.1, discuss what would be the appropriate measures of typicality and variation for this data. As homework, calculate these measures for each piece of data.

The next sub-section shows how we can use the mean and the standard deviation to expand from our sample and make statements about the population as a whole.

13.3.3 STATISTICAL INFERENCE

Generally in statistics we have samples from the population in which we are interested. If we have the data from the whole population we can make direct comparisons between the means. So if we counted the days of unauthorised absence from both Newcastle and Sheffield for a year and calculated the mean, these could be directly compared to show the difference between the two call centres. However, this is only true if we were only interested in that single year. If we wanted to compare more generally the two, we could say that the figures for that year were a sample of all years; in this case it is insufficient just to compare the two means. This is because, as we have seen above, there is variation around the mean, as expressed through the standard deviation.

To allow for this variation there are a number of statistical techniques we can draw upon. These rely upon the use of the **normal distribution**. The normal distribution is a theoretical probability distribution that is defined by two parameters: the mean and the standard deviation. In this case these are the population values and the notation is different: mean = μ and standard deviation = σ. The mean is the location parameter and the distribution is shaped around this, while the standard deviation is the shape parameter that defines the spread of the distribution. Its shape will be familiar to many – it is often called the bell-shaped curve, for obvious reasons as can be seen in Figure 13.10.

Figure 13.10 A normal distribution curve

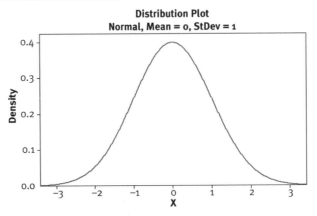

The distribution here is symmetrically centred around the mean and stretches to infinity (∞) in both directions. There are an infinite number of normal distributions as the mean can be any value and the standard deviation any positive value. Many natural phenomena follow normal distributions. The normal distribution is useful in statistical inference because through a piece of mathematically tricky samples that come from non-normal populations can be considered to be normal if we have a sufficiently large sample (the central limit theorem). This means that in many circumstances we can use the normal distribution rather than one of the many other distributions.

With probability distributions the area under the curve represents the probability of events occurring. Generally:

- Approximately 68.26% of the values of the random variable lie within $\pm 1\sigma$ of the mean.
- Approximately 95% of the values of the random variable lie within $\pm 1.96\sigma$ of the mean.
- Approximately 99% of the values of the random variable lie within $\pm 2.58\sigma$ of the mean.

This knowledge can be used to help make estimates of the population mean based on our sample. These estimates are called confidence intervals. If we have calculated the mean from our data, for example 2.6 days' unauthorised sickness absence as in the previous example, and we take another sample from the Newcastle call centre, it is highly unlikely that the mean would also be 2.6. However, we know that it would lie within a normal distribution, but we cannot know for certain where it would lie. In practice the population mean could be higher or lower than the mean for the sample we have taken. We can use the normal distribution to calculate the likelihood of where the population mean will lie. This is known as a *confidence interval*. We usually look at 95% or 99% confidence intervals based on the normal distribution; these take account of the sample mean and standard deviation and give an interval within which we can be 95% or 99% confident that the population mean will lie. Traditionally this was calculated by hand using the following formula:

$$95\% CI = \overline{X} \pm 1.96 \frac{s}{\sqrt{n}}$$

So for the Newcastle call centre this is:

$$95\% CI = 2.6 \pm 1.96 \frac{2.23}{\sqrt{10}} = 2.6 \pm 1.38$$

This means that the population mean for the Newcastle call centre lies between 1.22 and 3.98 with 95% confidence. This is usually written as (1.22 to 3.98).

The 99% confidence interval is calculated in the same manner with 1.96 replaced by 2.58. These values come directly from the standard normal distribution.

It should be noted, however, that with samples as small as 10 we would not use the normal distribution, but the t distribution. This gives slightly different results and compensates for the small sample size. Using the t distribution the 95% confidence interval for Newcastle becomes 1.0111 to 4.189. With samples over about 30 the difference between the two calculations is minimal. I have included calculations for the normal distribution here so you can see how it works.

All statistical packages will allow you to produce these easily, without doing the calculations yourself. It is good practice to always produce a confidence interval for the mean when you produce this figure. The point estimate, that is, the mean, does not take into account the variability in the data; the confidence interval does and therefore conveys more information. Confidence intervals can be calculated for proportions as well as means; all statistical packages will do these for you.

Interpreting the confidence interval requires care. The following two statements would be true of the confidence interval in the last example.

- I am 95% confident that the number of days' unauthorised absence taken by staff in the Newcastle call centre lies between 1.22 and 3.98 days.
- I am 95% confident that the estimate for the population mean number of days (2.6 from a sample of 10) unauthorised absence taken by staff at the Newcastle call centre is within plus/minus 1.38 days.

The following statement is not true, although it is commonly made:

- There is a probability of 0.95 that the population mean is between 1.22 and 3.98.

This is untrue as the population mean is a fixed, constant value, that is, it is a single number. The population value either will or will not fall in this interval. The probability that it does must either be one or zero; it does or it does not; it cannot be anything in between.

ACTIVITY 13.5

Calculating confidence

With the data collected in Activity 13.1, discuss, in groups, which pieces of data on which it would be appropriate to calculate confidence intervals. As homework, undertake these calculations.

13.3.4 HYPOTHESIS TESTING

The calculation of a confidence interval is useful as it allows us to quantify the interval within which a population parameter is expected to occur. However, this is often not sufficient because we may want to know if a specific value for the population parameter is likely. For example in a manufacturing environment, you might wish to know whether the cans of soft drink you have produced are actually filled to the level you have stated. Or you might have a target for performance and based on a sample you want to know whether this has been achieved.

Let us consider our previous example of unauthorised absence. We have seen that the mean number of days' unauthorised absence taken in the Newcastle call centre is 2.6 days. After benchmarking against competitors and the knowledge of the HR director, the company has set a target for the company of 2.5 days' unauthorised absence. Does this mean that the Newcastle call centre has missed this target? At first sight the answer is yes, we had a target of 2.5 and we achieved 2.6. However, we have already learned that we must consider the variation in our data. The hypothesis test allows us to do this.

All hypothesis tests are constructed in the same way, which provides an algorithm for us to follow. Traditionally this was done using statistical tables, which some of you may be familiar with.

- Formulate the *null* and the *alternative* hypotheses.
- Determine the significance level.
- Identify the rejection area.
- Determine the critical statistic.
- Calculate the test statistic value.
- Choose between the two hypotheses.

However, with statistical packages we do not need to take this first principles approach; instead we follow the following algorithm:

- Formulate the *null* and the *alternative* hypotheses.
- Calculate the *p value*, also known as the significance level.
- Choose between the two hypotheses.

In this chapter I will not show you how to do these tests from first principles, as in this age of a computer on everyone's desk this is no longer necessary.

The first stage is to formulate what are called null (denoted H_0) and alternative hypotheses (denoted H_1) that we can test. The logic of these tests is that we have a premise that the null hypothesis is appropriate for our problem. We will only reject this if we have sufficient evidence from our sample to do so, in which case we accept the alternative hypothesis test. In terminology of hypothesis testing we will have one of two outcomes:

- We reject H_0 and are therefore forced to accept H_1.
- Or we fail to reject H_0.

This may seem strange terminology but it has a clear and careful logic. If we fail to reject H_0 we are not saying that H_0 is true, but rather that we have insufficient evidence available to reject it. Think of this like a criminal proceeding: under English law you are asked to plead to any charge. The options are guilty or not guilty, and you are presumed not guilty until it is proven otherwise. Not guilty is the null hypothesis (H_0), and is presumed to stand until there has been sufficient evidence presented to the 'court' to show this not to be case – in which case the 'jury' reject the null hypothesis in favour of the alternative hypothesis (H_1), guilty.

We write the null hypothesis as follows:

$$H_0 : \mu = c$$

Where μ is the population mean and c is some constant. That is, the value we wish to test is true. So in the case outlined above we would look to test if the target of 2.5 days' unauthorised absence had been achieved.

$$H_0 : \mu = 2.5$$

The simplest form of alternative hypothesis is:

$$H_1 : \mu \neq c$$

This is known as a two-tailed test. The symbol $\neq$ simply means not equal to. So the alternative hypothesis states that the population mean does not equal the constant, c.

In the case of our example we would write this as:

$$H_1 : \mu \neq 2.5$$

In words, the null hypothesis states that the population mean number of days' unauthorised absence is 2.5; the alternative is that it is not 2.5.

In many cases this is a useful and informative test. However, in this case we might be less concerned if the number of days was less than 2.5, as this would be a positive. While if it is more than 2.5, this can be considered to be a poor outcome for the Newcastle call centre. In these cases we use what is called a one-tailed test.

For a one-tailed test we would write the null hypothesis as, if we are more interested in knowing the mean exceeds the value, c:

$$H_0 : \mu \leq c$$

and the alternative as:

$$H_1 : \mu > c$$

Or if we are interested in knowing if the mean is less than c, then the null hypothesis is:

$$H_0: \mu \geq c$$

And the alternative is:

$$H_1 : \mu < c$$

These are presented in some textbooks as

$$H_0 : \mu = c$$

$$H_1 : \mu > c$$

Or:

$$H_0 : \mu = c$$

$$H_1 : \mu < c$$

These are technically incorrect as they exclude the possibility of μ being either less than or more than c, respectively.

So in our case the two useful hypotheses would be:

$$H_0 : \mu \leq 2.5$$

$$H_1 : \mu > 2.5$$

In words, is the mean number of unauthorised days' absence in the Newcastle call centre less than or equal to 2.5 (the null hypothesis) or is it greater than 2.5 the alternative?

We then need to calculate the significance level, or p value. Statistical packages show the p value in different formats; some present it as a percentage, others show it as a number between zero and one. They will also quote different numbers of decimal places; do not be surprised to see $p = 0.000$. This is simply presenting the result to three decimal places on the zero to one scale.

You use statistical packages to make these calculations for you. For example in Minitab, you simply select:

Stat > Basic Statistics > 1 Sample t (if small sample)

Stat > Basic Statistics > 1 Sample Z (if large sample)

You then select the appropriate columns in your worksheet and click OK. The significance level produced by this test is $p = 0.890$. But what does this mean? We can use Table 13.7 to interpret this.

Table 13.7 Interpreting p values

p value	Also presented as	Interpretation
$p \geq 10\%$	$p \geq 0.10$	No evidence against the null hypothesis
$5\% \leq p < 10\%$	$0.05 \leq p < 0.10$	Slight evidence against the null hypothesis
$1\% \leq p < 5\%$	$0.01 \leq p < 0.05$	Moderate evidence against the null hypothesis
$0.1\% \leq p < 1\%$	$0.001 \leq p < 0.01$	Strong evidence against the null hypothesis
$p < 0.1\%$	$p < 0.001\%$	Very strong evidence against the null hypothesis

Our value of $p = 0.890$ clearly is greater than 0.10 and, therefore, we have no evidence to reject the null hypothesis. In words, we are saying that given the evidence we have available there is insufficient evidence to say that the population mean number of days' unauthorised absence in the Newcastle call centre is not 2.5, hence we appear to have reached our target. If we think back to our confidence interval for this data, which was 1.22 to 3.98, this hopefully makes intuitive sense. The confidence interval says that the population mean lies between these two values and this range contains 2.5, so it is a logical progression that we cannot have sufficient evidence that the mean is not 2.5.

If our target for unauthorised absence was only 1 day, we could rerun the test.

$H_0 : \mu \leq 1.0$

$H_1 : \mu > 1.0$

If we run the test with 1.0 day as the target value, we get a p value of 0.049. Comparing this to the values in Table 13.7, we interpret this test as having moderate evidence against the null hypothesis, and hence we reject the null hypothesis in favour of the alternative hypothesis, that there is a mean number of days' unauthorised absence greater than one day per year in the Newcastle call centre.

There are no hard and fast rules as to at which point you reject the null hypothesis. However, normally you would reject any null hypothesis with a p value of less than 5% or 0.05. It would also be normal to comment on a test that was in the range $5\% \leq p < 10\%$ ($0.05 \leq p < 0.10$) as showing some evidence against the null hypothesis, and you might choose to reject the null hypothesis, but you would have to state the p value to allow others to interpret your results themselves.

Comparison with a constant or target is useful; however, sometimes we wish to compare whether two samples come from the same population. If we have two samples, do they represent the same underlying population? So for example, if we had data for unauthorised absence from the Sheffield call centre, is this the same as Newcastle?

The following data is a sample of 10 records of unauthorised absence from the Sheffield call centre:

3, 7, 8, 2, 1, 3, 4, 5, 3, 2

This sample has a mean of 3.8 and a standard deviation of 2.25. Recall the same figures for the Newcastle call centre are 2.6 and 2.23. This suggests that there is a difference in the location (the mean) but they have similar variability (the standard deviation). Based on this, can we say that the two call centres have different levels of unauthorised absence?

We could establish this as a two-tailed hypothesis test, asking the question: are they different? First we establish the null and alternative hypotheses:

$H_0 : \mu_N = \mu_S$

$H_1 : \mu_N \neq \mu_S$

Here we are testing the null hypothesis of 'is the population mean for unauthorised absence in the Newcastle call centre (μ_N) the same as that for the Sheffield call centre (μ_S)?', against the alternative hypothesis that they are not the same.

You use statistical packages to make these calculations for you. For example in Minitab, you simply select:

Stat > Basic Statistics > 2 Sample t

You then select the appropriate columns in your worksheet and click OK.

This returns a p value of 0.247. If we again compare this with Table 13.7, this tells us that we have no evidence against the null hypothesis. In words, we have no evidence that the mean number of unauthorised days' absence at Newcastle and Sheffield are different.

For many people this appears counterintuitive; indeed, as you read this you might well be thinking, 'of course they are different!' One is 2.6 days and the other is 3.8 – clearly different. However, you are forgetting that these are samples from the whole workforce in each call centre and hence there is variability in the data. If we had data for the whole workforce and we were only interested in a single year, it would be sufficient just to compare the means. However, generally we do not have the data for the whole population, and so we need to perform the hypothesis test to account for the variability. Even if we had data for the whole workforce for a year, it could be argued that this is only a sample from one of potentially many years and we should look to perform a hypothesis test to confirm the difference.

Let us think about this a little more. If we calculate the 95% confidence interval for the data for Sheffield we get (2.4 to 5.2). Now recall this means that we are 95% confident that the number of days' unauthorised absence taken by staff in the Sheffield call centre lies between 2.4 and 5.2 days. If we compare this with the 95% confidence interval for Newcastle (1.22 to 3.98), we can clearly see that these overlap. This overlap means that given the variability in the sample, we cannot statistically tell these two call centres apart.

It should once again be noted that these are very small samples to be making comparisons upon. As the sample size increases it is likely that the variability in each sample will decrease and hence it will become easier to distinguish between the two call centres.

There is a third version of hypothesis test that is useful if you wish to compare before and after effects of an intervention on the same individual. This is called a *paired test*. It is called paired as you pair values from two samples.

To explain this, let's consider an example. Looking at the level of unauthorised absence at the Sheffield call centre, the HR manager believes there is a problem. Indeed, if you perform a hypothesis test against the target value of 2.5 days, a p value of 0.0340 is generated that shows moderate evidence against the null hypothesis, even though there is no statistical significance between the two call centres. Because of the perceived problem, a new procedure was introduced in 2012 to monitor absence and interview all staff who take unauthorised absence at the Sheffield call centre. The HR manager wishes to know whether this has been successful.

Table 13.8 contains absence data for 2011 and 2012 for the 10 members of staff in our original sample; hence, this shows their absence before and after the new procedure.

Table 13.8 Sample of unauthorised absence at Sheffield call centre

Employee	Unauthorised absence 2011	Unauthorised absence 2012
Adam	3	1
Chris	7	2
David	8	2
Ewan	2	0
Kyle	1	0
Liam	3	1
Michael	4	1
Nicholas	5	2
Stephen	3	1
Zach	2	0

The HR manager looks at this table and thinks that the new procedure has had an effect on the unauthorised absence and, indeed, inspection of the table strongly suggests this.

However, since you have done this course, you think that this should be further tested. Calculating the mean for 2012 you find it is 1 and the standard deviation is 0.82. Already the figures look very different.

The hypotheses are:

$H_0 : \mu_{2011} = \mu_{2012}$

$H_1 : \mu_{2011} \neq \mu_{2012}$

Here we are testing if the mean number of unauthorised days' absence for 2011 (μ_{2011}) is the same as that for 2012 (μ_{2012}), against a null hypothesis that they are different.

You use statistical packages to make these calculations for you. For example in Minitab, you simply select:

Stat > Basic Statistics > 2 Sample t

You then select the appropriate columns in your worksheet and click OK.

This calculates a p value of 0.000. Comparing this with Table 13.7, this shows very strong evidence against the null hypothesis. Hence, we reject the null hypothesis in favour of the alternative, that is, the population mean number of days of unauthorised absence has changed since the introduction of the new procedure.

You might be wondering why we performed a paired test; we have after all just seen a test for testing the two means. The reason is in statistics we always try to use all the evidence we have available as it makes the test more powerful. Since we know this data is for the same individual, it makes sense to make use of this knowledge. We could perform an appropriate test, assuming that these were not paired samples (adjusting for the heteroscedasticity, that is, the two samples have unequal variance). If we did this we get a p value of 0.004; comparing this with Table 13.7, this shows very strong evidence against the null hypothesis. So we would still reject the null hypothesis and accept the alternative, that they are different. However, you will note that the p value is larger, and with different data this could have produced different results if using the paired test.

ACTIVITY 13.6

Formulating hypotheses

With the data collected in Activity 13.1, discuss, in groups, what would be appropriate hypotheses to test. For example, testing whether males are on average taller than females. As homework, propose a series of hypotheses and test these.

13.3.5 TESTS OF ASSOCIATION

The last kind of hypothesis test we will look at is an example of what is known as non-parametric tests. The tests we have looked at so far use parameters from the data, the mean and the standard deviation. However, there are many occasions when we are not interested in a specific parameter of the data, such as the mean, but in the data as a whole. These tests are generally less powerful than parametric tests; however, they are still useful in circumstances when we only have rank ordering or preferences, such as the data on employee satisfaction provided in Table 13.3.

One of these X^2 is known as a contingency tables or tests of association. This is a type of hypothesis test, where we are looking to investigate whether two variables in our data are associated. Note the use of the word associated, which has a specific meaning. If two variables are associated it means that there is a connection between the two; however it is not a relationship. A relationship in statistical language means that there is a casual relationship between the two variables, that is A causes B. For example smoking causes lung cancer. While an association implies that there is a connection between the two, this is not causal, for example, if you drink you smoke more. While age could cause this difference, it might well be other factors like income and hence age is not causal. We will look at causal relationships in Section 13.3.

Test of association is a hypothesis test, where the null hypothesis is that there is no association between the two variables (they are independent) against an alternative hypothesis that there is an association between the two variables (they are not independent). The test works by calculating the values you would expect (E) if the variables were independent and compares these with the values observed (O) in the sample. You do not need to know how to do this manually as a good statistical package will do this for you. The two hypotheses are stated as follows:

$H_0 : O = E$

$H_1 : O \neq E$

You perform the test using a statistical package and generate a p value, as with the hypothesis test we have seen earlier. This p value is again interpreted with reference to Table 13.7.

Consider the data in Table 13.3, which shows the responses to one question in an employee satisfaction survey: how satisfied are you in your work? The responses from the Newcastle and Sheffield call centre are displayed separately. We looked at this graphically in Section 13.3.1. We noted that because of the different sizes of the two call centres we should look at the proportions or percentages as well as the absolute values. This suggested that there might well be an association between the call centre and how people responded to this question.

We construct the hypotheses:

$H_0 : O = E$ (outcomes are independent of call centre)

$H_1 : O \neq E$ (outcomes are not independent call centre)

We can use either Minitab or SPSS to conduct this test and calculate the p value. The p value is 0.000; comparing this with Table 13.7, it shows very strong evidence against the null hypothesis and hence we accept the alternative hypothesis. Hence, we accept that which call centre you work for and your response to the question about how satisfied you are in your work are not independent and therefore associated.

This does not mean that the call centre you work in causes the different responses to the question or the nature of the difference. However, the latter is possibly observable from Table 13.3, which suggests more people are dissatisfied in Sheffield than in Newcastle. The causal relationship might be related to the income figures presented in Table 13.5; however, we do not have the data in the necessary format to check this. To do so we would need to know how much an individual earned and how they responded to the question. If this data was available we could perform a more sophisticated version of the techniques presented in Section 13.3.

The use of these tests is very common in customer surveys to ascertain whether associations exist between the demographic information provided and how people respond to the questions. It can also be used to look for associations between how people responded to one question and see if that has an association with the answers to another question. So for example, if in our employee satisfaction survey we had asked the question 'how satisfied are you with your remuneration?', we could have linked the responses to this and the question 'how satisfied are you in your work?' This could have shown us if the two were associated.

This test has many uses that initially appear different but are conducted in exactly the same way. Let us look at another example. A member of staff at the Sheffield call centre has levelled an accusation of sexual discrimination against management as there are fewer female managers than male managers. Table 13.9 shows the breakdown of staff at the call centre by gender.

Table 13.9 Gender profile at Sheffield call centre

Level	Male	Female	Total
Manager	9	6	15
Supervisor	10	21	31
Customer service representative	210	260	470

This table appears to show an imbalance with only six female managers compared with nine male managers, 50% more. However, looking at supervisors, there are considerably more females in these positions. We can conduct a test of association to see if there is an association between gender and employment role.

We construct the hypotheses:

$H_0 : O = E$ (role is independent of gender)

$H_1 : O \neq E$ (role is not independent of gender)

You use statistical packages to make these calculations for you. For example in Minitab, you simply select:

Stat > Tables > Chi-Squared Test (Two Way Table in Worksheet)

You then select the appropriate columns in your worksheet and click OK.

The *p* value is 0.188; comparing this with Table 13.7, this shows no evidence against the null hypothesis and hence we accept that role and gender are not associated.

If the test had shown an association between gender and role, this does not mean discrimination had not occurred, just that we have no evidence that this has resulted in the distribution of roles in the Sheffield call centre. As students studying human resource management you will know that discrimination is a much more complex issue.

ACTIVITY 13.7

Testing hypotheses

With the data collected in Activity 13.1, discuss, in groups, which elements of this data you could test using the technique outlined above. As homework, construct some hypotheses with this data and test them.

In this section we have seen how we can use statistical tests to look for differences and associations between sets of data we have collected. In the next section we will look at models that can be used to establish relationships between sets of data and use this to forecast outcomes.

13.4 FORECASTING MODELS

Many different forms of forecasting models exist. Some try to look at past trends and project these into the future; these are known as time series models. These are used in many business contexts; however, they are complex to do well and as such beyond the scope of this chapter. One of the most common forecasting models is the regression model. This can also be used for establishing the strength of relationships between two or more variables. Several forms of regression model exist, from the simple to the complex. We will only explore the most simple; however, if you are interested in looking into these further, the 'Explore further' section will give you suggestions for places to start looking.

The simplest form of regression model is known as *linear regression*. Note that this model is only appropriate for continuous data; for discrete data it is best to consult a statistician as the models are more complex. As the name suggests, linear regression is based on the concept of a line, which is the simplest mathematical model available. The model looks at the available data and tries to plot a *best fit* line through this. Consider the data presented in Figure 13.11; this is presented in a graph known as a scatter plot.

Figure 13.11 Scatter plot showing length of service against average number of complaints

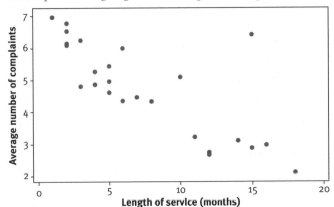

This shows information on a number of customer service representatives at the Newcastle call centre. One axis shows the number of months each has worked for the company and the other axis shows the average number of complaints received about each of them. Each dot represents the performance of an individual employee. If we look at the graph we can see there seems to be a trend: the longer someone has worked for the company, the fewer complaints received about them.

It is important to note the choice of axis for each variable. It might seem logical to assume that length of service impacts on the number of complaints. If someone has worked for the call centre for a longer period of time, they are likely to have undergone training and gained experience about the products and services and therefore able to help customers. If this is the case they are likely to receive fewer complaints. We can therefore say that the length of service has a causal relationship with the number of complaints received. It is less logical to think the other way around, that the number of complaints causes the length of service. We therefore put the length of service on the *x-axis* and use this to predict the number of complaints, which is placed on the *y-axis*. This point is important; the *independent* variable, or predictor, is always on the *x-axis* and the *dependent* variable, or predicted variable, is always on the *y-axis*.

In regression models we are trying to establish a direct mathematical relationship between the two variables; given this relationship we can predict, in this case, the level of complaints we would receive about an individual customer service representative, given we know how many months they have worked at the call centre. In linear regression we are trying to establish this relationship as a straight line. This is known mathematically as a *function* and is specified as:

$$y = ax + b$$

where *y* is the dependent variable and *x* is the independent variable. So we see that *y* is related to *x*. Hopefully you have seen something like this before at school. The two parameters of the linear equation are *a* and *b* (sometimes these are represented by different letters in different texts); *a* is known as the slope of the line and *b* is known as the intercept.

The intercept of a linear function indicates where the line would cross the vertical *y-axis*. More mathematically, you could say that *b* is the value that *y* takes if $x = 0$.

The slope (*a*) of a linear function indicates the relationship between a change in the independent variable (*x*) and a change in the dependent variable (*y*). The term *b* is also known as the gradient in some texts. In other words, it is the steepness of the straight line representing the function, if drawn on a graph.

To illustrate this, let us consider this in abstract through the following linear function:

$$y = 2x + 1$$

This tells us that if $x = 0$, then $y = 1$, the intercept. If $x = 1$, then $y = 3$ (2+1). If $x = 2$, then $y = 5$ and so on.

As the value of a increases, the slope of the graph becomes steeper and steeper, and hence y more rapidly for every x. This is known as a *positive* relationship: as x increases so does y. The relationship could also be *negative*, that is, a takes a value less than zero, in which case as x increases, y decreases; for example:

$$y = -2x + 1$$

This tells us that if $x = 0$, then $y = 1$, the intercept, as before. If $x = 1$, then $y = -1$ ($-2+1$). If $x = 2$, then $y = -3$ and so on.

If the relationship is positive then the line slopes upwards if drawn on a graph, and if the relationship is negative then the line would slope downwards. One further possibility exists, $a = 0$. What would this mean? If the slope is zero then there is no relationship between the two variables, that is, as x increases there is no change in y. Mathematically we would say that y is independent of x. This is an important point to which we will return later.

We have now established the basic model $y = ax + b$, but how is this useful to us? How can we create the relationship between the two variables in Figure 13.11? In order to do this we would need to be able to find the values for a and b; however, since both these can take a value, how do we know what is the best line to fit this data? In school you might have got a ruler and drawn what you think is the best fit by eye, then calculated a and b from this line. This, however, is insufficient for real problems; for one thing it is likely that two people would draw two different lines through the data.

It is possible to derive the values for a and b mathematically by hand, and indeed many textbooks will show you the formulas to do this. However, once again computers come to our rescue. The mathematical formulas find the values for a and b which produce the line that most closely fits the data; it is unlikely that it will fit precisely in any real-world problem. We will come back to this later.

You use statistical packages to make these calculations for you. For example in Minitab, you simply select:

Stat > Regression > Fitted Line Plot

You then select the appropriate columns in your worksheet and click OK. A graph like Figure 13.12 is then produced.

Figure 13.12 Fitted line plot showing best fit line for length of service against average number of complaints

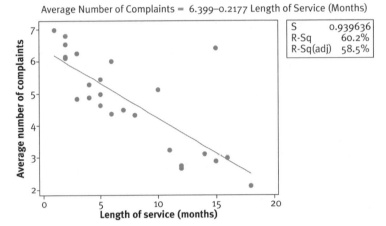

Average Number of Complaints = 6.399–0.2177 Length of Service (Months)

S	0.939636
R-Sq	60.2%
R-Sq(adj)	58.5%

This shows the best fitting line for the data and has the formula:

$$y = -0.218x + 6.40$$

We can use this to predict how many complaints we could expect to receive about an employee who has been with us for three months, that is, an average of 5.746 complaints per month.

We can also use the regression line to evaluate employees' performance. We know the level of complaints we would expect, given their length of service, given by the line of best fit. We can therefore compare individual employees against this line; if an employee is below this line, we would consider that they are 'over-performing' as on average we receive fewer complaints about them than is to be expected. Conversely, if an employee is above the line, they are 'under-performing' as we have received more complaints about them than would be expected. While small variations around the line are to be expected, larger ones are potentially a cause for concern.

 ACTIVITY 13.8

Working with data

Consider the individual in the top right-hand corner of Figure 13.12, with 15 months' service and 6.41 average complaints per month. As a manager, how would you react to this individual?

It should be noted that it is dangerous to use regression lines to predict outside the range of data you have since the relationship is not guaranteed to hold. For example, if you wished to assess an employee with 36 months' service, this is outside of the range of the original data; the model would predict –1.448 complaints; however, this is a negative number and therefore unrealistic, unless you consider commendations to be negative complaints. It is more likely that there is a baseline level of complaints that you would expect even from a long-serving member of staff.

Is creating the line of best fit sufficient in itself? How do you know how good a model the line is for the data? What is needed is some measure of the strength of the relationship that might exist between our two variables. The graph allows us to make a visual judgement of the strength of the relationship; however, this is very subjective. What is required is a statistical method of assessing the strength of this relationship.

Statistically the connection between the two variables is known as *correlation*. We can calculate the *correlation coefficient* (r) between the two variables that shows us clearly and objectively the strength of the relationship. Again many textbooks will show you a complex formula for calculating the correlation coefficient; however, in reality we use statistical packages to do this for us.

The correlation coefficient can take any value between 1 and –1. Table 13.10 helps us understand the strength of the relationship.

Table 13.10 Interpretation of the strength of a correlation

Correlation coefficient	Interpretation
$r = 1$	Perfect positive correlation
$0 < r < 1$	Positive correlation; however weakening as approaching zero
$r = 0$	No correlation, hence no relationship
$0 > r > -1$	Negative correlation; however weakening as approaching zero
$r = -1$	Perfect negative correlation

Positive correlation means there is a positive relationship between the two variables: as x increases so does y. Negative correlation is the opposite: as x increases y decreases. A correlation coefficient of zero means that the variables are unrelated. Perfect correlation, either positive or negative, is rare in real problems and any value approaching these shows a strong relationship. There is no rule as to what constitutes a strong relationship; however, in real problems values of r over 0.6 (positive or negative) show that the relationship is quite strong. Values approaching in on zero suggest that the two variables are only loosely related at best.

In our example $r = -0.776$. This shows that length of service is a reasonably good predictor of average level of complaints and that this is a negative relationship. The R^2 value shown in Figure 13.12 (60.2%) is simply the correlation coefficient squared and multiplied by 100, to give a percentage. This effectively shows the level of average complaints explained by length of service. This tells us that we have failed to explain nearly 40% of the reasons for complaints; however, this is still a good predictor.

It is worth noting that the correlation coefficient measures the strength of the relationship between the two variables; it *does not* measure cause and effect. The choice of variables to label x and y is based on the logic of the problem considered. In this example it is logical to assume length of service has a causal relationship on the average number of complaints. If we re-ran the statistics with the two axes swapped, we would still get the same value for r as the relationship still has the same strength; however, this would not be a logical cause and effect relationship. How could the number of complaints cause the length of service? This is a particularly important point as with modern software it is easy to run regression models and generate correlation coefficients; however, you need to think very carefully about the logical relationship between the variables and ensure you do this in the correct order.

ACTIVITY 13.9

Regression analysis

With the data collected in Activity 13.1, discuss, in groups, which elements of this data you could test using regression. As homework, undertake this analysis and think how you would explain this to someone who has not undertaken this course.

ACTIVITY 13.10

Translating figures Into words

Using the graphs and calculations you have prepared in Activities 13.1, 13.3, 13.4, 13.5, 13.6, 13.7 and 13.9, write a short report on the characteristics of your classmates.

13.5 CONCLUSION

We have seen in this chapter the importance of data for the modern manager (we are surrounded by it); the key is to use it effectively to help make better decisions, for your organisation and employees. Data can be used and misused by organisations and politicians to support their arguments, and it is the role of the manager to see through this and make the best choices possible.

Data can quickly and easily be turned into useful information through graphical approaches, and these allow us to make simple interpretations of what the data is telling us. However, it should be noted that these are simple interpretations of the data and are usually insufficient, in themselves, to be used to make decisions. With limited mathematical work we can summarise the data to provide measures of typicality and variability that tell us even more. With this summarised data we can perform simple statistical tests that allow us to say whether or not targets have been reached. Or to compare the performance of different sets of individuals, or indeed the same individuals before and after some intervention.

We have also seen how we can test for associations and relationships between variables; and further, in some cases we can establish the strength of the relationship. The tools and techniques presented in this chapter are only the tip of the iceberg of statistics – much more complex and sophisticated tools exist; however, they are all based on the same principles. Essentially, on the balance of probability, what do we believe to be the case?

One final note of caution: statistical tests do not do your work as a manager; they help inform your decisions and indeed provide information that might not be available through other means. In the end the job of the manager is to take all the information they have available, assess it in the light of their experiences and knowledge and make the decision.

EXPLORE FURTHER

For an interesting read on the power of numbers and how they are used and misused, try:

DILNOT, A. and BLASTLAND, M. (2007) *The tiger that isn't: seeing through a world of numbers*. London: Profile Books.

For more details on the tools and techniques demonstrated in this chapter, try either of these two books:

OAKSHOTT, L. (2012) *Essential quantitative methods: for business, management and finance*. 5th ed. London: Palgrave Macmillan.

WISNIEWSKI, M. (2010) *Quantitative methods for decision makers with MyMathLab Global*. 5th ed. London: Financial Times/Prentice Hall.

REFERENCES

ARISTOTLE (2004) *Nicomachean ethics*. London: Penguin Classics.

FAIRLIE, H. (1968) *The life of politics*. London: Methuen.

The Oxford English Dictionary (1979) Oxford: Clarendon Press.

CHAPTER 14

Interpreting Financial Information

MIKE ASHWELL

OVERVIEW

This chapter is designed to give you a basic but essential understanding of the content and significance of the three major types of financial statement, and to support the interpretation of key financial data in your internal company statements. You will find that the chapter is helpful in explaining basic accounting principles and how simple ratios can be calculated to compare the performance of companies. The key issue of corporate governance will be explained and linked with the roles and responsibilities of company officers. The controversial issue of fraud will be introduced, and the policy and operational implications for HR staff explored.

LEARNING OUTCOMES

By the end of this chapter, provided you engage with the activities, you should be able to:

- identify the three key financial reports and understand the key content and significance of those reports
- understand basic accounting principles and their importance
- gain a clearer understanding of the meaning of your internal company financial communication
- calculate simple financial ratios and use them to compare financial results
- explain the background to corporate governance issues and the resulting current best practice in determining the roles and responsibilities of senior company officers
- identify key risk areas for fraud, and the importance of fully documented fraud prevention policies and practices.

14.1 INTRODUCTION

Finance is a key aspect of modern organisations, and it is essential that all staff have a clear understanding to the appropriate level for their role. Finance issues touch all parts of the organisation, and it is important to understand the meaning and implications. If you imagine yourself in the early days of running a small business, the basic financial information that you will be seeking is:

- How much profit am I making?
- What am I worth?

- Can I pay my staff and my creditors' bills when they are due?

This key information is at the heart of financial accounting and reporting, and straightforward approaches to answering these questions will be fully explained. Some of the concepts and practices underlying these reports may seem challenging to non-finance specialists, and these ideas will be demystified. The potential problem arising if these processes are not applied correctly or legally has proved to be a challenge to financial authorities for centuries, and historic issues and remaining current debates will be highlighted.

14.2 KEY FINANCIAL REPORTS

In the UK, the format and content of external financial reports, in particular the published accounts of a company, are governed both by UK legislation and International Accounting Standards. Non-UK companies also have their own local standards, but there is an increasing international compatibility of accounting standards and presentation. In the case of companies above a minimum size, the accounts are reviewed and signed off by an independent firm of chartered accountants who signify that the accounts show a 'true and fair view' of the financial position of the company. While it is not important for the non-specialist to be familiar with the legislation and regulations surrounding the production of accounts, it is very valuable to have an understanding of the three key financial reports, particularly as sections of those reports, and the key principles behind them, are always present to some extent in internal financial reporting and communications. To gain an appreciation of the wider implications of financial reporting, you may wish to refer to the CIPD publication *Business Savvy: Giving HR the edge* (2012a).

It should also be remembered that there is a very wide range of users of published accounts. In addition to the obvious users such as investment analysts, investors, banks, customers, suppliers and competitors, other groups may also be important. Trade unions, for example, may employ financial analysts who, in addition to general trends, may look closely at the financial position of an individual company or group and make an independent assessment of their financial position and, for example, their ability to meet a given level of pay claim. Employees are also a major user of company financial information. In particular, they may use information in the following ways:

- as potential employees, to assess a company's financial prospects and ability to support a developing career
- as current employees, to assess their employment security or future prospects
- as past employees, to review the situation regarding benefits or pension funding.

14.2.1 INCOME STATEMENT

As with many financial terms, a number of alternative names for this report may be used, and you will see similar reports referred to as 'profit and loss accounts', or 'operating statements'. As we will discover in Section 14.3, your organisation may have a specific internal name for the report, but the key features, in terms of sales, costs and profit, will usually be easily recognisable.

The key elements of an income statement are as follows:

- the period to which it relates must be stated
- sales (or revenue or turnover – depending on the organisation)
- cost of sales
- expenses
- profit or loss.

For the purposes of this chapter we will not cover taxation, which can be considered to be a further deduction from profit. A basic income statement may be illustrated with a simple example.

Example 14.1: Income statement of a shoe retailer

If you are considering the income statement for a shoe retailer with a single high street outlet, the results for the month of January 2013 might appear as follows:

	£	£	
Sales		20,000	(shoes sold x price)
Cost of sales		12,000	(shoes purchased x price)
Gross profit		8,000	
Expenses			
Salaries	3,000		
Utilities	500		
Rent	1,000		
Administration	500		
Depreciation	250		
		5,250	
Net profit		2,750	

This report enables the business owner to identify clearly the level of profit or loss achieved in the month and to identify any variances with the result that was planned or expected.

In order to understand the details of the report, there must be some reference to basic accounting principles. The key principle for this purpose is that of 'matching'. This principle is intended to ensure a meaningful calculation of profits for each period by matching the revenues *earned* in each measurement period with the costs *incurred*. In the example above, this may be illustrated as follows:

- The business may sell some workwear shoes to companies on credit terms – for example, shoes may be purchased and delivered in January but there may be an agreement that the purchasers do not have to pay until 30 days after the date of the invoice. Clearly this will affect the timing of cash receipts, but the sales have taken place and should appear on the income statement for January.
- Cost of sales should reflect the costs of those shoes actually sold – for example, it should not include shoes which have been purchased by the business but are still in stock. If the stock of shoes at the beginning of January was £2,000, purchases of shoes were £13,000 and stock at the end of January was £3,000, then the cost of sales would be calculated as:

  - Purchases + Opening Stock – Closing Stock = Cost of Sales
  - £13,000 + £2,000 – £3,000 = £12,000

- The expenses should show those costs actually *incurred* in the period. This means that accounting adjustments known as accruals and prepayments must be made where appropriate.
- An *accrual* should be made where costs have been incurred but not yet charged in the accounts. For example, the shop may be preparing its January income statement on 5

February, but has not yet received its electricity bill for January. Clearly, electricity has been used, so an estimate, say £100, is added to the utilities costs, and is also shown in the balance sheet, which we will review later, as an accrual.

- A *prepayment* adjustment should be made where costs have been paid in advance, so that they are 'matched' correctly. For example, if the January administration costs included a prepaid insurance charge of £250 that related to insurance from February, the £250 should be removed from January costs and an entry made in the balance sheet for £250 shown as a prepayment.
- The final basic accounting adjustment that should be considered is for *depreciation*. When the organisation purchases fixed assets, such as cars, buildings, and fixtures and fittings, although the purchase may be recorded in the month that the items are acquired, they are not 'used up' in that month. A company car may have a life of four years, so the expense could be considered to be spread over that period – this is known as depreciation. If we assume that the shop purchased a company car in January for £12,000 with a life of four years, then the straight line depreciation method can be used to calculate an equal charge for the full 48 months – £250 per month. This is reflected on the income statement, and each monthly charge reduces the value of the asset on the balance sheet by the same amount.

14.2.2 BALANCE SHEET

Unlike the income statement, which covers a period of operation, the balance sheet relates to a single point in time, a 'snapshot', and reflects the accumulated wealth of the entity at that point. Income statements and cash flow statements show the movement from one balance sheet position to the next, as illustrated in Figure 14.1.

Figure 14.1 Key financial reports over time

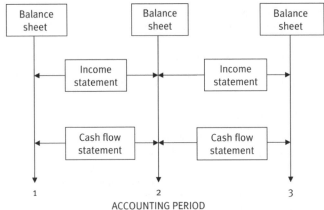

The balance sheet shows the assets of the business and the claims (liabilities) against the business. This can be readily illustrated with reference to an individual who has purchased a house using a mortgage or other form of loan. If we assume that the house is valued at £100,000 and there is a mortgage balance of £80,000, then the equity or capital that the homeowner has in the property is simply £100,000 – £80,000 = £20,000.

The balance sheet of a business is drawn up on exactly the same principles. The business will have a range of assets that it 'owns' and a number of liabilities that it 'owes' to others, with the balancing number being the 'equity' or ownership. The balance sheet equation may be illustrated as Assets – Liabilities = Capital.

The key elements of a simple business balance sheet are as follows:

- Assets (that is, things we OWN) are divided into:
  - *fixed assets* – which are items such as land, buildings, motor vehicles, plant and machinery, and fixtures and fittings, and apart from land are usually subject to depreciation as described in Section 14.2.1 above
  - *current assets* – which are items which are non-permanent and frequently changing – such as stocks, debtors, bank and cash balances, and prepayments.
- Liabilities (that is, things we OWE) are divided into:
  - *current liabilities* – which are day-to-day items and are expected to be settled within 12 months of the balance sheet date, for example creditors, accruals and bank overdrafts
  - *long-term liabilities* – due to be settled in more than 12 months of the balance sheet date, for example long-term loans.
- Capital (that is, the OWNER'S FUNDS) comprise shares or funds invested, and retained earnings (profits from previous years).

Let us assume that a trading entity starts as a small business with £4,000 of the owner's own money. At this point, it is easy to see that £4,000 in a bank represents what the business is worth, since the business owes nothing. The balance sheet 'equation' is therefore:

Bank   =   Capital
£4,000   =   £4,000

ACTIVITY 14.1

Exploring the balance sheet

Rewrite the balance sheet equation above after each of the following transactions:

1   The owner spends £1,000 of the money on a van.

2   The owner then obtains stock on credit of £2,000.

3   The owner introduces some more capital in the form of a computer at a cost of £3,000.

The equation will change at each step as follows:

1   After the owner spends £1,000 of the money on a van (another asset), the equation becomes:

Bank + Van   =   Capital
£3,000 + £1,000 =   £4,000

2   After obtaining the stock on credit the equation is a little different, since there is now a liability in the form of the supplier of the stock, but the balance on the capital account remains the same:

(Bank + Van + Stock) – Creditor   =   Capital
(£3,000 + £1,000 + £2,000) – £2,000   =   £4,000

3   After the further injection of capital, the equation becomes:

(Bank + Van + Stock + Computer) – Creditor   =   Capital
(£3,000 + £1,000 + £2,000 + £3,000) – £2,000   =   £7,000

In this last step the net worth of the business increased because of the introduction of new capital; whatever happens to one side of the net worth equation also affects the other side.

In addition, following mathematical principles, the equations can be manipulated. The last one would be exactly the same if it had been expressed as:

Bank + Van + Stock + Computer   =   Capital + Creditor

£9,000   =   £7,000 + £2,000

We can summarise this as follows:

Assets = Capital + Liabilities

OR

Assets – Liabilities = Capital

Non-current assets + Current assets – Capital + Non current liabilities + Current liabilities

OR

Non-current assets + Current assets – Capital – Non-current liabilities = Current liabilities

The balance sheet is a valuable document and gives a clear picture of financial strength at a point in time, but has a number of limitations:

- It can provide no details of what happened in the period.
- It can give little information about performance and cash flows in the period.
- As it contains purely historical data, it can offer little guidance about the future.

ACTIVITY 14.2

Fred Soul

Extract from the accounts of Fred Soul as at 30 September 2012.

Fred Soul: Trader	£
Premises	90,000
Bank overdrawn	2,000
Furniture	10,000
Van	6,000
Stock in trade	7,000
Loan	20,000
Trade creditors	3,000
Debtors	1,000
Bank	500
Equipment	2,000
Cash in hand	1,500
Capital	?

From the information provided, draw up a balance sheet for Fred Soul Limited.

Fred Soul: Balance sheet as at 30 September 2012		
	£	£
Fixed assets		
Premises		90,000
Furniture		10,000
Van		6,000
Equipment		2,000
		108,000
Current assets		
Stock in trade	7,000	
Debtors	1,000	
Bank	500	
Cash in hand	1,500	
	10,000	
Less current liabilities		
Bank overdrawn	2,000	
Trade creditors	3,000	
	5,000	
Net current assets		5,000
Total assets less current liabilities		113,000
Less long-term liabilities		
Loan		20,000
		93,000
Capital		93,000

Note that the key principle of 'balance' applies. The capital is equal to the assets minus the liabilities.

14.2.3 CASH FLOW STATEMENT

In order to obtain a full picture of what is happening financially in the business, we need to consider the third key financial report, which is the cash flow statement. In addition to answering the question 'can I pay my bills when they are due?', this statement provides valuable historical information on cash movements and can be used to generate useful forecasts to aid decision-making, as described in Chapter 15.

The cash flow statement is perhaps the easiest of the key reports to understand as it is very similar to your own personal bank statement. It is simply a record of cash balances and transactions. Note that for these purposes 'cash' extends far beyond notes and coins, which have only a limited place in most modern businesses, but also to bank deposits, both in local and foreign currencies, and short-term investments which may be readily converted into current bank balances.

In the example below, the business was started in January with capital of £10,000. This was clearly an input to the cash balance, as are the sales in January, February and March. The company has made loan and interest payments and incurred the direct costs of running the business. Expenses paid are also deducted. Total income and outgoings are summarised to produce information on the net cash flow. This is applied to the opening balance to calculate the closing balance for each period. Note that, as you would logically expect, the closing balance for each period *must* become the opening balance for the following period.

Table 14.1 Cash flow statement for first three months of a new business

All figures in £	Open	Jan	Feb	March
INCOME				
Sales		3,000	3,000	3,500
Capital in	10,000			
TOTAL INCOME	**10,000**	**3,000**	**3,000**	**3,500**
FINANCES / ASSETS				
Loan repayments		100	100	100
Interest paid		10	10	10
TOTAL FINANCES / ASSETS		**110**	**110**	**110**
DIRECT COSTS				
Materials		150	150	200
Direct labour		300	300	350
TOTAL DIRECT COSTS		**450**	**450**	**550**
EXPENSES				
Salary		1000	1000	1000
Office rent		200	200	200
TOTAL EXPENSES		**1,200**	**1,200**	**1,200**
OPENING BALANCE*	-	**10,000**	**11,240**	**12,480**
TOTAL INCOME	10,000	3,000	3,000	3,500
TOTAL OUTGOINGS	-	1,760	1,760	1,860
NET CASH FLOW*	10,000	1,240	1,240	1,640
ENDING BALANCE*	**10,000**	**11,240**	**12,480**	**14,120**

In addition to being used as a historical document, the same format may be used to produce a cash flow *forecast*, which is a very valuable business tool and will be described in Chapter 15.

14.3 UNDERSTANDING YOUR INTERNAL FINANCIAL REPORTS

You might ask the question, 'Why don't the financial reports issued in our internal communications look like any of the three reports described above?' The answer is probably that they are a lot closer than you might think. Remember that such reports are intended to show the key highlights of financial information and may therefore not include all the data, which is often a useful guide to show how the report works. For example, an internal income statement, using the basic data from our example from Section 14.2.1 above, might be shown as:

	£	£
	Budget	Actual
Sales	22,000	20,000
Gross profit	10,000	8,000
Expenses	6,000	5,250
Net profit	4,000	2,750

This shows the basic information, and compares it with budget, which is very useful, but is less easy to read as you are not able to check your understanding by running down the report using simple arithmetic. Even more confusing is the use of specific terminology in internal company reports. There are many such instances, but an example will help to illustrate the issue. Many companies use the term 'EBITDA' to describe a particular element of the financial performance target, and this is frequently quoted in boardrooms and used in internal communications at all levels. Unfortunately, many of those quoting the number do not know what the acronym stands for, or why this measure is considered to be important. It actually stands for 'earnings before interest, taxation, depreciation, and amortisation' (amortisation is just another form of depreciation). As these items are largely outside the control of local operational management, this can be seen to be a reasonable measure of the actual performance of local staff, as it takes into account items that are generally within their control. In the case of our shoe shop in Section 14.2.1, assuming that there is £50 interest included in the administration costs; the inclusion of an EBITDA line would create a report as follows:

	£	£
Sales		20,000
Cost of sales		12,000
Gross profit		8,000
Expenses		
Salaries	3,000	
Utilities	500	
Rent	1,000	
Administration	450	
		4,950
EBITDA		3,050
Depreciation	250	
Interest	50	
		300
Net profit		2,750

The net profit is the same, but the EBITDA figure has been calculated and may be compared with the plan or forecast data. It can be argued that EBITDA is not the best measure for staff communication as it includes the benefits of capital expenditure, but not the costs (as depreciation is eliminated).

Remember that internal reports often combine data from the income statement, balance sheet and cash flow statement, and you should therefore check any communication, in conjunction with the information on the three key reports given above, to ensure that you are clear on the sources and meaning of each line of data presented.

The simple example above illustrates the importance of understanding internal financial terminology. It is crucial that those involved in communicating such data, and this duty often falls on a large proportion of line managers, are able to explain the basic origins and importance of the data presented. This information should be readily available in the company, but if this is not accessible, a discussion with a member of the local accounting team would be advised.

ACTIVITY 14.3

Financial information in practice

Examine a recent copy of an internal financial communication for your organisation.

- Decide if the information provided relates to the income statement, balance sheet, cash flow statement, or some combination of these three.
- Do the reports add through to the totals or do they comprise individual information lines?
- What information is the report intending to convey?
- Is there a comparison with plans or budget numbers – is the performance better or worse than expected?

- Is there any terminology or use of acronyms that you do not understand?

Arrange to discuss any questions with your line manager, or if appropriate arrange to review with a local accounting contact. Obtaining a clear understanding of these issues will not only help your own understanding of the company financial position, but enable you to have meaningful discussions with your colleagues and team.

14.4 USING RATIOS TO EVALUATE FINANCIAL INFORMATION

In this section we interpret financial statements by using key ratios that are calculated from the balance sheet, income statement and cash flow statement, which we introduced in the previous sections of this chapter. After completing this section you should be able to undertake:

- classification of various financial ratios
- calculation and interpretation of important ratios
- utilisation of ratios in helping to assess financial performance
- description of the limitations of ratios as a tool of financial analysis
- production of reports analysing results over time or between entities by ratios.

14.4.1 PERFORMANCE MEASUREMENT

A financial statement is the final product of accounting activity. However, it tells us little about the business performance of an enterprise if we simply read these absolute numbers without analysis or comparison. To obtain more meaningful information requires us to do a financial analysis, which is a process involving reclassification and summarisation of information through the establishment of ratios and trends. This key point can be illustrated as follows:

A statement might be reported as: 'in 2012 John Smith ran 200 metres in 28.3 seconds' – this might sound like a good performance, but if we add a comparative statement – 'in 2009 Usain Bolt set the world record for 200 metres of 19.19 seconds' – we are better able to judge!

The objectives of a financial statement analysis are to review an organisation's financial position and returns in relation to risks, by forecasting the firm's future prospects. A popular technique used to analyse financial statements is *horizontal analysis* (or comparative analysis). Horizontal analysis examines changes in individual categories on a year-to-year or multi-year basis: a comparison of ratios between accounting periods over several years reveals direction, speed and extent of a trend(s). By using financial ratios, we can:

- express the relation of one figure to some other figures
- examine various aspects of financial position and performance
- conduct management planning, control and other management decisions, and
- inform investors for investment decision-making.

Vertical analysis is another useful tool. Using this method we examine an income statement or balance sheet in terms of percentages. By reducing the financial data to percentages, we eliminate the effect of the size of the business, as shown in the alternative name of 'common size analysis. The example below shows the income statements of two supermarket groups, a national chain and a local group. Clearly the national chain is far larger, but by reducing the data to percentages, we can examine the percentage of sales that comprises the costs and profits of each. By creating and examining such an analysis, a potential investor or lender can make a better-informed decision as to the use of their funds.

	HYPER PLC		LOCALSTORE LTD	
	£ million	%	£ million	%
Sales	120.0	100.0%	7.0	100.0%
Cost of sales	70.0	58.3%	4.4	62.9%
Gross profit	<u>50.0</u>	<u>41.7%</u>	<u>2.6</u>	<u>37.1%</u>
Expenses	30.0	25.0%	1.2	17.1%
Net profit	20.0	16.7%	1.4	20.0%

The vertical or common size analysis shows that, although Hyper PLC makes a higher percentage gross profit than Localstore Ltd, the smaller group appears to have a lower level of expenses, and hence returns a higher percentage gross profit.

14.4.2 CLASSIFICATION OF FINANCIAL RATIOS

Table 14.2 summarises major ratios which are commonly used.

Table 14.2 Key financial ratios

Type	Reflect	Examples
Profitability	Performance of company and managers	ROCE, ROE, gross and net profit margin
Efficiency	Efficiency of asset usage	Stock turnover period, average settlement period, and so on
Liquidity	Ability to meet short-term financial obligations	Current ratio, quick ratio and cash ratio
Gearing	Long-term solvency	Gearing ratio, interest cover ratio
Investment	Returns on shareholders' investment	EPS, PE ratio, dividend yield, dividend cover, and so on

14.4.2.1 Profitability ratios

Return on capital employed (ROCE)

ROCE examines the relationship between the size of the profit figure and the capital employed in the business. The ratio is designed to assess how efficiently a business is using its resources.

ROCE = profit / capital employed × 100%

Here, the profit is the net profit before interest and taxation. Capital employed comprises share capital plus reserves plus long-term loans.

ROCE can be used to compare with the firm's previous years' figures, its cost of borrowings, its own target ROCE as well as other companies' ROCE for a performance measurement.

Return on equity (ROE)

ROE is another ratio to measure business performance. It differs from ROCE; ROE focuses more on ordinary shareholders' return. Therefore, the ratio is more relevant for existing or prospective shareholders than management.

ROE = Profit after tax & interest & preference dividends / (ordinary share capital + reserves) × 100%

Here, the profit is the amount of profit which is available to the ordinary shareholders.

Gross profit margin (GPM) (used in the supermarket example above)

GPM relates the gross profit of the business to the sales generated for the same period:

GPM = gross profit / sales × 100%

GPM is a measure of profitability in buying and selling goods before any other expenses are taken into account. By comparing average GPM in the same sector, a low GPM may indicate a poor business performance and need a scope for improvement. A high GPM may evidence a good management but may attract more market entries into the industry sector.

Net profit margin (NPM)

NPM relates the net profit for a period to the sales during that period.

NPM = net profit before interest and tax / sales × 100%

NPM is a measure of net profit from trading operations before any costs of servicing long-term finance are taken into account. Different industry sectors have different types of NPM. For example, a supermarket usually has a low rate while a jewellery shop has a high one. There are a number of factors, such as competition, customer, economic climate and industry characteristics, which can influence the NPM ratio.

14.4.2.2 Efficiency ratios

Efficiency ratios are used to examine the ways in which various resources of the business are managed.

Stock (inventory) turnover

Stock turnover measures how well a company converts stocks into revenues. The ratio can be calculated in times or in days.

Stock turnover (times) = cost of sales / inventory

OR

Stock turnover (days) = Inventory / cost of sales × 365 days

Days increased (or times decreased) may indicate a lack of demand (outdated or obsolescence) for the goods or a poor inventory control. However, days increased (or times decreased) possibly resulted from a large stock quantity which is ordered with trade discounts. Similar with the net profit margin, stock turnover ratios could be significantly different between the different industry sectors. For instance, stock turnover ratios for milk in a supermarket are much lower than a building construction in a house developer company.

Accounts receivable collection period (ARCP)

ARCP measures the average number of days that accounts receivable are outstanding.

ARCP = trade receivables / credit sales revenue × 100%

OR

ARCP = trade receivables / credit sales revenue × 365 days

A number of factors may increase the ARCP ratio, such as a lack of a proper credit control, a firm's strategy of attracting more trade by extending credit period or conducting different terms for major customers, and so on. A decreased ARCP ratio usually indicates a good sign if the business is not in a cash shortage. However, an ARCP ratio could be decreased by using factoring of accounts receivables. In that case, the ARCP ratio provides little usefulness in measuring efficiency of credit control.

Accounts payable payment period (APPP)

APPP measures the average number of days that accounts payable are outstanding.

APPP = accounts payable / credit purchases × 365 days

A long payment period provides a business with a source of free finance. However, a long payment period may also indicate that the business has a liquidity problem. In addition, if the business is a slower payer of its payables, its reputation may be damaged and consequently supplies may be discontinued.

14.4.2.3 Liquidity ratios

Liquidity ratios are used to determine a company's ability to pay off its short-term debt obligations.

Current ratio

Current ratio measures the adequacy of current assets to meet short-term liabilities.

Current ratio = current assets / current liabilities

The higher the ratio, the more liquid the business. For most businesses, an ideal current ratio is at or higher than 1.5, although an appropriate level actually depends on the nature of the business. However, a high current ratio may result from a high level of inventory and/or receivables rather than cash and/or low liabilities. In this case, the quick ratio, described below, can be used to make a further analysis.

Some other factors need to be considered in terms of managing a current ratio. For example, an availability of further finance such as overdraft can compensate a relative current ratio. Seasonal nature of the business can also distort the interpretation of current ratio. For example, there is usually a high inventory level in a Christmas season for retailing firms. One more factor is the nature of long-term liabilities.

14.4.2.4 Nature of inventory: slow moving – quick ratio

Quick ratio (acid test ratio)

If the total value of inventory is significant against the total value of current assets and the nature of inventory is slow moving (that is, difficult to convert into cash), quick ratio is a more appropriate one to measure the liquidity.

Quick ratio = (current assets – inventory) / current liabilities

Quick ratio measures the adequacy of current assets (receivables and cash) to meet immediate liabilities. For most businesses, an acceptable figure is in a range of 0.7 to 1.0.

14.4.2.5 Gearing ratios

Gearing ratios are used to determine a company's ability to pay off its long-terms debt obligations.

Gearing

Gearing, or leverage, describes the mix of long-term funding provided internally (by shareholders) to that contributed externally (by lenders).

Gearing ratio = loan capital / total capital employed × 100%

Here, loan capital is long-term (non-current) loans. Capital employed is share capital plus reserves plus long-term loans. A high gearing ratio indicates a big proportion of money borrowed and therefore a big financial risk for the business to meet obligations.

Some disadvantages of a high ratio include:

- *financial risk* – capital repayment when due and interest burden
- *loan covenants* – restrictions on the firm's further loans and operating actions
- *shareholders' returns* – higher returns may be required from increased financial risks.

Some advantages of a high ratio include:

- *increase returns for shareholders* – cheap finance
- *tax relief* – loan interest is an allowable expense for taxation

- *no dilution of control* – each shareholder's proportionate share of the company remains intact.

Interest cover

Interest cover measures the amount of profit available to cover interest payable.

Interest cover ratio = operating profit / interest payable

Here, operating profit is the profit before interest and taxation.
A low interest cover means:

- a greater risk to lenders that interest payments will not be met, and
- a greater risk to the shareholders that the lenders will take action against the business to recover the interest due

14.4.2.6 Investment ratios

Earnings per share (EPS)

EPS is a measure of profitability: the portion of a company's profit allocated to each outstanding share of common stock.

EPS = earnings available to ordinary shareholders / number of ordinary shares in issue

EPS is important for the following reasons:

- It is a fundamental measure of share performance
- The trend of EPS shows the investment potential of a firm.
- It is a major component of the price/earning ratio.

Some limitations of EPS include:

- EPS is decreased by a new share issue in the short term, although the founded project is profitable in the long term.
- EPS is subjective as the earnings figure is subjective.
- EPS cannot be used to compare different companies.
- EPS is a historical figure based on historical accounts.

Price/earnings (P/E) ratio

P/E relates the market value of a share to the EPS.

P/E ratio = market value per share / earnings per share

The P/E ratio is a market confidence ratio:

- earnings multiple – the purchase of a number of years' earnings
- the higher P/E ratio, the faster the growth the market is expecting in the firm's future EPS
- useful in comparing different businesses.

Dividend yield ratio

The dividend yield ratio measures the cash return from a share to its current market value.

Dividend yield = dividend per share / market value per share × 100%

For investors the dividend yield ratio provides:

- how much dividends are paid by the company
- comparisons of various investment possibilities.

14.4.2.7 Trend analysis

By using financial ratios, a trend analysis can be performed by comparing current data with prior periods, to indicate the overall position or strength of a company. There are a number of methods which can be used in trend analysis such as 'scattergraphs' and other graphical techniques, time series analysis, and statistical regression (for example calculating the 'line of best fit) by using a computer program (see Chapter 13 for details).

14.4.2.8 Limitations of ratio analysis

Ratio analysis is an extremely important and valuable technique, but it does come with a 'health warning'. There are a number of potential limitations and issues. Most importantly, there is no standardisation of ratio calculations – these are not regulated in the same way as the production of published accounts, and a number of variations are used by different 'experts'. In comparing ratios, it is important to check that the methods of calculation are consistent, particularly if the ratios have not been calculated from the basic published accounts, but have been extracted from a number of sources. It is also vital that in addition to the headline financial results, the notes to the accounts are also examined to ensure that the content of each category, for example 'creditors', is similar. An example of a potential issue is that when comparing accounts of UK supermarkets, at least one included accounts for an in-house banking operation in recent years, and this would significantly distort the reported figure for creditors, unless the notes to the accounts were checked and the banking element of creditors removed.

 LORRY PLC

CASE STUDY 14.1

Using the figures given below, you are required:

1   To calculate relevant ratios for Lorry plc between 2010 and 2012:

    ● gross profit margin, ROCE, net profit margin; receivables collection days, payables payment days, stock turnover days; current ratio, quick ratio; gearing ratio, interest cover.

2   To analyse the performance of Lorry plc from 2010 to 2012.

The answers to this case study, and the IFRS and IAS summaries 2009, are available on the companion website.

Summarised income statement of Lorry Plc for the year ended 31 December

	2010	2011	2012
	(£m)	(£m)	(£m)
Revenue	840	981	913
Cost of sales	(554)	(645)	(590)
Gross profit	286	336	323
Expenses	(186)	(214)	(219)
Profit before interest	100	122	104
Interest	(6)	(15)	(19)
Profit before taxation	94	107	85

Summarised income statement of Lorry Plc for the year ended 31 December (continued)

	2010 (£m)	2011 (£m)	2012 (£m)
Taxation	(45)	(52)	(45)
Profit after taxation	49	55	40
Dividends	24	24	24

Summarised balance sheet as at 31 December

	2010 (£m)	2011 (£m)	2012 (£m)
Assets			
Non-current assets			
Intangible assets	36	40	48
Tangible assets	176	206	216
	212	**246**	**264**
Current assets			
Inventories	237	303	294
Receivables	105	141	160
Bank	52	58	52
	394	**502**	**506**
Current liabilities			
Trade payables	53	75	75
Other payables	80	105	111
	133	**180**	**186**
Net current assets	261	322	320
Non-current liabilities			
Long-term loans	74	138	138
Total net assets	399	430	446
Equity			
Ordinary share capital	100	100	100
Retained earnings	299	330	346
	399	**430**	**446**

14.5 KEY ISSUES IN CORPORATE GOVERNANCE AND THEIR IMPLICATIONS FOR YOUR ORGANISATION

Modern organisations in which HR professionals operate may take a wide range of forms. The public and 'not-for-profit' sectors have an increasingly varied range of organisations, ranging from central and local government, through NHS trusts, to charities and local enterprise partnerships. In the private sector, companies may range from businesses run by sole traders, through partnerships of various kinds, to limited companies. Each structure has a range of advantages and disadvantages which should be carefully considered when setting up the organisation. For further details, please refer to http://www.gov.uk/business-legal-structures.

Some of the key features are as follows.

A sole trader, for example an HR professional setting up as a consultant, has full control of the organisation. Decisions can be made quickly and since there is no extensive 'chain of command', there should be no problem with decisions and clarity of objectives. Sources of funding for such an organisation, however, could be relatively limited, as are resources to take on more work. Liabilities must be settled by the sole trader, even if this means liquidating personal valuables, or even their house.

A *partnership*, for example a firm of solicitors, operates within a partnership agreement, which clearly defines roles, responsibilities, and the way in which profits are shared. Wider resources and investment opportunities are available, compared with a sole trader, but clearly more care must be taken with communication and joint objectives. Originally, partnerships always had the downside of personal liability, but in appropriate circumstances, they may now be created as limited liability partnerships (LLP).

Limited liability companies, ranging from small private organisations to major multinational public limited companies (PLCs), have the advantages of a wide range of resources and funding opportunities, in particular the issue of shares, but of course may suffer from the many problems associated with a larger organisation. In particular, the area of corporate governance is a major concern, and this may be best explained by first considering the origins of limited liability principles.

Up to the eighteenth century in the UK and often much later in other countries, most companies were run by owner-managers who provided both the funding and the direction of the organisation, and their relatively small size meant that overall control could be exercised effectively. With the Industrial Revolution, huge companies were created in the iron and steel and textiles industries, supported by extensive organisations running railways and canals to provide a transport infrastructure. The funding for these companies could not be provided solely by individuals or small groups or proprietors, so the concept of share ownership became an increasingly popular method of funding. This introduced a fundamental change into the governance of companies, with the separation of ownership and control. Shareholders owned the company, but delegated control of the organisation to directors. This is illustrated by Figure 14.2.

Figure 14.2 Delegation of control

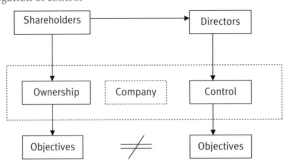

The key issue highlighted by Figure 14.2 is that there is no automatic guarantee that the objectives of the shareholders and directors will be the same. Mechanisms must be put into place to ensure that these are aligned, and to ensure the integrity of the management process in terms of its stewardship of the shareholders' funds.

In addition there is a general responsibility of the directors to ensure trust is present in the whole process. Without trust and confidence, there would be no investors and there would be a complete collapse in the market economy. While an overall failure of confidence has never occurred, over the centuries there have been a large number of individual corporate scandals and failures, and the most widely documented is perhaps that of Enron. We will consider this in some detail as it illustrates a number of key issues.

Enron Corporation was originally formed in 1985, principally around the transportation of natural gas, but the core activities quickly moved towards energy trading. The company clearly believed that the financial rewards in buying and selling financial contracts linked to energy were much higher than those earned by actually owning physical assets. Observers were generally very impressed by the transformation, and reported annual revenues grew from under $10 billion in 1990 to $101 billion in 2000. Unfortunately in August 2001, the situation started to unravel, as the CEO, Jeffrey Skilling, resigned and an increasing level of losses began to be reported, including major adjustments to previously reported information. Finally the company filed for bankruptcy in December 2001.

Subsequent investigations revealed a large number of errors and irregularities, many of which could be classified within the area of corporate governance failures. Some of those that are of the greatest relevance to this chapter are:

- Whereas the key role of a board of directors is to oversee corporate management to protect the interests of shareholders, the Enron board waived the conflict of interest rule to allow the chief financial officer to create private partnerships to do business with the company. This relationship appeared to increase Enron's reported profits by concealing some of its debts and liabilities.
- Enron created special-purpose entities which it did not include in its financial statements and could be used to conceal liabilities and losses.
- Enron directors and senior managers were heavily incentivised by share option schemes and bonuses to engineer increases in the share price, even though this may not be in the longer-term interests of the shareholders.
- One of the members of the internal audit team became very concerned about some of these practices and raised the matter with the CFO in his role as the head of the audit committee. As we will discuss later, this dual role is totally inappropriate. He simply asked for the matter to be left with him to investigate, which did not take place as he was at the heart of many of the various malpractices. A clear opportunity to address the problems was therefore lost.
- Finally, a much broader opportunity to question the practices rested with the 'independent' external auditors Arthur Andersen. This organisation was one of the largest accounting firms in the world. Their Houston office relied on Enron for a major proportion of its workload, as in addition to providing an audit service, Arthur Andersen performed many other accounting and advisory functions for Enron. The local partners failed to disclose the concerns that they had about Enron's accounts as they felt that to be removed as auditors would lose their other Enron work, and perhaps lead to the closure of the Houston office. Unfortunately, the ultimate outcome of their failures was the complete closure of the worldwide Arthur Andersen organisation!

Clearly this size of failure, combined with those, for similar reasons, of Worldcom, Parmalat, and so on, caused major concerns, and loss of confidence by investors. In the USA many urgent steps were taken including the passing of the Sabannes-Oxley Act (2002), which created a strict series of rules for accounts completion and reporting, including formal assertions by all levels of company management as to the accuracy and completeness of data provided. This Act applied to USA companies together with all their significant subsidiaries worldwide. In the UK, a variety of committees were formed, including the Cadbury Committee (1992), which defined corporate governance as 'the system by which companies are directed and controlled in the interest of shareholders and other stakeholders' (p14).

Financial reporting is the process by which directors meet the accountability requirements of the system of corporate governance. Directors report to shareholders regularly on their stewardship with a system of independent auditing providing a check on the 'truth and fairness' of those reports. There are a number of ways that the Cadbury report (1992) recommends that these objectives are addressed, particularly in the roles of executive and non-executive directors, and in particular their duties on key committees.

Executive directors should:

- ensure that managers are acting in the best long-term interests of the shareholders and other investors and stakeholders
- evaluate and influence – examine proposals, decisions, actions, provide feedback and offer direction
- initiate and determine – define the corporate mission, examine strategic options, make decisions.

As a result of the Cadbury report and other key findings, the oversight role of non-executive directors has been increasingly important. These are typically experienced business professionals whose key roles are to:

- provide independent advice and objectivity in monitoring executive management
- perform specialist tasks on particular committees or projects
- provide an external view of the business, improve board processes and effectiveness, and provide valuable external business connections.

The role of the director, whatever the size or structure of the organisation, is a crucial one, both in terms of fulfilling the legal requirements, and in terms of strategic and operational leadership. Further information on the roles and responsibilities of directors and other key company officers may be found on the Institute of Directors website at http://www.iod.com.

From a corporate governance viewpoint, two committees on which non-executive directors always serve are the remuneration committee and the audit committee. Clearly, it is very bad practice for a group of executive directors to be the sole decision-makers for their own remuneration packages, and the role of the remuneration committee, comprising almost exclusively non-executive directors, is to define and implement a transparent policy for remuneration. The policy and actual detailed remuneration of each director is disclosed in the annual report of the company. In determining the policy, the committee needs to consider such factors as:

- maximising the long-term returns to shareholders
- paying enough to attract suitable directors
- reflecting director performance with appropriate incentives
- using a range of measures to evaluate director and company performance, rather than simply share price or net profit (this topic is covered further in Chapter 15).

An example of the published remuneration policy for G4S, a major international security solutions group, which illustrates many of these features, is shown in Figure 14.3.

Figure 14.3 G4S Remuneration Report 2011

Remuneration policy

The policy for the remuneration of the executive directors and the executive management team aims to achieve:

- the ability to attract, retain and motivate high calibre executives;
- a strong link between executive reward and the group's performance;
- alignment of the interests of the executives and the shareholders; and
- Provision of incentive arrangements which focus appropriately on both annual and longer term performance.

In terms of market positioning, the overall objective is to achieve remuneration levels which provide a market competitive base salary with the opportunity to earn above market norms through the company's incentive schemes on the delivery of superior performance. A significant proportion of total remuneration is therefore related to performance, through participation in both short-term and long-term incentive schemes.

The audit committee is a very important body within the organisation and non-executive directors should play a key role, including the position of chairperson. The situation which occurred in Enron, where the FD chaired the audit committee and was able to 'filter' any complaints or issues, is clearly untenable. In the UK the Smith Guidance on Audit Committees (2003), produced by Sir Robert Smith, is annexed to the UK Corporate Governance Code. The Code provides that:

- The audit committee should consist of at least three independent non-executive directors, or two for companies outside the FTSE 350.
- The chairman of a smaller company may be an additional member of the committee provided he was regarded as independent when he was appointed chairman, but he should not chair the committee.
- The board should 'satisfy itself' that at least one member of the committee has recent and relevant financial experience.

The audit committee's main roles are detailed in the Code principles, which can be summarised as:

- to monitor the integrity of the company's financial statements and announcements
- to review internal financial controls and (unless there is a separate risk committee) risk management systems
- to monitor and review the internal audit function
- to recommend the appointment or replacement of external auditors and to review the effectiveness of their work
- to develop and implement policy on the use of the auditors for non-audit services.

Note that many of these provisions have a clear parallel with the problems encountered in the Enron and other major financial scandals.

The audit or risk committee also has a role in fraud prevention. It needs to be confident that there are opportunities throughout the company for employees to act as 'whistleblowers' and report improprieties and abuses. This may mean giving employees contact details for committee members for use if other avenues fail. Many companies have introduced confidential fraud hotlines for employees; others use an outside agency that can take calls and forward the information to the right person. As is covered in more detail in the next section, a fraud response plan will be needed to guide investigations into any allegations of wrongdoing.

ACTIVITY 14.4

Corporate governance in practice

1   Access the BP website and review the roles and responsibilities of the directors (www.bp.com/managedlistingsection.do?categoryId=9021801 &contentId=7040608):

- Identify the chair and members of the audit committee.
- Identify the chair and directors of the remuneration committee.
- Are these all non-executive directors as recommended?
- What else does the site say about corporate governance? (see http://www.bp.com/sectionbodycopy.do?categoryId=9021538&contentId=7077041)

2   Consider how this is addressed in other countries, for example review the corporate governance practices of the Methanex Corporation of Canada (http://www.methanex.com/ourcompany/governance.html). Note the similarities and differences to the BP practices.

3   Consider your own organisation.

- What is its legal structure?
- What is your role – does this have any legal implications?
- Is the organisation of an appropriate size and nature to have non-executive directors?
- Find their roles – audit/remuneration?
- Obtain a copy of the company accounts – are any views or policies on corporate governance stated?

14.6 WHAT IS FRAUD? HOW MIGHT IT BE PREVENTED?

14.6.1 WHAT IS FRAUD?

As Professor Michael Levi has stated: 'Fraud is a deceptively simple word covering very broad territory' (Levi 2012). Put simply, fraud is a way of obtaining money illegally via some form of deception, and may be a face-to-face activity or one conducted in an electronic system. It may take seconds to complete, or may take place over months or even years. The diverse and largely hidden nature of fraud means that the size of the problem is very difficult to quantify, but in 2012 the cost of fraud in the UK was stated to be £73 billion (Levi 2012). A significant proportion of this fraud takes place within organisations, and it is with this element that HR professionals should be particularly concerned – but who commits these offences, and how do they manage to carry them out? In addition to the material provided in the following sections, you may wish to refer to the CIPD 2012 report on this topic, *Managing Staff Fraud and Dishonesty* (2012b).

14.6.2 MANAGEMENT FRAUD

Further to the earlier discussion on corporate governance, some of the most significant frauds may be committed by the senior management of an organisation and involve such offences as deliberate misstatement of financial reports to overstate income or fail to disclose liabilities. Legislation under the Companies Act is becoming more prescriptive as to the accounts to be produced, and the role and responsibilities of directors, as noted in the corporate governance section.

14.6.3 EMPLOYEE FRAUD

This is an area of crucial significance to HR professionals. This category, again, has a wide scope, but primarily relates to the theft of money, goods or services. This may be carried out by employees or by third parties with the support of employees. Typical crimes might be:

- theft or misuse of company assets
- overcharging the company for goods or services received, or not provided
- deriving a benefit from a third party in return for orders or contacts placed
- falsely claiming overtime or expenses
- payment of fictitious employees.

While the purpose of this chapter is to raise awareness of these issues rather than provide a comprehensive guide, it is crucial to note that the investigation of suspected employee fraud must be handled with extreme care from the outset. The organisation should have a fully documented and approved fraud response plan, as part of an overall fraud policy, which must be put into place as soon as there are reasonable grounds to suspect that fraudulent activity has taken place. The size and scope of the suspected fraud will govern the nature of the response. In particular, careful steps must be taken to preserve forensic evidence, including securing of offices and electronic devices. Simply turning on a laptop which is turned off, or the reverse, could have a significant effect on the evidence available for use in any future court action; therefore the appropriate steps, as defined in a clear policy, must be followed. For many organisations, it may be appropriate for any significant investigation to be handled by an external specialist rather than internal HR and finance staff. The specialist should be fully aware of all the implications of the investigation, including the effects of the PACE (Police and Criminal Evidence Act) and the DPA (Data Protection Act).

14.6.3 PREVENTION OF INTERNAL FRAUD

While no system can guarantee to prevent internal fraud completely, Cave (2012) suggests that there are three key elements that are crucial:

- Adopting robust pre-employment screening practices – these can be considered to be the first line of defence against fraud and must consistently be applied. They should include such activities as the detailed review of application documents, full checks on such documents as to their validity, obtaining references including integrity statements, detailed sign-off before the employee is allowed access to the workplace and resources, and full communication and training on the organisation's 'code of conduct' with respect to fraud.
- Establishing an anti-fraud culture, including ongoing communication and training, full and consistent application of financial and procedural controls and, where appropriate, detailed risk assessments of employees or roles where the potential for fraud is a major concern.
- 'Setting the tone from the top': having a defined anti-fraud strategy and policy which is clearly endorsed by senior management, who are prepared to accept that 'it could happen here if we are not very careful' rather than being seen to deny the possibility of such issues, and ensuring that performance and reward schemes are rigorously defined and managed, and do not encourage fraud.

ACTIVITY 14.5

Exploring the risk of fraud in your organisation

Consider the potential risks of fraud in your own organisation.

Is there a clearly defined anti-fraud strategy and policy?

Do you know what steps you should take if a suspected internal fraud is reported to you?

ACTIVITY 14.6

Example of fraud detection

Review the report on the payroll data analysis (2010) undertaken by the UK auditors Deloitte on behalf of Shropshire Council: http://www.shropshire.gov.uk/committee.nsf/0/402CE3ECF970643C802577960031D7D8/$file/4%20Payroll%20Data%20Analysis.pdf

Consider the tests performed. Identify those which are intended to detect fraud by payroll

staff and employees, and which are to detect payroll processing errors. Do some tests have more than one objective?

Are there similar tests performed and recorded regularly in your organisation? If not, should this be taking place?

14.7 CONCLUSION

There are three key types of financial reports, each with distinct rules and purposes, which together can give an overall picture of the financial results and current position of an organisation. Financial reports are created using a clear set of accounting principles, and it is important to gain a basic understanding of these to enable you to gain value from reviewing them. Internal company financial communication may have a wide variety of format and content. You should make every effort to identify the basic messages from these reports, both for your own benefit and for that of your team or colleagues with whom you are sharing the communication.

Comparing financial data with that of other companies or other time periods is crucial to enable clear understanding of progress and issues. Ratios enable a wide variety of parameters to be compared and analysed. Current legislation and best practice has provided a clear framework for effective corporate governance, but it is crucial that company officials perform their roles ethically to ensure that these high standards are comprehensively and consistently applied. Despite all efforts to eradicate it, fraud is still present in most organisations, and it is crucial that HR teams are fully informed on the key risk areas, means of prevention and actions to be taken if it is suspected.

The key financial principles described in this chapter are fundamental to the understanding of financial reports and related activities. This provides an important building block on which to base an understanding of how financial resources can be effectively managed. Many aspects of this key business function are developed further in Chapter 15.

PAUSE FOR THOUGHT

Identify at least three things that you have learned by studying this chapter and engaging with the activities. How will your newly acquired knowledge and skills support your continuing professional development? What value do you expect your learning to have for your daily routines and your further career? In what area have you identified a need for further development and how are you planning to fill that gap? Address these issues in your learning journal and/or CPD log. You may also wish to discuss them with a peer, colleague, mentor or coach to aid your further development.

EXPLORE FURTHER

ELLIOTT, B. and ELLIOT, J. (2010) *Financial accounting and reporting*. 14th ed. Harlow: Prentice Hall.

GOWTHORPE, C. (2011) *Business accounting and finance for non-specialists*. 3rd ed. London: Thomson.

REFERENCES

BP BOARD GOVERNANCE PRINCIPLES: http://www.bp.com/sectionbodycopy.do?categoryId=9021538&contentId=7077041 [Accessed 29 June 2013].

CAVE, D. (2012) How to prevent internal fraud. In: A. DOIG (ed.). *Fraud: The counter fraud practitioner's handbook*. Farnham: Gower. pp429–44.

CIPD. (2012a) *Business savvy: giving HR the edge*. London: CIPD.

CIPD. (2012b) *Managing staff fraud and dishonesty*. London: CIPD.

COMMITTEE ON THE FINANCIAL ASPECTS OF CORPORATE GOVERNANCE. (1992) *Report with code of best practice (Cadbury Report)*. London: Gee Publishing.

INSTITUTE OF DIRECTORS: http://www.iod.com [Accessed 29 June 2013].

G4S REMUNERATION REPORT 2011: http://www.g4s.com/~/media/Files/Annual%20Reports/g4s_annualreport_2011.ashx [Accessed 20 June 2013].

LEVI, M. (2012) Trends and costs of fraud. In: A. DOIG (ed.). *Fraud: The counter fraud practitioner's handbook*. Farnham: Gower. pp7–18.

METHANEX CORPORATE GOVERNANCE PRINCIPLES: http://www.methanex.com/ourcompany/governance.html [Accessed 1 June 2013].

SARBANES-OXLEY ACT (2002) Pub. L. 107–204, 116 Stat. 745, (enacted 30 July 2002).

SHROPSHIRE COUNCIL PAYROLL ANALYSIS REPORT: http://www.shropshire.gov.uk/committee.nsf/0/402CE3ECF970643C802577960031D7D8/$file/4%20Payroll%20Data%20Analysis.pdf [Accessed 20 June 2013].

SMITH REPORT ON AUDIT COMMITTEES. (2003) http://www.icaew.com/en/library/subject-gateways/corporate-governance/codes-and-reports/smith-report [Accessed 20 June 2013].

UK GOVERNMENT BUSINESS LEGAL STRUCTURES: https://www.gov.uk/business-legal-structures [Accessed 29 June 2013].

Managing Financial Resources

Mike Ashwell

OVERVIEW

Chapter 15 builds on Chapter 14, intending to further the understanding of financial information and in particular its use as a key element of business decision-making. This is covered within the overall activity of management accounting. Management accounting is conducted primarily within organisations, and much of the information gathered is not disclosed to outside parties due to commercial sensitivity. An important exception is key information such as the business plan, for example, which will be shared with funders in support of an application for a loan or other financing. Management accounting has a wide scope, ranging from business plans and budgets, through performance reporting and measurement, to calculation of detailed costs. Unlike external financial reporting, there is no statutory requirement for organisations to maintain management accounts, but this chapter will demonstrate clearly the value of such information, and the risk to the business if this area is neglected or poorly applied.

LEARNING OUTCOMES

By the end of this chapter, provided you engage with the activities, you should be able to:

- identify the objectives and key elements of a business plan
- explain the purpose of a budget and identify the key steps in the budget process
- understand how different types of costs behave and the importance of this for business decisions
- understand the importance of cash management within an organisation
- evaluate a capital expenditure proposal using a variety of techniques
- understand the significance of performance monitoring within an organisation and the application of a range of measurement and control techniques
- have a clear appreciation of the value and application of management accounting information to the organisation.

15.1 INTRODUCTION

Management accounting is essentially a forward-looking activity – aiming to predict the future of an organisation by firmly establishing its current position and gaining a clear understanding of past events. The management information determined by this process has a key purpose – that of monitoring and controlling the progress of the organisation and enabling appropriate decisions to be made. Reference will be made throughout this chapter to the 'control loop' – the business process by which plans are established, decisions made, results gathered, and plans and decisions reviewed and evaluated. This process may be illustrated as shown in Figure 15.1.

Figure 15.1 Control loop

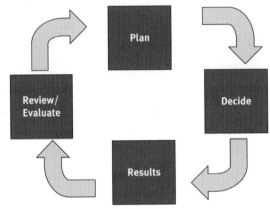

These decisions are usually taken at a variety of levels, from overall strategic issues to detailed pricing and costing choices for individual products or services. In the increasingly complex and fast-moving world of modern organisations, it is essential to establish and communicate a clear view of the overall strategy and direction of the organisation. This is the role of the business plan, with which we will commence our study of the management of financial resources.

15.2 BUSINESS PLANNING

One of the most difficult and time-consuming activities within an organisation is the establishment of a business plan. However, it is also an essential feature of business life – the old military saying 'if you fail to plan, you plan to fail' is still of the greatest relevance in today's organisations. There are a number of key questions addressed by the business plan, which are:

- It enables the business to be reviewed thoroughly in a logical and considered format. The key objectives and direction of the business can consequently be established.
- It provides targets and a framework against which the performance of the organisation may be monitored and controlled.
- It establishes the resources and the times when they are required to fulfil the agreed objectives.
- It provides a framework for communication with all employees about the business objectives and provides a 'common currency' for discussions on such issues.
- It enables current or potential investors in the business to gain a clear understanding of both the overall objectives and the detailed mechanisms by which these are planned to be achieved.
- It provides the framework on which annual budgets are based – and enables those budgets to be checked for consistency with the long-term aims.

The business plan should have a number of key components. These may be presented or combined in different ways according to the exact nature of the business, but the overall contents will always follow a similar pattern. The following structure is based on recommendations on the UK Government website www.gov.uk/write-business-plan:

1   The executive summary:

(a)   This should include a clear mission statement and the objectives of the business. A wide variety of mission statements are currently produced, ranging from a few words to several paragraphs. The best mission statements are lively and attractive and include key aspects of the product or service, the customers, the employees and the financial objectives of the organisation. A mission statement for Fusion 99, a fictitious restaurant, might look like:

> 'We aim to make Fusion 99 a great place to eat, combining a fun atmosphere with Eastern and Western influenced food. By serving delicious meals and retaining happy and motivated staff, we will delight our customers and develop an efficient and profitable organisation.'

(b)   The highlights and key points of the plan should also be presented. The objective should be to present information accurately, but in an attractive style and format which encourages the reader to examine the details of the plan. The summary should not include unsupported 'hype' as this may encourage unjustified expectations in the casual reader or simply cause an experienced evaluator to move on to a more realistic proposal.

2   The business overview:

(a)   key points in the business history and structure

(b)   details of the business products or services

(c)   key features of the industry or sector in which the business operates.

3   Markets and competitors:

(a)   overall size of the market, how it has been developed, and is anticipated to change in the future

(b)   target customers – current and proposed

(c)   competitors – evaluation of their number and size, with estimates of market shares

(d)   overall market environment and potential risks and opportunities.

4   Marketing and sales:

(a)   Given the factors established in Section 3 – Markets and Competitors – a clear description of the marketing strategy, including identification of customer needs, pricing policies and differentiation, promotion and selling techniques.

5   Business operations:

(a)   detailed analysis of the business operations and location(s)

(b)   facilities requirements for production/operations/logistics

(c)   management information systems – both to meet operational and statutory accounting requirements, and to provide management accounting information

(d)   IT infrastructure – to support financial information systems requirements and other applications, for example production control, design, and so on

(e)   an evaluation of the environmental implications of the business, including pollution controls, waste management and any necessary licences or consents.

6   HR requirements:

(a)   management structure, organisation and skills

(b)   employee numbers and structure and ongoing training and development requirements.

7   Financial forecasts:

(a)   These should be the direct and logical result of all the other elements of the plan and will include forecast profit and loss accounts, balance sheets and cash flow statements, together with the key additional assumptions used.

(b)   Detailed analysis should be provided for the first financial year, with clear summaries, with working papers available, for future years. Business plans typically cover 3–5 years, but in the case of industries with very long lead times for establishment of activities, for example a nuclear power station, a plan would extend over a much longer period.

ACTIVITY 15.1

Mission statement of your own organisation

Find the mission statement and objectives for your organisation (if you do not currently work or have no work experience, please move on to Activity 15.2) and consider the following questions:

- How easy was this to find?
- Is it publicly visible – websites, notice boards, prompt cards, communications, and so on?

- Does it address key aspects of the product or service, the customers, the employees and the financial objectives of the organisation?
- Is it employed to assist with agreeing or reviewing personal objectives, for example during personal development reviews?

ACTIVITY 15.2

Mission statements for major organisations

1   Find the mission statement – it may be listed as 'purpose', 'objectives' or 'vision' – for major organisations in the UK and overseas, for example:

- http://www.shell.co.uk/gbr/aboutshell/who-we-are-tpkg.html
- http://www.alcoa.com/global/en/about_alcoa/vision_and_values.asp

- http://www.coca-cola.co.uk/Mission_Vision_and_Values/

2   Consider:

- Is it clearly written and understandable by all stakeholders?
- Does it address key aspects of the product or service, the customers, the employees and the financial objectives of the organisation?

15.3 BUDGETS

15.3.1 BUDGET FUNDAMENTALS

Once an organisation has established a clear business plan, to operate effectively it should then create an annual budget. The budget for an organisation is a key part of the 'control loop' described in Section 15.1 above as well as a further building block in the management of an organisation. The budget should always be align[e] [with the] strategy and objectives and therefore fully consistent with the busin[ess; simply] achieving the budget may not move the organisation in the right direc[tion and lead] to sub-optimal behaviour. There are a number of key purposes fo[r the] budget:

- **Targets:** the most obvious purpose. Setting targets and agreeing acti[ons by which] they can be addressed. The targets may be in the form of costs, for e[xample a] Department budget of £20,000 per month, or may also include other measures, for example a Sales Department budget of 600 units per month.
- **Control:** by matching actual results, both financial and through other measures, with the agreed budget, management can identify divergences from budget at the earliest possible stage, take corrective action and monitor the effectiveness of this action.
- **Resources:** allocating resources and improving investments. In all organisations there are limits on resources, and the budget process enables the available resources to be aligned towards the key objectives. Resources issues can be identified in advance and crucial decisions made in a considered manner.
- **Co-ordination:** allowing the activities of departments or teams who interact within the business to ensure that their plans match. For example, the sales director may be planning to sell 5,000 units of a product during the budget year, but the process identifies that the production department can currently only manufacture 4,000 units in the period. This must be resolved by changing sales targets, revising production plans and resources, sourcing purchased products, or a combination of these actions.
- **Communication:** the budget document provides a sound basis on which to explain to employees the details of the organisation's objectives for the coming year and the role of themselves or their department/team in the achievement of these objectives.
- **Delegation and rewards:** by identifying key responsibilities of teams and individuals as part of the budget process, delegation may be effectively achieved and, where appropriate, this may be linked to an evaluation and reward process.

Given that the budget clearly has far-reaching impact on an organisation, it is vital that the budget process is effectively planned and managed. Successful organisations agree and communicate a budget timetable well in advance of the actual requirement and allocate clear responsibilities for each stage. As with all key activities, it is vital that the budget is demonstrated by management at all levels to be of crucial importance to the organisation rather than simply a necessary evil which must be despatched as quickly as possible. Each organisation will develop an appropriate process, but as Dyson (2010) suggests, a general process may be described as follows:

- Identify the current mission and objectives of the organisation and ensure that these fully reflect the latest position – they will form the keystone of the budget.
- Identify limiting factors, for example a production constraint, space limitation or pollution limit, which cannot be changed during the budget year.
- Prepare an initial forecast of the key factors – for example sales values/quantities and production/service quantities. Perform an initial match and resolve any fundamental discrepancies.
- On the basis of the agreed key data, prepare departmental cost and performance information.
- Prepare an initial budget – identify mismatches or shortfall in required profit or cash.
- Review the initial budget and agree management actions to resolve the issues identified. Where necessary, corrective actions must be communicated and resolved between departments/groups to ensure efforts are co-ordinated and not contradictory.
- Consolidate the updates to the budget and agree final approval – several iterations may be required before this point is reached!

- Communicate appropriate budget summary and details to all those affected. Senior management will require the full overview and details, but individuals may require a simple overview, together with the specific targets and impacts for their roles. This information can be effectively discussed during personal development reviews as an aid to objective-setting, monitoring and feedback.

15.3.2 BUDGET TECHNIQUES

The details of the budgets which are prepared in the process described above may be addressed by a number of different approaches. The two extreme approaches and a practical compromise are described below:

- The **incremental approach**, as described by Gowthorpe (2011, p386), was historically employed in public organisations and is still prevalent today. The approach is based on using the previous year's data and adding an agreed percentage for inflation. This approach may be made slightly more sophisticated by using a variety of percentages dependent on the data type, for example differing percentages for salaries, administration costs and IT costs. The advantages of this approach are that it is generally quick and simple, but it does not address changes to the internal and external environment of the organisation or its key objectives. It may also lead to pressure for managers to spend up to their budget level to ensure that the full value is subject to the inflation uplift for the following year.
- The **zero-based** or **bottom–up approach**, as described by ACCA (2013), starts with a 'blank sheet' and the budget is solely produced on the basis of the long-term objectives of the organisation and the means by which these can be addressed in the budget year. All items of sales and revenue are built up based on these objectives and the current environment with very limited initial assumptions. Clearly this should result in a very detailed and accurate budget, but is extremely time-consuming and there is a risk that key items may be omitted if there is not sufficient reference and validation with historic information.
- Best practice is to adopt a **practical approach** which is a combination of these two extremes. This involves the combination of overall organisational objectives and current environment with detailed knowledge of previous budgets and actual results. Where necessary, structural changes can be made to incorporate new departments or methods of working. The overall budget is checked for completeness and consistency against both long-term plans and previous history.
- Recent criticisms of the limitations of a fixed budget process have led to the development of **beyond budgeting** techniques, as described by Hope and Fraser (1999), where an organisation adopts a less structured approach that includes flexible targets in response to the ever-changing external environment. This has been adopted successfully by a number of major international organisations, such as Handelsbanken based in Sweden, but it has proved unsuccessful in others. The key issue has proved to be the increased requirement for very strong management to provide strong leadership and decision-making input to direct a fluid internal organisation with an absence of the traditional budget structure based on functional departments or 'silos'.

15.3.3 PRACTICAL BUDGET ISSUES

Without the effective engagement and co-operation of management and staff, budgetary control can be at best ineffective and at worst can cause demotivation and the opposite effects to those that were intended. Case Study 15.1 illustrates a number of these issues.

SNACKS LIMITED

CASE STUDY 15.1

Snacks Limited manufactures a variety of pre-packed food products. Responsibility for the manufacturing costs of each product is given to individual product managers. They have responsibility for the purchasing and production functions for their products but have no say in machine replacements or labour rates. The selling and distribution aspects are the responsibility of the sales manager.

The company has recently seen a large increase in both the demand for its products and the breadth of its own product range, and in order to effect better control has instigated a 'responsibility accounting' system.

This involves senior management in association with the accounts department setting predetermined budgets based on anticipated activity levels and costs. The budget is divided into 12 accounting periods and at the end of each of these the budget managers' individual performances are highlighted through the comparison of actual costs incurred in the period with the predetermined budgets. Any adverse variance in excess of 5% is required to be explained to senior management at the monthly management board meeting.

An example of such a performance report (for the De-Luxe sandwich department for month 5) is shown below:

Performance report

Production Centre: De-Luxe Sandwich Manager – E. Bowyer

Productive activity	Budget 6,000 units	Actual 8,000 units	Variance		
Costs	£	£	£		%
Sandwich fillings	3,000	3,900	900	Adverse	30
Bread	1,000	1,250	250	Adverse	25
Direct labour	800	950	150	Adverse	19
Indirect labour	500	500	–	–	–
Depreciation	200	200	–	–	–
Other attributable costs	300	310	10	Adverse	3
Selling and distribution	250	280	30	Adverse	12
Apportioned overhead	1,000	1,100	100	Adverse	10
Total	7,050	8,490	1,440	Adverse	20

The budget was prepared two months prior to the start of the year.

The manager concerned, Eddie Bowyer, is a little upset. He has just been heavily criticised for the adverse performance of this department. He has been with the company for 20 years, working his way up to manager from junior assistant, and has always felt he has given the company his best. He is now feeling rather disgruntled and is considering his future with the company.

Questions

1 What are the key issues that have upset Eddie Bowyer?

2 How could the report be improved to reflect the quantities of products that he has been required to make and the areas of cost that he can actually control?

3 Revise the report to illustrate your views.

4 Comment on problems that you have identified with the budget process and suggest improvements.

15.4 COST TYPES AND COST BEHAVIOUR

In order to make effective decisions, it is crucial that the behaviour of different types of costs is clearly understood. There are a number of different cost types and their nature is easily explained with reference to practical examples:

- **A fixed cost** does not change when there are changes in the level of activity. This level of activity may be defined in terms of production, sales or usage – but always in some form of units. A domestic telephone bill provides a helpful example. Most domestic telephone bills comprise two main elements, a line rental charge and a call charge. The line rental charge is a fixed cost. It does not vary with the number of call minutes. The line rental charge may be illustrated on a chart as shown in Figure 15.2.

Figure 15.2 A fixed cost

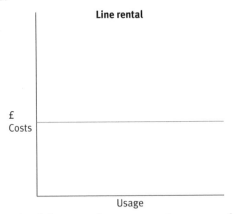

Many business costs are fixed, for example rent, rates, insurance, administration, salaries, and so on. These do not varying with changes in the level of activity or output of the organisation.

- A **variable cost** varies in proportion to the level of activity. Using our domestic telephone bill as an example, the call charges will usually be variable costs. Another indicator of a variable cost is that the cost is usually zero when the level of activity is zero – that is, when we make no calls we would expect no call charges. A variable cost is shown in Figure 15.3. Note that the cost line starts at the origin and steadily rises as usage increases.

Figure 15.3 A variable cost

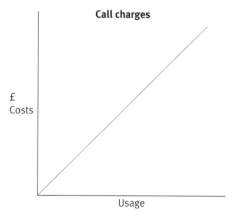

In a business, such items as raw materials and sometimes direct labour costs are variable costs.

- Some charges, such as the overall package for our domestic telephone, are combined so as to create an overall **semi-variable cost** – one that has both fixed and variable elements. This is illustrated in Figure 15.4, where the two elements of the charge are combined.

Figure 15.4 A semi-variable cost

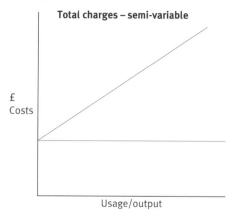

Figure 15.4 may also be used to illustrate the overall cost position of an organisation. Where, as is usual, the organisation has a combination of both fixed and variable costs, the overall fixed costs may be illustrated by the horizontal line and the variable costs by the slope. Note that even when there is zero usage or output, fixed costs are still incurred; therefore, the variable cost slope is added to the fixed costs, rather than starting at zero.

● A **stepped fixed cost** – in some circumstances, an organisation may have costs that are fixed until a certain output or usage level is reached, and then there is a step rise in costs. This may arise, for example, where a manufacturer has three distinct production bays in the factory, each of which can be used to produce 100 units per week. At demand levels between 0 and 100 units, heating and lighting is only required for one bay, between 101 and 200 units, two bays are used, and over 200 units three bays are used. The heating and lighting costs will therefore step up to the next cost level as each level of production is reached. Note that this is a distinct shift in costs, rather than a smooth progression as with variable costs. This is shown in Figure 15.5.

Figure 15.5 A stepped cost

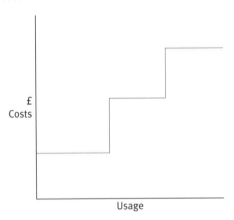

15.4.1 BREAK-EVEN POINT

The calculation of a break-even point for an organisation is very useful for management decision-making. 'The break-even point is the point at which no profit and no loss is made' (Gowthorpe 2011, p438). Any increase in output from that point should yield a measurable profit, whereas a decrease will produce a loss. The break-even point may be illustrated on a graph simply by adding a revenue line to our overall cost chart (Figure 15.6).

Figure 15.6 Total costs, total revenue, break-even

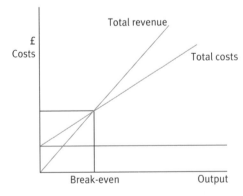

The point at which the revenue line intersects the total cost line is the break-even point, and the break-even level of output is simply shown by projecting that point downwards to the output axis. This shows the level of output required to break even. Practical business information requires a quicker and more accurate process than drawing graphs, and the break-even point may be readily found by calculation.

The break-even point can be calculated by first determining the contribution per unit sold. Contribution per unit is calculated as the sales (revenue) per unit, minus the variable costs per unit. The break-even point is then given by dividing the contribution per unit by the fixed costs.

For example, if a business made light fittings at a variable cost of £6 per unit and sold them for £10 per unit, the contribution would be £4 per unit. If the overall business fixed costs were £8,000 per annum, the number of fittings required to break even would be:

8,000 / (10–6) = 2,000 units

 ACTIVITY 15.3

Fixed costs, variable costs and break-even

As the owner of Woodlands Taxis, you are faced with intense competition in your local area, and you are worried because you do not know how many passenger miles need to be achieved in order to break even. You first need to confirm your understanding of fixed and variable costs, and break-even points.

Sketch a simple chart for the taxi firm, including labels on axes, showing:

- total costs – including both fixed and variable costs
- revenue
- break-even point.

Your fares are £2 per mile and you have the following annual costs:

Fuel	20p per mile
Insurance	£10,000
Drivers' wages – fixed contract	£50,000
Administration costs	£20,000
Depreciation of vehicles	£10,000

Part 1

Determine which of these items are fixed and which are variable.

Calculate how many passenger miles need to be driven to reach the break-even point.

Remember that the break-even point is calculated using the formula:

Break-even point = Fixed costs / Contribution per unit

Contribution per unit = Selling price per unit – Variable costs per unit

Part 2

Using the information in Part 1, how many passenger miles will be needed for you to make an annual profit of £10,000?

Part 3

You have been offered some more efficient vehicles for which the fuel cost will be only 10p per mile, but the total annual depreciation will be £30,000. How will this affect your break-even miles, and the miles required to make £10,000 annual profit?

15.4.2 SHORT-TERM DECISION-MAKING

It is important to note that the definition of fixed and variable costs described above is principally related to short-term decision-making. In the longer term, all costs may be considered variable, for example local authority rates are fixed in the short term, but in the longer term the organisation may choose to move or expand premises and hence the rates bill will change.

A clear understanding of cost behaviour is very valuable for managers making short-term tactical decisions about pricing or operations. A company may usually sell its products for £100 per ton, with variable costs of £60 per ton. If it has spare capacity and receives a short-term offer to purchase product at £80 per ton, the first instinct would be to refuse the offer as it is significantly below the usual price. The offer is, however, above the level of variable costs and hence every additional ton sold yields a contribution of £80 – £60 = £20 towards the existing fixed costs. If the offer was at £50 per ton, it should not be accepted as, in this case, each additional ton loses the company an additional £50 – £60 = £10 per ton.

15.5 CASH MANAGEMENT

The discussion of the cash flow statement in Chapter 14 demonstrated that this is a relatively simple financial statement, not unlike a bank statement that an individual receives for their bank current account. It may be tempting to think that if a monthly balance sheet and profit and loss account are available for an organisation, the cash flow statement is probably superfluous. This is very far from the truth, as many organisations have found to their cost.

It is also important to note that the meaning of the term 'cash' in this context extends far beyond notes and coins, which have only a limited place in most modern businesses, but also to bank deposits, both in local and foreign currencies, and short-term investments which may be readily converted into current bank balances.

In everyday conversation, the terms 'profit' and 'cash' are often used interchangeably, but in business they are very different, and this may be illustrated by two simple and contrasting examples:

1   Bob the builder has a one-man business as a jobbing builder, carrying out small construction work and repairs for householders, for which he insists on cash payment. The materials that he uses are bought on credit from a builders' merchant, nominally on 30 days' payment terms, although he usually manages to stretch that to 45 days or more. He always has plenty of cash and seems to be running his business successfully. At the end of the year, he takes his box of receipts and cheque book stubs to his accountant and is amazed to learn that he has actually made a small loss for the year. He has been underpricing jobs, but has not realised it because of favourable timing of his cash flows – generally receiving payment 45 days before paying his bills. He therefore has cash, but no profit.

2   Stadium Enterprises is a major building company specialising in the construction of sports stadia. They pride themselves in their construction skill and efficiency, and are delighted to be offered a two-year contract to build a football stadium. The contract price, at £20 million, looks fine, and all their projections indicate a healthy profit. They neglect to focus on the payment terms, however, which indicate that 40% of the contract value will be paid only on final completion. Work progresses very well on the contract, but with a high proportion of the overall expenditure being required in the first year of the project, the company runs up a large cash deficit, which had not been forecast, and is forced to go into liquidation. They have a good forecast profit, but no cash.

These examples clearly demonstrate that profit and cash are not the same and that an organisation must carefully monitor and manage its cash resources. There are many reasons for the divergence between profit and cash, and we will examine those that are of particular importance from a practical financial management viewpoint.

Organisations very frequently sell goods and services on credit terms. The sale will be recorded in the profit and loss account in the period in which the sale takes place, but in the cash flow statement in the period when the payment is received. It is vitally important that this time lag is recognised and closely monitored. It is also crucial that every reasonable effort is made to check the customer's ability to make payment when due – and the typical steps in this process, as described by Business Link, are as follows:

1   The organisation should have clear terms of sale which define precisely when payment should be received for invoices. These terms must not be ambiguous, for example 'payment in 30 days' is not sufficiently precise; 'payment into the designated bank account within 30 days of the date of product delivery' is much better as it is more exact. If an individual sales contract is made, these terms must be specifically referred to.

2   The organisation should have a detailed and consistently enforced credit management policy. This will include obtaining references and credit checks for new customers, and regularly monitoring the position of existing customers.

3   The credit management process for existing customers should include both periodic credit checks to ensure their ongoing credit worthiness, and could also include subscriptions to organisations providing business information, such as Dun and Bradstreet Limited, who provide both ad hoc information and ongoing customer monitoring and alerts.

4   Internally, the organisation's credit management policy and processes should include detailed monitoring of payments, at an individual customer level and for the organisation as a whole. One measure that is very frequently used is the accounts receivable collection period (ARCP) as described in Chapter 14, usually defined in numbers of days. This provides a very rapid measure of debt collection efficiency, for example, if the standard company payment terms are 30 days after delivery, and the ARCP shows a current value of 45 days, there is clearly a payment problem, which must be followed up urgently in detail. It may be just a few customers who are severely overdue or a general late payment problem.

5   If payments are severely delayed, the credit management policy should define a range and sequence of actions to be taken, for example stopping supply to the customer until payment is received, referring the company to a debt collection agency or direct legal action.

A second major variation between profit and cash is the purchase of goods and services on credit terms. Many of the principles that apply to this process are similar to those described above:

1   The organisation should establish a clear contract with the supplier, including a detailed description of the terms of payment.

2   The organisation should have a supplier payments policy and process which ensures that supplier payments are made on the due date, unless there is a documented dispute in process.

3   This may be effectively monitored using the accounts payable payment period (APPP) calculation described in Chapter 14. By reviewing the number of days yielded by this calculation, the organisation can identify overall supplier payment issues and focus on

the specific accounts where problems are arising. In practical terms, this often occurs, not as a deliberate company policy, but due to individual managers simply failing to approve and pass on invoices for payment. Clearly a simple training process, followed by effective monitoring, could address this issue.

4   In the short term, it might be argued that it is of benefit to the company's cash flow to delay payments to suppliers beyond the contractual due dates. This not only gives rise to problems of business ethics, but also can result in practical difficulties. Delay in payments may result in the company being placed on the supplier's 'stop list', with no supplies being made until payment is received. This may result in a number of problems, including disruption to business activities, due to the shortage of key materials or services, and an impaired credit rating, which may reduce the ability of the company to gain credit accounts with other suppliers.

The other key area where company managers can influence the variation between profit and cash is in the level of stocks held. By reducing stocks, the company may be able to improve cash flow, even though profit may be unaffected. As described in Chapter 14, the stock turnover, calculated as a number of days, can vary widely between different types of organisations. The key area of management decision-making and control in this area is to monitor and critically review the levels of stocks held, and make crucial decisions on stock-holding levels and possible alternative strategies. This requires accurate data, in terms of numbers of days' stock held for each item, clear information of the exact purpose and criticality of each stock item, and a good understanding of the supply chain and lead time for each item. Careful analysis of all these features may result in quite different decisions being made for the wide range of stock items. For example, a major manufacturer may identify three key stock areas:

1   An item in stock, costing £50,000 which is a unique spare part for a custom-built production line machine – to order and receive a replacement would take several months. Clearly, although the stock turnover of this item may be measured in years, rather than days, the value of cash tied up appears to be fully justified, to provide 'insurance' against major business disruption in the unlikely event of the failure of the installed part.

2   Production components, with a typical value of £500,000, which are delivered weekly by the supplier, with an average lead time of two weeks – the overall stock holding could be reviewed in detail, ensuring that the number of different components is rationalised, where possible, and agreement made to share the company production schedule with suppliers so that components could be delivered on a daily 'just-in-time' basis where this is beneficial.

3   Several hundred items of maintenance spares, with a total value of £100,000, and a stock turnover up to 60 days, all of which are readily available on a daily basis from a local supplier – this appears to be an example where, by making a specific agreement with the local supplier to hold stocks of a designated list of spares, the stock-holding effort and cash holding could be significantly reduced.

There are other reasons for differences between profit and cash, covered in Chapter 14, such as depreciation, provision for bad debts and company financing transactions which are significant for the organisation as a whole, but not within the remit of the day-to-day operational management of the organisation. By closely monitoring and managing the position with debtors, creditors, and stocks, the management of an organisation can significantly influence the cash flow statement of the organisation and be in a much stronger position to contribute to an accurate cash flow forecast. Further details on this topic are covered by Gowthorpe (2011).

Why is it so important that an organisation maintains an effective cash flow forecast?

1   To avoid surprises which can be costly both in direct terms and in lost opportunities – by having a clear forward view of its cash position, the company can identify, for example, that there will be a cash shortage of £50,000 for a week at the end of July, and appropriate steps can be taken to bridge that gap with a short-term loan or bank overdraft, which can usually be agreed more easily, and at better rates, than if it were a last-minute crisis request.

2   Similarly, the identification of a forecast cash surplus in a future period enables plans to be made to invest the cash at the best possible rates – again, these are likely to be more favourable when planned and agreed in advance.

3   Many transactions are now made in currencies which are not that of the usual company transactions, and by predicting such inflows and outflows, decisions can be made on currency sales and purchases and, where appropriate, these can be made in advance so as to hedge the exposure to exchange rate movements and remove uncertainty and risk.

15.6 CAPITAL EXPENDITURE EVALUATION

Capital investments are major long-term investments fundamental to the organisation. Dyson (2010, p427) notes that all entities would find it difficult to survive if they did not invest in some form of capital expenditure. Whereas many decisions have relatively short-term impacts, capital expenditure involves the appraisal of profits and cash flows generated, often over several years. The key objective of capital expenditure is to directly or indirectly generate extra profits for the business. Funds for capital expenditure are never unlimited; therefore, in considering the potential return on the investment, the opportunity cost should be taken into account. The opportunity cost is a measure of the return that could be earned if the funds were invested elsewhere.

In making decisions on capital expenditure, managers must make two linked decisions – whether the proposed project meets the basic criteria for financial return, and what is the ranking of the project among the other projects under consideration. Clearly if availability of capital was unlimited, all projects meeting the return criteria would be approved, but this is never the case, and a defined means of project ranking is crucial.

A number of evaluation techniques may be used to assess capital expenditure proposals. The techniques and process chosen by a company should be clearly documented, as illustrated later in this section, in some form of capital expenditure policy manual, to ensure that the approved processes are consistently followed, and decisions between expenditure requests are made logically and fairly. This section will examine the four most common techniques, all of which are widely used:

- accounting rate of return (ARR)
- payback
- net present value (NPV)
- internal rate of return (IRR).

15.6.1 ACCOUNTING RATE OF RETURN (ARR)

This method compares projected accounting profit for the project with the capital invested in the project or asset. The calculation is as follows:

Average expected return (accounting profit) / Average capital employed × 100 = ARR%

It should be noted that accounting profit for the project takes into account the depreciation of the assets, unlike the cash flow principle on which the other three evaluation techniques are based. The average capital employed is calculated by taking the initial expenditure at the start of the project, calculating the depreciated value at the end of each year, totalling each of the annual values for the life of the project, and dividing by the number of years, as follows:

	Accounting profit £'000	Capital employed £'000
Year 0		100
Year 1	20	80
Year 2	15	60
Year 3	10	40
Year 4	10	20
Year 5	5	0
Average accounting profit = 60 / 5 = £12,000		
Average capital employed = 300 / 6 = £50,000		
ARR = 12,000 / 50,000 × 100 = 24%		

This return may be compared with the minimum return required in the company's capital investment procedures, or with its return on capital employed, as calculated in Chapter 14. If the project return meets or exceeds the criteria, it is placed in a 'pool' to be compared with other projects whose return is calculated in exactly the same way. Projects with the highest returns are selected in descending order or returns, to the point where the organisation's capital budget is fully committed.

15.6.2 PAYBACK

Payback is a technique which is simple to understand and apply. It involves estimating the length of time it will take for the cash inflows from the project to exceed the initial outflow.

	Cash flow £'000	Cumulative £'000
Year 0	−100	−100
Year 1	20	−80
Year 2	30	−50
Year 3	30	−20
Year 4	20	0
Year 5	10	10

In this example, the project repays its capital costs by the end of year 4.

Using the payback technique has the advantage that it can be readily understood by non-financial staff and focuses on the payback in the early years of the project, thus reducing the effect of uncertainty. It does, however, ignore the time value of money, which will be explained in Section 15.6.3, and ignores potentially large cash inflows and outflows of cash after the payback period. This may be potentially misleading, particularly if there are major cash outflows at the end of the project, for example to remove major items of equipment.

15.6.3 NET PRESENT VALUE (NPV)

This technique uses the concept of the time value of money. The principle involved is that £1 now is more valuable than £1 in a month's time or £1 in a year's time. The net present value method therefore discounts all cash flows to the same terms, adjusting for the time value of money. This calculation is dependent on the choice of a discount rate. The company might choose to apply a discount rate that reflects the cost of borrowing, for example a bank rate of 4%, but few capital investment projects are risk-free, so the company is likely to apply a risk premium to give a total discount rate of, say, 10%.

Using the cash flows from the example in the previous section, the discount factor at a 10% rate is applied to each year's cash flow. Note that the discount factor increases each year, as £1 in five years' time is worth much less than £1 next year.

	Cash flow £'000	Discount factor (10%)	Discounted cash flow £'000
Year 0	−100	1.000	−100
Year 1	20	0.909	18
Year 2	30	0.826	25
Year 3	30	0.751	23
Year 4	20	0.683	14
Year 5	10	0.621	<u>6</u>
			−15

This calculation indicates that at the selected discount rate this five-year project has a negative discounted cash flow, and therefore should not proceed. If the value had been positive, the return would be compared with other potential projects, evaluated on the same basis, to provide a ranking list for access to the available capital. The NPV technique takes into account all cost and revenues over the full life of the project and hence should avoid issues around remediation costs, which are a significant problem with the payback method.

15.6.4 INTERNAL RATE OF RETURN (IRR)

Some organisations use the internal rate of return technique. This is best described as the inverse of the NPV method, in that using the cash flow information prepared on the same basis, a discount rate is calculated which brings the net value of the project to zero. For example, using a discount rate of 13% a project may have a negative net value of £10,000, at a rate of 12% the net value may be zero, and at a rate of 11% it may have a positive net value of £5,000. It can therefore be said that the IRR of the project is 12%. If the company discount rate was 10%, the project would qualify to be ranked for approval.

ACTIVITY 15.4

Evaluating capital expenditure

Examine the following cash flow information from a project proposal. The project is to extract gravel from a greenfield site, which must be returned to its original condition after five years. Note that there is a cash outflow in Year 5 which includes the expense of this remediation. Evaluate the project using both the payback and NPV methods described in this section. The company payback criterion is that a project must repay its capital cost within four years. The company uses a 10% discount rate for NPV calculations. The discount factors to be used can be taken from the example in Section 15.6.3 above.

	Cash flow £'000
Year 0	−200
Year 1	120
Year 2	80
Year 3	60
Year 4	50
Year 5	−120

Do both evaluation techniques yield the same decision? Consider why differences might arise.

15.6.5 CURRENT PRACTICE – TECHNIQUES ACTUALLY USED

Research shows that organisations often use a combination of approaches to decision-making on capital investment. Larger companies often use a payback criterion to 'weed out' projects that do not pay back sufficiently rapidly, and then apply IRR, NPV or ARR techniques to rank the shortlisted projects. Smaller companies often use the payback method to make their initial selections and then use a less formal process of management judgement to make the final choices. This judgement incorporates a view of the project risk, which is usually more formally incorporated in the discount rates by larger organisations. The key principle should be that a consistent approach is adopted to every proposed and approved project, and this is the purpose of the creation and implementation of a capital expenditure policy manual, which is described in the next section.

15.6.6 CAPITAL EXPENDITURE POLICY MANUAL

Such a manual is essential to ensure that capital investment proposals are correctly and consistently reviewed, and that once a decision has been made the ongoing investment process is fully managed and reviewed. The policy manual should include specifications for:

- an annually updated forecast of capital expenditures – to be included in the overall cash flow forecast for the organisation
- the appropriation steps – processes to follow and forms to be used
- the appraisal method(s) to be used to evaluate proposals, with a clear definition of the sequence and documentary evidence required
- the minimum acceptable rate(s) of return, or payback periods, on projects of various risk

- the limits of authority for approval of each defined project size
- the mechanism for reporting and control of capital expenditures
- the procedure to be followed when accepted projects will be subject to a post-completion audit and performance review after implementation.

15.6.7 POST-COMPLETION AUDITS

It is vital that capital expenditure projects are monitored from the approval stage through to final completion to provide evaluation and feedback on decisions. The post-approval audit plan should be established at the project authorisation stage. It should not be seen as threatening to managers as this would have an undesirable impact of deterring managers from putting forward all but the safest of investment schemes. It should have a very positive effect in that thorough and realistic project appraisal is undertaken before a project is finally proposed, as the sponsoring manager is clearly aware that both the decision process and the ongoing project costs and benefits will be thoroughly audited. By making a much more comprehensive database of reviews available to managers, this will improve the quality of decision-making by making past experience available to decision-makers – this is a significant contribution to knowledge management within the organisation.

A positive but sometimes unwelcome result of post-approval audits is that decisions can be made at an early stage to modify or even terminate a project which is not meeting its planned outcomes. Rather than this being the result of an ad hoc decision, it can be made with full explanation and justification.

There are some further practical difficulties with the post-approval audit process. One is simply the problem in isolating the specific costs, revenues and cash flows resulting directly from the project. This can be particularly difficult in a rapidly changing external environment, and some practical estimates may need to be made to enable a reasonable statement of the project performance, compared with the plan, to be produced. Post-approval audit may prove to be time-consuming and unwelcome to some managers, particularly when it is first introduced, but nevertheless it is an important tool to facilitate improvements in capital expenditure management and decision-making.

15.7 PERFORMANCE MONITORING

We have seen how budgets and budget monitoring and control are one aspect of the way that companies monitor their performance. As previously indicated, management accounting covers more than just financial data, and recent developments in performance monitoring have seen it adopt an expanded remit to cover much wider aspects of the organisation. Why should this be?

Current thinking is that traditional performance monitoring was unduly focused on budgetary financial control, which although it produced widely understood measures and information, concentrated on only a few aspects of the overall organisation. It was argued by Kaplan and Norton, among others, that a much wider view of the organisation and its strategy was required. They devised the balanced scorecard approach, which enabled managers to obtain a fast but comprehensive view of the business performance and the progress towards its strategic aims. The scorecard addresses the key areas of the organisation and shows how important the linkages are between those areas. The key areas initially chosen by Kaplan and Norton (1996) are as follows:

Financial – 'To succeed financially, how should we appear to our shareholders?'
Customer – 'To achieve our vision, how should we appear to our customers?'
Internal business processes – 'To satisfy our shareholders, what business processes must we excel at?'

Learning and growth – 'To achieve our vision, how will we sustain our ability to change and improve?'

These key areas are all clearly linked and are all targeted at the vision and strategy of the organisation. Kaplan and Norton intended the four initial areas to be indicative suggestions, and indeed other writers have added further dimensions, for example supply chain and technology. Once the key aspects of the scorecard have been devised, based on the mission and values that we discussed earlier in the chapter, a number of key objectives and measures for those objectives should be devised. Overall, this means that groups and individuals have specific targets that are directly aligned with the overall strategy of the organisation, and are not, as often happens, working hard but actually 'pulling in the wrong direction' through no fault of their own.

By identifying objectives and specific measures, and monitoring performance against targets, management have a clear picture of the overall success of the organisation and can readily identify areas where improvement is required. For each of these problem areas, an improvement project can be identified, and the total of these improvement projects should encompass all the initiatives in progress in the organisation. Any company initiatives not directly linked to the scorecard objectives are simply contributing to 'initiative overload' and should be removed.

An example of the application of the balanced scorecard approach to performance monitoring is as follows. If we analyse the mission statement from our imaginary restaurant, Fusion 99, as introduced in the Section 15.2, we might identify the key dimensions of the business as:

- customers
- operations
- human resources
- finance.

Within those dimensions, the objectives might be:

- delighted customers
- effective operations
- happy staff
- sustainable profits.

A range of measures and targets could be selected to monitor performance, for example:

- A weekly customer survey with a target of customers rating 'good' or 'excellent' at 95%.
- An employee turnover measure with a maximum target of 20% per annum turnover.

Several measures may be chosen to address each of the dimensions, but it is important that these should not proliferate so that the effect of each is devalued. A practical maximum of four measures per dimension is usually recommended. By monitoring performance against specific closely defined measures, the management of the organisation have a concise and accurate overall view of the progress of the organisation, and team leaders can provide clear briefings on their section's progress, with the knowledge that their objectives are fully integrated with the overall business strategy.

An example of an improvement project that might be identified is if the customer survey indicates a lower level of satisfaction than targeted. A multi-functional improvement team should be identified to analyse the areas of shortfall, recommend improvements and oversee their implementation. For example, a problem with the customer satisfaction results might be identified to relate to small portion sizes. Representatives of the finance, marketing and operations teams would meet to identify how this can be best resolved in the most effective way, in line with the overall organisation objectives. It might just require the purchase of smaller plates!

The argument is sometimes raised that not all objectives can be effectively measured, but the counterargument is that those that really cannot be measured are perhaps not appropriate objectives, or are at least very difficult to communicate to managers and individual staff.

The balanced scorecard (Kaplan and Norton 1996) is an example of a popular technique used for performance monitoring. It is widely used by commercial organisations and also in the public and other not-for-profit sectors. It also serves to illustrate the means by which finance closely integrates with other aspects of the organisation. Many performance measures are not finance based, but all of the items measured contribute directly or indirectly to the financial performance of the organisation. A good example of this will be illustrated in the following section on environmental management accounting, in which many non-financial measures are reported and monitored alongside the conventional financial measures as part of the overall management process of the organisation.

ACTIVITY 15.5

Developing Fusion 99's balanced scorecard

Examine the mission statement for Fusion 99, and the suggested objectives noted above, and create some additional measures and targets which could help to monitor the progress of the organisation towards its key objectives.

'We aim to make Fusion 99 a great place to eat, combining a fun atmosphere with Eastern and Western influenced food. By serving delicious meals and retaining happy and motivated staff we will delight our customers and develop an efficient and profitable organisation.'

ACTIVITY 15.6

Applying the balanced scorecard

Take the mission statement for your own organisation, identified in Activity 15.1, or for an alternative organisation, as identified in Activity 15.2, and consider the key dimensions of the

organisation – you should identify between four and six dimensions. Define the objectives, and hence measures and targets, that you consider to be appropriate.

15.8 ENVIRONMENTAL MANAGEMENT ACCOUNTING

Before the 1990s, environmental accounting was generally considered to be the preserve of a few specialist researchers, and environmental issues as a whole were examined by individuals or very small groups within major companies. The costs of pollution and waste were often not recorded against particular activities or departments, and were 'lost' in overheads. For example, costs of disposal of waste created throughout a manufacturing site were often collected and reported within a single transport or waste disposal department, rather than being identified as relating to specific production activities or products. Since these costs were not identified as being the responsibility of a specific manager, there was little incentive to reduce cost or environmental impact of the waste created. These specific issues are handled by environmental management accounting and are seen to be a key current concern for organisations, for a number of reasons, as noted by Gray and Bebbington (2001):

- *Regulations*: international, national and local environmental regulations are now in place with which organisations must comply, or risk major fines or restrictions on their ability to operate. The cost of fines or effect of restrictions could be prohibitive.
- *Customers and suppliers*: the overall supply chain is now much more environmentally conscious and companies may refuse to work with potential partners who, for example, are unable to offer the facility to return packaging for recycling.
- *Trade organisations*: having appropriate and auditable environmental procedures in place may be a condition of membership of a trade organisation which is vital to the company.
- *Cost benefits*: awareness and investigation of potential benefits, including cost savings, of waste reduction can yield a competitive advantage to the organisation.
- *Financing*: providers of finance, including banks and other financial institutions, are increasingly conscious of the importance of reviewing the environmental impact of their investments. Many shareholders, and potential shareholders, factor in environmental impacts to their investment decisions.

The role of management accounting in these processes is to enable the effects to be measured, using both financial and non-financial data. This is proving to be a significant challenge. Often environmental departments are not fully integrated with the cost structure of the organisation. Many environmental costs are hidden within overheads and are not attributed to the department actually generating the waste or pollution. Despite increasing focus on control and stewardship, many organisations do not fully track the flow of materials through their processes, and are simply unaware of all the losses and waste that are occurring. Many capital investment decisions do not follow the guidelines indicated earlier in this chapter, and hence do not include the overall lifetime costs of a project, including all pollution and remediation impacts.

Given these potential pitfalls, how should a modern organisation identify and handle environmental costs through its management accounting processes? Some key steps are as follows:

1   Analyse the flow of products and services through the organisation, so as to fully identify all costs of delivering products or services from the initial supplier through to the customer. Where these costs include elements of waste, these must be separately recorded against the operation and product or service to which they relate.

2   For companies using physical materials – use a mass balance process to accurately track flows of materials through the process, so as to identify where waste and pollution are occurring – this could also result in significant cost benefits.

3   Implement some form of reporting tool, such as the Rhône-Poulenc Environmental Index, through which all waste costs are reported back to the manager or department with which they originate, on the principle of 'polluter pays'. For example, rather than having overhead costs for waste disposal collected within a transport department, all such costs should be analysed and charged directly to the departments where these items originated, thus enabling the true cost of their product or service to be identified, and corrective action taken if required.

4   Analysing all capital expenditure proposals with full recognition of the overall lifecycle costs of the project.

Creating a budget for an organisation which recognises the key impacts of accounting for environmental costs and waste is thus a more complex activity, but the benefits in terms of management awareness and control should significantly outweigh the costs. By capturing environmental data within the routine management reporting of the organisation, decisions can be fully integrated into day-to-day operations, and annual company reporting, including environmental impacts, should prove to be easier and with more positive initiatives to be presented.

15.9 MANAGEMENT ACCOUNTING: KEY EMPLOYEE ATTRIBUTES

This chapter has illustrated a number of ways in which management accounting information is vital to the management and control of any organisation. In the current ever-changing environment, reliance on periodic financial accounting reports is not sufficient – an organisation needs to have effective measures, based on strategy, measures, budgets and forecasts, based on accurate, timely information. This vital information must be fully communicated to empowered and well-trained staff. An enlightening study by Dearman and Shields (2005) investigated how individuals in an organisation reacted to a fundamental change in the accounting principles used to determine product pricing. They found that:

- 78% of managers did not change their decision model
- 20% of managers changed their decision model in the right direction
- 2% of managers changed their decision model in the wrong direction.

Their conclusions on investigating these managers in detail was that those who reacted in the correct way to the change were those properly equipped to take on the change, that is:

- Unless people have the correct attributes, they are not likely to change their behaviour appropriately in response to change in management accounting.
- Because employees often lack enough of at least one of these attributes, many firms are not likely to realise benefits from change in management accounting.

This research indicates clearly that the implementation of one or more of the important management accounting techniques described in this chapter does not provide a guarantee of improvement in performance. Staff must have sufficient ability to understand both the details of the new techniques and their wider importance. They must be appropriately trained in the new techniques and their application. Most importantly, they should be sufficiently motivated to drive through the changes successfully.

15.10 CONCLUSION

Management accounting information is fundamental to the internal decision-making process of an organisation. The value of the information extends far beyond the traditional accounts department and is of essential importance both to the management teams within all departments, and to multi-functional teams working on projects or key initiatives. The all-encompassing nature of the financial and non-financial information provides the lifeblood of the control loop circulatory process described at the start of this chapter. The ever increasing rate of change in both organisations and the external environment in which they operate means that it is even more important that accurate and consistent information is available on a timely basis, to enable the decision-making processes to be swiftly but rigorously applied.

PAUSE FOR THOUGHT

Identify at least three things that you have learned by studying this chapter and engaging with the exercises and activities. How will your newly acquired knowledge and skills support your continuing professional development? What value do you expect your learning to have for your daily routines and your further career? In what area have you identified a need for further development and how are you planning to fill that gap? Address these issues in your learning journal and/or CPD log. You may also wish to discuss them with a peer, colleague, mentor or coach to aid your further development.

EXPLORE FURTHER

If you wish to explore further the management of financial resources, there are a range of activities and materials that can be recommended. There are a number of very helpful texts which expand on the key topics covered by this chapter and are particularly targeted at managers and students who are not finance specialists, but who aim to develop further their theoretical and practical knowledge of this key area. The works listed in the references section by Broadbent and Cullen (2003), Dyson (2010) and Gowthorpe (2011) should prove very useful in expanding on topics that are inevitably covered rather briefly in this general chapter. You may also want to explore Duncan Williamson's website, which introduces the key numerical techniques required for capital budgeting (see http://www.duncanwil.co.uk/invapp.html).

It is also strongly recommended that you take every opportunity to be involved in budgetary meetings and financial communication sessions within your organisation and that you volunteer for multi-functional project teams, where you will gain enormously from exposure to staff from across all specialisms, including finance. You should also consider taking part in business simulation activities, which will not only enhance your financial understanding, but will also develop your awareness of the linkages between finance and the other key business areas. There are many such 'games' that, although usually great fun, also have a very serious business and educational purpose. An example may be found at http://www.venturesimulations.co.uk

REFERENCES

ACCA. (2013) *Comparing budget techniques [online].* Available at: http://www.accaglobal.com/en/student/acca-qual-student-journey/qual-resource/acca-qualification/f5/technical-articles/comparing-budgeting-techniques.html [Accessed 27 June 2013].

BROADBENT, M. and CULLEN, J. (2003) *Managing financial resources.* Oxford: Butterworth-Heinemann.

CIMA GLOBAL. (2005) *A practitioner's guide to the balanced scorecard [online].* Available at: http://www.cimaglobal.com/Documents/ImportedDocuments/tech_resrep_a_practitioners_guide_to_the_balanced_scorecard_2005.pdf [Accessed 14 June 2013].

DEARMAN, D. and SHIELDS, M. (2005) Avoiding accounting fixation: determinants of cognitive adaptation to differences in accounting method. *Contemporary Accounting Research.* Vol 22, No 2. pp351–84.

DYSON, J. (2010) *Accounting for non-accounting students.* 8th ed. Harlow: FT/Prentice Hall.

GOWTHORPE, C. (2011) *Business accounting and finance for non-specialists.* 3rd ed. Stamford, CT: South-Western Cengage.

GRAY, R. and BEBBINGTON, J. (2001) *Accounting for the environment.* 2nd ed. London: Sage.

HOPE, J. and FRASER, R. (1999). Beyond budgeting: building a new management model for the information age. *Management Accounting.* Vol 77, No 1. pp16–21.

KAPLAN, R. and NORTON, D. (1996). Using the balanced scorecard as a strategic management system. *Harvard Business Review.* Vol 74, No 1. pp75–85.

MILLS, R. and KENNEDY, J. (1993) Experiences in operating a post-audit system. *Management Accounting.* Vol 71, No 10. p26.

CHAPTER 16

Effective Decision-making and Problem-solving

GILLIAN WATSON

OVERVIEW

Decision-making is a core managerial and leadership responsibility. Making a decision is to choose a course of action from a pool of alternative options. A decision, once made, commits resources required for its implementation. Decision-making is constrained by a number of factors over which managers do not always have full control. Decision-making becomes even more complex when it is at a group level or involves ethical considerations. To the manager or a leader, decision-making is not a matter of choice but a requirement and personal responsibility, which determines both the viability and profitability of the business. Continuous development of decision-making skills is a matter of priority for managers and other decision-makers.

An equally essential managerial responsibility is problem-solving. It involves finding the root cause of problem(s) through analysis, the exploration of possible solutions through evaluation and selection of the most suitable solution. Creative problem-solving skills enhance one's ability to resolve problems by stimulating imaginative thoughts to produce innovative remedies that ensure business survival. Creativity has been traditionally associated with the creative arts but has become a key quality that differentiates leading organisations from their less innovative counterparts in today's competitive business environment because it facilitates innovation, flexibility and competiveness. Creative problem-solving improves the quality of solutions to problems, motivates staff and enhances satisfaction of management.

Acquiring decision-making and creative problem-solving skills will enhance a manager's capacity to make effective decisions based on ideas that will gain acceptance and the resources needed to carry them through. In this chapter you will learn about such skills in the context of underpinning knowledge, creative methods, group approaches, techniques to deal with ethical dilemmas, and guidelines for communicating decisions.

LEARNING OUTCOMES

By the end of this chapter, provided you engage with the activities, you should be able to:

- understand decision-making and creative problem-solving
- understand and apply creative methods of decision-making and problem-solving

- understand the importance of developing mental skills to be creative and proactive
- understand ethical decision-making and problem-solving techniques and ways of resolving ethical dilemmas
- explain approaches to communicate and justify decisions and problem-solving options.

16.1 INTRODUCTION

Central to decision-making is choice among alternative courses of action. A decision is therefore a chosen course of action from alternatives (Harrison 1996). The choice is informed by the decision-maker's knowledge, their understanding of the issues at stake, and conviction of the solutions available. This means decision-makers determine the relative attractiveness of each option and select the 'best' to meet the decision-making criteria. Every decision option will lead to either a positive or negative outcome. It is possible to have a collection of decision options that provides positive outcomes to a different degree. The decision-making process is also constrained by financial and human resources, absence of requisite technology, the quality of data and information available, and relationships, legal and ethical considerations. Hence, the key issue in decision-making is the ability of the decision-maker to choose the option that offers the best outcome of all the options available. Effective decision-making aims at ensuring that the most efficient and effective decision is made by utilising the best information possible within a given timescale. It is also essential that the decision can be communicated and justified to respective stakeholders.

Creative problem-solving involves the application of imaginative thoughts to produce innovative remedies that create competitive advantage and ensure business survival (Titus 2000). At the operational level, it can motivate employees and increase the credibility of managers and decision-makers. The total effect of creative problem-solving techniques is improved satisfaction through the implementation of innovative ideas. It is therefore very important for decision-makers to acquire creative problem-solving skills to find solutions to complex problems, increase staff motivation and enhance organisational performance.

Many management writers have used creativity and innovation interchangeably but others (Heap 1989, Titus 2000) have argued that they are fundamentally different, albeit part of a continuous process. For example, Titus (2000) suggests that creativity results in the generation of new ideas. According to Heap (1989), creativity leads to the creation of new ideas but innovation relates to putting into practice the ideas produced from creativity. This means that creativity involves coming up with new ideas. It is then followed by a process of innovation which involves sorting out and applying the refined ideas within an organisational setting. Such a distinction is very important for a better understanding of the two key terminologies and how managers and decision-makers can take the correct steps to enhance their creative and innovative skills.

16.2 CREATIVE METHODS OF DECISION-MAKING AND PROBLEM-SOLVING

Managers and leaders within any sector of the economy will find it valuable to have a guide to decision-making and problem-solving. The associated skills and techniques allow them to reduce risks and enhance the rewards accrued from the decisions they make. For decision-makers to succeed and achieve the desired organisational objectives, it is important to resolve problems creatively. There are simple as well as complex decision-making and problem-solving tools and techniques. The proceeding discussion will cover six thinking hats (De Bono 2000) and lateral thinking (De Bono 2009, 2011), storyboard exercises, benchmarking creative leadership skills, mental imagery, mind-mapping (Buzan 2010, Keene 2013), Pareto analysis and the plus–minus–interesting (PMI) technique as key methods to enhance contemporary managers' decision-making and creative problem-solving capabilities. It will explain the nature and scope of these techniques, illustrate how they work and provide opportunity for practice and reflection.

16.2.1 DE BONO'S SIX THINKING HATS

The 'six thinking hats' technique, also known as 'De Bono's coloured hats', is noted as a key decision-making tool because it aids the decision-maker to look at making a decision from various perspectives. De Bono (2009) suggests the brain to be a self-regulating system and therefore we ought to educate the brain to think in different ways. Approaching decision-making from different perspectives does not come naturally when one has to make a decision. Rather, decision-makers are more inclined to stick to the status quo by adhering to what they know and believe works for them. This tool, therefore, comes in very handy to decision-makers as a good background skill that encourages them to explore all possibilities for a more comprehensive solution. By so doing, decision-makers are enabled to explore in addition to rational decision capabilities their creativity and intuitive abilities to deal with the problem at stake. It enables decision-makers to explore opportunities outside their comfort zone for solutions without overplaying the rational approach and being less defensive of the status quo. The six thinking hats technique is applicable to both group and individual decision-making.

Table 16.1 Description of De Bono's six coloured hat technique

Hat	De Bono's prescription
White	Always focus on data, information or facts available, explore knowledge gaps, draw lessons and attempt to bridge knowledge gap or find remedy.
Yellow	Stands for optimism and brightness and focuses on positive thinking, points to benefits and value of the decision, encourage forward-thinking and not giving up even when encountering challenges.
Black	Wear the hat of pessimism, play the devil's advocate, spot the weaknesses and dangers, minimise the tendency for complacency, enhance one's preparedness to resolve potential difficulties.
Red	Espouses expression of intuition, emotion and conviction, positive or negative feelings, reading into possible emotional and intuitive feedbacks from other people likely to judge the decision.
Green	Advocates creativity, creation of new ideas and perceptions, offers every idea an opportunity for consideration without initial criticism and possible elimination (see also discussion on lateral thinking).
Blue	Worn to manage the thinking process towards a consensus, usually associated with facilitators of the decision-making process at team meeting sessions, directs compliance with the directives on the thinking hats. For example, this hat will emphasise green hat to serve as a catalyst for creativeness.

Source: adapted from De Bono 2000

Using this tool means that a problem is considered from these six perspectives, and it therefore will prop up decisions and plans with a combination of ambition, skill in execution, sensitivity, creativity and good contingency planning. Hence, decisions made by exploring the six different points of view helps groups and individual decision-makers identify potential pitfalls, reduce the risk of a backlash and enhance the possibility of arriving at a viable solution to a problem. It minimises the tendency to becoming a victim of unforeseen possibilities by helping the decision-maker to test the waters.

CASE STUDY 16.1

AN ILLUSTRATION OF THE SIX THINKING HATS TECHNIQUE

The scenario

The management of an insurance company is considering whether to acquire a new office building. The economic indicators are all positive and the company is growing. They have subsequently employed many new staff and this is putting a lot of pressure on office space for staff. At a committee meeting to decide the way forward, the management team decided to use the six thinking hats technique as a planning tool.

Suggested application of the 'six thinking hats' to the above scenario

Assessing the issue with the *white hat*, the team analyses data at their disposal. The team reviews staff office allocation reports that confirm the need for more office space. They recognise that the time required to complete the new office acquisition will be adequate to solve the problem since the majority of the new recruits are starting in the next three months. The financial bodies are predicting increasing growth for at least the next three years in the light of the economic recovery and the reducing cost of credit.

Looking at the issue with the *yellow hat*, the team sees exciting moments ahead. The benefits likely to accrue to the business will outweigh the cost of acquisition as the economy and the business are all expected to grow. If there is any prospect of economic downturn, the company is not likely to suffer from acquiring the new office because they would have made significant profit in the three years of growth. They also have the option of freezing recruitment of new staff after three years.

When evaluating the problem from the point of view of the *black hat*, they have anxieties about how reliable the economic projections by the financial institutions are. Competitors could undercut prices and they can lose clients. Economic decline and intense competition may mean downsizing and hence the new office building would not be put to good use.

Thinking with the *red hat*, some members of the management team think acquiring the new office will mean many of the current middle managers located at their present office will have to be moved into the new office to manage the new staff, who are primarily client advisers. This change may not be well received by the affected middle managers, although analyses show that the acquisition is cost-effective.

With *green hat* thinking the management team focuses discussion around office arrangement and design to ensure efficient use and to offer a pleasant and safe working environment for staff. They further consider changes required to make their clients as comfortable as possible and the need to ensure that if the new office is to be rented out at some point, it will be attractive to other office users. They may also consider if the possibility of redesigning their current building to increase its capacity is a viable option. They may also explore office-sharing through flexible working arrangements.

The *blue hat* has been used by the meeting's chairperson to co-ordinate the step-by-step application of the different thinking styles. They may have needed to ensure that team members allow equal opportunity to contribute and share ideas and build consensus when all points have been expressed.

ACTIVITY 16.1

Applying the six thinking hats technique

Apply the six thinking hats technique to diagnose a case where you have been selected as the chairperson of a committee set up by your organisation to plan a redundancy programme in the wake of a global recession.

16.2.2 LATERAL THINKING

Lateral thinking is a way of thinking that explores non-conventional remedies and ideas to solve problems (De Bono 1970, 2009). It is a cognitive approach that sidelines the generally acceptable logical means of thinking in order to generate creative ideas. It has been characterised by bringing together unfamiliar elements, looking at the other side of the coin, re-combination and drilling out for new connections from existing ideas. Conceptually, it is similar to the 'green hat' thinking approach. In the context of problem-solving, lateral thinking espouses indirect rather than direct methods to provide solutions. Flexibility is one key element in lateral thinking. It is important to emphasise that lateral thinking principles do not seek to replace logical or traditional thinking methods in decision-making and problem-solving but play a complementary role. Some of the operative phrases that convey the differentiation between lateral and traditional logical thinking are:

- to think of as many solution options as possible and thus going beyond the obvious or the status quo
- to avoid sequence by approaching issues from several directions (order reversal) and then linking them up
- to break down problems into as many parts as possible to give equal attention to all parts
- to encourage cross-fertilisation of ideas where another person's idea is viewed as a different solution option from existing ones and not an opposing idea.

Thinking laterally leads to the creation of new mental representations as the problem-solver accepts all other suggested solution options that are treated as alternatives. Lateral thinking problems are encountered in everyday life. The popular case of describing a glass half full of water as being half empty is a typical lateral thinking example. Clearly, both views are correct and applicable. Hence, from the point of view of lateral thinking the two options are not opposing views but a collection of views that offer many decision options from a variety of creative ideas. Another interesting example is where, in a child custody case in the US, the judge, in deciding how much time the children involved will spend with the respective parent, ruled that the children will stay at their current address but parents will alternatively come in to spend time with them.

Lateral thinking is also very useful in solving problems in management practice. This is because management problems by their very nature can be approached from so many perspectives. Creative solutions to management problems mostly emanate from lateral rather than vertical thinking. De Bono (2011) maintains that creativity is a skill and, therefore, can be learned. However, according to De Bono (2011), the biggest obstacle to creativity is our poor thinking. Learning to think creatively can aid our overall decision-making, which in turn can enable us to 're-think the future' (De Bono 2011) in our attempt to make more creative decisions.

ACTIVITY 16.2

Hung parliament

The General Election in the UK in 2010 did not produce an overall majority for either of the major parties, which is commonly known as a 'hung parliament'. A new government can only be installed if a coalition government made up of two or more parties is formed. A hung parliament is a rare and undesirable scenario because new elections will have to be called until a party receives a majority or is able to from a coalition government.

Think about the threat of a hung parliament prior to the election in 2010 in the UK and the

solutions offered by contesting political party leadership. The popular position was for the electorate to ensure that they vote in such way that one party gains an absolute majority of 326 seats. Do you think the only solution was to avoid a hung parliament or were there other means of resolving this issue?

What decision will you make, regarding your political affiliation, in the next opportunity to vote for a new government in 2015, and what will be your main decision-making criteria?

ACTIVITY 16.3

Creativity is a skill

Go to YouTube and watch a presentation by Edward De Bono: http://www.youtube.com/

watch?v=UjSjZOjNIJg. What lessons can you take away from his contention that creativity is a skill that everyone can learn?

16.2.3 STORYBOARD EXERCISE

Organisations with a history of creativity and innovation are noted for encouraging the creation of ideas; they believe in attaining competitive advantage through innovation to meet their customers' needs (Twiss 1974). The receptiveness of organisations to creativity and innovation is important to unearth the potential of management and staff towards creative problem-solving. McAdam and McClelland (2002) have stressed the need for an organisation to build a culture which cherishes the continuous generation of ideas and which always seeks to reward creativity.

Storyboard exercise is a planning tool that helps users to explore their creative capabilities to generate ideas which are expressed in both words and pictures to bridge the gap between an existing state and an expected future state. A storyboard exercise covers a series of events that need to happen to ensure that the expected end state is achieved and is used in a number of diverse settings:

- in website design and video production to foster creativity
- as a planning tool for learners to help them organise their thoughts to achieve a learning outcome
- in project management to understand the various parts of the project and aids in rearranging sections of the project to achieve the total deliverables of their project

- in organisational change management to communicate through pictures the future desired state of the organisation.

The global pharmaceutical giant Glaxo's executive development programme epitomises a good example of a creative working environment in action. A key component of this development programme is to support their leaders to explore new ways of unearthing their creative potential to build cutting-edge competitive advantages (Godfrey 1998). For the purpose of illustration, Glaxo's Storyboard exercise is considered to point out building skills from a creative activity. The expected end state in this example was a successful management career at Glaxo (see Case Study 16.2).

CASE STUDY 16.2

 STORYBOARD EXERCISE (COURTESY OF GLAXOWELLCOME)

The objectives of the storyboard activity are:

1   to help participants express their future ambition

2   to allow them to see the gap between current and future state

3   to enable participants to generate some transitional steps

4   to encourage participants tap into their subconscious wisdom.

Table 16.2 The storyboard

The present	Transition 1	Transition 2
Transition 3	Transition 4	The future

Storyboard activity process

Step 1: Participants are supported by a facilitator to draw a picture of the future in the designated box on the storyboard.

Step 2: Participants then capture how things are at present in the box designated as the present on the storyboard.

Step 3: Transition steps are then drawn on the storyboard. It is important to note that the number of transition phases varies from one exercise to another. It is determined by both the issue to which the technique is being applied and the discretion of the individual or the team using it. In this particular case, Glaxo created four transitional stages.

Step 4: When the storyboard is fully completed participants are then invited to share their hopes, dreams and aspirations.

Lessons

During the sharing process participants within the group are offered the opportunity to assess commonalities and differences across their views and perceptions for the present and the future of the organisation. At the individual level, participants are led on a journey to explore 'transitional steps' towards the future.

ACTIVITY 16.4

Applying the storyboard exercise

Using an organisation you are familiar with, outline the benefits of the storyboard exercise to build creative skills.

16.2.4 BENCHMARKING CREATIVE LEADERSHIP SKILLS

Many organisations undertake skills audits to assess skills gaps for the continuing professional development of their staff. Leadership skills are important for managers and decision-makers because they influence acceptance and smooth implementation of decisions. One would come across various leadership attributes in management literature. Of special interest to this discussion are the common attributes for creative leadership developed by Peter Cook (1998).

Benchmarking leadership skills in terms of creativity is a relatively novel idea (Yamoah 2010) and was developed using the common attributes of creative leadership by Cook (1998). It provides you with an opportunity to assess your creative leadership ability and subsequently design a plan for further development. Based on Cook's (1998) six common creative leadership attributes, this exercise offers baseline criteria for personal assessment of and reflection on one's creative leadership skills. The six creative leadership attributes are presented in Box 16.1 as a general measure of creativity for business leaders and decision-makers.

Box 16.1: Creative leadership attributes

- ability to set a direction that excites others, rather than bland 'mission' statements
- ability to advocate, sense and move ideas around the organisation to attract resources and gain acceptance
- ability to espouse a tangible example to the concept that failure is a learning opportunity and encouraging risk-taking
- ability to build teams with a level of trust and conflict resolution
- capacity to enable others to make meaning and sense out of their environment
- competence to move rapidly from one role to another without losing credibility.

Source: based on Cook 1998

In terms of benchmarking, a professional can make a self-assessment on the scale of 1 (very low) to 5 (very high) across the six characteristics outlined above. For each attribute scored, the participant will have to cite at least two examples as evidence to support the score. A total score greater than or equal to 18 is deemed satisfactory creative ability, while a score below 18 suggests a need for improvement. It is, however, important to undertake a thorough analysis of the relative scores for each attribute to be able to identify specific competences that require improvement. It is also highly recommended for individuals engaging in this activity to involve others such as colleagues, peers, mentors, coaches or a line manager.

ACTIVITY 16.5

Applying creative leadership attributes

Carry out an assessment of your leadership skills using Peter Cook's (1998) six creative leadership attributes and design a personal creative leadership development plan for the next six months. It is always helpful to seek the co-operation of your line manager, mentor or a colleague for effectiveness of this activity.

16.2.5 MENTAL IMAGERY TECHNIQUE

Professionals adopting a proactive approach to decision-making and problem-solving tend to be more successful than their less proactive counterparts. Being proactive is to create one's own circumstance by undertaking entirely new events or changing existing ones, rather than waiting to react to situations as they occur (Bateman and Crant 1999). Self-awareness, conscience, independent will and creative imagination are important personal qualities that determine how proactive a person is (Pavlina 2004). Pavlina (2009, p3) further emphasises this point on proactivity when he relates this to personal growth: 'Genuine personal growth is honest growth. You can't take short-cuts through the land of make-believe.'

As described earlier, creativity is seen as the vehicle that generates innovative ideas to enable individuals to act proactively. Mental imagery technique is used to illustrate the importance of proactive problem-solving. It assumes that people in general (and decision-makers in particular) have a natural tendency to stick to the status quo. In Pavlina's (2009, p12) words: 'When you make decisions from a certain state of mind and act upon them, you reinforce the same state, thereby increasing the likelihood you'll respond similarly in the future.' Such a predisposition (which can be found in different cultures) has found expressions in popular phrases such as 'stick to the knitting', 'why re-invent the wheel', 'if it's not broken why fix it', and 'a bird in hand is worth more than two in the bush'. The limiting factor is the lack of capacity to 'think outside the box', that is, the inability to go outside the subjectively created boundaries, and as a result the better part of management knowledge is not used (Bennett et al 1999).

Behind this background, the proponents of mental imagery techniques advocate that creative and innovative solutions only emerge after an internal representation of the problem or issue is constructed. Therefore, the key to opening the door to stimulating imaginative thoughts is the ability to visualise and transcend beyond personal boundaries. It is viewed as the process of integrating the right- and left-brain thinking abilities (see also Chapter 11). This will then release thoughts across more divergent and creative ideas. Mental scenario rehearsal is regarded as a key activity within the technique since it has been found to improve mental imagery. Typical examples include:

1   Many athletes mentally practise their events either the night before the competition or minutes before they participate in the respective competition (McWhirter and McWhirter 1985).

2   Taking a mental walk through a presentation as part of preparation has proven to enhance the presenter's knowledge and the quality of responses to questions during the actual presentation session (Bennett et al 1999).

3   It is a common feature for an individual to mentally picture walking around the house to answer a question as to the number of windows there are in their house (Bennett et al 1999).

4   Many a prospective bride and groom have drawn on their mental imagery to visualise themselves at the altar (Moulton and Kosslyn 2009) and how their great day will look to ensure that everything is in place for the occasion.

These examples show that mental imagery is a common activity. However, in a business setting it seems that the benefits have been overlooked or not appreciated. This is because of the lack of understanding of its usefulness to creative decision-making and problem-solving. Mental imagery brings together a variety of cognitive processes such as opinions, perceptions, memory, voluntary and involuntary actions and thoughts (Hunt 1985) to indirectly observe a behaviour scenario. The direct effects of these processes are observed in the quality of ideas generated to solve problems.

Management decision-makers in particular will gain a lot from practising mental imagery. While management skills taught in the business schools follow the theoretical concepts of management functions, namely planning, controlling, organising, communicating, staffing, problem-solving and leading, in reality managers have undertaken a specific task within a constrained environment. Therefore, the development of mental imagery techniques can enhance management performance because it addresses real management challenges in a safe, convenient, not time-bound and relatively inexpensive manner.

 ACTIVITY 16.6

Applying mental imagery techniques

On the basis of your understanding about mental imagery write a brief outline on how imagery can help in your personal development. Indicate how imagery can help you overcome your personal assumptions and biases to become more creative in decision-making and problem-solving.

16.2.6 BUZAN'S MIND-MAPPING TECHNIQUE

Mind-mapping is an effective thinking tool to enhance creativity and communication for decision-making as well as problem-solving. It helps both individuals and organisations to improve learning, efficiency and productivity. The mind map is a graphical expression of connected thought processes that begins from a central point. Mind-mapping 'creates an exterior mirror of what is happening inside the mind during ideas generation, and repeats and mimics thought processes and amplifies the functions of the brain' (Buzan 2010, p31). Quoting Buzan, Keene (2013, p48) argues that 'normal linear note taking and writing will put you into a semi-hypnotic trance, while Mind Mapping will greatly enhance your left-brain cortical skills'.

The developing mind map in Figure 16.1 expresses the author's thoughts while generating ideas on what makes employees happy.

The developing mind map starts from a central image (a), which in this illustration is an image representing happy staff. The next stage (b) shows an initial four basic ideas on what makes employees happy. It then expands the four initial ideas to another level of branches shown in (c), and further sub-branches in (d) and (e). Examples of fully completed mind maps can be found at http://www.tonybuzan.com/gallery/mind-maps/

Figure 16.1 Graphical illustration of a developing mind map

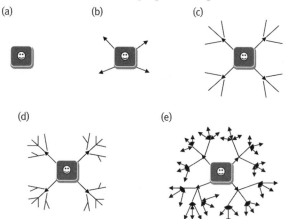

16.2.6.1 Key principles behind mind-mapping

Mind-mapping relies on research understanding of the nature and operations of the human brain and its potential to boost memory by enhancing receiving, holding, analysing and controlling information (Buzan 2010). Of special interest to this section are two such principles stemming from how the human brain thinks.

1   Mind-mapping is underpinned by the principle that the human brain thinks multilaterally and not linearly or sequentially like the computer (Buzan 2010). Therefore, a mind map follows the same pattern as the brain by creating branches outwards to form sub-branches and in so doing creating more ideas. The connection of thoughts in a multilateral thinking pattern of the brain is followed in mind-mapping. This is achieved through linking all ideas on the mind map and hence gains good understanding and insight through associations. Many people that have adopted the mind-mapping technique have found that word association is a key to generating more ideas. It is likened to online searches where finding and reading a piece of information leads to others. Mind-mapping applies this same principle to trigger avenues for linkages to ensure free flow of ideas.

2   Mind-mapping also relies heavily on the fact that human beings think with images and their associations and not in words, as presumed for so many years. It must, however, be emphasised that the period prior to print technology depended heavily on images, signs and symbols for communication. According to Buzan (2010), the words we use are just the vehicles that convey our images out from our own minds to other people's minds. This has been confirmed by many research findings that found the human brain is able to efficiently recognise images in three-dimensional space. Buzan (2010) further asserts that pictures are more important than words when it comes to the effective functioning of the mind because they make use of colour, form, line, dimension, texture, visual rhythm and imagination. This is the reason why mind-mapping places emphasis on the use of images instead of words.

ACTIVITY 16.7

Applying mind-mapping

Use plain paper and coloured pens for this exercise. On one paper write the name of your organisation or an organisation that you are familiar with in the middle. Write out around the name in the centre of the paper words that you associate with your organisation. On another piece of plain paper draw with the coloured pens an image of what the organisation looks like at the centre. Out of this image draw with different coloured pens thick branches to represent each of the words you associate with your organisation. On each branch draw an image that you think best represents the word you associate with that branch.

It is envisaged that the exercise in Activity 16.7 will give you a basic introduction to mind-mapping and will provide you with an opportunity to compare how your mind perceives what you have represented in words and images. The two sheets of paper are to ensure that you start both the word and image representations from the centre of the page.

Mind-mapping can be applied to personal life, learning and work. This section is interested in how the mind map technique application can improve work through management decision-making and problem-solving. It is particularly helpful to decision-making and problem-solving because it sets out needs, expectations, and preferences and challenges of the decision-maker. It ensures decisions are made on the basis of clear understanding of matters at stake. The following discussions will focus on how mind-mapping aids in making simple as well as complex decisions.

Mind-mapping technique follows a set of guidelines in making a simple dyadic decision involving clear-cut choices such as: Yes or No, Viable or Not Viable, Good or Bad, Beneficial or Not Beneficial, and Appropriate or Inappropriate.

The process begins with a central image, followed by drawing main branches and then sub-branches, as shown in the graphical illustration of a developing mind map in Figure 16.1. Having reported and expressed all ideas, emotions and thoughts across the main and all sub-branches of the mind map, five methods are used to arrive at a decision (see Buzan 2010, pp101–2), which are:

1   process-generated method

2   number-weighting

3   intuition

4   incubation

5   option if the weightings are equal.

In the *process-generated method* a decision emerges as the decision-maker gets a clearer picture from the ideas gathered and presented in the mind map. The decision becomes obvious from the detailed overview; this is dyadic decision-making. The *number-weighting method* is applied if a decision has not emerged at the end of the mind map development. With this method every specific word on all sides of the mind map is assigned a number from 1 to 100. Scores are then added for both 'yes' and 'no' sides. The side with the highest score wins. That is, the decision option corresponding to the highest score is adopted. When this second method does not work either, with the *intuition method* the decision-maker's gut feeling decides. Traditionally, intuition has been key in decision-making in crisis management, in situations of uncertainty and when there is a lot of data to be processed (Patton 2003, Novicevic et al 2002). What is unique with intuition application for decision-making through mind-mapping is that mind maps provide a large pool of information that serves as a background for an intuitive decision.

The decision-maker activates the *incubation method* when the first three have failed to yield a decision. It is a simple approach whereby the decision-maker takes a break to allow the brain to 'incubate' the idea. It is a fact that the human brain springs up ideas and decisions when at rest. It is expected that through such a resting phase a decision will emerge. Beyond incubation is a basic coin-tossing or balloting approach (*option if weightings are equal* method), which is used to make a choice because any of the alternatives is deemed satisfactory. The clue here is for the decision-maker to assess their reaction to the outcome of the coin-tossing or balloting, that is, whether your initial reaction is a feeling of disappointment or a relief to help you confirm if the outcome reflects your true feeling. Mind-mapping techniques do not rule out indecision after all the five methods have been exhausted. However, the occurrence of indecision is rare. If it happens, a third decision option, which is 'Continue thinking about the choice', ensues, in addition to Yes and No options, and therefore the nature of the decision is no more dyadic but a triadic (three-option) choice.

The key to using mind maps to tackle complex decisions is an improved ability to choose relevant 'basic ordering ideas' in a good time. Basic ordering ideas are the main branches that are drawn from the central image. Buzan (2010, p105) recommends choosing a maximum of seven basic ordering ideas because the average human brain 'cannot hold more than seven major items of information in its short-term memory'. He further recommends 11 basic ordering ideas that are helpful in developing good mind maps. The caution is that a maximum of seven can be chosen for each mind map and this means that you choose the ones that best reflect the subject.

The 11 basic ordering ideas suggested by Buzan (2010, p105) are as follows:

1   basic questions – how/when/where/why/what/who/which

2   divisions – chapters/lessons/themes

3   properties – characteristics of things

4   history – chronological sequence of events

5   structure – forms of things

6   function – what things do

7   process – how things work

8   evaluation – how good/worthwhile/beneficial things are

9   classification – how things are related to each other

10 definitions – what things mean

11 personalities – what roles/characters people have.

When you have mastered generating basic ordering ideas, the steps on how to create a mind map to aid decision-making covered earlier can then be followed to tackle complex decisions. Mind-mapping techniques can be applied to enhance many other management activities such as presentations and meetings. The coverage in this chapter serves as an introduction to draw the reader's attention to the enormous possibilities by developing mind-mapping skills.

ACTIVITY 16.8

Mind map about staff welfare

Imagine you have been consulted for advice by management on the key issues to be considered in the design of a new staff welfare package for your department. Outline the

relevant basic ordering ideas (main branches) to be drawn from the central image (staff welfare) that you find suitable for the design of a mind map.

16.2.7 PARETO ANALYSIS

This analytical technique thrives on the principle that the majority of the problems in organisations (especially in the area of quality management) are generated by a minority of issues which are the key causes of the entire problem (Craft and Leake 2002). It is expressed as the 80/20 rule, whose central idea is that when a decision-maker is able to identify the few major problems (20 per cent) and provide the appropriate solutions, it will enhance the chance of successfully dealing with the entire problem (Kock 2007). This tool is also referred to as the 'law of vital few' (Daniel 1983), and it was developed by the renowned quality management consultant J.M. Juran and named after Vilfredo Pareto, an eminent Italian economist (Craft and Leake 2002). Pareto analysis has been applied to other disciplines of study over time. In business, Pareto principles tie in nicely with the business idea that 80 per cent of an organisation's sales are generated from 20 per cent of its customers (Guerreiro et al 2008). Pareto analysis can be useful to both a decision-making team and a manager to ensure that they concentrate their efforts on the major key problems (Craft and Leake 2002). The technique becomes the important next step after a cause-and-effect analysis to determine how often the varieties of problems occur.

We will use the example in Case Study 16.3 to demonstrate how decision-makers can apply the principle to the decision-making process. This guides the reader through applying the tool to a typical decision-making scenario.

    LABOUR TURNOVER – AN ILLUSTRATION

CASE STUDY 16.3

A newly appointed human resource manager has found out that the organisation has experienced increased labour turnover for the past five years. In view of this she commissioned a piece of research to help identify the causes of the problem in order to address it.

Feedback from the survey conducted on current and some former employees indicated that seven causes (a, b, c, d, e, f, g), listed below, account for the high turnover rate. The accompanying scores on a scale of 1 to 20 also indicate the importance that the respondents attached to the factor as contributing to staff not completing their contracts with the organisation.

(a) Low morale due to lack of teamwork (2)

(b) Excessive bureaucracy (2)

(c) Poor communication between management and operational staff (3)

(d) Lack of performance incentives (3)

(e)   Absence of flexible working arrangement (1)

(f)   Limited opportunities to acquire new skills (17)

(g)   Absence of a clear staff development policy (13)

The causes identified in the survey were grouped under main three headings, namely:

(a)   Lack of staff training and development [Limited opportunities to acquire new skills (f) and Absence of a clear staff development policy (g)]

(b)   Poor reward system [Lack of performance incentives (d)]

(c)   Inappropriate work practices [Low morale due to lack of teamwork (a), Excessive bureaucracy (b), Poor communication between management and operational staff (c) and Absence of flexible working arrangement (e)].

Table 16.3 Causes of high turnover

Category	Complementary causes	Total score (%)
Lack of staff training and development	f and g	30 (73%)
Poor reward system	d	1 (2%)
Inappropriate work practices	a, b, c and e	10 (24%)

A careful observation of the nature of these causes shows that issues relating to staff training and development contribute largely to the high turnover rate. When the management team concentrates attention on continuous professional development, close to 73% of the problems will be resolved. It is also expected that when staff training and development help improve staff skills and confidence, their performance will also improve. With improved performance, management could afford an attractive reward package to help retain staff. This initial action could be followed up with a review of current work practices to embrace flexibility, improve communication and encourage better teamwork. Thus, by applying Pareto analysis the decision-maker can concentrate on training and development as an immediate priority instead of focusing attention on all the causes identified by current and former employees.

ACTIVITY 16.9

Applying Pareto analysis

Using the interview results presented in Table 16.4 below on a sample of 50 users and 20 staff members of an accident and emergency section of a health centre, apply Pareto analysis to determine the key causes/problems (20 per cent) to resolve. Recommend the important change(s) to be made, giving reasons for your suggestions.

Table 16.4 Possible causes of long waiting time

Possible causes of long waiting time	Percentage of total
Policies require excess information on users	01
Policies require complicated procedures	01
Too much paperwork	02
Not enough funding	02
Inadequate planning of activities	13
Inadequate policies	02
A&E personnel have no tea breaks	02
A&E personnel have other jobs	02
A&E personnel lack punctuality	06
A&E personnel have insufficient training	02
A&E personnel aren't motivated	01
A&E personnel are careless	01
A&E personnel don't follow the schedule	16
Users forget ID cards	01
Users don't follow instructions	02
Users are uncooperative	01
Delay in handing over data within the department	14
Outdated methods	12
Lack of automation	08
Procedures take too long	11

16.2.8 PLUS–MINUS–INTERESTING (PMI) TECHNIQUE

Plus–minus–interesting (PMI) is a straightforward but very useful tool which enables a decision-maker to judge the value of a decision option after assessing the positive and negative effects and the implications of the decision. Although it utilises subjective scores on pros and cons to evaluate decision implications, it highlights possible risks and benefits of a decision prior to its implementation (Mind Tools 2009, drawing on De Bono).

The following steps are used for PMI (Mind Tools 2009):

1   Draw a table with the headings 'plus', 'minus' and 'interesting'.

2   State all positive effects under the 'plus' column, negative effects under the 'minus' column and the implications of the decision under the 'interesting' column.

3   A trend may emerge at this stage to decide to go ahead with the decision or consider an alternative. The decision rule at this stage is to observe and compare the number of pluses and minuses.

4   If no clear trend emerges, consider assigning scores between 1 and 10; positive for points under the 'plus' column and negatives under the 'minus' column. State the total marks for positive and negative under 'plus' and 'minus' tables and state the total score under 'interesting' as well.

5   Sum up the scores, which will reflect either a 'strong positive' or 'strong negative' score to inform decision direction.

Consider the example in Case Study 16.4 to illustrate the use of the PMI technique.

CASE STUDY 16.4

HOSPITALITY SERVICES – AN ILLUSTRATION

A growing hospitality services provider in the Midlands is deciding where to locate a branch in south-east England. The choice is between a big city and a rural setting, and managers are inclined towards a big city branch. A PMI table is designed under the headings 'plus', 'minus' and 'interesting'.

Table 16.5 PMI table to aid location decision-making for a hospitality services provider

Plus	Minus	Interesting
Vibrant business environment in the city (+7)	High property rental and council tax (–4)	Attract more customers? (+4)
Easier to partner and network with related businesses (+4)	More noise pollution (–2)	Increased profit level? (–1)
Good transport and communication facilities (+6)	No countryside attractions (–2)	Staff relocation? (–2)
	Less space like packing restrictions (–2)	
+17	–10	+1

The PMI table score reads 17 (plus) – 10 (minus) + 1 (interesting) = (+8).

By referring to the steps suggested by Mind Tools (2009) above, the PMI table is interpreted as follows: firstly, without recourse to the scores, we assess whether a clear decision emerges after completing the 'plus', 'minus' and 'interesting' columns. Comparing the three points raised under 'plus' and the four under 'minus', it does not appear there is a clear decision. This is because minuses such as less parking space and noise pollution could be controlled to a large extent. We will now move to the second stage, where we will factor the score into making a decision. The PMI table score shows a positive balance of eight (8). We conclude that, for this hospitality services provider in the Midlands, the benefits of locating the south-east England branch in a big city outweighs locating in a rural setting.

ACTIVITY 16.10

Applying the PMI technique

Imagine the appraisal report on the middle managers of your organisation has revealed an urgent need for postgraduate study in management to enable them to take up senior management positions in the future. There is the need for management to choose between granting postgraduate study leave (full-time) and a part-time (day release plus weekend) option. Design a PMI table to reflect the possible 'plus', 'minus' and 'interesting' factors and suggest an option to management.

16.3 CREATIVE TEAM-BASED DECISION-MAKING AND PROBLEM-SOLVING TECHNIQUES

All the techniques discussed so far can be used in both individual and team/group contexts. The following discussion on creative team-based decision-making and problem-solving will consider exclusively techniques that are only applicable in a team or group setting, since in contemporary organisations the majority of decisions are made by more than one individual.

Creative knowledge is essential for new products and services development and solving complex business problems. One way of achieving these is through the use of problem-solving teams (McFadzean 2002). However, creative team-based decision-making presents a different challenge to decision-makers because of the need to have a cutting-edge decision and also build consensus among the entire team. Two key features of creative and team-based decision-making and problem-solving techniques are:

1   It has the elements of creativity and innovation embedded in it (Cook 1998).

2   It presents a broad acceptability among all stakeholders (team) to facilitate its implementation (McAdam and McClelland 2002).

This is the reason why creative team-based decision-making tools and guidelines are essential in enhancing decision-makers' skills. Group decision-making is constrained by a struggle for recognition, feeling of intimidation on the part of quieter team members (often leading to non-contribution), destructive attitudes and excessive criticisms. To illustrate this point we will explore the following examples of group decision-making approaches and guidelines:

1   stepladder technique

2   brainstorming skills

3   group decision facilitation skills.

16.3.1 STEPLADDER TECHNIQUE

This group decision-making technique helps minimise the tendency for team members not to contribute to the decision-making process (Orpen 1995, Mind Tools 2009). Through this technique team members are given the opportunity to make inputs into decision-making in their individual capacities before any group interaction begins. The stepladder technique thus ensures that the decision-making process is more enriched with a diversity of ideas (Orpen 1995).

16.3.1.1 How to apply the stepladder technique

This is a straightforward tool that follows four simple steps to apply (see Orpen 1995, Mind Tools 2009):

1   *Task administration prior to group meeting*: At this first stage the issue for discussion is given out in good time for each member to think through it and develop a solution option.

2   *Group formation stage*: Forming the groups begins with two members who discuss and come up with their decision option.

3   *Additional member introduction*: A third member is introduced to the existing two-member group. The new member shares their ideas and the three collectively discuss and select a decision option. A fourth member is then introduced and the process is repeated, and this continues until all team members have joined

4   *Final collective decision-making stage*: At this stage the whole group engages in a final discussion and the final decision is taken.

 ACTIVITY 16.11

Applying the stepladder technique

As part of a four-member group, apply the stepladder technique above to explore the challenges that global economic recession poses to human resource management. Provide specific examples to support your point of view. Make recommendations as to how human resource practitioners can face these challenges through continuing professional development.

16.3.2 BRAINSTORMING SKILLS

Brainstorming is an important technique used to generate verbal ideas by groups or teams involved in decision-making and solving problems (see also Chapter 11). The rules outlined below illustrate the key features, merits and demerits of brainstorming. The rationale for brainstorming is to ensure total involvement of all group members in the decision-making process. Its usage is traced back to Alex Osborn's *Applied Imagination*, published in 1962.

Osborn's rules for brainstorming, as cited in Stech and Ratliffe (1985), are:

1   *Criticism is ruled out*: Both positive and negative evaluation of ideas must be withheld during the brainstorming process.

2   *"Free-wheeling" is encouraged*: The wilder the idea, the better. It is much easier to tame down than to think up an idea.

3   *Quantity is encouraged*: The greater the number, the greater the likelihood that several ideas will be workable.

4   *Combinations of ideas are encouraged*: The participants may combine two or more stated ideas in still another idea.

5   *'Hitchhiking' is encouraged*: This involves suggesting an idea similar to or triggered by someone else's idea.

Brainstorming is noted for generating a lot of ideas while being relatively inexpensive and requiring relatively moderate amounts of time. Creating many ideas without first screening is seen as a big limitation of the brainstorming technique as its use is limited to small, homogenous teams. You may also come across 'brainwriting' as another technique for group decision-making, and it differs from brainstorming because the former encourages silent generation of ideas in writing while the latter requires a verbal discussion of ideas with others (Wilson and Hanna 1990).

16.3.3 GROUP DECISION-MAKING AND PROBLEM-SOLVING FACILITATION SKILLS

Group decision-making and problem-solving is important (see also Chapters 8 and 11) but thrives only on excellent group facilitation skills, which are often scarce in contemporary organisations. Some of the characteristics associated with disorganised decision-making groups are lack of direction and focus, boredom, apathy, and lack of motivation and commitment. However, there is also evidence that the role of facilitation among UK businesses is changing (Berry 1993) and that decision-makers involved in group decision-making and problem-solving need to be conversant with tested facilitation guidelines.

A useful example of such guidelines for facilitating a group problem-solving session is that of Nelson and McFadzean (1998), which covers the tasks and responsibilities of the facilitator during: pre-planning session, group session, post-session report and post-session. They suggested that during pre-planning sessions the facilitator should be conversant with problem-solving techniques, consult on agenda and structure it accordingly, design standards and meeting procedure and understand group dynamics. At the group session, the facilitator should promote teamwork, be flexible, neutral and give feedback from the previous session. At this stage communication and presentation skills are important for the success of the session. The post-session report should entail the outcome of the session and issues to be followed up and an implementation timetable. A post-session review is also suggested for the facilitator to reflect on the meeting and find out areas that may need to change for future sessions.

ACTIVITY 16.12

Team facilitation

Investigate the team facilitation activities undertaken in your organisation or an organisation with which you are familiar.

- Tabulate team facilitation activities undertaken by your decision-making team or management team under the headings: pre-planning session, group session, post-session report and post-session review.
- Report on any difference in activities between your team or management team and that suggested by Nelson and McFadzean (1998) and explain why there are differences in activities.

Let us now consider the competences of a group facilitator in more detail. In addition to knowing and understanding the variety of activities involved in group facilitation, group facilitators (ideally) need to know what the salient attributes of an effective team facilitator are. Knowing them helps the team leader or facilitator to carry out a self-assessment on the specific attributes, discover gaps and then improve their facilitation practice. This is pertinent because many organisations continue to appoint senior managers on the basis of their qualification and experience in the organisation and not necessarily their management experience and, for that matter, team facilitation skills. Hence, it is widely assumed that once a person is appointed to a managerial position they will be able to effectively facilitate meetings and group discussions, and associated skills are not commonly offered in training programmes. Mosaic Management Consulting Group's key team facilitation competences (Nelson and McFadzean 1998) outlined in Box 16.2 is a good example to study.

Box 16.2: Facilitator competences

- *Understanding context*: Understanding of problem-solving theories, methodologies and techniques, business environments, particular problem situation and why it is so, learning processes, and group dynamics.
- *Technical competences*: Time management, planning and preparation, management and use of visual aids, managing physical environment, management and use of computer-based group

decision support tools, the use of integrated software packages to feed back/present information and produce post-group session reports.

- *Rational competences*: Objectivity, judgement, makes rapid and quality decisions and is specific.
- *Interpersonal competences*: Communication (verbal and non-verbal), active listening and hearing, clarifying, questioning, summarising, persuasiveness, emphatic, respectful, elicitation of information, observation, presentation and feedback.
- *Task process competences*: Development of a structured group problem-solving agenda, guidance and support throughout the whole problem-solving process, flexible – going with the flow, process intervention management, and action and results orientation – establishing expectations; maintaining focus; pacing and congratulating people.
- *Human process competences*: Establish trust, conflict resolution and management, management of internal group relations – treating people as equals; recognising and respecting differences; addressing people's fears; and positively confronting difficult issues.
- *Personal characteristics*: Ability to learn, friendliness, tact, sensitivity, sincerity, intellectual agility, genuineness, sense of humour, self-awareness, modesty, emotional stability, humanity and integrity.

ACTIVITY 16.13

Developing team facilitation skills

Justify the inclusion of understanding context and personal characteristics as essential elements to consider in developing team facilitation skills.

16.4 ETHICAL CONSIDERATIONS IN DECISION-MAKING

Contemporary decision-makers are facing many challenges which are exacerbated when the decisions to be made and problems being resolved involve ethical considerations. Hence, decision-makers require as much understanding and skills to help solve ethical dilemmas which they encounter regularly in their daily work. In fact, ethical decision-making techniques have not received a lot of attention in management training programmes, and the majority of discussions has centred on general ethical guidelines and research findings on the views of decision-makers on the subject.

For an illustration, we will consider conclusions of an ethical decision-making strategies model (Holian 2002, p866, and 2006, p1122), which is based on practising managers' experiences of and views on ethical decision-making. This model is very useful because the study on which it is based combined intensive case studies involving over 200 managers and in-depth interviews of 39 managers from 32 organisations in Australia. The model categorises skills related to ethical decision-making and problem-solving into four categories, which are:

1 judgement

2 integrity

3 courage

4 humanity.

A combination of these skills leads to four distinctive ethical decision-making approaches, namely: legalistic, entrepreneurial, navigation, and worried modes (Holian 2002).

Figure 16.2 Holian's model on ethical decision-making strategies

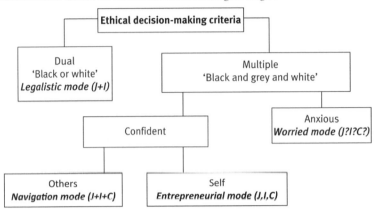

Key: J = Judgemental; I = Integrity; C = Courage
Source: adapted from Holian 2002, p866

16.4.1 MODEL INTERPRETATION

When a decision-maker is faced with making an ethical decision in which the issues involved are clear (dual – black or white), the best option to consider is the *legalistic mode*. Under this condition, managerial elements at play are judgemental and have integrity. When the issues are not clear-cut, the decision-maker may assume the *entrepreneurial mode* and make a decision by combining the three elements of judgement, integrity and courage. The other option under this scenario is to take the *navigation mode* by involving others to decide. The *worried mode* ensues when the decision-maker is anxious because the issues are not clear.

Examples of high-profile management decisions that made the headlines in the first quarter of 2010 in the UK include:

- 400 Cadbury workers were made redundant one week after Kraft took over Cadbury with the promise to keep the factory open in the UK. Clearly, the new management would have taken a look at the ethical implications of their decision, which fell within the multiple (black and grey and white) domain. They decided, however, to apply the entrepreneurial mode knowing very well the consequences of their actions. Kraft management could have reclined into a worried mode by delaying making a decision.
- Another example is the resignation of Lord Triesman – former England Football Association (FA) boss – over bribery accusations by Spain and Russia, though in a private conversation. Once the issue was out, it was clearly in a black and white domain. Thus, the FA's trustees rightly compelled him to leave. If he had persisted, they would have exercised a legalistic mode to get him out to save the FA and England's bid to host the 2018 World Cup.
- The court ruling on a British Airways (BA) cabin crew strike as illegal on technical grounds is another interesting case reflection. Consider how the elements (judgement, integrity, courage and humanity) informed given that (1) BA management resorted to seeking a court order to restrain cabin crew from embarking on a strike and (2) the decision by the cabin crew union to embark on a strike at the time of peak holiday travel of BA passengers.

Decision-makers within the worried mode are challenged by generating decision options because they focus more on the ethical problems rather than finding solutions. Whereas judgement and integrity are classified as prime requirements for ethical decision-making, courage is seen as a necessary precursor. Excessive use of the legalistic mode for ethical decision-making could be problematic because of the fact that it cannot be said in all cases that any course of action that is legal is also ethical. The rule of thumb here is for managers and decision-makers making decisions that are sensitive with ethical ramifications to temper judgement and integrity modes with courage and humanity to minimise worry, delays and resentment towards ethical decisions.

Ethical decisions are also influenced by the prevailing conditions, which include perceived opportunity to commit an unethical act, perceived incentive to the individual for committing an unethical act (magnitude of personal gain envisaged if the unethical act is committed), and perceived chance of being caught (Perri et al 2009). According to Perri et al (2009), decision-makers need to recognise that their personal views and ideas about business ethics play a key role in helping them resolve ethical dilemmas in decision-making and problem-solving. One way of ensuring that personal ethical opinions do not unduly influence decisions is for managers to review their ethical positions in line with corporate and industry ethical standards.

ACTIVITY 16.14

Sample scenario for practice

You are the executive director of a human resource management consultancy. Numerous recruitment agents regularly contact your organisation to encourage the placement of their professionals with leading financial institutions whose recruitment and selection is handled by your consultancy. Your organisation has just placed three professionals from a new recruitment agent with two leading financial institutions. The new agent passed by your office, and as a way of showing his appreciation for placing his professionals, and knowing you are a big fan of the hometown professional football team Sunderland, offers you a ticket to Sunderland's next home game. Bear in mind that your company's code of practice prohibits any employee from accepting gifts beyond a value of £20 and that there is almost no chance that anyone would find out about you accepting the ticket with the face value of £40. Given the circumstances, would you accept the offer? Please indicate your choice from among the following alternatives and give reasons for your answer.

1. Definitely yes	2. Probably yes
3. Probably no	4. Definitely no

16.5 APPROACHES AND GUIDELINES TO COMMUNICATING DECISIONS

A creative and innovative decision which can be described as 'good' may not succeed if it is poorly communicated and justified to stakeholders. Management is in essence an act of communication: management processes are linked to the receipt of information and its valid interpretation, which results in effective decision-making (David 1995). According to Nelissen and Van Selm (2008), satisfaction with management communication is strongly related to staff responses (positive or negative) to organisational change (see also Chapter 12). Effective communication is vital for all aspects/stages of decision-making and problem-solving. Keeping in line with basic tenets of communication such as ensuring relevance, accessibility, and being as precise as possible is always a sensible thing to do when communicating decisions. But it must be emphasised that different decisions may require different approaches to communication and justification. Sample guidelines and admonitions to communicating decisions are explored in this section.

There are more traditional means of communicating decisions across businesses and work groups, such as letters, minutes, memos and reports. In contemporary organisations, electronic systems (email, intranet, information platforms) have become the most common means of communication. Hence, a conscious effort is required by decision-makers to ensure a good balance between modern means of communication and the more traditional ones because of an overdependence on electronic systems to the detriment of more personal interaction. Decision-makers, therefore, must be at the forefront of efforts to develop personal communication skills to enable them to participate effectively in information exchange (Connolly 1996). Core interpersonal skills essential in the decision communication mix include listening, questioning and giving feedback to ensure that all stakeholders accept joint ownership of the decision (Connolly 1996).

Another discipline that can potentially enable modern decision-makers to effectively communicate their decisions is communication ethics. It is a vehicle that provides a language to build trust in shared knowledge and in relations between organisations and people (Beckett 2003). Being conversant and skilful in communication ethics will help decision-makers to be able to evaluate their decisions for their ethical content. The result of such an evaluation will inform choice of language and other communication processes to ensure clarity and acceptability of decisions.

Effectively communicating decisions among business teams is absolutely essential. In terms of cost, speed and time, modern communication methods have considerable advantage over the traditional ones. Yet, it still appears the simple personal communication skills such as taking ample time to listen and offer the appropriate feedback are extremely effective to achieve corporate ownership of decisions for successful implementation. This highlights the need for decision-makers to be conversant with the use of both modern and traditional communication methods. A good blend is recommended.

ACTIVITY 16.15

Reviewing communication

In the light of the above discussion, undertake a review of the communication methods used by your organisation in communicating decisions and make recommendations for improvement.

ACTIVITY 16.16

How do the techniques and skills covered in this chapter relate to your job role and responsibilities?

Can you identify specific area(s) of your work that could benefit from the application of any of the skills and techniques covered in this chapter?

Which of these techniques, tools and guidelines would you recommend to your colleagues, work group or organisation to be incorporated or adopted for their continuing professional development?

Reflect on the potential benefits that your knowledge and acquisition of specific decision-making and problem-solving techniques could bring to bear on your professional career and organisational development.

Using the skills pool identified across the various techniques and tools covered in this chapter, carry out a decision-making and problem-solving skills audit. Identify the skills that you possess at present and others that you think are lacking and classify as 'decision-making and problem-solving skills gap'.

Set out a decision-making and problem-solving skills and techniques development plan for yourself by outlining which skills you require, when you need them, and how you can acquire them and master their use. Indicate how you intend to monitor your skills acquisition and implementation plan to ensure progress.

16.6 ENTREPRENEURS: AN INSIGHT

Much of this chapter has been concerned with creativity in decision-making and problem-solving to enhance an organisation's effectiveness. An area where creativity is most apparent is in entrepreneurship, be it as an individual or as part of a group of individuals starting a new venture or as part of an organisation's ethos. Hence, several theorists have established significant similarities between creative and entrepreneurial skills (Whiting 2011, Fillis and Rentschler 2010), which organisations can utilise to be more creative.

A recent research report published by the CIPD extols the virtues of entrepreneurial endeavour, reminding us that in the current economic climate there is a need for individuals 'to consider working in different ways and [to] fuel their creative business juices' (McCartney and Garrow 2013, p2). Their research spanned 500 people who set up their own businesses and found that the 'key challenges that entrepreneurs face include the difficult economic climate (65 per cent), working long hours (54 per cent), managing financial issues (52 per cent) and a general lack of funding (52 per cent)'. However, for the purposes of this chapter, we look at the ten tenets of entrepreneurial practice in organisations to determine the skills, attributes and activities that entrepreneurs highlight as part of their daily lives.

Table 16.6 Key insights: ten tenets of entrepreneurial practice

Purposeful profit: it's okay to care	The entrepreneurial leaders we spoke to have a genuine desire to make a sustainable difference to their local communities and beyond and instil these values throughout their organisations. This clearly distances them from the sometimes unacceptable and uncaring face of larger corporates. Often a general dissatisfaction with current practice spurs them to try new things and lead in different ways, and there is a shared emphasis on doing business in a responsible way, showing respect for people, communities and the environment.
One part entrepreneurial, twenty parts reach and impact	Entrepreneurial organisations are not limited by their size, resource or money. Their entrepreneurial leadership and practices enable them to punch far above their weight. And, by catalysing with other elements, they create more value; clever use of social media, smart networking and multiple strategic alliances all significantly amplify their impact and reach.
But the best hold on to their intimacy and togetherness	Even though their outward reach and impact is impressive, the best entrepreneurial organisations deliberately maintain a strong sense of intimacy with both employees and customers. They know that it is this culture of intimacy and togetherness that sets them apart from many of their competitors, and they do all that they can to enhance this as they develop and grow by disregarding hierarchy, providing all employees with opportunities for real business involvement and decision-making and facilitating bottom–up innovations.

Entrepreneurial spirit driving growth	**Fiercely protect the integrity of their brand** While entrepreneurial organisations excel at extending their reach through partnerships and collaborations, one thing they never compromise is the integrity of their brand. A key way of protecting their brand is by creating a shared sense of organisation purpose and values internally and externally. Partners, collaborators and charity recipients are therefore carefully chosen around their synergy and alignment with the organisation's existing values and brand. Entrepreneurs themselves are often 'super-connectors', continuously introducing like-minded contacts to one another in a way which reflects very positively on their own business and brand.
Agility through clever use of deep and deliberate co-creation with customers' expertise	Entrepreneurial organisations understand the importance of keeping on their toes and being agile. They know they cannot afford to rest on their laurels, and as their business develops they need to ensure that scanning the horizon for emerging trends, competitors and new opportunities becomes first nature. But it is often the clever way in which they seek out and use both their employees' and customers' expertise which ensures their agility.
Deep and deliberate co-creation with customers	Building on this use of expertise, where entrepreneurial organisations really stand out is in their deep co-creation with clients and customers. This involvement goes way beyond simple one-sided communication to active involvement in shaping and even sponsorship of business strategy. Client engagement can include regular events, competitions, product testing, focus groups and feedback, and it facilitates excitement about products and loyalty to the brand. Entrepreneurial organisations really listen to their customers and draw on their ideas and requirements to keep the business and brand fresh. Many even recruit from their customer pools, where it is ethical to do so, because they have shared values and will act as genuine brand ambassadors.
Employees as individuals	In entrepreneurial organisations employees are treated as individuals rather than one big group. There is a clear awareness of where individual strengths lie and people are encouraged to play to their strengths as much as possible. Entrepreneurs have a massive appetite for developing themselves and their employees. They are also aware of the potential of talent clusters – connecting individuals inside and outside the organisation, with similar interests or needed skills, to work on projects.

Sense of stretch and fun	Entrepreneurial organisations inspire a sense of stretch and fun – a 'work hard and play hard' culture. Leaders place high expectations on their employees – there is no room for mediocrity and work ethic is particularly important. At the same time, fun is vital to their success. While most organisations talk about creating fun working environments, very few actually achieve this. Entrepreneurial organisations know the importance of making this a reality. Some put the fun into their office design; others are creative around working practices, while some get the social side of things right. All place particular importance on ensuring people are happy in their work environment and well supported so they are able to find that 'sweet spot'.
Head space for innovation	A common theme across all the organisations involved in this research is the emphasis they place on employee innovation. Even when entrepreneurial organisations are at their busiest, they deliberately protect time and space for employees to innovate because they know that this is central to their success. Whether that is by supporting intrapreneurs in some of the larger organisations or innovation days and cross-team working in some of the smaller organisations featured. More often than not this activity is bottom–up, not top–down, because employees working daily with customers on the front line have the creative sparks or ideas that could really make a difference.
Go forward with failure	Finally, fear of failure does not stop entrepreneurial organisations from doing things differently and innovating. In fact very little, if anything at all, holds back the entrepreneurial leaders and organisations we spoke to. They recognise that in order to create and innovate some failure is inevitable and realise the great potential in learning from mistakes and failures and even publicising these as part of the learning process.

Source: reproduced with permission from McCartney and Garrow 2013, pp4–7

From this research McCartney and Garrow (2013) have defined several attributes that are exhibited by successful entrepreneurs. Specifically, such individuals:

- are determined and passionate
- are continually alert to new opportunities
- look for purposeful profit
- are dissatisfied with current practice
- take calculated risks
- are commercially and financially astute
- play to people's strengths
- are super-connectors
- co-create with customers
- protect innovation
- are proud of failure
- out-think their size.

Table 16.7 shows a further three elements that depict the attributes used by entrepreneurs when they are in a particular situation: they are intrapreneur, leadership and talent managers.

Table 16.7 Attributes exhibited by entrepreneurs

Intrapreneur practices that work	• Find ways of supporting grass-root innovations – bottom–up. • Not all employees can/will want to be intrapreneurs – think about your approach to selection and whether your organisation can support intrapreneurs. • Get intrapreneurs in front of the right decision-makers. • Connect workers to one another – 'speed dating for innovators'. • Aid connections and collaboration in larger or distributed organisations through social media tools (online profiles, blogs, wikis). • Ensure intrapreneurs share their projects and success more widely – innovation breeds innovation. • Don't forget the failures too – there is great learning to be had from these, so don't hide them away. • As a manager, try to widen and amplify your intrapreneurs' thinking and give them space to innovate. • Adapt training schedules to include topics and skills which enhance intrapreneurs' expertise. • Finally, think about and anticipate the approach you'll take if employees want to develop an idea.
Leadership: entrepreneurial practices that work	• Successful entrepreneurial leaders need persistence and a positive mindset. • Listen to, involve and engage your customers (through, for example, events, product feedback and competitions). • Make your customers part of your creativity strategy. • Take time out for innovation days and for learning from others. • Put something back into the community. • Work can be fun – create an environment where people love to work. • Build strategic alliances with organisations and entities that share your values. • Create partnership arrangements that work for you.
Talent management: entrepreneurial practices that work	• Focus on the quality of hires (shared values, work ethic, work enjoyment). • Sell to candidates what makes your company unique. • Let candidates know that there will be real opportunities for business involvement and decision-making – 'if they have a great idea it could be on the shelf in nine months' time'. • Use your networks, customers and social media to get the best recruits in a cost-effective way. • Get the well-being and performance balance right – don't expect the impossible. • Find the individual's 'sweet spot'. • Encourage your talented people to share their knowledge and network inside and outside of the organisation. • Recruit for the business you are aiming to be before you get there.

Source: reproduced with permission from McCartney and Garrow 2013

ACTIVITY 16.17

Review your entrepreneurial skills and attributes

Review your entrepreneurial skills and attributes by considering Tables 16.6 and 16.7.

1　Have you found any similarities to yourself? Justify your answer.

2　Do you intend to develop any of the attributes or skills using a PDP process? If so, what is your rationale for this?

3　Consider your own workplace. Can you observe any colleagues who display any of the entrepreneurial attributes? If so, how has their career progressed? What positions do they currently hold? Which positions do you expect them to hold in future?

16.7 CONCLUSION

This chapter has shown that the amount and variety of decision-making skills and techniques that a manager or a decision-maker possesses determines the level of achievement of organisational and career goals. This chapter has covered the six thinking hats and lateral thinking, storyboard exercise, benchmarking creative leadership skills, mental imagery technique, mind-mapping technique, Pareto analysis and plus–minus–interesting (PMI) technique as key creative techniques of decision-making and problem-solving. It has also explored exclusively team-based techniques comprising the stepladder technique, brainstorming skills and group facilitation skills.

Guidelines and techniques beneficial to resolving ethical dilemmas and communicating decisions have also been addressed as well as the creative ability commonly exhibited by entrepreneurs and entrepreneurial organisations. Clearly, placing decision-making and problem-solving skills acquisition and practice at the centre of continuing professional development is the best way forward for management professionals and organisations to achieve corporate success, career aspirations and sustainability.

PAUSE FOR THOUGHT

Identify at least three things that you have learned by studying this chapter and engaging with the activities. How will your newly acquired knowledge and skills support your continuing professional development? What value do you expect your learning to have for your daily routines and your further career? In what area have you identified a need for further development and how are you planning to fill that gap? Address these issues in your learning journal and/or CPD log. You may also wish to discuss them with a peer, colleague, mentor or coach to aid your further development.

EXPLORE FURTHER

Books and other literary works by E. Paul Torrance provide a good source of materials for further reading on lateral and creative thinking.

The 80/20 Principle: The secret to achieving more with less by Richard Kock (2007), 2nd edition, is recommended for further reading on the 80/20 principle.

Wilson and Hanna's book *Groups in Context* (1990) is a good source for further reading on brainwriting.

Papers in the *Journal of Communication Management* are also recommended for further reading, particularly Beckett (2003).

REFERENCES

BATEMAN, T. and CRANT, J.M. (1999) Proactive behaviour: meaning, impact, recommendations. *Business Horizons.* Vol 42, No 3. pp63–70.

BECKETT, R. (2003) Communication ethics: principle and practice. *Journal of Communication Management.* Vol 8, No 1. pp41–52.

BENNETT, R.H., WHEATLEY, W.J. and MADDOX, E.N. (1999) The mind's eye and the practice of management. *Management Decision.* Vol 32, No 2. pp21–9.

BERRY, M. (1993) Changing perspectives on facilitation skills development. *Journal of European Industrial Training.* Vol 32, No 2. pp21–9.

BUZAN, T. (2010) *The mind map book.* Harlow: Educational Publishers LLP.

CONNOLLY, C. (1996) Communication: getting to the heart of the matter. *Management Development Review.* Vol 9, No 7. pp37–40.

COOK, P. (1998) The creativity advantage. *Industrial and Commercial Training.* Vol 13, No 5. pp179–84.

CRAFT, R.C and LEAKE, C. (2002) The Pareto principle in organizational decision making. *Management Decision.* Vol 40, No 8. pp729–33.

DANIEL, E.A. (1983) Quality control of documents. *Library Trends.* Vol 41, No 4. pp644–708.

DAVID, W. (1995) *Managing company wide communication.* New York: Chapman & Hall.

DE BONO, E. (1970) *Lateral thinking: creativity step by step.* New York: Harper & Row.

DE BONO, E. (2000) *Six thinking hats.* Rev. and updated ed. London: Penguin.

DE BONO, E. (2009) *Lateral thinking: a textbook of creativity.* London: Penguin.

DE BONO, E. (2011) Available at: http://www.youtube.com/watch?v=UjSjZOjNIJg [Accessed 18 October 2013].

FILLIS, I. and RENTSCHLER, R. (2010) The role of creativity in entrepreneurship. *Journal of Enterprising Culture (JEC)*. Vol 18, No 1. pp49–81.

GODFREY, S. (1998) Are you creative? *Journal of Knowledge Management*. Vol 2, No 1. pp14–16.

GUERREIRO, R., BIO, S.R. and MERSCHMANN, E.V.V. (2008) Cost-to-serve measurement and customer profitability analysis. *The International Journal of Logistics Management*. Vol 19, No 3. pp389–407.

HARRISON, W.G. (1996) A process perspective on strategic decision making. *Management Decision*. Vol 34, No 1. pp46–53.

HEAP, J. (1989) *The management of innovation and design*. London: Cassell.

HOLIAN, R. (2002) Management decision making and ethics. *Management Decision*. Vol 40, No 9. pp862–70.

HOLIAN, R. (2006) Management decision making, ethical issues and 'emotional intelligence'. *Management Decision*. Vol 44, No 8. pp1122–38.

HUNT, M. (1985) *The universe within*. New York: Simon & Schuster.

KEENE, R. (2013) *The man who introduced the world of mind maps: the official biography of Tony Buzan*. Croydon, Surrey: Filament Publishing.

KOCK, R. (2007) *The 80/20 principle*. London: Nicholas Brealey.

MCADAM, R. and MCCLELLAND, J. (2002) Individual and team-based idea generation within innovation management. *European Journal of Innovation Management*. Vol 5, No 2. pp86–97.

MCCARTNEY, C. and GARROW, V. (2013) *Entrepreneurial spirit driving growth*. Research report: July. London: CIPD.

MCFADZEAN, E. (2002) Developing and supporting creative problem-solving teams, part 1 – a conceptual model. *Management Decision*. Vol 40, No 5. pp463–76.

MCWHIRTER, J. and MCWHIRTER, M. (1985) Increasing human potential. *Personnel and Guidance Journal*. Vol 62. pp135–43.

MIND TOOLS. (2009) *Essential skills for an excellent career [online]*. Available at: http://www.mindTools.com [Accessed 4 December 2009].

MOULTON, S.T. and KOSSLYN, S.M. (2009) Imaging predictions: mental imagery as mental emulation. *Philosophical Transactions of the Royal Society Biological Sciences*. Vol 364. pp1273–80.

NELISSEN, P. and VAN SELM, M. (2008) Surviving organizational change. *Corporate Communications: An International Journal*. Vol 13, No 3. pp306–18.

NELSON, T. and MCFADZEAN, E. (1998) Facilitating problem-solving: facilitator competences. *Leadership and Organisation Development Journal*. Vol 19, No 2. pp72–82.

NOVICEVIC, M.N., HRENCH, T.J. and WREN, D.A. (2002) 'Playing by the ear' … 'in an incessant din of reasons'. *Management Decision*. Vol 40, No 10. pp992–1002.

ORPEN, C. (1995) Using the stepladder technique to improve team performance. *Team Performance Management*. Vol 1, No 3. pp24–7.

PATTON, J.R. (2003) Intuition in decisions. *Management Decision.* Vol 41, No 10. pp989–96.

PAVLINA, S. (2004) *Be proactive [online].* Available at: www.stevepavlina.com [Accessed 17 March 2010].

PAVLINA, S. (2009) *Personal development for smart people: the conscious pursuit of personal growth.* London: Hay House Publishing.

PERRI, D.F., CALLANAN, A., ROTENBERRY, P.F. and OEHLERS, P.F. (2009) Education and training in ethical decision making. *Education and Training.* Vol 51, No 1. pp70–83.

STECH, E. and RATLIFFE, S. (1985) *Effective group communication.* Lincolnwood, IL: National Textbook Company.

TITUS, P.A. (2000) Marketing and the creative problem-solving process. *Journal of Marketing Education.* Vol 22, No 3. pp225–35.

TWISS, B. (1974) *Managing technological innovations.* London: Pitman.

WHITING, B.G. (2011) Creating and entrepreneurship: how do they relate? Posted online 22 December 2011. Article first published in *Journal of Creative Behaviour.* Vol 22, No 3. pp178–183, Sept. 1988.

WILSON, G. and HANNA, M. (1990) *Groups in context.* New York: McGraw-Hill.

YAMOAH, F. (2010) Effective decision-making and creative problem-solving. In: WATSON, G. and REISSNER, S.C. (eds). *Developing skills for business leadership.* London: CIPD. pp419–48.

Applying Skills for Business Leadership

STEFANIE REISSNER AND GILLIAN WATSON

OVERVIEW

So far, each chapter of this textbook has covered a distinct skill set, from self-management, interpersonal, quantitative, subject specific to key transferable skills. In a business context, however, such skill sets will be interlinked and therefore need to be applied in conjunction with others. This chapter has been specifically designed to provide you with opportunities to test and hone your skills in relation to real-life business scenarios in the form of case studies. The cases relate to the skills covered in a number of chapters and also raise important issues that contemporary organisations are facing, which you may know from other elements of your studies.

LEARNING OUTCOMES

By the end of this chapter, provided you engage with the case studies and activities, you should be able to:

- analyse complex business situations
- apply business and people skills to complex business situations
- decide what course of action to take and justify your answer.

17.1 INTRODUCTION

Studying theory is one thing and applying it in practice is often another. While there may limited opportunities for you to practise your newly acquired skills while studying with this book (particularly if you are studying full-time), working on real-life business scenarios is a good way to apply theory; the use of case studies has a long tradition in business and management education because of that. This chapter contains nine specifically developed case studies to give you the opportunity to practise the wide range of skills developed throughout this book in a real-life context. Each case study was developed from management and organisational practice and has a true background, even though details may have been altered to protect the identities of individuals and organisations featured therein.

As in real business situations, each case study provided in this chapter relates to more than one skills area and, therefore, more than one chapter of this textbook. The cases give you an opportunity to apply a mix of skills to real-life business scenarios, experiencing for yourself how difficult it can be to manage and lead in an increasingly complex world. The case studies vary in length, type, content and context to appeal to different audiences and situations. We encourage you to use as many case studies as you can in independent study to deepen your understanding of complex business scenarios and your development of the skills covered in this textbook. Practising your knowledge and skills in this way will be a fruitful way to prepare for your first or new job.

17.2 REDEPLOYMENT IN A PUBLIC–PRIVATE PARTNERSHIP

17.2.1 INTRODUCTION TO CASE STUDY 17.1

In England there has been an increasing trend to 'improve efficiency and value for money … by the application of private-sector management techniques and processes' to public sector service delivery (Ferlie et al 2003, pS9). There has been a range of models including private finance initiatives (PFI) and other 'co-operative institutional arrangements between public and private sector actors' (Hodge and Greve 2009, p33) that take the form of strategic partnerships, as NorthService Ltd in Case Study 17.1 below.

Such partnership organisations are essentially manufactured by those driving the deal, typically those in charge of the respective partner organisations, with a strong focus on opportunities for enhanced business performance. However, partnership organisations bring characteristic challenges to those leading and managing them, from overcoming different ways of operating to specific clauses in the partnership contract as highlighted below. This case study most closely relates to the skills covered in Chapters 6, 8, 9, 10, 16 and 18.

CASE STUDY 17.1

NorthService Ltd is a company created as a result of a public–private partnership, in which a local authority has entered into a long-term partnership with a private sector partner to achieve the following:

1   transformation and delivery of support services (for example HR services to the local authority and other businesses)

2   protection of a large number of employees who were TUPE (Transfer of Undertakings (Protection of Employment)) transferred (that is, on their original terms and conditions) in their substantive roles and are guaranteed opportunities for personal development

3   guaranteed year-on-year efficiencies and savings for the local authority

4   bring about regeneration and job growth in an area where unemployment and social deprivation is high and aspirations of local residents are low.

The challenge NorthService Ltd faces is to meet these four objectives and to grow the organisation in its own right by bringing in new business from external organisations. Achievement of these objectives will inevitably mean that, because of successful implementation of transformation activities, some roles will become redundant and that the affected employees will still need to be protected and developed. Trade union presence is strong within NorthService Ltd and as a group who represent employees they are engaged with regularly.

Also within the partnership contract, there is a 'no compulsory redundancy' agreement in place for all TUPE'd employees and a guarantee that the local authority will see transformation and efficiency saving in service delivery (year on year). The modernisation and streamlining of day-to-day practices and operations within the transferred service areas will happen as a result of the implementation of new technology, removing the need for manual processes.

However, after successful implementation of organisational transformation activities such as business process re-engineering (BPR), the business will still need to cover the cost of those people whose roles had become redundant and redeploy them into the right areas of the business.

Employees' values, beliefs, attitudes and practices are more aligned to traditional public sector culture. These typically include:

- The focus of employee activity is delivering services for the local community, but not necessarily at the most competitive price.
- The general ethos is that what employees do is for the common good as opposed to any financial gain (for example for shareholders).
- Operate in a 'blame' culture and covering their own backs, as opposed to feeling empowered, taking responsibility and ownership for issues and providing well-thought-out appropriate solutions.
- Poor formal communication: grapevine is used as a key source of information, as opposed to extensive and varied communication approaches to reach and engage as many employees as possible.
- Culture of mistrust and suspicion in the new business where employees have got used to being micro-managed and their focus is on inputs, for example time recording as opposed to output, for example what work is actually done.
- Poor employee performance was not tackled effectively, and 'just good enough' was deemed on the whole to be acceptable.

Questions

Imagine that you have recently been appointed to a senior management role reporting directly to the chief executive officer of NorthService Ltd. Part of your remit is to understand the operating parameters and the nature of the contractual agreement between the local authority and its private sector partner and to develop a redeployment pool for employees whose roles will no longer exist as a result of transformation activities.

Specifically, you will need to:

- Produce a high-level briefing paper for the CEO that sets out your approach in how you will strategically and operationally implement the redeployment pool, including who the key stakeholders are that you need to engage with and why.
- Set out how you would resource the pool with a focus on your approach to recruitment and selection and learning and development of the employees.
- Set out how you would manage performance, recognising the need to shift culture and practices from the traditional public sector towards a more private sector model.
- Set out what the benefits would be of your approach from the perspectives of an individual who is part of the redeployment pool as well as the benefits of your approach to the business.

Source: Case Study 17.1 and the accompanying questions have kindly been provided by Darryl Warden and Kathryn Atkinson in collaboration with Stefanie Reissner. More details about NorthService Ltd. are available in the book *Storytelling in Management Practice: Dynamics and implications*, authored by Stefanie Reissner and Victoria Pagan, Routledge, 2013.

ACTIVITY 17.1

Reflection on Case Study 17.1

Critically reflect on your learning from Case Study 17.1 in relation to your future career.

- What have you learned about the business scenarios described in this case study? How will your learning inform your professional practice?

- What lessons will you take from this case study? What will they enable you to do differently in your professional practice?
- What skills required in this business scenario do you already possess and which need to be developed (further)? Why?

17.3 MANAGERIAL BEHAVIOUR LEADS ORGANISATIONAL CHANGE

17.3.1 INTRODUCTION TO CASE STUDY 17.2

Since the start of the economic crisis in 2008, UK organisations have been facing testing economic times. While for many it has been a question of survival, for others the challenge has been to adapt business strategy, management capability and product/service portfolio in increasingly uncertain financial circumstances. Individually owned businesses such as APD in Case Study 17.2 rightly consider ways in which they can develop their workforce to build management capability from within to guide the organisation through difficult times. This case study most closely relates to the skills covered in Chapters 5, 6, 7, 8, 9, 11, 12 and 16.

CASE STUDY 17.2

ADAPTING TO A CHANGING ENVIRONMENT

APD are a small business in the north of England providing services nationally to the public sector and employing 20 staff. They have enjoyed success over the past 20 years, with steady growth, diversification of services provided and developing expertise within a largely stable workforce. For the most part this has been under the sole direction of the MD, Michael, with some assistance through part of that time of a deputy who has since moved on. Since his deputy's departure several years ago, Michael has taken on a considerable amount of work – regular board meetings, leading special projects, being the face of the company at events, and managing an increasingly diverse portfolio of activity and staff back at the office.

Despite a testing economic climate, APD has continued to exploit new opportunities and maintain their strong reputation. However, with the financial state within their customer base looking increasingly uncertain, Michael realises that it is time for a change. Times have been good but unless they position themselves for a more difficult context, they are in danger of rapidly losing ground. Juggling the range of responsibilities is proving too much for one person, from maintaining customer service, developing new products, identifying and pursuing opportunities, managing staff and budgets, and marketing the business. In short, they have become too big for a single leader to cope with.

Developing new management

Four of the current staff had, to some extent, existing positions of responsibility but no formal management role. Michael proposed a new structure with these four assuming positions on a new management group which he chaired. Michael was committed to developing the staff and, taking advice, agreed that a core part of the reorganisation will be a management development programme. Simply giving them new roles seemed insufficient to ensure effective performance of the management.

Myself and a colleague were engaged to develop and deliver a bespoke development programme to provide the new management group with a sense of identity and purpose, a set of core managerial and leadership skills and approaches, a culture of empowerment to enable all staff to flourish, and a new sense of drive and effectiveness to position the business to thrive in the new economic and political climate. My focus on organisational psychology and my colleague's focus on coaching allowed us to offer a portfolio approach tailored to the business's needs.

Personality profiles developed for the four staff showed they were in fact a reasonable spread (in MBTI terms INTJ, ESTP, ENFP, ESFJ and ENTJ for the MD) with a lot to offer across the business – these profiles informed various aspects of the later development. However, this diversity also led to some tensions with different attitudes and approaches. An early part of the development programme established a series of group sessions during which they discussed and agreed principles for the management group and undertook various activities around key themes. They identified cohesion of the group, mutual support, trust and openness as key elements to their success as an effective management group leading change.

Involving the team

Early on the managers were encouraged to take an active role in a development day for the whole business on leadership. In part, the day was designed to enable more junior staff to recognise their potential in taking responsibility and leadership, regardless of their status or job description.

As part of this day, each of the management group presented their 'pitch' to the rest of the staff on their leadership approach. This was prepared in advance through a series of sessions exploring issues around leadership 'brand'. However, the term brand was uncomfortable with some, giving connotations of an artificial construction of an image, or 'spin', so the focus instead was on an authentic description of their real capabilities and aspirations for themselves and the business. The managers reported that the 'pitches' in front of the team proved very useful as a public statement, giving them a sense of ownership and commitment to the new management structure. Previously, little had been said openly about the change, even though it was common knowledge among the staff.

The drama of an evolving programme

The content for the programme evolved, responding to the needs of the group as they established themselves and settled in to their new roles. An initial, more formal, programme of development topics gave way to a more organic approach, including at times giving the managers a break from development to focus on their day-to-day work. The group sessions varied from exploratory and discursive to more formal skills development. Interspersed were a series of profiling instruments to inform them individually and as a group on various aspects of their current and future behaviour. Examples include personality, approaches to conflict, leadership styles and character strengths.

Some of the development sessions involved the use of drama-based learning, whereby an actor played a character within a work-based scenario and each of the managers interacted with the character to explore their approach and practise alternative approaches in a safe environment. One of these topics was conflict – exploring the nature of relationships at work, how situations escalate to conflict and how this can be prevented or managed. Another theme was around line management, exploring developmental and performance conversations with staff.

The importance of reflection

A coaching approach to management was encouraged, based on the principles that managers can be most effective if they can empower and enable other staff to achieve their potential. This seemed particularly relevant to their context, where there was an expectation of taking responsibility, pursuing new opportunities, developing new ideas, and continually pushing the boundaries of their business.

The group sessions also proved to be a valuable opportunity to reflect on situations that had not gone so well. They were encouraged to speak openly about how the situation affected them, what they had expected, and how they would like it to have been different. These proved important points in the group's development, giving an opportunity to voice previously unexpressed views, give open and honest feedback, more fully understand each other's behaviour, and look to a constructive future.

Alongside the group sessions we provided one-to-one coaching sessions for each of the managers, identifying individual strengths and areas for development, setting behavioural goals, and exploring their current and potential future performance. A range of techniques was employed in the coaching, including solutions-focused models to maintain a clear focus on a positive future outcome, while developing practical small steps of action that could be achieved. Another technique was drawn from cognitive behavioural coaching (CBC), exploring in detail the cognitive, behavioural, emotional and physiological responses to situations, and identifying appropriate

interventions to change behaviour patterns.

Changing behaviour

Behaviour patterns were a focus for several aspects of the development. Our experience, backed up by theory, tells us that much of an individual's behaviour is habitual, learned and formed over time based on past experiences. No matter how objective and professional a manager tries to be, inevitably they will fall into a behavioural pattern at some point, one that may not be helpful for the situation. Using CBC techniques, we helped the managers identify these patterns, then challenge and modify them, or at the very least increasing awareness of the pattern. Simply recognising when they were about to slip into a habit often gave the managers the opportunity to pause and reflect, and respond more appropriately.

We felt this was important for a number of reasons:

1 As an individual, behaviour patterns can be sticking points for implementing change in your own performance. This was frequently cited by Michael, expressing some frustration that some behaviours were not changing as fast as he would like. Part of the development also involved managing expectations about what was realistic at this level of intervention, and over what timescale.

2 Managerial behaviour patterns strongly influence the nature of inter-relationships at work and the corresponding culture within the business. It was noted in feedback from other staff that a shift to a more coaching style of management led to more open conversations, trust and improved relationships with managers.

3 Individual change is symptomatic of organisational change – if staff within the business recognise that their managers are responding to them and to the situation, they are more likely

to model this behaviour, recognise the importance, and contribute to a joint commitment to the broader change objectives. In reality of course across such a group, the behaviours modelled are not always consistent, and some tensions are still being worked through across the managers, particularly around their line management styles.

A new norm

Twelve months on, the management team is well established, the business is moving forward with key strategic projects, finances remain secure, and the image and reputation of the business is strengthening, particularly with the recent successful completion of a number of high-profile projects for new customers. The development programme and coaching continues at a reduced level of intensity, picking up on themes that arise through work projects and activities.

Source: Case Study 17.2 and the accompanying questions have kindly been provided by Dr Robert Allen, Director at Hapsis Innovation Ltd, in collaboration with Stefanie Reissner.

Questions

Consider the following questions, which you may want to discuss in a small group.

1   What were the key moments in this change process and why?

2   How important is managerial behaviour to organisational change? Justify your answer.

3   What do you think of Michael's approach to changing the business? What would you have done differently?

4   How appropriate do you think the bespoke programme was to meet the business needs? Justify your answer.

5   How effective would such a development-led approach be in other business contexts? Consider your answer in relation to a business or industry context with which you are familiar.

6   To what extent do you believe individual behaviour can really be changed?

7   Which aspects of the development approach or techniques mentioned do you think were most useful?

8   How does this scenario relate to theoretical change models studied in this book and beyond?

ACTIVITY 17.2

Reflection on Case Study 17.2

Critically reflect on your learning from Case Study 17.2 in relation to your future career.

● What have you learned about the business scenarios described in this case study? How will your learning inform your professional practice?

● What lessons will you take from this case study? What will they enable you to do differently in your professional practice?

● What skills required in this business scenario do you already possess and which need to be developed (further)? Why?

17.4 COLLABORATION AND LEADERSHIP: THE UNIVERSITY OF SUNDERLAND AND ONE WATER

17.4.1 INTRODUCTION TO CASE STUDY 17.3

Increasing interconnectedness of business over the last 20 years has led to recognition of the needs of other business and organisations. A rising number of business and not-for-profit organisations have begun to engage in corporate social responsibility, some at a generic (and arguably somewhat superficial) level and others with clear objectives in mind. The collaboration between the University of Sunderland and One Water outlined in Case Study 17.3 is one of the latter initiatives in which the university community engaged in development work in one of the poorest countries in Africa that would not have been possible otherwise.

Case Study 17.3 examines the potential achievements of inter-organisational collaboration and the impact of partnership working between change agents in one organisation and innovative leadership in the other. It relates most closely to the skills covered in Chapters 9, 11 and 12 and has an international dimension.

CASE STUDY 17.3

THE UNIVERSITY OF SUNDERLAND

The University of Sunderland's vision to be recognised as one of a new generation of great civic universities is expressed thus:

- to be innovative, accessible, inspirational and outward-looking
- with international reach, and
- with great local impact.

The university has long been aware of its social responsibilities and in many areas goes beyond what is expected of an organisation. It has been on a journey towards corporate social responsibility for a number of years; however, for many years the university had not taken conscious leaps forward. A new outlook began to emerge in 2006 as its corporate social responsibility principles became more apparent. Under these corporate social responsibility principles, an organisation's internal and external practices can influence their employees, customers, partners, community and environment in a positive manner. It is this positive change and influence of staff members and the further implications for partners that this case study addresses.

Between 2006 and 2009 a number of work strands began to link together from the point of view of the individuals and the disparate examples of good practice already taking place throughout the institution. Further work ensued which bound many of these elements of good practice together with new initiatives; this helped to foster a corporate culture underpinned by ethical principles and one which gave a good grounding for the corporate social responsibility (CSR) ethos.

One initiative that exemplifies this change in corporate consciousness is the ongoing collaboration between the university and One Water.

One Water

In 2003 the compassion and imagination of Duncan Goose was stirred when he read about the 1 billion people around the world who do not have access to clean drinking water. He drew up his own business vision and left his job in 2004 to work full-time on getting his new project off the ground.

Tichy and Ulrich (2008) refer to a new breed of transformational leaders who develop a vision, gather support and buy-in from stakeholders, and guide their organisation into institutionalising a clear value base. In 2005 the vision of Duncan Goose became a reality when the first bottles of One Water began to roll off the production line. One Water is a not-for-profit organisation which aims to deliver clean drinking water for some of the people hardest hit by a shortage of drinkable water.

The revenue generated via the sale of bottles of One Water funds mechanical spinning wheels known as 'PlayPumps' in different regions of Africa. The effect of children using these PlayPumps is that in the villages they can draw clean water from below ground, as opposed to the practice of the children having a long return walk of several miles to collect unclean water from rivers. This ready access to clean water brings significant health benefits to villages and to the children's ongoing education.

Working in partnership

The University of Sunderland achieved Fairtrade status in 2006. The policy not only covered every cup of tea and coffee in the university's outlets, but also a range of innovative sport and leisure goods. The fairtrade branding extended to catering concessions, with the university's Greggs Bakery outlet becoming the first fairtrade Greggs in the UK. The success of this arrangement led to Greggs embracing fairtrade across all its outlets within a two-year period. Fairtrade status proved extremely popular with students and staff alike and became part of the university branding. The university was a key contributor to the City of Sunderland achieving fairtrade status in 2007.

The two main drivers behind the university's fairtrade profile, Catering Manager Sharon Olver and Equality and Diversity Manager Paul Andrew, wished to go a step further in ethical sourcing and also saw the potential benefits to the university and its wider communities. In early 2007 they asked Duncan Goose to deliver a guest lecture on the story of his new company and invited an audience

drawn from the university and region. In this lecture Duncan outlined the philosophy and impact of his organisation. It was very well received and paved the way for the university to strike an initial catering contract with One Water. Within six months, One Water became the sole water supplier for all the university's hospitality and retail outlets.

Zadek (2001) asserts that 'partnerships are a means of getting things done that individuals would be unable to achieve alone'. The collaboration between the two organisations proved fruitful for both parties.

In 2009 the university achieved the installation of its first water wheel, or PlayPump, funded solely by the sale of One Water at its outlets. In collaboration with One Water, the PlayPump was installed in the village school in Lerato, Lesotho, Southern Africa. Lerato is a village in which 20 per cent of children are orphans due to the high prevalence of HIV/Aids. The clean water is greatly assisting with the treatment of the disease. It is also enabling the children, who used to spend three hours per day collecting water from elsewhere, to spend more time at school.

The Principal of the School, Ms Malikhoele Letsie, commented in 2009:

> The PlayPump has made a dramatic impact not only on the pupils of Lerato Primary School, but the wider community, too. Thanks to the support of Sunderland University, they now have a reliable source of fresh, clean drinking water, which means that rather than spending hours every day collecting water, children can go to school, learn and also have fun!

The PlayPump captured the imagination of staff and students alike. To highlight this, a group of self-funded drama students visited Lerato School to see the PlayPump for themselves and carried out drama workshops with the schoolchildren.

Simply by buying the water, the students had appreciated their own contribution to the water wheel. Moreover, they recognised the role of their university in making this happen.

To both internal and external stakeholders, the university is now seen as a socially responsible and fair organisation. In the 2009 staff survey, 81 per cent of staff rated the university as a responsible organisation, compared with 56 per cent in 2007. This brings benefits to the organisation in terms of employee commitment and also places It strategically in terms of being seen as a good business partner. Cannon (1994) asserts that 'when competing for resources, firms with a good corporate reputation in the wider society will find themselves in an advantageous position'.

Leadership styles

In an organisation's structural context, Middleton (2007) argues that many organisations operate in silos. They need leaders who can see across the whole organisation and make the sum of the parts greater than the whole. These leaders understand the value of networks which extend beyond the traditional confines and they know how to lead them. Her concept of 'leading beyond authority' is not about pre-existing perceived levels of authority. It is about earning legitimacy with ideas that resonate, and using an approach that means that people and organisations willingly grant authority to turn the ideas into deliverable objectives.

At the university, Paul Andrew and Sharon Olver had acted as change agents in their institution, leading beyond authority by turning one-off initiatives into general practice and helping to formally embed ethical principles into corporate culture. Significantly influenced by their input, the University of Sunderland in 2009 launched its first corporate responsibility statement, which set out ethical organisational values and outlined how it is making a difference to its stakeholders.

This was the second CSR statement issued by a UK university, the first to be international in scope, and placed the institution at the forefront of CSR developments in higher education. Within 12 months the CSR principles were embedded into the university's Corporate Plan 2009–10 to 2013–14.

The leadership style at One Water is reflected in the work of Collins (2001), who explored the role of leadership in turning an organisation's performance from mediocre to excellent. This 'good to great' leadership is epitomised at its highest level by the executive, 'who builds enduring greatness through a paradoxical blend of personal humility and professional will'. The impact of the personal leadership of Duncan Goose meant that by 2009 One Water had become a global organisation, with sales in four continents across the world. Distribution of One Water has progressed from small sympathetic organisations to national supermarket chains and their partnership initiatives now involve a number of global organisations. In 2010 the One Water product range has expanded to include vitamin water, condoms, toilet tissue and handwash, with over 500 clean water projects extending across the African continent.

An ongoing relationship

The relationship between the University of Sunderland and One Water has benefited from both taking what Goyder (1998) describes as an inclusive approach to internal and external stakeholders. 'The *inclusive approach* differentiates Tomorrow's Company from Yesterday's Companies. Tomorrow's Company values reciprocal relationships, understanding that it can improve outcomes. It works to build relationships with customers, suppliers and other key stakeholders, through a partnership approach.' The two organisations fit Goyder's description as companies of tomorrow, ones that have clear values that encourage commitment and deliver successful business partnerships.

Their relationship was further strengthened with the awarding of an honorary doctorate from the university to Duncan Goose in 2009. The recognition was returned with Duncan making a public endorsement of the university's approach to corporate social responsibility in One Water's Annual Review 2009, which is circulated to business partners and to a range of UK and worldwide organisations. With a second PlayPump being installed in 2010, the collaboration between the University of Sunderland and One Water is now an integral part of both organisations' operations.

Source: Case Study 17.3 and the accompanying questions were kindly provided by Paul Andrews (Diversity Manager, University of Sunderland) in collaboration with Gillian Watson.

Questions

1   Analyse the motives for the collaboration between the University of Sunderland and One Water. What are the potential benefits and pitfalls for both organisations?

2   Analyse the leadership qualities of both Duncan Goose and Paul Andrew. Which ones were crucial in designing, implementing and maintaining the collaboration between the University of Sunderland and One Water? Justify your answer.

3   Conduct some research into corporate social responsibility and consider how the concept helps to explain the importance of the collaboration described here.

4   Evaluate what impact the collaboration between the University of Sunderland and One Water had on both organisations as well as on other stakeholders.

ACTIVITY 17.3

Reflection on Case Study 17.3

Critically reflect on your learning from Case Study 17.3 in relation to your future career.

● What have you learned about the business scenarios described in this case study? How will your learning inform your professional practice?

● What lessons will you take from this case study? What will they enable you to do differently in your professional practice?

● What skills required in this business scenario do you already possess and which need to be developed (further)? Why?

17.5 HEALTH AND SAFETY DAY – A TEAM-BUILDING EXERCISE

17.5.1 INTRODUCTION TO CASE STUDY 17.4

Socio-political changes such as the end of Apartheid in South Africa in the 1990s have had significant impact on business organisations in terms of strategy, operations and staffing. Racial discrimination under Apartheid has produced unique team dynamics in which different groups within the organisation would work with one another while avoiding others. Competitive pressures and adherence to international standards, however, require South African businesses to make their teams more inclusive to improve working climate and business performance.

Steel Corp., the organisation featured in Case Study 17.4, has organised regular health and safety days to encourage different (and previously segregated) groups of employees to mix and have fun together with an aim to improve team dynamics, working climate and business performance. The case study is most closely related to the skills covered in Chapters 1, 8, 9, 11 and 12, and it has an international dimension.

CASE STUDY 17.4

It is a glorious spring day, warm and sunny. Scores of people have gathered in small groups on a giant lawn, many sitting in a camping chair in front of small tents in which traditional South African stews are bubbling away in the midst of a wave of delicious smells. It is a friendly and relaxed atmosphere with people chatting, visiting those in the neighbouring tents and also playing football or rugby. In the background is Steel Corp., one of South Africa's biggest steel companies. It is Health and Safety Day on which production is staffed at minimum levels (and only to keep the machinery going) to allow the majority of employees to have a fun day with a serious message. This message is that Steel Corp. employees have to work together as a team to improve relationships between different groups of employees, to improve their mediocre health and safety record and, most importantly, to improve productivity.

Steel Corp. is experiencing a difficult transition – the transition from an exclusive, racially divided organisation to a more inclusive and team-based one that is profitable, effective and efficient. The firm was founded shortly after the Second World War and thrived under the Apartheid regime, providing work for many white men from the local community. Black manager Adam recalls that 'Steel Corp. was a purely Afrikaans-dominated company influenced by ideas of racial segregation and discrimination. All managers were white and Afrikaans was the official company language, even though many blacks didn't understand the language. The perception was that a black guy is inferior and useless and not going to survive. At certain colour lines, your job

prospects would end, that was that. You would spend the rest of your life slaving away at the furnaces.'

After the end of the Apartheid regime South Africa began a transition to a more inclusive, democratic society and Steel Corp. had to follow suit. There is more than one official company language now, including English and the most widely spoken native South African languages. Social facilities such as canteens are open to all employees, regardless of their position and their ethnic origin. An increasing number of black employees are being promoted to supervisory and managerial positions as a result of the Government's Employment Equity programme, which prescribes that organisational hierarchies have to mimic the country's ethnic composition (that is, 80 per cent black, 15 per cent white and 5 per cent Asian). Employees like Adam have much-improved job prospects and do not face any major obstacles to the top of an organisation's hierarchy.

However, this transition has been painful for Steel Corp. employees and the local community. In the course of only a few years, 65 per cent of employees from all ethnic groups were made redundant in an attempt to make the company more profitable in a very competitive environment. The efforts have paid off, and Steel Corp. has become a respected player in the global steel industry. It is a leaner organisation that operates like a business and not a charity like in the past, as many employees acknowledge today. However, unemployment in the local community is high and few former Steel Corp. employees have found alternative employment. Many white employees are facing a glass ceiling when striving up the career ladder but lack better prospects elsewhere. Adam's experiences of job prospects ending at a certain colour line, it seems, have become a reality for those who previously dominated supervisory and managerial positions. It is therefore not surprising that relationships between different ethnic groups in the plant remain difficult, with many falling back on old prejudices.

After a successful turnaround in financial terms, Steel Corp. management is devoting much energy to softer aspects of their business. Teamwork, particularly in multi-disciplinary teams across hierarchical boundaries, has become more prevalent and decision-making has become more participative. However, the greatest challenge to these efforts is to rid employees of the baggage of the past, that is, to overcome old prejudices with regard to racial segregation and discrimination. This baggage was visible on Health and Safety Day: white employees would visit former colleagues in other tents, while black employees would do the same – strictly along previous colour lines. The football teams would be almost exclusively black, while the rugby teams would be almost exclusively white. The friendly and relaxed atmosphere that characterised Health and Safety Day, however, might have been the first step to a more inclusive and team-oriented way of working at Steel Corp. where every employee is given a fair chance, regardless of their background and ethnic origin.

Source: Case Study 17.4 has been provided by Stefanie Reissner, deriving from her research into organisational change and learning. More details are available in her book *Narratives of Organisational Change and Learning: Making sense of testing times*, Edward Elgar Publishing, 2008.

Questions

1   How would you describe group dynamics on Health and Safety Day? Which kind of group – formal or informal – is the most cohesive and therefore very difficult to change in an organisation required to turn around its fortunes?

2   How have the levels of power and authority of white employees and black/Asian employees respectively changed over time? What can managers do to promote a different balance of power in organisations?

3   Evaluate the benefit of measures such as Health and Safety Day to promote teamwork and cross-cultural understanding. What other measures might complement or perhaps even replace Health and Safety Day?

4   What role do leaders have in a transition like the one that Steel Corp. has been going through? What knowledge and skills do they require?

ACTIVITY 17.4

Reflection on Case Study 17.4

Critically reflect on your learning from Case Study 17.4 in relation to your future career.

● What have you learned about the business scenarios described in this case study? How will your learning inform your professional practice?

● What lessons will you take from this case study? What will they enable you to do differently in your professional practice?

● What skills required in this business scenario do you already possess and which need to be developed (further)? Why?

17.6 THE KEYSTONE DEVELOPMENT PROJECT AT INTERCONTINENTAL HOTEL GROUP (IHG)

17.6.1 INTRODUCTION TO CASE STUDY 17.5

In all organisations there is scope for further development, regardless of whether they are successful or struggling, large or small, national or international. Such development potential can relate to strategic, operational or people matters and requires careful attention to make the organisation as successful as it can possibly be. At InterContinental Hotels Group (IHG) a pertinent issue was the higher than desirable turnover among its general managers, and Case Study 17.5 outlines how the organisation sought to tackle it. The case relates most closely to the skills covered in Chapters 1, 6, 11, 16 and 18.

CASE STUDY 17.5

IHG BUSINESS EMPLOYEE DEVELOPMENT OFFERING

InterContinental Hotels Group (IHG) is a hotel organisation comprising 3,557 hotels globally. IHG comprises seven brands, namely Holiday Inn, Holiday Inn Express, Crowne Plaza, InterContinental Hotels, Staybridge Suites, Hotel Indigo and Candlewood Suites. The hotel portfolio comprises a mixture of business models including franchised, managed and company-owned hotels. The 53 properties to which this case study refers are the 'owned' UK and Ireland estate.

To help deliver the IHG core purpose 'Great Hotels Guests Love', the company is committed to developing employees to help them excel today in their current role as well as prepare them for future roles. The training offer across all hotels includes:

● facilitator-led training with specialist IHG trainers and IHG subject-matter experts
● online learning through our partners Harvard Business online; eCornell; E-Advisor; Rosetta Stone® – language learning; Element K – technology and management training; and Risk – online modules
● leadership development at Ashridge executive education business school.

Such a commitment to employee development formed part of the element which secured the business a 2010 *Sunday Times* '25 Best Big Companies to Work For' award, which is based on surveys from employees within large companies in the UK and officially recognises companies that 'Provide their people with an outstanding place to work' (Times Online 2010).

Historical background to the case

This very successful organisation has an excellent track record in developing its staff; however, along with other major hotel groups trading in the UK, it was experiencing some labour turnover issues. This was slight in regard to numbers, although significant in regard to loss of talent, particularly in its general manager population.

As a result of labour turnover within the general manager population of InterContinental Hotels Group (IHG) over a 12-month period (the causes of which are explained fully later), the business incurred cost to refill the positions. As a result IHG recognised that immediate action was needed to reduce recruitment costs; this was one of the primary motivators for change. The senior staff were keen to highlight how heavily recruitment agencies were being used for senior management recruitment, a realisation therefore of how much exceptional talent the business might be losing. Even more concerning was that in the majority of cases, these senior managers were moving to market sector competitors. At board level, it was decided that action needed to be taken in order to retain those employees who were performing well and of key value to the business. Subsequently, the following strategy was adopted:

- ban on the use of agencies (only with authorisation from the area general manager were positions permitted to be advertised using agencies)
- investment in succession planning software was being purchased
- re-launch of the existing outdated talent management matrix was to be collated and aligned to individual PDPs (personal development plans), mobility and performance reviews.

Introduction of a development programme to support 'Growing Our Own' general manager talent

The company had identified that there was a need to train and develop the existing operations manager population with the aim of creating a 'bank of home-grown talent' that could move up to general manager level. This would present the company with the opportunity to promote internally through a structured succession plan.

The task

A project leader was appointed and was tasked to design and implement an internal development programme, named **Keystone**. It was envisaged that the project's success would result in an increase in general manager positions being filled internally.

Expected programme return on investment (ROI)

By the end of the project the following results were anticipated:

- At the end of the 18 months, a 'high impact' development programme would be embedded into the business.
- This would result in 15 per cent of general manager positions being filled by internal candidates in the two years following completion of the programme (dependent on vacancies within the business).

The programme would support the development of the operations manager population, and would furnish them with the core skills and knowledge needed in the role of general manager.

The problem

Despite all of this investment, philosophy and opportunity, between 2007 and 2008, several resignations from the general manager population, from a total of 53, were received. Interestingly, all leavers had secured new positions within the hospitality sector. Subsequent analyses of exit interviews from these employees revealed that there were four key factors for their decisions to leave (Figure 17.1). The main reason for leaving was a 'belief' that IHG offered limited career progression or individual development opportunity. More in-depth probing and questioning with existing managers revealed that they were disillusioned by vacancies being filled externally and internal candidates being rejected as well as weak, unsubstantiated feedback being given when feedback had been requested. These findings fully support Charan et al (2001) and Hirsh's report (2000), which highlighted the need for developing internal talent as opposed to 'buying it in' as key to career planning. Secondly, those interviewed said the company offered marginal structure to GM development and the PDP process was a, quote, '*paperwork exercise*'. Priding itself in strong employee engagement survey scores and low labour turnover (LTO), the business was concerned at these findings.

Figure 17.1 Staff perceptions of personal development planning

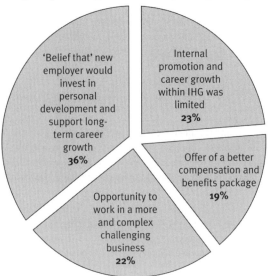

Primary research conclusions

Competitor analysis findings and primary research in the business resulted in the following conclusions; they identified:

- IHG needed to address comments made by the exiting GMs relating to succession planning opportunity and personal development.
- Investment and provision of a structured development route for GMs could have significant ROI benefits to all stakeholders.
- Such a programme would be most effective if delivered as 'off job' training.

- Existing GMs believed that all of the subjects identified were critical to success, and therefore the syllabus should contain all of them.
- As competitors weren't offering development programmes specifically aimed at talent management (TM), there could be potential benefit to IHG working on TM and talent development as a recruitment tool.
- Action needed to be taken to reduce the risk of business being lost through GM tacit and intellectual knowledge.

Recommendations and actions

The preliminary research conclusions helped to inform the business case for moving forward. This was presented to the executive team for approval and backing. With this approved, an inaugural meeting was held with the objective of creating working parties to use a knowledge management (KM) approach to communicate the subject content. This delivery model was purposely selected primarily as it would give ownership for the writing and delivery of the modules to the specialists in the business, aiming to achieve the best results and for the delegate to be tutored by the experts in each subject. Colleagues therefore were enlisted according to individual skills, competencies and subject knowledge, matched to the needs of each module. Volunteers were plentiful; at the risk of sounding pessimistic, the author would propose that this was largely due, initially, to the high-level sponsorship from senior management and the subsequent opportunity to profile oneself. Keystone was a great platform to be noticed! However, as awareness and momentum grew, the motivation completely changed to a genuine commitment and desire to do a great job.

From the inaugural planning meeting the programme was given its identity. It was decided to call the project **Keystone**. The thought process behind this was that the 'keystone' of a building is the stone that supports the rest of the structure; therefore this programme would support the business. A logo to market the programme was designed (Figure 17.2).

Figure 17.2 Logo 'Building for the Future'

Over the following months the working parties designed their specialised assigned programmes.

Programme nomination and selection

As Keystone's main objective was to provide the business with a 'pipeline' of next generation GM talent, the target audience for the programme were operations managers (Ops). As this population are best known, and their performance reviewed by their direct report who is the GM, GMs were asked to nominate potential candidates aligned to success criteria.

It was clear that this process was vital to the success of the programme. Selecting the right delegates would be a major factor in achieving a successful outcome in relation to the project. It was imperative that the selection process was fair, had clearly defined eligibility and success criteria and was challenging enough to attract *high-potential* candidates. Delegates were required to have reached an overall score in their last performance review of level 4 (defined as **strong** – employee demonstrates effective performance in this competency and exceeds on some occasions). This was set as minimum entry criterion, effectively eliminating weaker candidates from applying and increasing the chances of those accepted to be successful in securing a GM position within the 18-month duration of Keystone. Nominations then needed to be supported by the candidate's general manager, HR manager, area general manager and the vice president of operations. This ensured that everyone had 'bought in' and committed to the candidate's nomination.

A short interview and presentation by each candidate based around the title 'What will I do to give return on investment to the company if I am selected for Keystone?' This process proved to be very challenging in several ways: firstly, due to the company's financial results being released late, the review process was subsequently held up (the financial results are needed to score performance objectives, which form part of the review process). As the criteria required the nominee to achieve a score of 4 in their annual performance review, there was a time laps while waiting for the review process to be completed. This was in place to prevent any tampering with the scores.

Note: for those candidates not successful getting onto the programme, one-to-one feedback was given to identify areas of development, and direction to help them to be successful in the future.

Keystone – the programme

Over the subsequent 18 months, the Keystone delegates attended nine modules. After each module delegates were set an assignment in order to consolidate the module learning and to put learning into practice. Consequently there was a strong emphasis on continuing professional development and reflective learning. The purpose of this was to make each learner take responsibility for their own development and to link their learning experience to business needs (ibid).

To support CPD and to enable all learners to have a 'helpline', each delegate was assigned a trained mentor from the business. The aim of offering this long-term tailored relationship (CIPD 2010) was to allow the learner or 'mentee' access to ongoing support, outside of the Keystone modules, and allowing the mentee the opportunity to reap all of the benefits of access to a personal mentor. Mentors and mentees attended awareness sessions, which followed Alred et al's (1998) three-step model to make sure the relationship was steered to success:

1   exploration – to explore issues which are identified by the mentee

2   new understanding

3   action planning.

The results: ROI and programme achievements – evaluation of programme objectives

- The programme would result in 15 per cent of general manager positions being filled by internal candidates in the two years following completion of the programme (dependent on vacancies within the business).
- At the end of the 18 months, a 'high impact' development programme would be embedded into the business.

On completion of the programme all of the delegates and all those involved in Keystone were invited to attend the Graduation Ball to celebrate the successes of the programme and the 'feeling' was that the programme had been a huge success.

Twenty-two delegates completed the programme. The original programme objective/target of 15 per cent of delegates becoming GMs had been exceeded; in fact, 25 per cent of the delegates were promoted to GM positions (5 of the 25 delegates).

Some of the other successes were: two delegates were offered GM positions externally (arguably not a business success, but success for the individuals). One of the delegates was successful in securing a general manager position covering maternity leave for 12 months, four delegates were promoted to larger, more challenging and complex business model hotels, in the same role, or moved into corporate roles (two individuals) aligned to their PDPs.

One delegate confidentially informed the project leader that he had been offered a position with a competitor hotel group but had declined because of the prospects that Keystone would offer her, and that she is working on her personal development plan. The remaining 12 delegates stayed in their current roles. However, all were given programme exit interviews and attended an additional day's 'debrief', which was devoted to the individual's career plan being formulated with the objective of the delegate fully understanding their career plan and exited the programme motivated and with a clear vision for the future. It was of vital importance that these delegates felt they had been successful and had benefited from the programme.

Keystone – set up for success and the results

It is important to acknowledge that Keystone was, by its design, created to be a success. The programme manager was selected because of her tenacity and creativity, coupled with networking and impact and influencing people skills as well as a proven track record in project management and a background in leadership development. From the business perspective, delegates were selected using a set criterion of behavioural competencies and attitudes, as well as demonstrating potential skill ability and a desire to become general managers. From the outset all of the resources needed to elevate challenges were provided to ensure that there were no barriers to success, and this also included allowing the rare and valuable commodity of time to plan, deliver and evaluate.

As previously discussed, the high-level sponsorship was undoubtedly a critical contribution factor to Keystone. Throughout the programme senior management were visible: they opened the programme and told the delegates of their vision for Keystone and the commitment from the company

Source: Case Study 17.5 and the accompanying questions were kindly provided by Debee Forster in collaboration with Gillian Watson.

Questions

1 From a talent management perspective, evaluate the Keystone programme's aims.

2 Comment on how participants were recruited for the development. What impact did this have on the success of the programme?

3 Do you agree that the objectives were met: why/why not?

4 Evaluate the value of the programme from the participant point of view (there are distinct pluses and minuses here); in particular, consider their career development.

5 Evaluate the level of support given by executive/senior managers to the Keystone project.

6 Evaluate the success of the initiative. What criteria do you use to measure its success?

7 Where should they go from here? What decisions need to be taken? What criteria for decision-making will you use?

 ## ACTIVITY 17.5

Reflection on Case Study 17.5

Critically reflect on your learning from Case Study 17.5 in relation to your future career.

● What have you learned about the business scenarios described in this case study? How will your learning inform your professional practice?

● What lessons will you take from this case study? What will they enable you to do differently in your professional practice?

● What skills required in this business scenario do you already possess and which need to be developed (further)? Why?

17.7 EXPERT BANK

17.7.1 INTRODUCTION TO CASE STUDY 17.6

As more and more businesses operate in different countries, an increasing number of managers have international management responsibilities. While some organisations organise their international operations in such a way that managers have a relatively permanent position for a particular term in the host country (usually three or five years), in others, such as Expert Bank, managers tend to have only an oversight function. In practice, this means that managers are based at headquarters and travel regularly to the different subsidiaries for which they are responsible. In between visits, contact is mainly made through email, telephone and conference calls. Such limited personal interaction between managers and their subordinates can pose particular challenges in some countries, as Case Study 17.6 demonstrates. The case study relates most closely to the skills covered in Chapters 1, 8, 9, 11, 12, 16 and 18 and has an international dimension.

CASE STUDY 17.6

Expert Bank is an international commercial bank with its headquarters in Germany. It has specialised in supporting the international operations of their corporate clients – typically small and medium-sized manufacturing firms seeking to sell German technology abroad. Expert Bank will accompany this core client group on all steps on their way into operation internationally through providing financial advice as well as offering the necessary financial products for this process, either as own products or together with partners.

For this purpose, Expert Bank has established small units of local finance experts in the developing markets of this world, among others in India. The Indian unit, which is the focus of this case study, accounts for about 50 per cent of market share in the product field export finance and therefore contributes significantly to Expert Bank's performance. The Indian unit is headed by Gurjeet Singh, a very experienced and well-networked finance expert in his early 50s. He is a self-motivated and very sales-oriented professional, making him the ideal candidate for this role. Gurjeet Singh is supported by a secretary looking after administrative matters and, as typical in India, by an office boy who does the errands.

Traditionally, Expert Bank's core client group only sought to sell their products in India, which involved export financing and the accompanying bank-to-bank services required for such deals. Gurjeet Singh is an expert in this field and has developed considerable know-how and expertise over his many years in banking. His unit is doing extremely well and has reached the upper limits of its capacity. However, there is a trend among German manufacturers to expand their international operations. Many choose to set up their own distribution networks in their target markets while others venture into setting up production facilities for purchasing in the Indian markets. This requires new and different financial products and services (for example new current accounts, investment financing), which would stretch Gurjeet Singh's unit beyond capacity.

Gertrude Muller is Gurjeet Singh's manager at German headquarters and very happy with his performance. She is an economist by training and has managed Expert Bank's international operations for the last 15 years. It is Gertrude Muller's task to take the Indian unit forward as Expert Bank cannot afford to lose the new opportunities presented by their clients' expansion plans and the associated potential for Expert Bank's own expansion in India. This involves expanding Gurjeet Singh's unit to create new capacity for the new products and services to be offered.

Her many years in international management have taught Gertrude Muller that she will have to tread carefully to achieve her goal. Although she has only been responsible for the Indian unit for the last two years (and therefore did not have a close relationship with Gurjeet Singh), she is aware that she cannot just hire an additional member of staff for Gurjeet Singh's unit to look after the new products and services. The reason is that Gurjeet Singh would be offended by having to work with a probably younger and less experienced employee and concerned about losing his knowledge and expertise to them, thereby reducing his own market value as export finance expert. This is a crucial concern for Gurjeet Singh because the value of employees in India is measured by their knowledge of the market, their knowledge of the customers, their know-how and expertise in their field of specialism as well as their network of contacts. Gertrude Muller is therefore well aware that Gurjeet Singh is a much sought after finance expert that competing organisations would be more than welcome to hire. If Gurjeet Singh was to leave Expert Bank, they would lose a major part of the export finance business in India – a risk that they can ill afford in the present economic climate. She needs to find a way to expand the Indian unit without losing Gurjeet Singh in the process.

Source: Case Study 17.6 and the accompanying questions have been provided by Stefanie Reissner in collaboration with 'Gertrude Muller'.

Questions

1 Imagine you are Gertrude Muller. How would you go about resolving this dilemma? How would you approach it – on your own, with the help of your colleagues (all international managers themselves) or in consultation with Gurjeet Singh?

2 Using the creative decision-making and problem-solving techniques discussed in Chapter 16 and drawing on your knowledge of international issues introduced in Chapter 1, identify the different options

that Gertrude Muller has. Discuss these options and their viability with a peer or in small groups and devise an action plan. Justify your decisions at all stages.

3 Consider how you will approach this dilemma from a management and leadership perspective – will you discuss your options with Gurjeet Singh or will you make that decision on your own and communicate it to him? Devise a strategy of how to communicate with Gurjeet Singh. If this case study is being used in a classroom setting, the discussion between Gertrude Muller and Gurjeet Singh might be brought to life through role-play.

ACTIVITY 17.6

Reflection on Case Study 17.6

Critically reflect on your learning from Case Study 17.6 in relation to your future career.

● What have you learned about the business scenarios described in this case study? How will your learning inform your professional practice?

● What lessons will you take from this case study? What will they enable you to do differently in your professional practice?

● What skills required in this business scenario do you already possess and which need to be developed (further)? Why?

17.8 DEVELOPMENT INTERVENTION AT GULP HOTELS

17.8.1 INTRODUCTION TO CASE STUDY 17.7

Organisations seeking to operate in a premium segment of their market need to attend to the quality of their products or services. In many cases, this means that staff – both managers and front-line employees – require continuing professional development to stay at the top of their game. As Case Study 17.7 demonstrates, it can be a considerable challenge to resolve the problems resulting from a neglect of staff development and management attention. The case study consists of three parts, which build on one another. It relates most closely to the skills covered in Chapters 1, 6, 9, 15, 16 and 18.

CASE STUDY 17.7 – PART 1

Gulps Hotel are a small hotel chain that has 12 establishments, predominantly in the north of England; however, there are two hotels in the south of England and a further two in Scotland. They are all between four and five stars and consequently quality is central to the company ethos. Madeline is the newly appointed development and quality adviser; she is a university graduate who completed her studies at master's level. She has worked for other hotel chains in the past.

The hotel group has two regional managers which split the areas into the North and Scotland, and the Midlands and the South, the former having seven hotels under their control and the latter five. The northern regional manager has designated Madeline's first task – or indeed problem – which he wants her to resolve: the hotel experiencing problems is in Newcastle. He tells her that the hotel manager is nearing retirement (in eight months' time); therefore, in his opinion, there needs to be a planned change regarding the management of the facility. Furthermore, there may need to be a progression process enabling career development for some of the staff; the hotel chain has had a practice of appointing the assistant manager to the post.

Certainly somewhat vague information is given to Madeline; however, she is undaunted and always ready for a challenge. The information is as follows:

- Bookings have remained unchanged over the last year, although the rest of the group has enjoyed a small rise.
- Unlike other hotels in the region of a similar star rating, they have few bookings for special events such as conferences, occasional parties, weddings, and so on.
- Complaints have grown over the last three months, some of which include:

- rooms being unclean when guests arrive
- misplaced luggage
- unanswered telephone calls to the hotel or potential customers having to wait long periods before calls are being answered
- bills being incorrect.

Having stayed at the hotel for two days, Madeline concludes that:

- The manager is extremely complacent about the service offered.
- The assistant manager has been given no real responsibility for a particular area of work or a particular function and has been used very much as an office junior.
- The assistant manager has been employed at the hotel for 2.5 years, has a business degree and is very eager and interested in all aspects of the business.

Questions

Given the somewhat limited information provided in the case study:

1 What do you identify as major areas of training and development need?

2 What additional information would you seek?

3 What intervention(s) would you consider implementing and what strategies would you adopt?

4 Plan how you would evaluate whether your interventions will be effective.

Discuss and evaluate the case in groups and arrive at a consensus for moving forward.

CASE STUDY 17.7 – PART 2

Madeline has examined the situation in the hotel at Newcastle. It is tellingly obvious to her that she must discuss her findings with the hotel manager. At first the hotel manager is reluctant to acknowledge any of the issues Madeline has brought up. However, during the session the assistant manager walks into the office highlighting another problem, which fortunately is a minor consideration. The assistant manager joins the discussion and Madeline wished she had thought to ask her to attend in the first place. From that point on the discussion goes well, with the hotel manager agreeing with Madeline that there are quality and customer care issues that need to be resolved. She is also concerned that because of the volume of customer complaints, any development in that area will just address the 'tip of the iceberg'. Nonetheless, customer care remains the primary concern. With that in mind Madeline, having consulted with her manager, agrees to a regime of staff training. This will effectively develop the whole workforce in customer care issues. They have allocated £3,500 for this task. Madeline considers running the training programme herself as she has had experience of running such courses.

The staff complement of the hotel is as follows

1   receptionists: 2 full-time and 3 part-time

2   cleaners: 10 part-time and 1 full-time cleaner/supervisor

3   porters/caretakers: 4 full-time

4   bar staff: 2 full-time, 4 part-time and 1 full-time drinks manager

5   kitchen staff: 3 chefs, 6 assistants, 6 ancillary staff – all are full-time under a head chef

6   restaurant staff: 6 full-time and 8 part-time waiters – all under a head waiter

7   administrative staff: 4 full-time – reporting directly to the hotel manager

8   maintenance staff: 1 full-time, 2 part-time.

- 9.00am to 5.00pm (A shift)
- 5.00pm to 1.00am (B shift)
- 1.00am to 9.00am (C shift).

Madeline has to make a decision: if she decides to take on the training herself, she will have the task of designing, implementing and evaluating how effective the customer care programme has been.

Questions

1   What would you do?

2   Devise an implementation plan for training the hotel's workforce.

3   Design the customer care training sessions.

4   Plan an evaluation strategy.

5   Consider the cost of your training plan – can it stay within the budget?

6   Calculate the full learning cost.

7   Consider the cost–benefit analysis of carrying out this extensive training programme.

APPENDIX 17.1 CALCULATING LEARNING AND TRAINING COST

From Reid et al (2004, p106):

The following tables depict the type of items that could be used to calculate each element of the training process.

Table 17.1 Examples of learning cost

Payment to employees
The cost of materials wasted, sales lost or incorrect decision-making
Supervision/management costs in dealing with problems of incompetence
Cost of reduced output/service/sales
Cost attributed to accidents caused by lack of knowledge and 'know-how'
Costs resulting from employees learning • Work too difficult • No planned learning • No prospects You may think of others as appropriate to a particular circumstance/environment

Table 17.2 Examples of training cost

People cost	Wages or salaries of the trainees Managers' salaries while training/coaching Fees to external providers Fees to external assessors Travel and subsistence
Equipment cost	Training equipment and aids Depreciation of training buildings and equipment
Administration cost	Wages and salaries of administration – back-up staff Postage and telephone calls Office consumables Systems and procedures Room hire
Materials cost	DVDs, downloads Distance learning packages Materials used in practical sessions Protective clothing Books and journals You may think of others as appropriate to a particular circumstance/environment

CASE STUDY 17.7 – PART 3

Madeline has come to a decision: the problems at the Newcastle Gulp Hotel are too deep to be solved by a customer care training programme, which only gave each member of staff one training session. The problems are widespread and the skill level of some staff must be a question. As Madeline delivered several of the training sessions herself, she knows the complexity of the overriding problems as well as the general staff attitude to any development plan.

Madeline has therefore unearthed some disturbing characteristics of the hotel's practice:

1   Staff usually receive no feedback on their tasks or have any reference made to their abilities, thus there is no individual or group performance record; for this reason the hotel management cannot possibly know how well it is doing.

2   Staff are not encouraged to develop new skills, nor are they expected to pass on their skills to other less experienced staff.

3   Staff at times make suggestions for improvements, for example reporting a problem or improving a service, but they are not listened to and consequently nothing gets done.

Because of her close involvement with the customer care training course, all the staff at the hotel believe it is Madeline's job to solve all their problems and that all issues have a training solution. As the hotel manager remarked, 'Madeline, you did such a good job dealing with "customer care"!'

Madeline feels extremely pressured and also believes she has been 'trapped' at Newcastle long enough. After all, she has another 15 hotels to oversee, and her family bemoans the fact that she is never at home. For Madeline the journey across the Pennines seems to get longer and longer. However, she still needs to complete her work here. There is a growing imperative to use the skills, knowledge and experience of the hotel staff to ensure all have an opportunity to develop and learn – after all, they cannot rely on Madeline for everything.

Questions

1   Madeline is feeling a great deal of pressure. What steps can she take to overcome this?

2   What practical suggestions do you have to help Madeline enable the hotel to make the best use of its skill base?

3   Develop a training plan for either:

● the administrative and reception staff
● the deputy manager, or
● the cleaners.

4   Develop a strategy to ensure that the other hotels in the business have a career/succession plan.

Source: Case Study 17.7 and the accompanying questions have been provided by Gillian Watson.

ACTIVITY 17.7

Reflection on Case Study 17.7

Critically reflect on your learning from Case Study 17.7 in relation to your future career.

● What have you learned about the business scenarios described in this case study? How will your learning inform your professional practice?

- What lessons will you take from this case study? What will they enable you to do differently in your professional practice?
- What skills required in this business scenario do you already possess and which need to be developed (further)? Why?

17.9 CONCLUSION

This chapter has provided a series of case studies on the basis of which you can practise vital managerial and leadership skills. The case studies highlight that complex business scenarios require thorough analysis, robust decision-making and often the support of others. Such business scenarios can only be tackled effectively with an appropriate mix of business and people skills to ensure continuing survival and success of the organisations in question. As management professionals you will have to deal with multiple stakeholders as well as unique team/organisational dynamics to enable your organisation to thrive in an increasingly competitive business environment. The skills covered in this textbook and the case studies presented in this chapter will help you with this.

PAUSE FOR THOUGHT

Identify at least three things that you have learned by studying this chapter and engaging with the activities. How will your newly acquired knowledge and skills support your continuing professional development? What value do you expect your learning to have for your daily routines and your further career? In what area have you identified a need for further development and how are you planning to fill that gap? Address these issues in your learning journal and/or CPD log. You may also wish to discuss them with a peer, colleague, mentor or coach to aid your further development.

REFERENCES

ALRED, G., GARVEY, B. and SMITH R. (1998) *Mentoring pocketbook*. Alresford: Management Pocketbooks.

CANNON, T. (1994) *Corporate responsibility*. London: Prentice Hall.

CHARAN, R., DROTTER, S. and NOEL, J. (2001) *The leadership pipeline: how to build the leadership-powered company*. San Francisco, CA: Jossey-Bass.

CIPD. (2010) *Mentoring [online]*. Available at: http://www.cipd.co.uk/subjects.lrnanddev/coachmntor/mentor.htm?IsSrchRes=1 [Accessed 20 May 2010].

COLAN, L.J. (2008) *Engaging the hearts and minds of all your employees: how to ignite passionate performance for better business results*. London: McGraw-Hill.

COLLINS, J. (2001) *Good to great*. New York: HarperCollins.

FERLIE, E., HARTLEY, J. and MARTING, S. (2003) Changing public service organizations: current perspectives and future prospects. *British Journal of Management*. Vol 14, No S1. ppS1–S14.

GOYDER, M. (1998) *Living tomorrow's company*. London: Gower.

HIRSH, W. (2000) *Succession planning demystified.* Report 372. Brighton: Institute for Employment Studies.

HODGE, G.A. and GREVE, C. (2009) PPPs: the passage of time permits a sober reflection. *Institute of Economic Affairs.* Vol 29, No 1. pp33–9.

MIDDLETON, J. (2007) *Beyond authority: leadership in a changing world.* Basingstoke: Palgrave Macmillan.

ONE WATER. (2009) Press release. 9 June. Available at: http://www.Onedifference.org/water.

REID, M.A., BARRINGTON, H. and BROWN, M. (2004) *Human resource development: beyond training interventions.* 7th ed. London: CIPD.

TICHY, N.M. and ULRICH, D.O (2008) The leadership challenge – a call for the transformational leader In: J.S. OTT, S.J. PARKES and R.B. SIMPSON (eds). *Classical readings of organisational behaviour.* Belmont, CA: Thomson-Wadsworth.

TIMES ONLINE. (2010) *Top 25 big companies to work for [online].* Available at: http://business.timesonline.co.uk/tol/business/career_and_jobs/best_100_companies/article7029136.ece [Accessed 20 May 2010].

UNIVERSITY OF SUNDERLAND. (nd) Corporate social responsibility [website]. Available at: http://www.sunderland.ac.uk/university/social/

UNIVERSITY OF SUNDERLAND. (nd) Annual review 2008/09 [online]. Available at: http://www.sunderland.ac.uk/dvc/dvc-sureview.pdf [Accessed 30 May 2010].

UNIVERSITY OF SUNDERLAND. (nd) Corporate Plan 2009/10 – 2013/14 [online]. Available at: http://www.sunderland.ac.uk/dvc/dvc-uoscorporateplan.pdf [Accessed 30 May 2010].

ZADEK, S. (2001) *The civil corporation.* London: Earthscan Publications.

CHAPTER 18

Consolidating Leadership Skills: Project Management and your Development

GILLIAN WATSON AND KEVIN GALLAGHER

OVERVIEW

Perhaps you have never considered yourself to be a 'project manager' but in many working situations today project management is likely to be an area that you are involved in, either as a project team member or in the *role* of a project manager. Project management is no longer the sole preserve of large construction projects – any complex, one-off organisational undertaking may use project management techniques. Increasingly, projects are also focusing upon internal change within organisations, so are clearly of importance to HR strategic change initiatives. Developing your skills as a project manager will therefore be beneficial to your career development and may be particularly so if you are considering managing your career, as such skills will broaden your personal portfolio.

LEARNING OUTCOMES

By the end of this chapter, provided you engage with the activities, you should be able to:

- define the scope of project management
- understand the concept of hard and soft changes
- recognise organisational change management projects
- analyse the four phases of projects
- apply stakeholder analysis to projects
- draw typical project organisational structures
- construct Gantt charts
- argue the importance of employee engagement in successful projects
- explain the nature of culture and virtual teams within multinational project teams
- analyse typical communication barriers within such project teams
- outline the concept of talent management
- apply various aspects of career enhancement, with particular reference to links with personal and professional development, personal performance and progression.

18.1 INTRODUCTION

This final chapter is structured in two sections and brings together many of the skills covered in previous chapters of this book. Part 1 covers project management as a specific subject area by exploring how a typical project may be tackled. We want to highlight that no matter what your job title is, you are likely to be involved in projects (that is, complex, one-off undertakings), either in a supporting or leading role. Typical projects include: setting up a new company operation; amalgamating sites; organisational restructuring; a new staff development programme; introduction of a quality assurance system, and so on. While we will introduce you to specific project management techniques, you will need to use many of the skills covered in earlier chapters of this book, in particular team dynamics, negotiation, change management, leadership, problem-solving and decision-making.

Specifically, Section 1 discusses the different phases of a project, stakeholder analysis, organisational structure, project control, project team as well as learning, training and change. It illustrates project management with the Mountech Gear case study, in which a 'green' project will be implemented across three countries. Projects are synonymous with change and there are clear links to corresponding requirements in professional development. The case study highlights the need for particular aspects of professional development for various staff members, thus giving typical examples of CPD. You are encouraged to then consider the importance of CPD within your own professional context and your own CPD in particular. You may wish to include your course of study and the skills outlined in this book as part of this process.

Section 2 covers career development with a focus on talent management, career enhancement and continuing professional development, with a special emphasis on what you can do now that your studies with this book have come to a close.

PART 1: PROJECT MANAGEMENT

18.2 WHAT IS PROJECT MANAGEMENT?

Project management as a subject discipline has its roots in large civil engineering and construction projects, complex military projects (for example missile development) and oil exploration. With advances in information technology, the advent of large IT projects has also featured prominently in the project management literature. The emphasis within these areas has been based upon ensuring that the project runs to budget, on schedule, and delivers optimal performance. Within such industries the role of a dedicated project manager has emerged, and some organisations have even created a dedicated department with specialists working on different aspects of project management, such as project planning.

Project managers have access to computer software to assist them in co-ordinating a multitude of information in the most efficient manner; they may also use sophisticated project management systems (such as PRINCE – **Pr**ojects **in** **C**ontrolled **E**nvironments – see Maylor (2005, p399)). A growing research culture is supplying academic papers for consideration by both academics and practitioners. The *Project Management Body of Knowledge* (often referred to as 'PMBOK' (Project Management Institute 2007)) heralded a milestone in this quest for information with which to expand the project manager's command of the discipline. The Project Management Institute (www.pmi.org) offers a comprehensive website for professional managers. Key academic journals are the *International Journal of Project Management* and the *Project Management Journal*. If you are already a professional project manager, skip the first part of this chapter. However, many of you will not be in such jobs and it is for you that this chapter is written, for if you are involved in a complex, one-off undertaking at work, you are probably *doing the role* of the project manager. Consider the following statement from one of project management's gurus, Jeffrey Pinto:

> At one time, project management was almost exclusively the property of civil and construction engineering programs where it was taught in a highly quantitative, technical manner. ... Project management today is a holistic 'management' challenge requiring not only technical skills but a broad based set of people skills as well. Project management has become the management of technology, people, culture, stakeholders, and other diverse elements necessary to successfully complete a project. (Pinto 2007, pxvii)

Then consider what Harvey Maylor, another well-respected project management author, says:

> Many managers have not recognised that they are project managers, despite the statistics from those who study such things that the average manager now spends upwards of 50 per cent of their time on projects or project-related issues. Their line responsibilities (finance, marketing, design) involve them in a variety of day-to-day activities plus longer-term projects. ... The more enlightened organisations will provide a basic skills grounding in the best way to run projects, and help, coach and mentor individuals in recognising and developing their project roles. (Maylor 2005, p10)

18.2.1 PROJECT DEFINITION – A MORE DETAILED CONSIDERATION

Something which you do every day as part of your normal activities, such as producing goods or services, is *not* a project; it is a *process*. So if you are an accountant producing the usual end of month accounts, a sales manager selling your usual range of products, or a university lecturer marking students' scripts, you are engaged in your normal, everyday work activities. We would not describe these as projects. Now, that is not to say that accountants, sales managers or university lecturers do not become involved in projects, nor that they cannot be project managers. Pinto (2007, pp3–5) describes a project in the following terms:

> A project is a unique venture with a beginning and end, conducted by people to meet established goals within parameters of cost, schedule, and quality.

[that are]

1   complex, one time

2   developed to resolve a clear goal(s)

3   customer-focused

[and]

4   are ad hoc endeavours with a clear lifecycle

5   are responsible for the newest and most improved products, services and organisational processes

6   provide a philosophy and strategy for the management of change ... crossing functional and organisational boundaries.

Here are a few real examples that illustrate some of the scale and scope of project work:

● a major construction project: the Lesotho Highlands Water Project – a hydro-electric construction project in the mid-1980s (Gallagher 2006)

- introduction of Quality Assurance System ISO 9001 to an organisation
- amalgamation of two NHS hospitals within the same trust
- GP's surgery IT project to locate all patients records and communication hub
- Tempus project – university staff developing managers in Egypt.

Considering points 1–6 above (Pinto 2007), the Lesotho Highlands Water Project (LHWP) is typical of the large, complex projects that you would automatically tend to think of when the word 'project' is mentioned. The LHWP was unique in terms of the terrain, requirements of construction – for example number of dams and their location – the political situation (this was a project between the adjoining countries of Lesotho and South Africa) and costs were applicable only at that time. Its goal was to provide South Africa with water and Lesotho with electricity and revenue. The customers were the governments and ultimately the peoples of these countries. It had a definite start and end date; many amendments/alterations were made along the way as the project developed to overcome unforeseen circumstances. It remains one of the most technologically advanced examples of tunnelling in the world (the series of waterways and tunnels built to pipe the water). Although not a 'change project' as such, in a political sense it crossed boundaries with its mutual benefits.

The introduction of ISO 9001, on the other hand, is something that many organisations have done. However, each organisation is unique and must analyse its own operations. It is true that it must ensure that its systems then meet the requirements of the ISO 9001 system and use accepted standards – but *how* it does this is not prescribed. For instance, it is a requirement for the organisation to ensure that it has a customer feedback system in place, but the exact set-up is not dictated, rather the emphasis is upon satisfying criteria such as the system's ability to identify problem areas. So, although this sort of project is not likely to have the same scale of unknowns as the previous example (the LHWP) it will still have many lesser unknowns. Experienced ISO 9001 consultants may advise or assist organisations and thus cut down some of the 'guesswork', but there is still a great deal of work to be done, least of all in ensuring that staff 'buy in' to the new system.

The amalgamation of two hospitals into one is, again, something that various NHS trusts have done over recent years, usually from a service efficiency viewpoint. However, no two situations are the same. There is a start and end date, ad hoc arrangements must be made and arrangements for the amalgamation are often intricate. In such cases there may be resistance from various quarters – staff objecting to the move, the possibility of staff grades restructuring and redundancies, and patients objecting to the loss of their 'local' hospital.

The GP's surgery IT support system is typical of the gradual linking of patient/customer information for monitoring and control purposes. Establishing and implementing the system is a one-off activity. Such systems have various 'users' as 'stakeholders' (more on these later): the GP, practice nurses, local hospitals and the patients. Such systems replace the traditional paper record cards and communication methods for arranging appointments and requesting repeat prescriptions, and even queries to the GP or practice nurses; however, this requires the patient to 'buy in' to the system and to be trained to use it – part of the project.

The last example shown relates to a 'Tempus' project. Tempus is the European Union's programme which supports the modernisation of higher education in the Partner Countries of Eastern Europe, Central Asia, the Western Balkans and the Mediterranean region, mainly through university cooperation projects' (Executive Agency Education, Audiovisual and Culture 2009). This particular example concerned a UK and an Egyptian university devising a project for the management development of staff working for the Suez Canal Authority in Egypt. This was not that complex a project but it was very customer-oriented and, more significantly, it was aimed at point 6 (Pinto 2007) as organisational change was a major requirement.

18.2.2 HARD AND SOFT CHANGES

Occasionally some projects are purely technical in nature; for instance, a construction company carrying out yet another project is just doing what it always does. The challenges it faces will be different but will relate to technical matters. Such changes are sometimes called 'hard' changes. However, many changes in other sorts of organisations affect the end-user (the customer) and those working for the organisation. Take, for instance, the hospital amalgamation project outlined above; the operation of the amalgamated hospital will be changed but there are also many other changes of leadership, communication and working behaviours. Such changes are sometimes called 'soft' changes.

In reality many projects embody both hard and soft changes. IT projects sometimes receive bad press for introducing technical improvements without sufficient consideration for staff development in the new processes, but they are far from being alone in this regard. This view is backed by research, with one study stating that 'human factors [of] change management (the most important factor identified), internal staff adequacy, training, project team, consultants, prioritization/resource allocation, ownership, senior management support' are the source of a staggering 57 per cent of difficulties and obstacles in the implementation of certain types of IT project implementation (Legris and Collerette 2006, p65).

18.2.3 ORGANISATIONAL CHANGE MANAGEMENT PROJECTS

It is not possible to discuss project management without also considering 'change'. From a traditional project point of view (Briner et al 1996, p126) projects are dynamic, and thus change within the project is to be expected. These authors suggest that the project team carries out successive cycles of plan–do–review with the project team and discuss and agree revisions to plans with relevant stakeholders. Construction projects are characterised by updated plans (it is very important to give all plans a clear issue status so that everyone is working to the same documents).

Going a stage further, some projects only have provisional plans in place as the final outcomes are unknown. In particular, IT projects which involve the creation of software are examples of what Cockburn (2002) describes as incremental learning, as the team progresses towards its final goal through a succession of developmental stages during design and implementation.

Some projects, however, are deliberately established to bring change to the ways in which organisations behave or the behaviours of people within them – that is, internal change projects. Others have this as a 'knock-on' effect of some primary technical change. When people talk of 'managing change' they are often referring to these sorts of changes. Thus quality systems projects such as ISO 9001 incorporate the technical changes relating to documenting systems and adhering to quality standards but to *work* they need to bring about an *attitude change* to quality – that quality is not the sole responsibility of the quality manager but of everyone in the organisation, from the managing director downwards. This is an example of *organisational change*.

ACTIVITY 18.1

My projects

1   Make a list of various projects that you have been involved in over the last two years. Now, select a maximum of three projects.

2   Describe each project with a sentence, outlining its main aim(s).

3   Next, list hard and soft aspects of these projects.

4   Would you describe any of them as having significant organisational change aspects? Explain.

    leader, other) was in each of these projects?

5   Finally, what do you think your role(s) (for example team member, specialist, project

18.2.4 PHASES OF PROJECTS

The project management writers appear to agree that there are four main stages to any project. Pinto (2007, p11) uses the terms 'Conceptualization, Planning, Execution, and Termination', while Lockyer and Gordon (2007, p4) refer to 'Conception, Development, Realisation, and Termination'. These stages overlap each other as projects progress from one stage to the next. This basic framework can be used to great effect to analyse various aspects of projects – for instance the people involved at each stage – and is a feature of research into project management.

Let us take the writing of this book as a project to illustrate each of the four stages.

18.2.4.1 Conception

The beginning – an idea is born. This book is a natural accompaniment to the new CIPD standards, providing a core text for *Developing Skills for Business Leadership*, so the idea of producing a book is hardly a surprise. However, the exact format of such a book is very much open to further ideas. Like many projects, a *business case* has to be put forward and agreed before further development can take place. In publishing terms this means the acceptance of a *book proposal*. Typical questions reflect those of any business project:

1   What is the *scope* of the project? In other words, what areas will it cover, what depth, what size (for example aim of the book, level and type of book, intended readers, outline of content)?

2   Who is likely to be involved (for example, in this case, two editors and a team of contributors)?

3   How does the project case compare with the competition (for example other existing books, books about to be published)?

4   What is the financial case for the project (for example projected sales versus costs)?

5   How does the project 'fit' the publisher's business strategy (for example is this the sort of book the publisher wishes to be associated with)?

6   What are the likely timescales involved (for example writing of drafts and reviews of chapters, and so on)?

7   Contracts are signed outlining who is responsible for various aspects of the project and the overall output and completion date (for example between the publisher, the editors and the contributors).

18.2.4.2 Development

Hopefully the book proposal is accepted by the publishers. However, acceptance of a project proposal should never be taken for granted, especially in new product development, where many projects 'bite the dust' at this initial stage. If not already done so, at this point a project manager(s) will be appointed. In the case of our book example there are various levels of project management and leadership. From the editors' point of view they are acting as project manager for the writing of the book; however, the publisher will assign a commissioning editor to liaise with the writers and to co-ordinate their activities into a bigger plan of which the writing is only one (though important) part. Other aspects of the book 'project' involve editing, typesetting, printing and marketing of the book. If we consider for the sake of this example the actual research and writing of the book (as opposed to its publication) and the author as a 'project manager', typical issues for the development stage are as follows:

1   appointment of project manager and team if not decided already (for example sole author, editor, multiple authors, and so on)

2   meeting of project team to discuss how the project will be developed (for example meeting of the writing team)

3   a project plan (for example any headings for the various sections and chapters, how it links together, content outline, who is doing what)

4   a project schedule (for example when will various chapters be ready in draft and final form).

18.2.4.3 Realisation

This is the stage at which the project is carried out. Progress will be monitored against the plan. Sometimes things do not go according to the plan and corrective action will have to be taken. Sometimes the planner will have built in a certain amount of 'slack time' – a buffer zone – to the project. In the 'book project' example this is the time at which the chapters are researched, written and submitted to the review process and then subsequently revised before final submission to the publisher.

18.2.4.4 Termination

At this stage of the project the end is in sight! However, the client still needs to accept the work has been carried out to the agreed standard. This phase is characterised by official signing off to accept the work and the handing over of the completed work to the client. For the authors in the book project this is initially when the final submission is accepted by the publisher, but for the publisher this is when the book is finally published and available to readers. This stage should also be one of celebration (or relief!) within the project team (Legris and Collerette 2006, p73). It also marks an opportunity for a more analytical review of the whole project and lessons learned and, perhaps, ideas for the next project!

ACTIVITY 18.2

Project phases

Choose a project with which you are familiar. Break it down into the four phases of conception, development, realisation and termination, and make notes.

18.3 STAKEHOLDER ANALYSIS

A project stakeholder is any individual, group or organisation that may have an interest in, an input into, or be affected by the project, either directly or indirectly. The obvious stakeholders are the client/customer for whom the project is being delivered and the project team who are the providers. Stakeholders have varying degrees of influence and the project manager needs to be aware of this. Some writers (for example Briner et al 1996, p83) divide stakeholders into 'internal', 'external' and 'customer', whereas others (for example Pinto 2007, p40) refer only to 'internal' and 'external', though he places the client as an external stakeholder. In both cases, however, 'internal' refers to those who are carrying out the project and 'external' to those outside of the project manager's organisation.

Both of these models reflect the traditional view of projects, for instance as carried out by a construction company for a client; for a modern change management project the 'client' is within the organisation and is therefore an 'internal' stakeholder. There is the additional argument that the project provider should involve the customer much more within the workings of the project team, especially at the conception/design phase, to align more closely with the end-user needs (Legris and Collerette 2006, p71). In some cases there will be other projects between the project organisation and the customer and a closer working relationship may be beneficial. As Rowlinson and Cheung (2008, p611) state:

> ... project managers, traditionally have been seen to attempt to mollify stakeholders while focusing their attention on the details of the project management rather than to empower stakeholders to have a significant input to the project ... this change in attitude to stakeholders marks a culture change in the real estate and construction industry, brought about by an increased emphasis on relationship management.

For these reasons, Figure 18.1 has placed the client/customer within the 'inner circle' of stakeholders.

Figure 18.1 Project stakeholders

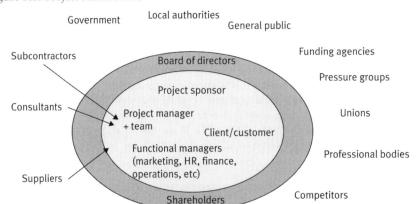

Also within this inner circle are the project manager and team, the person who approves or supports the project (the project sponsor) and other senior functional managers within the organisation who are supplying staff to the project. As you would expect, the board of directors are positioned fairly close in the next layer as the management team are accountable to them. Shareholders of course own the company and have a clear interest, though perhaps not always immediate influence. Consultants may provide specialist advice to project teams and subcontractors may be employed for the duration of the project to carry out certain aspects of work, so clearly input to the success of the project. Suppliers too may be closely linked to the project, particularly if they have to deliver to quality standards set by the project team and client.

Those other stakeholders outside of these circles such as government, local authorities, competitors and the general public may be regarded as not directly related to the project (in effect the 'external stakeholders' referred to earlier) but may still have considerable influence. You should note, therefore, that Figure 18.1 is only intended to give a *general indication* of the stakeholder relationships and influence – particular projects may have stakeholders who, for one reason or another, hold a lot of influence.

ACTIVITY 18.3

Health and well-being awareness day

Case Study 18.1 considers how a large university went about organising a staff and student awareness day for health and well-being (names have been changed). You are asked to:

1   Read the case study and then draw a stakeholder diagram. (You may think of other possible stakeholders who are not mentioned in the case.)

2   Next, you are asked to consider the viewpoints of the various members of the project team – in this case the Health and Well-being Committee – in terms of how they might assess the value of the awareness day. For this you might wish to consider the work of Anderson (see CIPD

2007a, p8, and reference at the end of this chapter for further details), who suggests that there is a variety of approaches to 'assessing learning contribution'. In particular you may wish to think about the following three aspects:

- 'Return on investment' – that is, costs versus benefits for the awareness day.
- 'Return on expectation measures' – that is, did/will the awareness day actually meet the expectations of staff, students, and the Health and Well-being Committee?
- 'Benchmark' – does this raise the university's standing for its health and well-being policy, particularly when compared with other universities?

NORTHERN UNIVERSITY

CASE STUDY 18.1

Northern University is a large university. It has four faculties: Business, Education, Arts and Health Sciences. Recently it has established a health and well-being committee. The committee is led by the health and well-being officer (Margaret), who is keen to promote health and well-being awareness among staff and students. The activities of the committee are linked to the university's policy on health and well-being; also, the committee is responsible for monitoring health and well-being statistics (including absence levels and sick leave), feeding these as reports to senior university management.

Other members of the committee are as follows: university occupational health nurse (Sarah); disabilities and equality officer (Jim); HR representative (Judith); union representative (Malcolm); health and safety officer (Peter); student

counselling officer (Stuart); faculty representatives (various members from academic staff and administrative support) for Business, Education, Arts and Health Sciences.

The committee has decided that awareness day should achieve three main aims: to raise awareness among staff and students that they need to be more proactive in caring for their physical and mental well-being; to offer a range of quick, on-the-spot health checks; to promote what the university has to offer in terms of its health and sports services.

The awareness day will be widely advertised in all faculties via posters and emails. The event will be held in a large, centrally located hall on the main campus. A series of stalls will be set up – student counselling, the external group MIND, the British Heart Foundation, the local aquatics centre, the university sports club, student union giving advice on clubs and societies, university nurse, and the local Weight Watchers group. There will also be the opportunity to try out some yoga, meditation and head massage treatments.

18.4 PROJECT ORGANISATIONAL STRUCTURE(S)

Working in project teams is a different experience from working in a functional environment dedicated to one particular activity such as sales, HR, marketing, finance or operations. In these functional environments you will work with others above, below and side on to you but in the same discipline. For instance, a university lecturer may work in the business school's economics department of teaching staff. The same lecturer may meet with the economics department to discuss the latest developments in the field of economics and other teaching-related matters. She may be line-managed by the head of the economics department, being appraised by this person, agreeing work allocation, and reporting sickness/requesting holidays. The benefits of this arrangement relate to professionalism, research and staff development – in this case within the field of economics.

However, suppose that a *project group* is established to consider the 'student experience' in year 1. This project group is likely to include a range of staff, cutting across academic disciplines. Our economics lecturer might then find herself as the only one from the economics department. She may well find herself making decisions with others in the group who are at different levels in the organisation's hierarchy. The project group will have its own *project leader*. Suddenly she finds herself with two bosses – her functional (economics department) boss and, now, her project boss. She is in a matrix organisation, though this is rarely shown on an organisational chart for ad hoc projects. The textbooks often show this form of organisational structure as the *usual form* for a construction company – hardly surprising as carrying out projects is what construction companies do for most of the time. Figure 18.2 shows typically how a construction company operates as a matrix structure.

In Figure 18.2 the functions are those of design, purchasing and construction (there could be more – the diagram shows only part of a possible structure). The circles represent individual members of staff. In the example shown, design engineers report to the design director, quantity surveyors report to the purchasing director and site engineers report to the construction director. However, they are also in project teams and report to the appropriate project manager. Of course a member of staff may in fact occupy two or more circles if they work on more than one project. Also, project managers might have more than one project.

Figure 18.2 Typical project management organisational structure

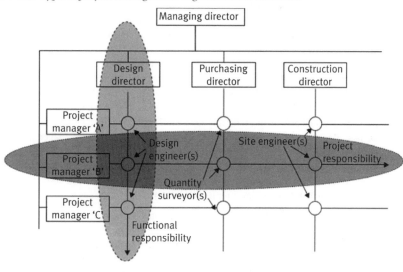

Question: is having two bosses confusing?

The answer to this question is that it can be. There needs to be an agreement regarding which of the two bosses the member of staff reports to for specific purposes. There should not be direct overlap as this can lead to contrary directives to the member of staff; nor should there be any gaps where the member of staff does not know where to go for direction.

Question: what about power differences between functional and project bosses?

This is a good question. The power relationship can actually determine if the structure is one which has project managers as co-ordinators but where real power still lies with the functional managers (Maylor (2005, p224) calls this a 'lightweight' matrix) or as powerful project managers who draw on project team members through a process of secondment from the functional areas (Maylor (2005, p224) classifies this as a 'heavyweight' matrix).

MEDICAL PRACTITIONERS PROJECT – STAFF DEVELOPMENT

CASE STUDY 18.2

Read the following case study and answer the questions given at the end of it.

You are the External Activities Manager for Sheerwater Business School, part of Grandpool University, reporting directly to the Head of School. The business school offers a range of degrees and other qualifications. Whereas the majority of business school income is generated from individual full- and part-time students who attend the business school on conventional qualification routes, your job involves you in new 'product'

development for companies and government bodies. In other words, you help create and sell various staff development and educational packages unique to particular companies or industries.

You sometimes rely upon the involvement of academic tutors drawn from across the subject disciplines at the university. These academic tutors are normally specialists in their own teams (for example law, human resource management, operations management) who work in the university teaching students on degree programmes; any work they do for you is thus additional to their normal workload, although they are paid a fee by the university for the additional work. This fee would cover development costs – that is, cover time which they, as academic staff, spent in developing the staff development package; it would also be usual for the same staff to deliver the programme of study and receive a fee whenever they did this (this is regarded as the main incentive). However, team leaders still need to agree that their specialist tutors can work for you; team leaders tend to regard the business school and the teaching of degrees as of prime importance and anything else, such as work for you, as secondary. Team leaders report to the Head of School.

You recently have been approached by the HR manager of a local hospital to establish a new staff development programme for some of their senior staff (senior nursing managers and specialist managers in charge of areas such as eye surgery, cancer care, x-ray department, and so on). The aim of this development programme is to deliver a mix of human resource management, law, operations management and IT skills. These are managerial and IT skills which have not traditionally been provided by the hospital's own staff development (training has been provided for specific skills in nursing, eye surgery, and so on).

At the moment only these broad titles (for example 'human resource management module') have been suggested and there are no guidelines yet on possible educational content, but you do know that there will be four modules (human resource management, operations management, law, computer skills); in other words, you have an 'open page' as to what to include in the programme. However, you have been asked to somehow involve the hospital's own HR staff in the development process to put your business school's managerial and IT skills into a health context. Students will be assessed throughout the programme; this is something else you need to think about.

You have six months to get the programme operational, but other than the initial contact with the hospital, nothing has yet been done. Once you have established the programme and checked that it is running properly, the project, in terms of new product development, is complete. The first thing you intend to do is create a development team for the new programme.

Questions

1 Who would you include in your (new product) development team? Why?

2 Draw a matrix organisational structure for the new product development team.

3 How do you envisage the hospital HR staff contributing to the development of the modules/programme?

18.5 PROJECT CONTROL

Perhaps one of the most well-known control instruments of project management is the Gantt chart. We will focus on this, although you should be aware that there are other, more advanced techniques which lie beyond the scope of this book. Named after Henry Gantt (1861–1919), one of the founding figures of the scientific management approach in the early twentieth century, the Gantt chart is now firmly established. The basic Gantt chart breaks down a project into its component activities and shows these as line bars mapped against a timescale. Its simplicity means that it is easy to understand yet it is surprisingly effective at communicating, at a glance, start and end dates of activities and, to some extent, the logical connection between dependent activities. Gantt charts can be used in various ways: to assist in the planning of a project; to allocate resources – including staff; and to monitor actual progress against the plan. The Gantt chart should be the starting point for anyone interested in project scheduling. Figure 18.3 shows a Gantt chart for the writing of a textbook by a lead author and team of authors. We will use this example to elaborate on some of the practical pointers you may encounter in your own projects.

In this example there is an initial conception phase, which ends with the agreement between author and publisher for the scope of the book. The authoring team has a lead author and authors 2, 3 and 4 (normally we would give their names!). Each author has responsibility for researching a set of chapters and writing drafts. These are then submitted to the publisher, who arranges for them to be reviewed anonymously and returned to the authors. The authors then revise their chapters, as appropriate, and resubmit to the publisher (for the sake of simplicity only one cycle of reviewing has been shown). Other activities need to be carried out. Note that the lead author has decided to press ahead with research on chapters 1, 2 and 3 even before signing the contract – that is his choice. However, all other authors are only asked to start by the lead author after the contract has been signed. You should note that the Gantt chart is a useful tool but it is only that – it is dependent upon the skill of the person creating it to include all activities and to give appropriate timescales. An experienced scheduler may build in some 'slack', that is, leeway on key tasks that lie on the 'critical path' – those activities that if delayed will results in a delay to the overall completion date of the project. There is still a place for intuition and improvisation on the part of the project manager (Sadler-Smith and Leybourne 2006).

This example has been prepared on a standard Microsoft Excel spreadsheet, although it could have easily been drawn on squared graph paper. You do not need anything more advanced than this for relatively small projects. You will see that, for the purpose of the chapter, activities have been grouped into the project phases (conception, development, realisation and termination) described earlier. However, you do not need to do this. That said, this approach lends itself to inserting 'milestones' to indicate key points in the project (for instance, signing the contract). If you scan the whole diagram you will observe a general trend from left to right of successive activity completion; this makes it easier for you to visualise the sequential logic of activities but is not essential – placing the initial book outline at the bottom of the list of activities may look strange but the activity bar would still appear on the chart in weeks 1 and 2, which is correct.

You will note that this 'project' has been planned from the point of view of the lead author and his team of authors. The publisher will have a more inclusive Gantt chart, viewing the project as bigger than the writing (author) stage, for instance including activities such as typesetting, proof reading, printing and marketing.

If you want to make dependent activities more obviously linked to one another, you could add a connecting arrow from the end of one activity to the beginning point of the next one which follows logically on from it – for instance, after a chapter has been reviewed by the publisher/reviewer it then needs to be revised by the author in the light of the reviewer's comments. In terms of timescale we have simply used week number, but you could use calendar weeks. Also a two-week period has been blocked out for some sort of national holiday when it is assumed no work will be done (not always the case!).

Figure 18.3 A typical Gantt chart for writing a textbook

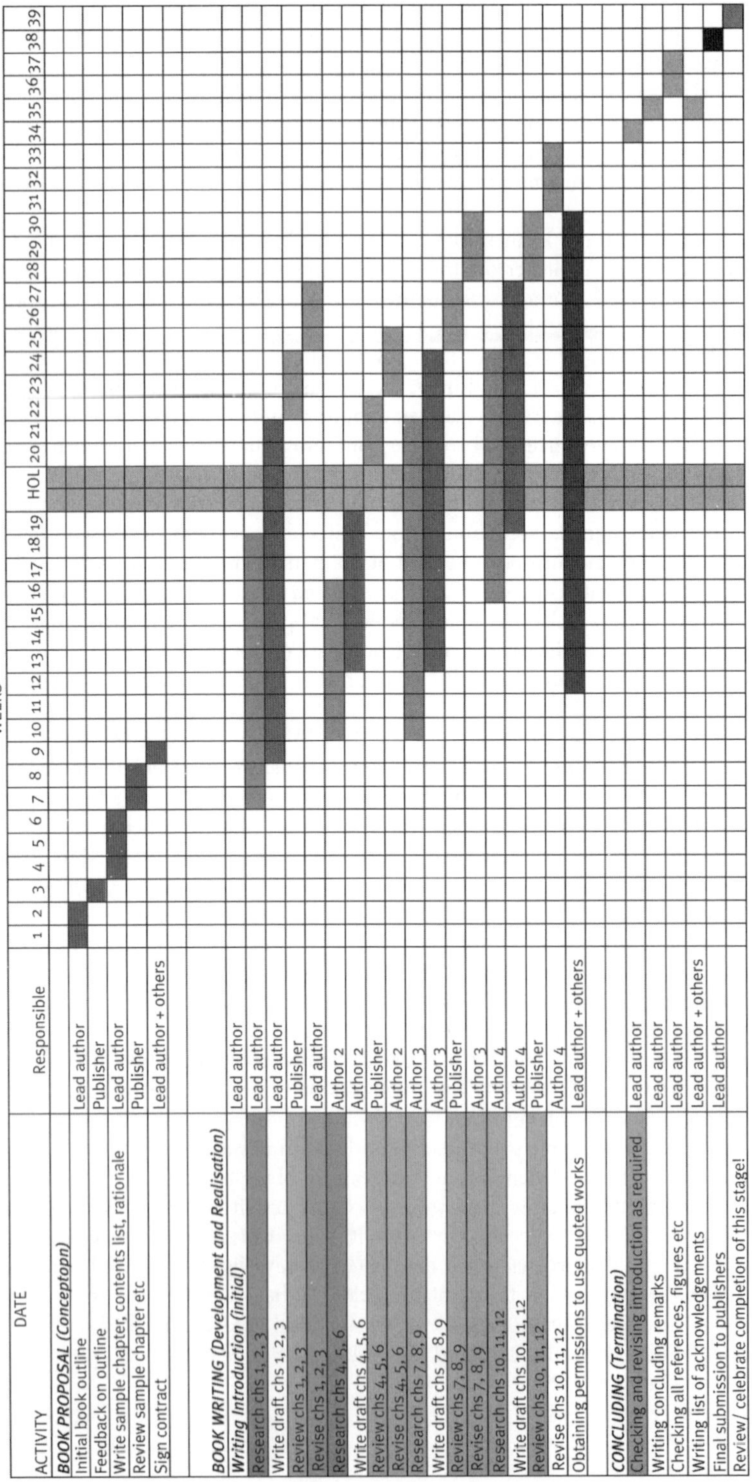

The headings given for the Gantt chart in Figure 18.3 will suffice for simple charts. However, you may wish to add further columns to add more detail – for instance resources used, start and end dates and duration of activities. You may then have a chart with headings as laid out in Figure 18.4, which shows part of a house renovation project.

Figure 18.4 More detailed headings for a Gantt chart

Activity No	Activity (or task)	Resource	Start date	End date	Duration of activity	Week 1	Week 2	Week 3	Week 4 etc
23	Sand wooden floor	Sanding machine	4 May 2013	5 May 2013	2 days				

For more complex projects you may wish to use project software. A study by Ali et al (2008, p11) showed that the most commonly used project management tool was Microsoft Project, with 75 per cent of the study's respondents using this software, 10 per cent using Primavera Project Management and the remainder using other software such as Timesheet, Excel and database applications. Presently (September 2013) you can download trial versions of Microsoft Project Professional 2013 from the website http://www.microsoft.com/project/en/us/default.aspx, which has Gantt charts as one of its features. One of the advantages of using such software is that you can now use the sort of MS drawing tools you are familiar with in, say, MS Office, and produce very professional-looking charts that you can cut and paste into your documents.

18.6 PROJECTS IN CONTEXT

This section uses the Mountech Gear case study, outlined in Case Study 18.3, to provide the context for further discussion on employee engagement and other important people factors within projects.

MOUNTECH GEAR

CASE STUDY 18.3

Background information

Mountech Gear was founded in 1972 by Jeremy Burnes and Christopher Child as a company which manufactured waterproof jackets and trousers for outdoor pursuits such as walking, climbing and skiing. Operations were fairly small scale, all production being carried out in a factory unit in Northumberland. Gradually the market grew and so did the business. However, in the late 1980s and 1990s competition from overseas manufacturers cut profit margins drastically, and eventually in 2000 the decision was made to relocate manufacturing operations to Dongguan in China. This proved a successful move and recently (2009) the company has bought a new production plant, again in Dongguan, which has long had a tradition of textile manufacture and is now home to many industrial and business parks. Production centres on two lines – down products (that is, sleeping bags and insulated, down jackets) – and waterproofs (that is, mountain jackets and trousers manufactured from high-tech fabrics). Alex Burnes, daughter of the founder Jeremy, is now the managing director of the company. Her father

Jeremy and his business partner Christopher Child have now both retired from running the business but still sit on the board of directors. In 2005 the company bought out a struggling business in Stuttgart, Germany which manufactured alpine climbing axes. Since then they have injected money into this part of the business and it is now beginning to show a profit; its main two lines are ice tools (for example ice axes) and climbing harnesses. Upon acquiring this business the company effectively consisted of two divisions: the Dongguan division was re-named MG-Wear and the Stuttgart operation given the name of MG-Climb. Head office remained in Sunderland in the UK. Currently products from MG-Wear are sold within China and throughout Europe, while MG-Climb distributes within Europe and has a new outlet in Colorado, USA. The organisation chart is shown in Figure 18.5.

Figure 18.5 Organisation structure of Mountech Gear

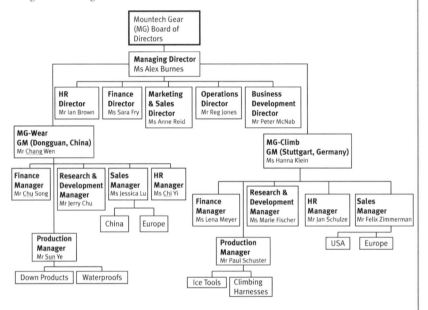

Profiles of key players at head office

Alex Burnes: Managing Director

Alex is in her mid-40s. As daughter of one of the founding partners she has been immersed in the business for most of her working life. A keen walker and skier, she has a ready appreciation of the outdoor leisure market – always on the lookout for new opportunities, attending conferences worldwide and with an eye on technical developments. Easily bored. She has a strong bond to 'her' company (she is a major shareholder). She is a professional manager who has held a variety of senior posts prior to this and has been involved in a number of company mergers. Tough. Admired and feared in equal measure by staff. By coincidence she is an old university acquaintance of Mr Chang (the head of MG-Wear in Dongguan) from their time spent in Edinburgh on their MBA programme in 1996.

Ian Brown: HR Director

Keen to show his worth as a new director to the company. Rather fastidious about detail. Responsible for all major aspects of HR policy including health and safety, management development and selection and recruitment. Recently has spent much of his time with MG-Climb (Germany) assisting Peter McNab (see below) in overseeing the introduction of new quality assurance procedures. Previously worked within a university HR department as a senior manager. Considers this his 'big break' into industry. Not an active outdoors person as such but is an avid football supporter and coaches a local team. In his early 40s.

Sarah Fry: Finance Director

An ambitious high-flyer in her early 30s. Graduated with 1st class honours from a prestigious university and head-hunted for a major financial consulting group before joining the company. A keen skier.

Anne Reid: Marketing and Sales Director

An extrovert with an enviable list of contacts. Does not always play 'by the rules' but achieves results. Has a natural affinity for picking up on what people are looking for in a product; believes very much in promoting 'lifestyle'. Mid 50s but shows no sign of slowing down. Owns a chalet in Chamonix and is a vibrant party host.

Reg Jones: Operations Director

Previously operations manager for the UK manufacturing plant, now shut down. Although ostensibly in a strategic role, tends to take too much of a 'hands-on approach' with operations, particularly with MG-Wear in Dongguan, which replaced the UK facility. Early 50s. Tends to adopt a paternal attitude to the production manager there – Mr Sun Ye. Less close to Paul Schuster, the operations manager in Stuttgart, partly because he is used to working with textiles, rather than what he calls 'ironmongery' (ice axes, and so on).

Peter McNab: Business Development Director

Reports directly to Alex Burnes. Does not have a department other than secretarial support. Has a strategic role in growing the business. Often involved as a project manager. Last major project overseeing the introduction of a new quality assurance system to MG-Climb. Early retiree from project management in petro-chemical industry, and financially secure, returned to the business world for 'one more challenge'. Now in his early 60s. An open and enquiring mind. Sees himself as a 'fixer', applying his knowledge and skills and then moving on. Keen to keep up with any new developments – technical, social and environmental. Meets socially with Alex Burnes and their respective partners.

Introducing the 'green project'

It was during their visit to Dongguan during the 2009 opening of the new manufacturing site that Alex Burnes and Peter McNab were invited to attend a conference being hosted in the prestigious Songshan Lake Science and Technical Industry Park (a friend of Mr Chang owned a company there). They were pleasantly surprised with the mix of high-tech and research companies located within a spacious (by Chinese standards) area, laid out among pleasant waterways and greenery. They were even more impressed to learn that the industry park had gained an award for the environmental management system ISO 14001 in 2003. Further, Dongguan City was encouraging investors and had other systems in place, including what it called 'talent policies'. This trip fired their imaginations. Alex felt sure that she could convince the board of directors to agree to a 'green project' for the company, involving MG-Wear, MG-Climb and head office in one co-ordinated push. Peter McNab was equally keen. They had noticed that the Research and Development Manager, Jerry Chu, was keen to emulate the practice of Songshan Lake. They were not so sure of the other MG-Wear staff as they had kept rather a low profile, other than Mr Chang, who seemed to generally be very agreeable. However, they suspected that their views would be largely dictated by their departmental/team considerations. From his work with MG-Climb Peter McNab favoured inviting the HR Manager Jan Schultze as 'change manager' for the Stuttgart operation, though he would have to discuss this further with the head of the division, Hanna Klein.

18.6.1 EMPLOYEE ENGAGEMENT

This section will draw on a recent CIPD (2010a) research study, *Creating an Engaged Workforce*, drawing on its data and findings to inform the Mountech Gear case study. The data collected in the study was from 5,291 questionnaires and 180 interviews. The CIPD (2010a) report measured three dimensions of engagement: emotional or affective engagement; intellectual or cognitive engagement; and social engagement, as follows:

- **intellectual engagement**, or thinking hard about the job and how to do it better
- **affective engagement**, or feeling positively about doing a good job
- **social engagement**, or actively taking opportunities to discuss work-related improvements with others at work.

The report also differentiated between:

- the *extent of engagement* – the strength of feeling engaged – and
- the *frequency of engagement* – that is, how often individuals experience engagement.

For the purposes of this section (which relates to the case study) we are only considering 'the extent of engagement'. The CIPD researchers defined engagement as: 'being positively present during the performance of work by willingly contributing intellectual effort, experiencing positive emotions and meaningful connections to others' (CIPD 2010a, p5). This definition has resonance with other writers (Kahn 1990, May et al 2004, Schaufeli and Bakker 2004, Truss et al 2006) as it highlights the view that engagement involves intellectual, emotional and behavioural dimensions (CIPD 2010a).

Strong employee engagement in the Mountech Gear case study will be required for the 'green project' to be a success. Managers at Mountech Gear should bear the following questions in mind:

- How do employees add value?
- Have employees expressed optimistic and constructive views about their work?
- Can employees influence a positive outcome to the 'green project', for example by holding meaningful discussions with others about the task and celebrating the gains and improvements?
- How are any positive responses related to the campaign and how are these communicated to staff? (For example if it is shown that a 'switch off' (electricity)

initiative is working it will be evident by the reduction in the electricity bill the company has to pay; this would be cause for sharing the good news.)

Table 18.1 includes some of the main findings of the CIPD (2010a, p2) study that may assist our analysis of the case study by offering an agenda for engaging Mountech Gear's employees.

Table 18.1 Engaging the workforce

Types of engagement	Outcome of the study
Engagement across different organisational contexts	● Comparisons across employee groups reveal a variety of interesting differences with respect to demographics and job types. ● Women are more engaged than men. ● Younger workers are less engaged than older workers. ● Those on flexible contracts are more engaged. ● Managers are more engaged than non-managers.
Strategies for engagement	● Organisations can implement a range of workplace strategies that impact upon levels of engagement. ● Meaningfulness is the most important driver of engagement for all employee groups. ● Two-thirds of all respondents in our study find meaning in their work. ● Senior management vision and communication is a key driver of engagement, whereas senior management effectiveness is negatively related to employee engagement. ● Positive perceptions of one's line manager are strongly linked with engagement.
Outcomes of engagement	● Employee engagement is associated with a range of positive outcomes at the individual and organisational levels. ● Engaged employees perform better. ● The majority of our respondents were rated 'good' in their last appraisal. ● Engaged employees are more innovative than others. ● Engaged employees are more likely to want to stay with their employer.

ACTIVITY 18.4

Engagement

Consider the following questions in relation to the case study:

1   What does engagement mean to Alex Burnes and Peter McNab, who are tasked with overall control of the project?

2   How can they manage the engagement with staff?

3   What are the consequences of engagement for organisations?

4   What are the consequences of success and failure for the organisation?

5   How does engagement in the case relate to some of the other individual characteristics mentioned in Table 18.1?

6   How is engagement related to employee voice and representation – do they have a choice, and how will the initiative be communicated?

18.6.2 THE PROJECT TEAMS: THEIR MULTICULTURAL NATURE AND COMMUNICATION PROBLEMS WHEN WORKING VIRTUALLY

18.6.2.1 Team groupings

As you will have realised from the Mountech Gear case study, various groupings are likely to emerge as distinct teams, with each one having an individual in a change leadership role. If we take into account the executives as well as the change managers, one approach is for each team to cascade into another, as shown in Figure 18.6.

Figure 18.6 Senior and next level team configuration

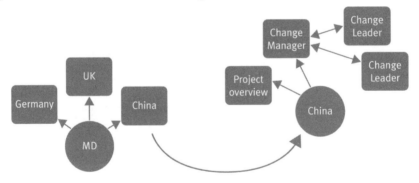

In Figure 18.6 the managing director (Alex Burnes) is co-ordinating an executive team (with Peter McNab as the overall project co-ordinator) that includes directors from the UK head office, and the German and Chinese operations. This team will oversee the project and will act as sponsors (see Section 18.2). Cascading to each of the countries (China is shown by itself in the diagram for clarity but a similar situation will exist for Germany and the UK head office), there will be other teams required to make the project work. The diagram shows someone in the Chinese operation (MG-Wear) with an overview of the whole project – this will probably be Mr Chang, Head of MG-Wear. The change manager whose task it is to push the change through will probably be Mr Jerry Chu, who was identified in the case study as a likely, enthusiastic and able candidate, to take this forward. Figure 18.6 also shows 'change leaders' – these are key individuals who wish to 'champion' the change in their particular areas of expertise or departments.

Another team is also possible, and in fact, desirable – a virtual team of change managers, who communicate with each other at a distance. For the purpose of the case study we may assume that in addition to Jerry Chu in China, Peter McNab will take on this role himself in the UK head office (in addition to his overall project co-ordination role), and Mr Jan Schultze (HR manager) in the Stuttgart office.

Figure 18.7 The project and change manager team (who will be working virtually)

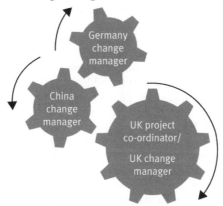

The virtual team (see Chapter 8) will have its own characteristics as well as cross-cultural and communication variables, adding to the complexities of accomplishing the task. Each country's change manager will have their own project team who are not working in a virtual capacity. The challenge is to manage the external and internal interaction between and within each team or grouping and to manage the overall process of engagement.

ACTIVITY 18.5

Challenges and barriers

1   Describe what you see as the main challenges facing the various teams.

2   What specific barriers to success do you see as being significant?

18.6.2.2 Communication across cultures

We will assume that part of your answer to the questions in Activity 18.5 included concerns related to communicating across cultures. Therefore, the examination of salient literature may help you analyse these issues. In our case it should be remembered that the UK head office has been working with the factories in both China and Germany for some years. However, the combination of all three countries working together has not been prevalent. Therefore, this spirit of co-operation is very new to all concerned, particularly the two head managers of the Chinese and German operations, who have in the recent past seen each other as rivals and have been known to disagree; indeed, on one occasion Mr Chang had walked out of an executive board meeting believing he had 'lost face' after being challenged by Ms Klein to revisit his year-end figures.

The issue of culture and national culture are important factors as they could be barriers to co-operation. Browaeys and Price (2008) inform us that culture operates on three levels or layers: artefacts and attitudes, norms and values, and basic assumptions. The first layer can be seen, such as artefacts, rituals and behaviours; the second, an underlying variable, can be addressed through investigation (interviews/questions) and surveys; the third, however, is more problematic as basic assumptions can only be inferred and interpreted (Schneider and Barsoux 2003). Schein suggests these basic assumptions are 'shared solutions to universal problems of external adaption (how to survive) and internal integration (how to stay together) – which have evolved over time and are handed down from one generation to the next' (Schein 2004, p14). Tayeb (2003, p13) refers to national culture as 'a constant thread' which runs 'through our lives which makes us distinguishable from others, especially those in other countries'.

From a Chinese perspective, relationships are valued and are seen as the channel to success, and from a business point of view, so too is the building up of networks of strong relationships. Drawing on connections (Luo and Chen 1997) outside the immediate family (Child 1994) is referred to as 'guanxi' (Browaeys and Price 2008). Central to these relationships is aspects of trust and having confidence in the other person. Individuals in the 'guanxi' network will grant favours, although they will expect favours in return. This, Browaeys and Price (2008) suggest, reflects village life in China. Mountech Gear is no different from many other Western companies in being affected by this well-established process operating within the business context. Chow (2004) highlights that some of the problems organisations may experience in doing business in China are a lack of understanding of these fundamental issues of culture. Chen (1995) states that guanxi and 'face' are intertwined in this patrimonial society (Child 1994). The preservation of face (Lockett 1988) also forms part of the four central values identified as key to understanding the Chinese culture and in turn are part of Confucian ideology. The other two are a configuration towards groups and respect for age and hierarchy, particularly male hierarchies (for example Mr Chang in the case study). 'Face' (mianzi), Child (1994) suggests, is a concept that relates to an individual's position, social standing and moral character. Therefore, importance is placed on how one is viewed by others as individuals will jealously guard their public reputation as this is used to influence the decisions of others (Browaeys and Price 2008). Therefore, direct confrontation is frowned upon, and it can even be construed as damaging as it may result in a diminishment of prestige. Again this links to Confucianism, which distinguishes people as social beings, each having their own place in the hierarchy of relationships (Michailova and Worm 2003). Consequently, doing business in China entails maintaining good relationships and being respectful of culture: Alex Burnes and Mr Chang have such a relationship, formed when they studied their MBA and MSc respectively, at a British university in 1996.

ACTIVITY 18.6

Project relationships

1   What positive aspects of relationships within Mountech Gear you detect?

2   There are also some problematic elements here: do you see them as insurmountable or can you see how they can be overcome?

3   Investigate how the business cultures of the UK and Germany differ from China. We suggest you reflect on the work of Geert Hofstede and Fons Trompenaars.

Earley and Mosakowski (2000) proposed that if multicultural teams are used for transnational project development they can eventually outperform monocultural teams (Ochieng and Price 2010). Weatherley (2006) contends, however, that project success is difficult even when teams are co-located, and this is made more problematic when geographically dispersed, dissimilar culture groups are used. We may conclude from this that developing virtual, multicultural project teams is extremely demanding, yet, if it is accomplished, these teams are incredibly effective at achieving their goals. Emmit and Gorse (2007) report that often problems with communicating factual data in project teams have been addressed by the development of higher specification computers, better hardware and software, and better global telecommunication. They also maintain, however, that many issues are left unaddressed in respect to teams that are both multicultural and working virtually. Examples may range from a lack of face-to-face communication, causing misunderstanding, to difficulties in developing relationships that may lead to a breakdown in trust and confidence (Weatherley 2006).

This is particularly worrying in respect to the case study as it is essential that the various project teams communicate successfully and work well together. There is no guarantee that because communication and reporting structures have worked with head office in the past, they will do so in the future – especially with the culturally diverse make-up of the 'green project' teams. These teams will need to establish their own versions of good practice and communications. Indeed, they will need to acquire what Ochieng and Price (2010, p451) suggest must be developed in such circumstances, which are: 'cultural sensitivity and the ability to manage and build future capabilities'.

In their research, Marquardt and Hovarth (2001) recognised that by harnessing the energy and synergy of people from various backgrounds, organisations can benefit, as together these individuals stimulate creative ways of thinking in addressing the challenges and problems they encounter in project-based undertakings. Pearson and Nelson (2003) help us to summarise the implementation issues of the 'green project' when they discuss, in general, the challenges facing project and change managers as: 'developing team cohesiveness; maintaining communication richness; dealing with coordination and control issues; handling geographical distance and dispersal of teams: and managing cultural diversity, difference and conflicts' (in Ochieng and Price 2010, p452).

The issue of communication-related risk factors (Lee-Kelley and Sankey 2008) are singled out by Reed and Knight (2010, p423) from their research advice, and comments from participants are highlighted thus:

- Particularly in large projects, communication is essential for efficient co-ordination.
- Lack of communication can lead to people 'not being on the same page' and 'working at cross purposes'.
- Lack of communication can lead to confusion that can add more cost and more time.
- Having good communication with your client and group members is very important when working on any project.
- False starts from misunderstandings are expensive in terms of time and resources and they also create bad feeling within a team.
- Meeting overload is also a risk; projects that meet too much and work too little also suffer from poor morale.

ACTIVITY 18.7

Implementation issues in Mountech Gear's 'green project'

1   Create a plan of how you would engage the project team as a virtual team.

2   What processes or rules would you like to see occurring?

3   How will you deal with the cultural issues?

4   Use the lists supplied above to discuss whether the comments highlighted will pose problems or help with ideas for managing this situation.

18.6.3 DEVELOPING THE WORKFORCE

Learning has always been a key component of how and why the business has prospered; whenever times have been hard, they have still encouraged training and development. This ethos was founded by Alex's father, and the organisation is noted for its commitment to its employee development. Their current development strategy has been influenced by the work of Harrison (1997, 2009), where she highlights the need for the whole business environment to be considered along with the business strategy and in line with the people development strategy. This has led to an increase in the organisational skills base in all three countries. Furthermore, management development has also not been neglected, as several of the existing staff have been funded to take bachelor and/or master's degrees at local universities; they also have a strong in-house training arm. However, the 'green project' offers new challenges as this particular initiative is about winning hearts and minds to engender change rather than training individuals in job-skill activities.

Figure 18.8 Mountech Gear development strategy model

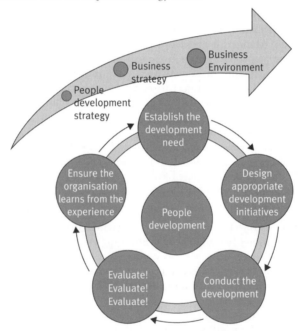

The opportunities for learning and development for many, if not all, of the participants in the 'green project' are immense. Likewise, staff in the whole organisation have the prospect of enhancing their understanding and appreciation of 'green/carbon-footprint' issues through training and engaging – then participating in the activities and initiatives the change managers will provide. The organisation as a whole will have to budget significant resources to make the project a success. Their overall strategy and their development strategy, therefore, must be calculated to recoup some of their money and/or to exploit this initiative in other ways.

Figure 18.9 Matching strengths with opportunities

ACTIVITY 18.8

Matching strengths with opportunities

1   Analyse the strengths, weaknesses, opportunities and threats facing Mountech Gear with respect to:

- their overall business strategy
- their development strategy.

Note: the analysis is stylised in triangular sections (in Figure 18.9) so that emphasis can be given to opportunities and strengths, which are placed centrally and higher up the pyramid respectively. In conducting this analysis,

therefore, take the weaknesses and threats a step further by ensuring you consider how to overcome these problematic concerns. Or are they insurmountable?

2   Using the development cycle from the organisational development strategy, map out the types of activities in which various sections of staff will need to engage.

3   List the resource implications for this process (you may wish to explore the scale of costs associated with such a budget).

18.6.4 JOURNALING

Loo (2002, p61) cites 'journaling' as a reflective learning devices for project managers (in our case we can add change managers) or indeed any management activity. He contends that reflective learning journals 'are useful tools that can help staff learn as individuals as well as members of a team' (Loo 2002, p66; see also Chapter 1 for details). The three-stage model of Scanlon and Chernomas (1997) can be adapted to help our purposes here. The model highlights the first stage as being *awareness*: without this the whole process of reflection cannot begin. The second stage they cite as individual *critical analysis* of the situation; this stage involves critical thinking, evaluation and self-examination, while continuing to become more self-aware. The third stage involves the creation of a *new perspective* or outlook that in itself is based on the previous critical analysis, the application of new knowledge to the problem or situation under the reflective gaze. The model seems to be consistent with Boud et al's (1985) model of reflection, as well as exhibits elements of Schön's model (1987). Using elements of these three models, and journaling in particular, we may represent three stages of a reflective process which could be used by the change managers in the Mountech Gear case study, as shown in Figure 18.10.

Figure 18.10 Three-stage reflection used at Mountech Gear

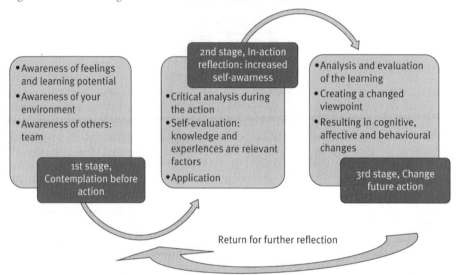

- Awareness of feelings and learning potential
- Awareness of your environment
- Awareness of others: team

1st stage, Contemplation before action

2nd stage, In-action reflection: increased self-awarness

- Critical analysis during the action
- Self-evaluation: knowledge and experiences are relevant factors
- Application

Analysis and evaluation of the learning
- Creating a changed viewpoint
- Resulting in cognitive, affective and behavioural changes

3rd stage, Change future action

Return for further reflection

Loo (2002) contends that the expectation of an individual engaged in reflective practice is that they will become more effective in their job roles as both an individual and team member; in essence, reflective practice engenders change, and changes are adaptive. Therefore, during this adaptive process learning will have occurred. Reflective journals are part of this process.

Earlier in this book (see Chapter 1) we highlighted learning logs as relevant in assisting reflective practice and facilitating the collection of evidence of competence for portfolio or continuing professional practice purposes. Some of these previous models may be worth re-visiting as they lead the reader to pose or answer certain questions. Loo's work gives a similar perspective when he poses several questions that he suggests help individuals stay focused when journaling. These questions are (Loo 2002, p62):

1   What was the learning situation or event?

2   What have I learned and how have I learned it?

3   How do I feel (good and bad feelings) about what I have learned?

4   How could I have learned more effectively/efficiently?

5   What actions can I take to learn more effectively/efficiently?

6   In what ways do I need to change my attitudes, expectations, values and so on to feel better about learning situations?

Keeping a log, as we have stated previously, is a tool to aid reflection: journaling takes the process to a deeper stage as it expects the writer to create an articulated narrative that is born out of the critical thinking and reflection on a specific learning event or a learning experience occurring over a period of time. For details, please refer to Chapter 1.

ACTIVITY 18.9

Journaling

1   Considering the case study, how can keeping a learning journal help the change managers and the change leaders?

2   Why would the company encourage such activity?

18.6.5 LEARNING AND TRAINING IN THE GREEN PROJECT CASE STUDY

There is a significant amount of work for project/change managers and change leaders to do. They need to decide on a focused model for their development process, a training model and a vehicle whereby they communicate with their colleagues. Review of the project at various stages is essential, and this will form part of the course of action any project would take (highlighted in Section 18.2.2 above). However, they will need to be mindful of budgetary constraints, cultural differences and similarities, consider the relevant literature for change and conduct a development process that adds value to the organisation.

The CIPD (2009) report on *Promoting the Value of Learning in Adversity* suggests a critical framework for ensuring learning and development is positioned, and its implications thought through, to offer maximum sustainable value. The model in Figure 18.11 highlights the testing issues those who seek to develop staff must contemplate.

Figure 18.11 Levels of LTD provision

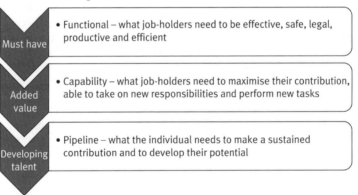

Source: CIPD 2009, p20

Finally, we must recognise that learning is for everyone, and as far as the case study is concerned, learning, training and development is a key aspect that will support a successful outcome to the project.

ACTIVITY 18.10

Developing the workforce

1 Using relevant literature sources, plan each stage of the development process:

- learning needs
- design
- delivery
- evaluation
- organisational development.

2 Plan a learning process that caters for ongoing talent management of key individuals.

3 Plan a presentation to senior managers to show how the workforce will be included in the development and communication process.

4 How will you evaluate the success of the learning, training and development aspects of the project?

18.6.6 CHANGE MANAGEMENT COMPETENCES

The case study has stated that certain staff will be designated as change managers (see also Chapter 12). They are distinct from the project manager as they take on what Gareis (2010) describes as second-order change. This level of change relates to 'discontinuous, deep structural and cultural change' (Gareis 2010). According to Crawford and Hassaner Nahmias (2010), second-order change requires a more insightful approach than first-order change. They cite first-order change as practised by project managers as direct, straightforward with a rational style, whereas skills needed for second-order change, they suggest, require a different approach which includes astuteness, sensitivity and interpersonal skills. Change managers focus on communication and engagement, encourage others to believe in the change, identify charismatic champions, train and develop staff, affect organisational culture, defuse opposition and manage the gambit of stakeholder expectation (Crawford and Hassaner Nahmias 2010). Their research indicates that to be successful in this role a range of personal competences are required which are directly linked to the change activities on which change managers embark. These are: stakeholder management, leadership, team selection and development, planning, communication, decision-making and problem-solving, cultural awareness and project management skills (Crawford and Hassaner Nahmias 2010).

18.6.7 SUMMARY OF PART 1

In this part we have covered a range of project management-related topics, bringing together a wide range of skills that you will have built while studying this book. You should now be aware that projects are very widely used, and you are likely to be either directly involved in carrying them through to completion, or indirectly involved by dealing with their organisational impact. You have been introduced to some of the language of project management, such as 'project phases', 'stakeholders' and 'Gantt charts', and should be able to use these techniques in a basic, but nonetheless useful, manner.

You have also explored further other areas introduced in previous chapters, particularly the management of change. Culture has also featured strongly in this section of the chapter, illustrated through the Mountech Gear case study, which focused on the design and implementation of its 'green project'. Virtual teams have been discussed as part of this analysis. Much has been made of the human side of project management, with the importance of employee engagement being selected for particular emphasis. We expect that this case study will have highlighted the many skills required for the successful management of projects.

PART 2: THE WAY FORWARD: MANAGING YOUR TALENT AND CAREER

Part 1 above has focused on project management as an outlet in which managers and staff alike can practise and improve a wide range of skills. In Part 2, we take a more personal approach, looking at how you can manage your talent and develop your career more effectively.

18.7 MANAGING YOUR TALENT

The concept of talent management was born out of ongoing skill deficiencies, shifting demographics, increased workforce diversity and work–life balance initiatives (CIPD 2013), which make it increasingly difficult for organisations to attract employees whom they believe will enhance the business. Organisations, therefore, continue to try to either attract talented employees from outside of the organisation or develop them internally. But what does 'talent' actually mean and what can organisations do to attract and retain talented employees? Let us consider two recent definitions.

> Talent consists of those individuals who can make a difference to organisational performance either through their immediate contribution or, in the longer term, by demonstrating the highest levels of potential. (CIPD 2013, p2)

Talented employees, therefore, are those who have the right knowledge, skills, attitudes and behaviours (see Chapter 5 for a discussion) to contribute to the organisation's success. What it means to have the 'right' attributes depends on the organisation, the industry in which it operates and the type and nature of the work. A specialist engineer will require different knowledge, skills, attitudes and behaviours than an HR specialist, for example. Nevertheless, both can contribute to building a high-performance workplace in their own way.

But what can an organisation do to manage such 'talent'? The CIPD (2013, p2) offers the following definition:

> Talent management is the systematic attraction, identification, development, engagement, retention and deployment of those individuals who are of particular value to an organisation, either in view of their 'high potential' for the future or because they are fulfilling business/operation-critical roles.

Hence, talent management consists of what contemporary organisations do to develop, retain and attract talented individuals. It is important that such efforts are part of a planned strategy on talent and that management systems are adopted to measure the return on this investment (for instance through a cost–benefit analysis). The term '"talent" may be used to encompass the entire workforce of an organisation' (Caplan 2011, as cited in CIPD 2013), thereby bringing a more inclusive view to organisational approaches to develop and retain their people. Many organisations employ talent managers (regardless of whether they carry that title or simply fulfil that role) to seek out talented individuals, nurture them and encourage them to engage with the current and future skill requirements of the organisation.

The process adopted to engage in the talent perspective reflects what the CIPD describes as the 'talent management loop'. Here they focus on four areas: attracting, developing, managing and evaluating talent (Figure 18.12).

Figure 18.12 Talent perspective: the management loop

Source: reproduced from CIPD 2013 with kind permission

The talent perspective denotes the particular strategy an organisation envisages as in keeping with their philosophy and as appropriate to their economic circumstances at a particular point in time. For example, an organisation may not be able to afford to adopt talent management across the board in testing economic times. Box 18.1 depicts the CIPD overview of the talent management loop.

Box 18.1: Talent management loop

Attracting talent

The ability to attract external talent depends upon how potential applicants view the organisation, the industry or sector in which it operates and whether they share the values of that organisation. The creation of an attractive employer brand is an important factor in recruiting external talent. More information can be found in our factsheet on this topic.

Developing talent

Talent development should be linked to other learning and development initiatives, including both informal as well as formal learning interventions. Participants on talent management programmes tend to value coaching, mentoring and networking particularly highly, especially, according to our research, the opportunity to meet senior people in the organisation.

Managing talent

Investment in management and leadership development will positively impact on talent retention. The process of succession planning in particular helps many organisations in identifying and preparing future potential leaders to fill key positions, while secondments may also play a useful role.

Tracking and evaluating talent management

Evaluation of talent management is difficult, requiring both quantitative and qualitative data that is valid, reliable and robust, but necessary to ensure that the investment is meeting organisational needs. One method could involve the collation of employee turnover and retention data for key groups such as senior management postholders or those who have participated in high-flyer programmes.

> Ultimately, organisational success is the most effective evaluation of talent management.
>
> Source: reproduced from CIPD 2013 with kind permission

Therefore, after appointment of staff, organisations are actively seeking to develop talented individuals and protect their investments by retaining them. They realise that there must be a planned procedure for managing and challenging individuals with high potential; in other words, to manage their talent. It is therefore our contention that you should do the same for yourself – manage your own talent by taking the initiative. We therefore encourage you to continue to develop or enhance your skills levels by seeking out experiences that enhance your 'human capital', even though they may be unpaid. Your motivation, however, is crucial to this endeavour, and we recommend you take a proactive attitude.

Table 18.2 gives suggestions for you to reflect upon in terms of managing your own talent:

Table 18.2 Talent management – learning points

Illustration	Therefore	Outcome
Talent is specific	Give your own definition for managing your talent.	This is the start of your journey; use your definition to keep your focus.
Create a strategic plan	The plan enables you to map out what is possible and achievable.	It offers an opportunity to reflect on your aims and adjust your thinking accordingly.
Produce overarching learning outcomes	Review your learning needs: what skills do you believe you will/should develop and enhance?	Allows for greater focus and more detailed reflection.
Gain support	This falls into three categories: Personal – find support from your friends, family and colleagues. Organisational – find out if your current employer (or one to which you have applied) has a good training and development record. Conduct a cost–benefit analysis of your plans – can you rely on financial support from your current employer or will you be self-funding?	Ensure you have the commitment and resources to develop your strategy.
Focused departmental support	Discuss your development with your line manager. Gain their commitment to act as a coach or mentor.	Act on the advice if you judge it is appropriate. Consider how you add value.
Self-help	Take the opportunities that are offered if you decide they are interesting and appropriate.	Develop an attitude that sustains you on the journey.

Box 18.2 illustrates a perspective of how another successful organisation is using talent management to enhance its business as well as enhancing the careers of its employees.

Box 18.2: What you can learn from L'Oréal: Totally worth it

Isabelle Minneci has helped cosmetics giant L'Oréal make its HR as innovative as its R&D – and it's paying off. Unless you spent 2012 in a cave, you couldn't have missed the debut of BB cream on British shores. It was the biggest beauty sensation in years: a 'wonder cream' to 'cut your morning beauty routine in half', screamed *Cosmopolitan*, praising the way it reduced the appearance of blemishes and gave tired complexions a dewy glow.

As chemists across Britain braced themselves for the arrival of hordes of miracle-hungry shoppers, L'Oréal – the largest cosmetics company in the world – was racing to be first to market with its Nude Magique BB brand. And that meant unleashing the French-owned firm's full innovative might, not only in product development but right across the organisation.

Minneci says her 38-strong HR department's role is pivotal to unleashing and 'animating' the talent that creates such bankable products. 'We believe that the success of L'Oréal comes from its people, so the HR function is at the core of our strategy,' she says. 'Our motto is: "We want to be number one in beauty, but also in growth."'

Her people-centric strategy seems to be playing its part. It helped produce a 5.5 per cent rise in like-for-like sales in 2012, following similar growth in 2011. 'We are very fortunate to be in a market that's growing – partly because there is an eternal quest for beauty,' says Minneci, who has been with the business for more than a decade. 'Even in economically tough times, people always need something for their own pleasure. We are constantly focusing on consumer insights and needs.'

Minneci says one of the key challenges for her team is to 'constantly develop the skills of our organisation'. To ensure HR is close enough to its employees to identify where support, training and strategic development are needed, its structure resembles a multi-armed sub-continental goddess with manicured fingers reaching into every part of the business. There is an HR lead for each British division (professional, consumer, luxury and pharmaceutical products) and heads of HR for four regional distribution centres, as well as a group-wide corporate HR function located in London.

But Minneci says this multi-faceted structure doesn't slow the march of change – locating HR close to the talent means it can nurture people throughout their careers by 'knowing them well'. But what does delivering those principles actually mean?

Get closer

'To ensure that the HR function is at the core of the business strategy, you need proximity and to know your employees. In some companies you have one HR person for 1,000 employees. For us, the average ratio is 1:200 or 1:300 max,' says Minneci. This enables HR to understand employee needs. 'Then you can see the best way to develop people and truly work on their career progression.'

This proximity helped Minneci spot skills gaps as the company geared up to embed more digital capability across the business. Although L'Oréal's marketers were already highly skilled in digital communications and technology, she says, this wasn't the case in every function. 'Digital is important everywhere. If I take HR as an example, we have more and more social media activity in our recruitment strategy,' she says. To ensure staff could be developed, HR dedicated 15 per cent of its training budget to digital.

The effectiveness of this approach is evident in staff retention. For example, over a quarter of senior managers in the consumer division started out as graduates at the business.

Connect your staff

Siloed working is not conducive to innovation or collaborative working. At L'Oréal the staff dots are joined through regular team and company meetings, communications around 'career week' and other initiatives or emails highlighting job-swap opportunities. 'The point is to get people talking and experiencing different parts of the organisation,' says Minneci. 'We also offer staff the chance to shadow members of the management team. L'Oréal is such a big organisation that you can be working in your brand and not see what the rest of the business is doing. So we are constantly talking about our brands and our results.' Members of HR from different parts of the business also meet up and talk regularly to share ideas and experiences.

Engage your ears

'Listening to what our staff think is key to making them feel valued as well as gleaning new ideas for more efficient ways of working,' Minneci says. HR partners with the communications team to ensure that employees know which initiatives are being put in place for their benefit. The business holds regular mini-polls, which take the form of an employee meeting where they vote anonymously in real time on questions on a big screen (a little like the audience voting system on *Who Wants to be a Millionaire?*).

'Our employees love it because they feel it is much more transparent. We are not hiding anything and we are seeing the successes but also the more challenging results,' she says. Such feedback has also led to a current project to amalgamate the HR systems staff use, so they only have to login once to access key information.

Be responsive

For innovation to thrive and remain part of the culture, it must be clear that suggestions and feedback don't just disappear into the ether.

It's important for people to know HR has acted on their suggestions, Minneci says, so areas that staff identify as needing improvement are designated as 'change management programmes' for HR. 'We constantly measure our progress on these areas and relay it back to employees.' When a staff survey found that people felt managers were 'not close enough to their employees', HR developed a programme to boost management skills. It led to improved employee survey scores in the area. In its most recent poll, L'Oréal scored above its peers in the sector and above the UK national norm for management scores, specifically when it came to the statement 'my direct manager encourages new ideas and new ways of doing things'.

Recruit early and often

'For us, the war for talent is ongoing. It's about getting the next generation of employees. Because we are a growing business, we have a constant need for new recruits,' Minneci says.

When you are promoting people from within the business, you're constantly needing to fill roles, she says. This opens up more generic jobs within the organisation, which are perfect for graduates. The employer has 34 graduates and 100 interns in the business at all times. This pipeline of fresh talent underpins L'Oréal's ability to renew its innovative culture. 'For us, it's an opportunity to detect talent. Seventy per cent of graduates come from internship programmes. We can recruit them before they have finished their degree. We work very much in advance in terms of talent recruitment.'

Source: excerpt reproduced with permission from Churchard 2013

ACTIVITY 18.11

L'Oréal

After having read the passage in Box 18.2, answer the following questions:

1   Compare and contrast the stance L'Oréal take on talent management in relation to your organisation or one with which you are familiar:

- get closer
- connect your staff
- engage your ears
- be responsive
- recruit early and often.

2   Consider a cost–benefit analysis approach – is the point of view L'Oréal takes economically sound? Why or why not?

- Develop an argument for and against.
- Would this work in an organisation with which you are familiar?

18.8 CAREER ENHANCEMENT

From the passage above we have set out certain strategic considerations regarding managing talent. The next step is to review what you can accomplish in terms of your own career enhancement. You should note that the concept of 'career' is wide ranging; for instance, Collin (2010, p258) asks us to conceptualise career as: 'the experience of continuity and coherence while the individual moves through time and social space'. This may sound rather like a time traveller/'Dr Who' definition (!), but the point is that your career is ideally *coherent* (that is, linkages from one job to another over time, see also Chapter 5) and is more than just a series of tasks – it also involves your experience with people.

Career development and enhancement is of consequence both to the individual and the organisation in which they work. To enhance your career, constructively, it is useful to view its development in an organisational context. Recalling that organisations employ people to manage talent and careers, the CIPD (2003, p1) gave the following definition of career management: 'Planning and shaping the progression or movement of individuals within an organisation by aligning employee preferences and potential with organisational resourcing needs.'

Certainly organisations are concerned about their 'talent pool', while individuals are mindful of the job market and ensuring they gain development opportunities. Both, however, are interested in progression, and it is therefore incumbent on both to think about future needs. On the one hand, an organisation must retain and build new talent by putting the right people in the right place and fostering development, thereby increasing their talent pool. On the other hand, individuals will seek an outlet for their knowledge, skills and abilities as well as seeking to learn and grow with a view to future ambitions. While these aspirations are necessary and (at least on the surface) even harmonious, the two perspectives can create conflicting interests. However, they can also initiate opportunity if you choose an organisation that values what you bring to your role.

ACTIVITY 18.12

Critical reflection on your career development

We have asked you to do this exercise in Chapter 1 and, now that you have been developing your knowledge and skills over the course of your studies, it may be a good time to do so again.

1   Consider your career from the first time you entered employment. Analyse the periods

or events of critical importance for representing one of the following:

- worst growth period
- best growth period
- static period – how did this change?
- working for a particular company or individual
- meeting a specific individual
- participating in a particular training or development event
- being at the right place at the right time!

2   How much of this was planned or happened by chance?

3   Discuss your finding within a group and share your experiences.

4   In the future, do you intend that your career development should be left to chance?

You may want to compare this reflection with the one you did in Chapter 1 and, where appropriate, discuss the results with a peer, colleague or mentor.

Career enhancement is often influenced by individual performance systems, which help us focus on career enhancement by relating to individual performance in a managed way. Many of these systems are not perfect as they are not always perceived by all to be equitable. However, most value an appraisal process as 'a well-established practice that drives decisions about pay, promotion, terminations, transfers and training needs' (CIPD, 2010b, p31) – in effect, the decisions that can make or break careers (see also Chapter 10 for a discussion of performance management). Activity 18.3 is based upon a CIPD study (McMahon 2010, p31).

 ACTIVITY 18.13

Performance systems as they relate to career opportunity

CIPD performance management suggestions	Your response and basis for discussion
1 Review the system: It's farcical to expect performance management systems devised years ago to remain effective. Would you expect it of your IT, marketing or financial management systems? Given the current emphasis on such practices as coaching, mentoring, 360-degree feedback, competencies, and so on, systems should not be allowed to remain static and become ritualistic, as they will quickly fall into disrepute and be neglected. A full formal evaluation exercise is central to attaining an ongoing successful system.	Where do you and your organisation stand on this point? What influence do you have? Or, how can you influence decisions?

CIPD performance management suggestions	Your response and basis for discussion
2 Engage the managers: The support of management is crucial to a successful system. This can be secured by involving managers in the system's (re)design process and ensuring that they are reviewed on their performance management responsibilities. It also helps to secure feedback on the system's effectiveness, making sure the process and any associated training is conducive to upward feedback to identify where it's not being prioritised.	Are you or your managers involved in the system? Why, why not? Are there opportunities to give feedback?
3 Address interpersonal and interviewing skills: Subjectivity, interpersonal skills and human judgements are inherent to the process of good performance management. Appropriate training, incorporating coaching and interviewing techniques, will help here. Reviews should start from jointly agreed objectives, focus on factual performance data rather than style or personality, encourage self-assessment and provide an appeal mechanism.	Does your appraisal system rest on subjectivity? Is appropriate development given to enhance your skills?
4 Define the objectives: Performance management encounters difficulties when addressing a number of objectives. For example, when used for reward-related decisions, any developmental impetus it is intended to have is threatened. Playing judge and counsellor at the same time is highly problematic. It is best to opt for a combination of agreed, consistent and compatible objectives. Where this is not feasible, some organisations opt to conduct separate interviews at separate times of the year for the separate purposes. Furthermore, many organisations are now concentrating on non-financial measures and assessing key competencies.	Describe your organisation processes. Are key objectives set and relevant competencies developed/measured?
5 Remember to follow up: The manager who promises to provide additional resources or some form of personal development option is unlikely to enhance the system's reputation (or their own) by persistently failing to deliver. In the long run, the system is judged by the extent to which recommendations arising from review meetings actually materialise.	Is there a formalised follow-up process? Do you follow up if your manager does not?

CIPD performance management suggestions	Your response and basis for discussion
6 Minimise paperwork: Managers already feel inundated with paperwork and so resent the additional and often extensive form-filling associated with performance management systems. This is exacerbated by the fact that the forms are not 'living documents', but remain stored in the archives of the HR department. So it is important to remember that the purpose of performance management is to motivate the employee for the purpose of improving organisational performance – not to generate more paperwork.	Give your analysis of this issue. Are you motivated by the current system practised in you organisation?
What can the organisation do with regard to any of the above?	What can you do in connection with any of the above?

Source: reproduced with permission from McMahon 2010, p31

It may be time for organisations to rethink these issues, especially in current economic times where many companies are finding increasing pressures to survive. However, from an individual's perspective, being alert to these problems is essential because of the skills and talent people acquire, they will need a job/career where these attributes can be expressed. Otherwise the whole process may be career-demotivating rather than career-enhancing. Let us now consider where your career may lead you (Activity 18.14).

 ACTIVITY 18.14

Career pathway

Choose a career pathway (for example human resources) and investigate how that career can be enhanced, that is, what attitudes and qualifications are necessary for the individual to be of value to the organisation. What career avenues are open to HR professionals?

You may want to consult the CIPD Profession Map introduced in Chapter 1 to guide you and assess which area offers the best fit for your knowledge, skills, attitudes and behaviours.

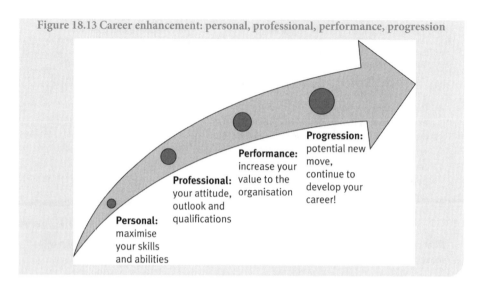

Figure 18.13 Career enhancement: personal, professional, performance, progression

Career enhancement, we suggest, consists of four important variables: personal development, professional development, managing your performance and progression. It is, however, important that the individual takes an active role in their own career enhancement. The 'personal' element encourages us to maximise skills and abilities, 'professional' aspects might include our general outlook and positive attitude to doing a good job. While part of this may include an individual's qualifications, another important part is the way in which their knowledge, skills, norms, attitudes and behaviours work together and in conjunction with the organisation, as discussed in Chapter 5. The notion of adding value is prevalent in many organisational recruitment and employee engagement texts; an individual's own 'performance', therefore, can hold the key to their ability to progress. Lastly, there is the issue of 'progression', which to some extent is optional as some individuals may choose not to progress for personal reasons. However, we take the view that most people using this textbook will be seeking (further) career enhancement as well as opportunities for career advancement. Therefore, progress may include actively seeking the next internal promotion, a sideways development move or a new project, and/or employment in another organisation that offers a challenge and is an all-important, enhancing step.

18.9 CONTINUING PROFESSIONAL DEVELOPMENT

Much has been written about CPD throughout this book and, therefore, this section only seeks to expand and conclude upon some of the prevalent themes. In-company or professional CPD may have many specific elements that usually differ from one organisation or professional body to another. However, we can expect that some of the more general features of CPD will remain, including:

- A requirement that time be allocated to this investment and that different activities are considered to be of equal value or importance as others.
- The development itself should be owned and managed by you, the learner, although there may be organisational and/or professional body support.
- Your development should emanate from your current situation and learning needs (such as your work role) or be forward-looking (that is, focusing on your goals and aspirations).

- Objectives should be set for all development activities which encompass both your individual aims as well as those of the organisation. Keep them clear and focused.
- Ensure reflective practice is emphasised to support other, more formalised development activities.
- Actively search for ways to improve performance; ensure you develop continuously.

Most professional bodies encourage individuals to be credited with formal qualifications alongside informal and self-directed learning. Rothwell and Arnold (2005) suggest that, unfortunately, active engagement in CPD by individuals and organisations is not always matched by the supposedly high value members of professional bodies (such as the CIPD) place on CPD. Nonetheless, they continue to form a clearly established characteristic of the contemporary organisation as well as the 'professional career' (Kanter 1989, p508), and you are in the driving seat of your own professional development.

ACTIVITY 18.15

Review your learning plan

Using the examples provided in Chapter 1, draw up a learning plan and scrutinise it by answering the following questions:

1 Do you have goals that you wish to achieve next week/month/year?

2 Do you have an unambiguous view of the priorities?

3 Do you have specific objectives?

4 Does your plan need adjustment or are you on course to achieve your stated goals?

5 When will you revisit your plan?

Such a strategic and thoughtful approach to your learning – whether in formal study or at the workplace – can help you focus your continuing professional development and career management on what really matters to you.

18.9.1 SUMMARY OF PART 2

Part 2 has outlined the important concept of talent management, illustrating how it might be applied through the use of case studies and encouraging you to consider your own CPD and career enhancement. It has shown how you might analyse your career enhancement, with particular reference to links with personal and professional development, personal performance and progression.

18.10 CONCLUSION

Chapter 18 has been a challenging chapter. The first part not only introduced the area of project management skills but also sought to integrate these with the skills developed in previous chapters. It has shown through a range of activities how leaders and managers need to develop a wide array of attributes and skills. In the Mountech Gear case study you were challenged to research certain areas of work and to think critically; in answering questions relating to this case you have had to reflect about working cross-culturally in a virtual team configuration and how to communicate with distinct groups of people: in effect, you have practised a range of solution-oriented techniques to managing and leading work-based decisions and situations.

The second part of this chapter has picked up issues originally discussed earlier in the book to aid the management of your talent and development of your career. The ideas expressed here have given a contemporary perspective of the rewards and challenges relating to the vital journeys of engagement and development by both individuals and organisations. Effective approaches to managing your talent can have substantial benefits to your overall career, your personal finances and your satisfaction, and we can only encourage you to take a strategic approach to the development of your career. It is now your turn to continue to practise the skills that you have developed while studying this book and to actively manage your talent and the enhancement of your career.

18.11 CONCLUDING REMARKS AND RECOMMENDATIONS

These concluding remarks will serve as a conclusion to the textbook as a whole. At this stage you should ask yourselves several fundamental questions:

1   Why have I engaged with this text?

2   What have I learned?

3   How will I apply what I have learned?

4   When will I feel confident to employ any new skills and techniques?

The purpose of this book has been to enhance your learning using active engagement and participation throughout. In short, we have taken you through a process of learning that encouraged reflective thinking when applying and experiencing the cases and activities. Many of the chapters have asked you to examine your own current practices and to self-critique and self-evaluate. The intention has been to give you a much deeper insight into what attributes you currently possess and those you may wish to enhance still further. A further point when considering yourself is that of self-confidence. Personal experience provides a route for experimentation, allowing you to learn from your own experience as well as from the experiences of others; we hope that the activities you have experienced throughout this book have helped to raise your confidence levels and serve as an impetus for your future skills development.

EXPLORE FURTHER

COCKBURN, A. (2002) *Agile software development*. London: Addison-Wesley. The book considers incremental learning in software projects and is also interesting for its discussion of software development teams.

A rather brief but practical book for some additional tips and pointers to other sources of information specific to projects is:

DEEPROSE, D. (2001) *Smart things to know about managing projects*. Oxford: Capstone. Read the chapter on Power vs Persuasion.

Still regarded by technical-oriented project managers as one of the key textbooks to read is: KERZNER, H. (2009) *Project management: a systems approach to planning, scheduling, and controlling*. 10th ed. Hoboken, NJ: Wiley. Interestingly, it devotes a whole chapter to culture – Chapter 19: 'Managing cultural differences'.

For cross-cultural issues, we recommend you read the works by Geert Hofstede and Fons Trompenaars and subsequent applications.

REFERENCES

ALI, A.S., ANBARI, F.T. and MONEY, W.H. (2008) Impact of organizational and project factors on acceptance and usage of project management software and perceived project success. *Project Management Journal.* Vol 39, No 2. pp5–33.

BOUD, D., KEOGH, K. and WALKER, D. (eds) (1985) *Reflection: turning experience into learning.* London: Kogan Page.

BRINER, W., HASTINGS, C. and GEDDES, M. (1996) *Project leadership.* Aldershot: Gower.

BROWAEYS, M.-J. and PRICE, R. (2008) *Understanding cross-cultural management.* Harlow: FT/Prentice Hall.

CAPLAN, J. (2011) *The value of talent: promoting talent management across the organization.* London: Kogan Page.

CHEN, M. (1995) *Asian management systems: Chinese, Japanese, and Korean styles of business.* London: Thunderbird.

CHILD, J. (1994) *Management in China in the age of reform.* Cambridge: Cambridge University Press.

CHOW, I.H. (2004) The impact of institutional context on human resource management in three Chinese societies. *Employee Relations.* Vol 26, No 6. pp626–42.

CHURCHARD, C. (2013) What you can learn from L'Oréal: Totally worth it. *People Management.* 23 August.

CIPD. (2003) *Managing employee careers: issues, trends and prospects.* Survey report. London: CIPD.

CIPD. (2007a) *The value of learning: a new model of value and evaluation [online].* Available at: http://www.cipd.co.uk/NR/rdonlyres/94842E50-F775-4154-975F-8D4BE72846C7/0/valoflearnnwmodvalca.pd [Accessed 30 July 2013].

CIPD. (2007b) *Talent management [online].* Research insight. Available at: http://www.cipd.co.uk/NR/rdonlyres/B513502C-8F42-419C-818C-D3C12D87E0D3/0/talentmanage.pdf [Accessed 29 September 2013].

CIPD. (2009) *Promoting the value of learning in adversity [online]* . Available at: http://www.cipd.co.uk/hr-resources/guides/promoting-value-of-learning-adversity.aspx [Accessed 29 September 2013].

CIPD. (2010a) *Creating an engaged workforce [online].* Available at: http://www.cipd.co.uk/hr-resources/research/creating-engaged-workforce.aspx [Accessed 18 October 2013].

CIPD. (2010b) *Innovative learning and talent development [online].* Available at: http://www.cipd.co.uk/hr-resources/research/learning-talent-development-recession-recovery.aspx [Accessed 29 September 2013].

CIPD. (2013) *Talent management: an overview [online].* Revised September 2013. Available at: http://www.cipd.co.uk/hr-resources/factsheets/talent-management-overview.aspx [Accessed 20 September 2013].

COCKBURN, A. (2002) *Agile software development.* London: Addison-Wesley.

COLLIN, A. (2010) Learning and development. In: J. BEARDWELL and T. CLAYDON (eds). *Human resource management: a contemporary approach.* 6th ed. London: Prentice Hall, pp235–82.

CRAWFORD, L. and HASSANER NAHMIAS, A. (2010) Competencies for managing change. *International Journal of Project Management.* Vol 28, No 4. pp405–12.

EARLEY, P.C. and MOSAKOWSKI, E. (2000) Creating hybrid team cultures. *Academy of Management Journal.* Vol 43, No 1. pp26–49.

EMMITT, S. and GORSE, C.A. (2007) *Communication in construction teams.* Oxford: Taylor & Francis.

EXECUTIVE AGENCY EDUCATION, AUDIOVISUAL AND CULTURE. (2009) *Tempus [online].* Available at: http://eacea.ec.europa.eu/tempus/index_en.php [Accessed 29 September 2013].

GALLAGHER, K. (2006) *The Lesotho Highlands Water Project.* CIPD Case Studies Club. London: CIPD.

GAREIS, R. (2010) Designing changes of permanent organisations by process and projects. *International Journal of Project Management.* Vol 28, No 4. pp314–27.

HARRISON, R. (1997) *Employee development.* London: IPD.

HARRISON, R. (2009) *Learning and development.* 5th ed. London: CIPD.

KAHN, W.A. (1990) Psychological conditions of personal engagement and disengagement at work. *Academy of Management Journal.* Vol 33, No 4. pp692–724.

KANTER, R.M. (1989) Careers and the wealth of nations. In: M.B. ARTHURS, C.T. HALL and B.S. LAWRENCE (eds). *Handbook of career theory.* Cambridge: Cambridge University Press, pp505–21.

LEE-KELLEY, L. and SANKEY, T. (2008) Global virtual teams for value creation and project success. *International Journal of Project Management.* Vol 26, No 1. pp51–62.

LEGRIS, P. and COLLERETTE, P. (2006). A roadmap for IT project implementation. *Project Management Journal.* Vol 37, No 5. pp64–75.

LOCKETT, M. (1988) Culture and the problems of Chinese management. *Organisation Studies.* Vol 9, No 4. pp475–96.

LOCKYER, K. and GORDON, J. (2007) *Project management and project network techniques.* 7th ed. Harlow: Pearson.

LOO, R. (2002) Journaling: a tool for project management training and team building. *Project Management Journal.* Vol 33, No 4. pp61–6.

LUO, Y. and CHEN, M. (1997) Does guanxi affect company performance? *Asia Pacific Journal of Management.* Vol 14, No 1. pp1–16.

MARQUARDT, M.J. and HOVARTH, L. (2001) *Global teams.* Palo Alto, CA: Davies-Black.

MAY, D.R., GILSON, R.L. and HARTER, L.M. (2004) The psychological conditions of meaningfulness, safety and availability and the engagement of the human spirit at work. *Journal of Occupational and Organizational Psychology.* Vol 77, No 1. pp11–37.

MAYLOR, H. (2005) *Project management.* 3rd ed. Harlow: Pearson.

MCMAHON, G. (2010) How to… manage performance. *People Management.* 6 May. p31.

MICHAILOVA, E. and WORM, V. (2003) Personal networking in Russia and China: blat and guanxi. *European Management Journal.* Vol 21, No 4. pp509–19.

OCHIENG, E.G. and PRICE, A.D.F. (2010) Managing cross-cultural communication in multicultural project teams. *International Journal of Project Management.* Vol 28, No 5. pp449–60.

PEARSON, J.C. and NELSON, P.E. (2003) *Human communication.* New York: McGraw-Hill.

PINTO, J.K. (2007) *Project management: achieving competitive advantage.* Upper Saddle River, NJ: Pearson.

PROJECT MANAGEMENT INSTITUTE. (2007) *A guide to the project management body of knowledge: PMBOK Guide.* Project Management Institute.

REED, A.H. and KNIGHT, L.V. (2010) Effect of a virtual project team environment on communication-related project risk. *International Journal of Project Management.* Vol 28, No 5. pp422–7.

ROTHWELL, A. and ARNOLD, J. (2005) How professionals rate 'continuing professional development'. *Human Resources Management Journal.* Vol 15, No 3. pp18–32.

ROWLINSON, S. and CHEUNG, Y.K. (2008) Stakeholder management through empowerment. *Construction Management and Economics.* Vol 26, No 6. pp611–23.

SADLER-SMITH, E. and LEYBOURNE, S. (2006). The role of intuition and improvisation in project management. *International Journal of Project Management.* Vol 24, No 6. pp483–92.

SCANLON, J.M. and CHERNOMAS, W.M. (1997) Developing the reflective teacher. *Journal of Advanced Nursing.* Vol 25, No 6. pp1138–43.

SCHAUFELI, W.B. and BAKKER, A.B. (2004) Job demands, job resources, and their relationship with burnout and engagement: a multi-sample study. *Journal of Organizational Behaviour.* Vol 25, No 3. pp293–315.

SCHEIN, E.H. (2004) *Organization cultural and leadership.* 3rd ed. San Francisco, CA: Jossey-Bass.

SCHNEIDER, S.C. and BARSOUX, J.L. (2003) *Managing across cultures.* 2nd ed. Harlow: FT/Prentice Hall.

SCHöN, D.A. (1987) *Educating the reflective practitioner.* San Francisco, CA: Jossey-Bass.

TAYEB, M. (2003) *International management.* Harlow: Pearson.

TRUSS, K., SOANE, E.C. and EDWARDS, C. (2006) *Working life: employee attitudes and engagement 2006.* London: CIPD.

WEATHERLEY, S. (2006) *Managing multicultural project teams [online].* Available at: www.gdsinternational.com/infocentre/artsum.asp?
lang=en&mag=182&iss=149&art=25863 [Accessed 4 July 2010].

Index